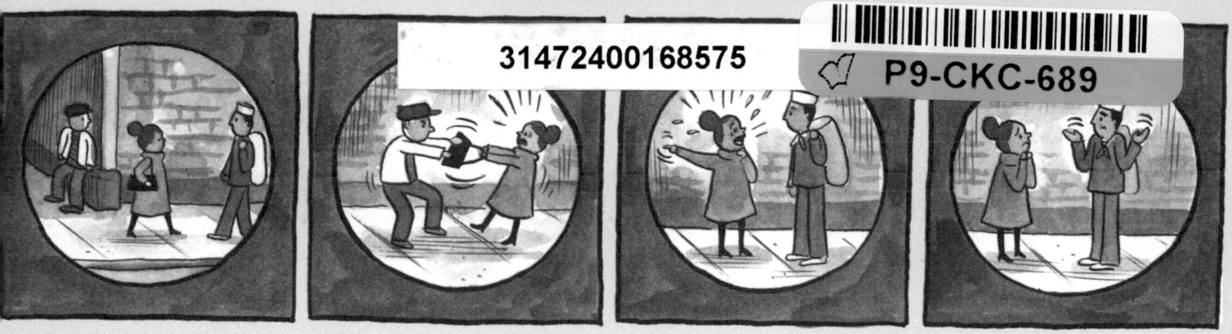

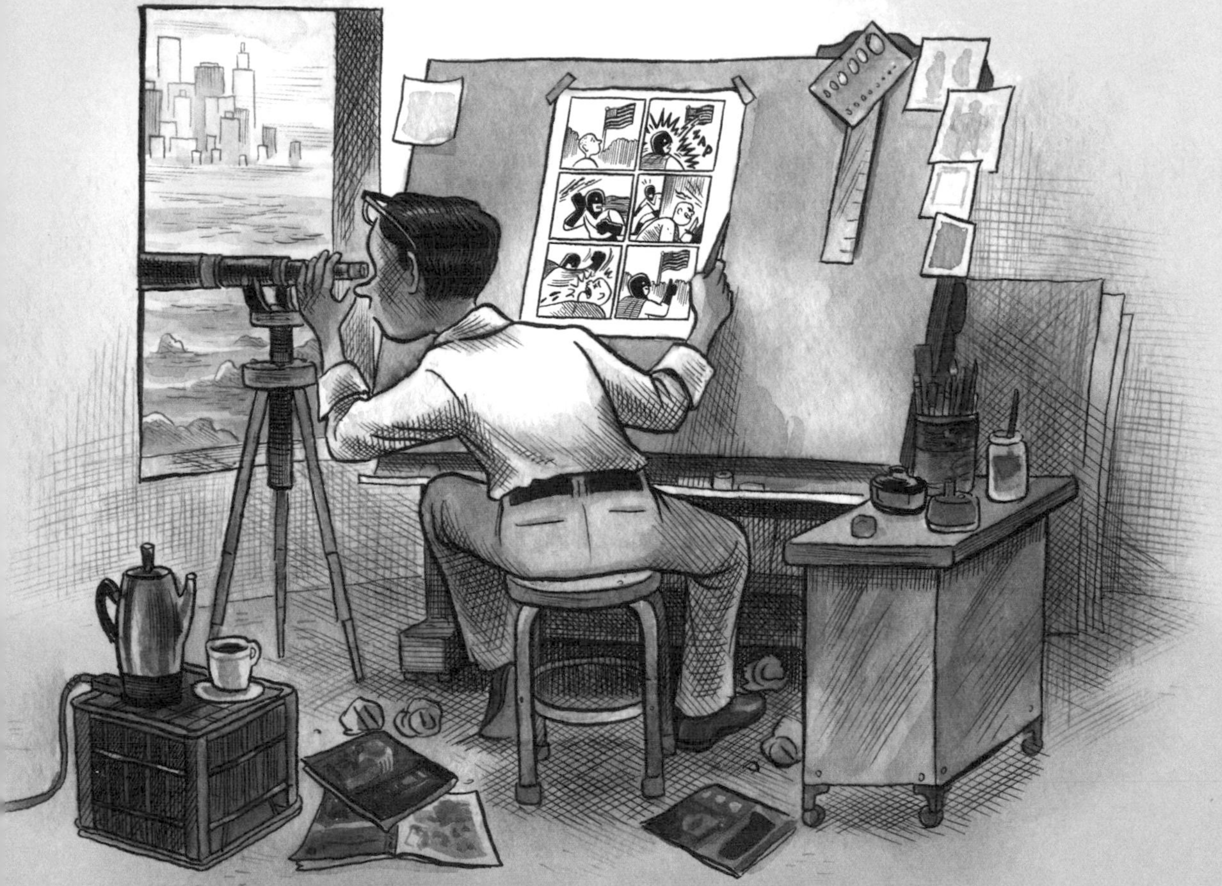

DATE DUE

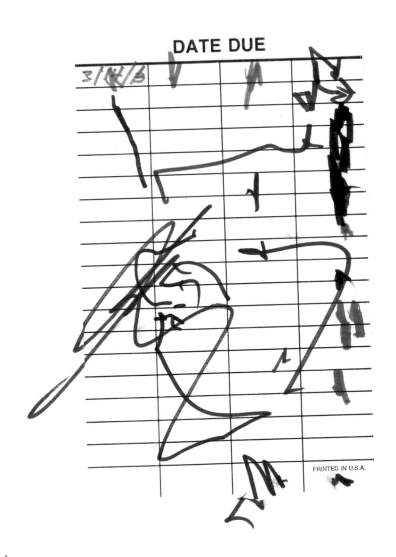

THE BEST AMERICAN

Comics 2013

GUEST EDITORS OF
THE BEST AMERICAN COMICS

2006 HARVEY PEKAR
2007 CHRIS WARE
2008 LYNDA BARRY
2009 CHARLES BURNS
2010 NEIL GAIMAN
2011 ALISON BECHDEL
2012 FRANÇOISE MOULY
2013 JEFF SMITH

THE BEST AMERICAN

Comics

2013

EDITED *and with an*

INTRODUCTION *by* Jeff Smith

JESSICA ABEL & MATT MADDEN,
series editors

HOUGHTON MIFFLIN HARCOURT
BOSTON ▪ NEW YORK   2013

www.hmhbooks.com

Library of Congress Cataloging-in-Publication Data is available.

ISBN 978-0-547-99546-5

Book design: Robert Overholtzer   Cover design: Kate Beaton   Endpaper art: Laura Park

PRINTED IN THE UNITED STATES OF AMERICA

DOC 10 9 8 7 6 5 4 3 2 1

Permissions credits are located on page 382.

Contents

Foreword

Right at the outset, some news from us: this is our last volume as series editors of the *Best American Comics*. We are currently living in France on an extended residency in Angoulême (home of one of the biggest comics festivals in the world and a generally comics-friendly city) and will be concentrating on producing some of our own work in the years to come. The very capable Bill Kartalopoulos will succeed us. We've got mixed feelings as we draw to the close of this, our sixth and last volume of the *Best American Comics,* but we're happy to have had the opportunity to run this series for so long and to work with so many fantastic guest editors and cartoonists.

When we began our run on the series back in 2008, we joyfully dived into the business of collecting vast numbers of North American comics to read and assess. That big old pile has become a mountain in the last few years, and it threatened to overwhelm us. Nonetheless, we feel a bit of melancholy at the idea of *not* walking around comicons picking up boxes of little colorful books we'd never seen before.

It's worth asking: Why do we need a new anthology every single year that purports to pick out the best? Don't the best rise to the top in any case? And hasn't everyone already read them by the time this appears? How surprising can it really be? From a certain angle you could argue that *BAC* is too obvious or predictable: you'll find here excerpts from and stories by most of the truly well-known and excellent cartoonists of our day. Hardcore comics fans (especially of the indy comics variety) will certainly have read a lot of those pieces. (At the same time, we're pretty confident that each volume contains at least a surprise or two for even the most encyclopedic comics readers.) But the audience for *BAC* is much broader than that. For us, the most important audience for this book is those of you who are coming to comics for the first time or after a long pause in reading. What *BAC* excels at is offering a sampler of many of the most exciting comics coming out in North America in a given year. If you're an assiduous comics reader, and you've gotten complacent about the amazing times we live in, just try to imagine that you'd never heard of Chris Ware or Jim Woodring or Alison Bechdel and that you then open up one of these volumes and come across them for the first time. We like to think we've provided that experience for many readers out there.

And then there's the way that, over time, the series captures a sense of the strong and diverse comics world. Each guest editor has his or her own preferences, but averaged over time, you can really get a picture of the richness of comics in America and a sense of who the interesting artists here are. If you also take into account the nuggets assembled in the list of Notable Comics in the back of each volume, *BAC* is a striking compendium of what's been going on out there in the last six years (eight years from the beginning of the series). That's the beauty of revisiting the idea of "what's best?" with different input every year. You create a kind of tapestry of art and information that simply can't come out of a single volume or short-run anthology, no matter how good. And we can afford to take all kinds of chances on little-known artists, knowing we'll be back next year, and get to pick anew from the greats. They're not going anywhere. We have color, we have page-count, we have distribution. All of that is very good for comics, and wonderful for the new and for the veteran comics reader.

That said, we would never claim to have caught everything worth catching. Especially when it comes to comics on the web, there's an enormous amount of material out there and discoverability is a huge problem. We published our first true webcomic (meaning a comic designed originally to be read online, as opposed to print comic posted online) in 2011—by Kate Beaton, who we're proud to have as our cover girl . . . ahem, Strong Female Character this time around (Google "Kate Beaton" and "Strong Female Character" if you're curious about this joke)—at which time the webcomics explosion was well established among the gag-a-day crowd, but hadn't made a huge dent in the rest of the comics world. What a difference two years make. This year, we could barely keep up with the tsunami of great stuff published online. Or more often, online, then offline, then online again. It's a series editor's nightmare: when and where was this thing first published? Such basic info is often very hard to come by. And with comics buried in apps, PDFs, and .cmx files, not to mention Facebook pages and blogs, actually getting a sense of what's out there is virtually impossible at this point. Bill K, *bonne chance* say we from our outpost in France!

In a parallel track to our work on BAC, we've been teaching comics at the School of Visual Arts in New York, among other places, and we have written two textbooks on making comics, *Drawing Words & Writing Pictures* and *Mastering Comics*. Comics education is surging, with new programs popping up all over the country and all over the world. It's just beginning, but we're already seeing the effects in the variety of subject matter coming into comics, the more diverse backgrounds of creators, and the remarkable skill and passion shown by those who devoted years of formal study to the art. And BAC has an important role to play in the classroom, functioning de facto as an annually updated reader for many classes devoted to the study of comics. We've even heard of our forewords being assigned as homework! (Hi, kids, and sorry, this won't take much longer!)

We've said it before, but it's worth repeating: we're especially proud of our work on the Notable comics lists, and in republishing and publicizing them. The work that actually appears in BAC is great every year, but it can't possibly cover all that's good out in the American comics world. With the additional one hundred or so titles in the back of each volume (and online in user-friendly linked format at bestamericancomics .com and dw-wp.com), one can put together a truly decent annual reading list.

Finally, we are very proud to have had a hand in choosing our guest editors (with the exception of Lynda Barry, who was already lined up when we took on the job), including a few who are yet to come. This series would not be anywhere near as good as it is without the passionate and eclectic guest editors we've managed to wrangle into agreeing to work with us. It is not an easy job. As much as we get worn out by reading through so many hundreds of comics, we are at least spared the final judgment: the Solomonic choices the guest editor has to make are truly painful at times. In selecting candidates for the job, we have tried to find a balance of backgrounds and tastes to keep the series surprising and lively. We're particularly pleased that half the guest editors we've worked with have been women, especially since they have all lamented (correctly, alas) the continuing lack of diversity in this series and in the medium as a whole.

This year, of course, our guest editor is Jeff Smith. Working with Jeff has been a great pleasure, both because he's an excellent editor, hitting deadlines and staying in contact, but also because, as is well known, he's pretty much the nicest guy in comics. We are both huge fans of his work and were very excited to feature *RASL* in a previous volume. This time around, it's his turn to choose, and his selections reflect a strong, cohesive aesthetic marked by powerful storytelling and accessible, welcoming art. That said, in some ways, the selections in this volume are even more diverse than what we've seen before, even as the end result is as well integrated and complete-feeling a volume as we've had in the past. We're sorry to see this collaboration end, and hope we'll get to work with him in some capacity again sometime.

The Best American Comics 2013 represents a selection of the outstanding comics published in North America between September 1, 2011, and August 31, 2012. As series editors, we search out and review comics in as many formats and publications as we can find, from hand-produced minicomics to individual pamphlet issues to graphic novels and collections to webcomics. Our goal is to put as much interesting and worthwhile material in front of our guest editors as they can stand to read through.

This includes works that we consider excellent by reasonable objective standards, but it also certainly includes comics we have a particular fondness for, as well as left-field choices that may not be our cup of tea but that we feel may turn out to be someone else's "best"—and in particular the guest editor's.

Guest editors will sometimes seek out material on their own, as well. The guest editor makes the final selections from this large and varied pool of titles. Idiosyncrasy is encouraged. One of the things we love most about this series is the way it changes from year to year. Each volume is indisputably the best of that year—as seen through one particular pair of eyes.

The job of the series editor is to seek out as much great stuff as possible every year but it's not a task one person (or even two!) can handle alone. We depend on advice and submissions from publishers and artists. Here are the submission guidelines: Comics eligible for consideration must have been published in the eligibility period either on paper on electronically, in English, by a North American author, or one who makes his or her home here. As this 2013 volume hits the shelves, the deadline for the 2014 volume will have already passed and Bill will be on to collecting for the 2015 volume, whose eligibility window is September 1, 2013, to August 31, 2014. A note about webcomics (and comics on the web): We did our best to find what's out there, and we relied on friends, blogs, and "best of" lists to track down important work, but on Bill's behalf we'd like to especially encourage you web cartoonists and publishers to send us submissions either on paper or digitally. Printed submissions can be sent to the address below. Digital submissions can be made in the form of a PDF of the comics published in the eligibility window, with each comic labeled with the exact date it was published online. Better yet, you might make a sub-selection of what you consider your best strips from the year or send a self-contained continuity, as long as it appeared in the eligibility period. You can mail a CD of the PDF to us or e-mail a download link to bestamericancomics@hmhpub.com.

All comics should be labeled with their release date and contact information and mailed to the following address:

Bill Kartalopoulous
Series Editor
The Best American Comics
Houghton Mifflin Harcourt Publishing Company
215 Park Avenue South
New York, NY 10003

Further information is available on the Best American Comics website: bestamerican comics.com

We'd like to thank all the amazing guest editors we've had the honor of working with these past six years: Lynda Barry, Charles Burns, Neil Gaiman, Alison Bechdel, Françoise Mouly, and Jeff Smith. Your dedication, sensitivity, and thoughtfulness—extending beyond the comics selections to cover and endpaper artists and the design and feel of the whole book—have made each volume excellent in its own way, and it's been an honor and a thrill for us to collaborate with you. We'd also like to thank the design and production team that has worked with us for all of these volumes, in particular: David Futato, who designs the book's interior, Christopher Moisan, who art directs the covers and endpapers, and Beth Burleigh Fuller, who oversees it all and makes sure we don't hit any icebergs. We'd also like to thank the series of in-house editors we've worked with: Anjali Singh (who also invited us aboard in the first place), Meagan Stacey, Johnathan Wilber, and our current editor, Nicole Angeloro. And we'd like to again acknowledge the important groundwork laid by the first editor and series editor, Meg Lemke and Anne Elizabeth Moore. Thanks also to our assiduous, meticulous, and just super-nice studio assistants for this year's volume, Li-Or Zaltzman, Kou Chen, and Wyeth Yates; as well as, as always, to all the artists and publishers from all over who sent in submissions.

We're ready to move on to new projects and, most important, to get back to being authors ourselves. Nonetheless, we are going to miss this job (after all, who can really complain about being paid money to read comics?!) and the front-row seat it gave us to all the great comics that are coming out in North America in recent years. We're proud of the work we've done, and we are very excited to see how the series develops under the guidance of Bill and guest editors to come. We look forward to whatever surprises the next volume has for us when we pick it up in a bookstore in the fall of 2014.

JESSICA ABEL and MATT MADDEN

Introduction

The boxes started arriving around Thanksgiving and kept coming in waves over the next twelve months. Cartons stuffed with comics from the previous year; anthologies, comic books, trade paperbacks; monster batches of indies and self-published stuff; secret passwords to online comics, and last, a mother lode of big, gorgeous, hardcover graphic novels. For an entire year, my studio was piled from one end to the other with stacks and stacks of comics in every shape, size, and genre; running the gamut from glorious, amateur, DIY silk-screened minicomics to professionally designed 500-plus-page marvels from major New York publishing houses.

How great is that? The nine-year-old in me loved every minute of having those piles around, and as guest editor for *Best American Comics,* it was my job to read the hell out of them. I swear, there was one day I sat on the floor with a glass of milk and a plate of cookies and did nothing but read comics all day. Of course, some days there were fewer cookies and milk, and more bourbon, but in any case, a good time was had.

So what *is* a comic? In these days of graphic novels, albums, stapled booklets, self-published 'zines, and webcomics, readers are presented with an impressive array of new and tempting formats, more than at any other time in comics history. But comics are more than the object itself, surely. Are comics, then, the sum of their subjects—such as superheroes, or talking animals, or literary tales of modern life and quiet desperation? No, those are genres. I would say that comics are the art form itself: The art of taking still drawings and making them move by using emotion, skill, characters, settings, and placement to keep the thing alive, panel after panel. This is a rare talent among the cartoonists of the world, but when you find it, it's treasure. And you will find treasure in this book.

As I slowly worked through the stacks, it was humbling and a little overwhelming to see the range of talent and relative youth of the creators. In terms of art, imagination, format, and opportunities, there are no limits. I'd say comics have broken out of the box, but no one remembers where the box is. We are truly in a golden age.

How did we ever get here? For those of us from that ancient generation of cartoonists that entered the field in the '80s and early '90s (from whom all the guest editors of this series so far have come), this is exactly what we were striving for—and now it is here. "It" being comics that are the original vision of an author, being read by the widest possible audience.

I wonder if you can imagine how impossible the book that you hold in your hands is.

Not that long ago, comics were considered children's fare, beneath notice at best, and at worst the territory of the outsider. Even as a kid, I knew that was ridiculous . . . but then, I was an outsider, so my opinion didn't count.

Prior to the underground comix of the '60s and '70s, making comics was akin to a factory job; a writer, or penciler, inker, or letterer worked to fill the pages of a magazine devoted to a company-owned character, usually a superhero or a funny animal. Not that there weren't artists in the industry at that time—quite the opposite, there were some outright geniuses toiling their way into fans' hearts.

But in the collection that follows, you won't find a single comic that was done on someone else's time. Every piece is the artistic output of an author or a pair of collaborators with a unique voice. That's an astonishing thought in a field once considered commercial, ephemeral, and disposable.

The Age of the Cartoonist (the artist who writes and draws his or her own work) has arrived. There are no rules or boundaries other than imagination and skill. The democratization brought about by self-publishing, the small press, and the Internet has brought with it an influx of outside influences. No longer the province of company-dictated stories and characters, or restrained by conventional ideas of what a comic book is or who it should be read by, the field has exploded to encompass every known topic. From the early days of avant-garde reactionary tales about sex and drugs to fiction and autobiography, documentary and historical reporting, humor and adventure, and just plain surrealism, comics have become idiosyncratic expressions that are transcendent and human.

I suppose (and hope) that the above statement is obvious in 2013, but I like saying it anyway.

As the art form flowers, the cartoonists are blossoming as well, which has, happily, lead to longer, more complex works—which brings us to the limitations of a "best of" anthology like this. Longer means you have to excerpt. Excerpting from a longer novel isn't the perfect way to present a work, but when it had to be done, I tried to find a succinct portion to represent the piece honestly and effectively.

And of course, I have limitations. I'm just another cartoonist and this compilation reflects my tastes—even though I'm pretty wide-minded, this is a much broader field than it was twenty years ago, and I've done my best to create an enjoyable flow through a variety of themes, genres, and styles. My main criteria: originality; grasp of the tools and syntax of panel-to-panel progression; and most important, if the thing surprised me, it was in.

I'd like to thank the series editors Jessica Abel and Matt Madden for all their help and support. Their knowledge and dedication to the art form has no bounds.

So get yourself a glass of milk (or a bourbon), because in front of you awaits wit, style, danger, curiosity, philosophy, metaphysical visions, love, angst, sex, betrayal, and cutting-edge ocular techniques all folded into this thing—this *experience*—we call comics.

JEFF SMITH

THE BEST AMERICAN

Comics 2013

6

Alison Bechdel

Mirror

FROM THE GRAPHIC NOVEL *Are You My Mother?*

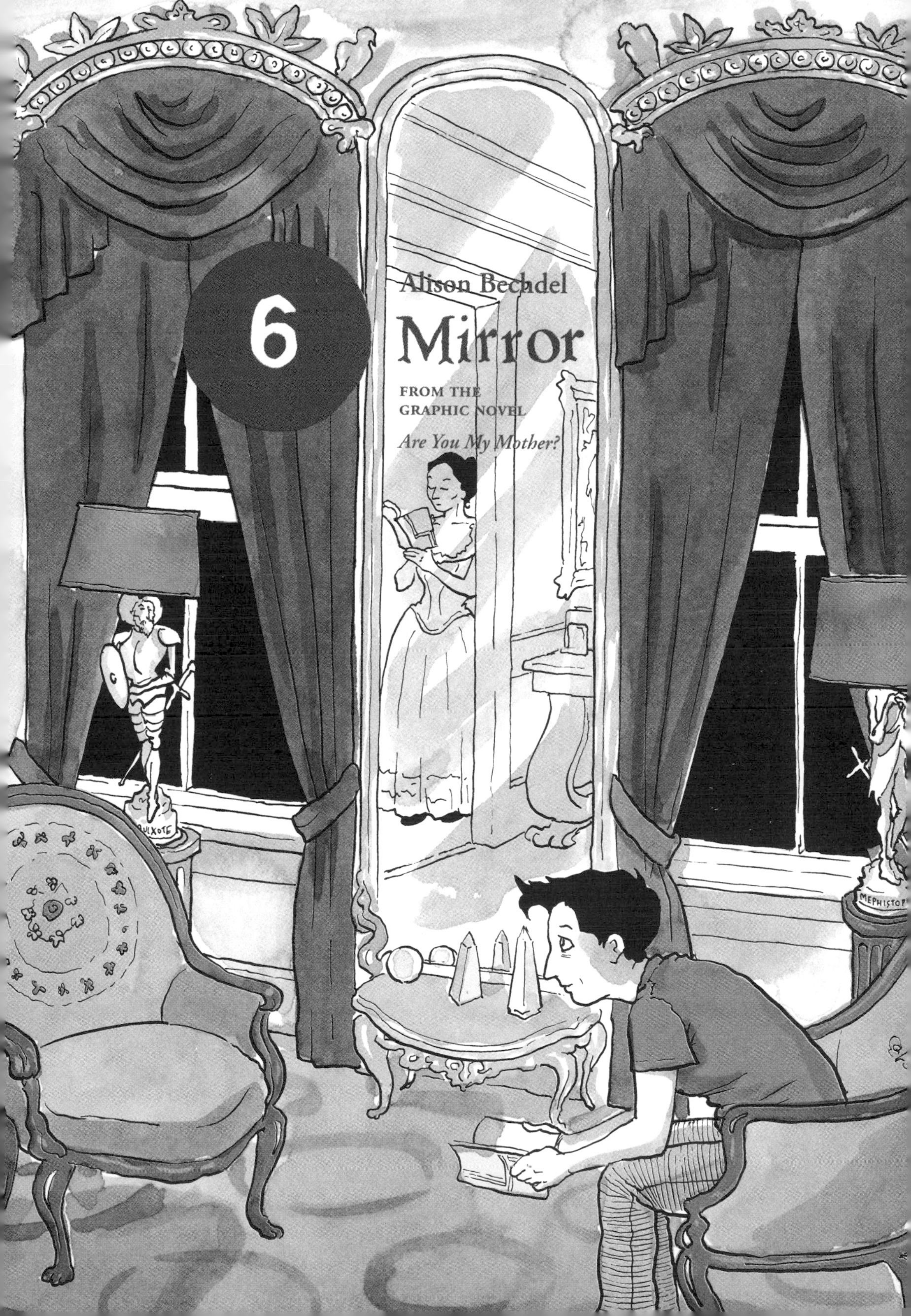
QUIXOTE
MEPHISTOP

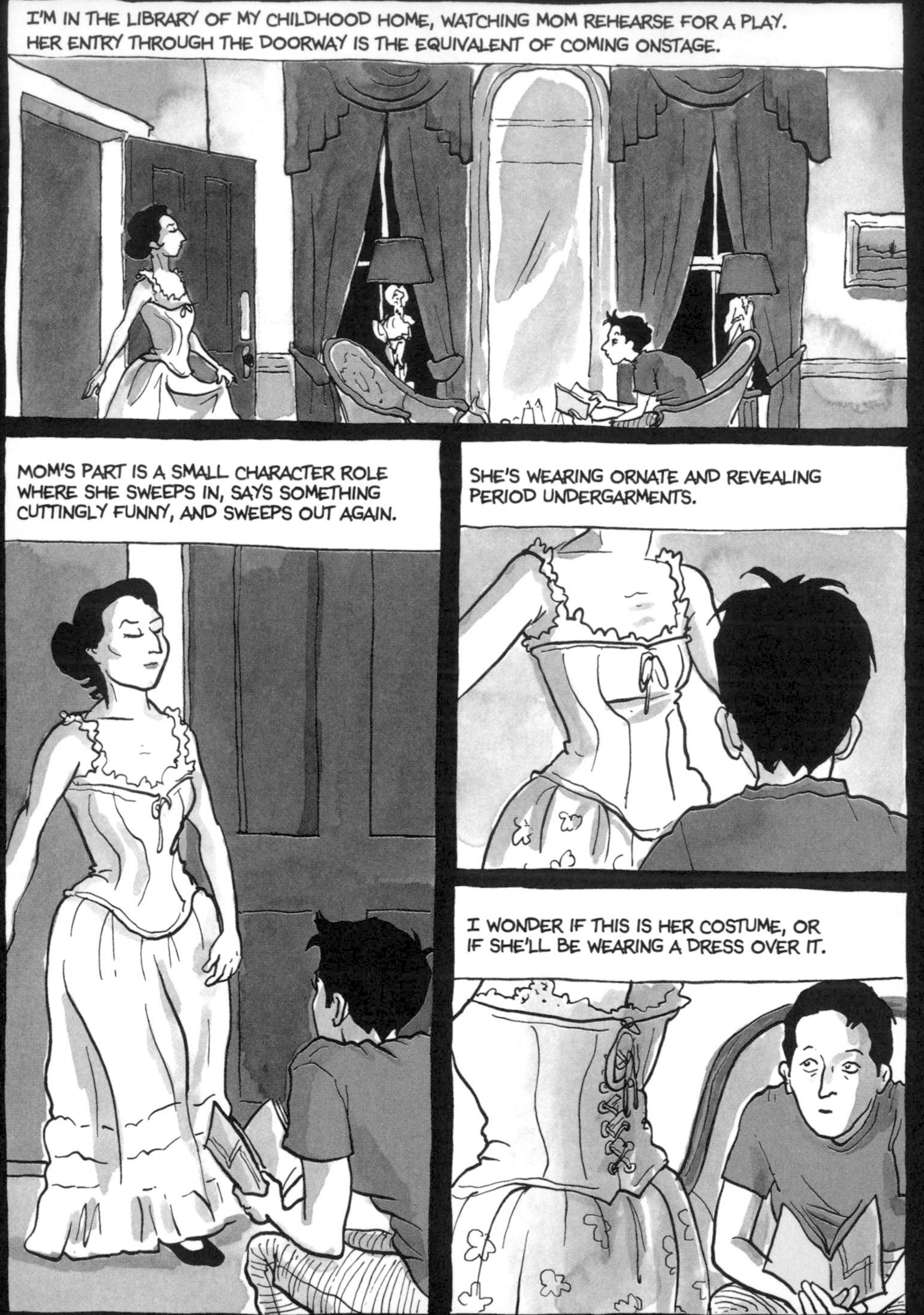
I'M IN THE LIBRARY OF MY CHILDHOOD HOME, WATCHING MOM REHEARSE FOR A PLAY. HER ENTRY THROUGH THE DOORWAY IS THE EQUIVALENT OF COMING ONSTAGE.
MOM'S PART IS A SMALL CHARACTER ROLE WHERE SHE SWEEPS IN, SAYS SOMETHING CUTTINGLY FUNNY, AND SWEEPS OUT AGAIN.
SHE'S WEARING ORNATE AND REVEALING PERIOD UNDERGARMENTS.
I WONDER IF THIS IS HER COSTUME, OR IF SHE'LL BE WEARING A DRESS OVER IT.

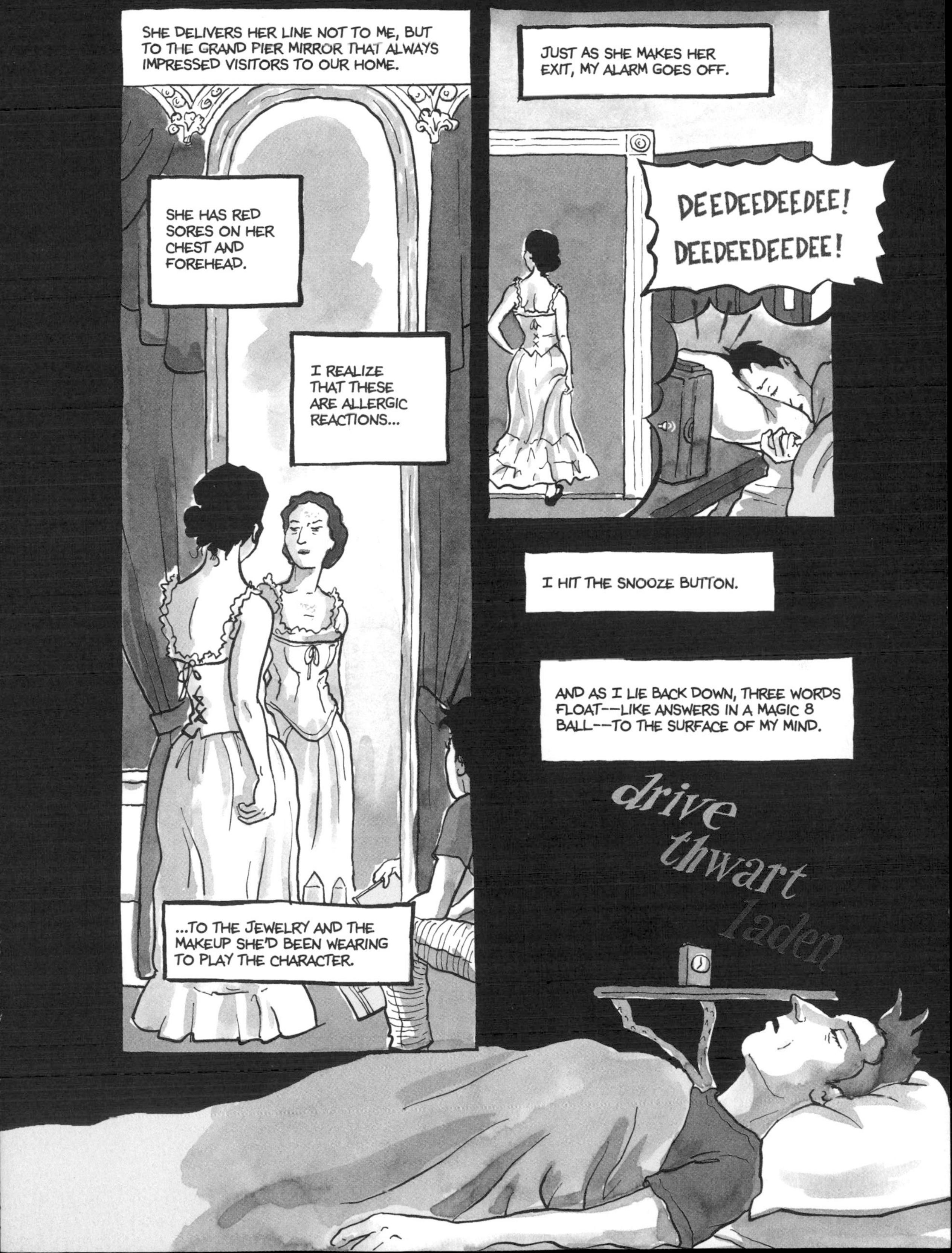
SHE DELIVERS HER LINE NOT TO ME, BUT TO THE GRAND PIER MIRROR THAT ALWAYS IMPRESSED VISITORS TO OUR HOME.
SHE HAS RED SORES ON HER CHEST AND FOREHEAD.
I REALIZE THAT THESE ARE ALLERGIC REACTIONS...
...TO THE JEWELRY AND THE MAKEUP SHE'D BEEN WEARING TO PLAY THE CHARACTER.
JUST AS SHE MAKES HER EXIT, MY ALARM GOES OFF.
DEEDEEDEEDEE! DEEDEEDEEDEE!
I HIT THE SNOOZE BUTTON.
AND AS I LIE BACK DOWN, THREE WORDS FLOAT--LIKE ANSWERS IN A MAGIC 8 BALL--TO THE SURFACE OF MY MIND.
drive
thwart
laden

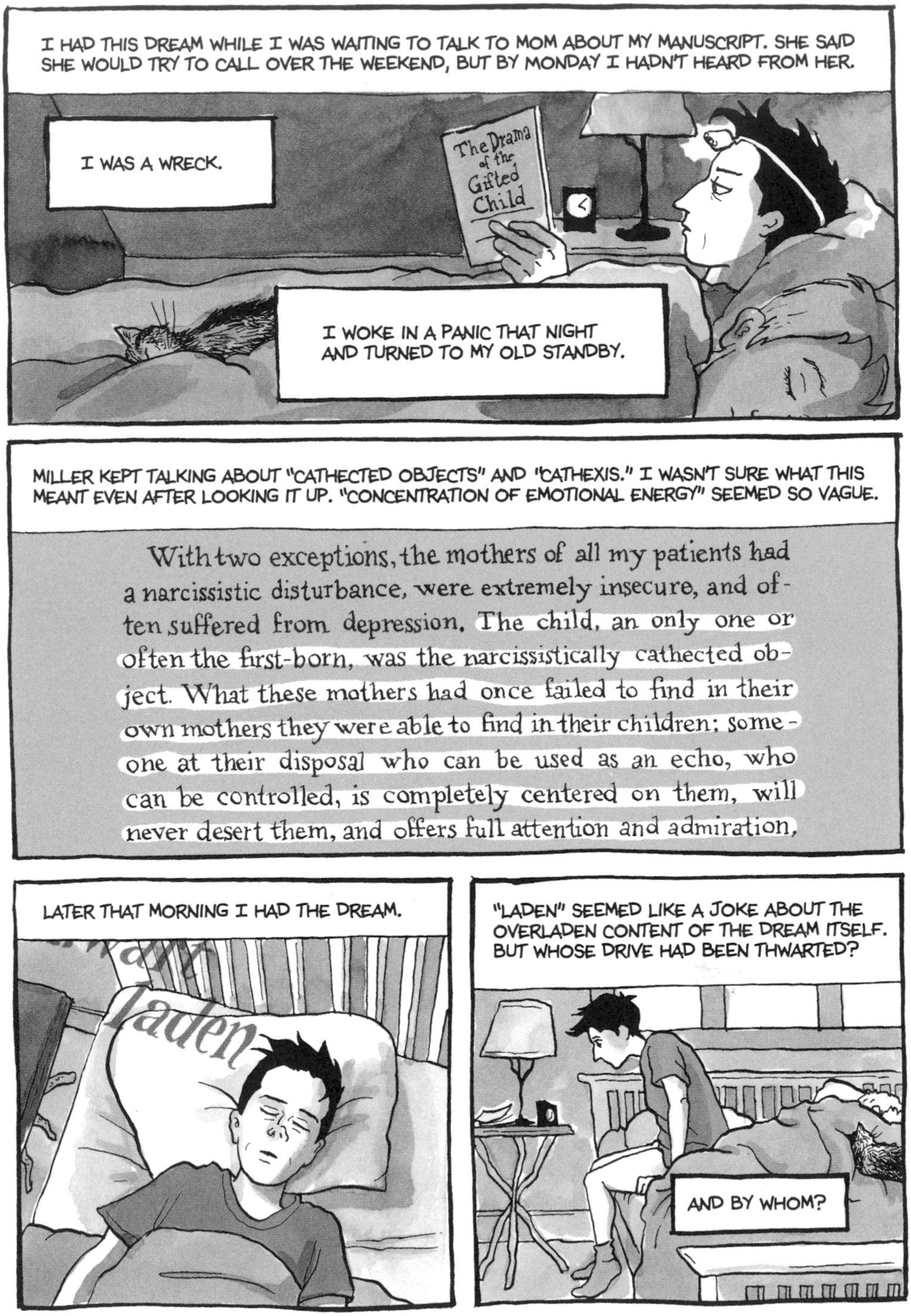
I HAD THIS DREAM WHILE I WAS WAITING TO TALK TO MOM ABOUT MY MANUSCRIPT. SHE SAID SHE WOULD TRY TO CALL OVER THE WEEKEND, BUT BY MONDAY I HADN'T HEARD FROM HER.
I WAS A WRECK.
The Drama of the Gifted Child
I WOKE IN A PANIC THAT NIGHT AND TURNED TO MY OLD STANDBY.
MILLER KEPT TALKING ABOUT "CATHECTED OBJECTS" AND "CATHEXIS." I WASN'T SURE WHAT THIS MEANT EVEN AFTER LOOKING IT UP. "CONCENTRATION OF EMOTIONAL ENERGY" SEEMED SO VAGUE.
With two exceptions, the mothers of all my patients had a narcissistic disturbance, were extremely insecure, and often suffered from depression. The child, an only one or often the first-born, was the narcissistically cathected object. What these mothers had once failed to find in their own mothers they were able to find in their children: someone at their disposal who can be used as an echo, who can be controlled, is completely centered on them, will never desert them, and offers full attention and admiration,
LATER THAT MORNING I HAD THE DREAM.
laden
"LADEN" SEEMED LIKE A JOKE ABOUT THE OVERLADEN CONTENT OF THE DREAM ITSELF. BUT WHOSE DRIVE HAD BEEN THWARTED?
AND BY WHOM?

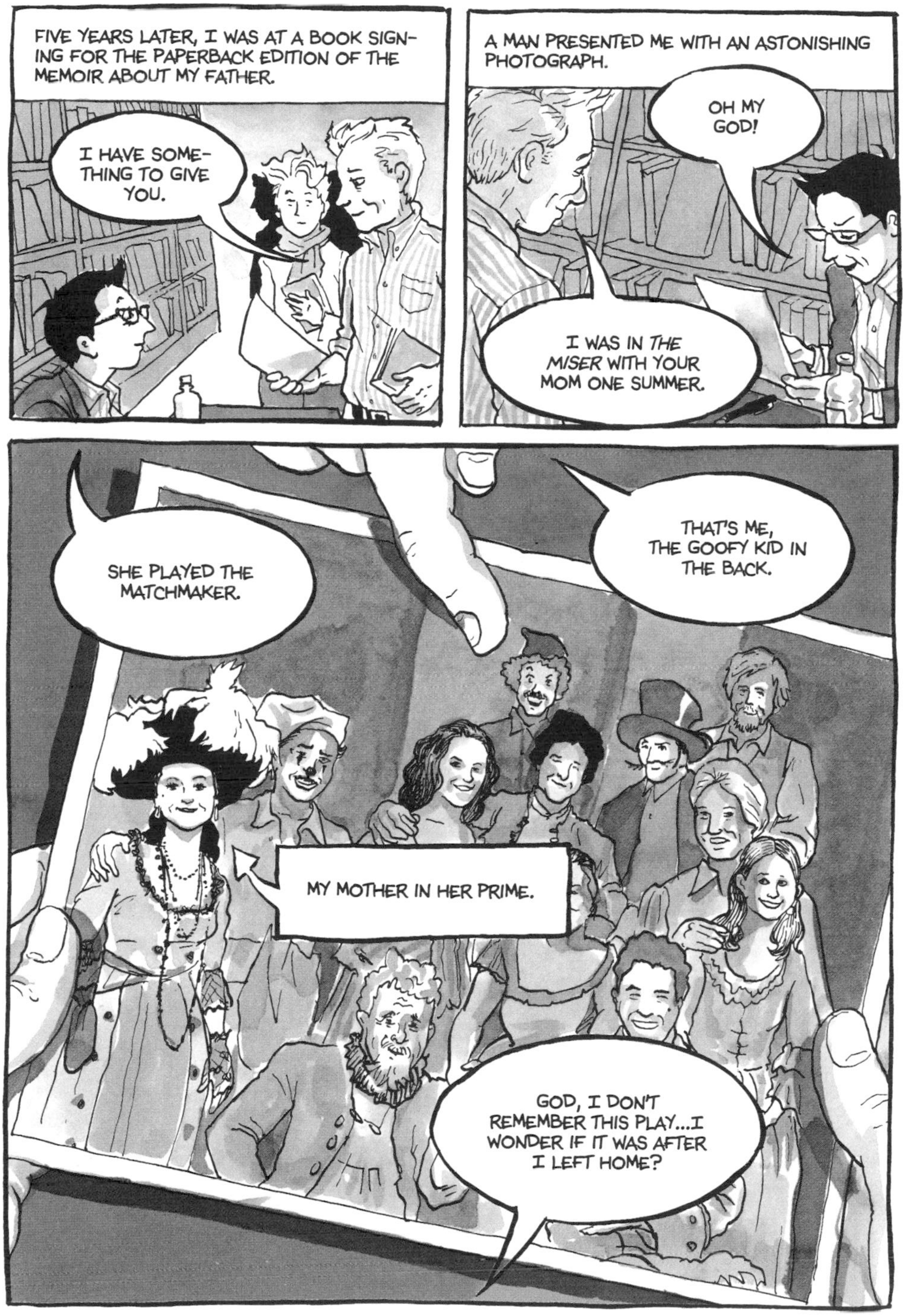
FIVE YEARS LATER, I WAS AT A BOOK SIGNING FOR THE PAPERBACK EDITION OF THE MEMOIR ABOUT MY FATHER.
I HAVE SOMETHING TO GIVE YOU.
A MAN PRESENTED ME WITH AN ASTONISHING PHOTOGRAPH.
OH MY GOD!
I WAS IN *THE MISER* WITH YOUR MOM ONE SUMMER.
SHE PLAYED THE MATCHMAKER.
THAT'S ME, THE GOOFY KID IN THE BACK.
MY MOTHER IN HER PRIME.
GOD, I DON'T REMEMBER THIS PLAY...I WONDER IF IT WAS AFTER I LEFT HOME?

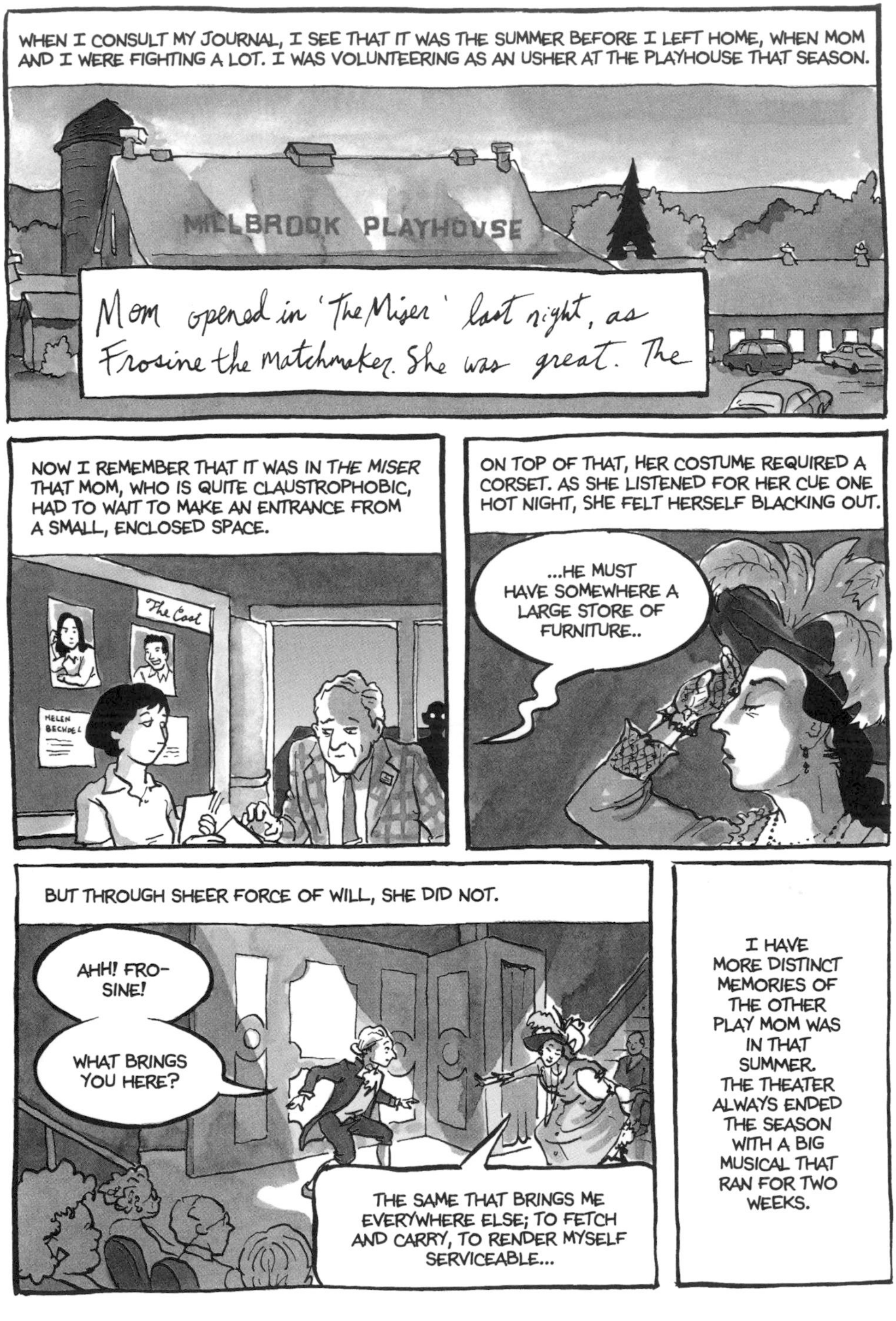

WHEN I CONSULT MY JOURNAL, I SEE THAT IT WAS THE SUMMER BEFORE I LEFT HOME, WHEN MOM AND I WERE FIGHTING A LOT. I WAS VOLUNTEERING AS AN USHER AT THE PLAYHOUSE THAT SEASON.
MILLBROOK PLAYHOUSE
Mom opened in 'The Miser' last night, as Frosine the matchmaker. She was great. The
NOW I REMEMBER THAT IT WAS IN *THE MISER* THAT MOM, WHO IS QUITE CLAUSTROPHOBIC, HAD TO WAIT TO MAKE AN ENTRANCE FROM A SMALL, ENCLOSED SPACE.
The Cast
HELEN BECHDEL
ON TOP OF THAT, HER COSTUME REQUIRED A CORSET. AS SHE LISTENED FOR HER CUE ONE HOT NIGHT, SHE FELT HERSELF BLACKING OUT.
...HE MUST HAVE SOMEWHERE A LARGE STORE OF FURNITURE..
BUT THROUGH SHEER FORCE OF WILL, SHE DID NOT.
AHH! FRO-SINE!
WHAT BRINGS YOU HERE?
THE SAME THAT BRINGS ME EVERYWHERE ELSE; TO FETCH AND CARRY, TO RENDER MYSELF SERVICEABLE...
I HAVE MORE DISTINCT MEMORIES OF THE OTHER PLAY MOM WAS IN THAT SUMMER. THE THEATER ALWAYS ENDED THE SEASON WITH A BIG MUSICAL THAT RAN FOR TWO WEEKS.

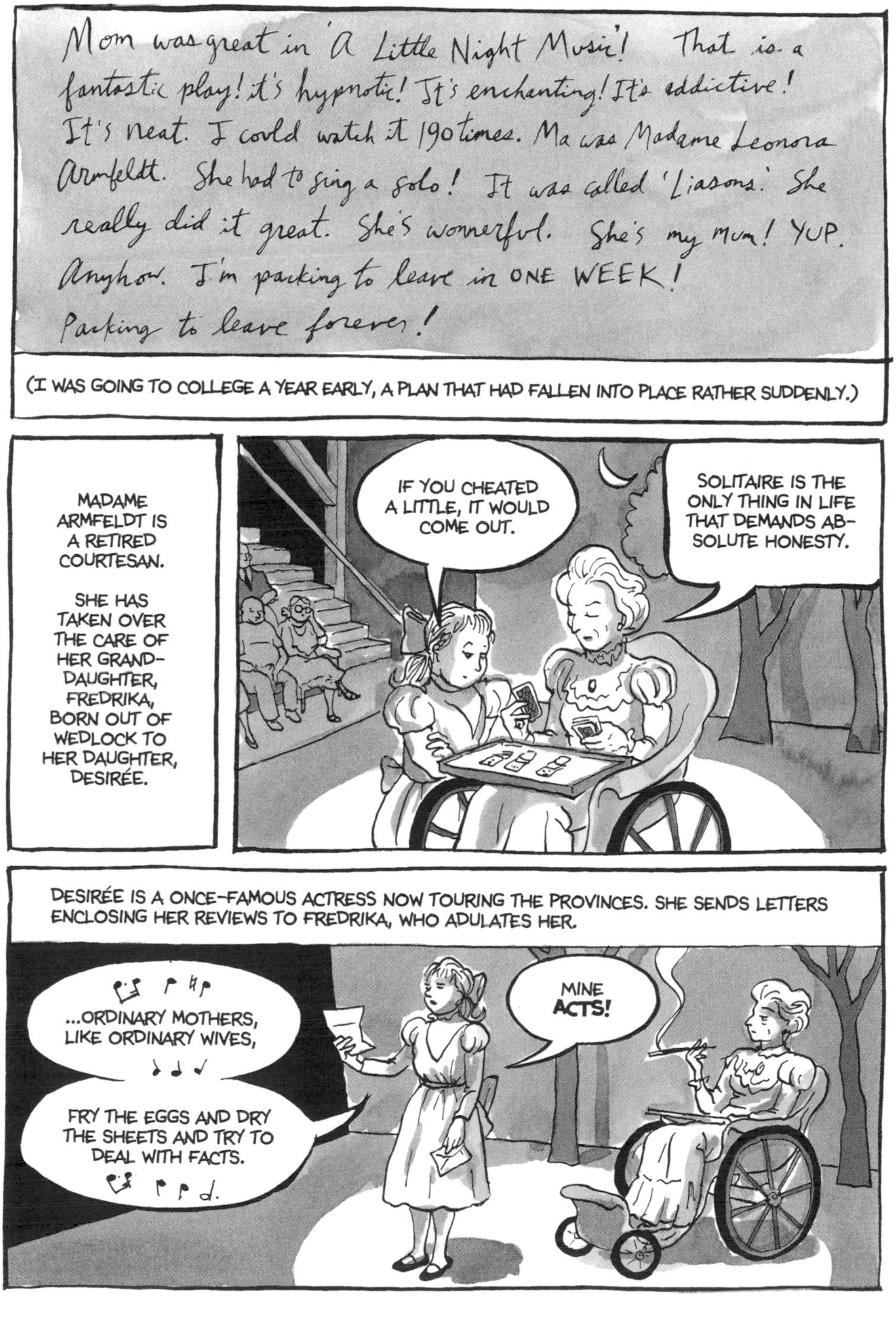
Mom was great in 'A Little Night Music'! That is a fantastic play! it's hypnotic! It's enchanting! It's addictive! It's neat. I could watch it 190 times. Ma was Madame Leonora Armfeldt. She had to sing a solo! It was called 'Liasons.' She really did it great. She's wonnerful. She's my mum! YUP. Anyhow. I'm packing to leave in ONE WEEK! Packing to leave forever!
(I WAS GOING TO COLLEGE A YEAR EARLY, A PLAN THAT HAD FALLEN INTO PLACE RATHER SUDDENLY.)
MADAME ARMFELDT IS A RETIRED COURTESAN.
SHE HAS TAKEN OVER THE CARE OF HER GRAND-DAUGHTER, FREDRIKA, BORN OUT OF WEDLOCK TO HER DAUGHTER, DESIRÉE.
IF YOU CHEATED A LITTLE, IT WOULD COME OUT.
SOLITAIRE IS THE ONLY THING IN LIFE THAT DEMANDS AB-SOLUTE HONESTY.
DESIRÉE IS A ONCE-FAMOUS ACTRESS NOW TOURING THE PROVINCES. SHE SENDS LETTERS ENCLOSING HER REVIEWS TO FREDRIKA, WHO ADULATES HER.
...ORDINARY MOTHERS, LIKE ORDINARY WIVES,
FRY THE EGGS AND DRY THE SHEETS AND TRY TO DEAL WITH FACTS.
MINE ACTS!

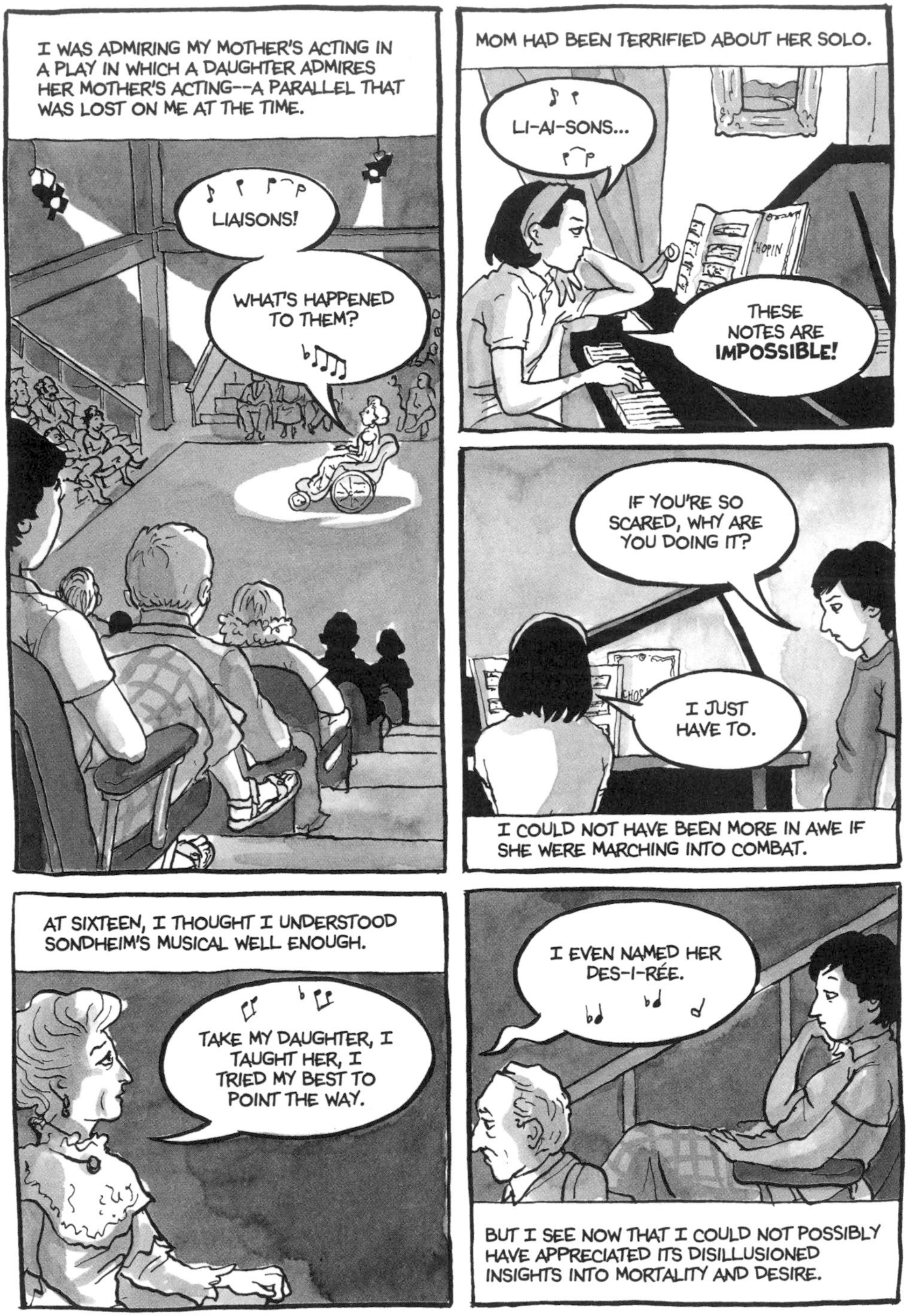
I WAS ADMIRING MY MOTHER'S ACTING IN A PLAY IN WHICH A DAUGHTER ADMIRES HER MOTHER'S ACTING--A PARALLEL THAT WAS LOST ON ME AT THE TIME.
LIAISONS!
WHAT'S HAPPENED TO THEM?
MOM HAD BEEN TERRIFIED ABOUT HER SOLO.
LI-AI-SONS...
CHOPIN
THESE NOTES ARE **IMPOSSIBLE!**
IF YOU'RE SO SCARED, WHY ARE YOU DOING IT?
I JUST HAVE TO.
I COULD NOT HAVE BEEN MORE IN AWE IF SHE WERE MARCHING INTO COMBAT.
AT SIXTEEN, I THOUGHT I UNDERSTOOD SONDHEIM'S MUSICAL WELL ENOUGH.
TAKE MY DAUGHTER, I TAUGHT HER, I TRIED MY BEST TO POINT THE WAY.
I EVEN NAMED HER DES-I-RÉE.
BUT I SEE NOW THAT I COULD NOT POSSIBLY HAVE APPRECIATED ITS DISILLUSIONED INSIGHTS INTO MORTALITY AND DESIRE.

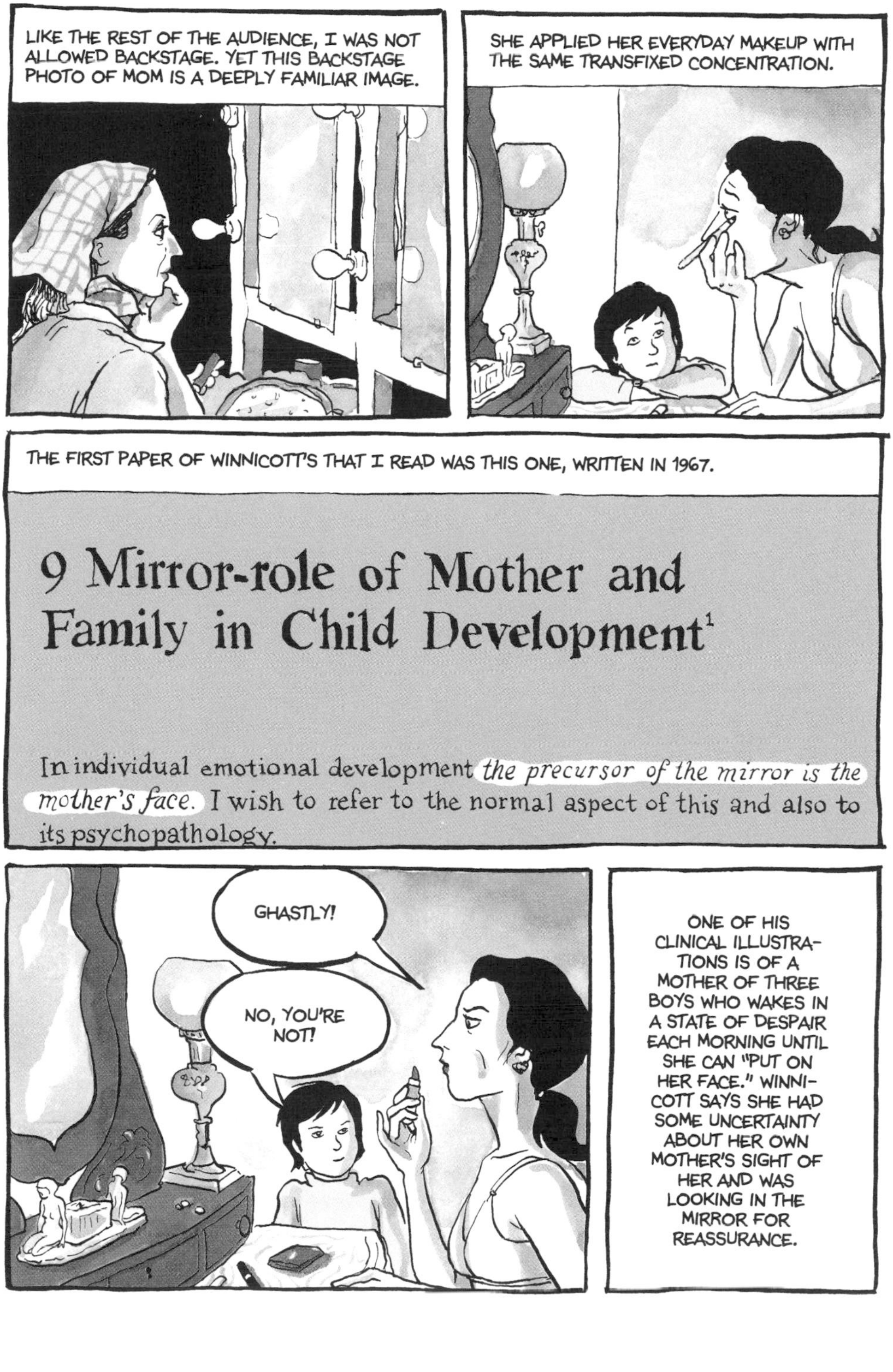
LIKE THE REST OF THE AUDIENCE, I WAS NOT ALLOWED BACKSTAGE. YET THIS BACKSTAGE PHOTO OF MOM IS A DEEPLY FAMILIAR IMAGE.
SHE APPLIED HER EVERYDAY MAKEUP WITH THE SAME TRANSFIXED CONCENTRATION.
THE FIRST PAPER OF WINNICOTT'S THAT I READ WAS THIS ONE, WRITTEN IN 1967.
9 Mirror-role of Mother and Family in Child Development[1]
In individual emotional development the precursor of the mirror is the mother's face. I wish to refer to the normal aspect of this and also to its psychopathology.
GHASTLY!
NO, YOU'RE NOT!
ONE OF HIS CLINICAL ILLUSTRATIONS IS OF A MOTHER OF THREE BOYS WHO WAKES IN A STATE OF DESPAIR EACH MORNING UNTIL SHE CAN "PUT ON HER FACE." WINNICOTT SAYS SHE HAD SOME UNCERTAINTY ABOUT HER OWN MOTHER'S SIGHT OF HER AND WAS LOOKING IN THE MIRROR FOR REASSURANCE.

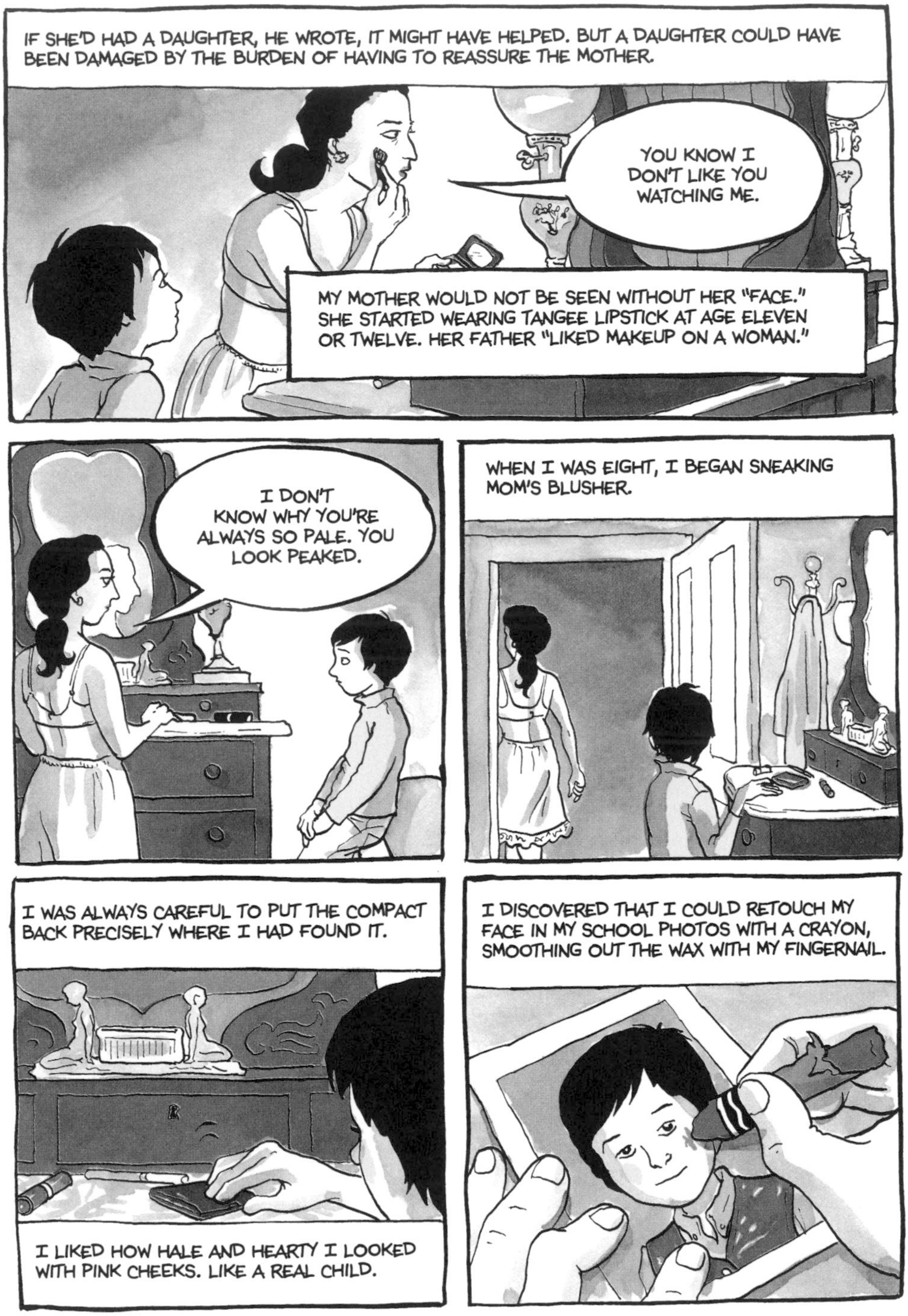
IF SHE'D HAD A DAUGHTER, HE WROTE, IT MIGHT HAVE HELPED. BUT A DAUGHTER COULD HAVE BEEN DAMAGED BY THE BURDEN OF HAVING TO REASSURE THE MOTHER.
YOU KNOW I DON'T LIKE YOU WATCHING ME.
MY MOTHER WOULD NOT BE SEEN WITHOUT HER "FACE." SHE STARTED WEARING TANGEE LIPSTICK AT AGE ELEVEN OR TWELVE. HER FATHER "LIKED MAKEUP ON A WOMAN."
I DON'T KNOW WHY YOU'RE ALWAYS SO PALE. YOU LOOK PEAKED.
WHEN I WAS EIGHT, I BEGAN SNEAKING MOM'S BLUSHER.
I WAS ALWAYS CAREFUL TO PUT THE COMPACT BACK PRECISELY WHERE I HAD FOUND IT.
I LIKED HOW HALE AND HEARTY I LOOKED WITH PINK CHEEKS. LIKE A REAL CHILD.
I DISCOVERED THAT I COULD RETOUCH MY FACE IN MY SCHOOL PHOTOS WITH A CRAYON, SMOOTHING OUT THE WAX WITH MY FINGERNAIL.

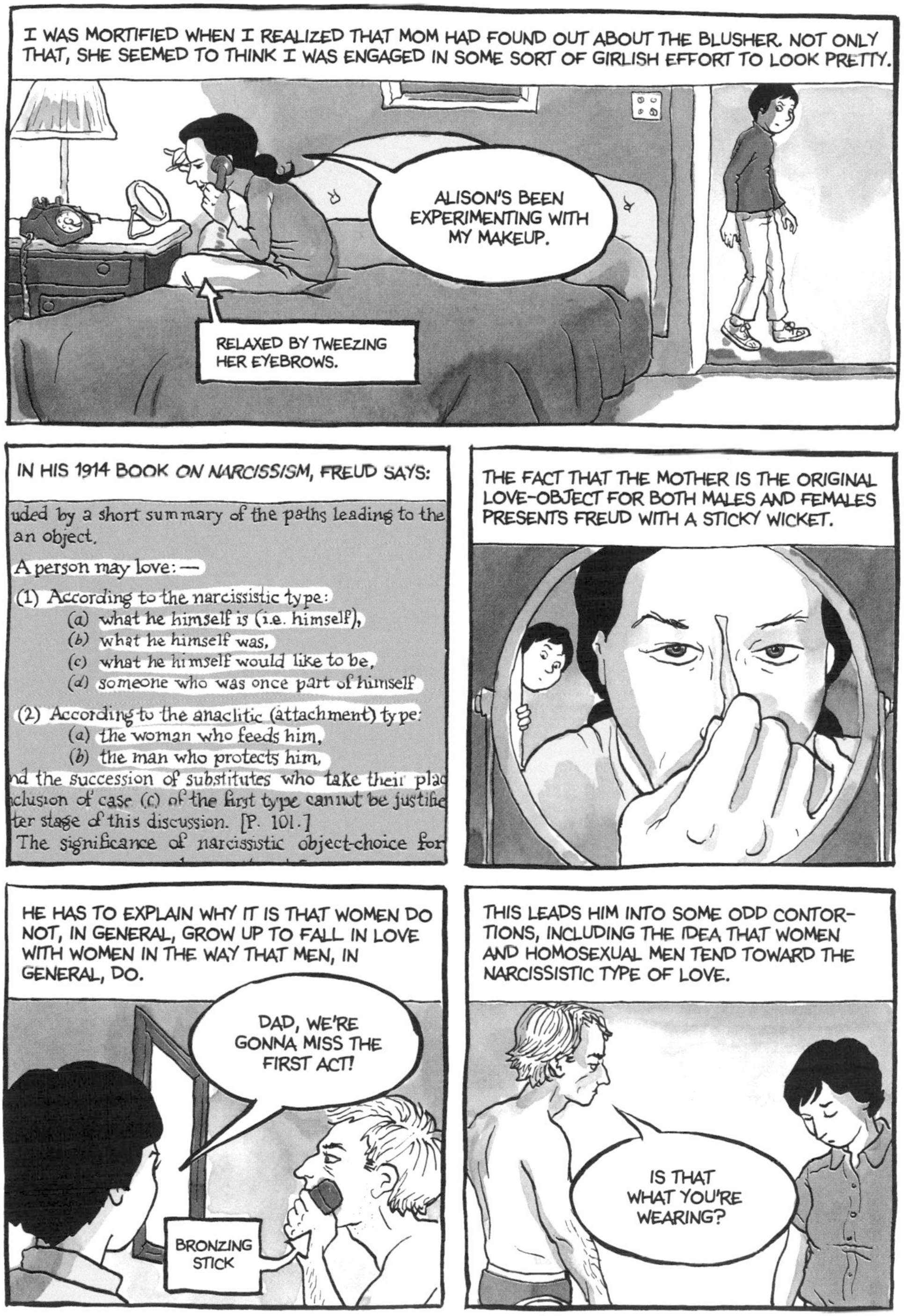
I WAS MORTIFIED WHEN I REALIZED THAT MOM HAD FOUND OUT ABOUT THE BLUSHER. NOT ONLY THAT, SHE SEEMED TO THINK I WAS ENGAGED IN SOME SORT OF GIRLISH EFFORT TO LOOK PRETTY.
ALISON'S BEEN EXPERIMENTING WITH MY MAKEUP.
RELAXED BY TWEEZING HER EYEBROWS.
IN HIS 1914 BOOK *ON NARCISSISM*, FREUD SAYS:
uded by a short summary of the paths leading to the
an object.
A person may love:—
(1) According to the narcissistic type:
(a) what he himself is (i.e. himself),
(b) what he himself was,
(c) what he himself would like to be,
(d) someone who was once part of himself
(2) According to the anaclitic (attachment) type:
(a) the woman who feeds him,
(b) the man who protects him,
nd the succession of substitutes who take their plac
clusion of case (c) of the first type cannot be justifie
ter stage of this discussion. [P. 101.]
The significance of narcissistic object-choice for
THE FACT THAT THE MOTHER IS THE ORIGINAL LOVE-OBJECT FOR BOTH MALES AND FEMALES PRESENTS FREUD WITH A STICKY WICKET.
HE HAS TO EXPLAIN WHY IT IS THAT WOMEN DO NOT, IN GENERAL, GROW UP TO FALL IN LOVE WITH WOMEN IN THE WAY THAT MEN, IN GENERAL, DO.
DAD, WE'RE GONNA MISS THE FIRST ACT!
BRONZING STICK
THIS LEADS HIM INTO SOME ODD CONTORTIONS, INCLUDING THE IDEA THAT WOMEN AND HOMOSEXUAL MEN TEND TOWARD THE NARCISSISTIC TYPE OF LOVE.
IS THAT WHAT YOU'RE WEARING?

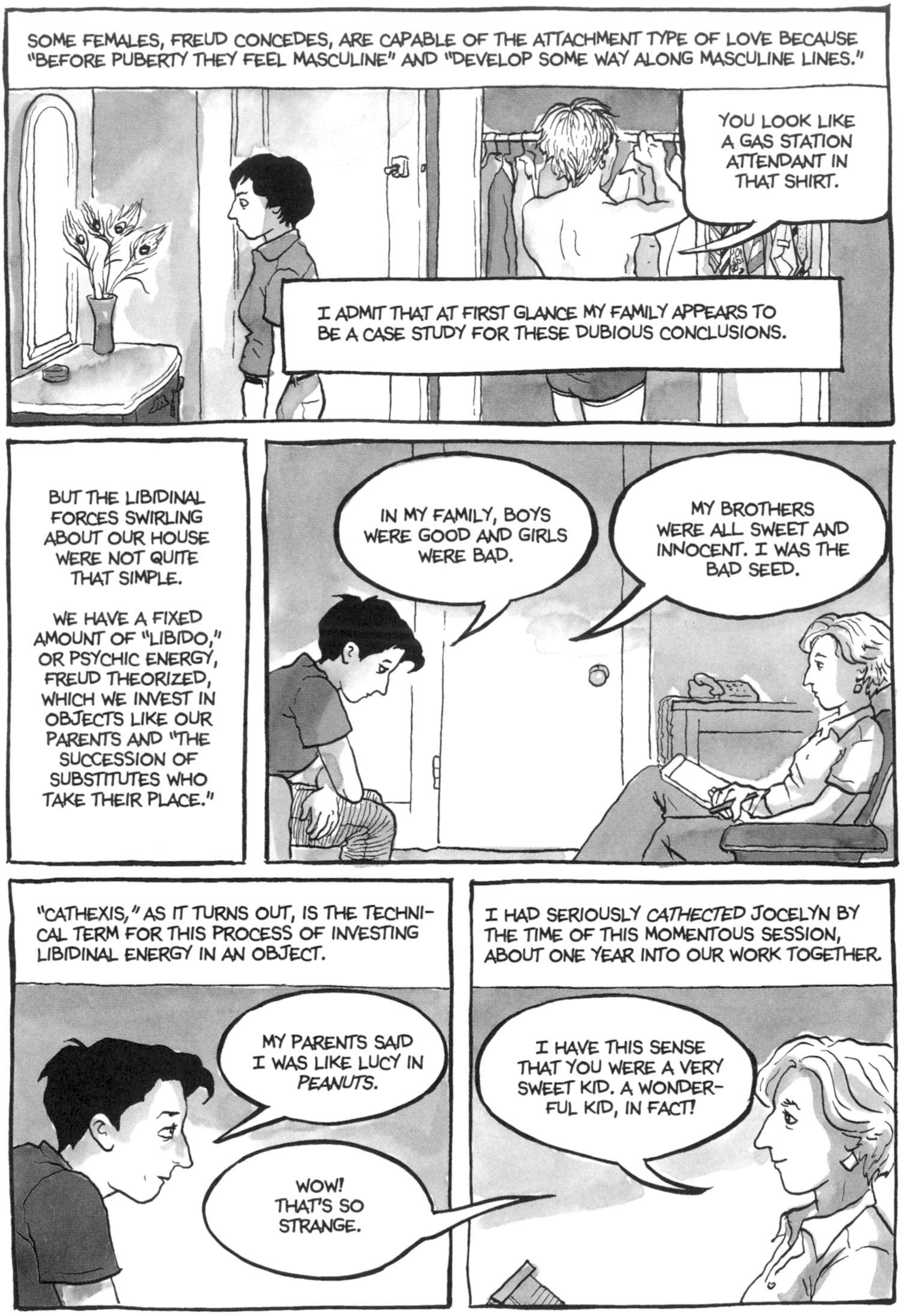

SOME FEMALES, FREUD CONCEDES, ARE CAPABLE OF THE ATTACHMENT TYPE OF LOVE BECAUSE "BEFORE PUBERTY THEY FEEL MASCULINE" AND "DEVELOP SOME WAY ALONG MASCULINE LINES."
YOU LOOK LIKE A GAS STATION ATTENDANT IN THAT SHIRT.
I ADMIT THAT AT FIRST GLANCE MY FAMILY APPEARS TO BE A CASE STUDY FOR THESE DUBIOUS CONCLUSIONS.
BUT THE LIBIDINAL FORCES SWIRLING ABOUT OUR HOUSE WERE NOT QUITE THAT SIMPLE.
WE HAVE A FIXED AMOUNT OF "LIBIDO," OR PSYCHIC ENERGY, FREUD THEORIZED, WHICH WE INVEST IN OBJECTS LIKE OUR PARENTS AND "THE SUCCESSION OF SUBSTITUTES WHO TAKE THEIR PLACE."
IN MY FAMILY, BOYS WERE GOOD AND GIRLS WERE BAD.
MY BROTHERS WERE ALL SWEET AND INNOCENT. I WAS THE BAD SEED.
"CATHEXIS," AS IT TURNS OUT, IS THE TECHNICAL TERM FOR THIS PROCESS OF INVESTING LIBIDINAL ENERGY IN AN OBJECT.
MY PARENTS SAID I WAS LIKE LUCY IN *PEANUTS*.
WOW! THAT'S SO STRANGE.
I HAD SERIOUSLY *CATHECTED* JOCELYN BY THE TIME OF THIS MOMENTOUS SESSION, ABOUT ONE YEAR INTO OUR WORK TOGETHER.
I HAVE THIS SENSE THAT YOU WERE A VERY SWEET KID. A WONDERFUL KID, IN FACT!

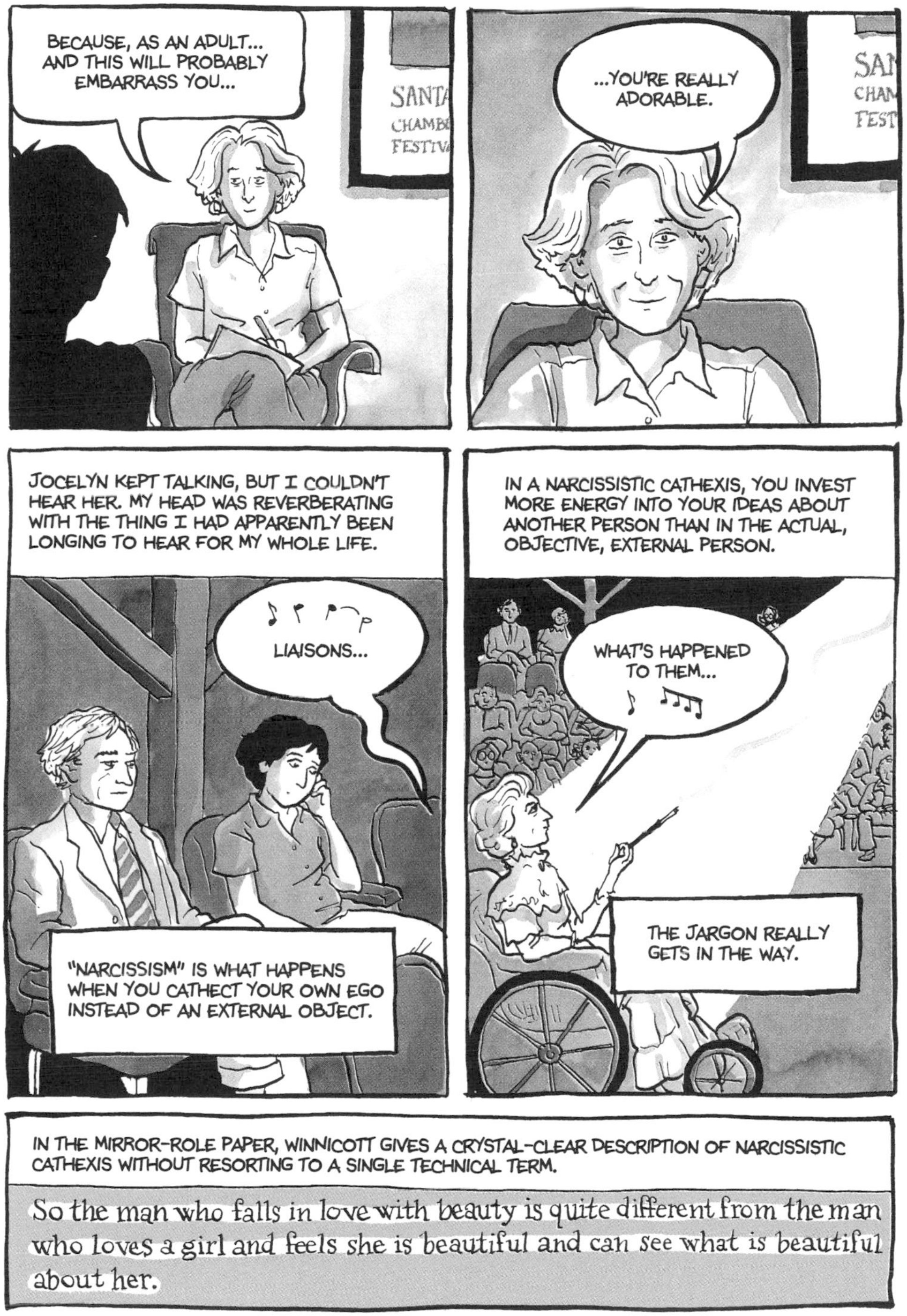
BECAUSE, AS AN ADULT... AND THIS WILL PROBABLY EMBARRASS YOU...
...YOU'RE REALLY ADORABLE.
JOCELYN KEPT TALKING, BUT I COULDN'T HEAR HER. MY HEAD WAS REVERBERATING WITH THE THING I HAD APPARENTLY BEEN LONGING TO HEAR FOR MY WHOLE LIFE.
LIAISONS...
"NARCISSISM" IS WHAT HAPPENS WHEN YOU CATHECT YOUR OWN EGO INSTEAD OF AN EXTERNAL OBJECT.
IN A NARCISSISTIC CATHEXIS, YOU INVEST MORE ENERGY INTO YOUR IDEAS ABOUT ANOTHER PERSON THAN IN THE ACTUAL, OBJECTIVE, EXTERNAL PERSON.
WHAT'S HAPPENED TO THEM...
THE JARGON REALLY GETS IN THE WAY.
IN THE MIRROR-ROLE PAPER, WINNICOTT GIVES A CRYSTAL-CLEAR DESCRIPTION OF NARCISSISTIC CATHEXIS WITHOUT RESORTING TO A SINGLE TECHNICAL TERM.
So the man who falls in love with beauty is quite different from the man who loves a girl and feels she is beautiful and can see what is beautiful about her.

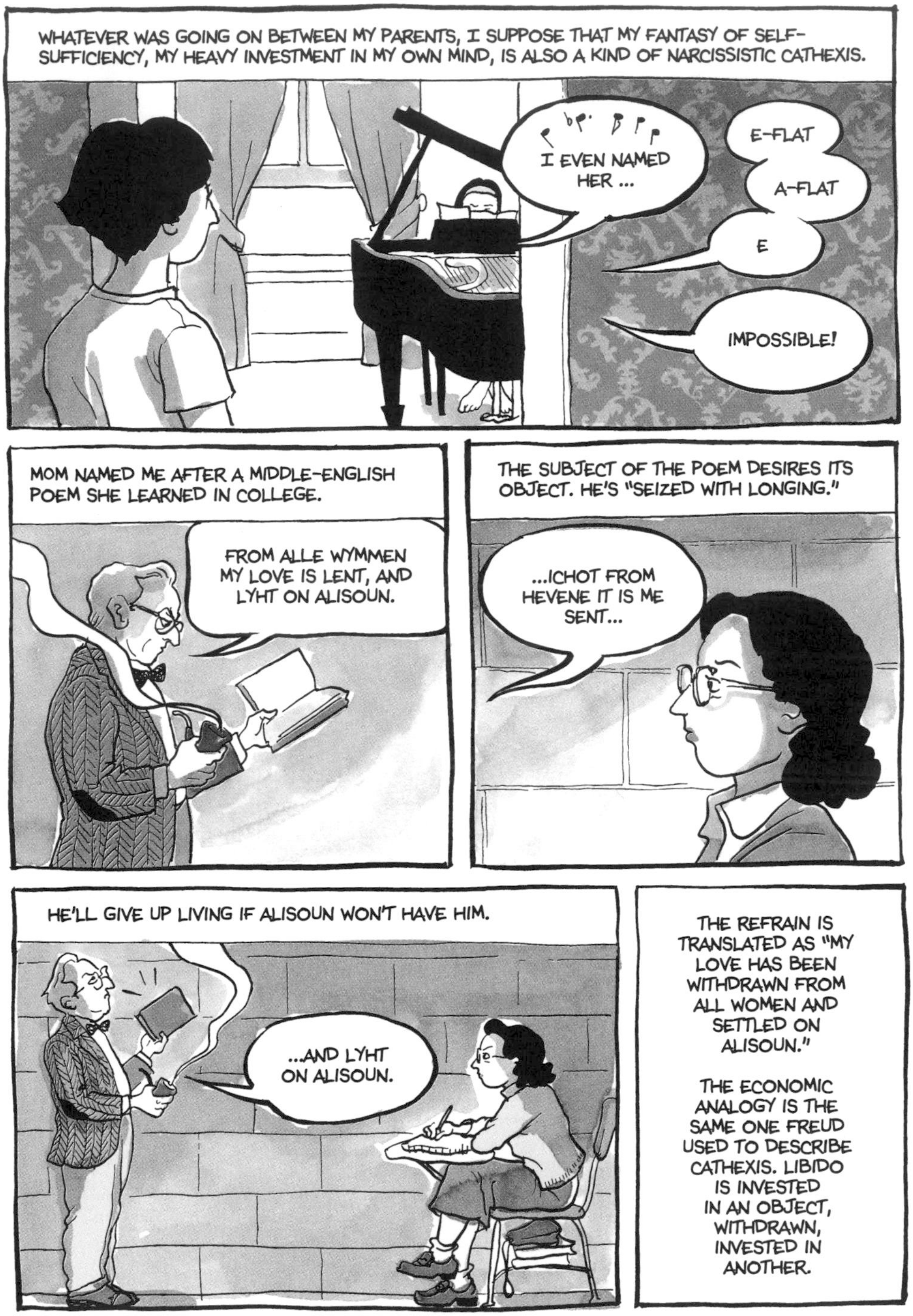
WHATEVER WAS GOING ON BETWEEN MY PARENTS, I SUPPOSE THAT MY FANTASY OF SELF-SUFFICIENCY, MY HEAVY INVESTMENT IN MY OWN MIND, IS ALSO A KIND OF NARCISSISTIC CATHEXIS.
I EVEN NAMED HER ...
E-FLAT
A-FLAT
E
IMPOSSIBLE!
MOM NAMED ME AFTER A MIDDLE-ENGLISH POEM SHE LEARNED IN COLLEGE.
FROM ALLE WYMMEN MY LOVE IS LENT, AND LYHT ON ALISOUN.
THE SUBJECT OF THE POEM DESIRES ITS OBJECT. HE'S "SEIZED WITH LONGING."
...ICHOT FROM HEVENE IT IS ME SENT...
HE'LL GIVE UP LIVING IF ALISOUN WON'T HAVE HIM.
...AND LYHT ON ALISOUN.
THE REFRAIN IS TRANSLATED AS "MY LOVE HAS BEEN WITHDRAWN FROM ALL WOMEN AND SETTLED ON ALISOUN."
THE ECONOMIC ANALOGY IS THE SAME ONE FREUD USED TO DESCRIBE CATHEXIS. LIBIDO IS INVESTED IN AN OBJECT, WITHDRAWN, INVESTED IN ANOTHER.

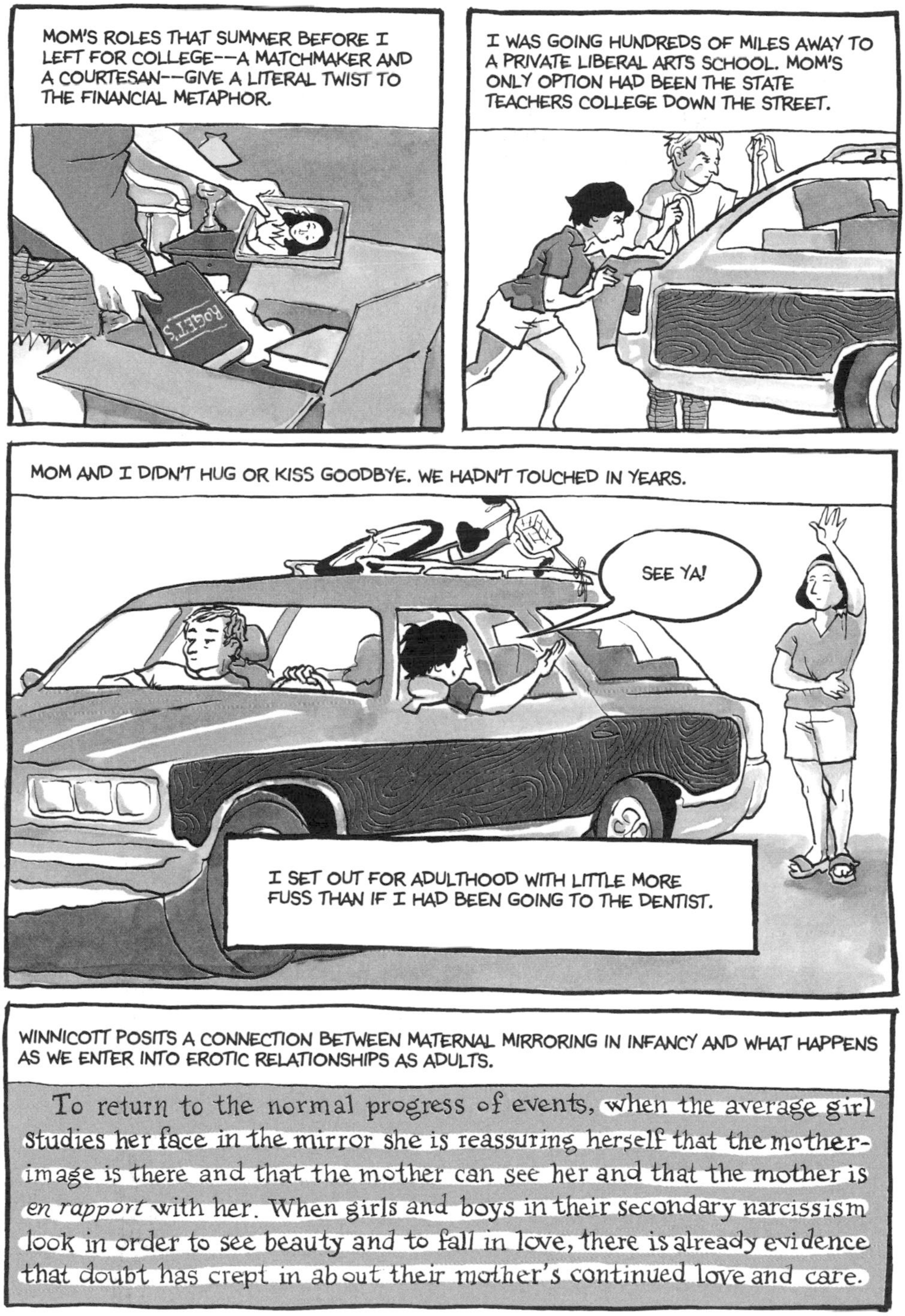

MOM'S ROLES THAT SUMMER BEFORE I LEFT FOR COLLEGE--A MATCHMAKER AND A COURTESAN--GIVE A LITERAL TWIST TO THE FINANCIAL METAPHOR.
ROGET'S
I WAS GOING HUNDREDS OF MILES AWAY TO A PRIVATE LIBERAL ARTS SCHOOL. MOM'S ONLY OPTION HAD BEEN THE STATE TEACHERS COLLEGE DOWN THE STREET.
MOM AND I DIDN'T HUG OR KISS GOODBYE. WE HADN'T TOUCHED IN YEARS.
SEE YA!
I SET OUT FOR ADULTHOOD WITH LITTLE MORE FUSS THAN IF I HAD BEEN GOING TO THE DENTIST.
WINNICOTT POSITS A CONNECTION BETWEEN MATERNAL MIRRORING IN INFANCY AND WHAT HAPPENS AS WE ENTER INTO EROTIC RELATIONSHIPS AS ADULTS.
To return to the normal progress of events, when the average girl studies her face in the mirror she is reassuring herself that the mother-image is there and that the mother can see her and that the mother is *en rapport* with her. When girls and boys in their secondary narcissism look in order to see beauty and to fall in love, there is already evidence that doubt has crept in about their mother's continued love and care.

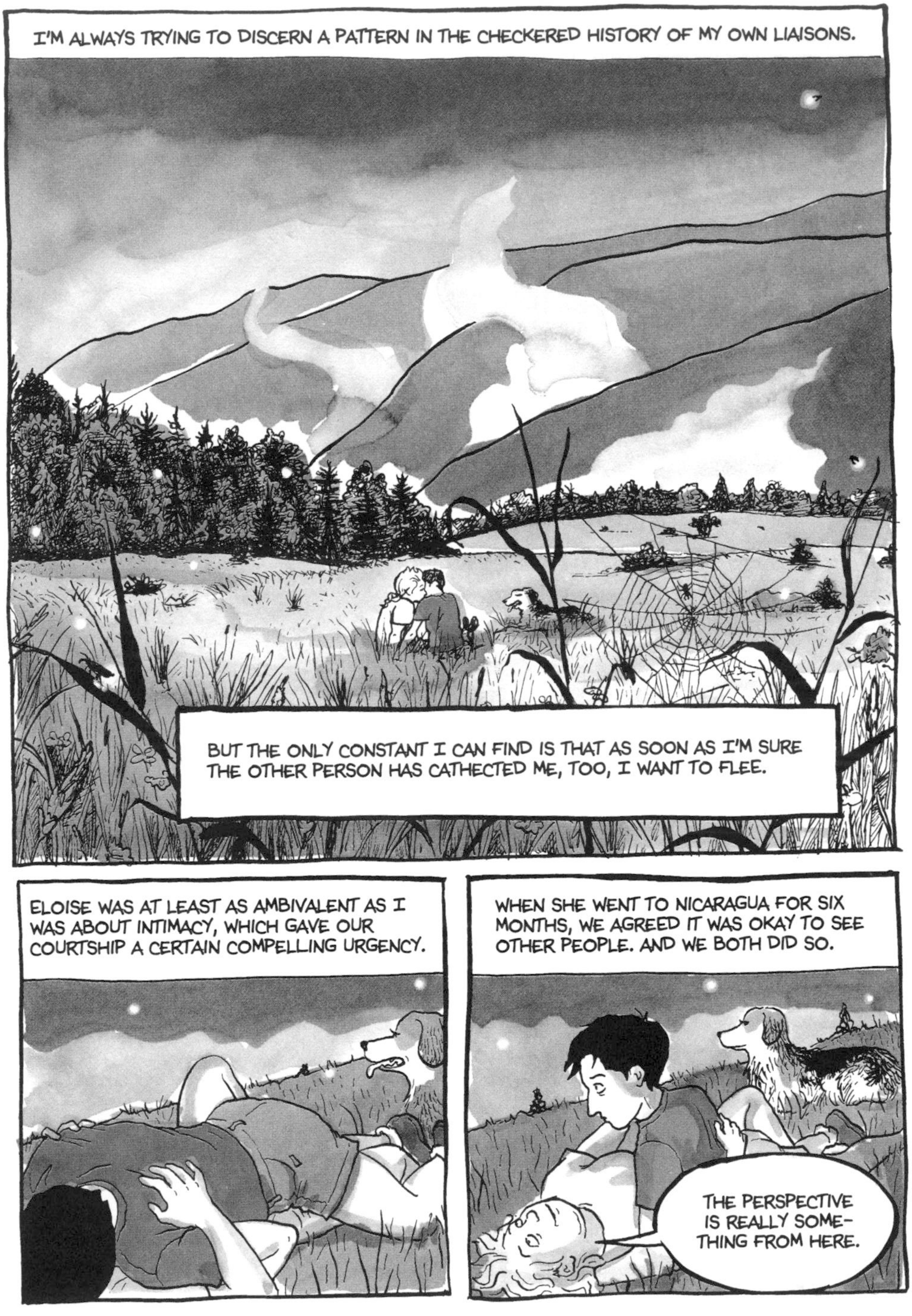
I'M ALWAYS TRYING TO DISCERN A PATTERN IN THE CHECKERED HISTORY OF MY OWN LIAISONS.
BUT THE ONLY CONSTANT I CAN FIND IS THAT AS SOON AS I'M SURE THE OTHER PERSON HAS CATHECTED ME, TOO, I WANT TO FLEE.
ELOISE WAS AT LEAST AS AMBIVALENT AS I WAS ABOUT INTIMACY, WHICH GAVE OUR COURTSHIP A CERTAIN COMPELLING URGENCY.
WHEN SHE WENT TO NICARAGUA FOR SIX MONTHS, WE AGREED IT WAS OKAY TO SEE OTHER PEOPLE. AND WE BOTH DID SO.
THE PERSPECTIVE IS REALLY SOME-THING FROM HERE.

WHEN SHE RETURNED, WE ENDED THESE DALLIANCES, BUT REMAINED LIVING APART. SHE WOULD VISIT ME IN THE CITY, I WOULD VISIT HER IN THE COUNTRY.

SEE?

OUR RELATIONSHIP PROGRESSED WITH EXTREME DELIBERATION.

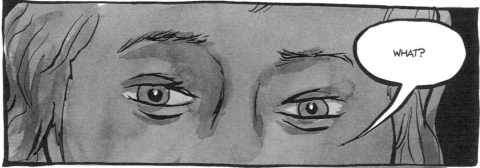

IT WAS A FULL YEAR, FOR EXAMPLE, BEFORE WE REACHED THIS PARTICULAR BENCHMARK:

WHAT?

I LOVE YOU.

AND EVEN THEN, I WAS ACUTELY UNCLEAR WHAT I MEANT BY IT.

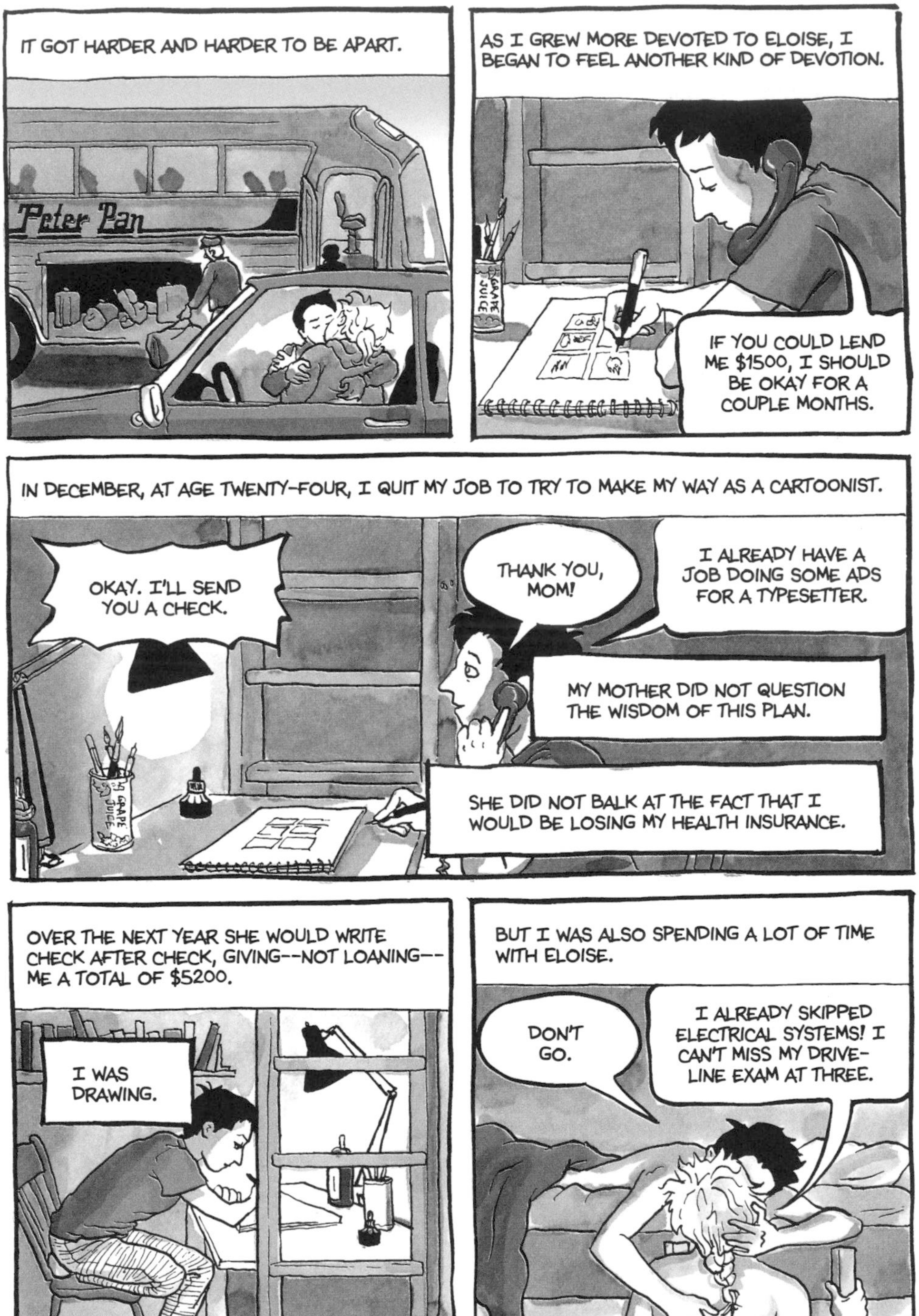
IT GOT HARDER AND HARDER TO BE APART.
Peter Pan
AS I GREW MORE DEVOTED TO ELOISE, I BEGAN TO FEEL ANOTHER KIND OF DEVOTION.
GRAPE JUICE
IF YOU COULD LEND ME $1500, I SHOULD BE OKAY FOR A COUPLE MONTHS.
IN DECEMBER, AT AGE TWENTY-FOUR, I QUIT MY JOB TO TRY TO MAKE MY WAY AS A CARTOONIST.
I ALREADY HAVE A JOB DOING SOME ADS FOR A TYPESETTER.
OKAY. I'LL SEND YOU A CHECK.
THANK YOU, MOM!
MY MOTHER DID NOT QUESTION THE WISDOM OF THIS PLAN.
GRAPE JUICE
SHE DID NOT BALK AT THE FACT THAT I WOULD BE LOSING MY HEALTH INSURANCE.
OVER THE NEXT YEAR SHE WOULD WRITE CHECK AFTER CHECK, GIVING--NOT LOANING--ME A TOTAL OF $5200.
I WAS DRAWING.
BUT I WAS ALSO SPENDING A LOT OF TIME WITH ELOISE.
DON'T GO.
I ALREADY SKIPPED ELECTRICAL SYSTEMS! I CAN'T MISS MY DRIVE-LINE EXAM AT THREE.

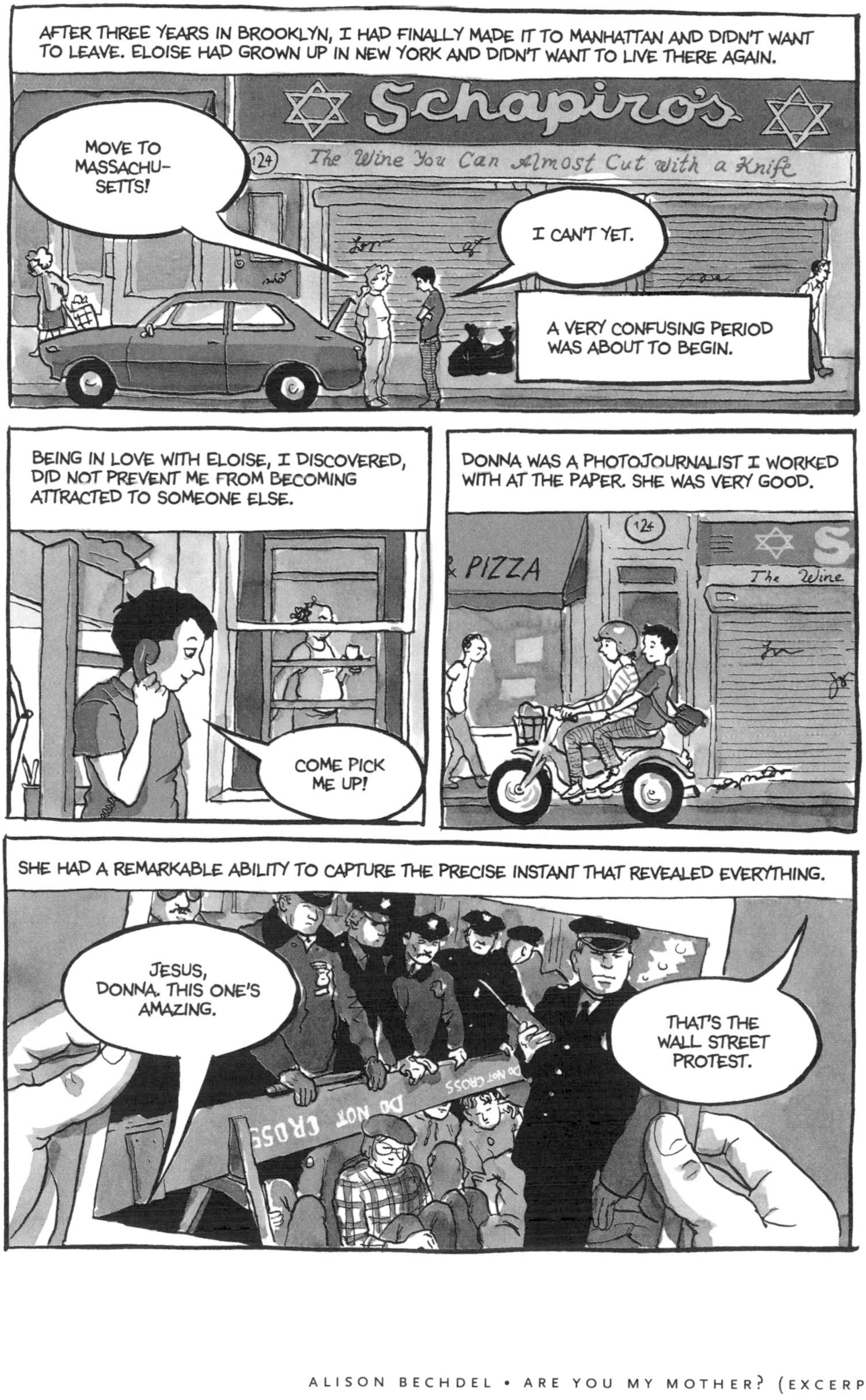
AFTER THREE YEARS IN BROOKLYN, I HAD FINALLY MADE IT TO MANHATTAN AND DIDN'T WANT TO LEAVE. ELOISE HAD GROWN UP IN NEW YORK AND DIDN'T WANT TO LIVE THERE AGAIN.
Schapiro's
124
The Wine You Can Almost Cut with a Knife
MOVE TO MASSACHU-SETTS!
I CAN'T YET.
A VERY CONFUSING PERIOD WAS ABOUT TO BEGIN.
BEING IN LOVE WITH ELOISE, I DISCOVERED, DID NOT PREVENT ME FROM BECOMING ATTRACTED TO SOMEONE ELSE.
COME PICK ME UP!
DONNA WAS A PHOTOJOURNALIST I WORKED WITH AT THE PAPER. SHE WAS VERY GOOD.
124
& PIZZA
The Wine
SHE HAD A REMARKABLE ABILITY TO CAPTURE THE PRECISE INSTANT THAT REVEALED EVERYTHING.
JESUS, DONNA. THIS ONE'S AMAZING.
THAT'S THE WALL STREET PROTEST.
DO NOT CROSS

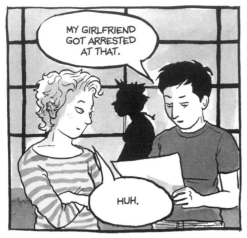

MY GIRLFRIEND GOT ARRESTED AT THAT.
HUH.
OMIGOD, THAT'S HER ! UNDER THE BARRICADE!
Springfield Technical College
A FEW WEEKS LATER, DONNA AND I KISSED AND SLEPT TOGETHER BUT DID NOT HAVE SEX.
I'M IN A MONOGAMOUS RELATIONSHIP.
I THINK I'M ATTRACTED TO YOU BECAUSE YOU'RE UNAVAILABLE.
I TOLD ELOISE, OMITTING SOME DETAILS.
I'M SO FUCKED UP.
I THINK IT'S ABOUT MY CONFLICT OVER WHETHER TO MOVE OR NOT.
THE NEXT TIME SHE CAME TO THE CITY, WE HAD A BAD FIGHT.
MAYBE IT WOULD HELP IF I HAD A SHELF HERE FOR MY STUFF.
A SHELF?
ELOISE SUGGESTED THAT WE SEPARATE FOR THREE WEEKS WHILE I FIGURED THINGS OUT.
OKAY.

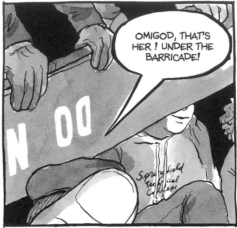

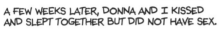

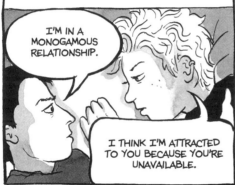

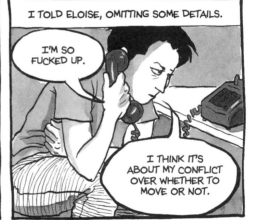

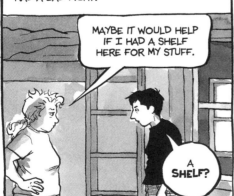

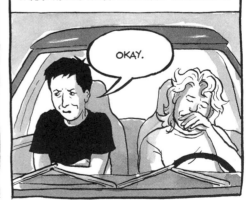

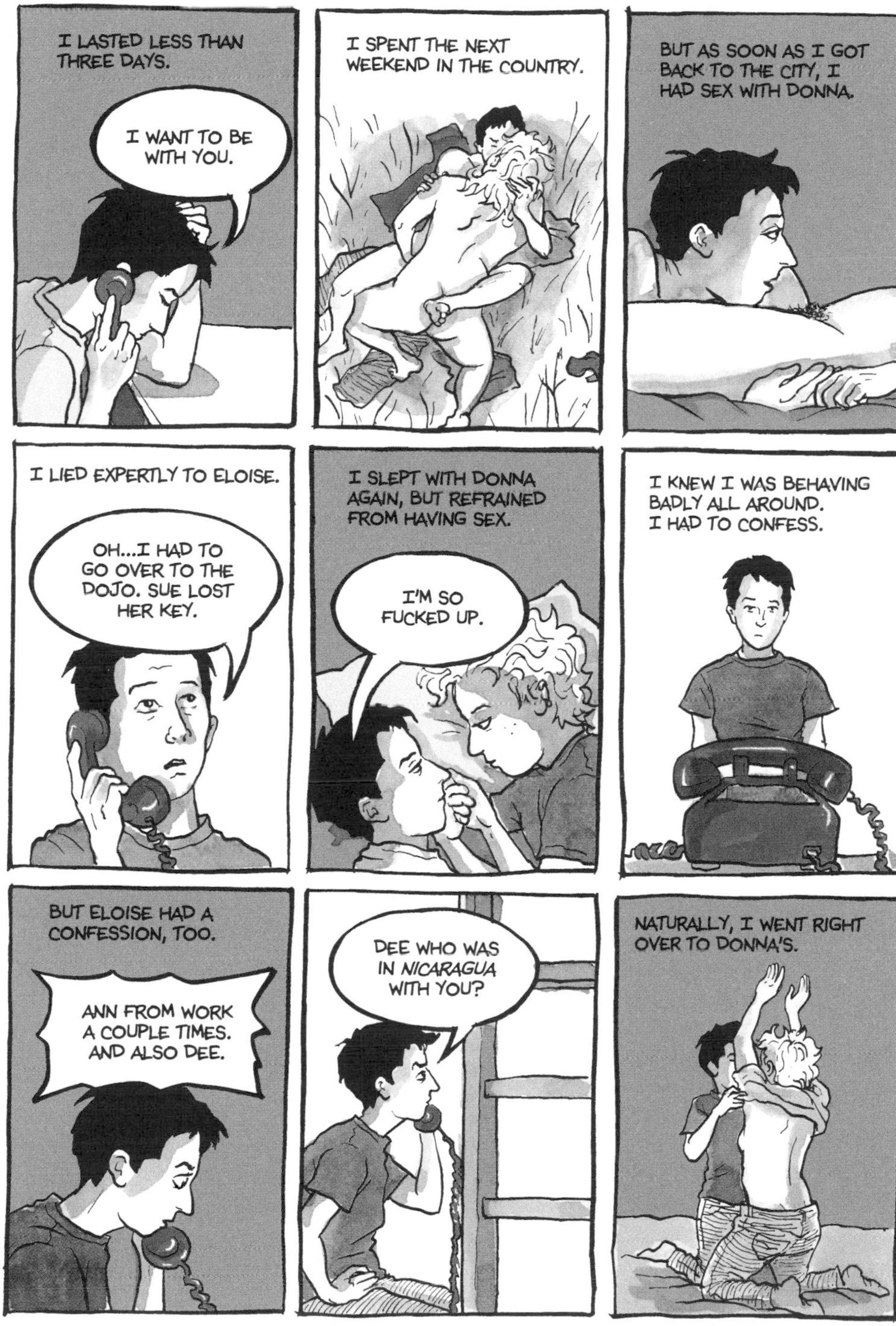
I LASTED LESS THAN THREE DAYS.
I WANT TO BE WITH YOU.
I SPENT THE NEXT WEEKEND IN THE COUNTRY.
BUT AS SOON AS I GOT BACK TO THE CITY, I HAD SEX WITH DONNA.
I LIED EXPERTLY TO ELOISE.
OH...I HAD TO GO OVER TO THE DOJO. SUE LOST HER KEY.
I SLEPT WITH DONNA AGAIN, BUT REFRAINED FROM HAVING SEX.
I'M SO FUCKED UP.
I KNEW I WAS BEHAVING BADLY ALL AROUND. I HAD TO CONFESS.
BUT ELOISE HAD A CONFESSION, TOO.
ANN FROM WORK A COUPLE TIMES. AND ALSO DEE.
DEE WHO WAS IN *NICARAGUA* WITH YOU?
NATURALLY, I WENT RIGHT OVER TO DONNA'S.

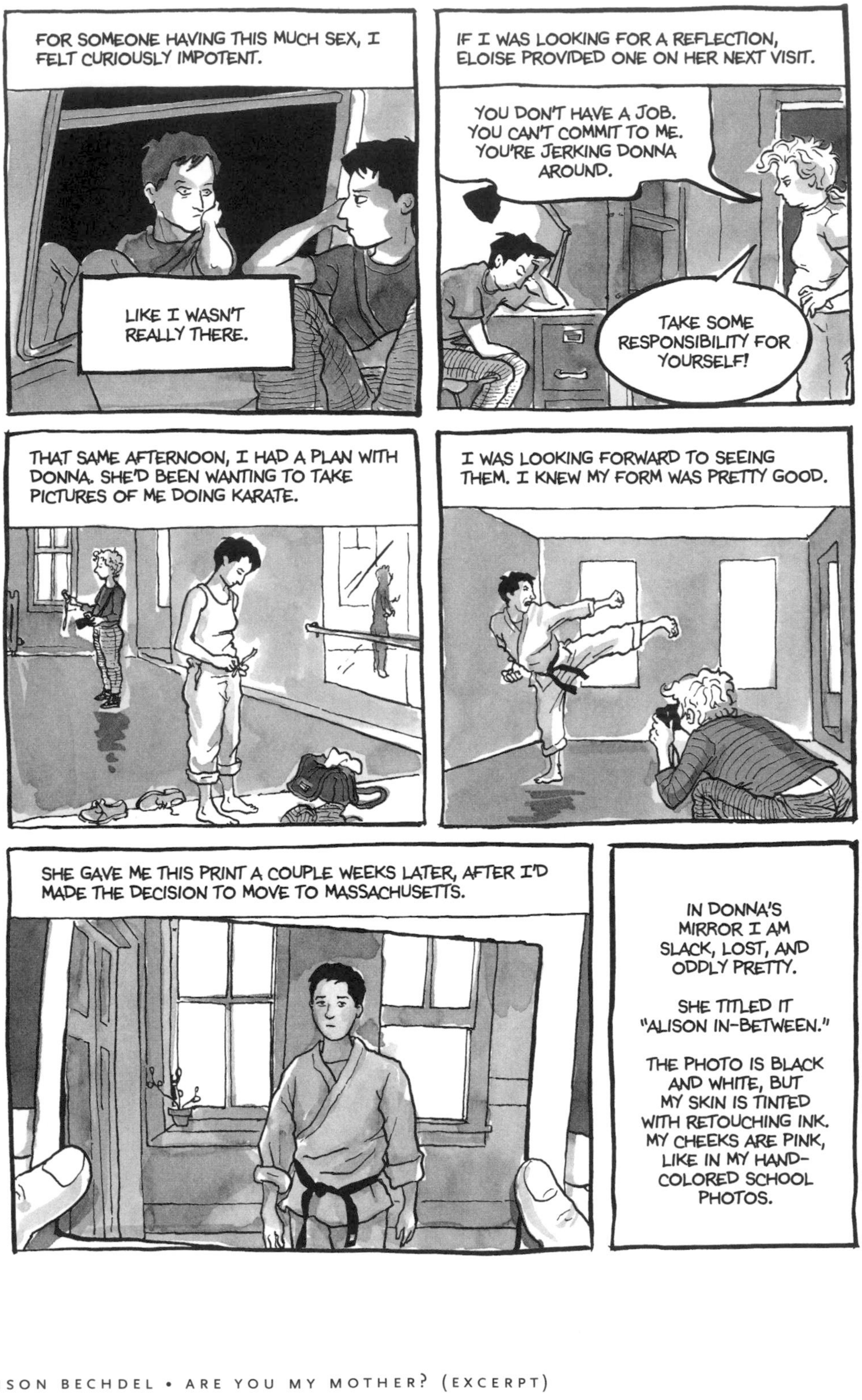
FOR SOMEONE HAVING THIS MUCH SEX, I FELT CURIOUSLY IMPOTENT.
LIKE I WASN'T REALLY THERE.
IF I WAS LOOKING FOR A REFLECTION, ELOISE PROVIDED ONE ON HER NEXT VISIT.
YOU DON'T HAVE A JOB. YOU CAN'T COMMIT TO ME. YOU'RE JERKING DONNA AROUND.
TAKE SOME RESPONSIBILITY FOR YOURSELF!
THAT SAME AFTERNOON, I HAD A PLAN WITH DONNA. SHE'D BEEN WANTING TO TAKE PICTURES OF ME DOING KARATE.
I WAS LOOKING FORWARD TO SEEING THEM. I KNEW MY FORM WAS PRETTY GOOD.
SHE GAVE ME THIS PRINT A COUPLE WEEKS LATER, AFTER I'D MADE THE DECISION TO MOVE TO MASSACHUSETTS.
IN DONNA'S MIRROR I AM SLACK, LOST, AND ODDLY PRETTY.
SHE TITLED IT "ALISON IN-BETWEEN."
THE PHOTO IS BLACK AND WHITE, BUT MY SKIN IS TINTED WITH RETOUCHING INK. MY CHEEKS ARE PINK, LIKE IN MY HAND-COLORED SCHOOL PHOTOS.

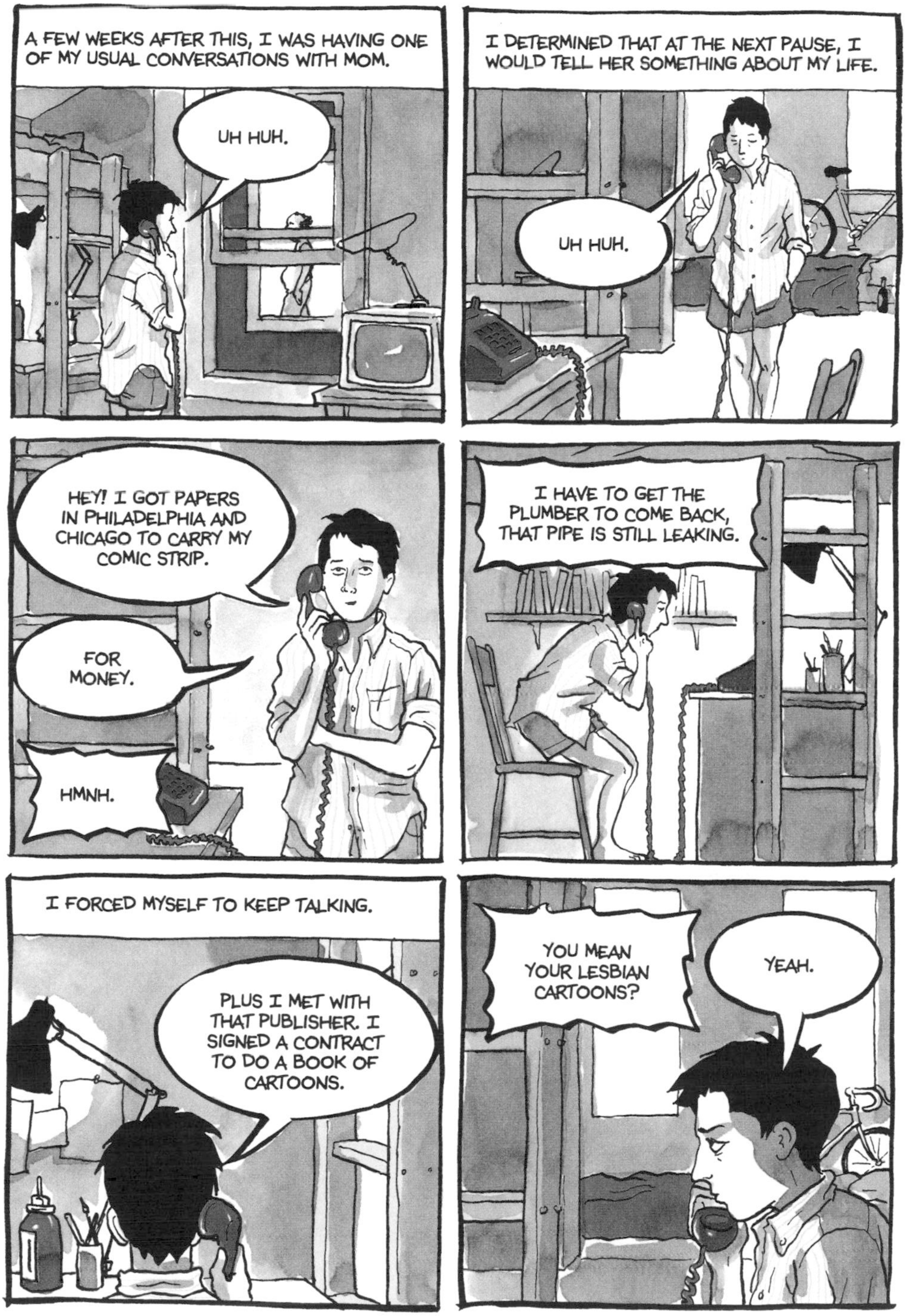
A FEW WEEKS AFTER THIS, I WAS HAVING ONE OF MY USUAL CONVERSATIONS WITH MOM.
UH HUH.
I DETERMINED THAT AT THE NEXT PAUSE, I WOULD TELL HER SOMETHING ABOUT MY LIFE.
UH HUH.
HEY! I GOT PAPERS IN PHILADELPHIA AND CHICAGO TO CARRY MY COMIC STRIP.
FOR MONEY.
HMNH.
I HAVE TO GET THE PLUMBER TO COME BACK, THAT PIPE IS STILL LEAKING.
I FORCED MYSELF TO KEEP TALKING.
PLUS I MET WITH THAT PUBLISHER. I SIGNED A CONTRACT TO DO A BOOK OF CARTOONS.
YOU MEAN YOUR LESBIAN CARTOONS?
YEAH.

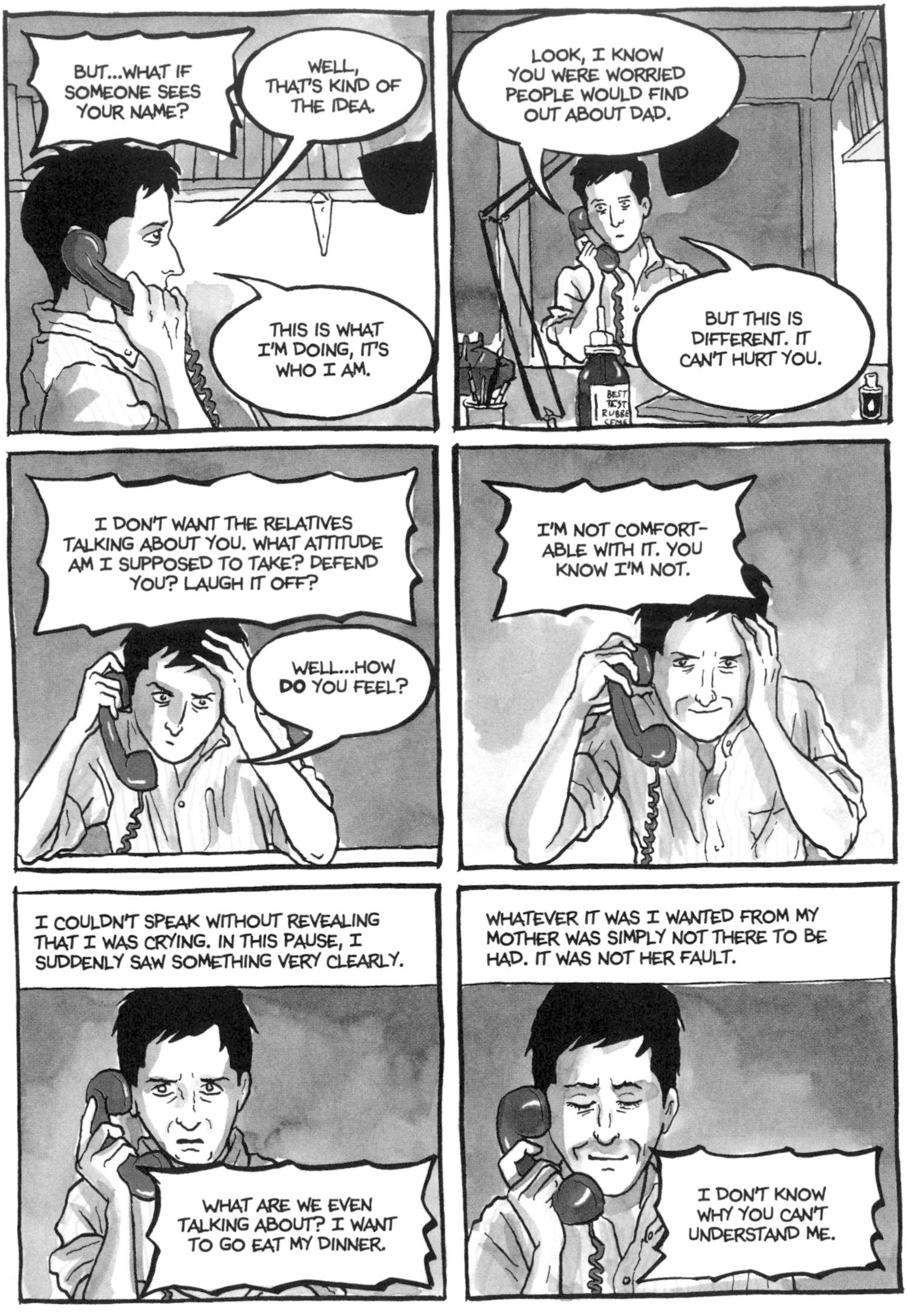
BUT...WHAT IF SOMEONE SEES YOUR NAME?
WELL, THAT'S KIND OF THE IDEA.
THIS IS WHAT I'M DOING, IT'S WHO I AM.
LOOK, I KNOW YOU WERE WORRIED PEOPLE WOULD FIND OUT ABOUT DAD.
BUT THIS IS DIFFERENT. IT CAN'T HURT YOU.
I DON'T WANT THE RELATIVES TALKING ABOUT YOU. WHAT ATTITUDE AM I SUPPOSED TO TAKE? DEFEND YOU? LAUGH IT OFF?
WELL...HOW **DO** YOU FEEL?
I'M NOT COMFORT-ABLE WITH IT. YOU KNOW I'M NOT.
I COULDN'T SPEAK WITHOUT REVEALING THAT I WAS CRYING. IN THIS PAUSE, I SUDDENLY SAW SOMETHING VERY CLEARLY.
WHAT ARE WE EVEN TALKING ABOUT? I WANT TO GO EAT MY DINNER.
WHATEVER IT WAS I WANTED FROM MY MOTHER WAS SIMPLY NOT THERE TO BE HAD. IT WAS NOT HER FAULT.
I DON'T KNOW WHY YOU CAN'T UNDERSTAND ME.

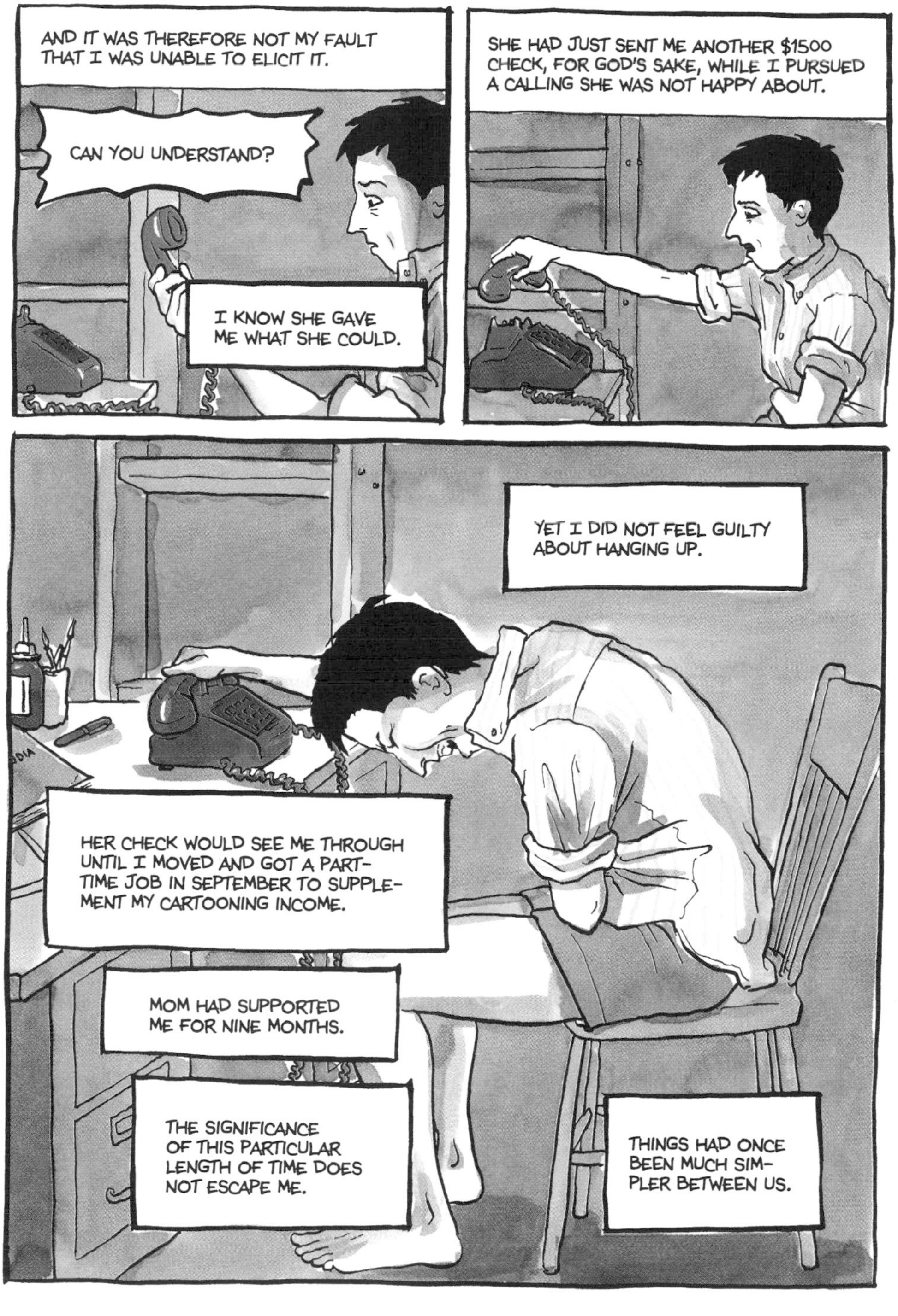
AND IT WAS THEREFORE NOT MY FAULT THAT I WAS UNABLE TO ELICIT IT.
CAN YOU UNDERSTAND?
I KNOW SHE GAVE ME WHAT SHE COULD.
SHE HAD JUST SENT ME ANOTHER $1500 CHECK, FOR GOD'S SAKE, WHILE I PURSUED A CALLING SHE WAS NOT HAPPY ABOUT.
YET I DID NOT FEEL GUILTY ABOUT HANGING UP.
HER CHECK WOULD SEE ME THROUGH UNTIL I MOVED AND GOT A PART-TIME JOB IN SEPTEMBER TO SUPPLEMENT MY CARTOONING INCOME.
MOM HAD SUPPORTED ME FOR NINE MONTHS.
THE SIGNIFICANCE OF THIS PARTICULAR LENGTH OF TIME DOES NOT ESCAPE ME.
THINGS HAD ONCE BEEN MUCH SIMPLER BETWEEN US.

Brandon Graham

The Speaker

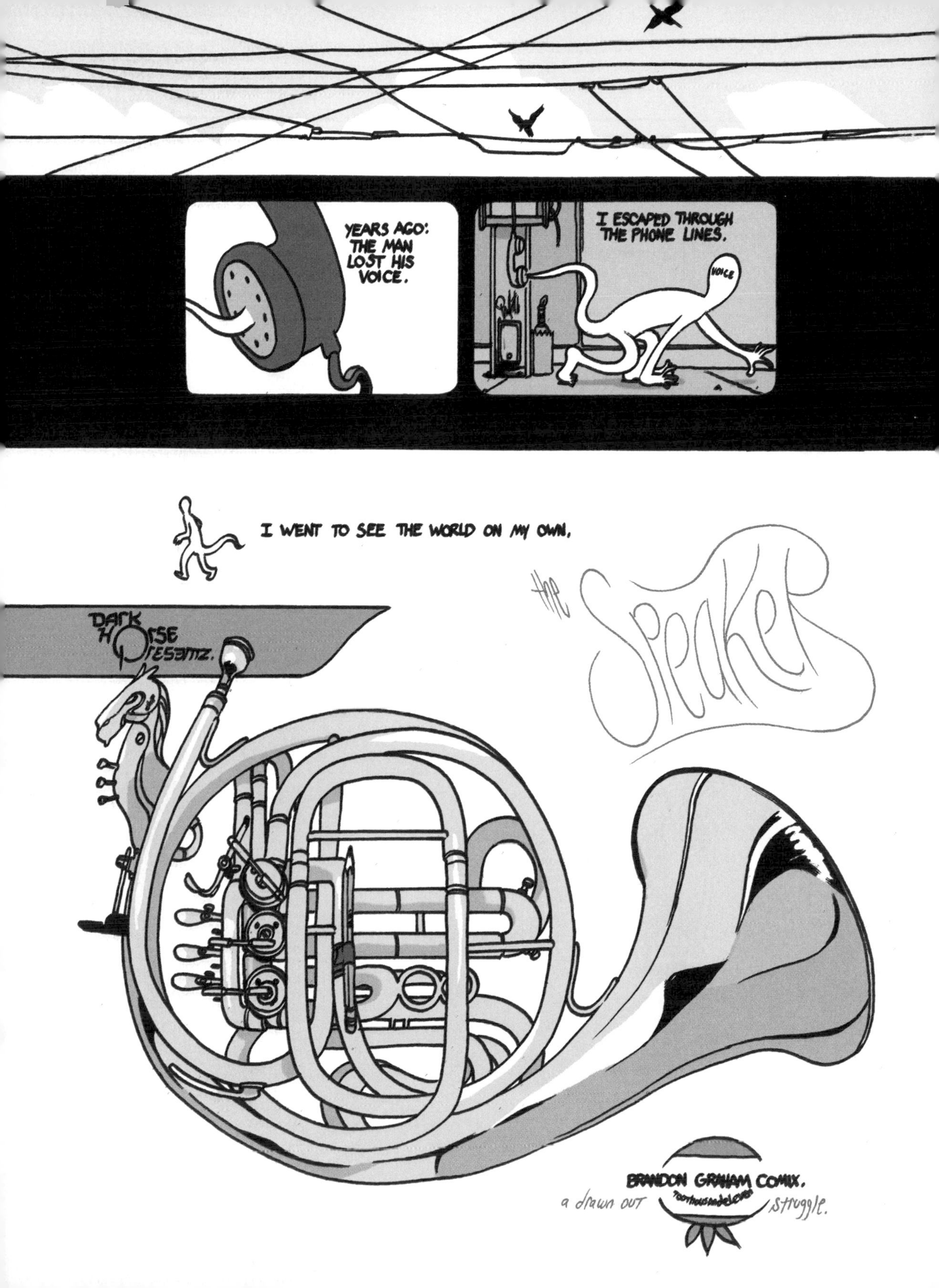

YEARS AGO: THE MAN LOST HIS VOICE.
I ESCAPED THROUGH THE PHONE LINES.
VOICE
I WENT TO SEE THE WORLD ON MY OWN,
the Speaker
DARK HORSE PRESENTZ.
BRANDON GRAHAM COMIX.
a drawn out twothousandeleven struggle.

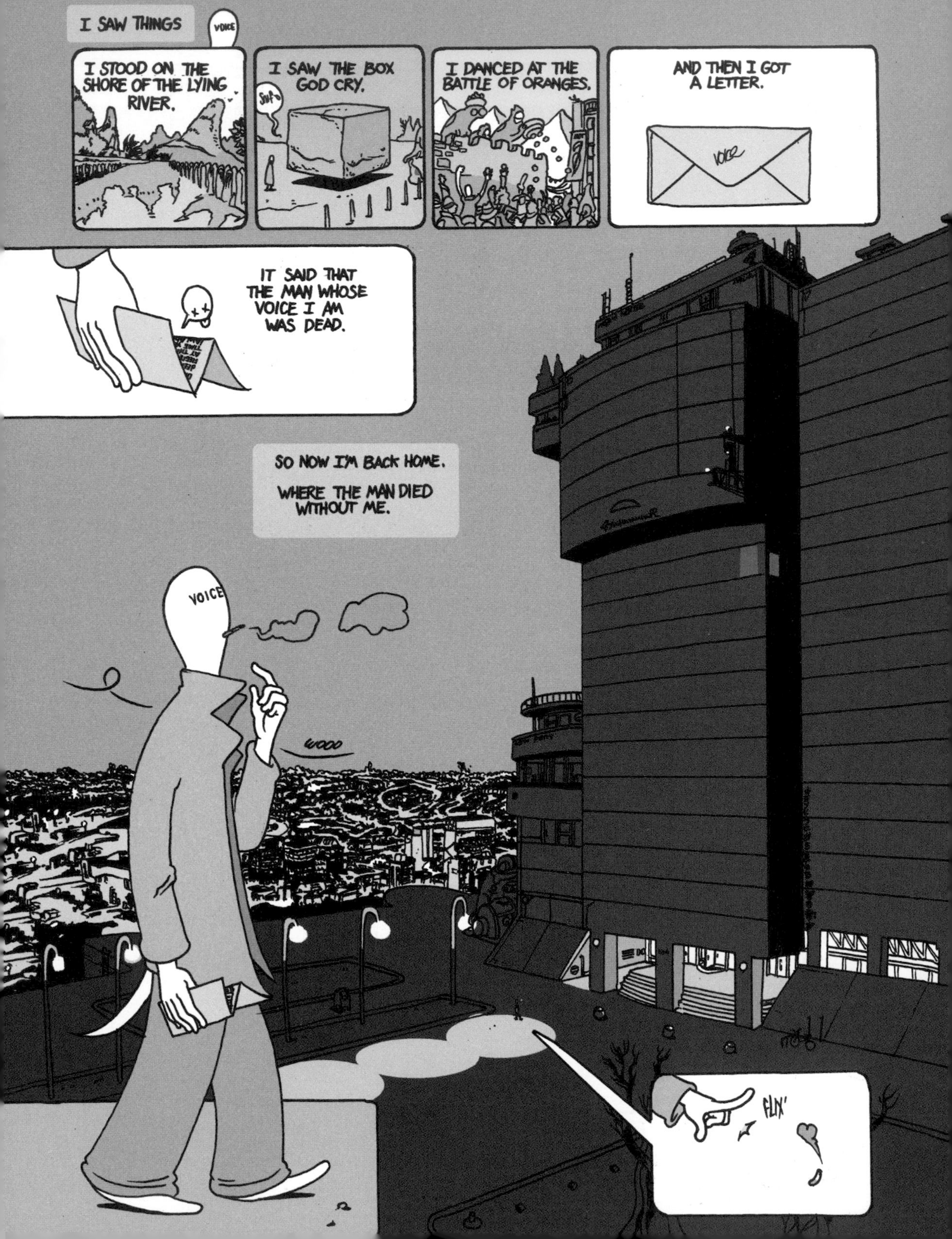

I SAW THINGS
VOICE
I STOOD ON THE SHORE OF THE LYING RIVER.
I SAW THE BOX GOD CRY.
I DANCED AT THE BATTLE OF ORANGES.
AND THEN I GOT A LETTER.
VOICE
IT SAID THAT THE MAN WHOSE VOICE I AM WAS DEAD.
SO NOW I'M BACK HOME.
WHERE THE MAN DIED WITHOUT ME.
VOICE
WOOO
FLIX'

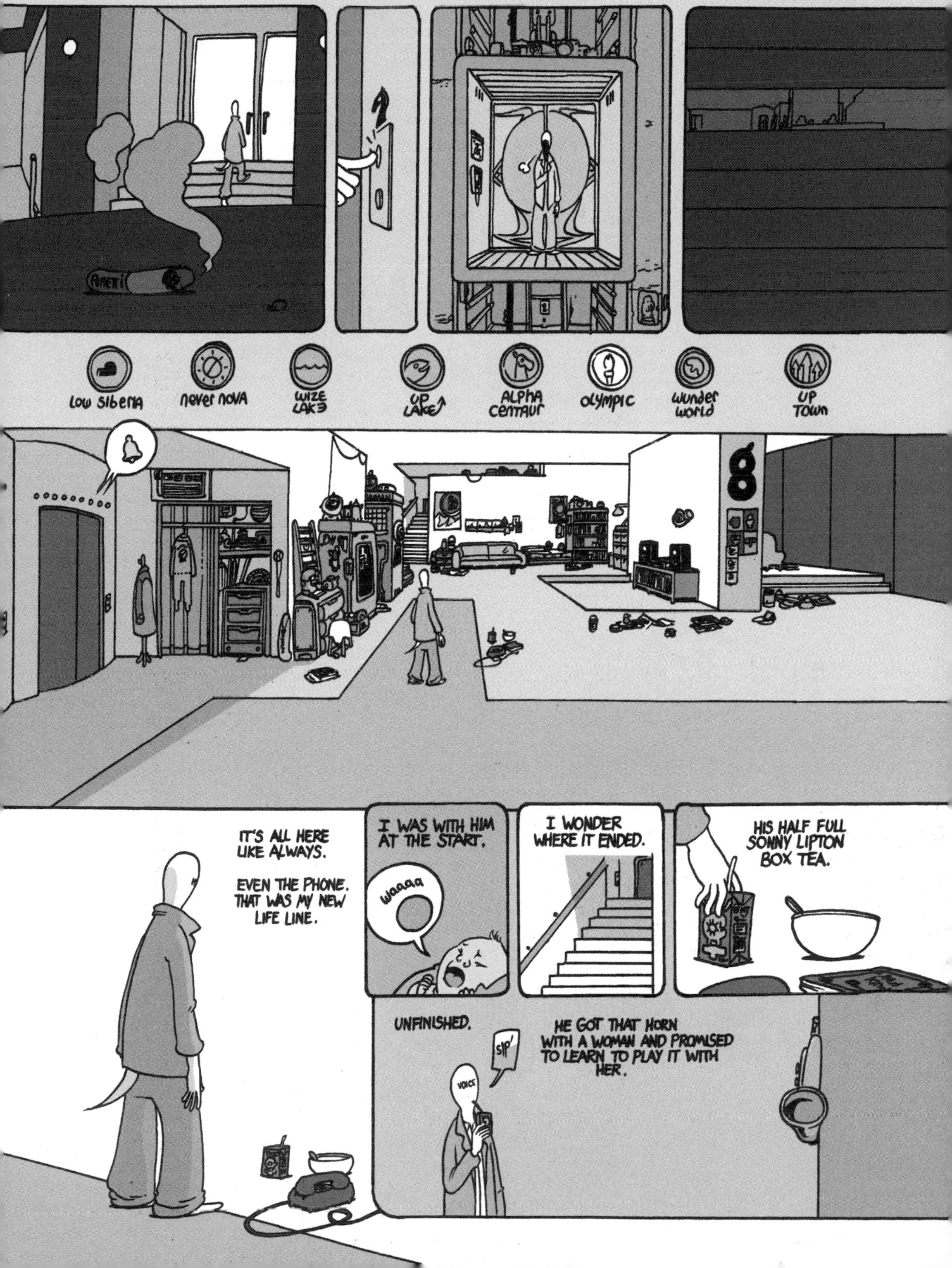
low siberia
never nova
wize lake
up lake
alpha centaur
olympic
wunder world
up town
IT'S ALL HERE LIKE ALWAYS.
EVEN THE PHONE. THAT WAS MY NEW LIFE LINE.
I WAS WITH HIM AT THE START.
Waaaa
I WONDER WHERE IT ENDED.
HIS HALF FULL SONNY LIPTON BOX TEA.
UNFINISHED.
sip
VOICE
HE GOT THAT HORN WITH A WOMAN AND PROMISED TO LEARN TO PLAY IT WITH HER.

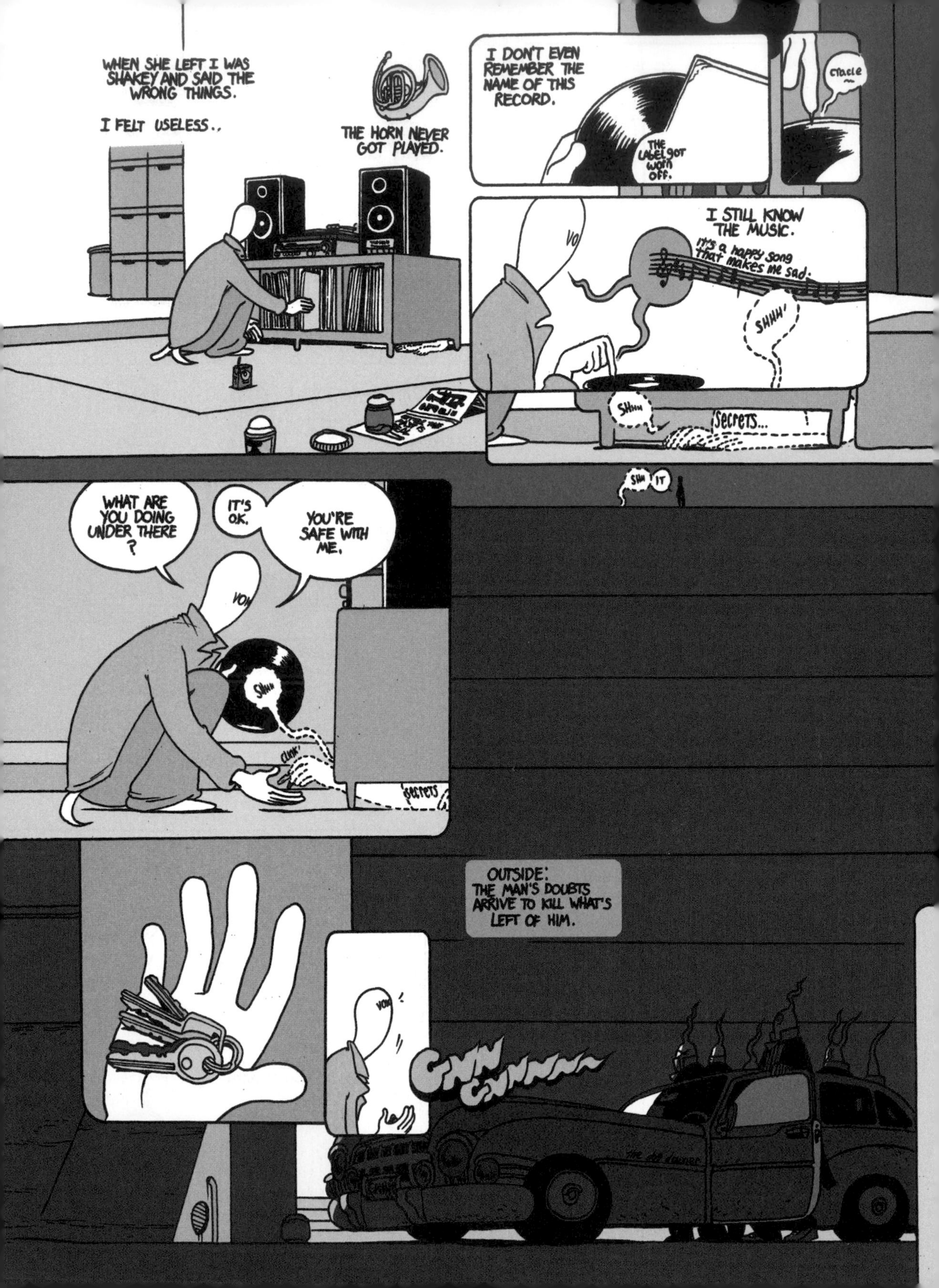
WHEN SHE LEFT I WAS SHAKEY AND SAID THE WRONG THINGS.
I FELT USELESS..
THE HORN NEVER GOT PLAYED.
I DON'T EVEN REMEMBER THE NAME OF THIS RECORD.
THE LABEL GOT WORN OFF.
crackle
I STILL KNOW THE MUSIC.
it's a happy song that makes me sad.
SHHH'
SHHH
secrets...
SHH
IT
WHAT ARE YOU DOING UNDER THERE ?
IT'S O.K.
YOU'RE SAFE WITH ME.
SHHH
CLINK'
secrets
OUTSIDE: THE MAN'S DOUBTS ARRIVE TO KILL WHAT'S LEFT OF HIM.
GNN GNNNNN

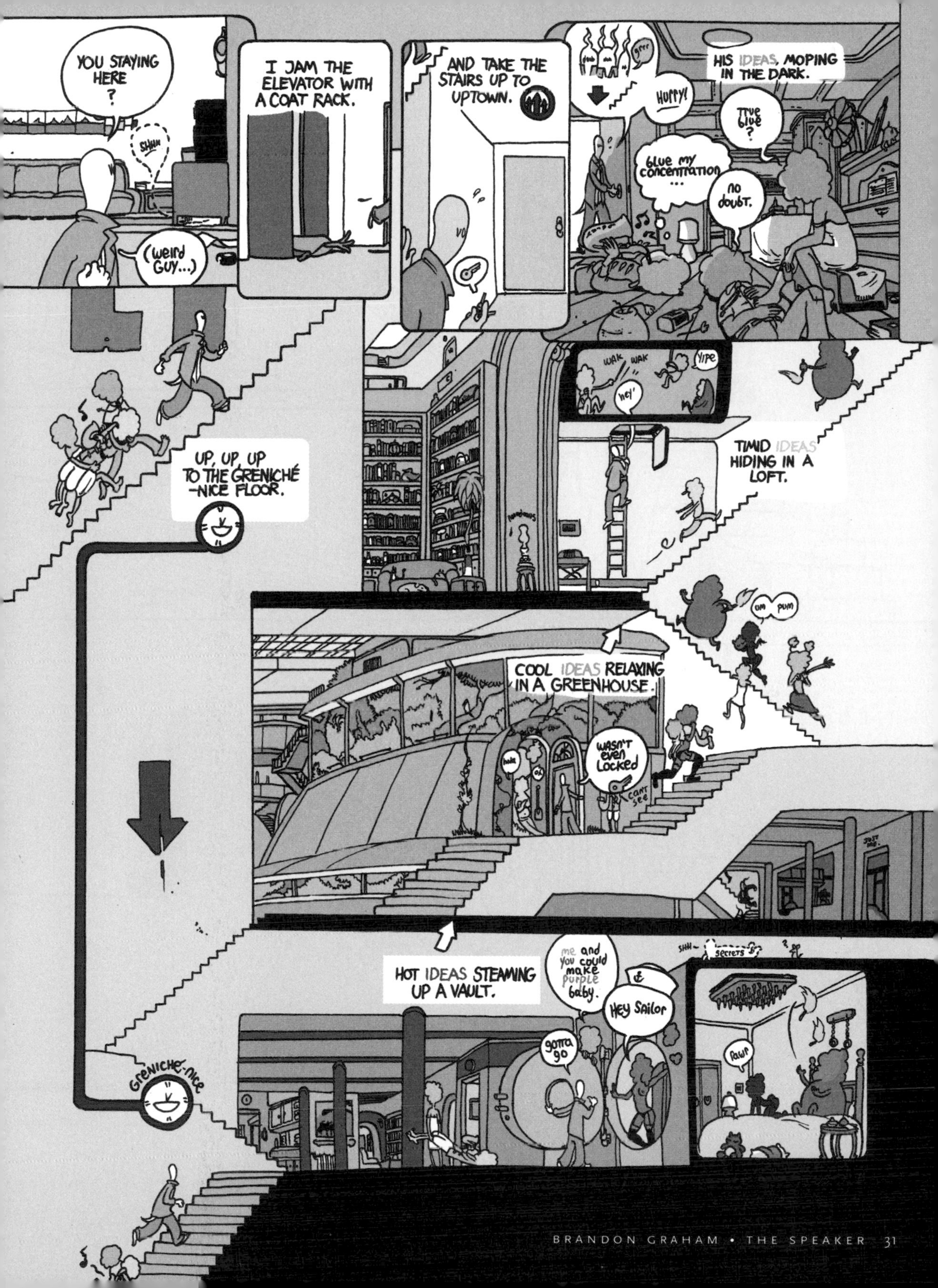
YOU STAYING HERE ?
SHHH
(weird GUY...)
I JAM THE ELEVATOR WITH A COAT RACK.
AND TAKE THE STAIRS UP TO UPTOWN.
HIS IDEAS, MOPING IN THE DARK.
Hurry!
True blue ?
blue my concentration ...
no doubt.
WAK WAK
Yipe
hey'
TIMID IDEAS HIDING IN A LOFT.
UP, UP, UP TO THE GRENICHÉ -NICE FLOOR.
COOL IDEAS RELAXING IN A GREENHOUSE.
wasn't even Locked
can't see
HOT IDEAS STEAMING UP A VAULT.
me and you could make purple baby.
Hey Sailor
gotta go
SHH~ secrets
Rawr
Greniche-nice

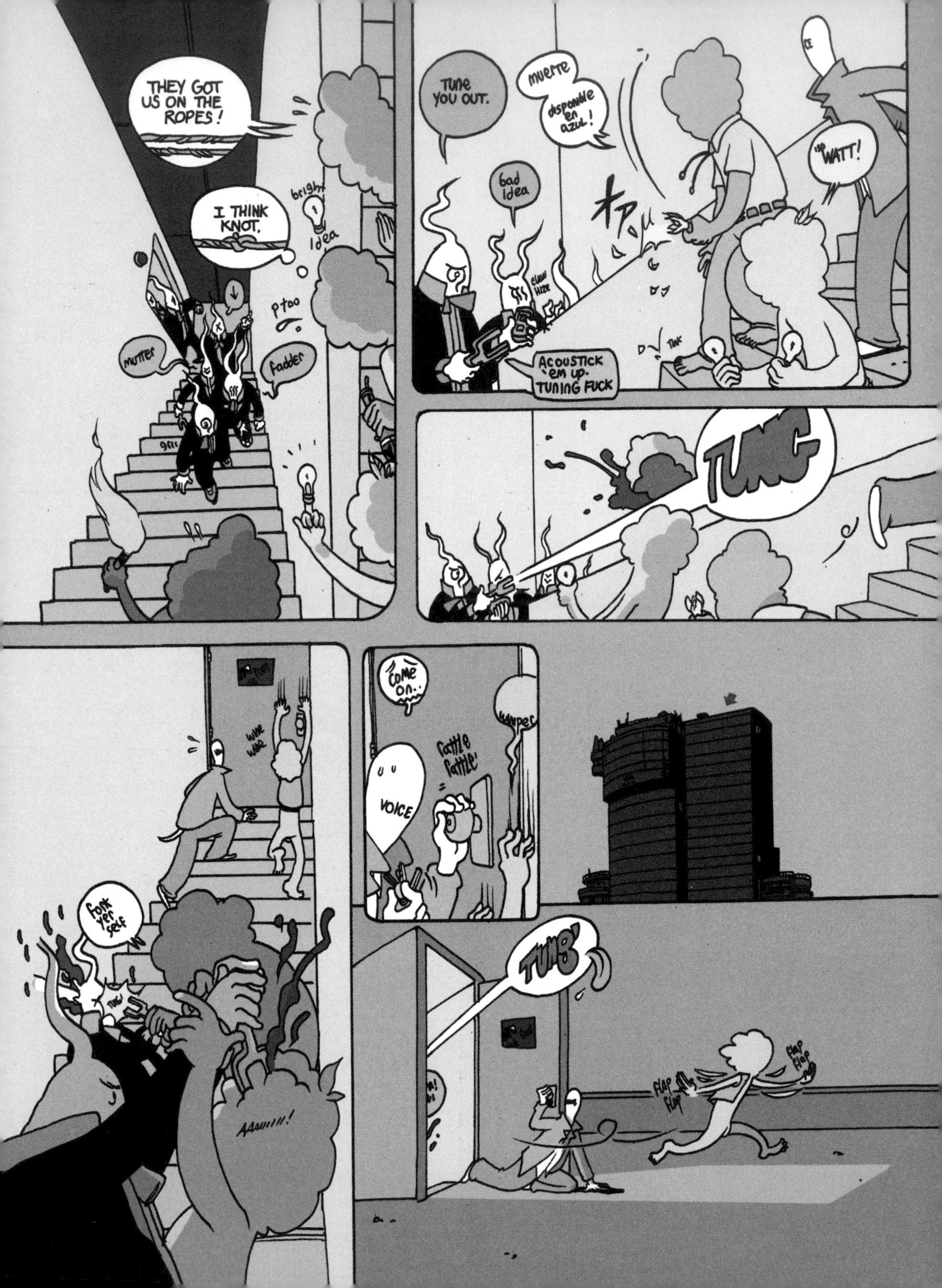
THEY GOT US ON THE ROPES!
I THINK KNOT.
bright idea
ptoo
mutter
fadder
TUNE YOU OUT.
muerte
disponible en azul!
bad idea
ACOUSTICK 'em up. TUNING FUCK
WATT!
TINK
TUNG
fork yer self
AAAIIIII!
come on..
rattle rattle
VOICE
TUNG
flap flap
flap flap

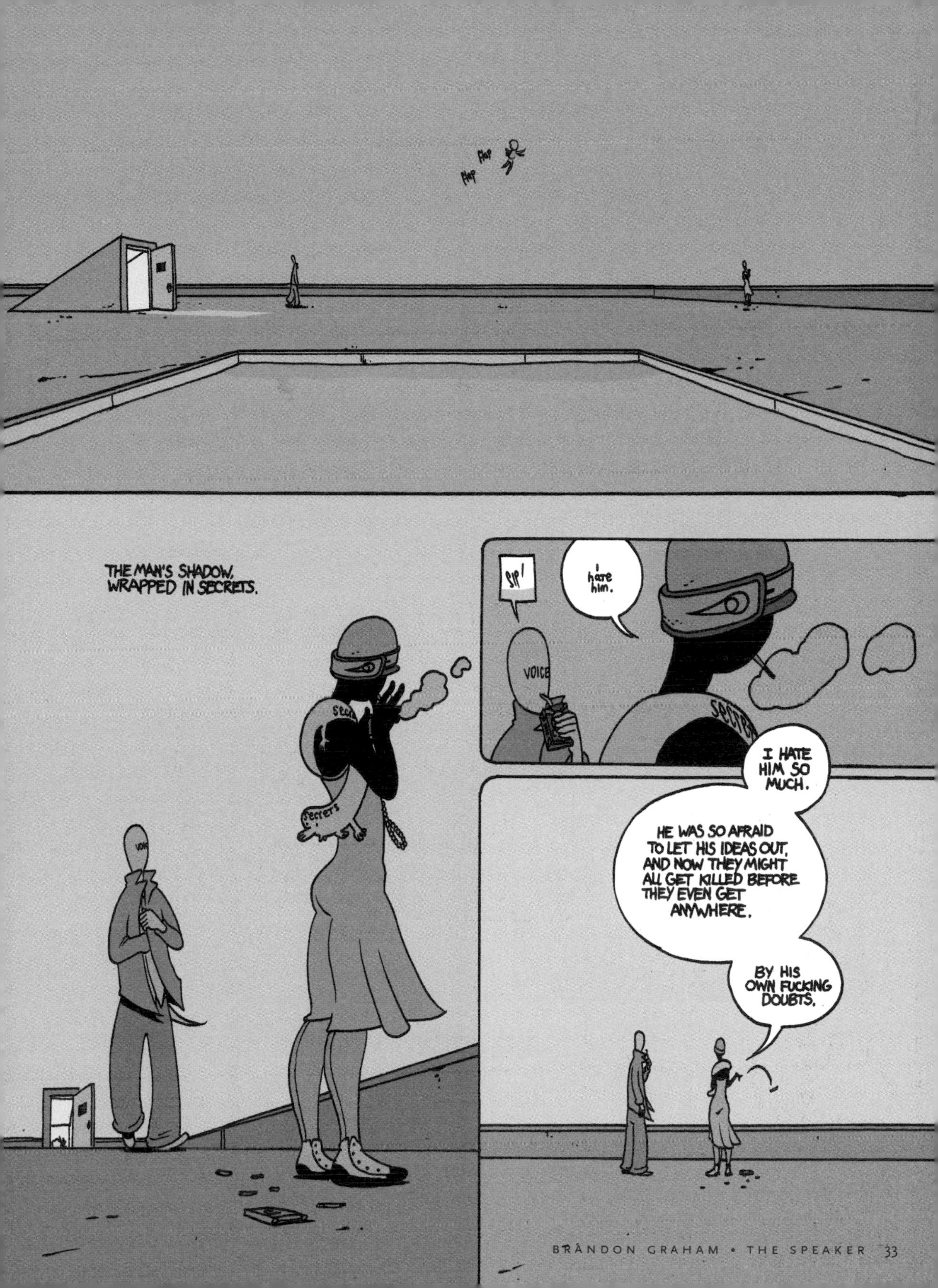
FLAP
FLAP
THE MAN'S SHADOW, WRAPPED IN SECRETS.
SECRETS
SIP!
i hate him.
VOICE
SECRETS
I HATE HIM SO MUCH.
HE WAS SO AFRAID TO LET HIS IDEAS OUT, AND NOW THEY MIGHT ALL GET KILLED BEFORE THEY EVEN GET ANYWHERE.
BY HIS OWN FUCKING DOUBTS.

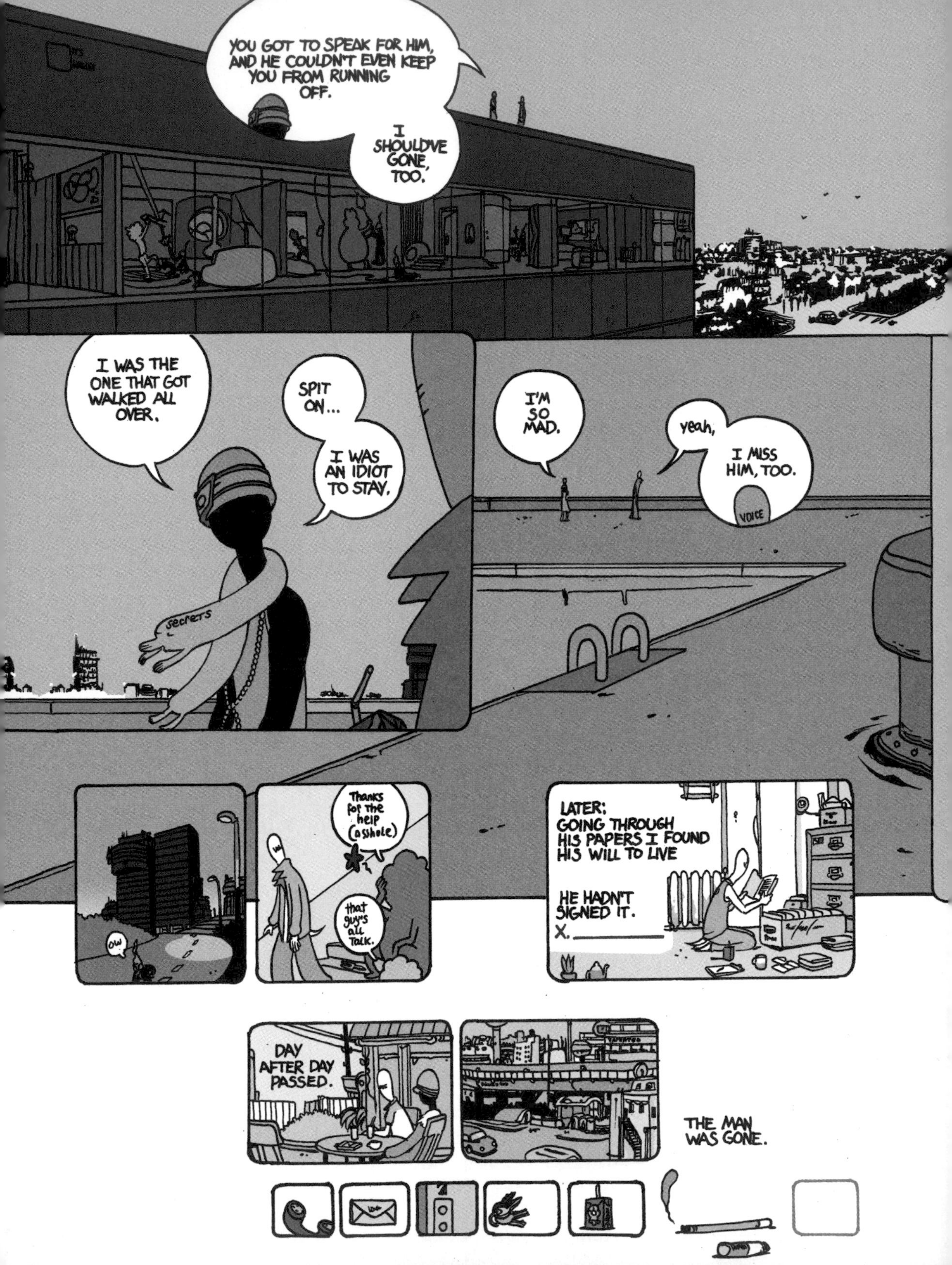
YOU GOT TO SPEAK FOR HIM, AND HE COULDN'T EVEN KEEP YOU FROM RUNNING OFF.
I SHOULD'VE GONE, TOO.
I WAS THE ONE THAT GOT WALKED ALL OVER.
SPIT ON...
I WAS AN IDIOT TO STAY.
secrets
I'M SO MAD.
yeah,
I MISS HIM, TOO.
VOICE
OW
Thanks for the help (asshole)
that guy's all talk.
LATER: GOING THROUGH HIS PAPERS I FOUND HIS WILL TO LIVE
HE HADN'T SIGNED IT.
X.
DAY AFTER DAY PASSED.
THE MAN WAS GONE.

Jesse Jacobs

THE DIVINE MANIFESTATION OF A SINGULAR IMPULSE

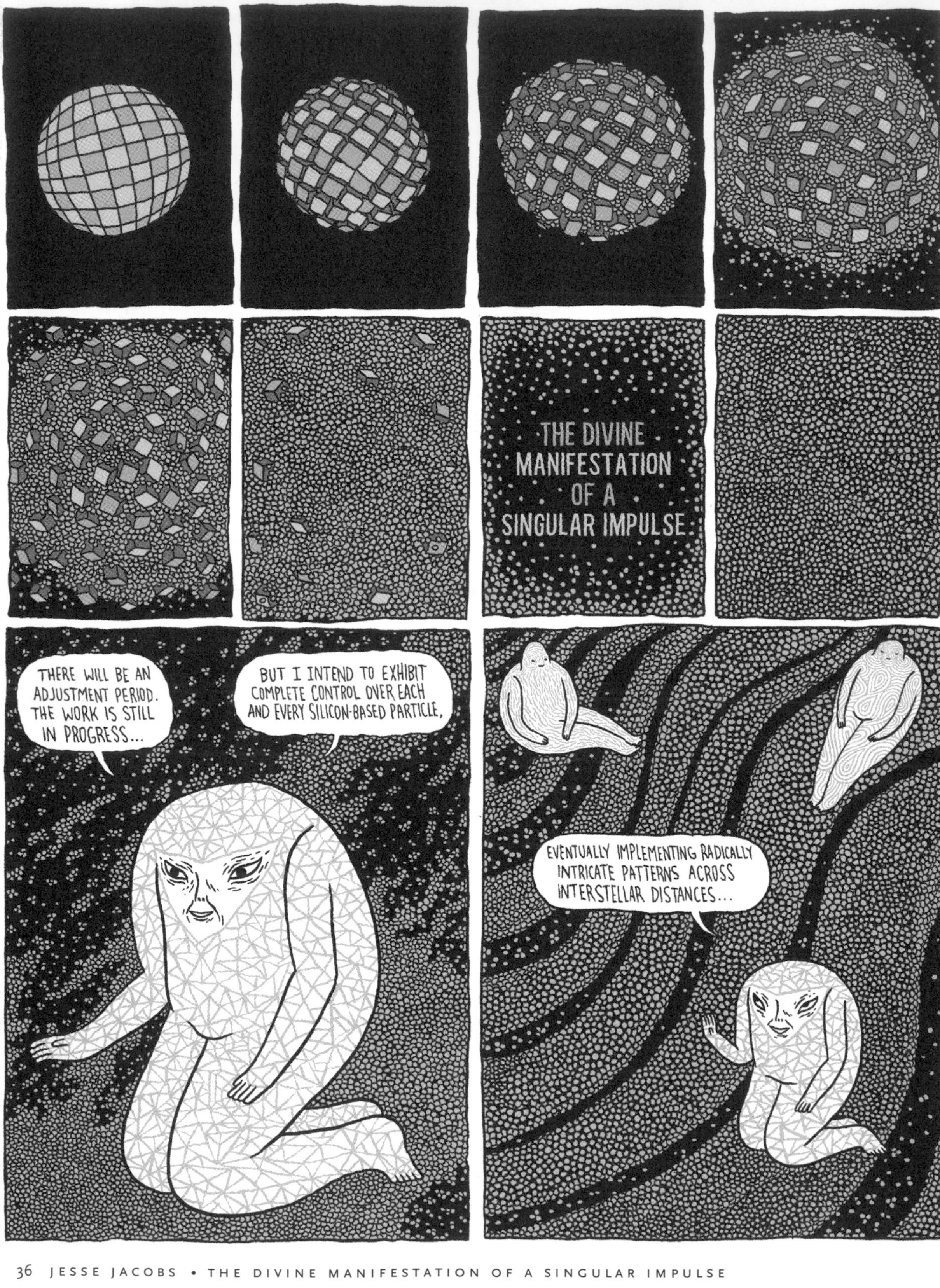
THE DIVINE MANIFESTATION OF A SINGULAR IMPULSE
THERE WILL BE AN ADJUSTMENT PERIOD. THE WORK IS STILL IN PROGRESS...
BUT I INTEND TO EXHIBIT COMPLETE CONTROL OVER EACH AND EVERY SILICON-BASED PARTICLE,
EVENTUALLY IMPLEMENTING RADICALLY INTRICATE PATTERNS ACROSS INTERSTELLAR DISTANCES...

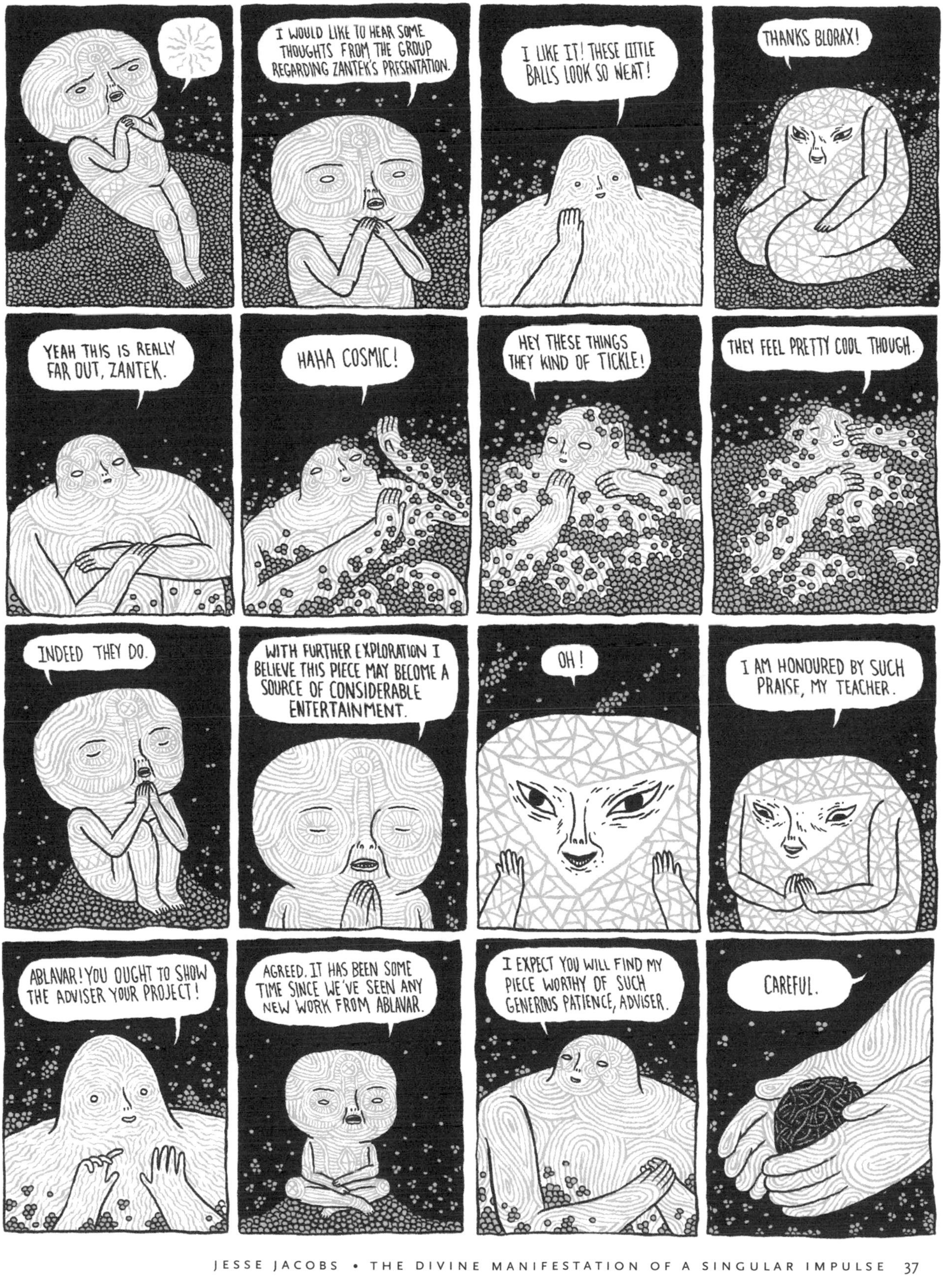
I WOULD LIKE TO HEAR SOME THOUGHTS FROM THE GROUP REGARDING ZANTEK'S PRESENTATION.
I LIKE IT! THESE LITTLE BALLS LOOK SO NEAT!
THANKS BLORAX!
YEAH THIS IS REALLY FAR OUT, ZANTEK.
HAHA COSMIC!
HEY THESE THINGS THEY KIND OF TICKLE!
THEY FEEL PRETTY COOL THOUGH.
INDEED THEY DO.
WITH FURTHER EXPLORATION I BELIEVE THIS PIECE MAY BECOME A SOURCE OF CONSIDERABLE ENTERTAINMENT.
OH!
I AM HONOURED BY SUCH PRAISE, MY TEACHER.
ABLAVAR! YOU OUGHT TO SHOW THE ADVISER YOUR PROJECT!
AGREED. IT HAS BEEN SOME TIME SINCE WE'VE SEEN ANY NEW WORK FROM ABLAVAR.
I EXPECT YOU WILL FIND MY PIECE WORTHY OF SUCH GENEROUS PATIENCE, ADVISER.
CAREFUL.

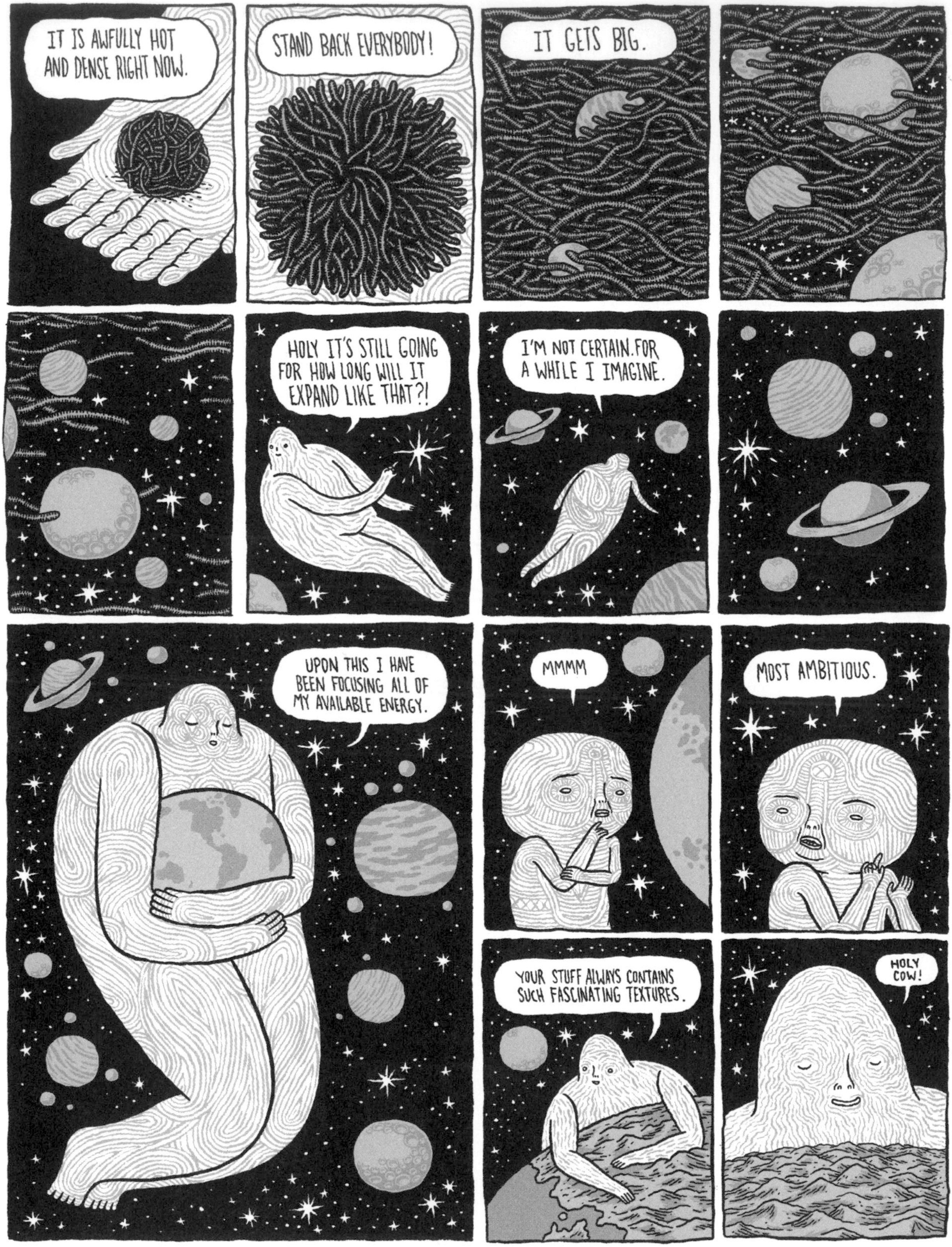
IT IS AWFULLY HOT AND DENSE RIGHT NOW.
STAND BACK EVERYBODY!
IT GETS BIG.
HOLY IT'S STILL GOING FOR HOW LONG WILL IT EXPAND LIKE THAT?!
I'M NOT CERTAIN.FOR A WHILE I IMAGINE.
UPON THIS I HAVE BEEN FOCUSING ALL OF MY AVAILABLE ENERGY.
MMMM
MOST AMBITIOUS.
YOUR STUFF ALWAYS CONTAINS SUCH FASCINATING TEXTURES.
HOLY COW!

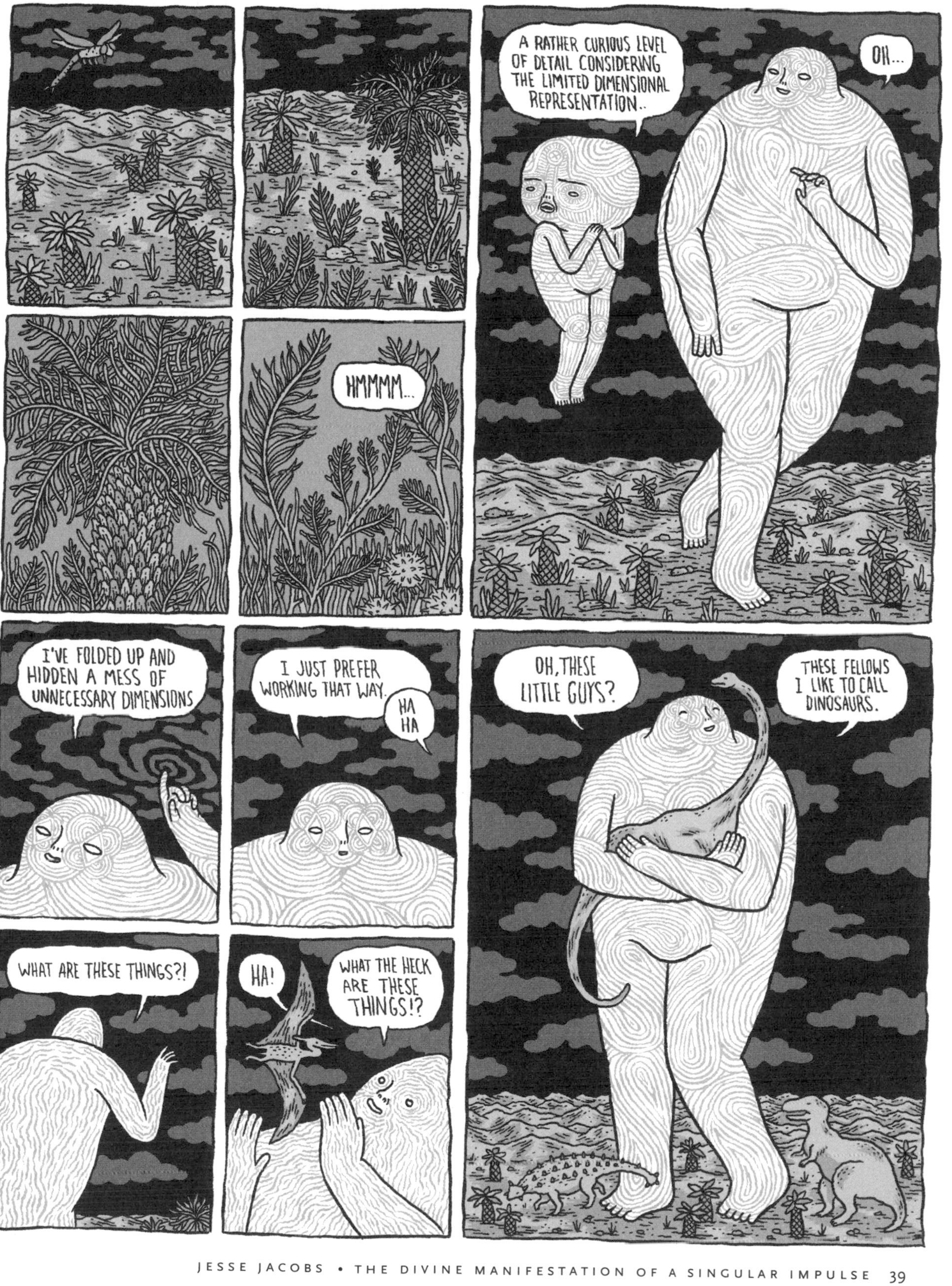
HMMMM...
A RATHER CURIOUS LEVEL OF DETAIL CONSIDERING THE LIMITED DIMENSIONAL REPRESENTATION..
OH...
I'VE FOLDED UP AND HIDDEN A MESS OF UNNECESSARY DIMENSIONS
I JUST PREFER WORKING THAT WAY.
HA HA
OH, THESE LITTLE GUYS?
THESE FELLOWS I LIKE TO CALL DINOSAURS.
WHAT ARE THESE THINGS?!
HA!
WHAT THE HECK ARE THESE THINGS!?

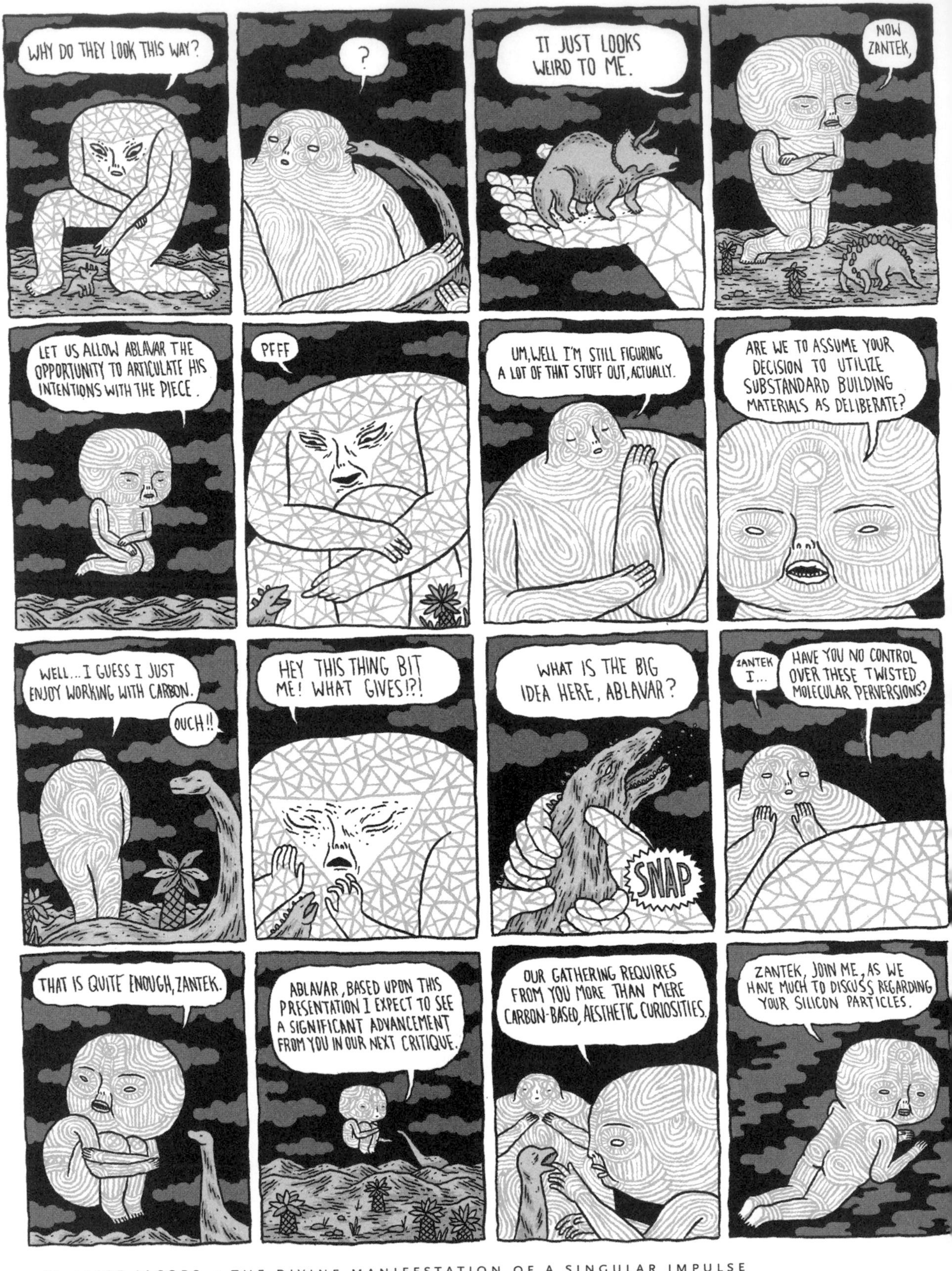
WHY DO THEY LOOK THIS WAY?
?
IT JUST LOOKS WEIRD TO ME.
NOW ZANTEK,
LET US ALLOW ABLAVAR THE OPPORTUNITY TO ARTICULATE HIS INTENTIONS WITH THE PIECE.
PFFF
UM, WELL I'M STILL FIGURING A LOT OF THAT STUFF OUT, ACTUALLY.
ARE WE TO ASSUME YOUR DECISION TO UTILIZE SUBSTANDARD BUILDING MATERIALS AS DELIBERATE?
WELL... I GUESS I JUST ENJOY WORKING WITH CARBON.
OUCH!!
HEY THIS THING BIT ME! WHAT GIVES!?!
WHAT IS THE BIG IDEA HERE, ABLAVAR?
SNAP
ZANTEK I...
HAVE YOU NO CONTROL OVER THESE TWISTED MOLECULAR PERVERSIONS?
THAT IS QUITE ENOUGH, ZANTEK.
ABLAVAR, BASED UPON THIS PRESENTATION I EXPECT TO SEE A SIGNIFICANT ADVANCEMENT FROM YOU IN OUR NEXT CRITIQUE.
OUR GATHERING REQUIRES FROM YOU MORE THAN MERE CARBON-BASED, AESTHETIC CURIOSITIES.
ZANTEK, JOIN ME, AS WE HAVE MUCH TO DISCUSS REGARDING YOUR SILICON PARTICLES.

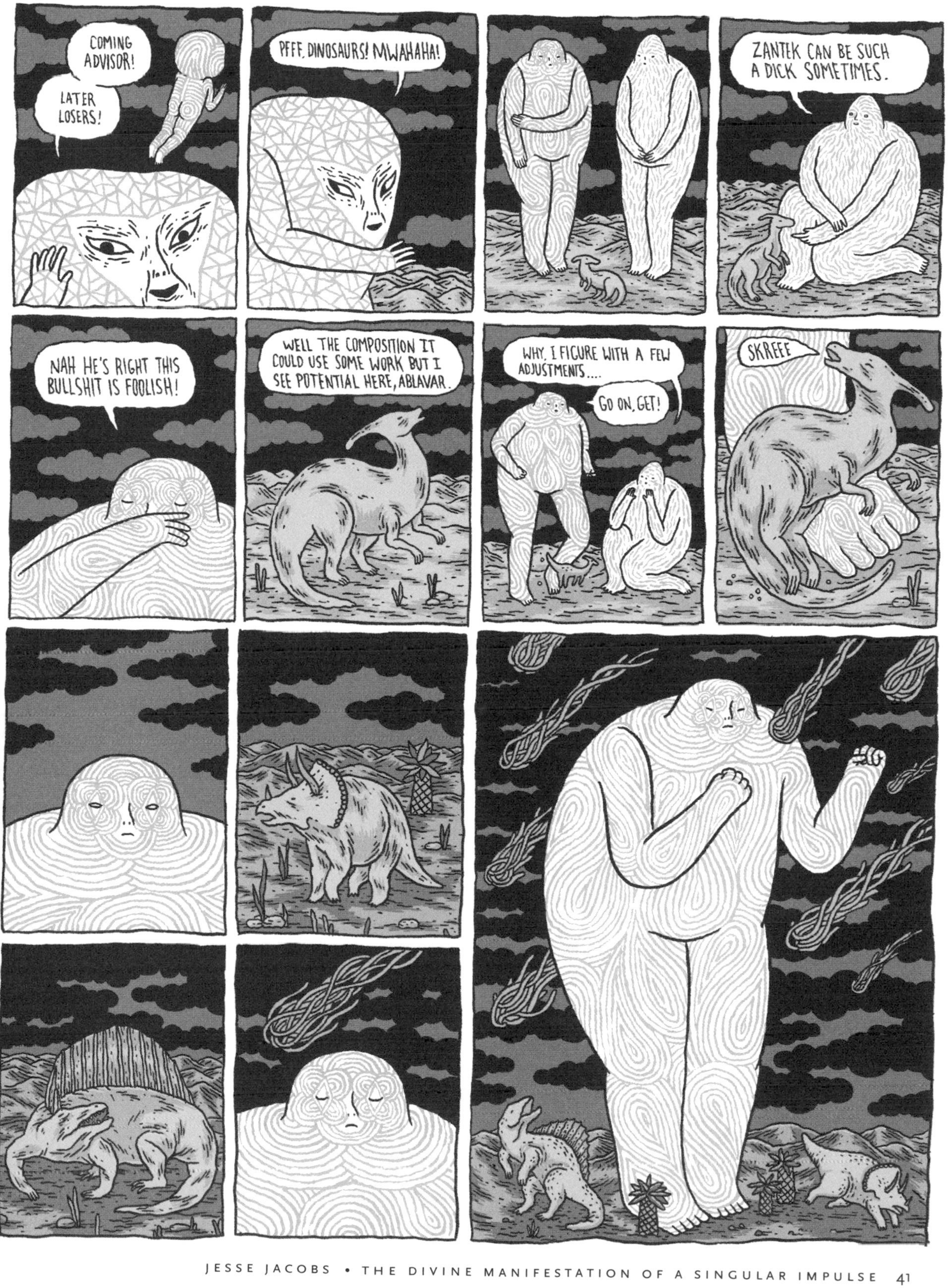
COMING ADVISOR!
LATER LOSERS!
PFFF, DINOSAURS! MWAHAHA!
ZANTEK CAN BE SUCH A DICK SOMETIMES.
NAH HE'S RIGHT THIS BULLSHIT IS FOOLISH!
WELL THE COMPOSITION IT COULD USE SOME WORK BUT I SEE POTENTIAL HERE, ABLAVAR.
WHY, I FIGURE WITH A FEW ADJUSTMENTS....
GO ON, GET!
SKREEE

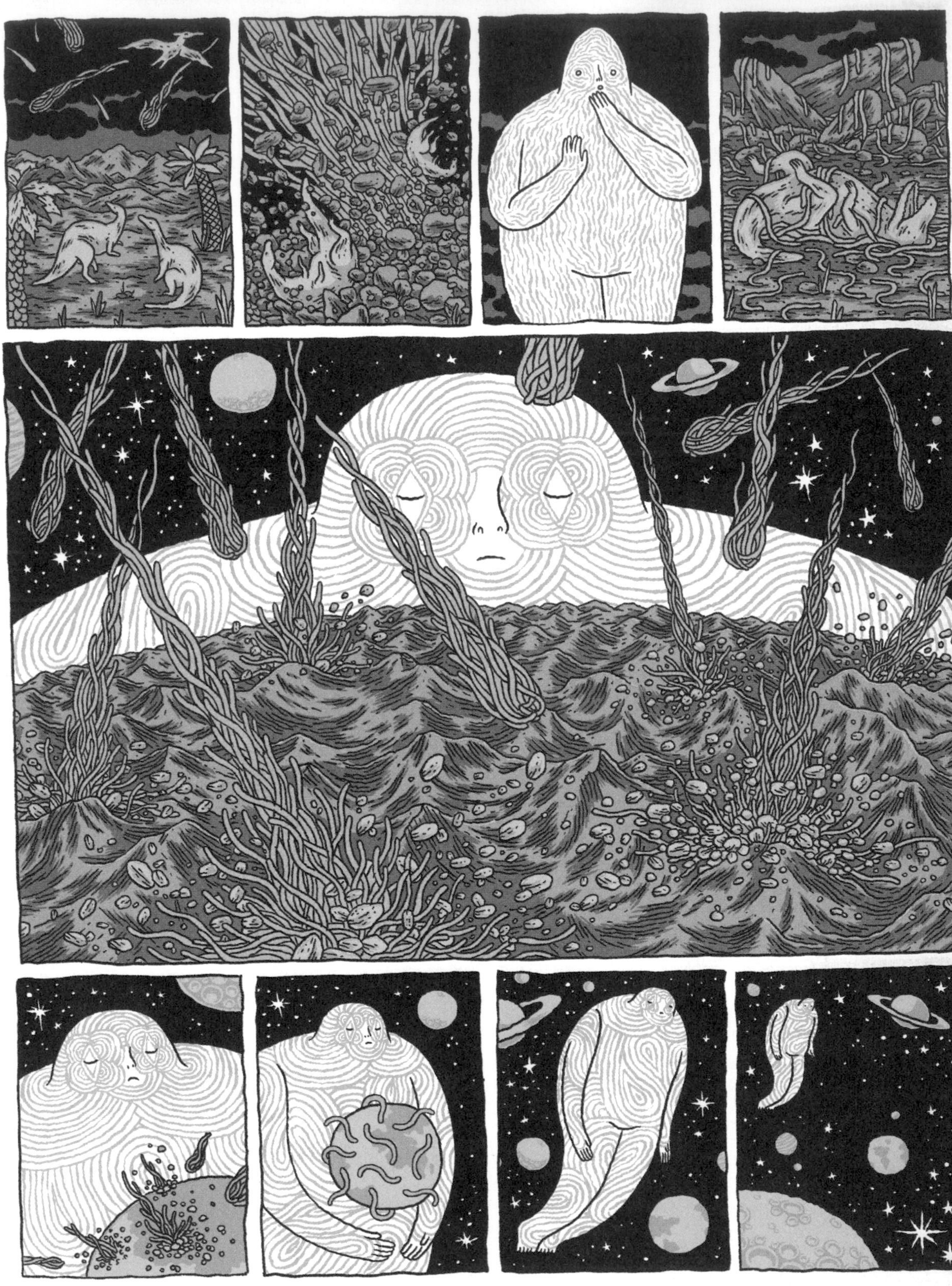

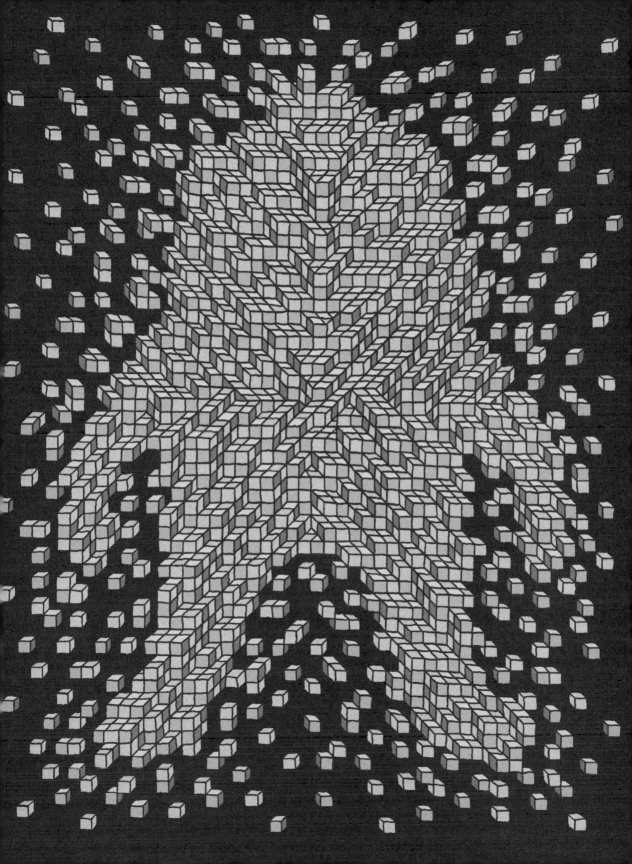

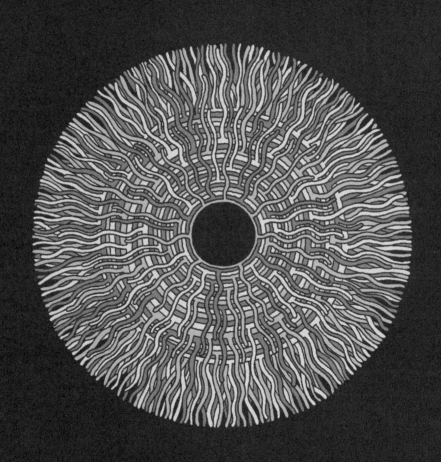

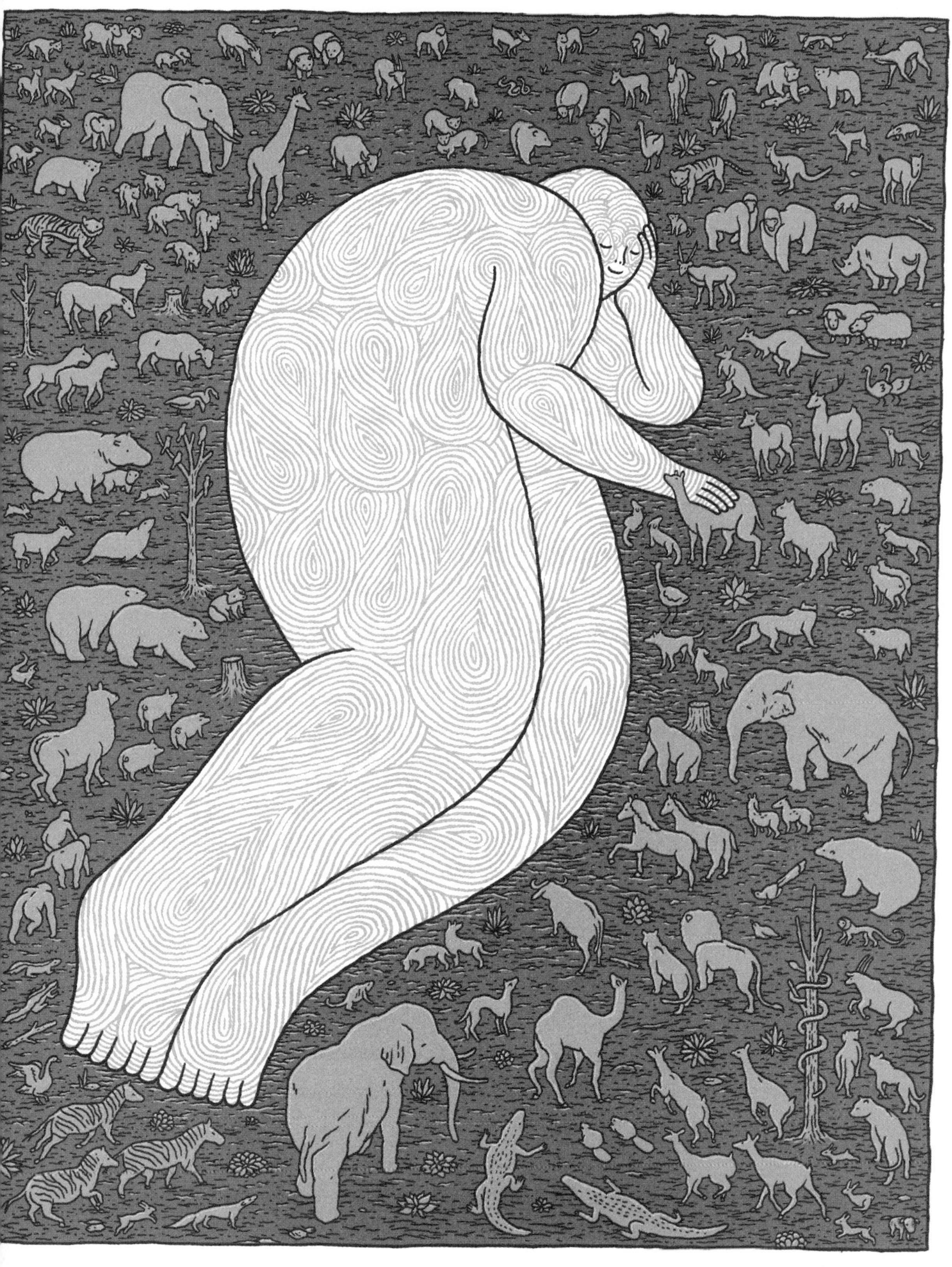

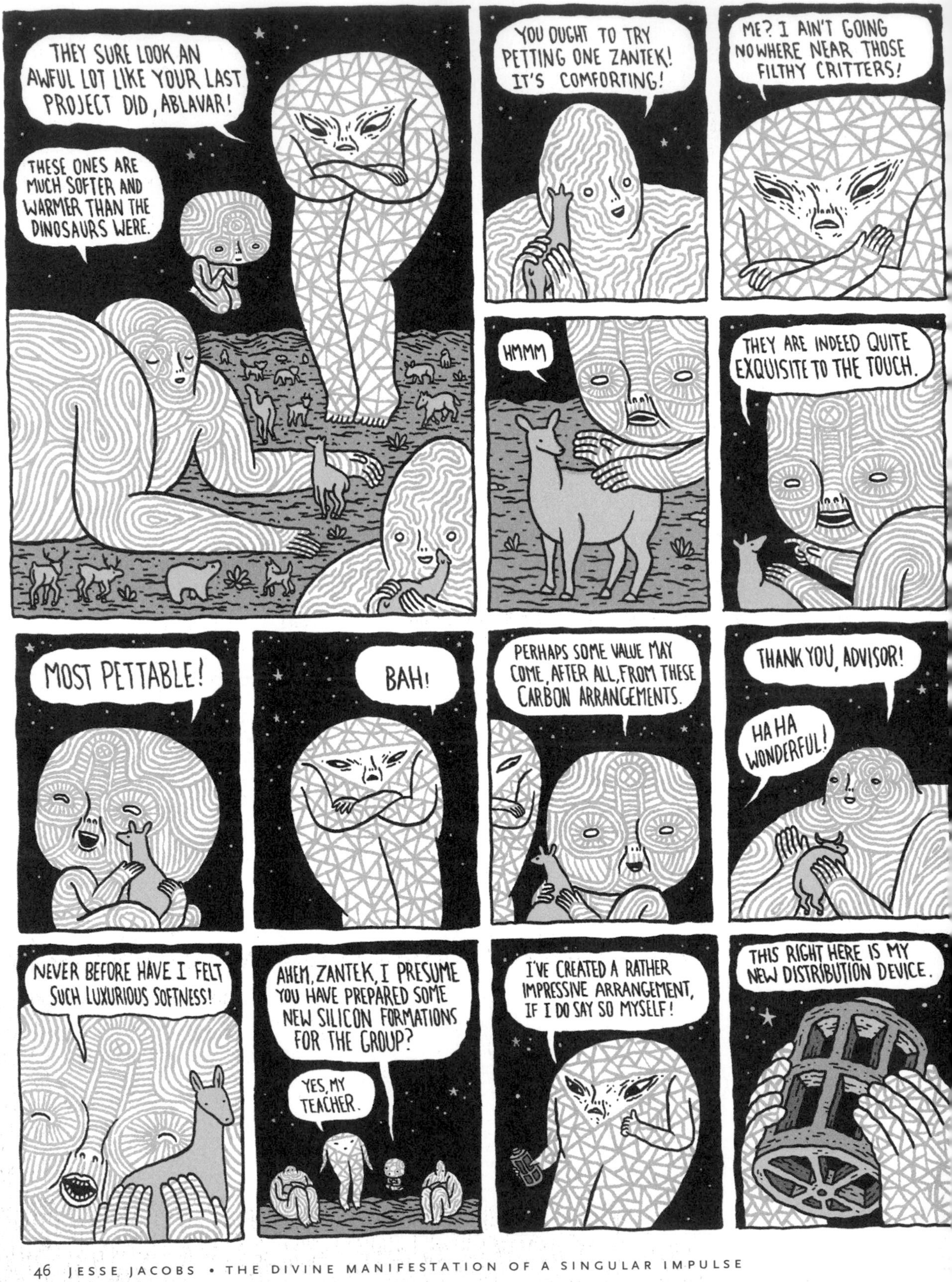

THEY SURE LOOK AN AWFUL LOT LIKE YOUR LAST PROJECT DID, ABLAVAR!
THESE ONES ARE MUCH SOFTER AND WARMER THAN THE DINOSAURS WERE.
YOU OUGHT TO TRY PETTING ONE ZANTEK! IT'S COMFORTING!
ME? I AIN'T GOING NOWHERE NEAR THOSE FILTHY CRITTERS!
HMMM
THEY ARE INDEED QUITE EXQUISITE TO THE TOUCH.
MOST PETTABLE!
BAH!
PERHAPS SOME VALUE MAY COME, AFTER ALL, FROM THESE CARBON ARRANGEMENTS.
THANK YOU, ADVISOR!
HA HA WONDERFUL!
NEVER BEFORE HAVE I FELT SUCH LUXURIOUS SOFTNESS!
AHEM, ZANTEK, I PRESUME YOU HAVE PREPARED SOME NEW SILICON FORMATIONS FOR THE GROUP?
YES, MY TEACHER.
I'VE CREATED A RATHER IMPRESSIVE ARRANGEMENT, IF I DO SAY SO MYSELF!
THIS RIGHT HERE IS MY NEW DISTRIBUTION DEVICE.

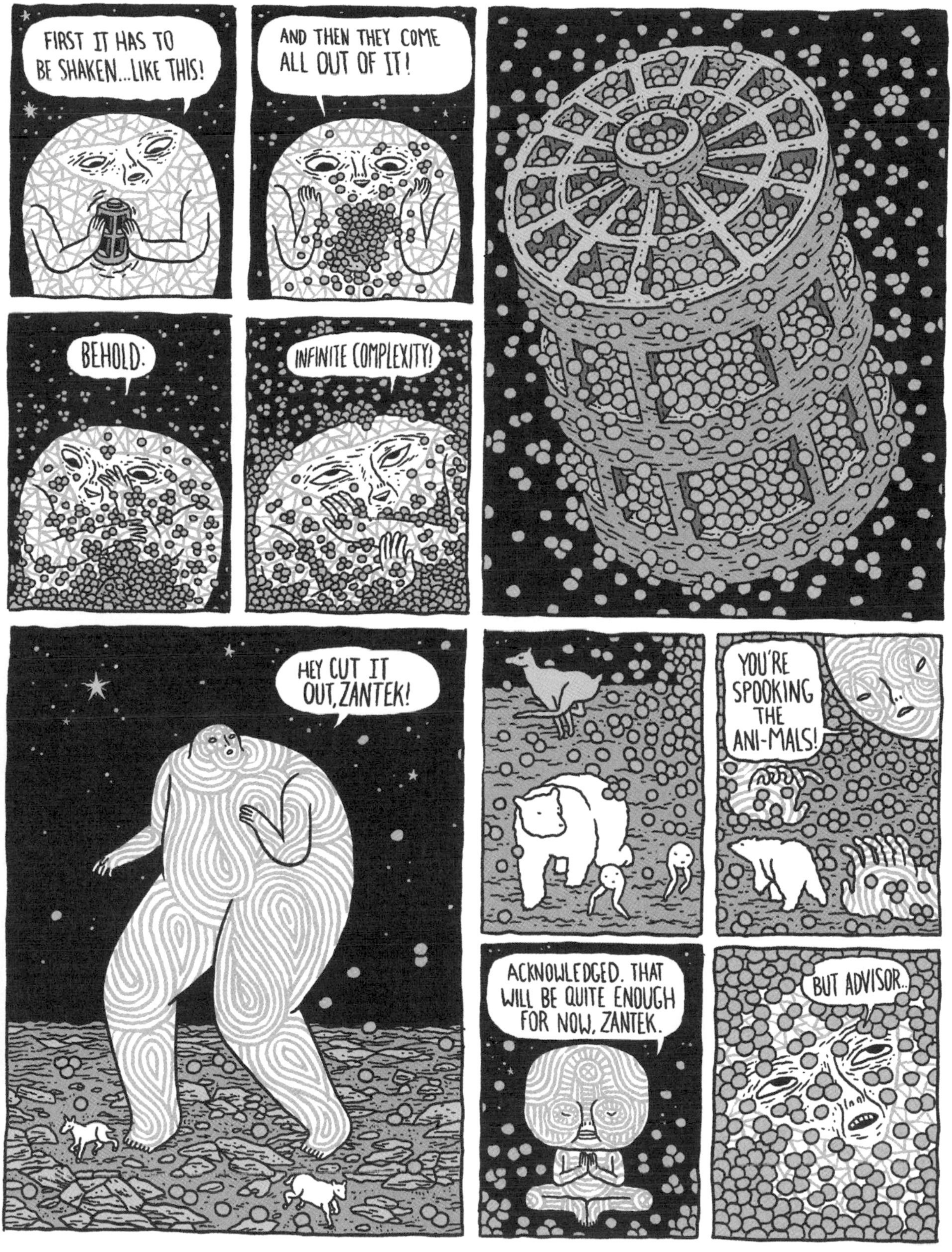
FIRST IT HAS TO BE SHAKEN...LIKE THIS!
AND THEN THEY COME ALL OUT OF IT!
BEHOLD:
INFINITE COMPLEXITY!
HEY CUT IT OUT, ZANTEK!
YOU'RE SPOOKING THE ANI-MALS!
ACKNOWLEDGED. THAT WILL BE QUITE ENOUGH FOR NOW, ZANTEK.
BUT ADVISOR..

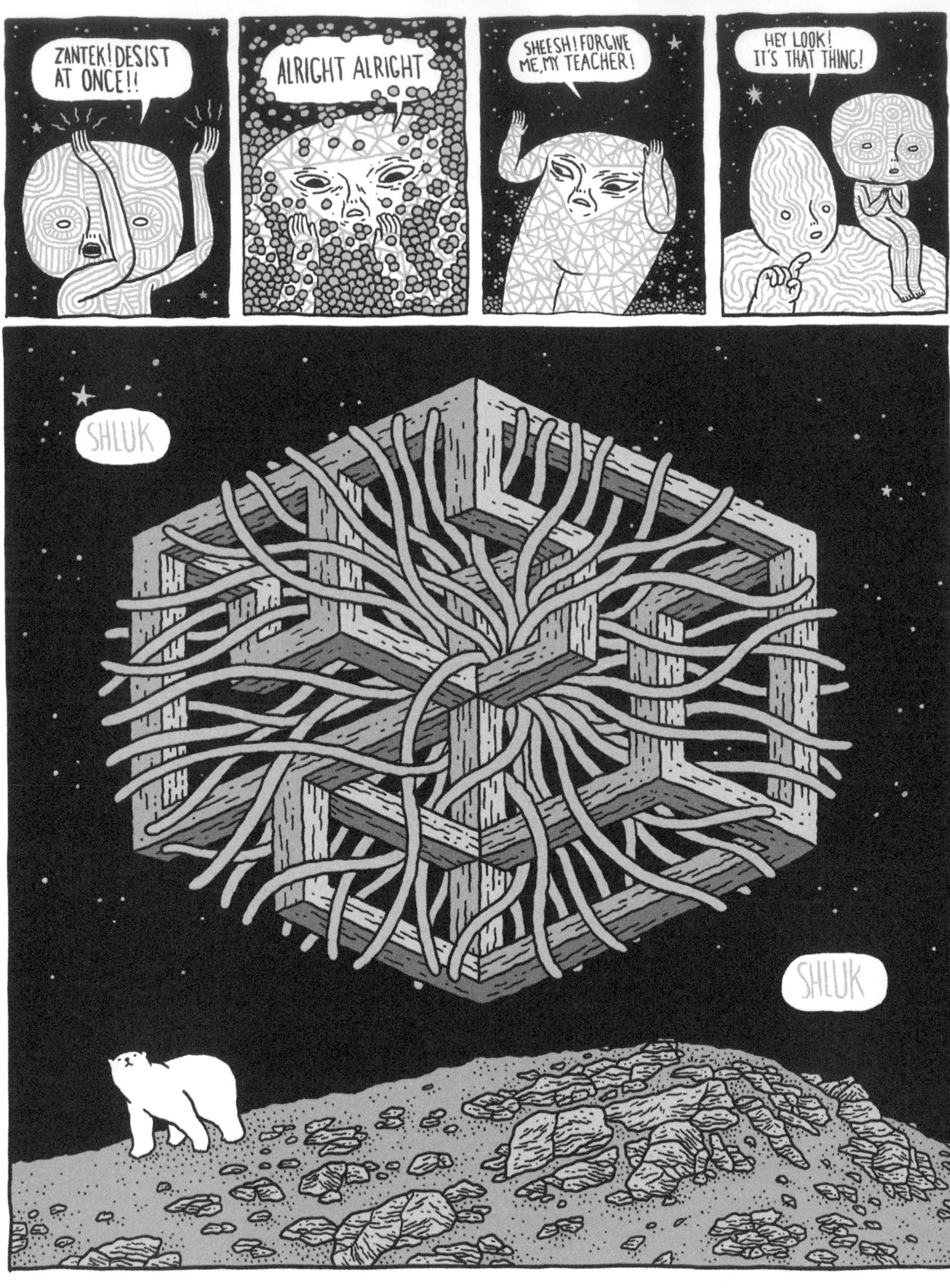
ZANTEK! DESIST AT ONCE!!
ALRIGHT ALRIGHT
SHEESH! FORGIVE ME, MY TEACHER!
HEY LOOK! IT'S THAT THING!
SHLUK
SHLUK

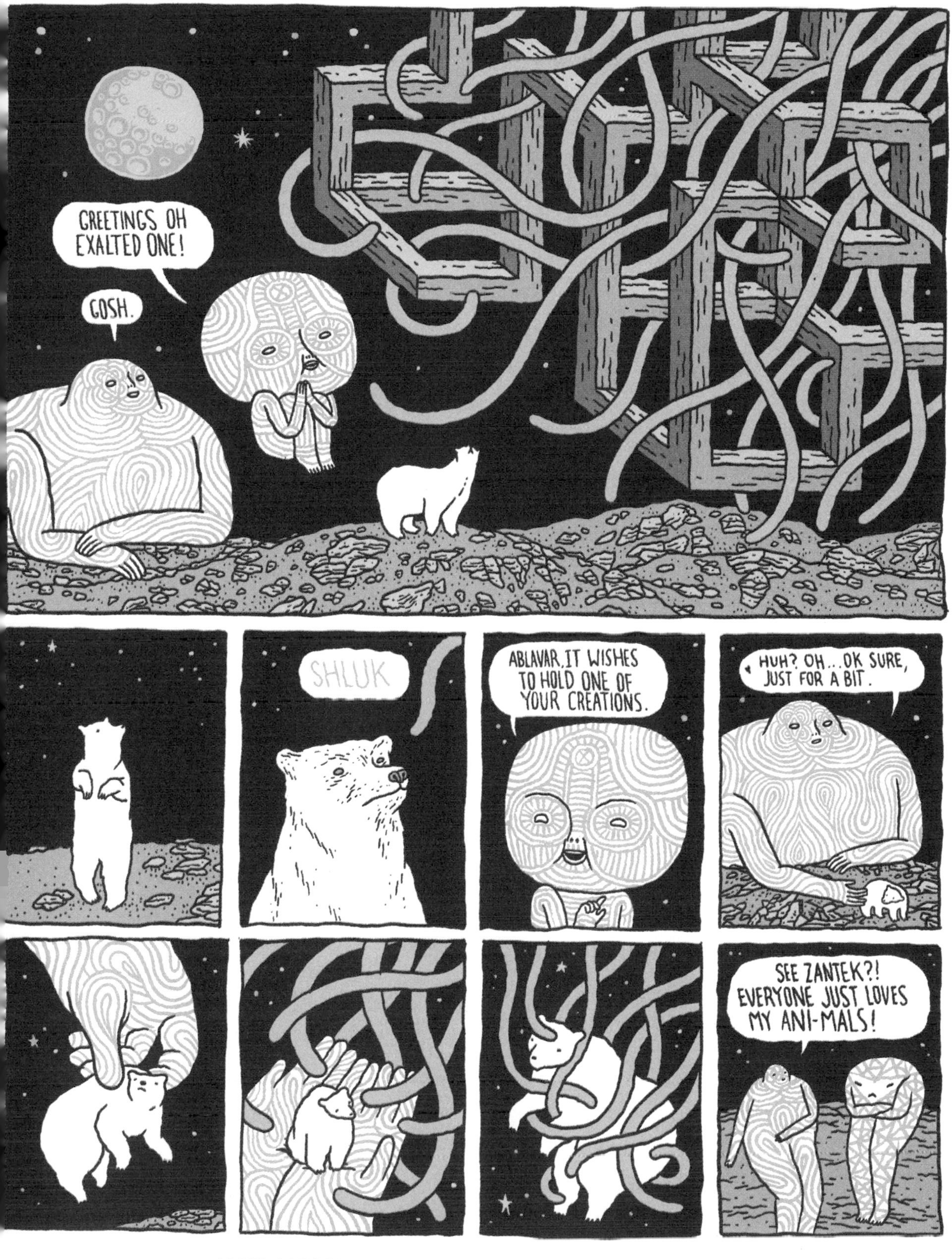
GREETINGS OH EXALTED ONE!
GOSH.
SHLUK
ABLAVAR, IT WISHES TO HOLD ONE OF YOUR CREATIONS.
HUH? OH...OK SURE, JUST FOR A BIT.
SEE ZANTEK?! EVERYONE JUST LOVES MY ANI-MALS!

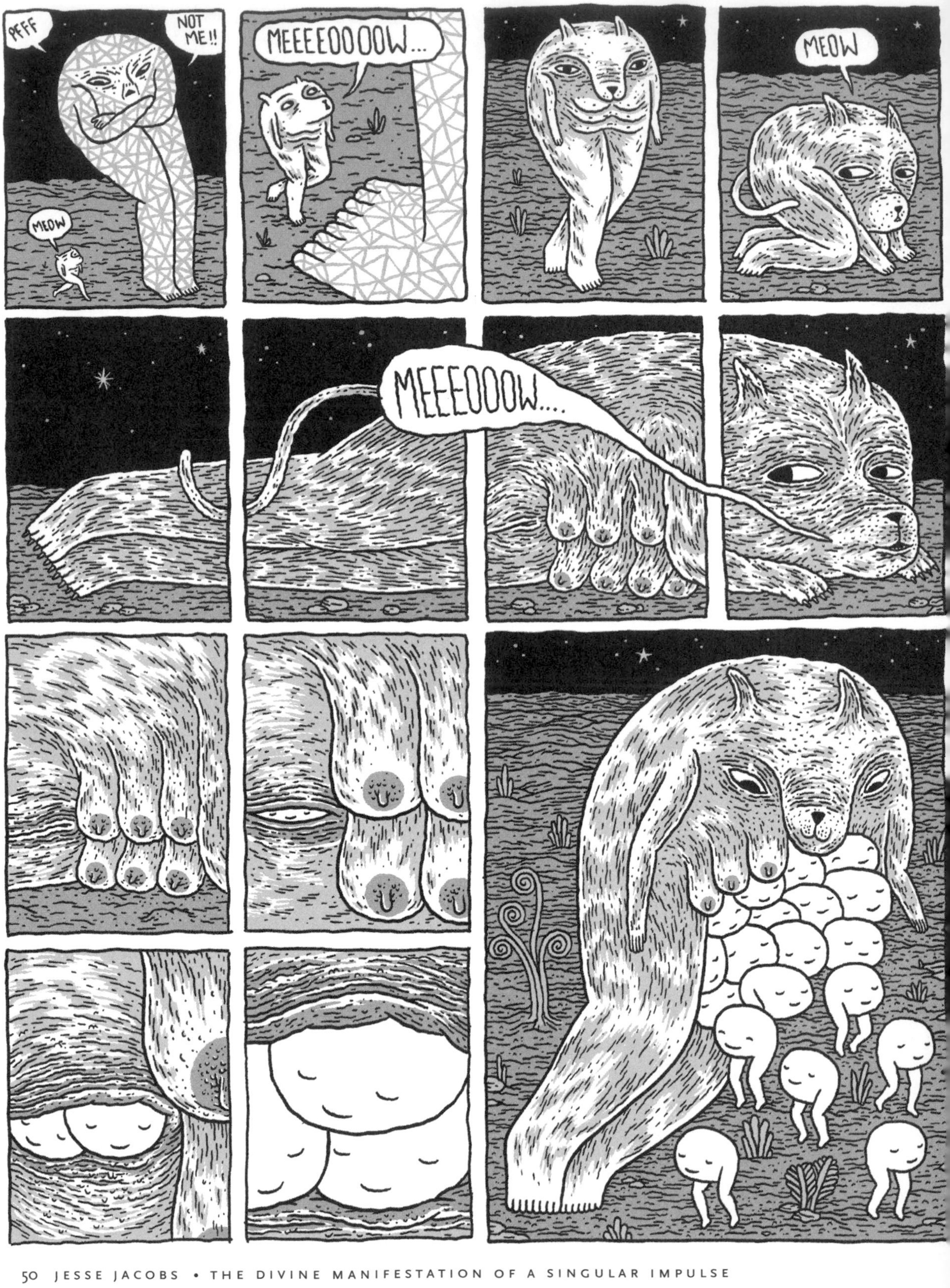
PFFF
NOT ME!!
MEOW
MEEEEOOOOW...
MEOW
MEEEOOOW....

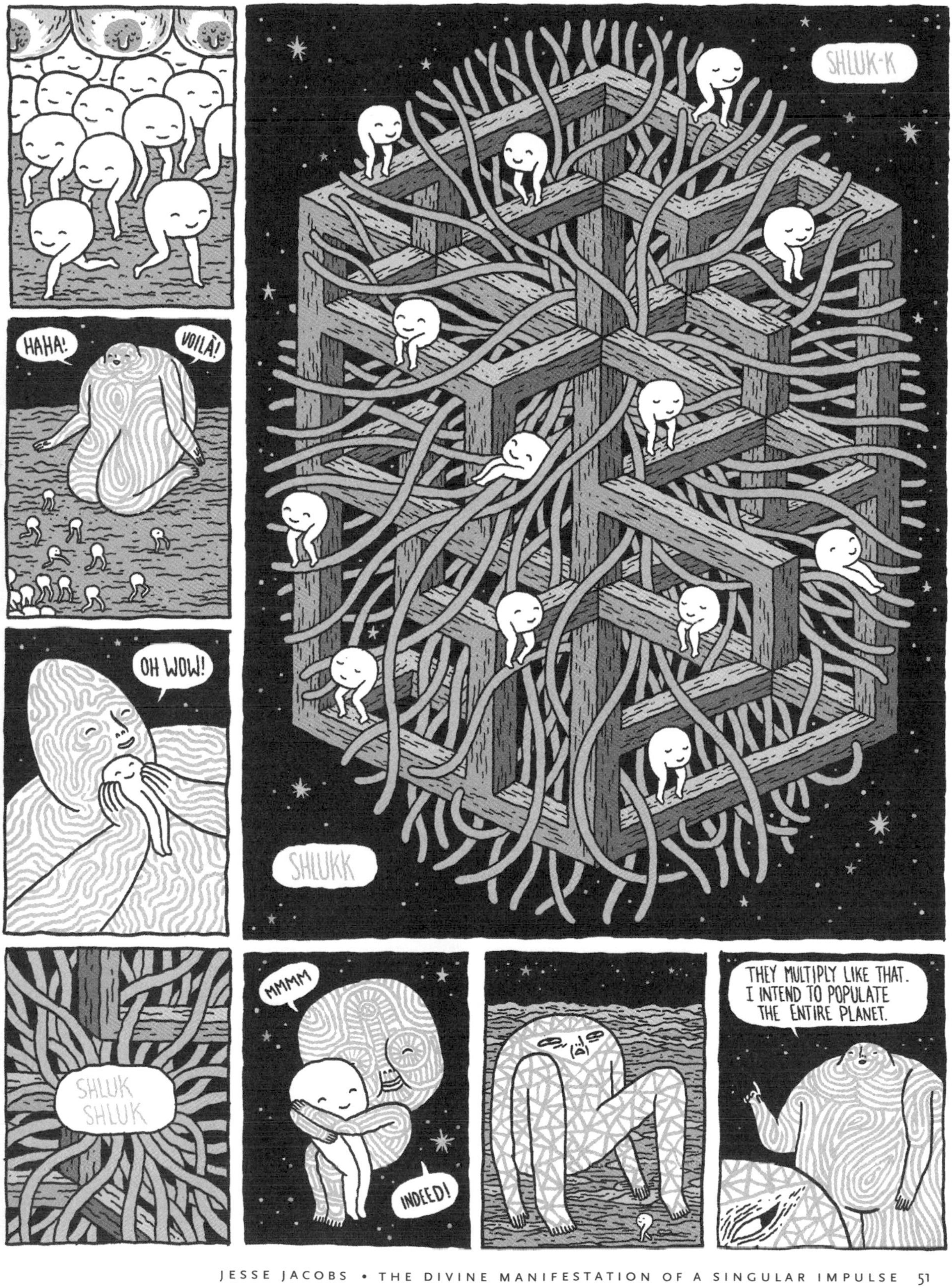
HAHA!
VOILÀ!
OH WOW!
SHLUK-K
SHLUKK
SHLUK
SHLUK
MMMM
INDEED!
THEY MULTIPLY LIKE THAT.
I INTEND TO POPULATE
THE ENTIRE PLANET.

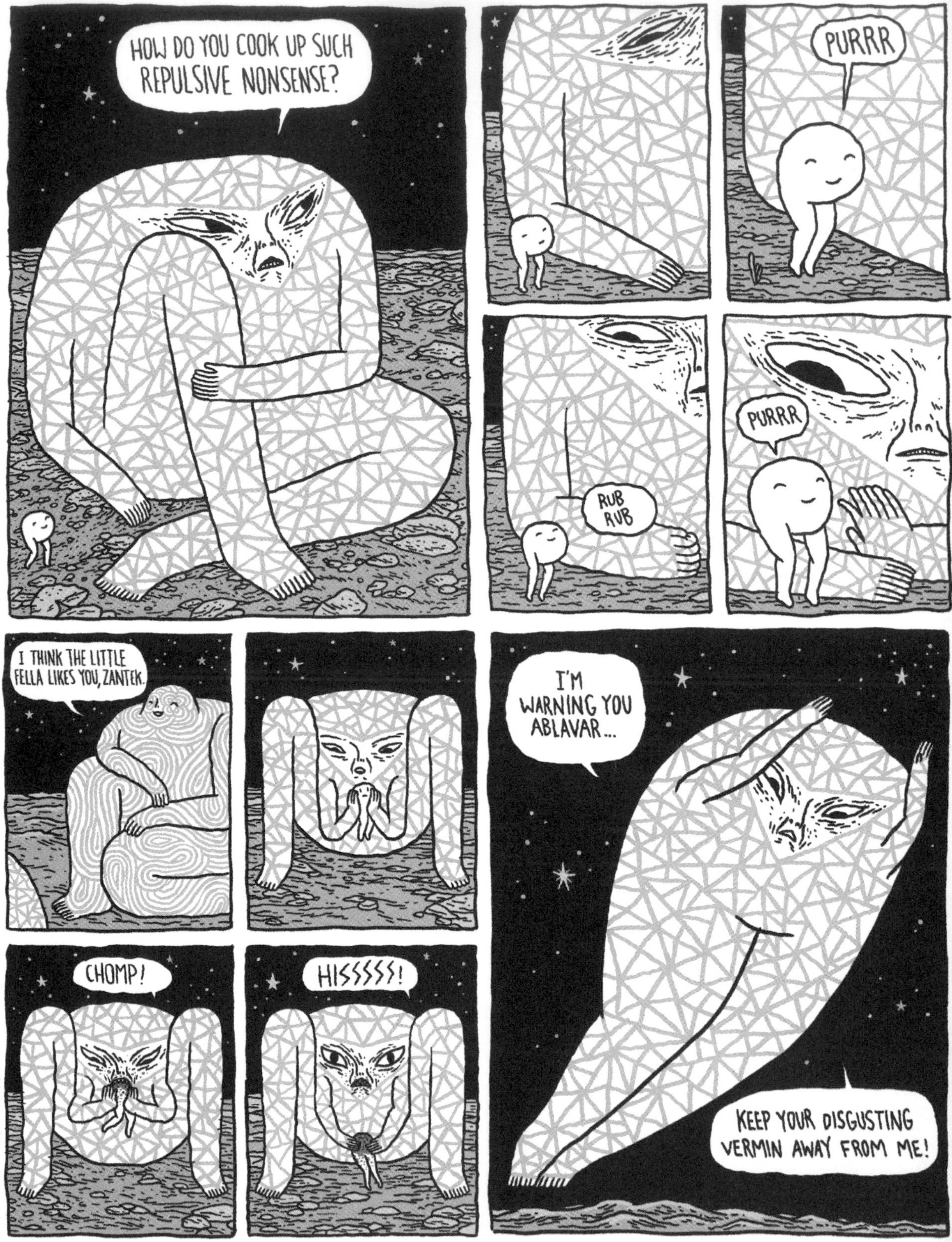
HOW DO YOU COOK UP SUCH REPULSIVE NONSENSE?
PURRR
RUB RUB
PURRR
I THINK THE LITTLE FELLA LIKES YOU, ZANTEK.
I'M WARNING YOU ABLAVAR...
KEEP YOUR DISGUSTING VERMIN AWAY FROM ME!
CHOMP!
HISSSSS!

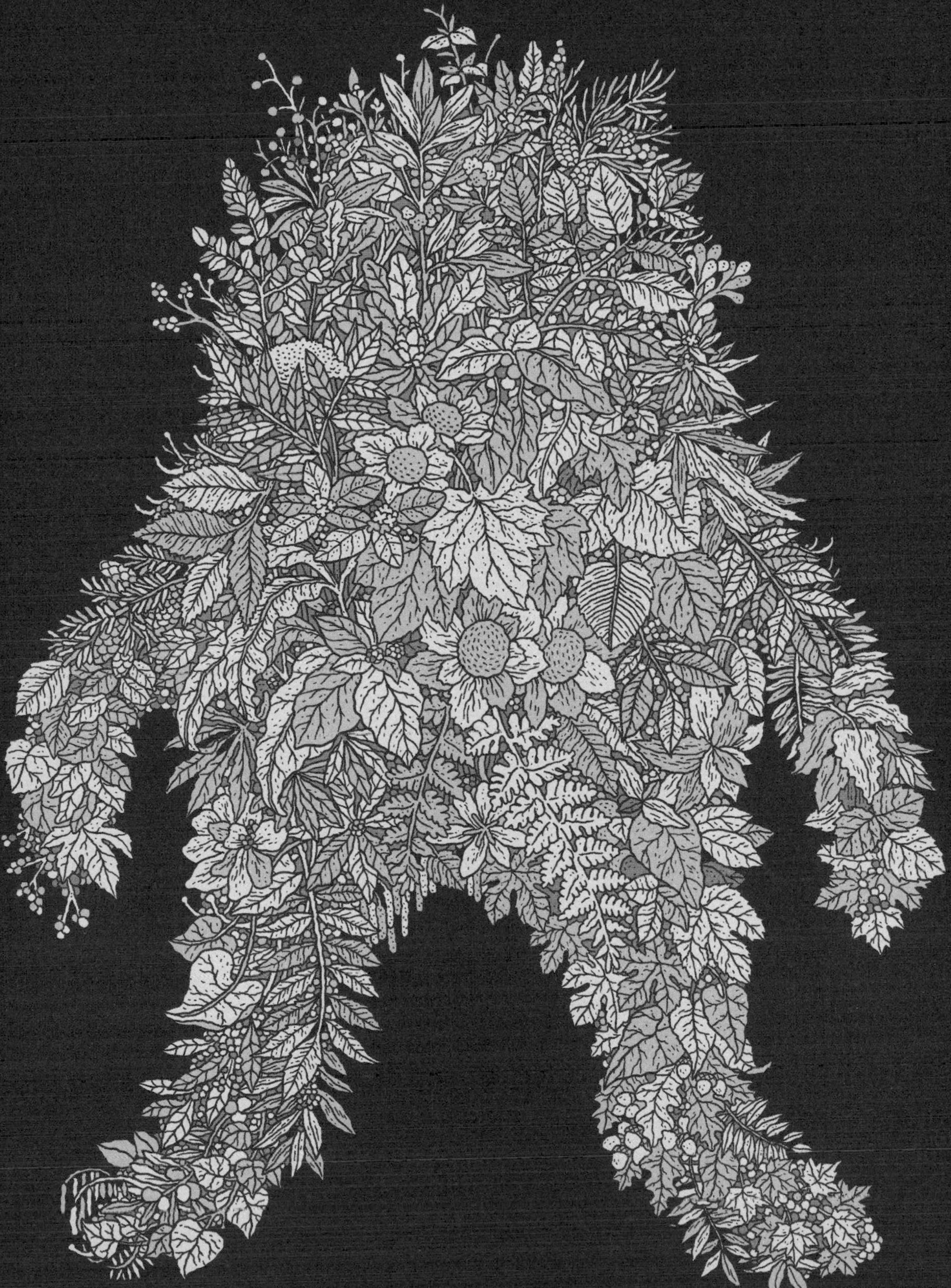

SAM ALDEN

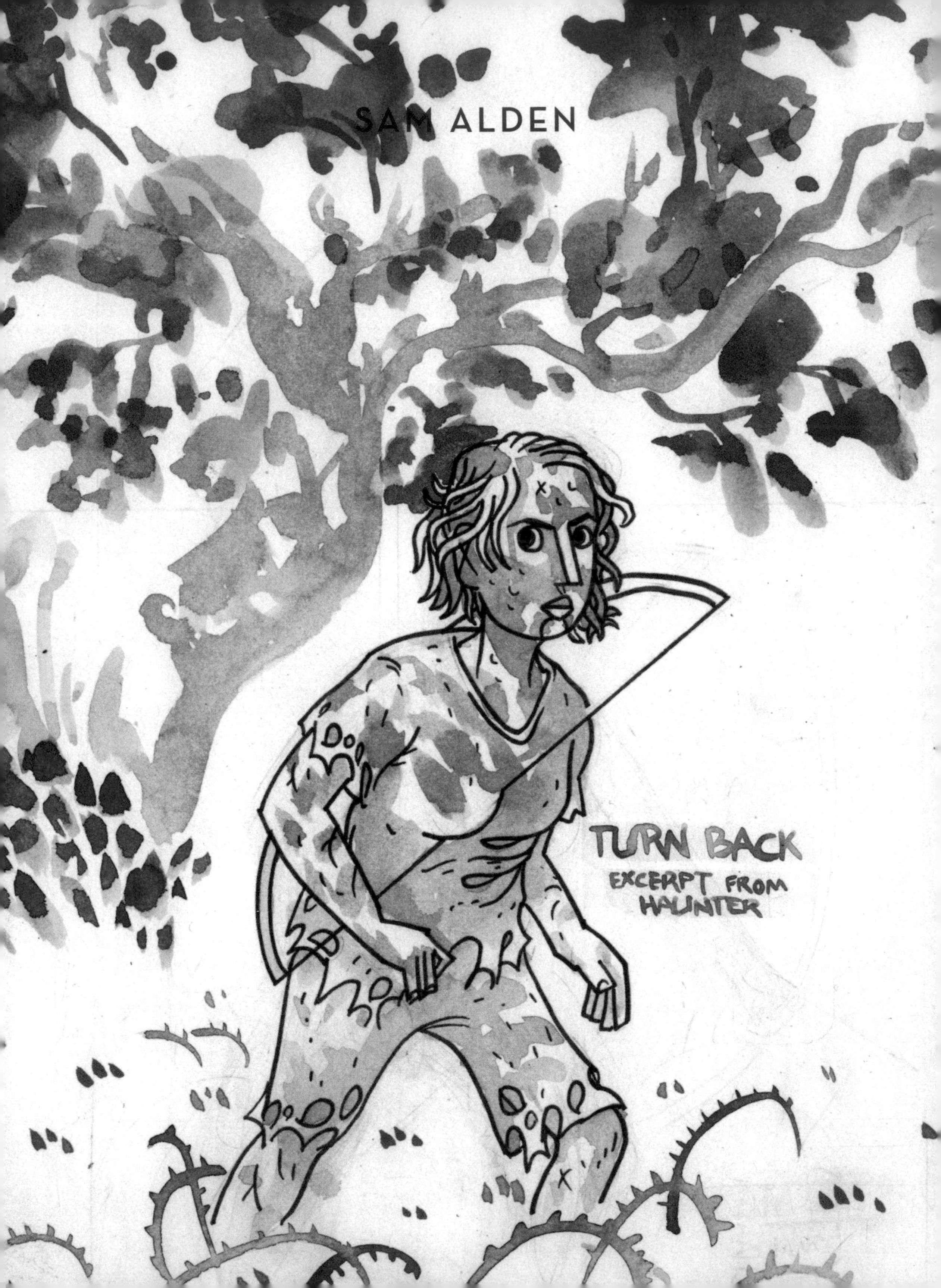
TURN BACK
EXCERPT FROM
HAUNTER

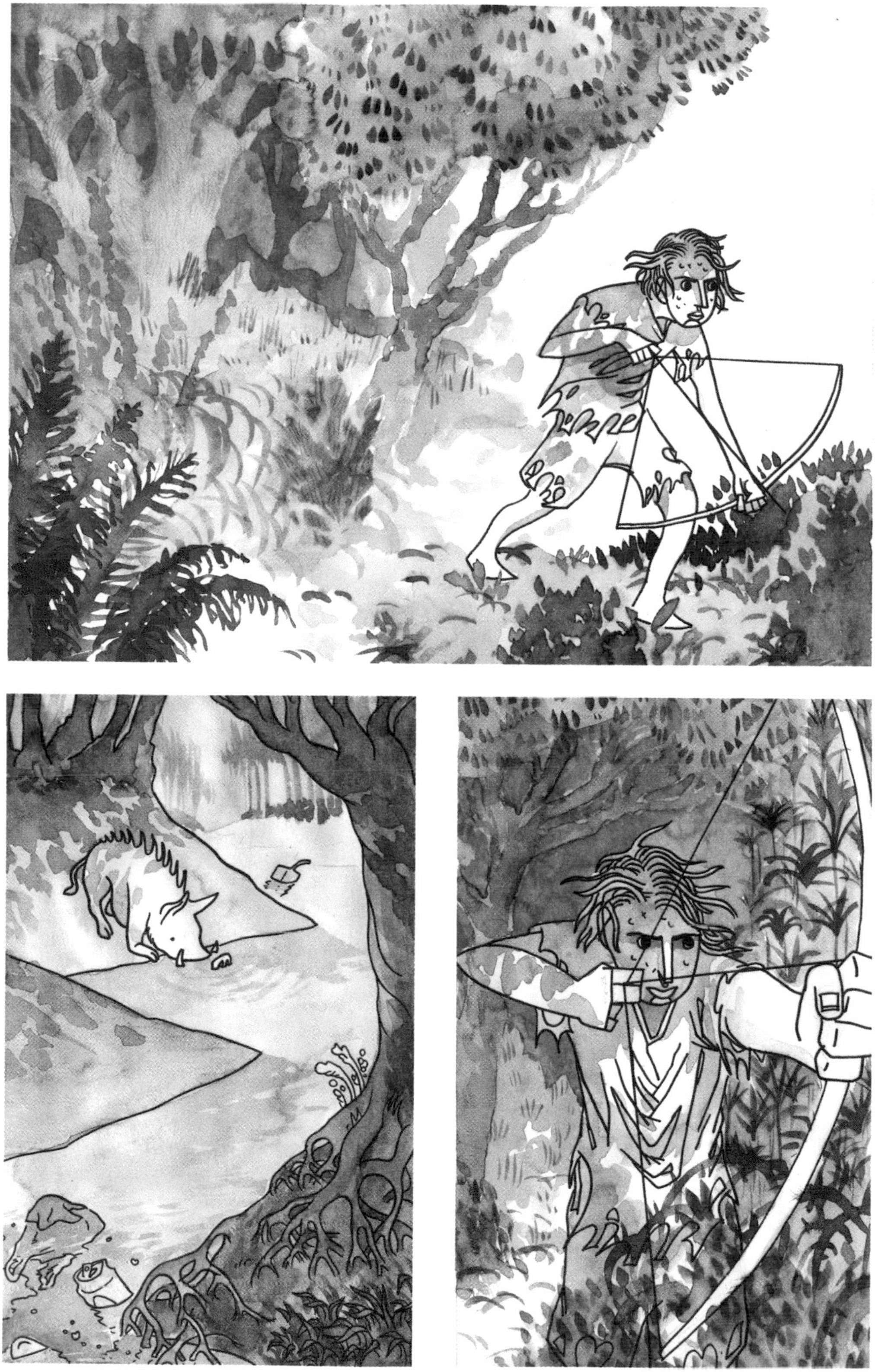

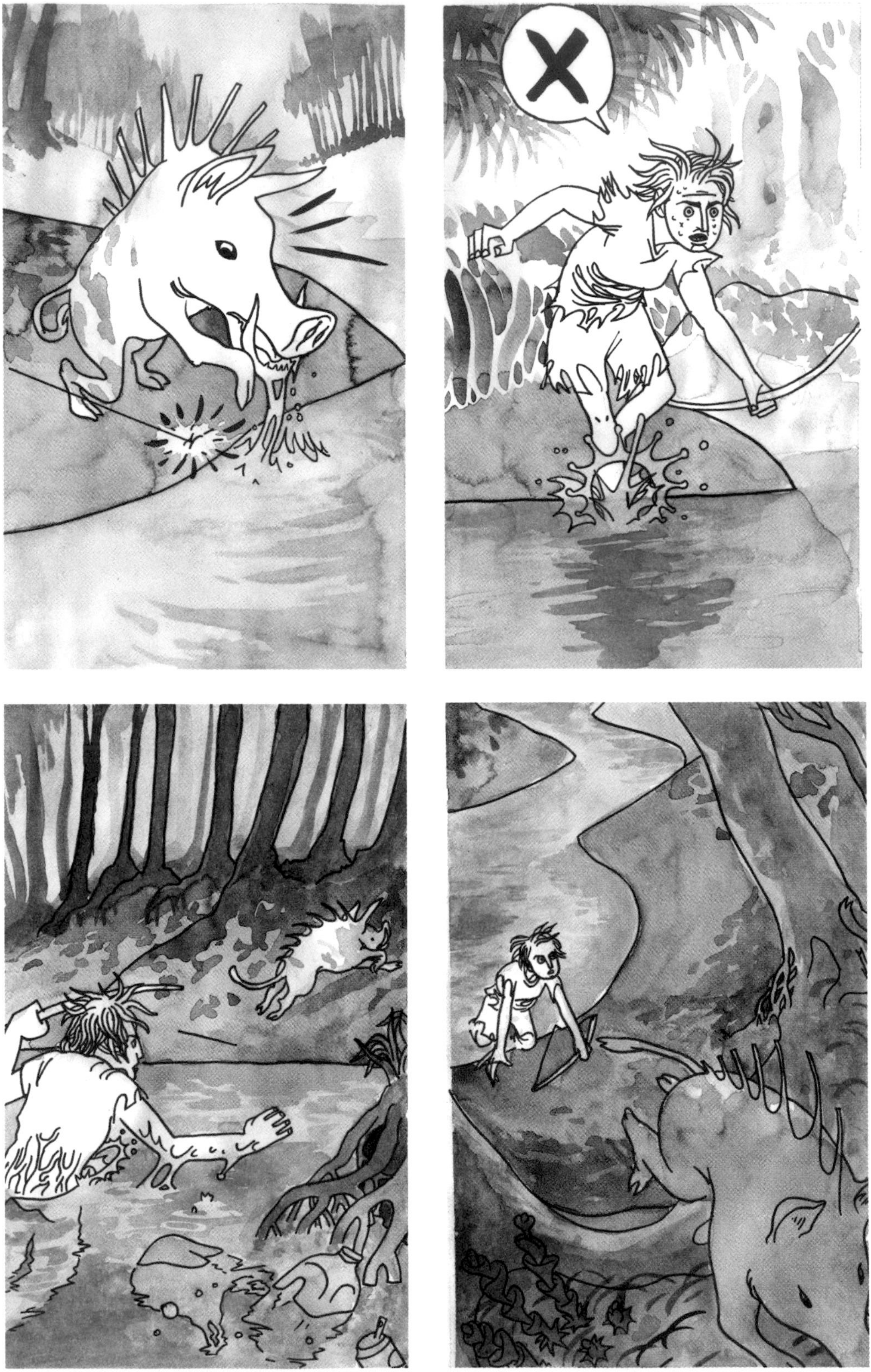

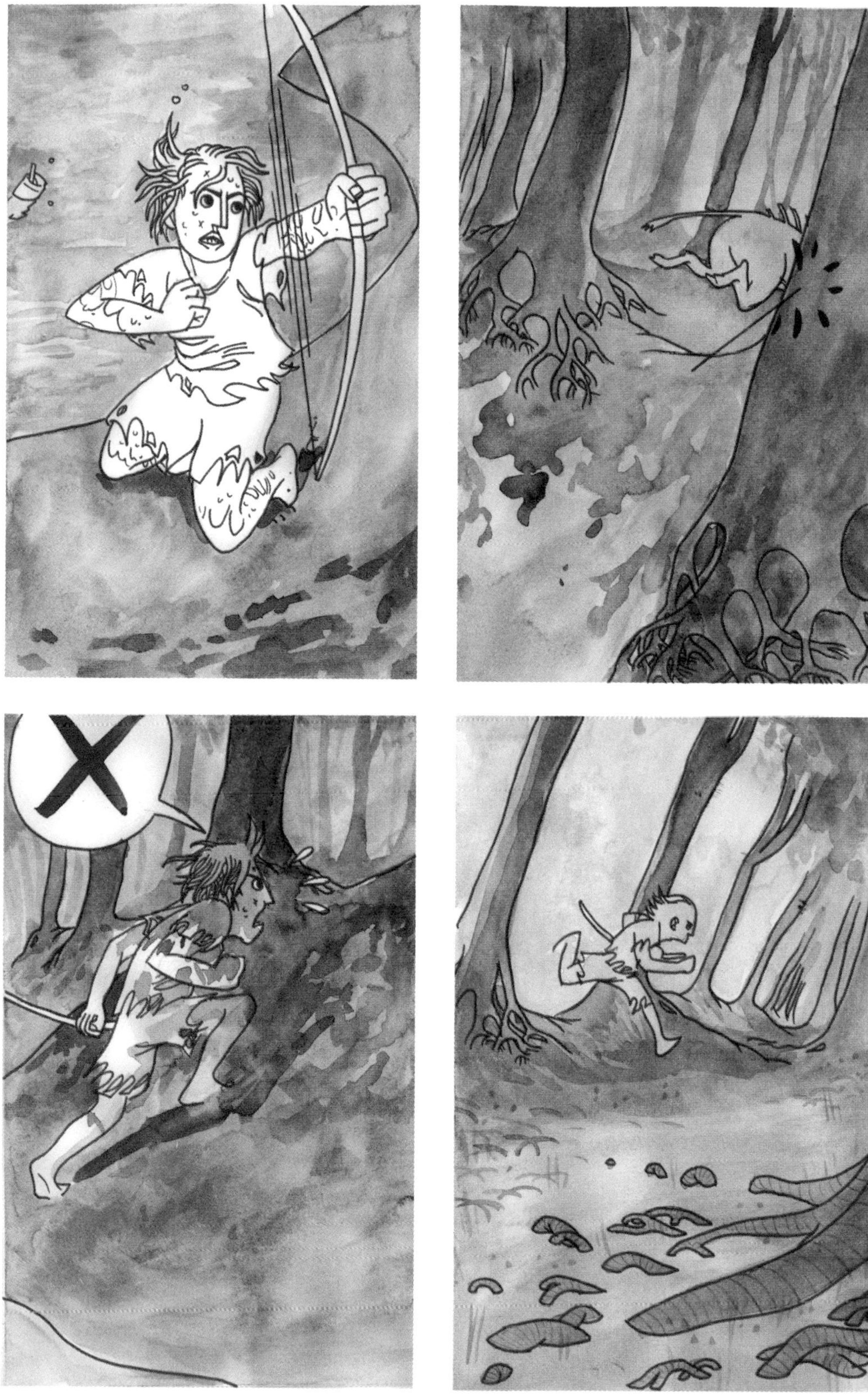
X

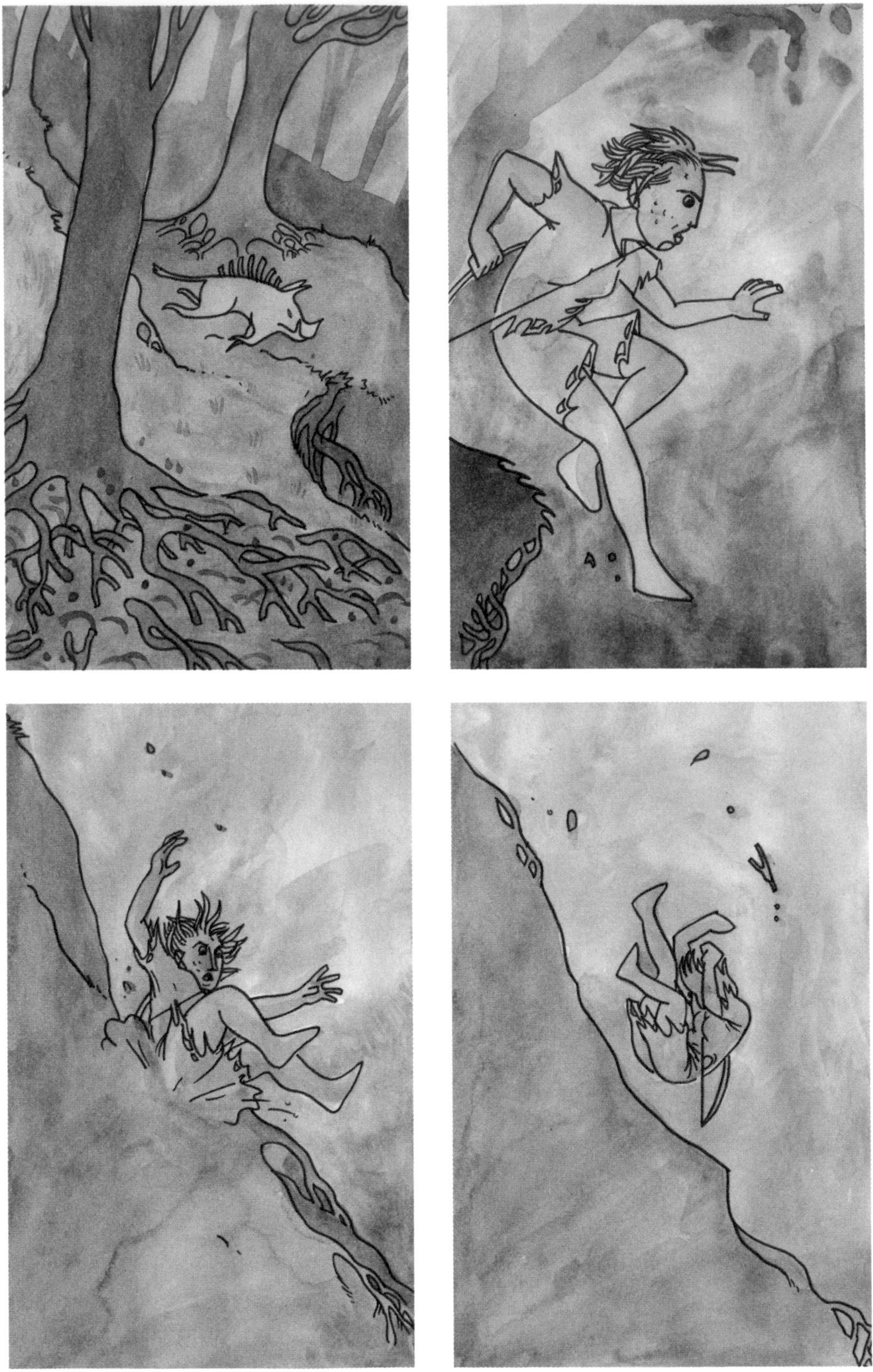

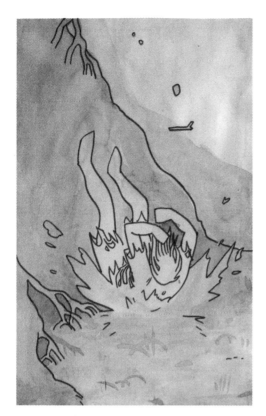

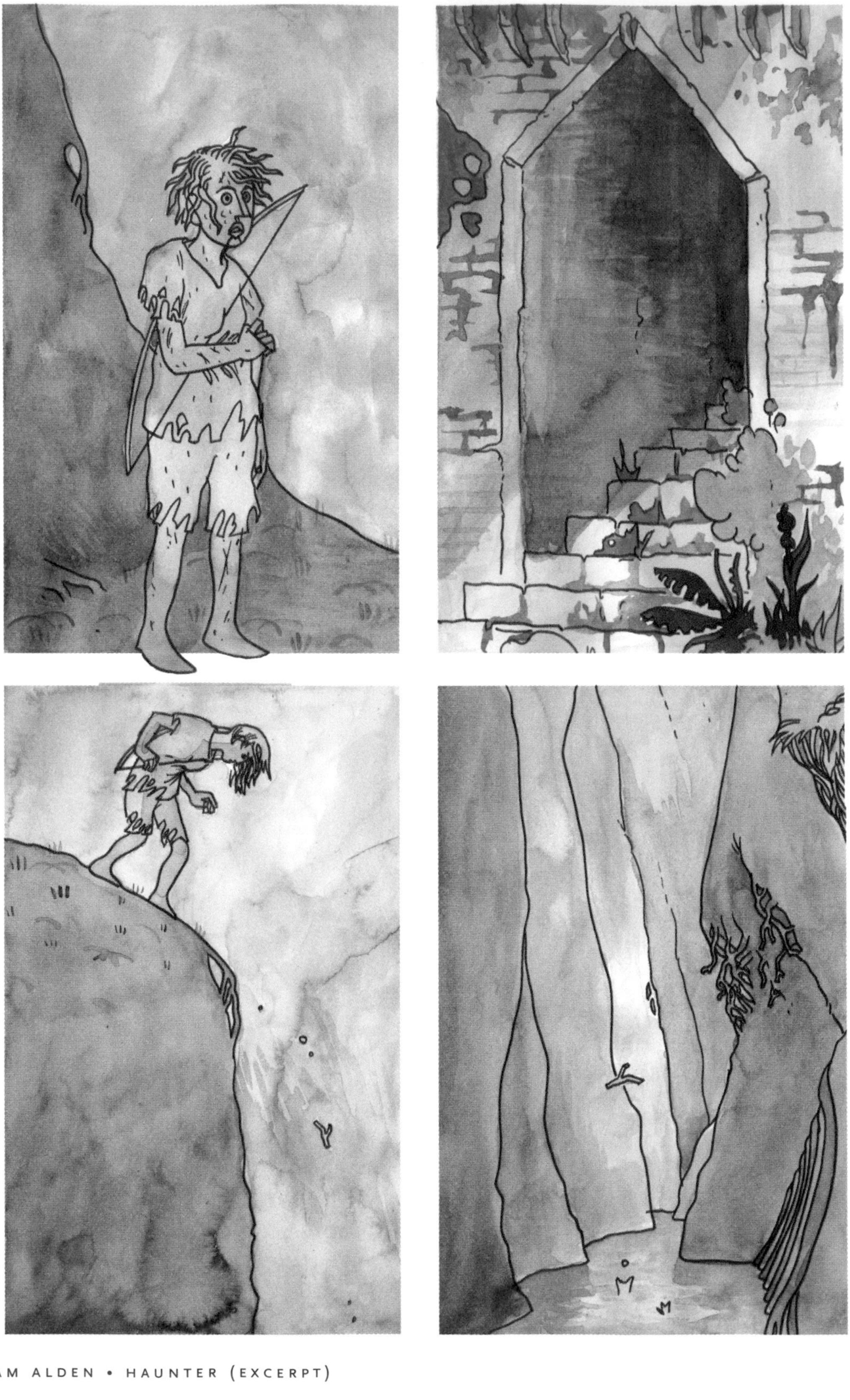

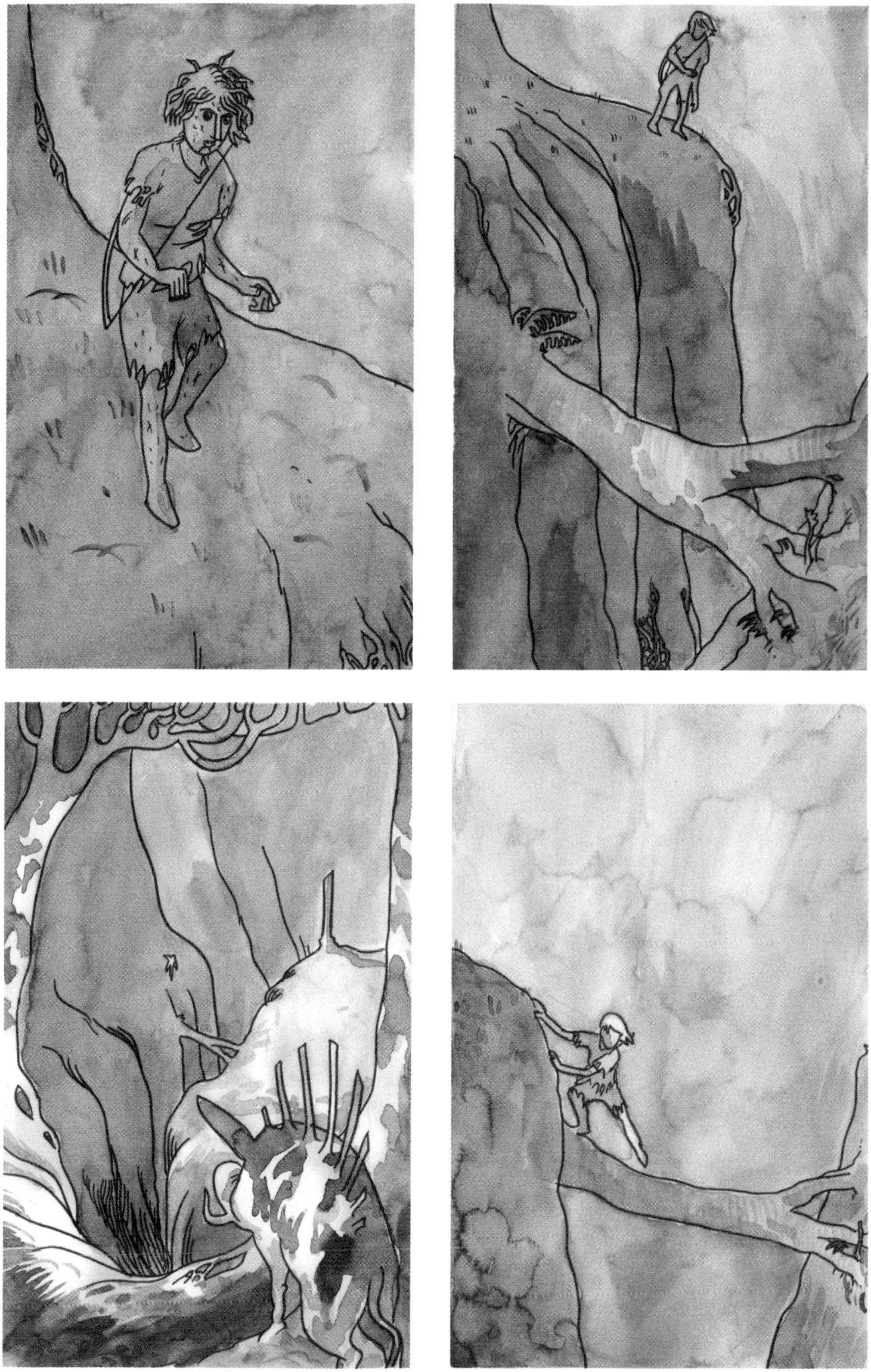

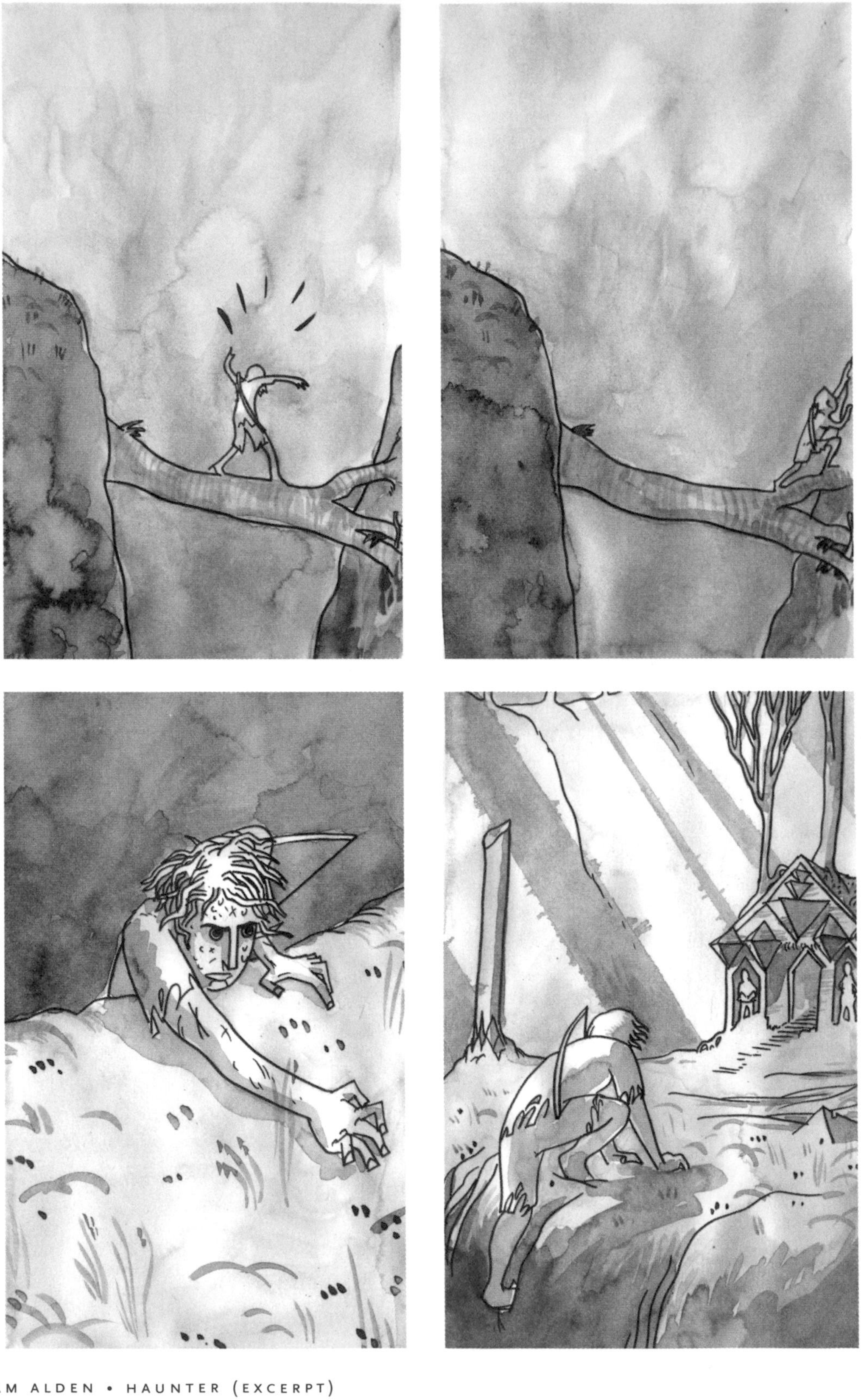

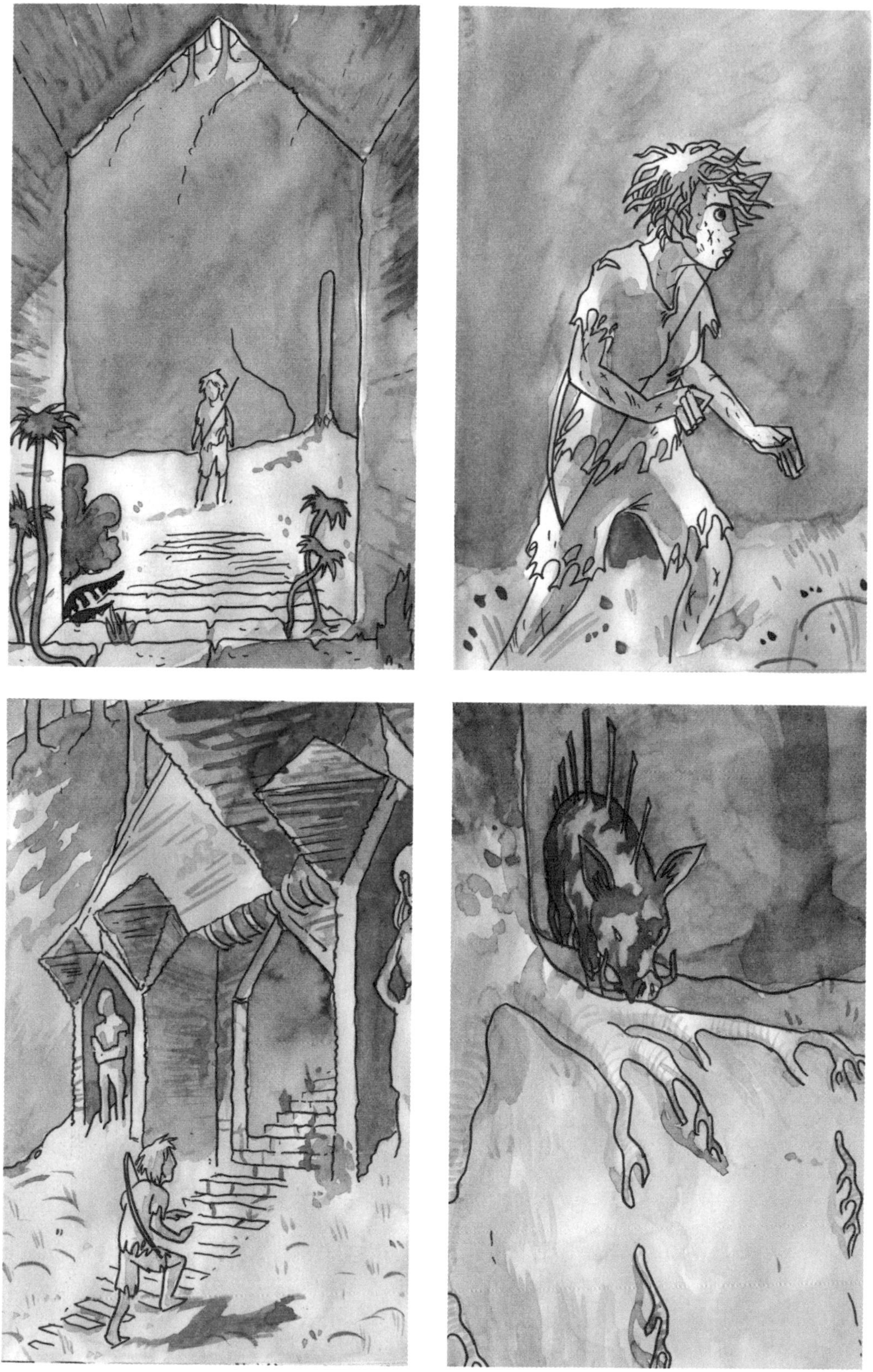

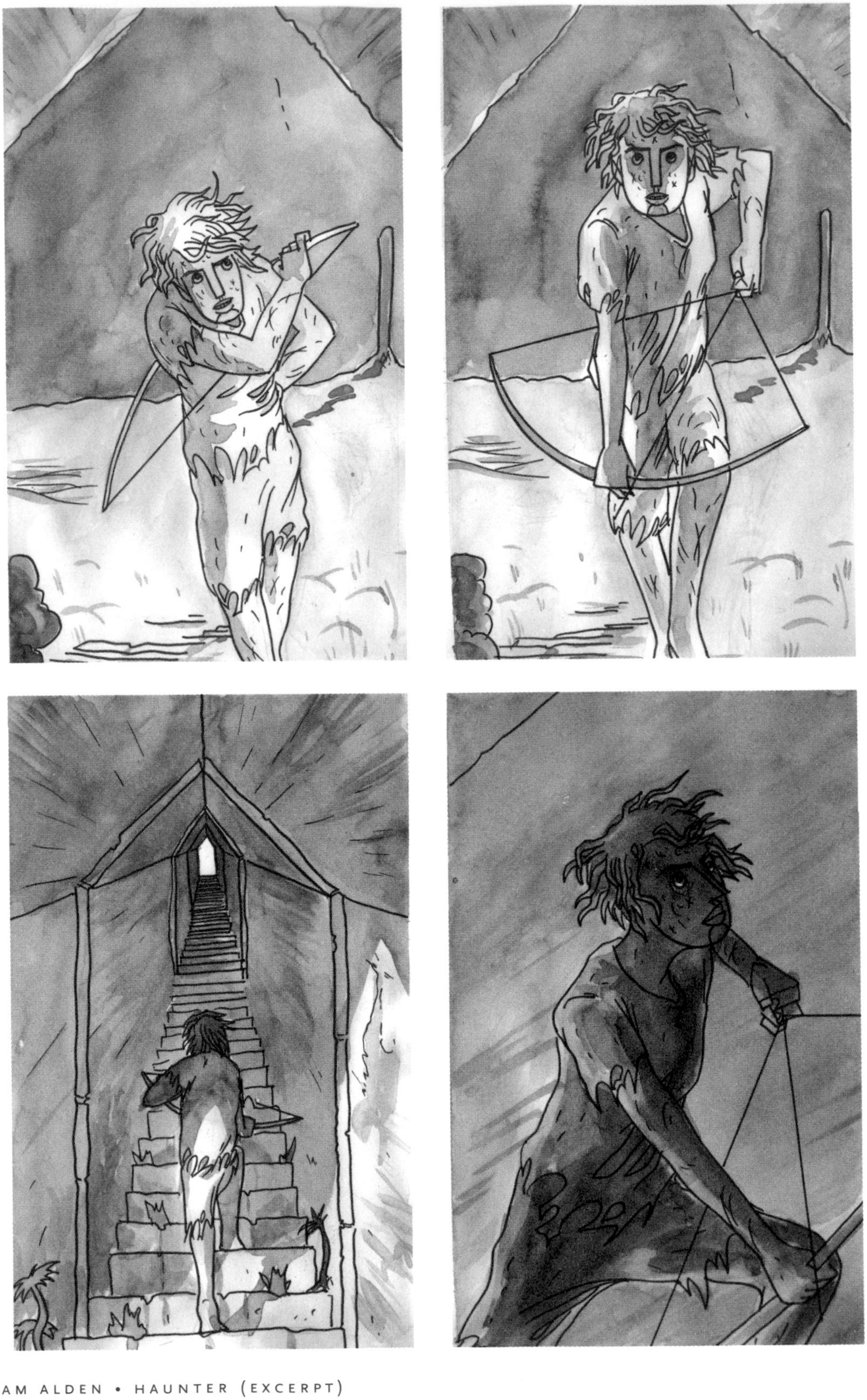

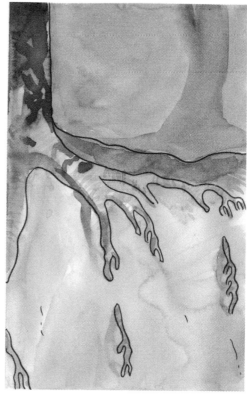

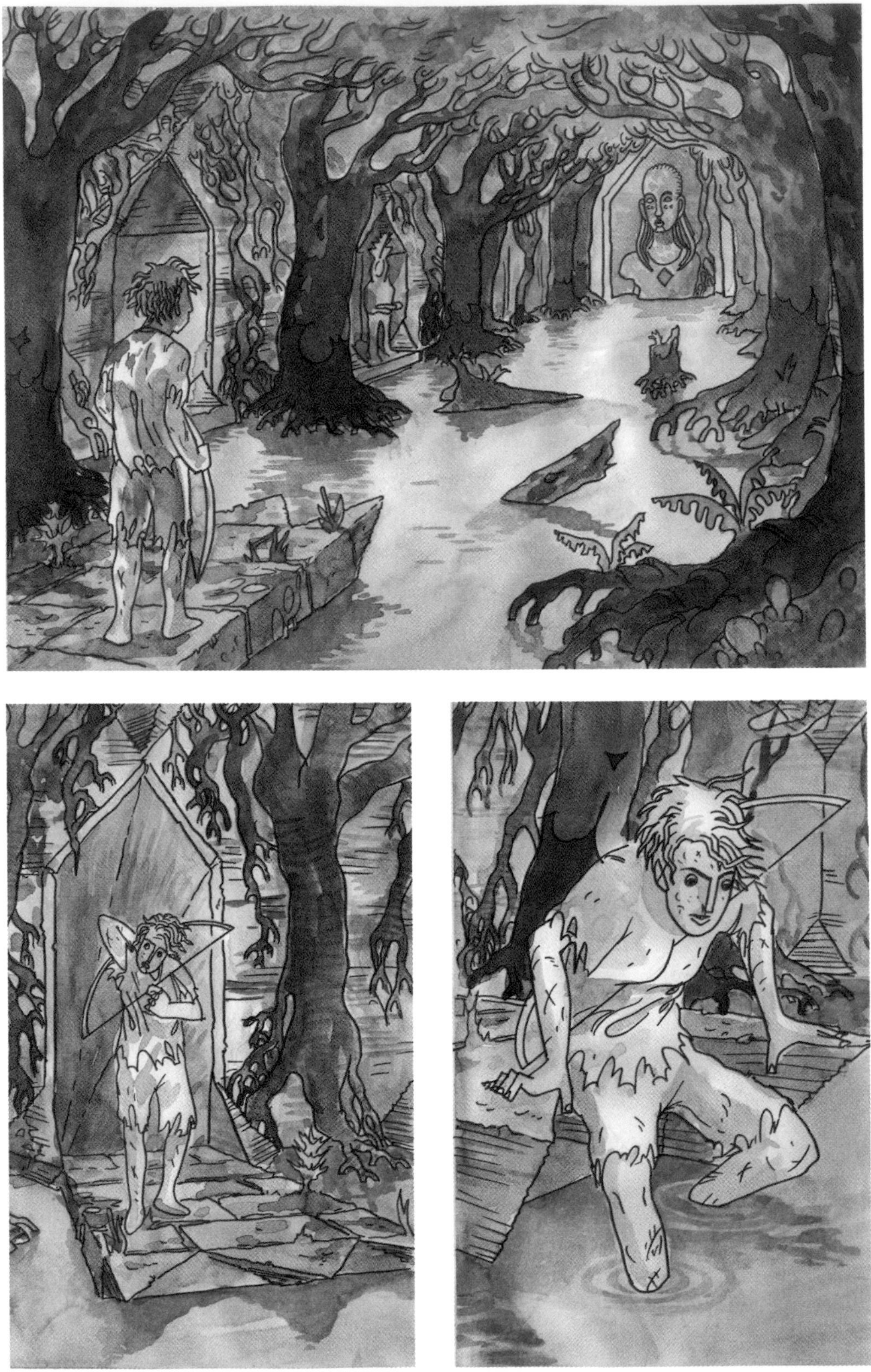

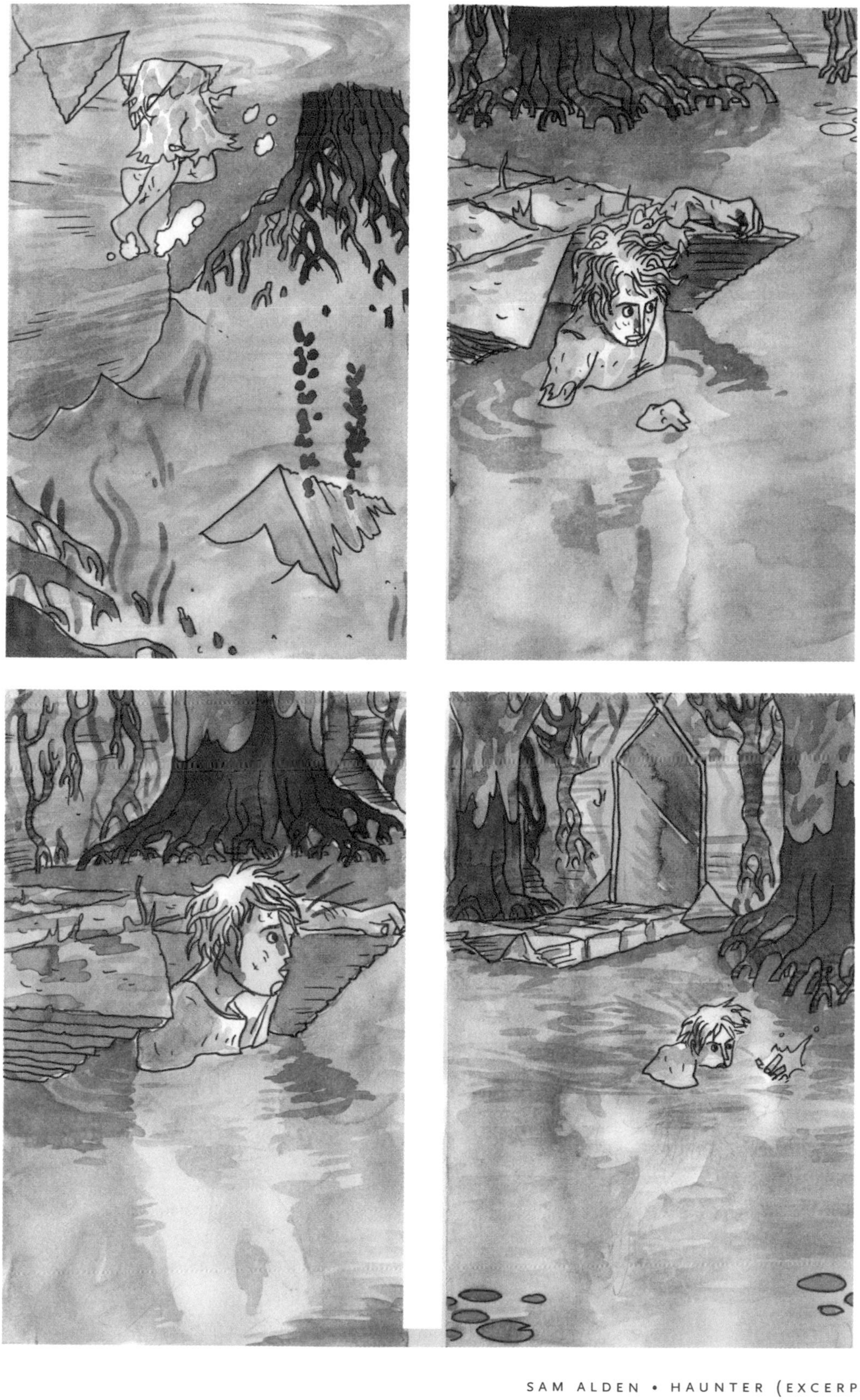

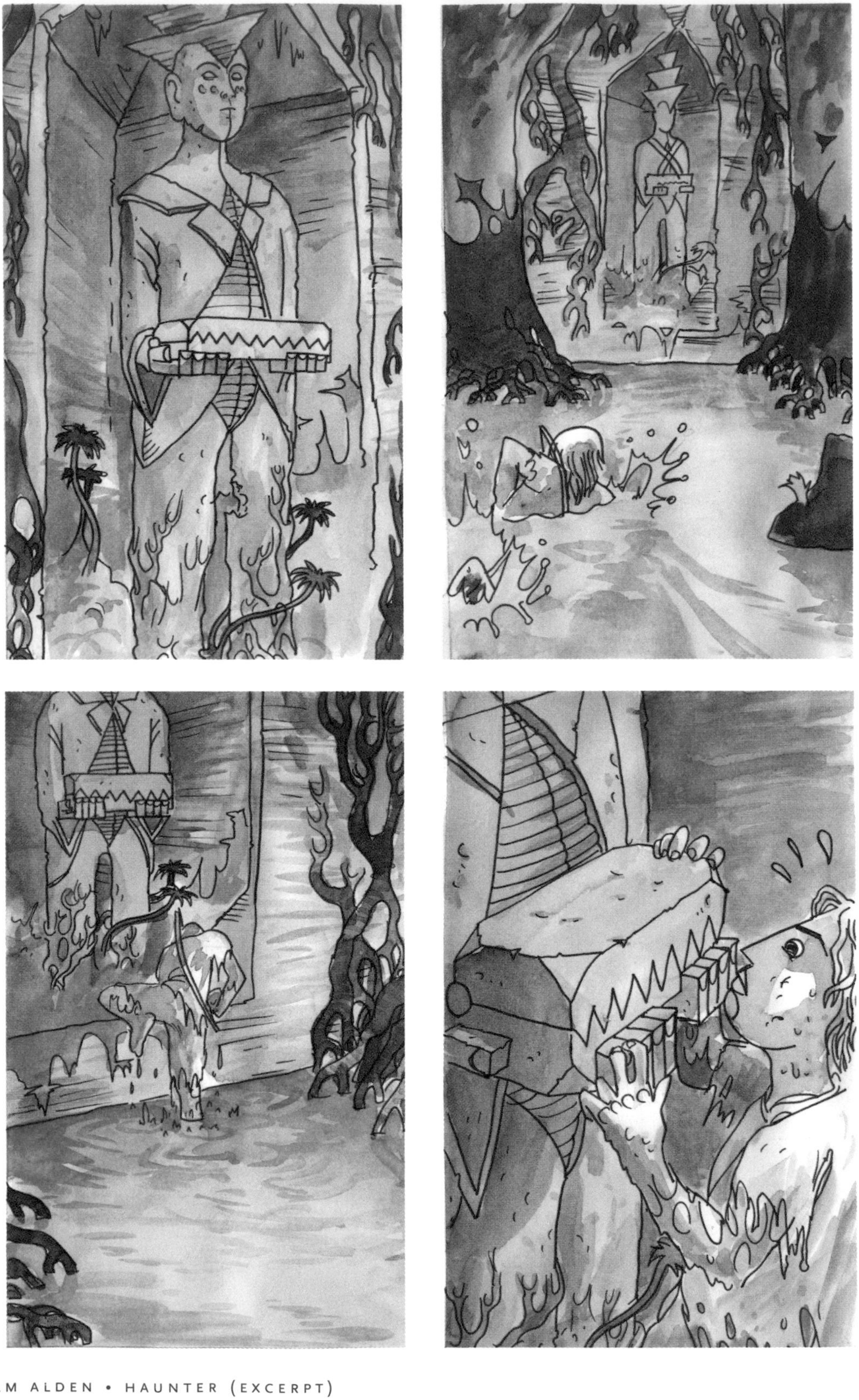

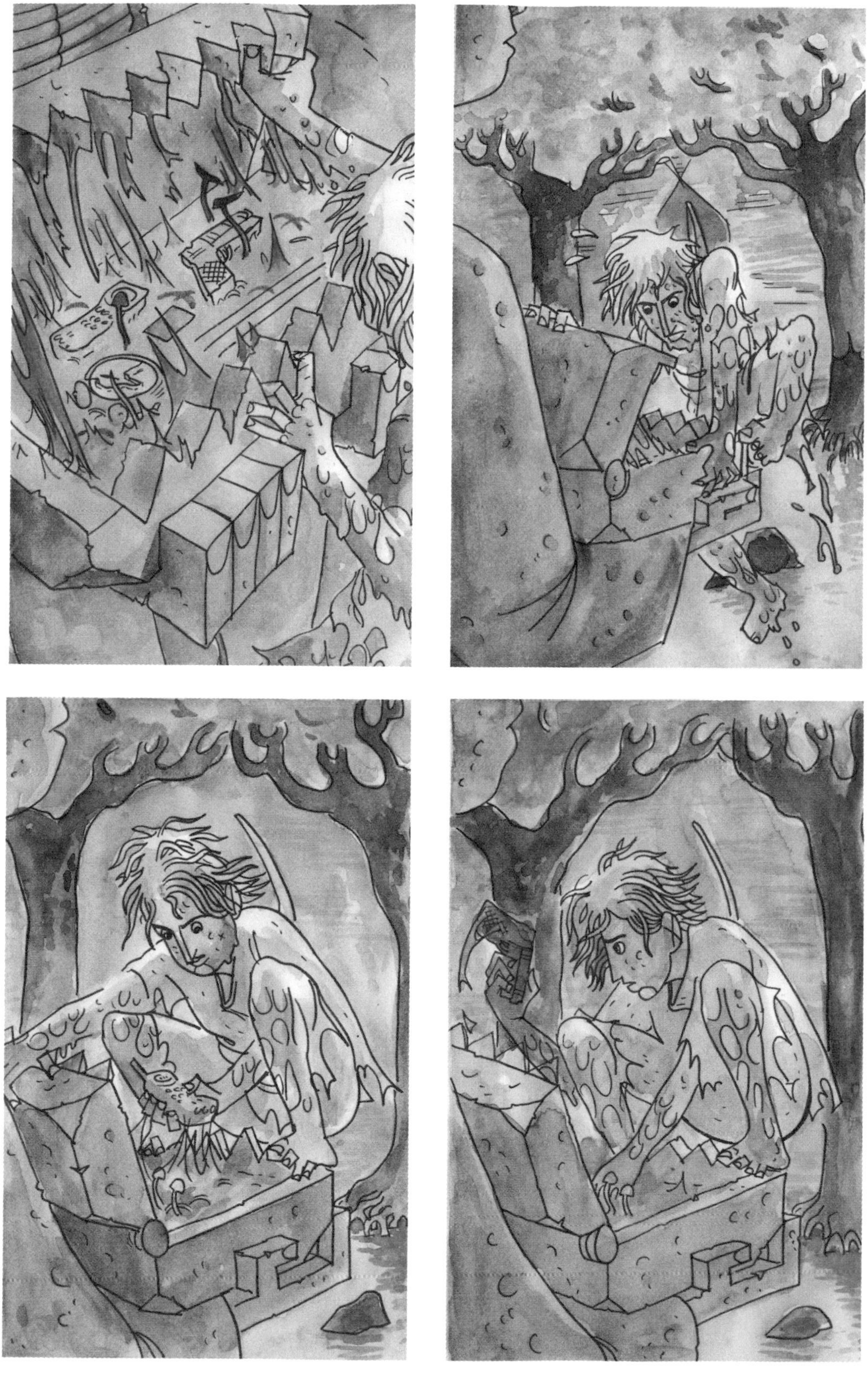

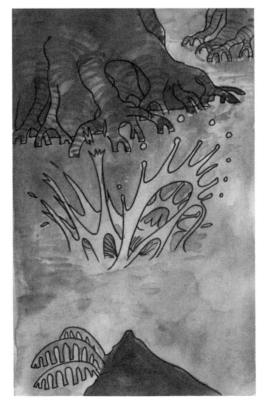

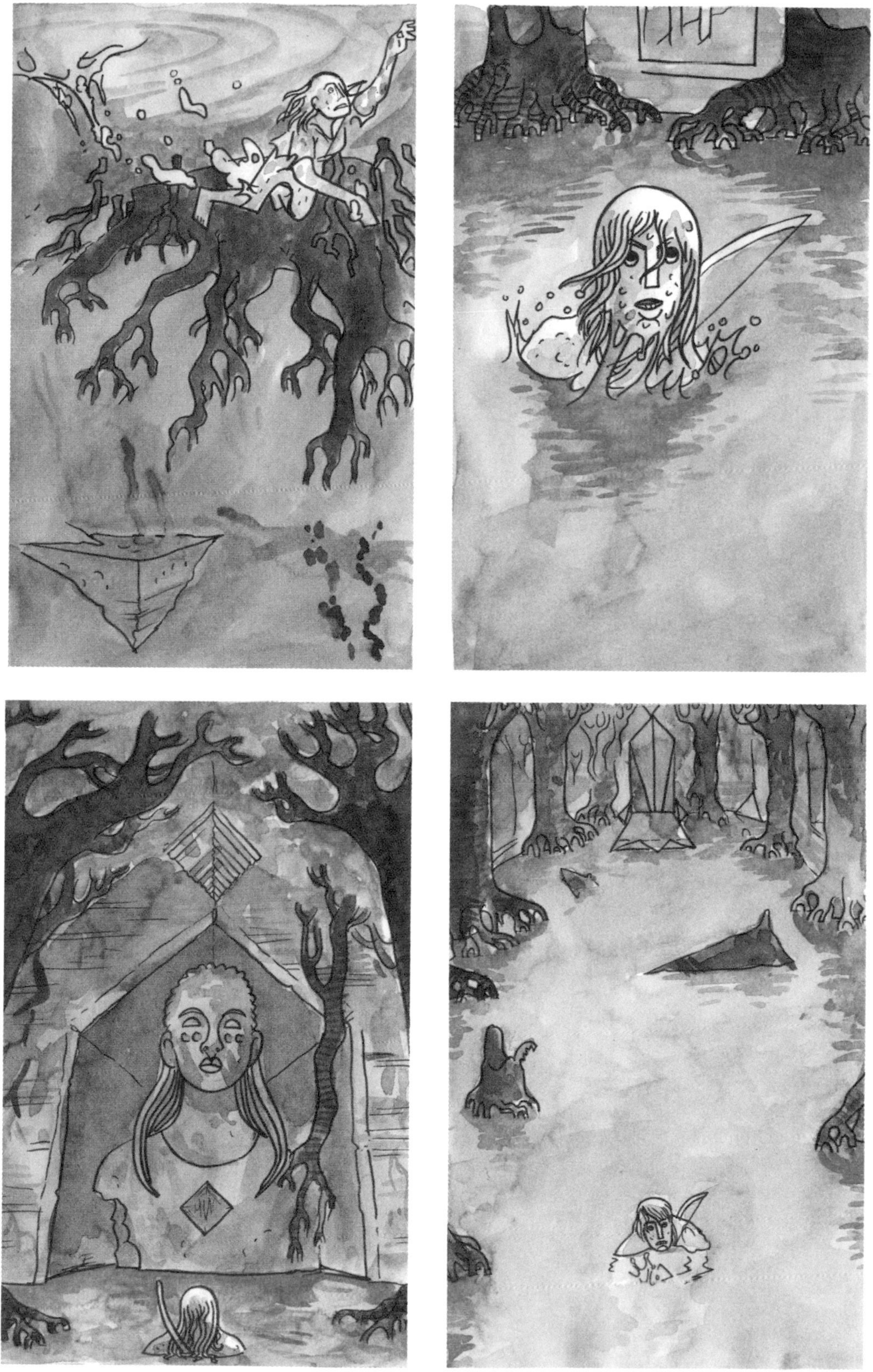

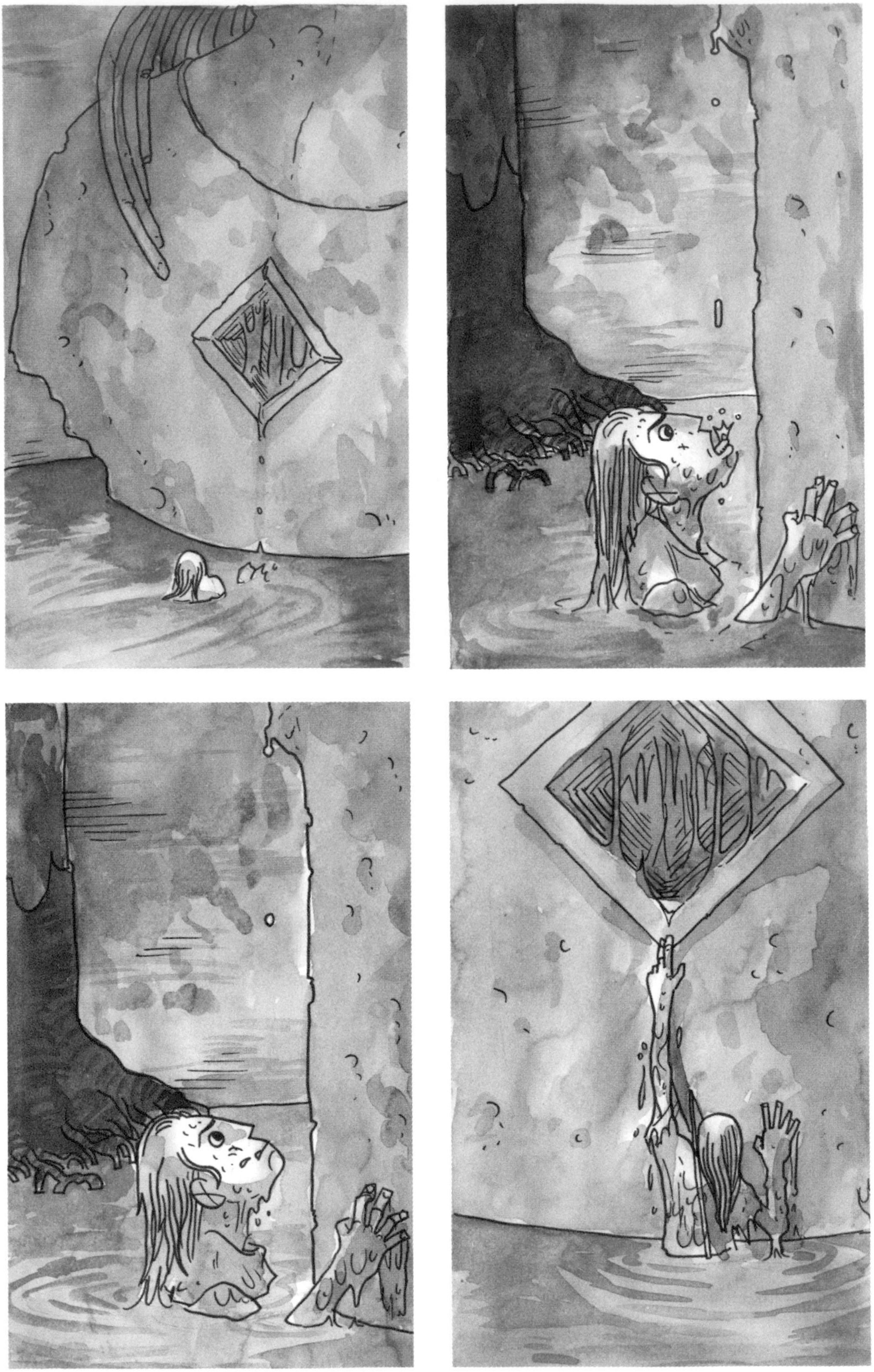

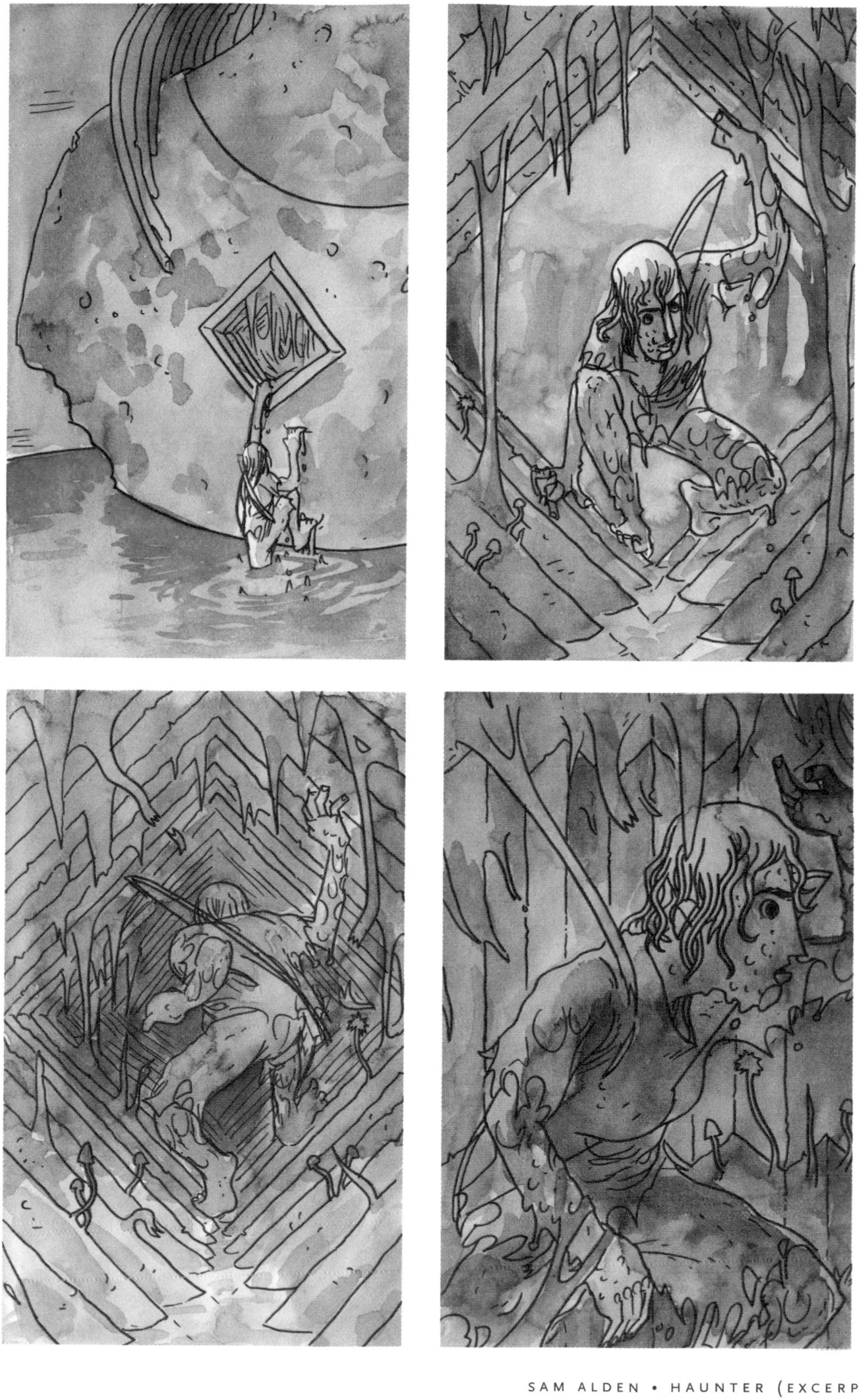

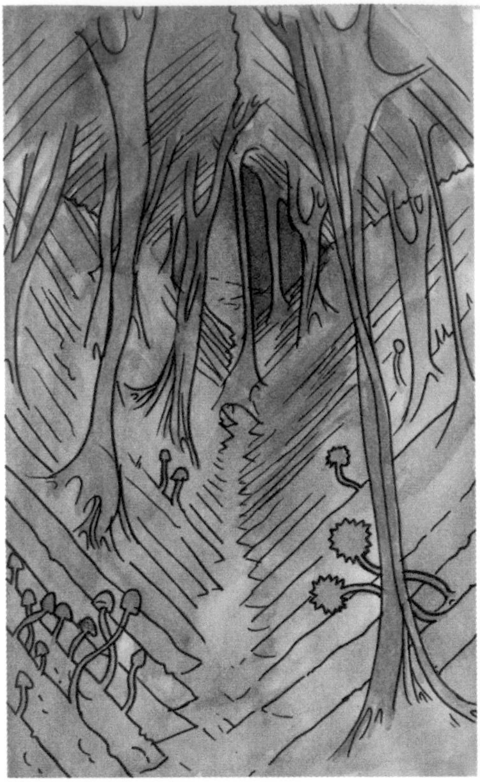

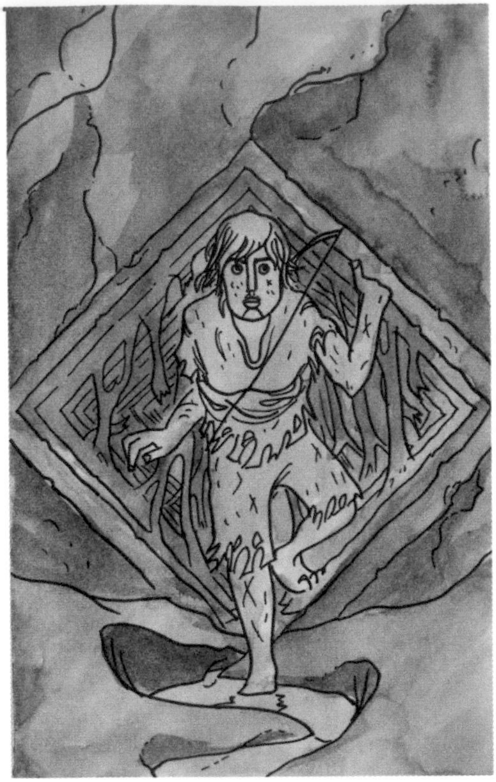

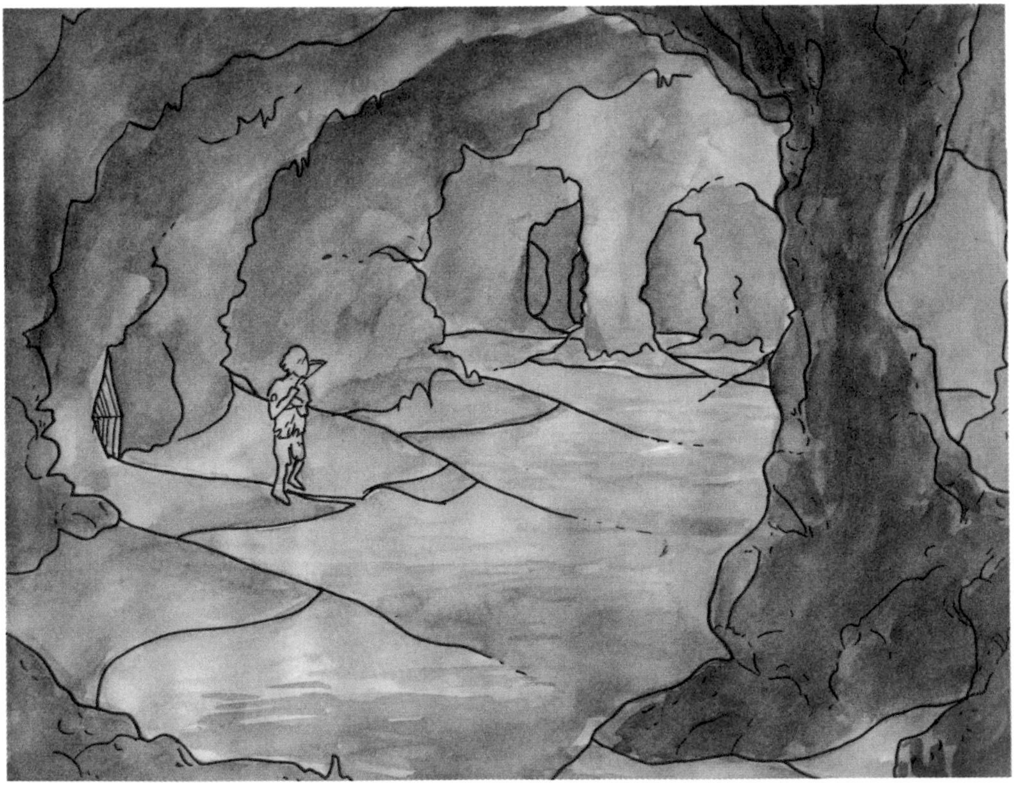

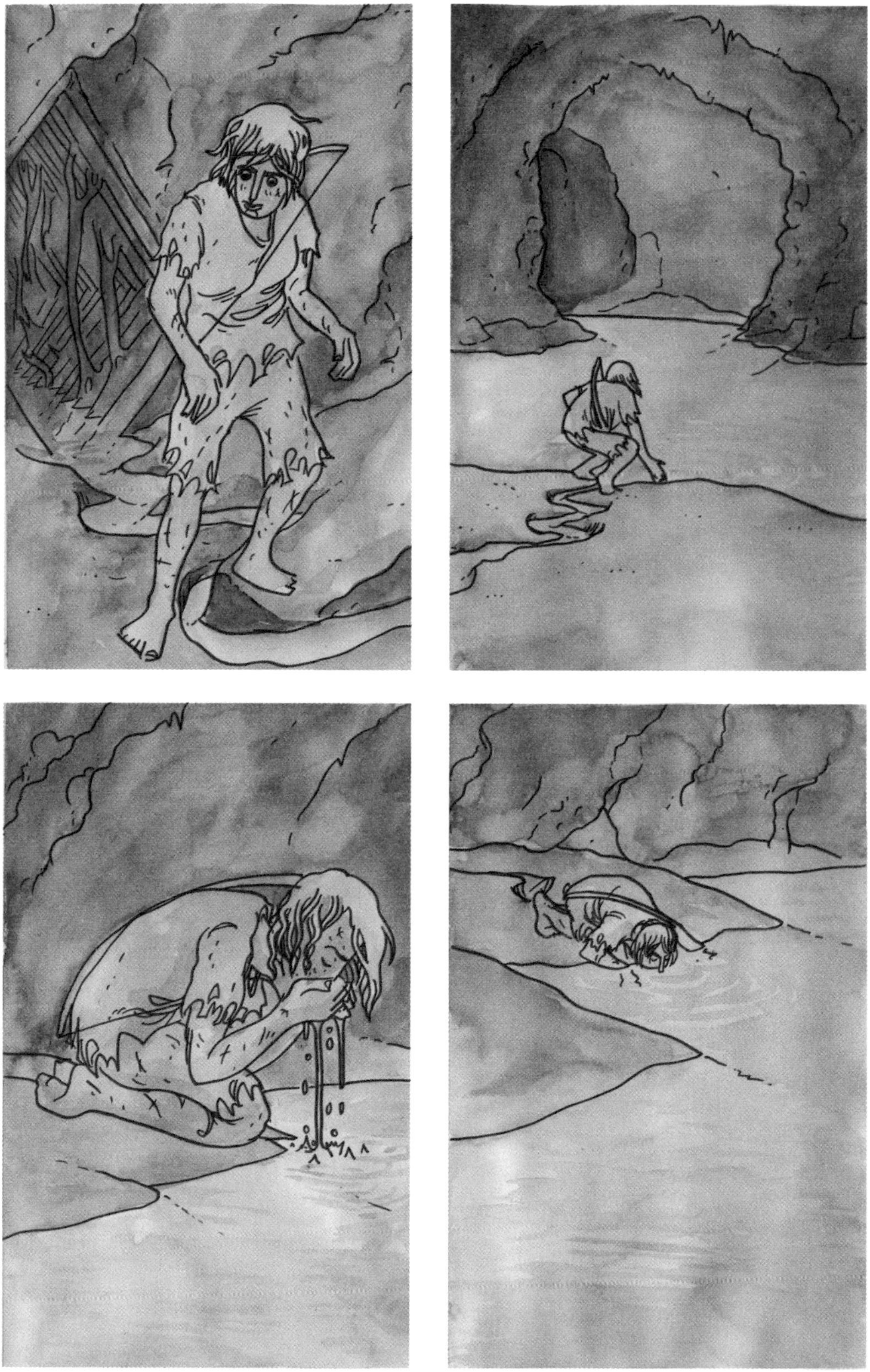

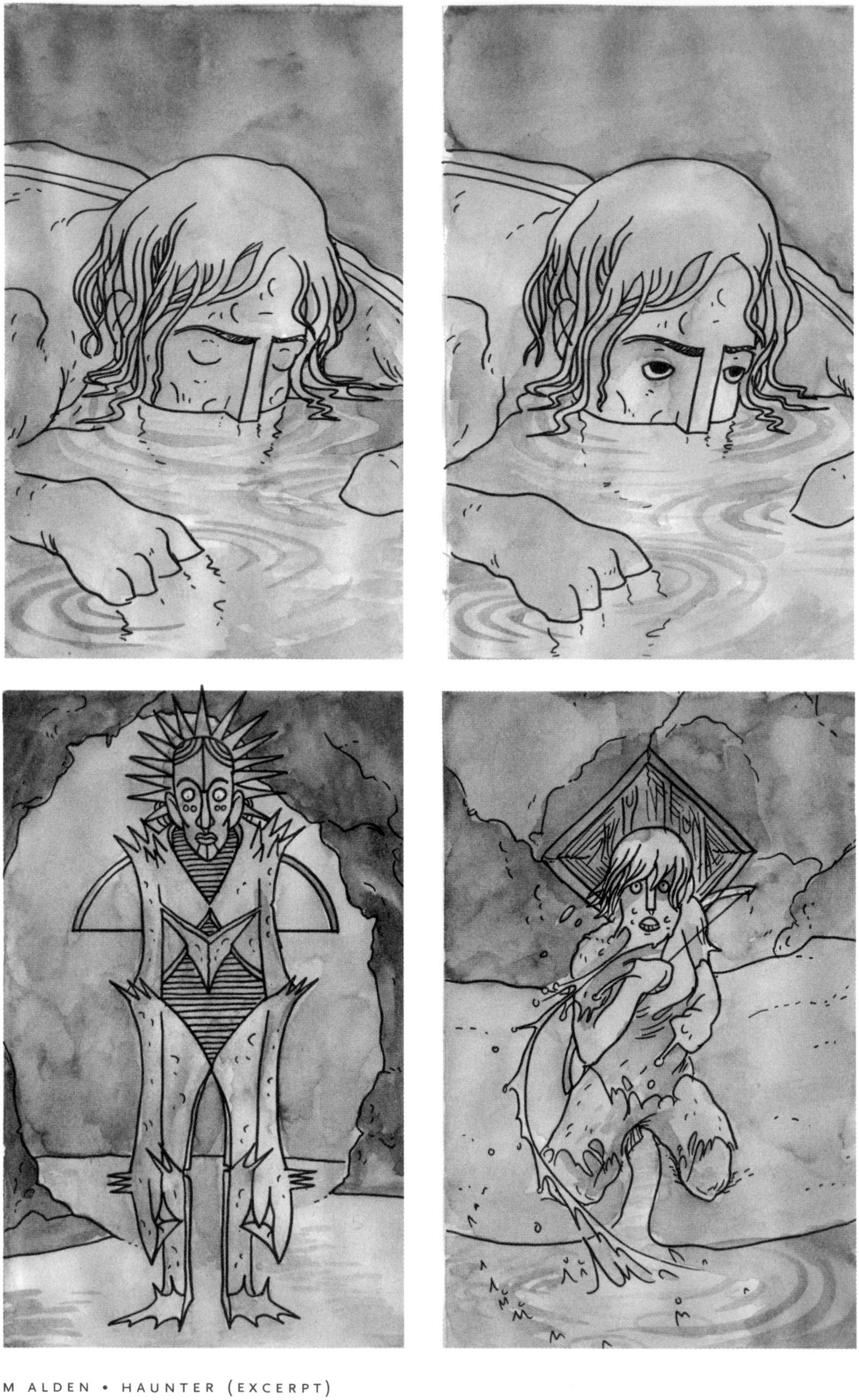

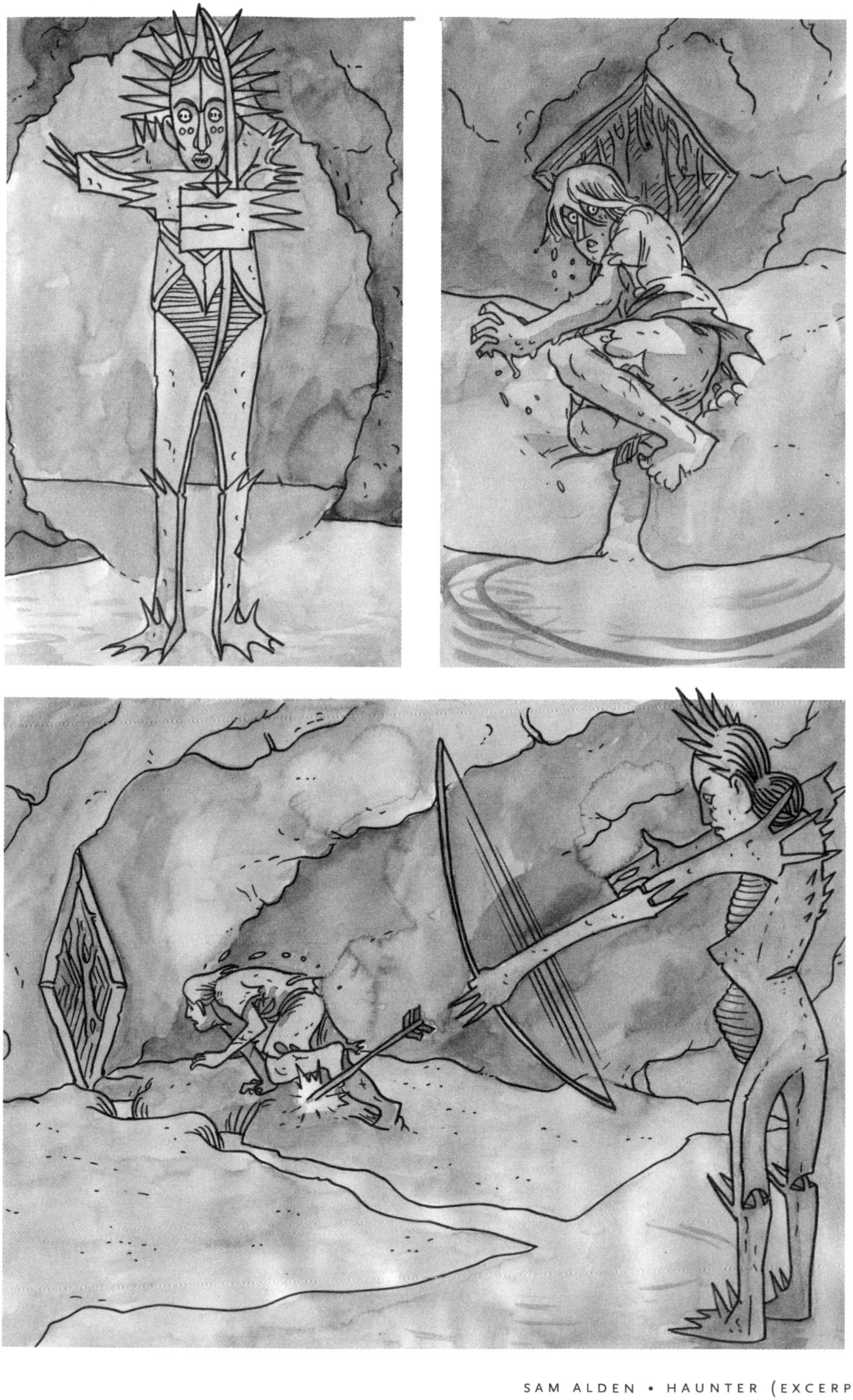

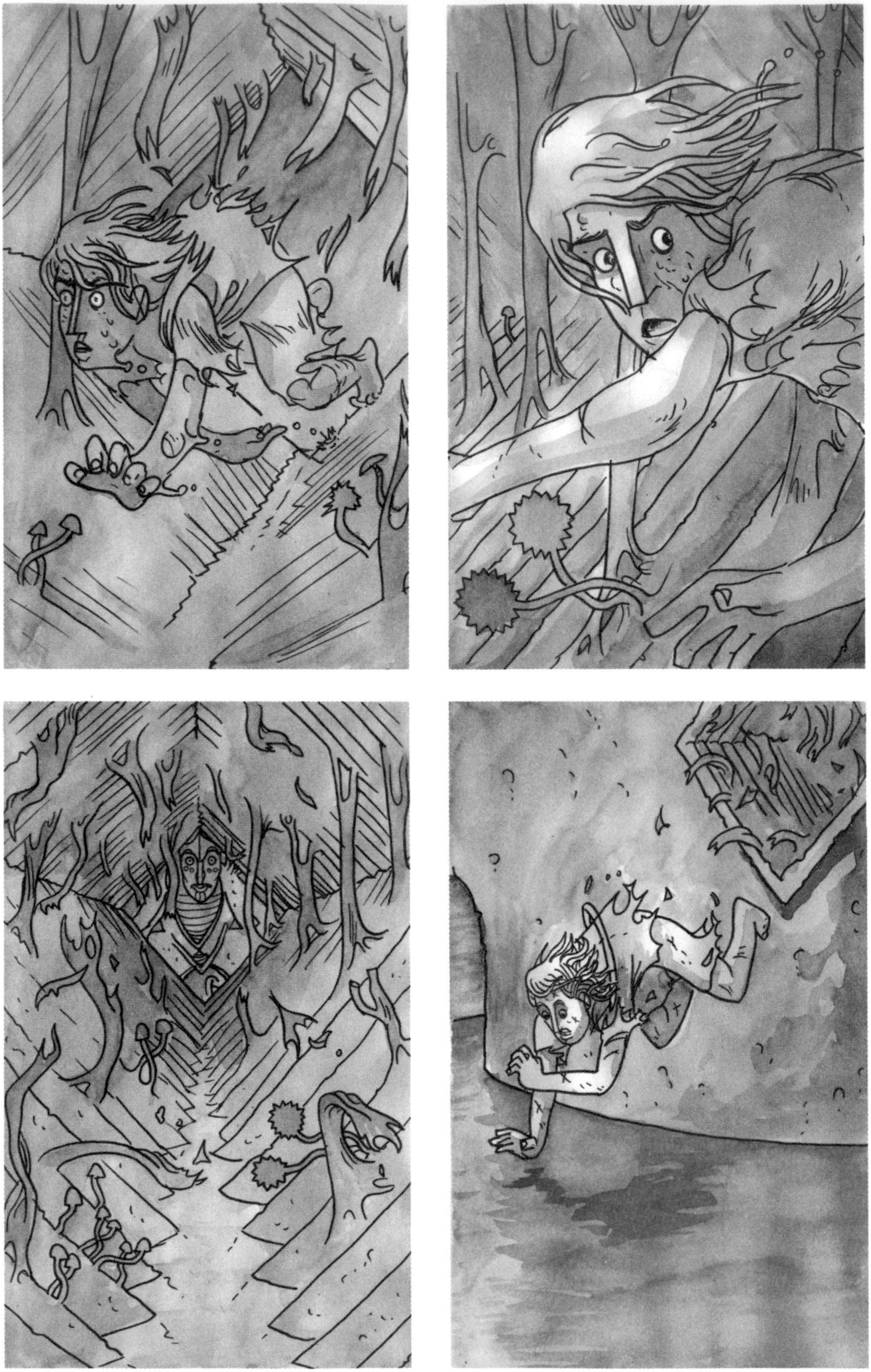

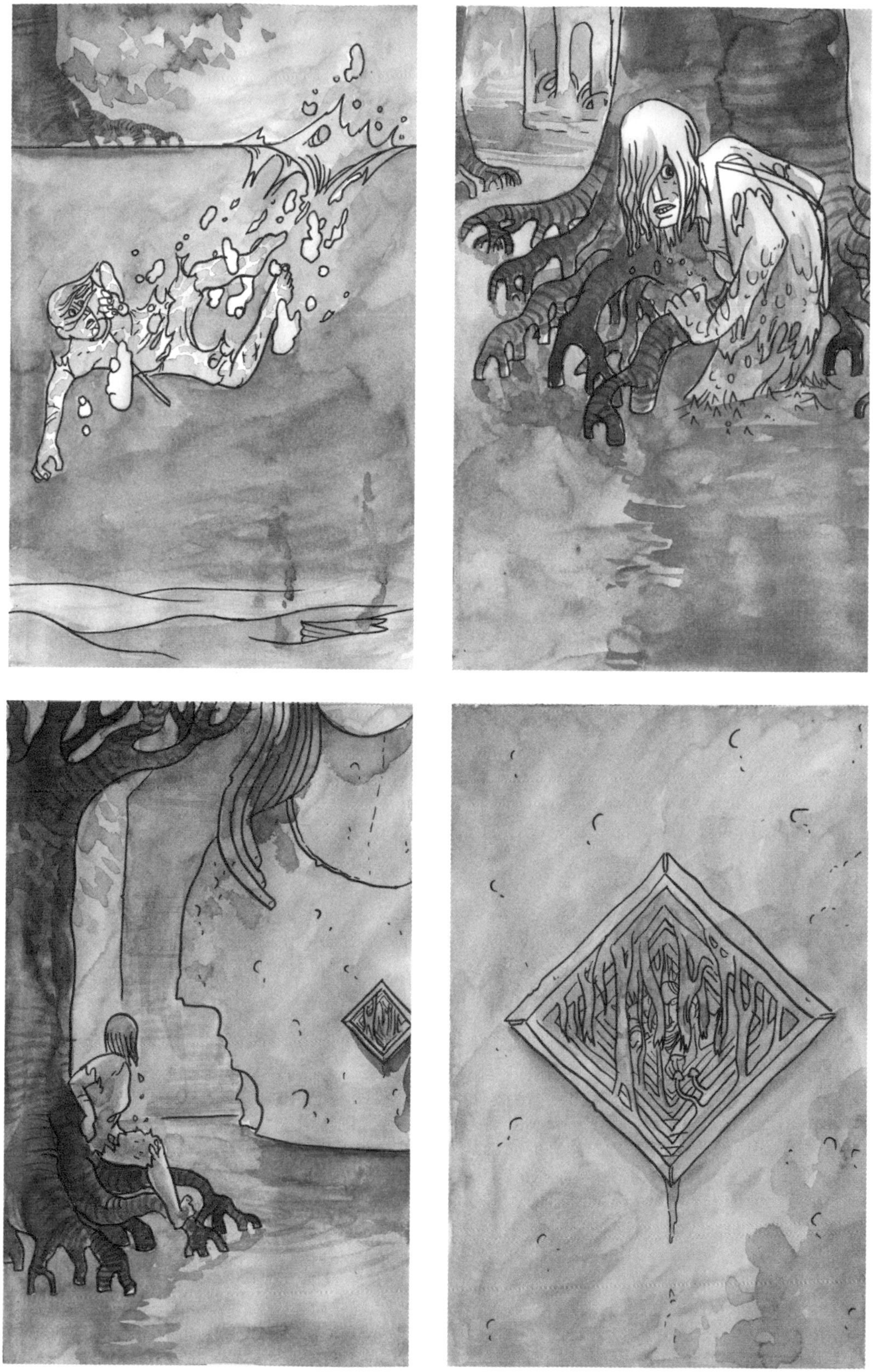

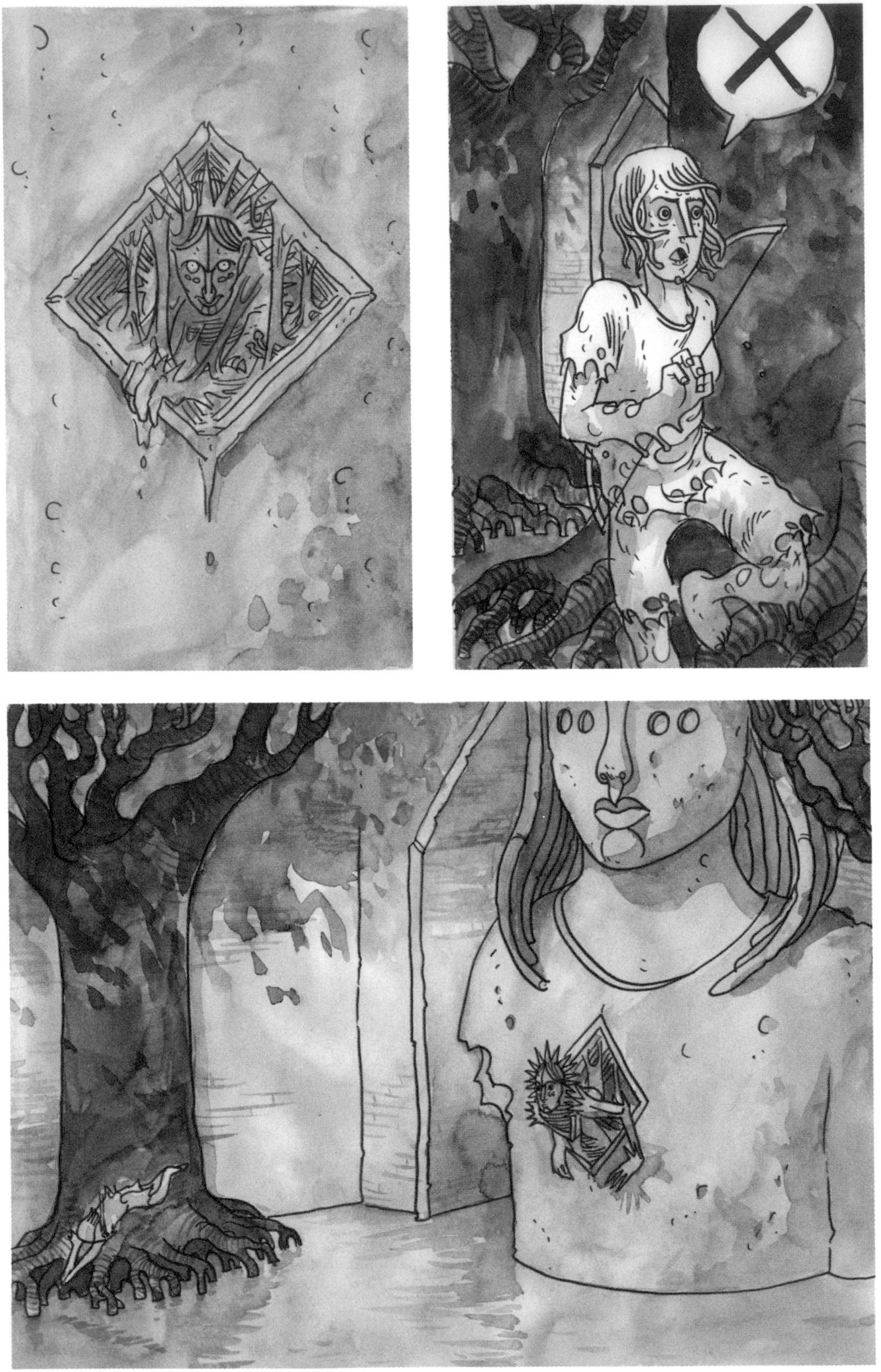

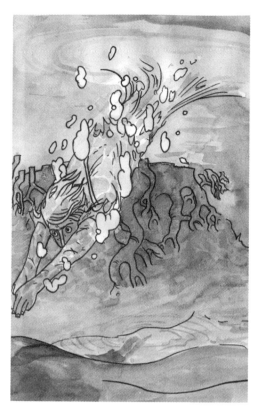

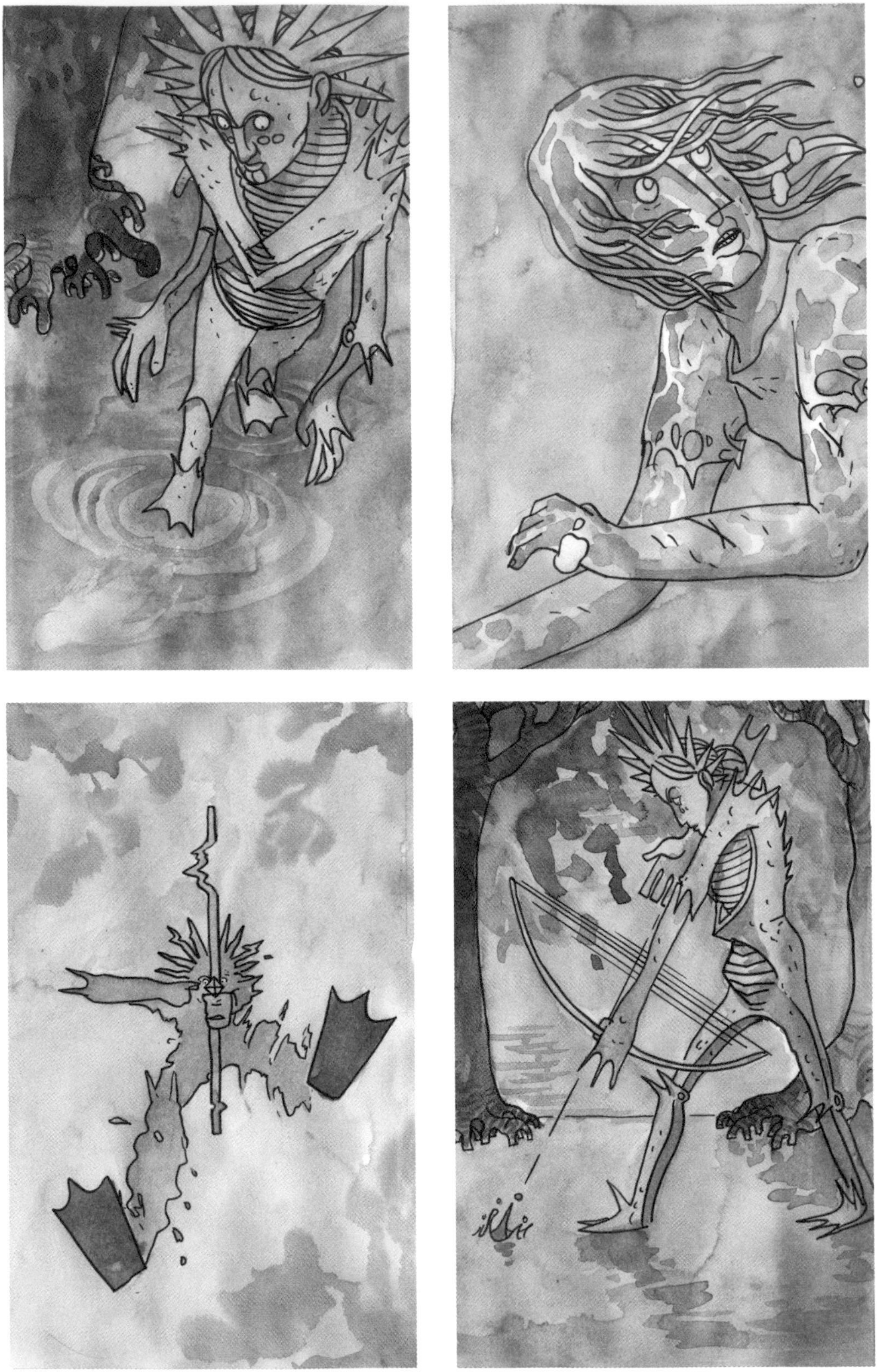

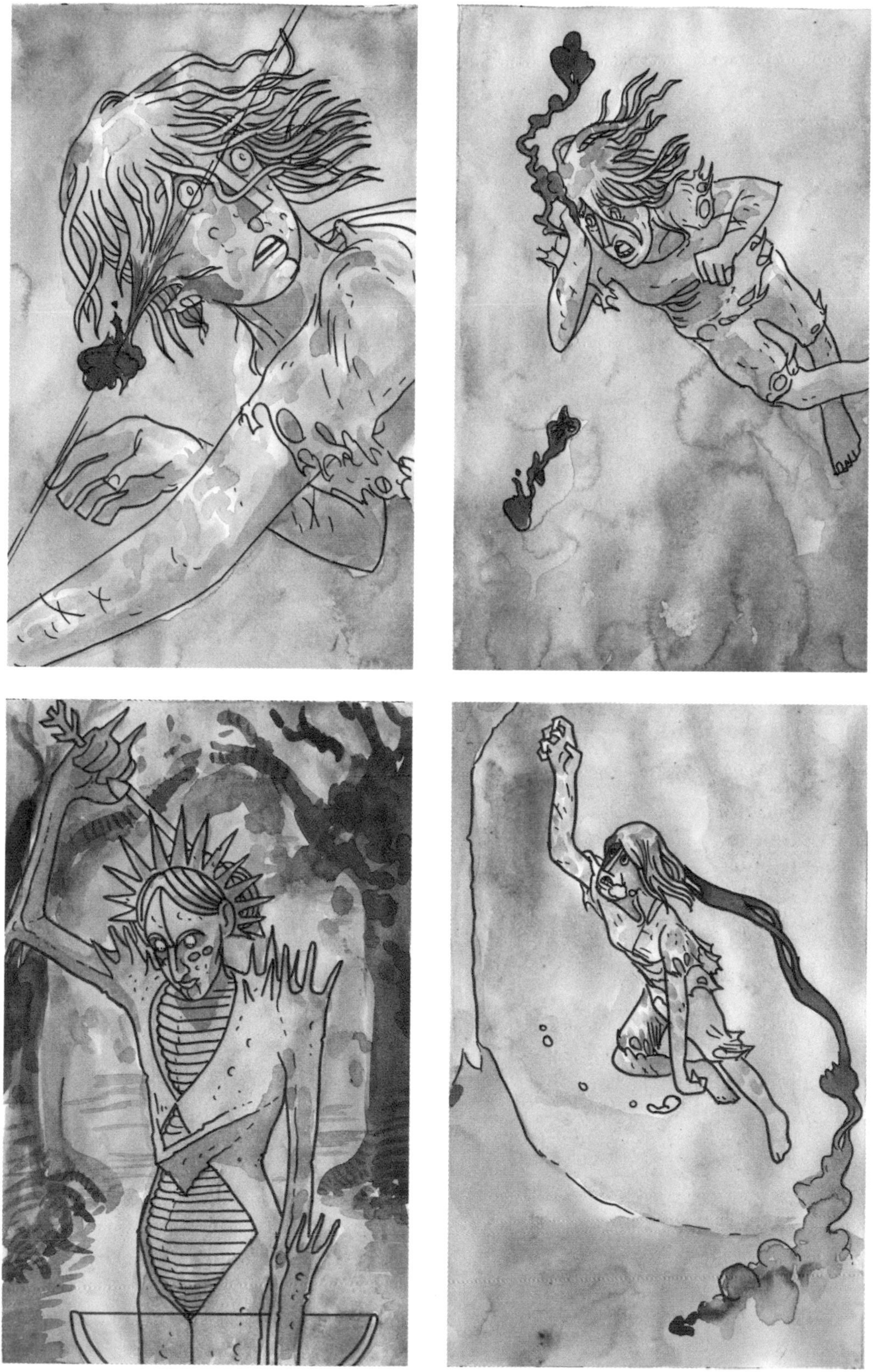

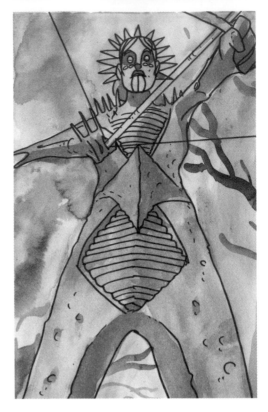

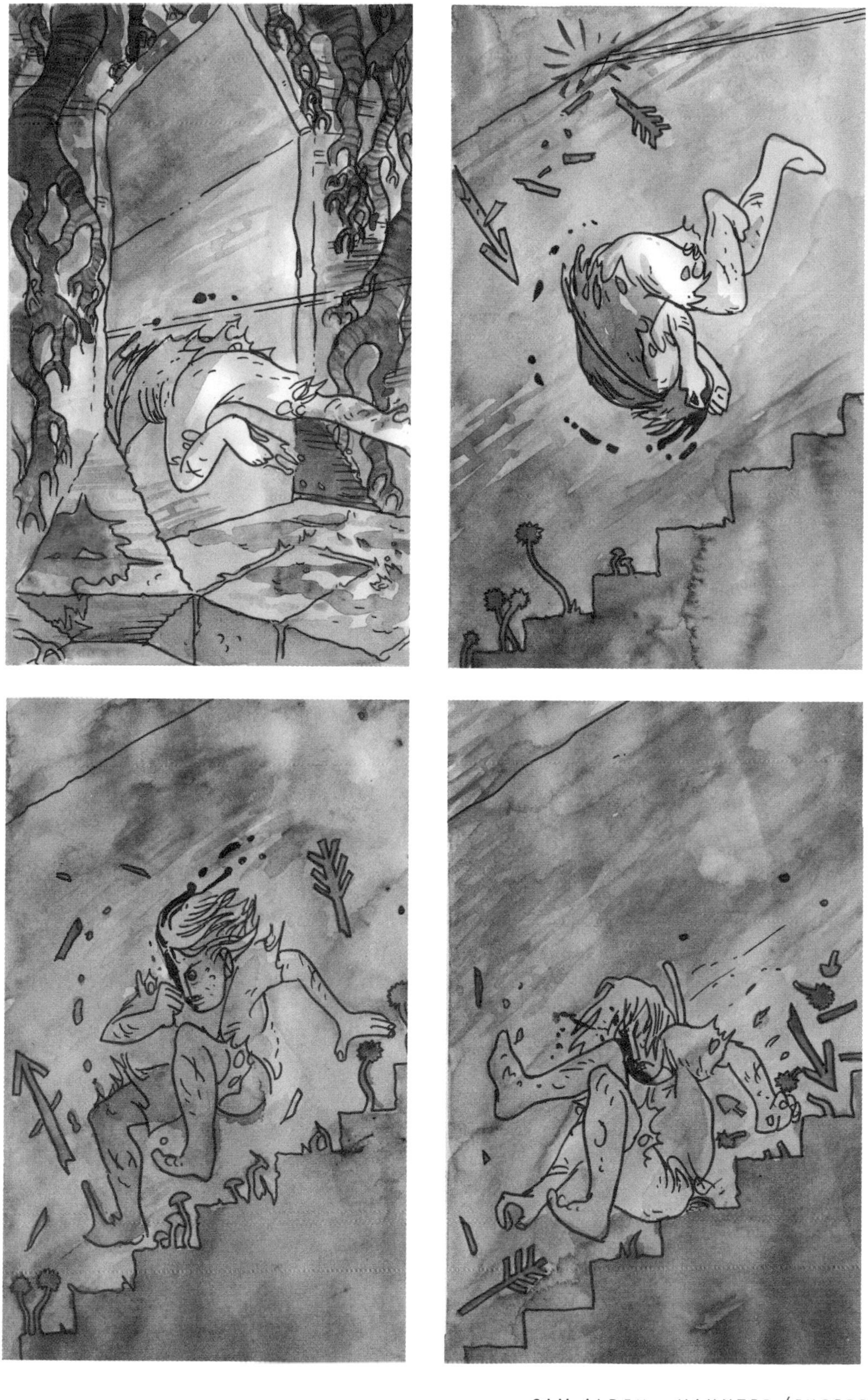

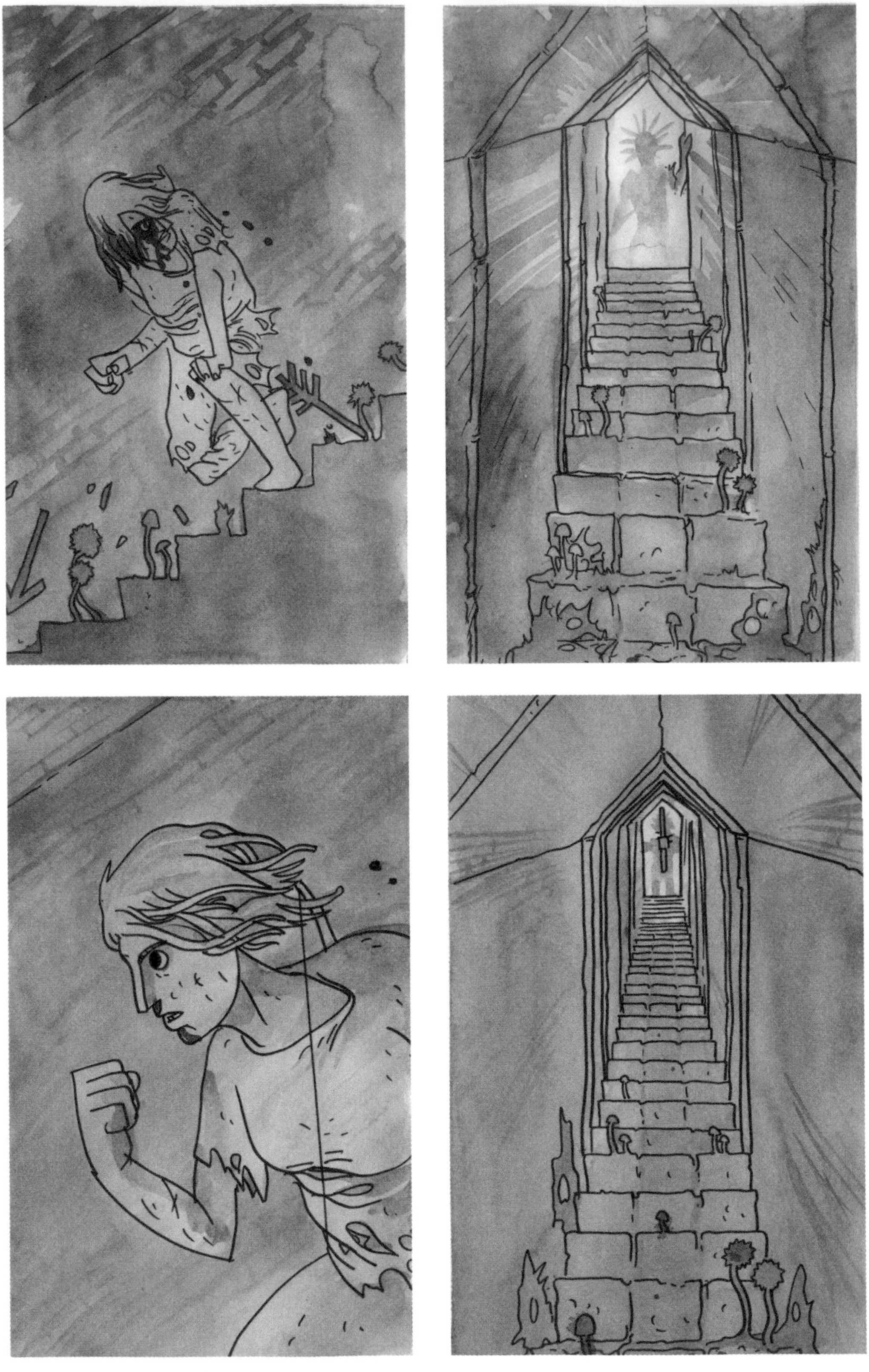

MICHAEL DeFORGE

MANANANGGAL

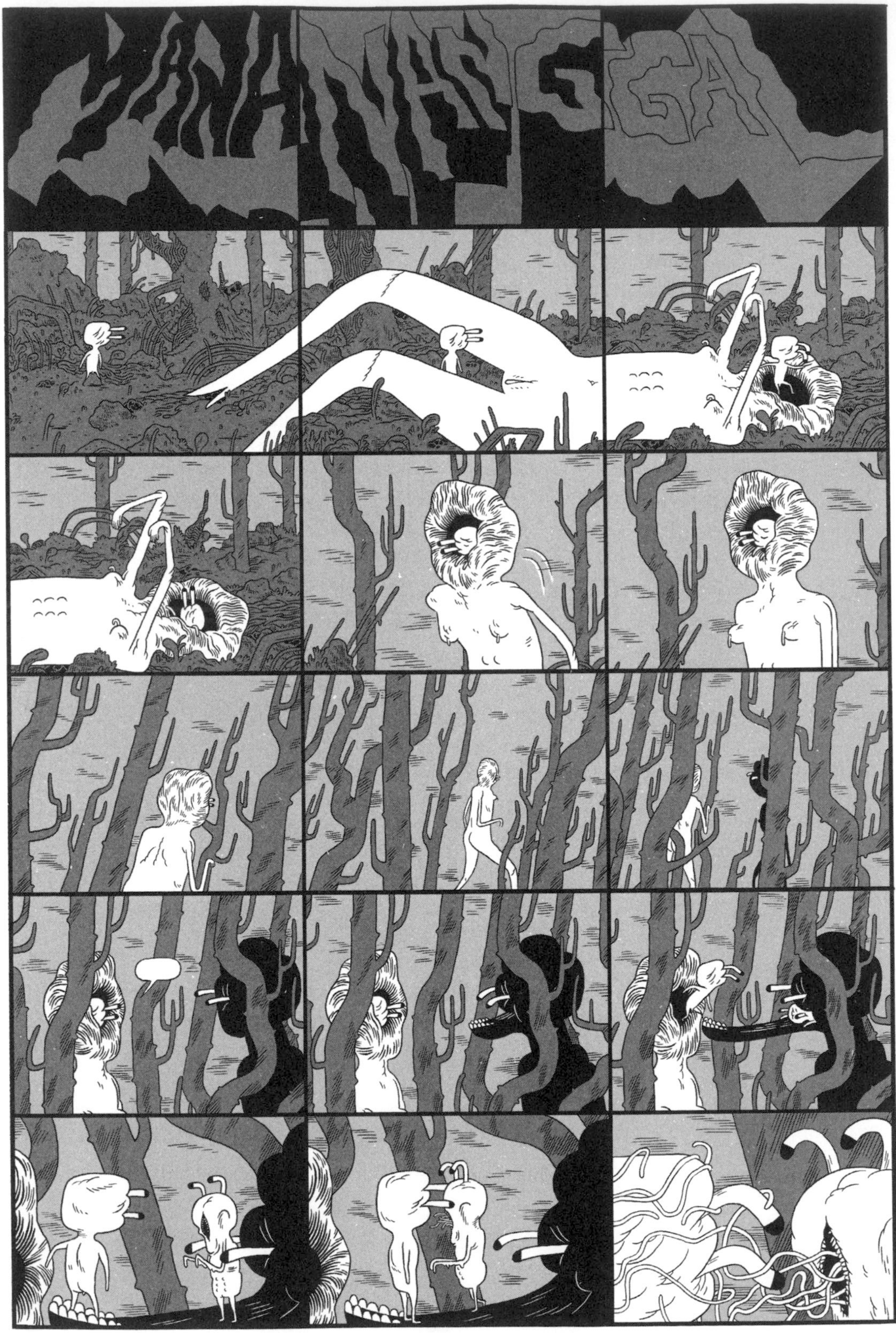

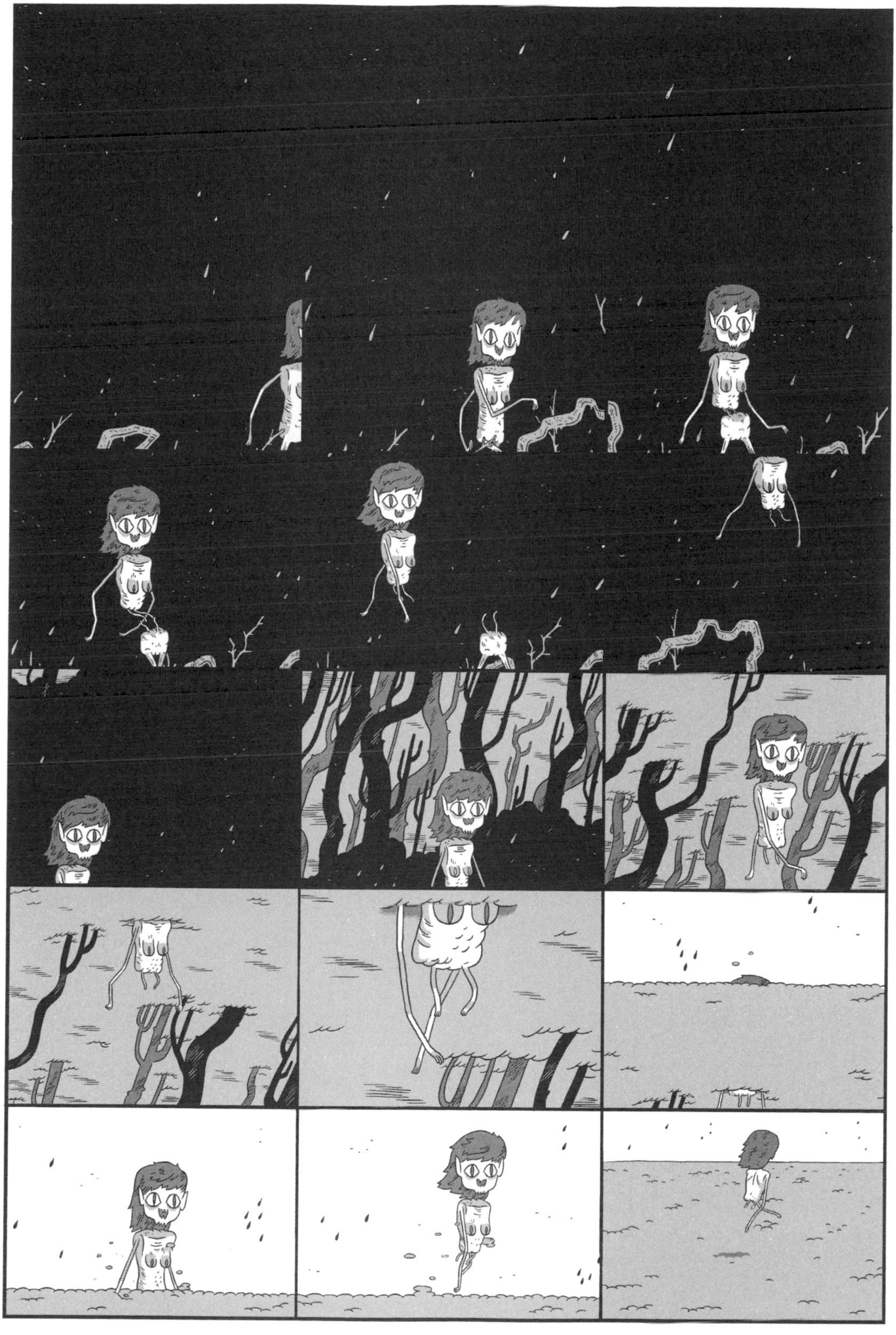

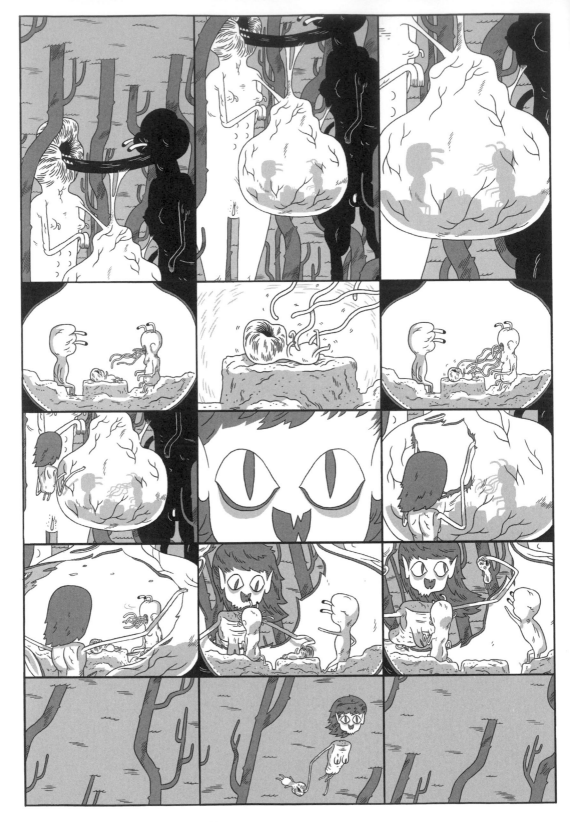

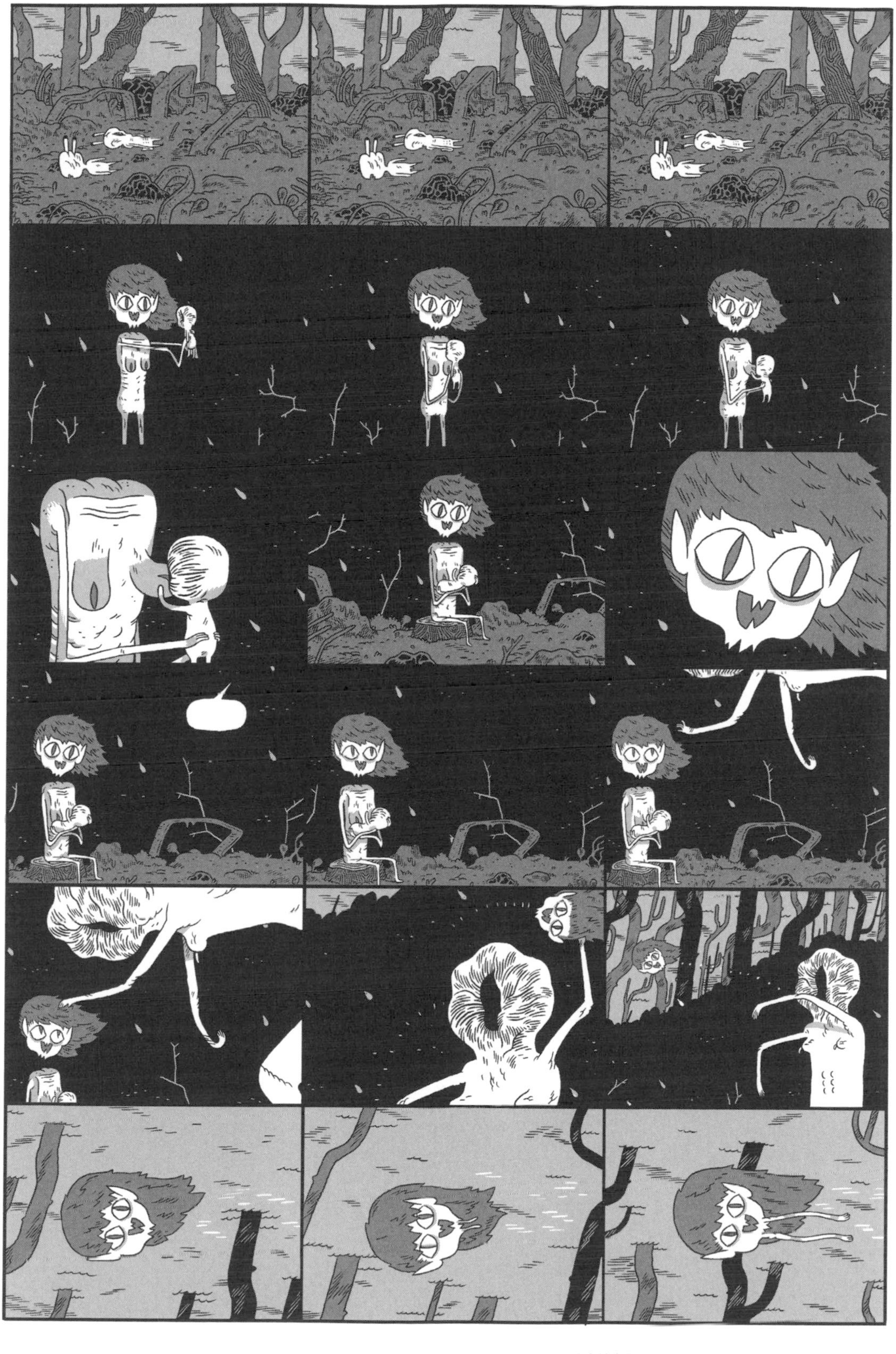

The Good Wife

By Sophie Goldstein

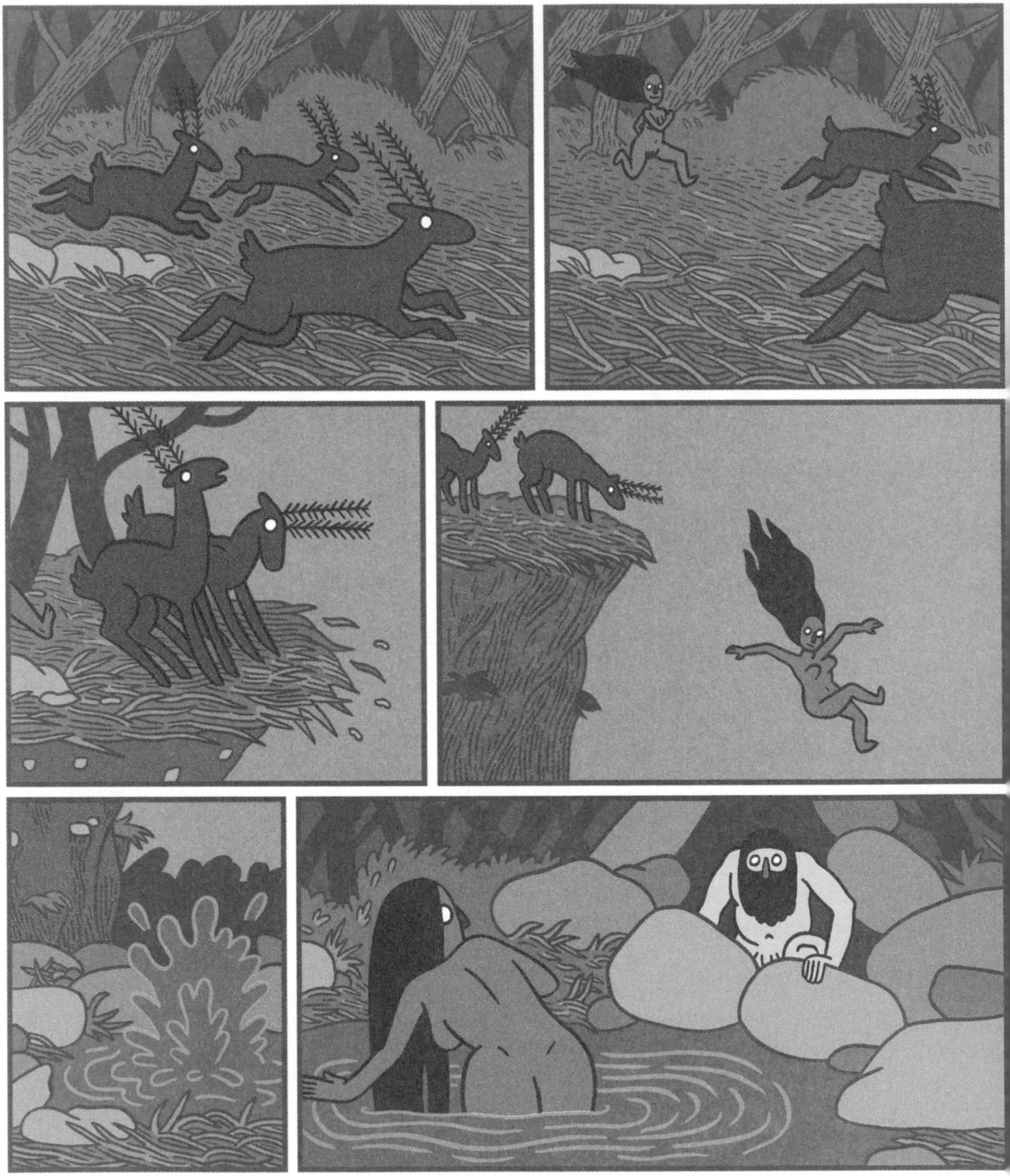

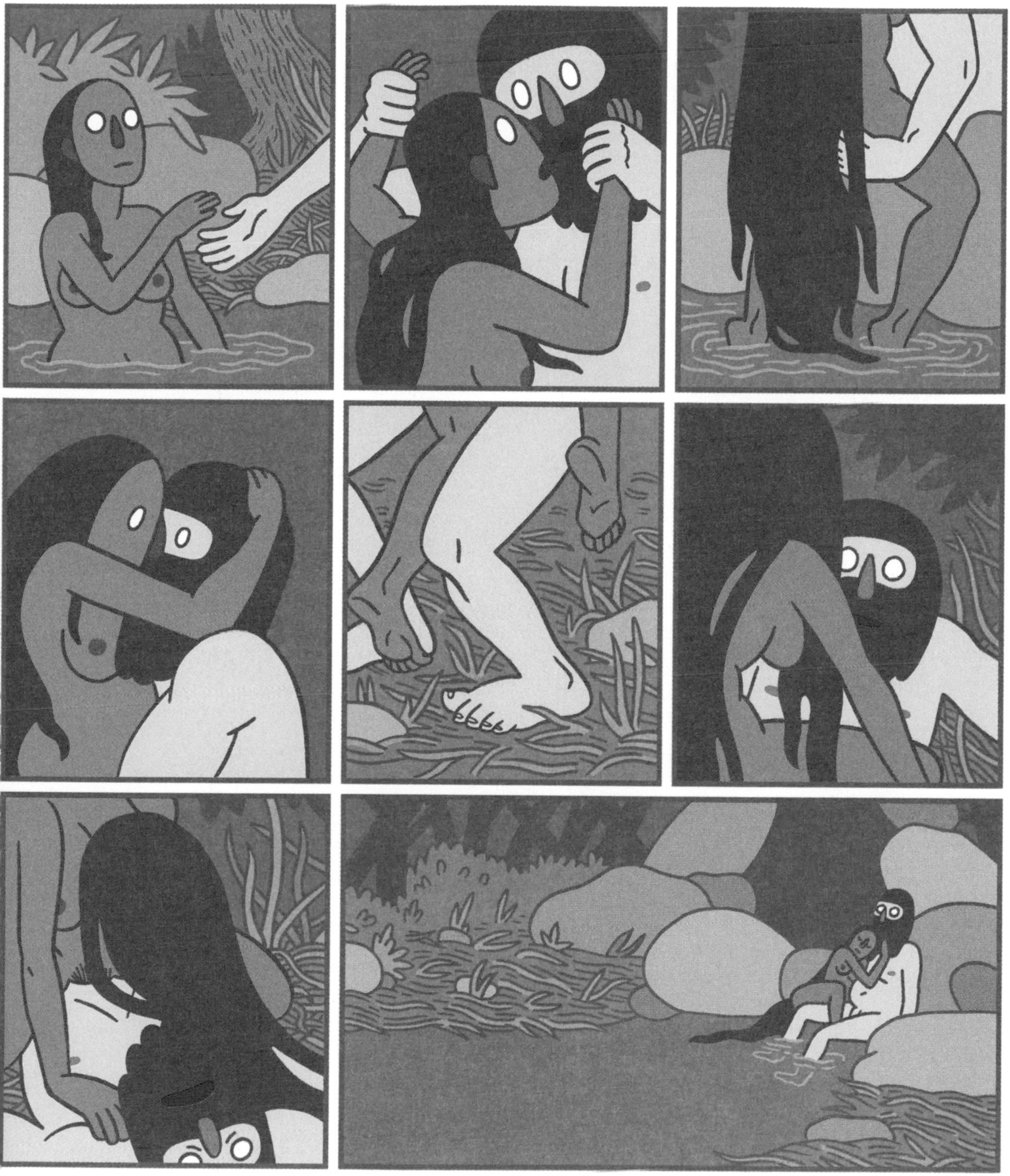

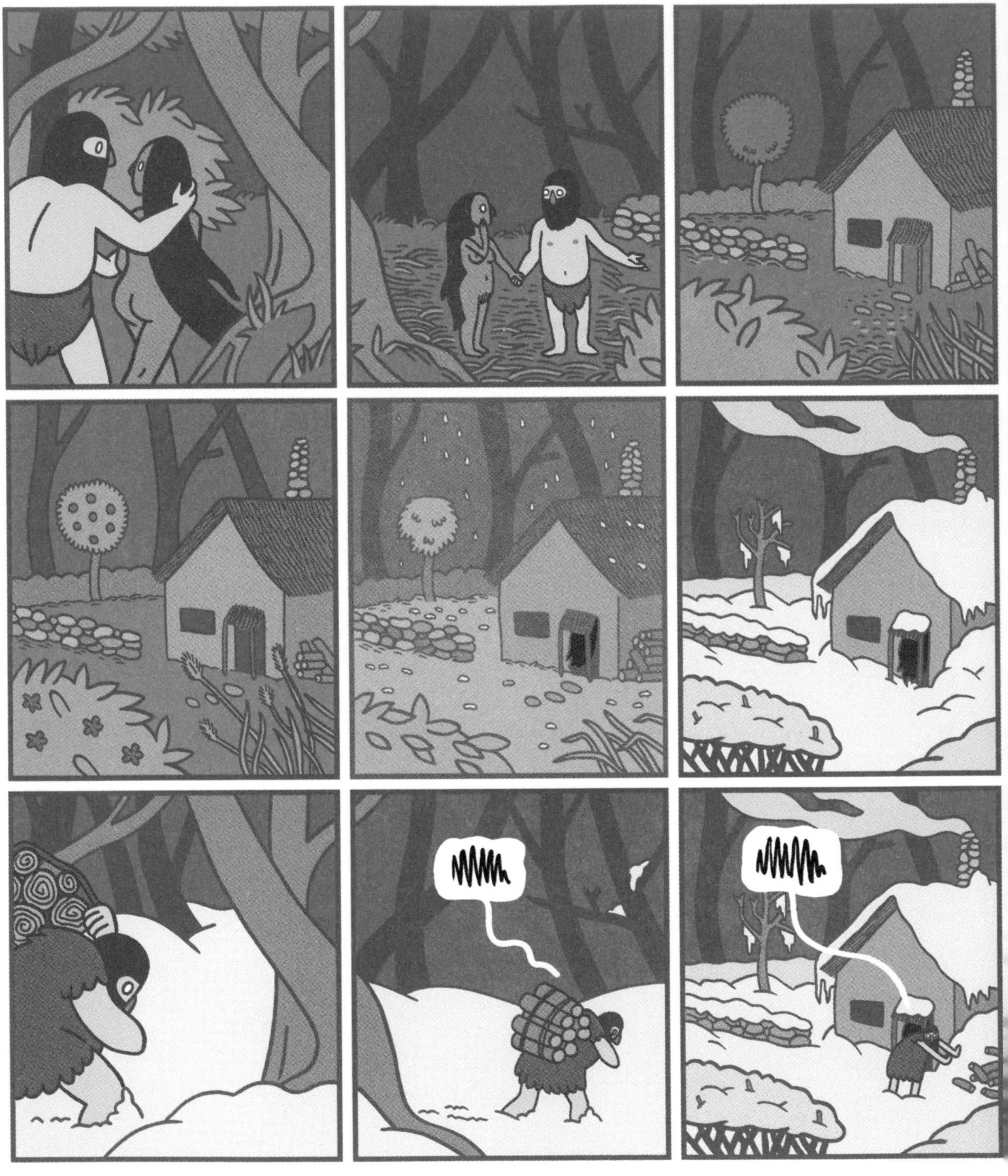

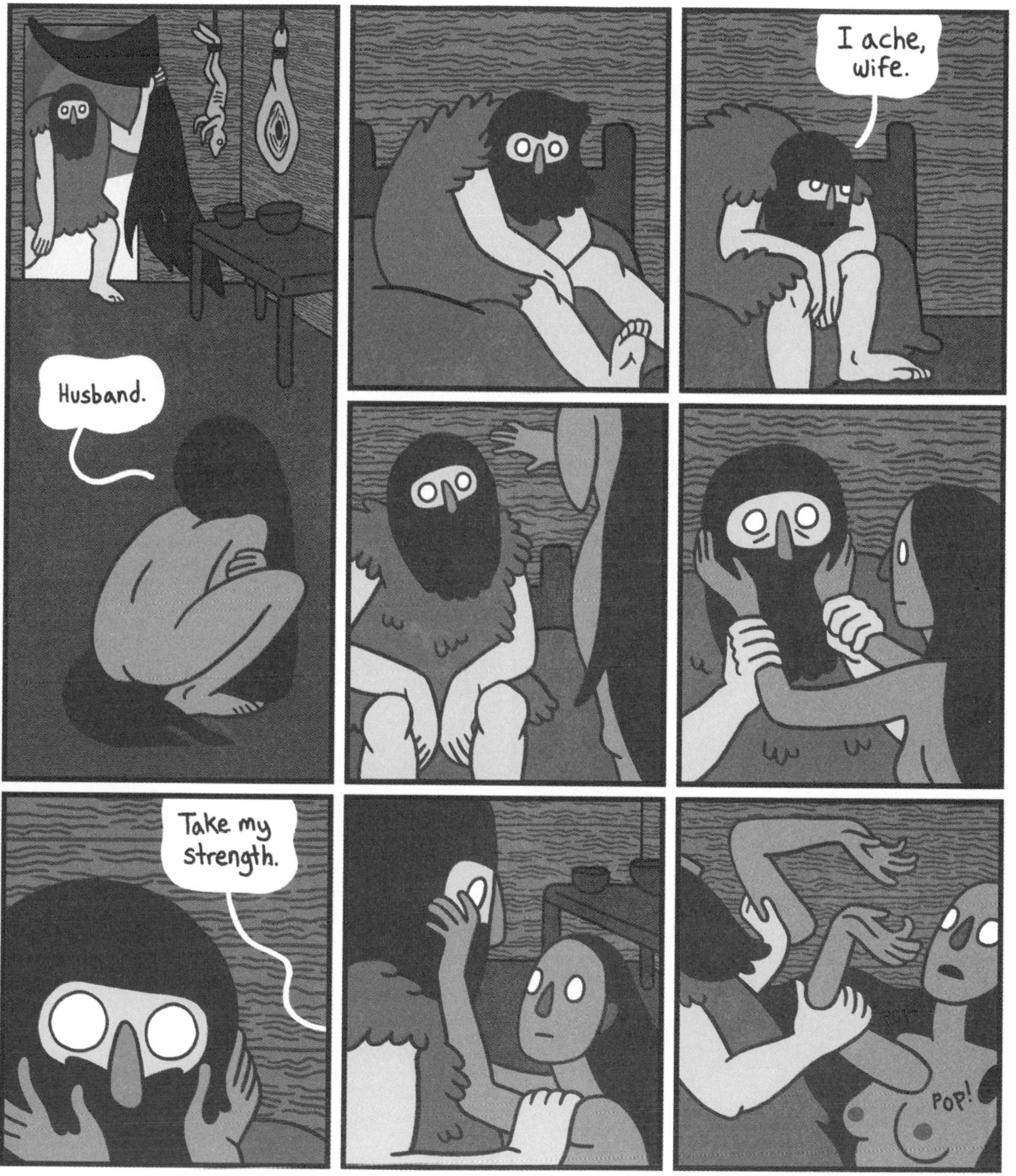
I ache, wife.
Husband.
Take my strength.
POP!

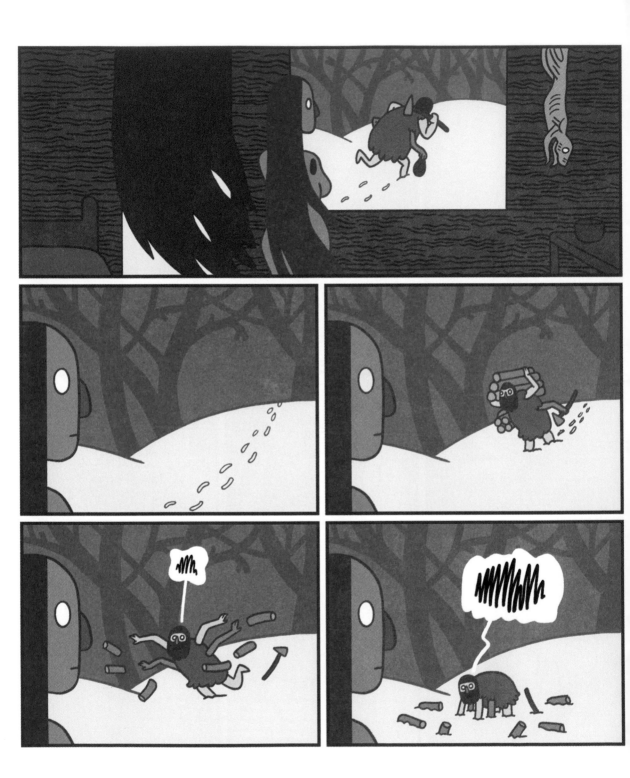

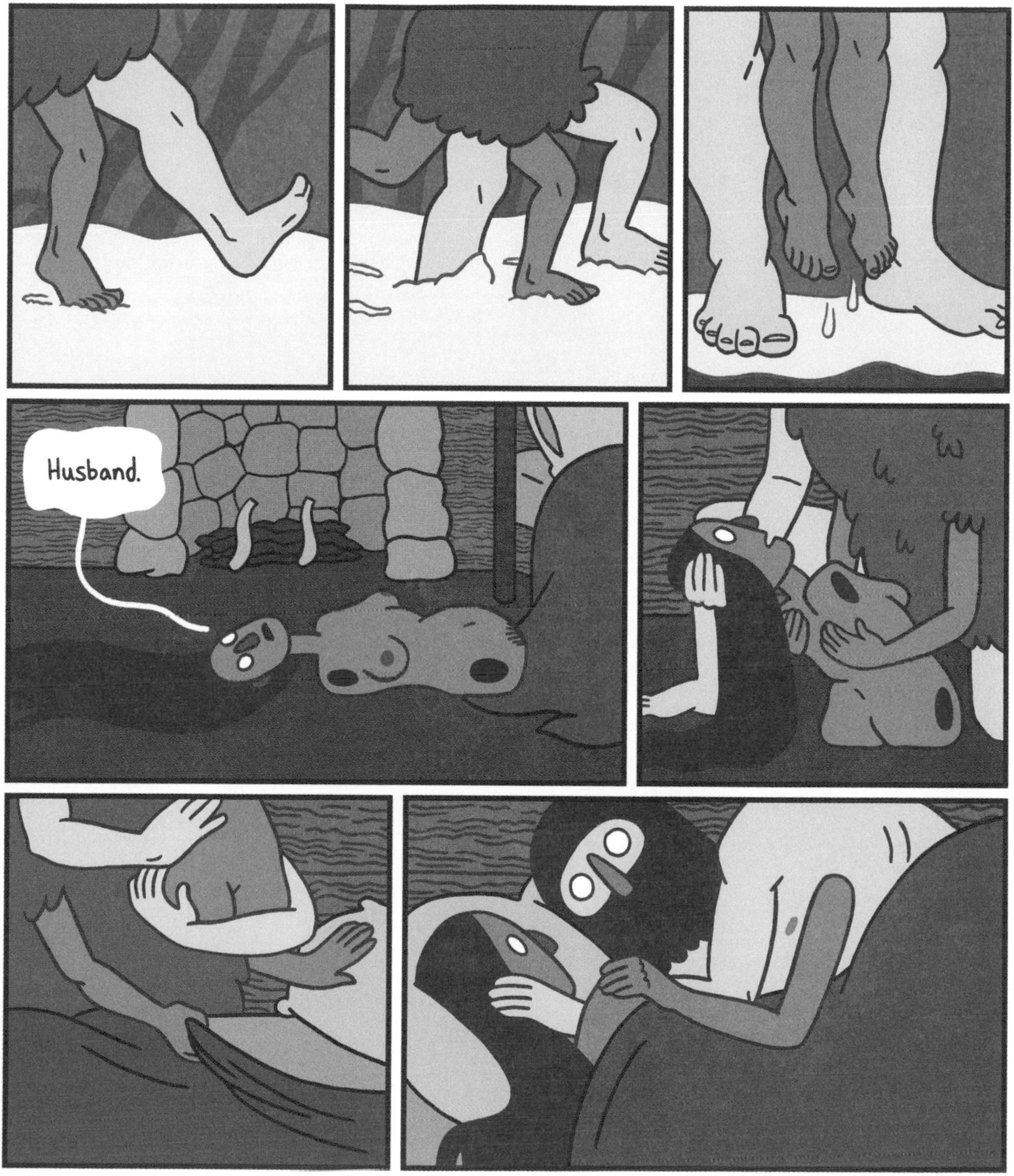
Husband.

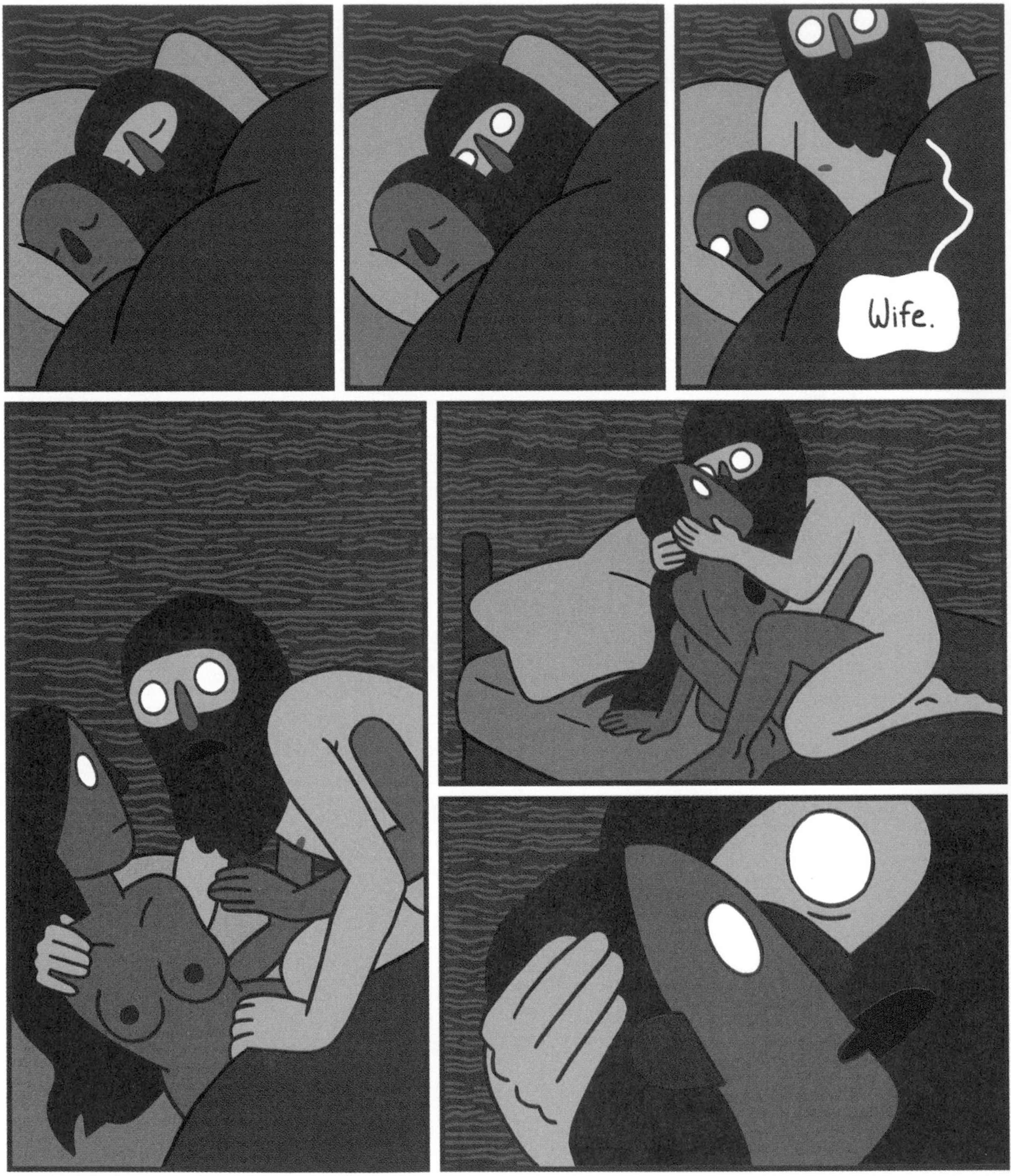
Wife.

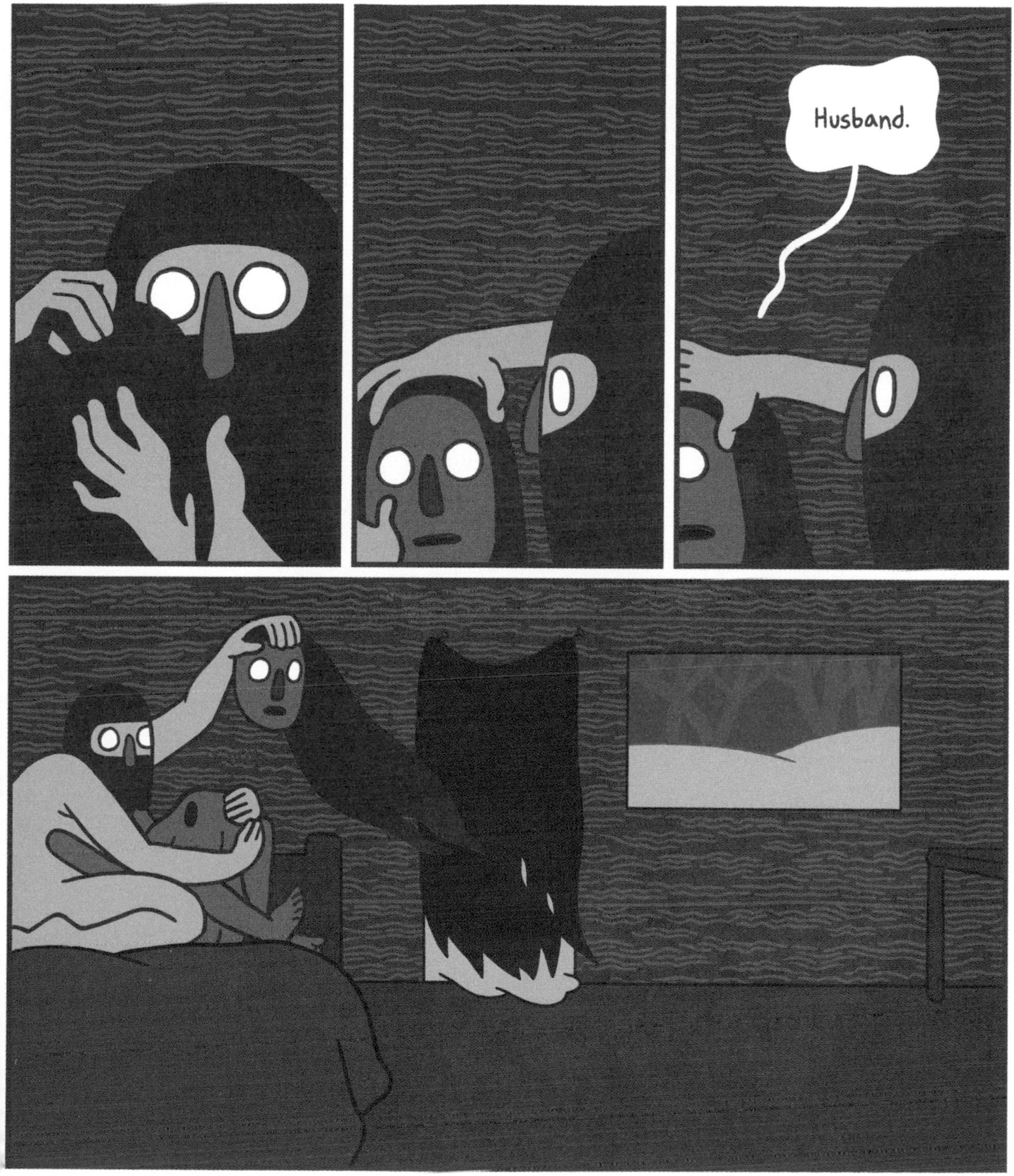
Husband.

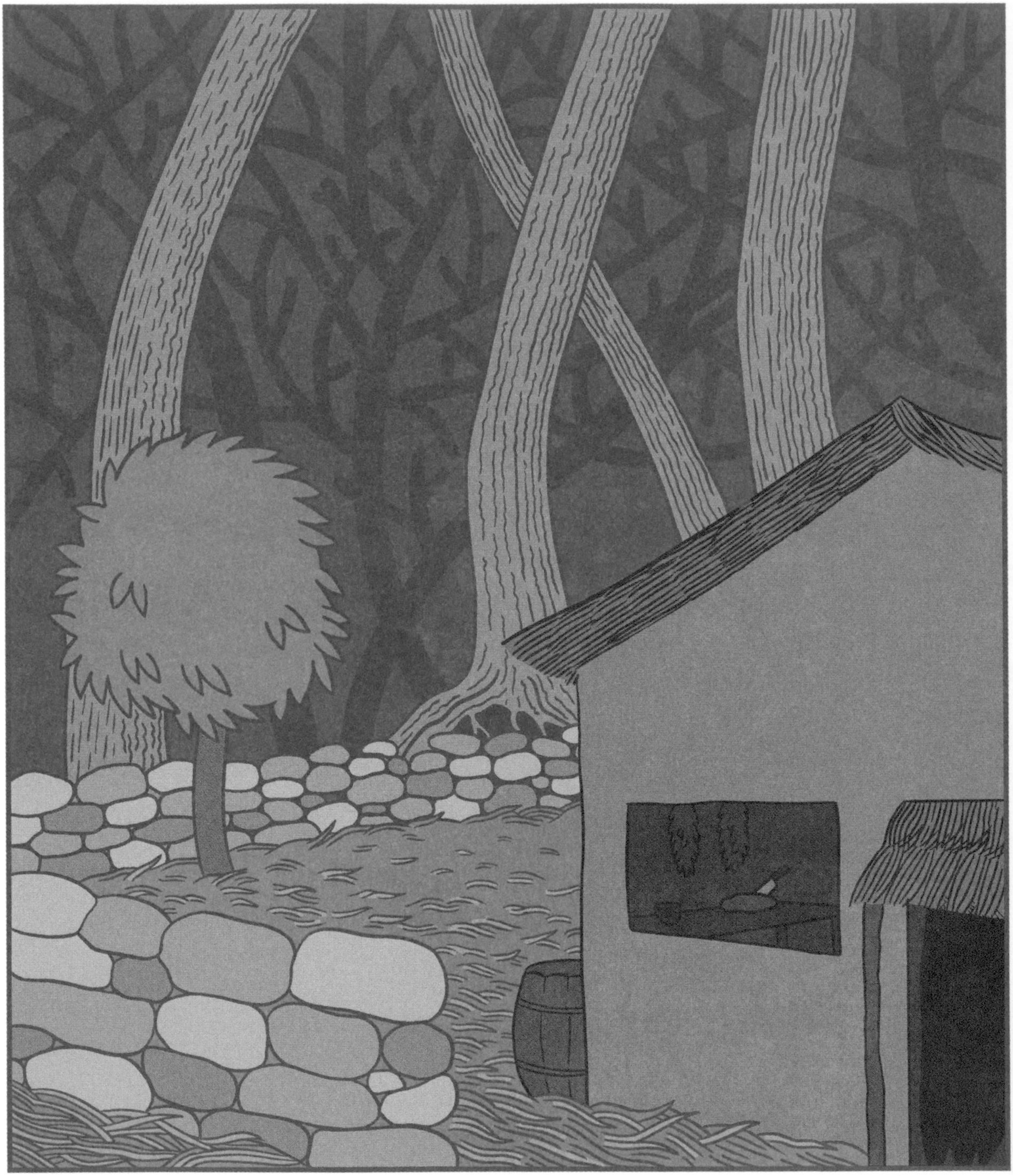

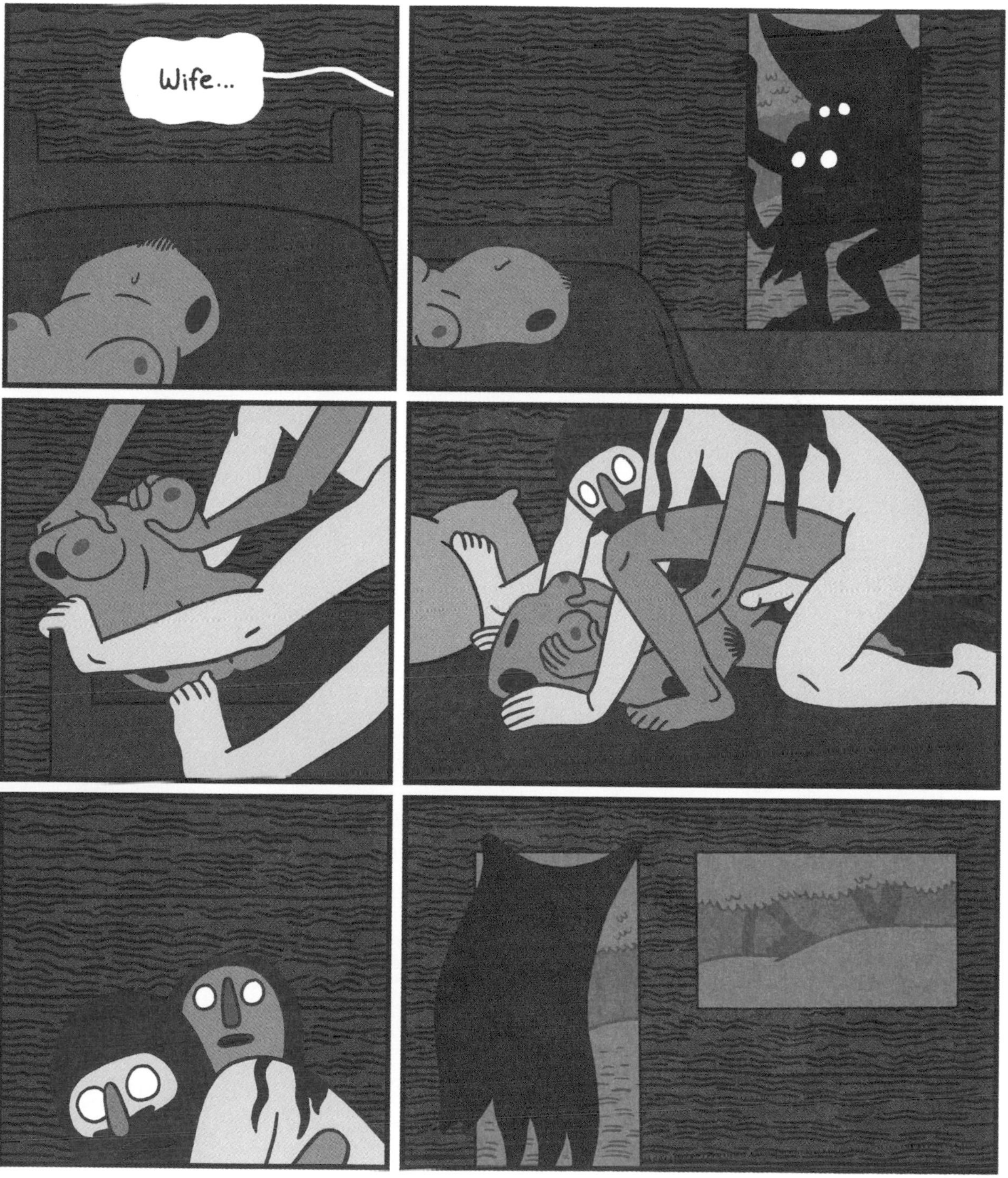
Wife...

Craig Thompson

70 Nights
of Pleasure

excerpt from
Habibi

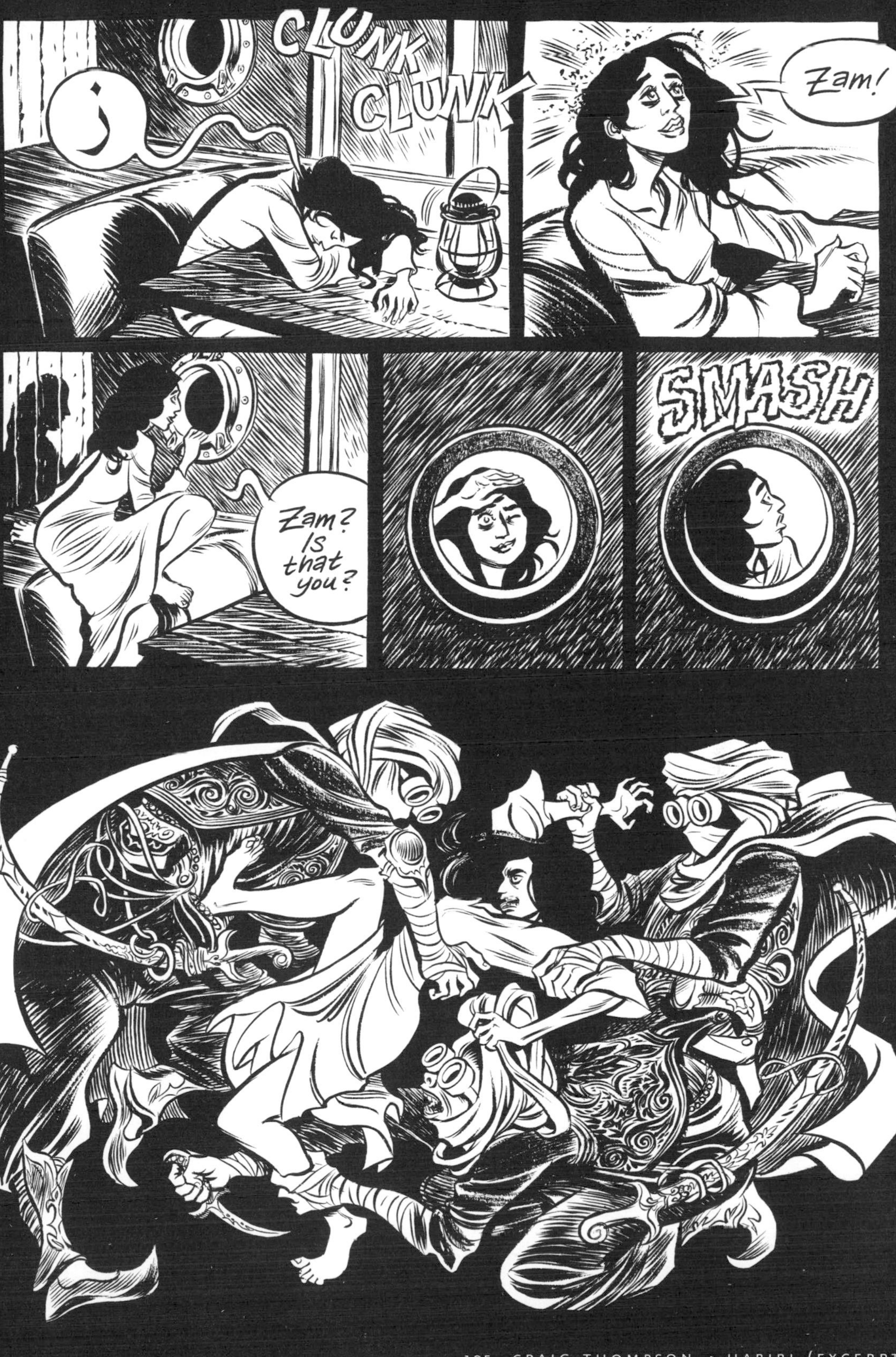
ز
CLUNK CLUNK
Zam!
Zam? Is that you?
SMASH

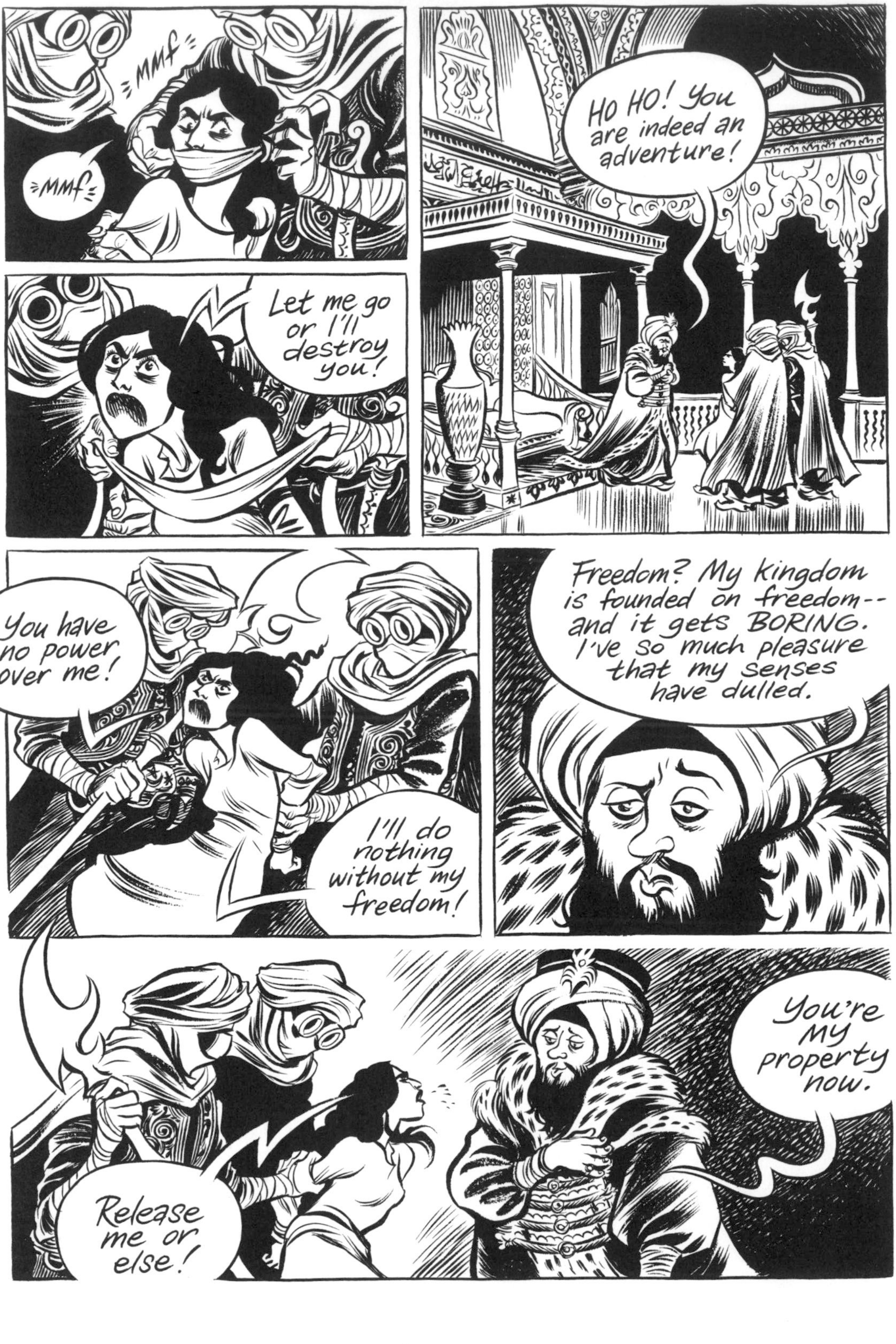
MMf
MMf
HO HO! You are indeed an adventure!
Let me go or I'll destroy you!
You have no power over me!
I'll do nothing without my freedom!
Freedom? My kingdom is founded on freedom-- and it gets BORING. I've so much pleasure that my senses have dulled.
Release me or else!
You're MY property now.

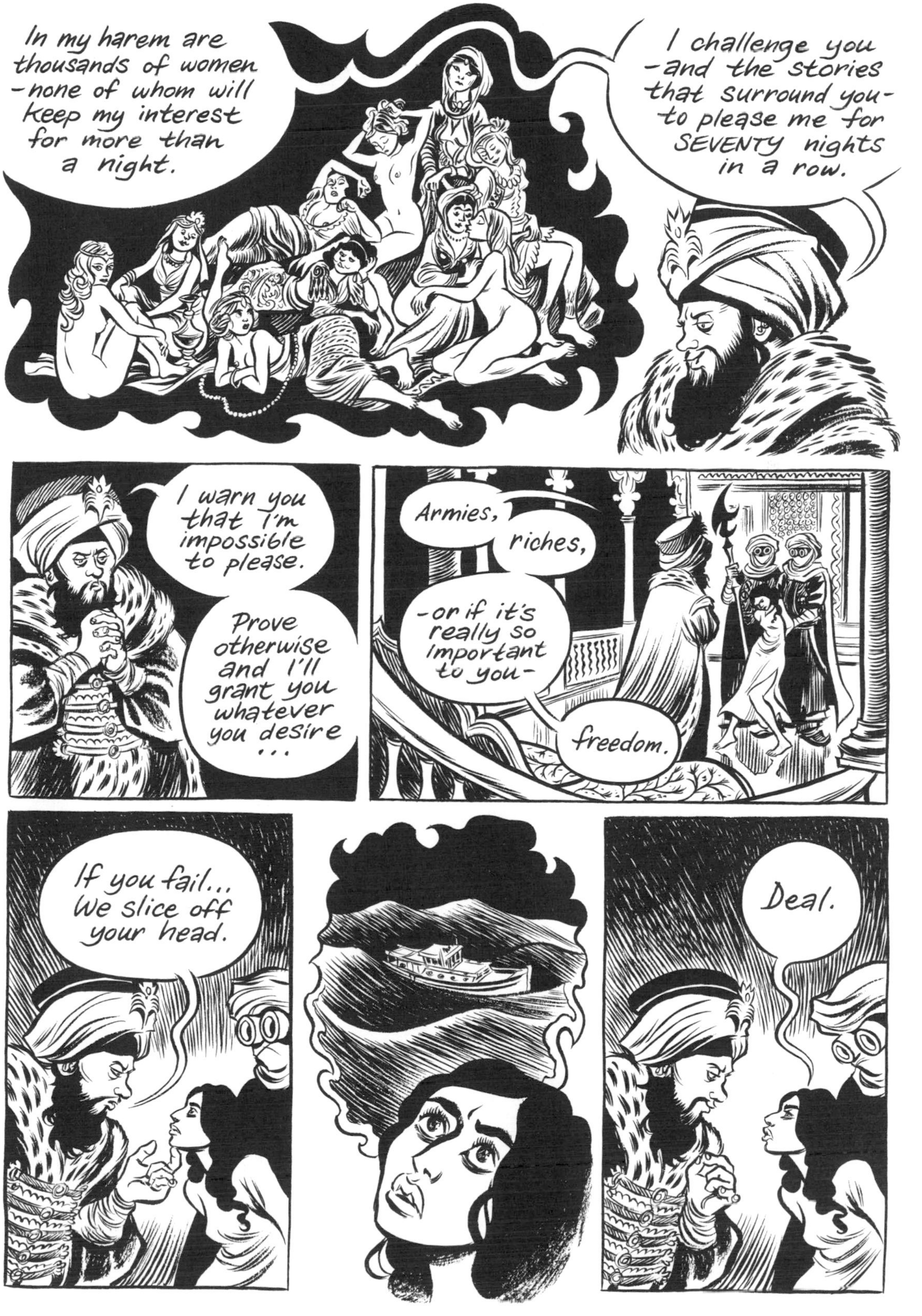
In my harem are thousands of women -none of whom will keep my interest for more than a night.
I challenge you -and the stories that surround you- to please me for SEVENTY nights in a row.
I warn you that I'm impossible to please.
Prove otherwise and I'll grant you whatever you desire . . .
Armies,
riches,
-or if it's really so important to you-
freedom.
If you fail... We slice off your head.
Deal.

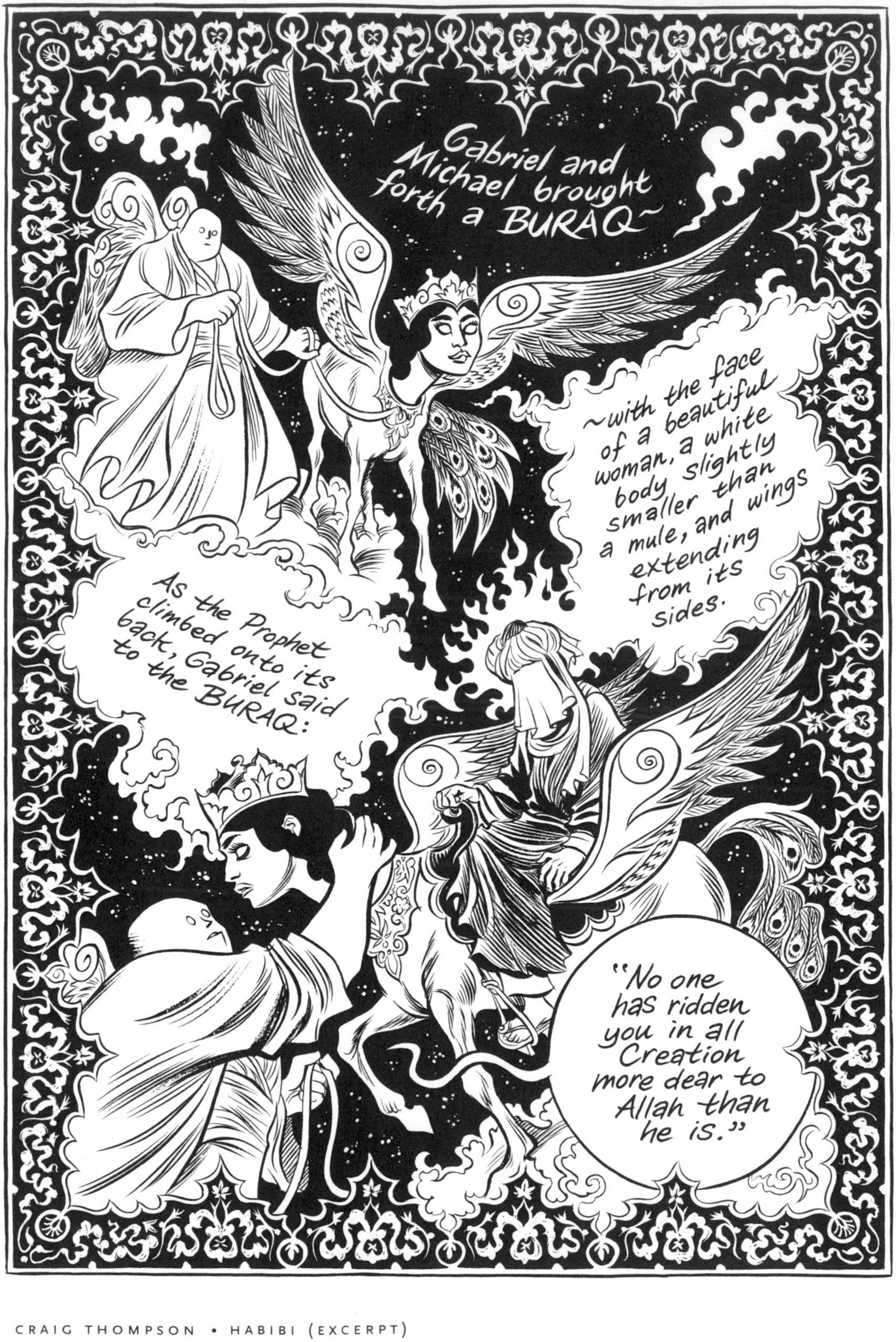
Gabriel and Michael brought forth a BURAQ~
~with the face of a beautiful woman, a white body slightly smaller than a mule, and wings extending from its sides.
As the Prophet climbed onto its back, Gabriel said to the BURAQ:
"No one has ridden you in all Creation more dear to Allah than he is."

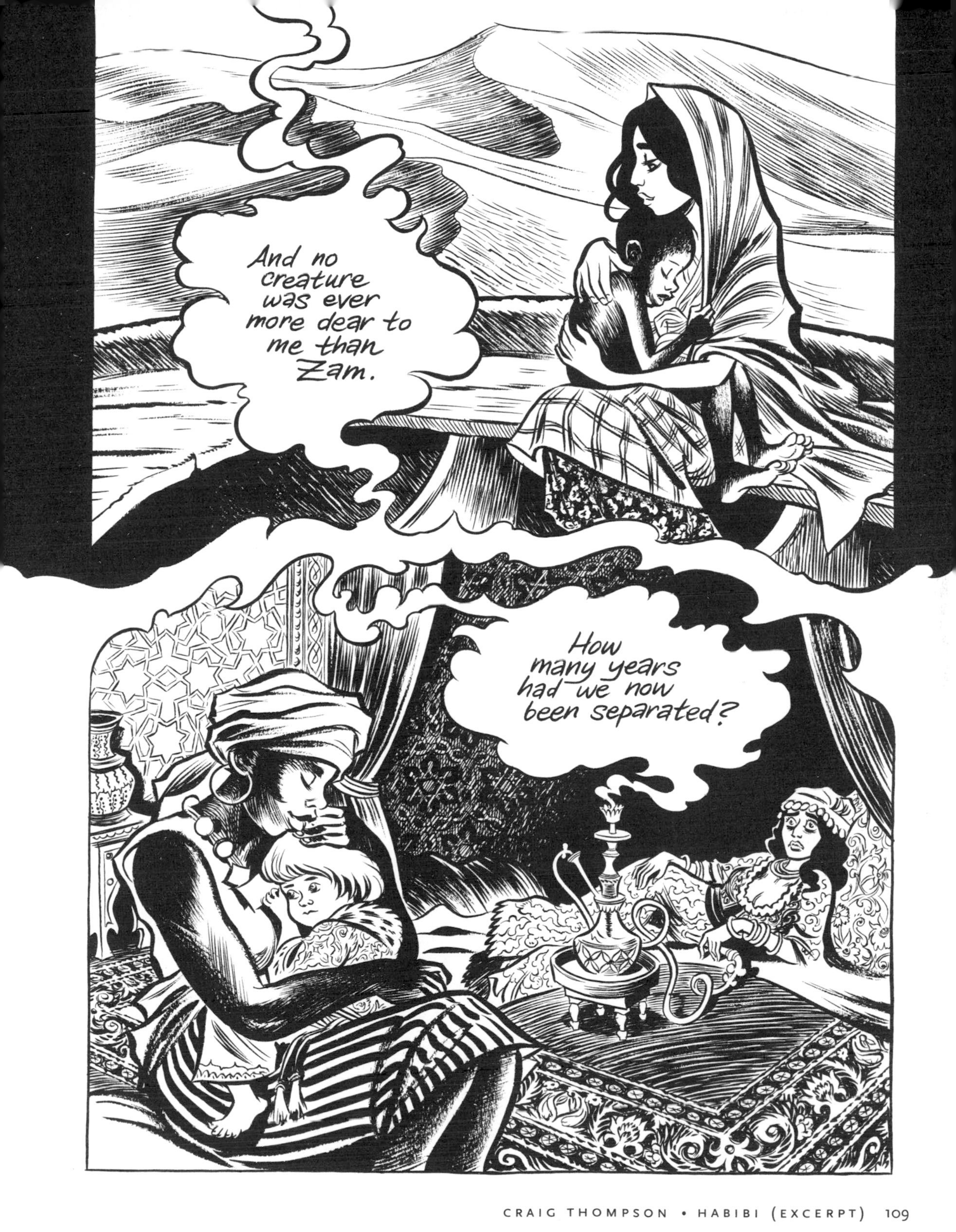
And no creature was ever more dear to me than Zam.
How many years had we now been separated?

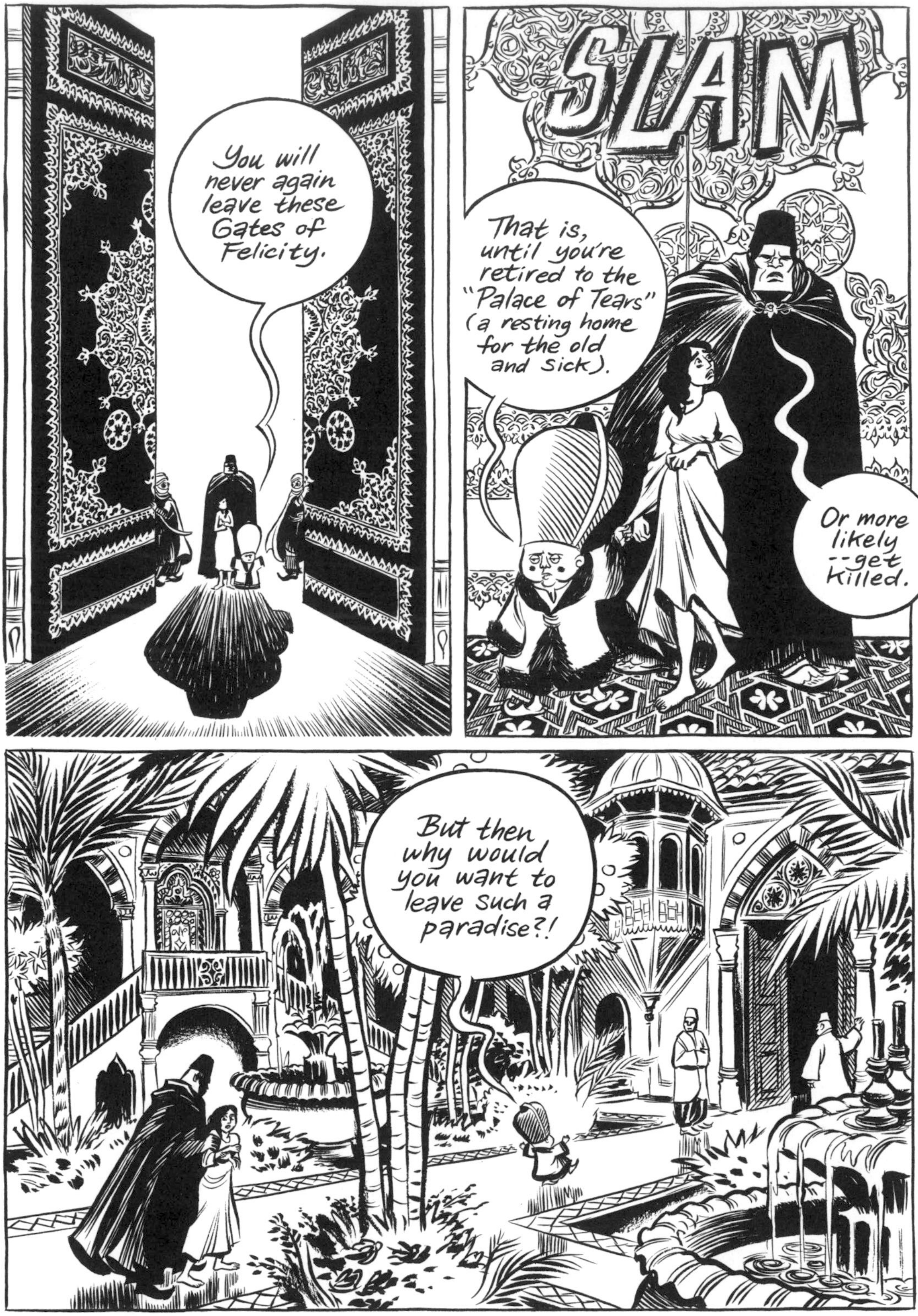
You will never again leave these Gates of Felicity.
SLAM
That is, until you're retired to the "Palace of Tears" (a resting home for the old and sick).
Or more likely --get killed.
But then why would you want to leave such a paradise?!

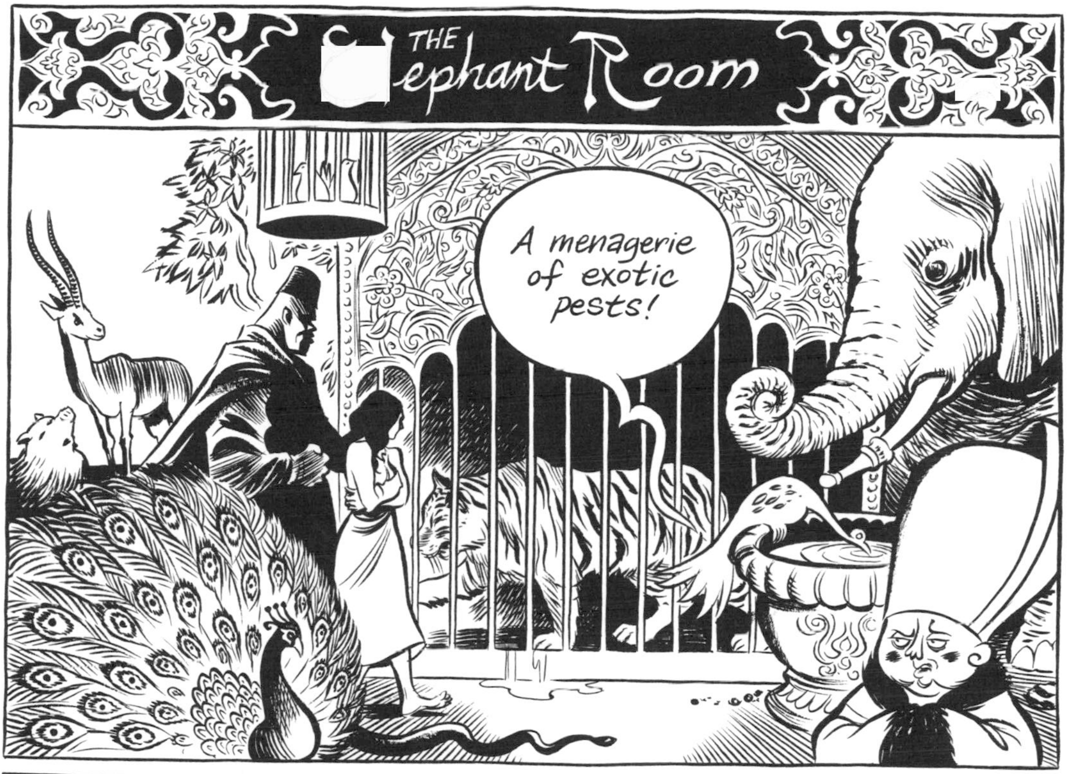
THE
ephant Room
A menagerie of exotic pests!

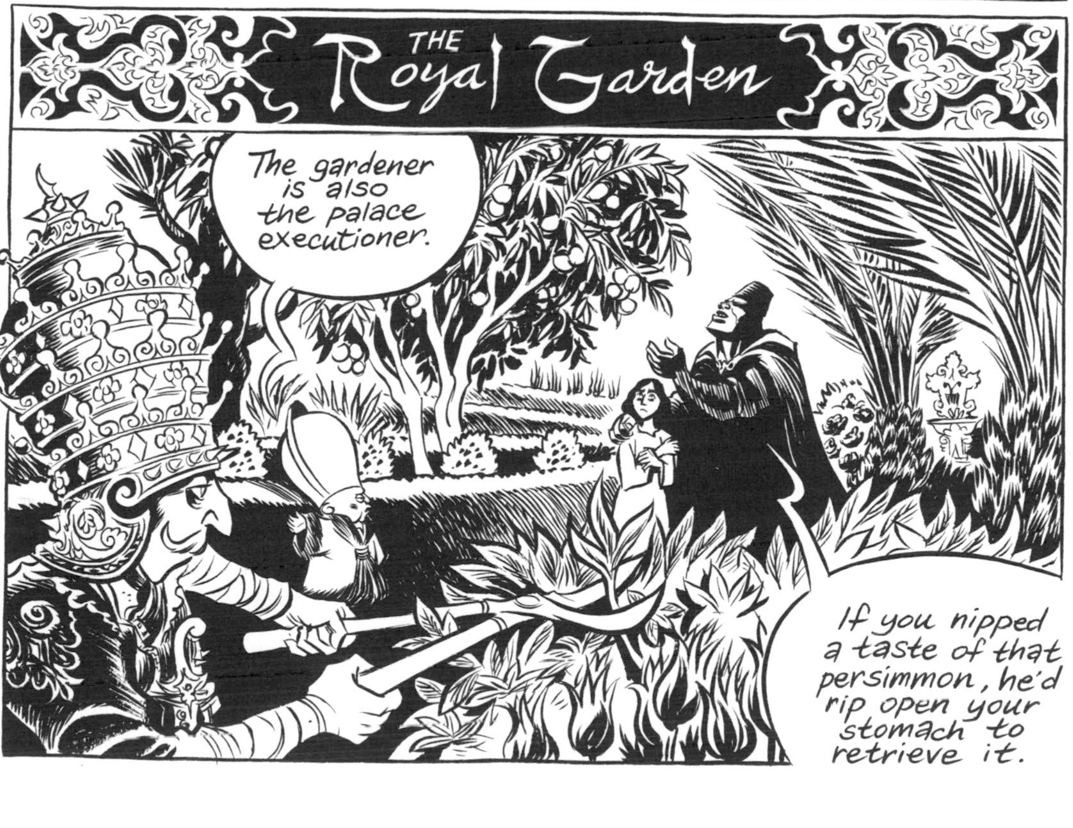
THE
Royal Garden
The gardener is also the palace executioner.
If you nipped a taste of that persimmon, he'd rip open your stomach to retrieve it.

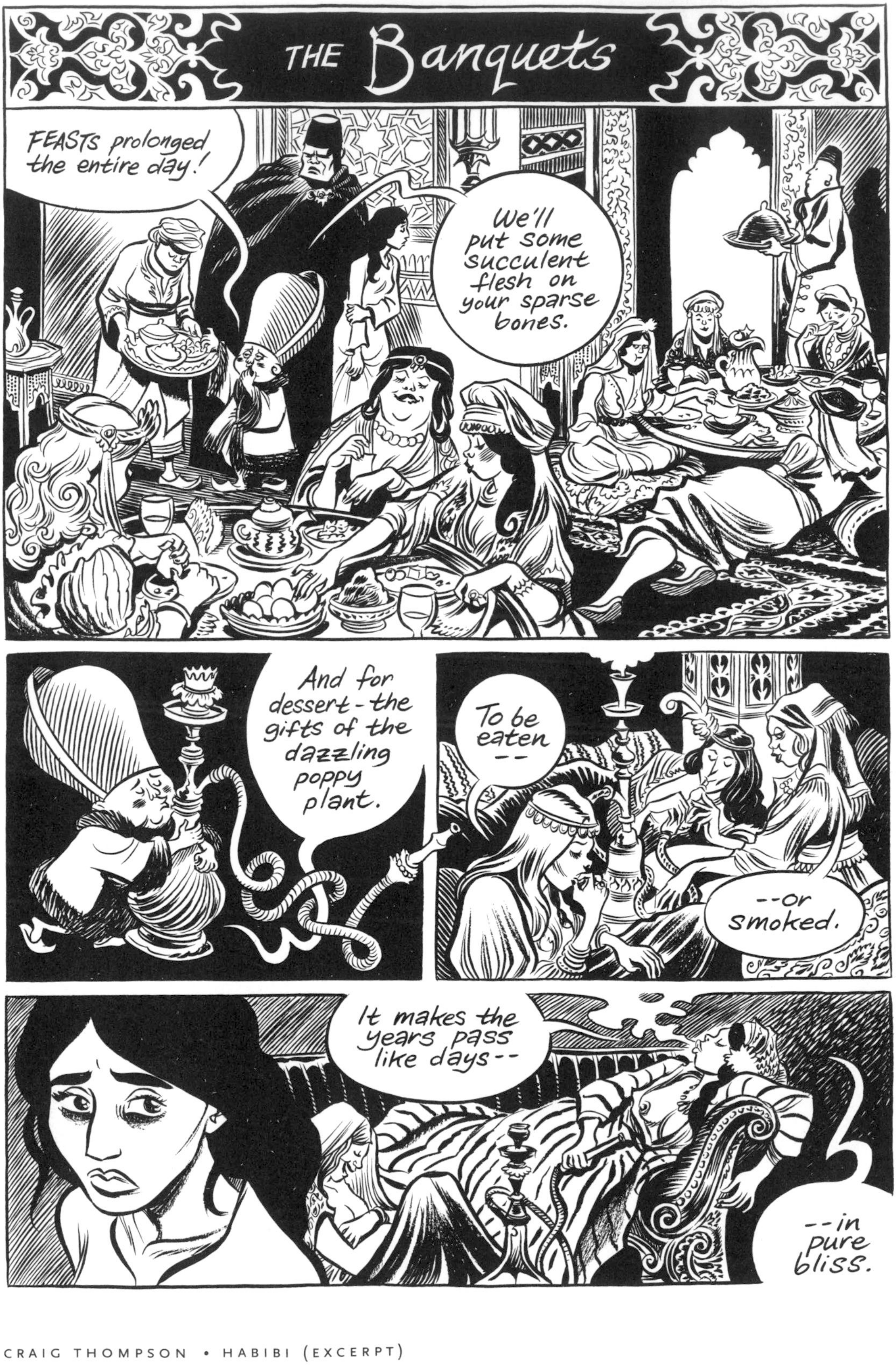
THE Banquets
FEASTS prolonged the entire day!
We'll put some succulent flesh on your sparse bones.
And for dessert - the gifts of the dazzling poppy plant.
To be eaten --
--or smoked.
It makes the years pass like days--
--in pure bliss.

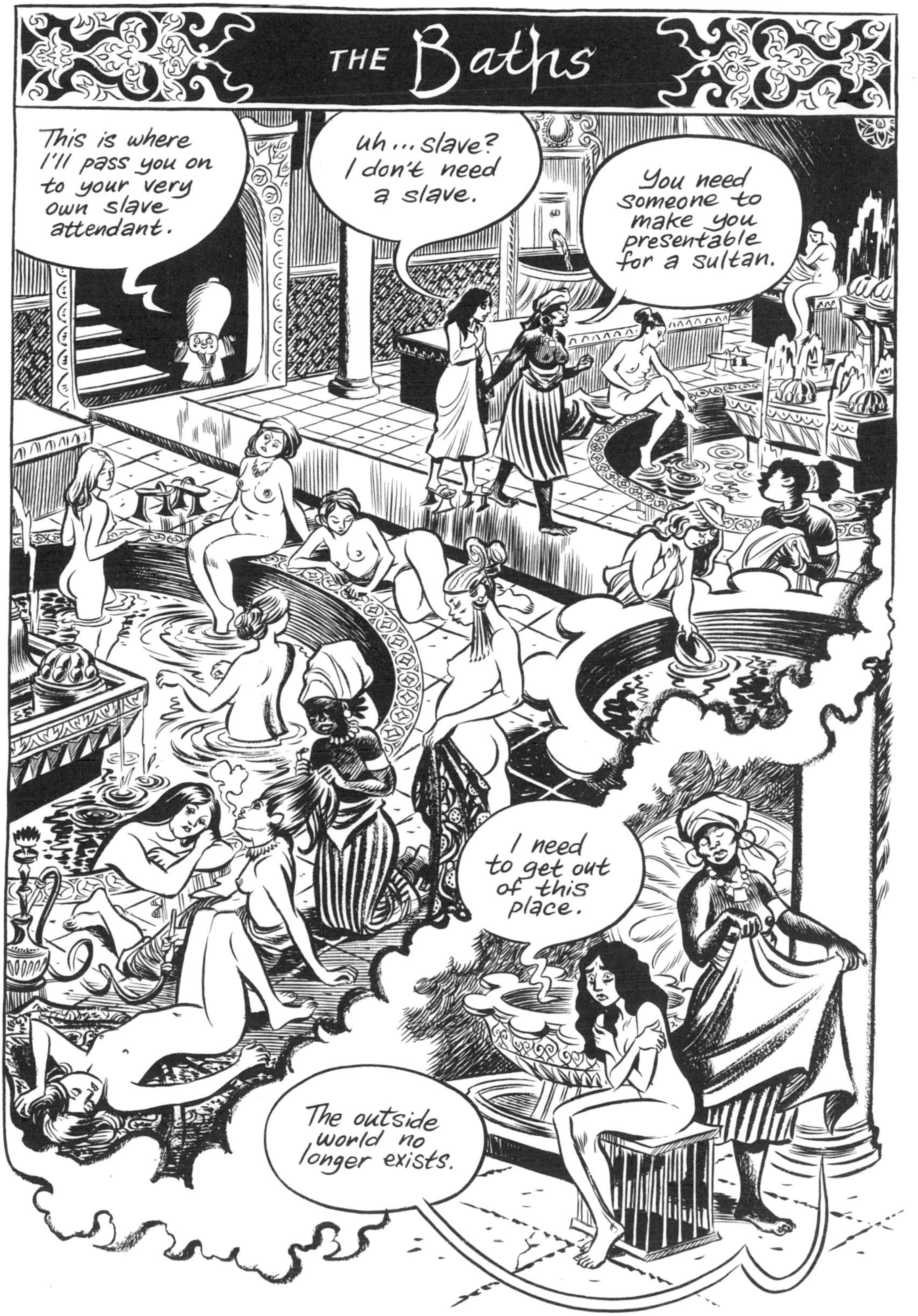
THE Baths
This is where I'll pass you on to your very own slave attendant.
uh... slave? I don't need a slave.
You need someone to make you presentable for a sultan.
I need to get out of this place.
The outside world no longer exists.

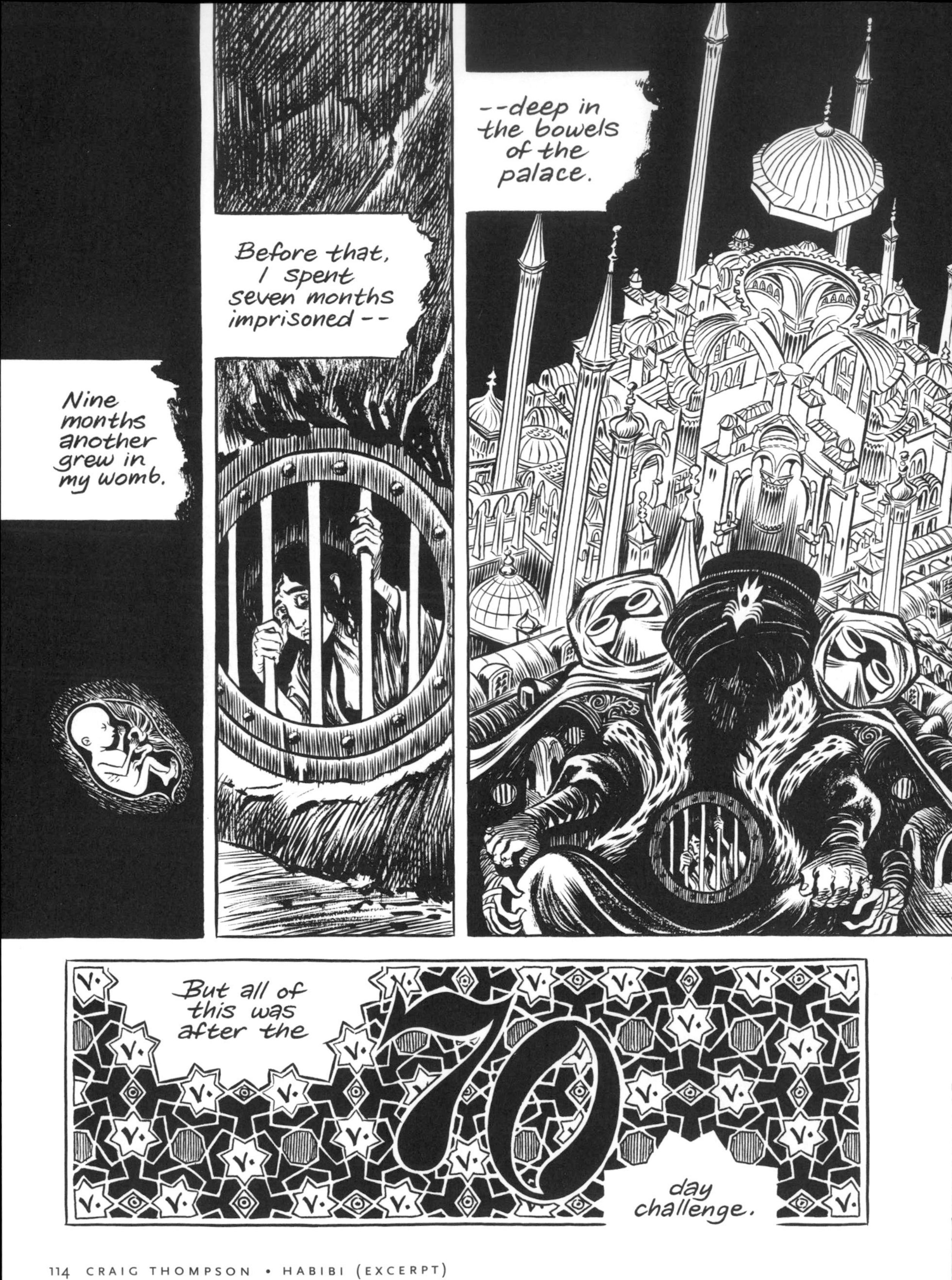
Nine months another grew in my womb.
Before that, I spent seven months imprisoned --
--deep in the bowels of the palace.
But all of this was after the
70
day challenge.

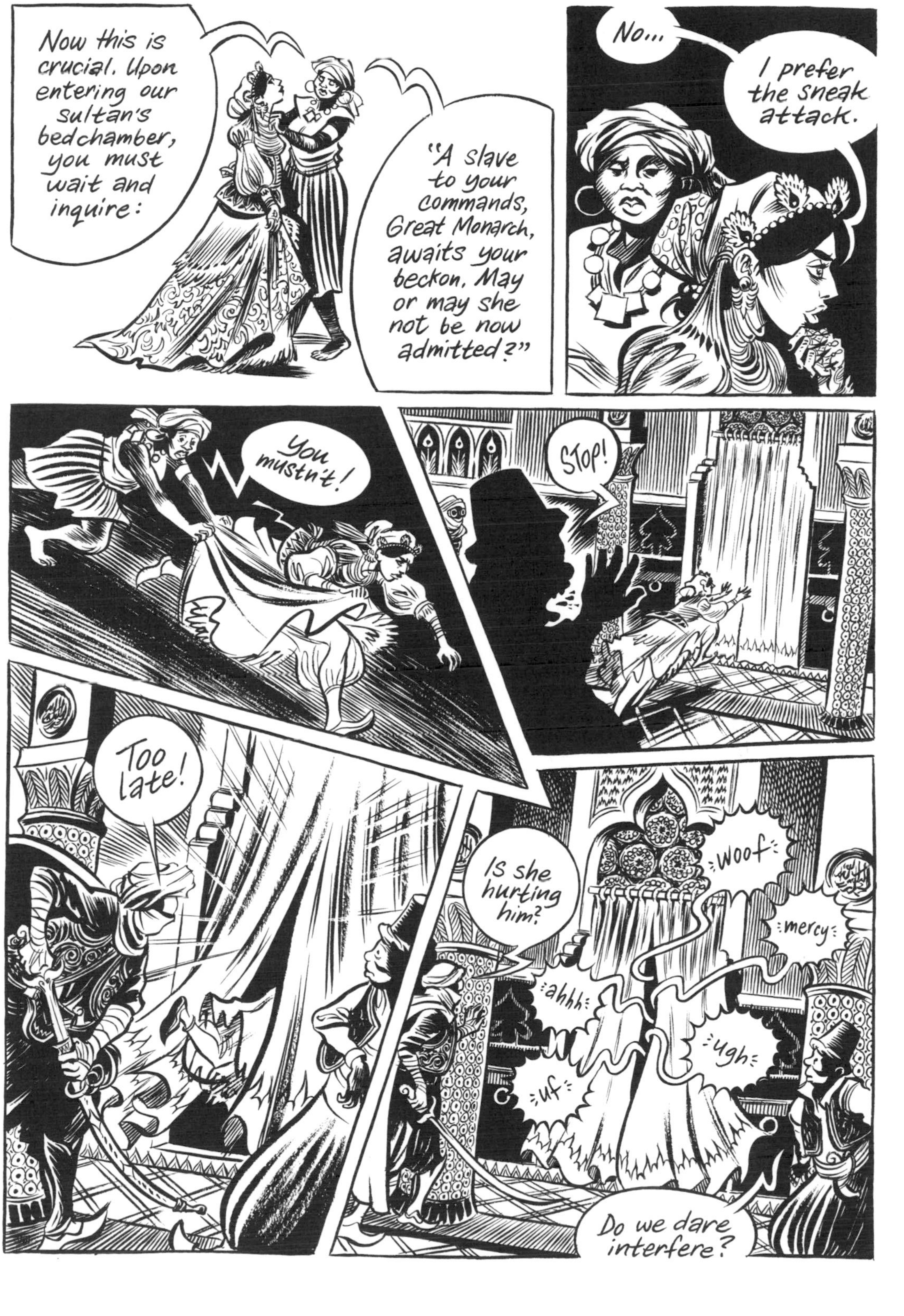
Now this is crucial. Upon entering our sultan's bedchamber, you must wait and inquire:
"A slave to your commands, Great Monarch, awaits your beckon. May or may she not be now admitted?"
No...
I prefer the sneak attack.
You mustn't!
STOP!
Too late!
Is she hurting him?
woof
mercy
ahhh
ugh
uf
Do we dare interfere?

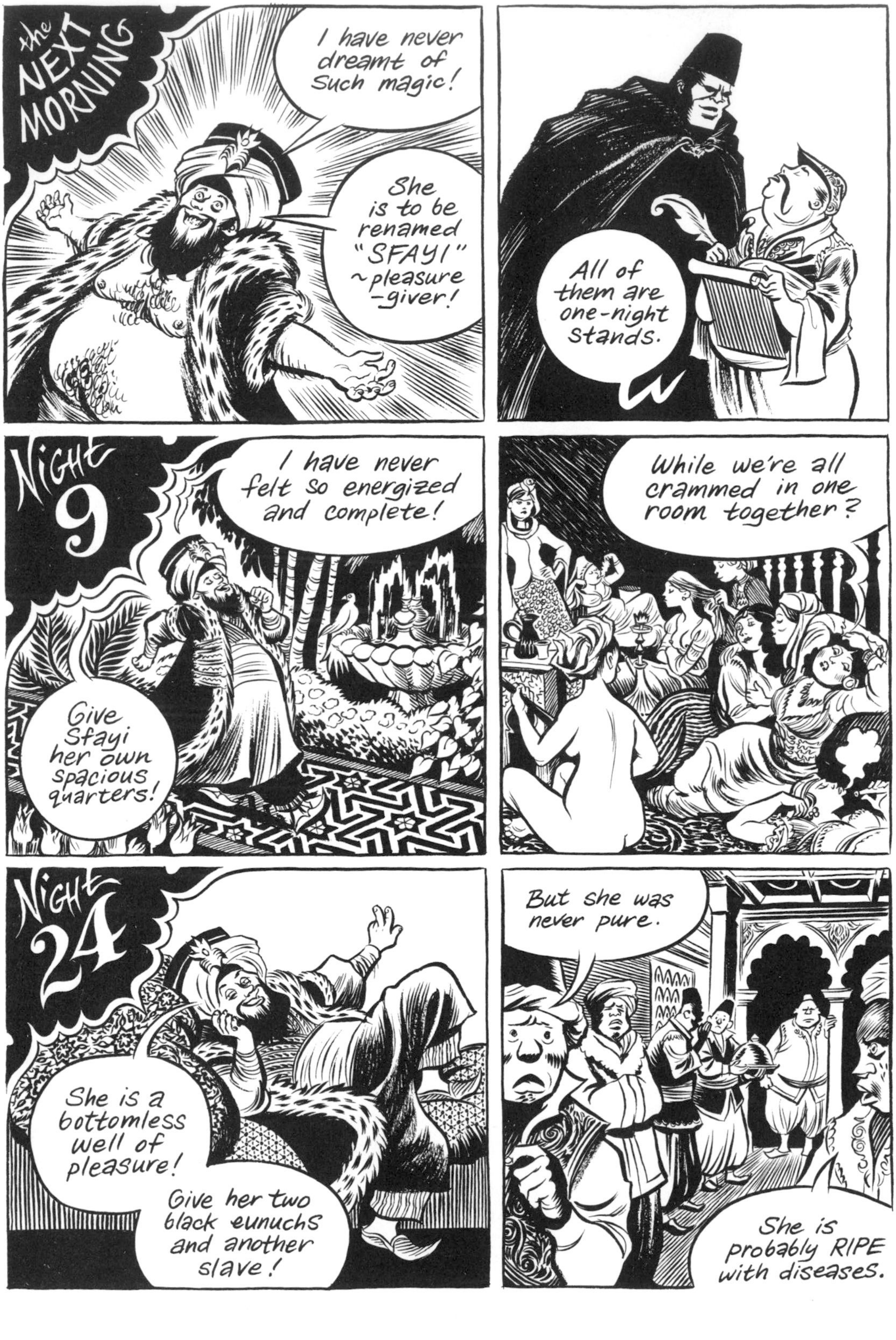
the NEXT MORNING
I have never dreamt of Such magic!
She is to be renamed "SFAYI" ~pleasure-giver!
All of them are one-night stands.
NIGHT 9
I have never felt so energized and complete!
Give Sfayi her own spacious quarters!
While we're all crammed in one room together?
NIGHT 24
She is a bottomless well of pleasure!
Give her two black eunuchs and another slave!
But she was never pure.
She is probably RIPE with diseases.

NIGHT 39

Sfayi is my only aphrodisiac!

Give her clothes and jewelry and a generous allowance!

She is a threat.

No matter what, keep her from getting pregnant.

NIGHT 54

Could this be LOVE?

We most certainly hate her.

Myself, Hyacinth, and two other attendants are loyal to her.

But the rest of us eunuchs find her filthy!

NIGHT 69

She is "Ikbal" ~ GLORIFIED. Have all others bow to her.

Have her STRANGLED in the middle of the night.

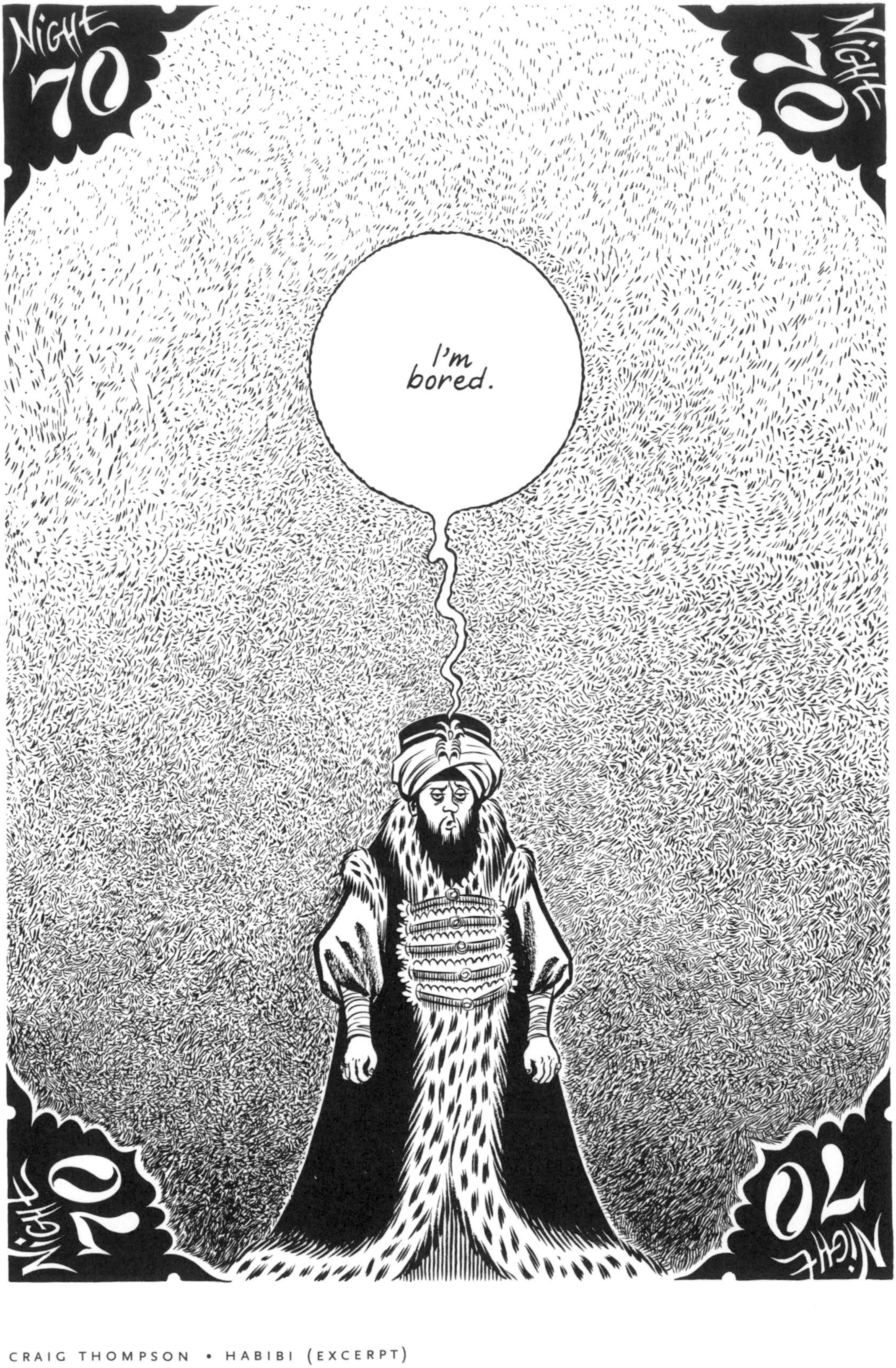
NIGHT 70
NIGHT 70
NIGHT 70
NIGHT 70
I'm bored.

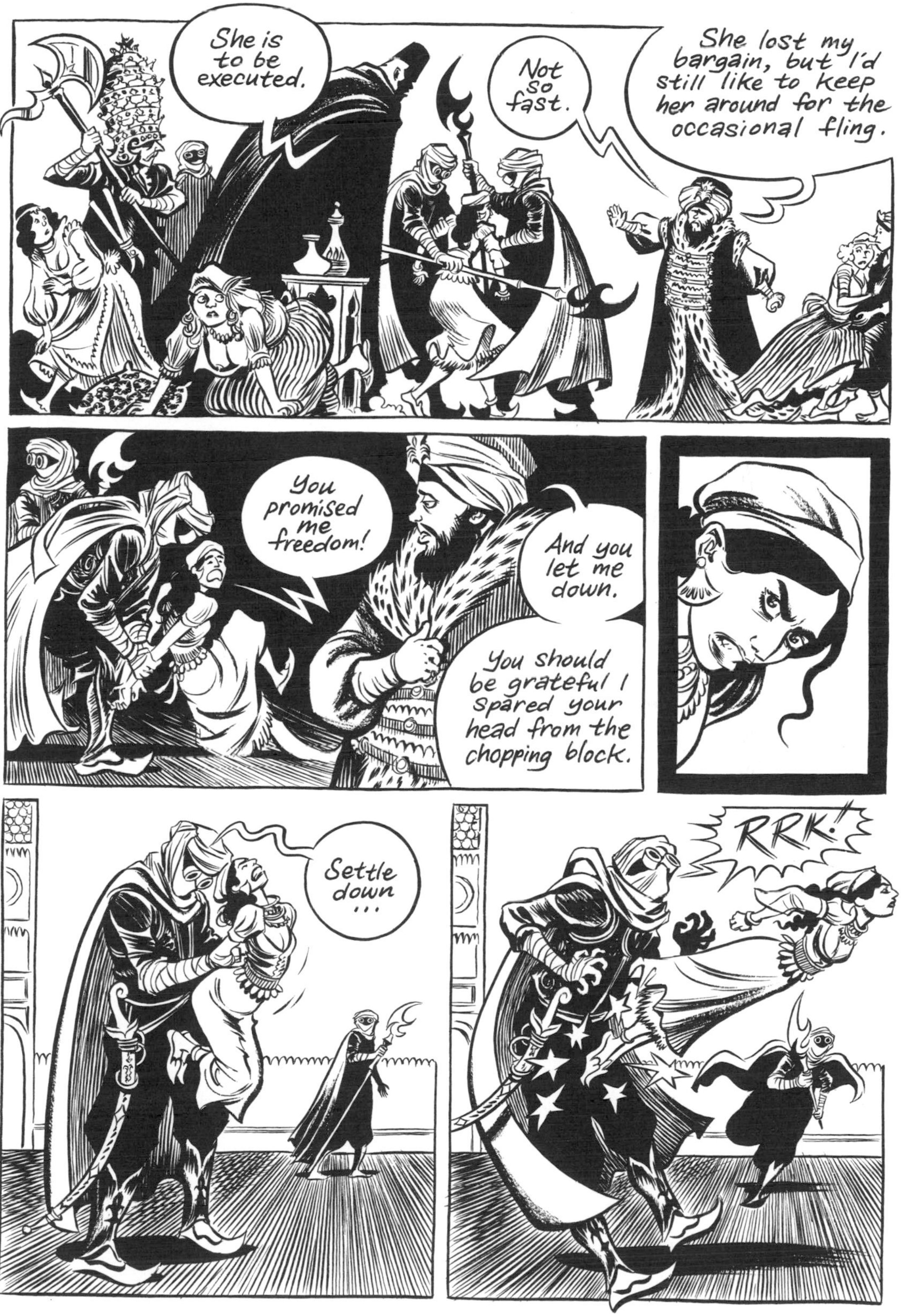
She is to be executed.
Not so fast.
She lost my bargain, but I'd still like to keep her around for the occasional fling.
You promised me freedom!
And you let me down.
You should be grateful I spared your head from the chopping block.
Settle down ...
RRK!

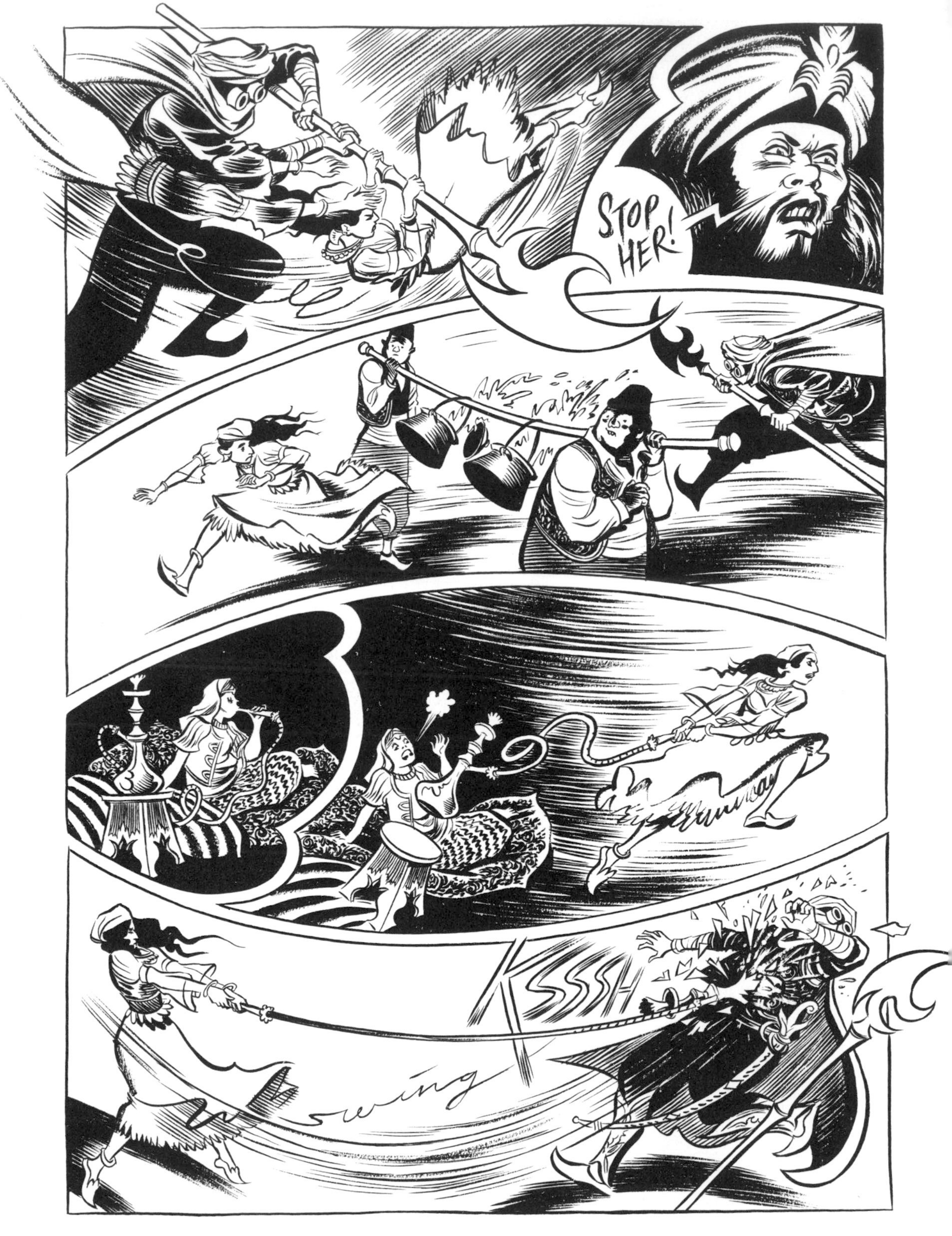
STOP HER!
KSSSH
swing

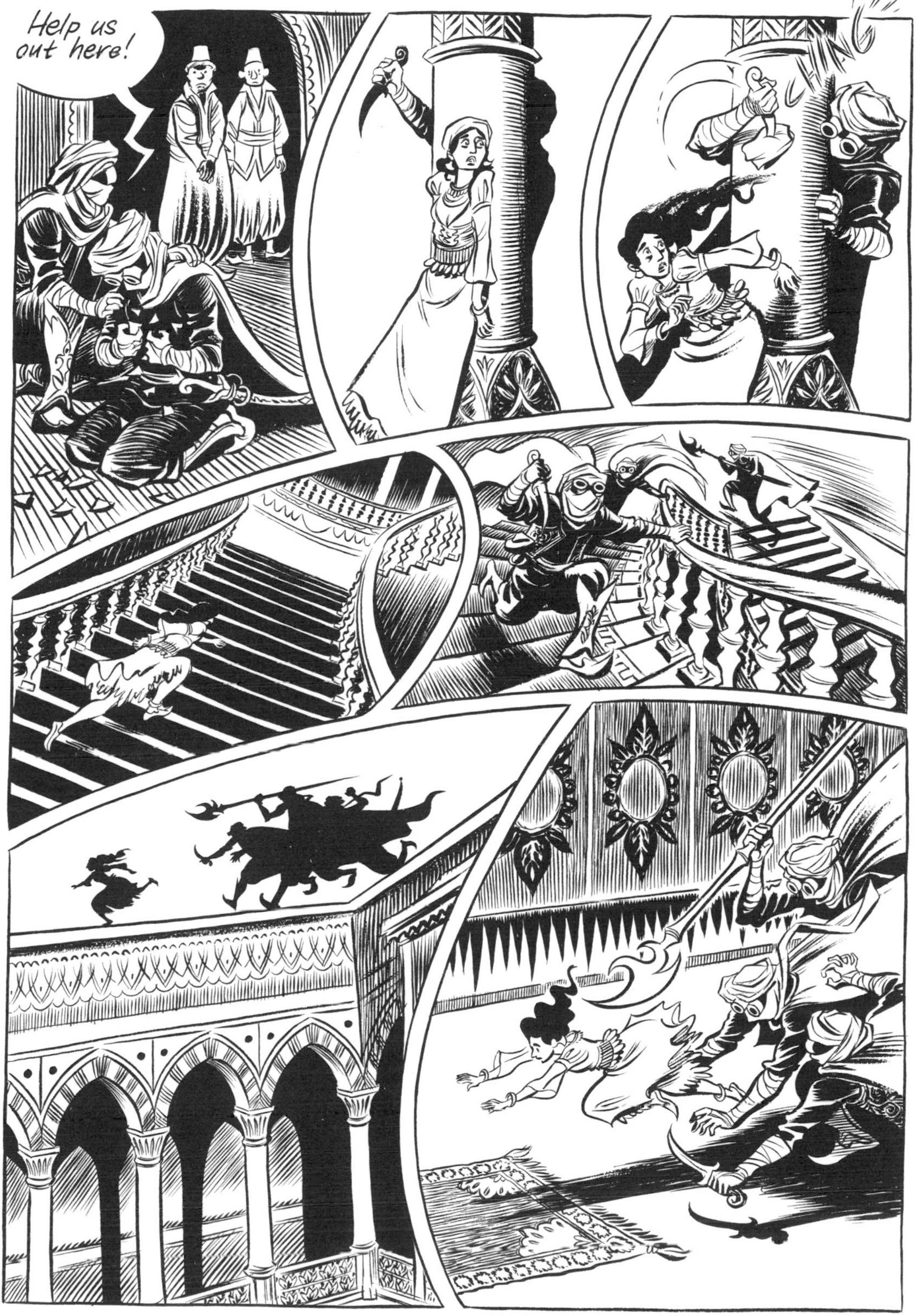
Help us out here!
KLANG

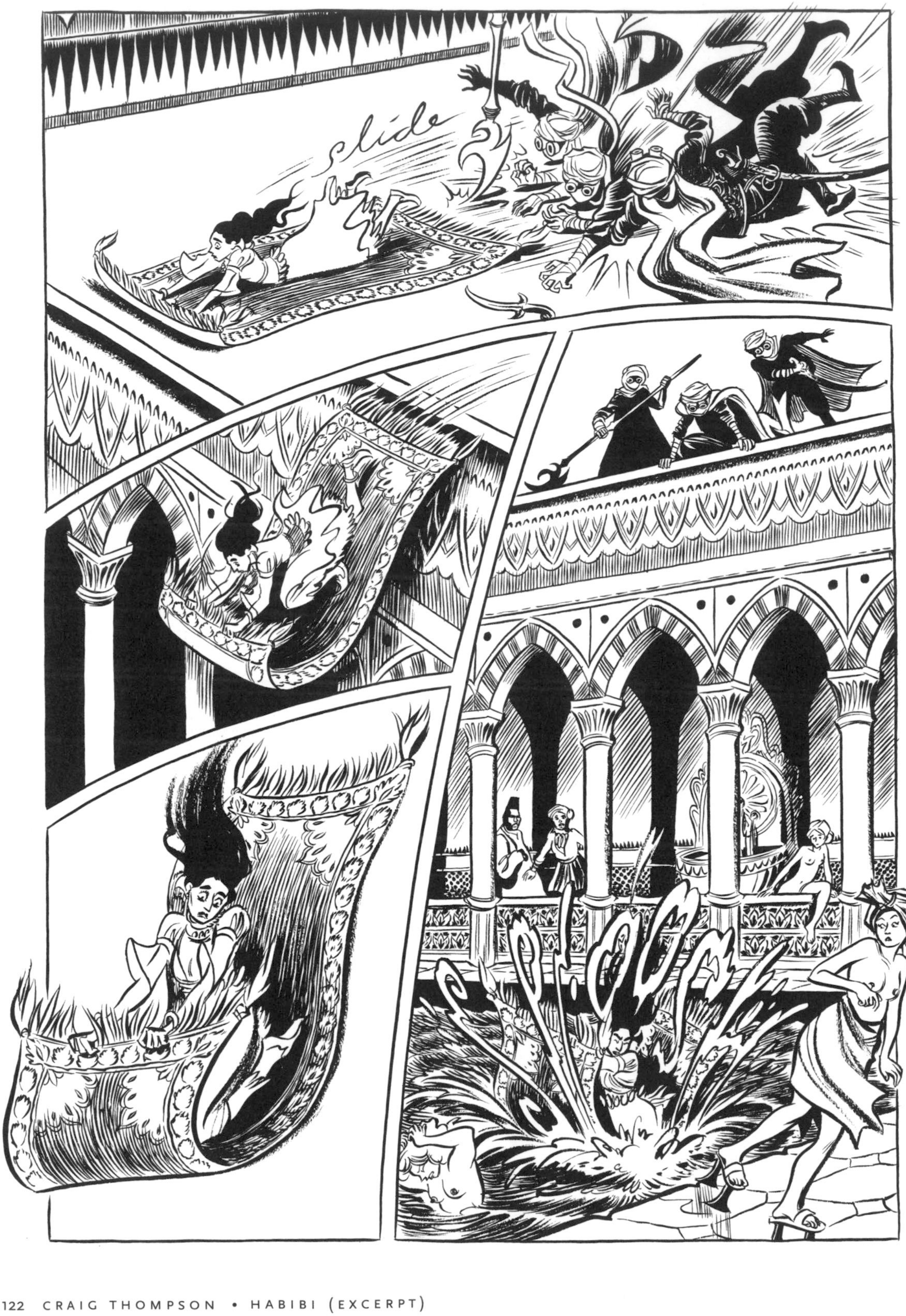
slide

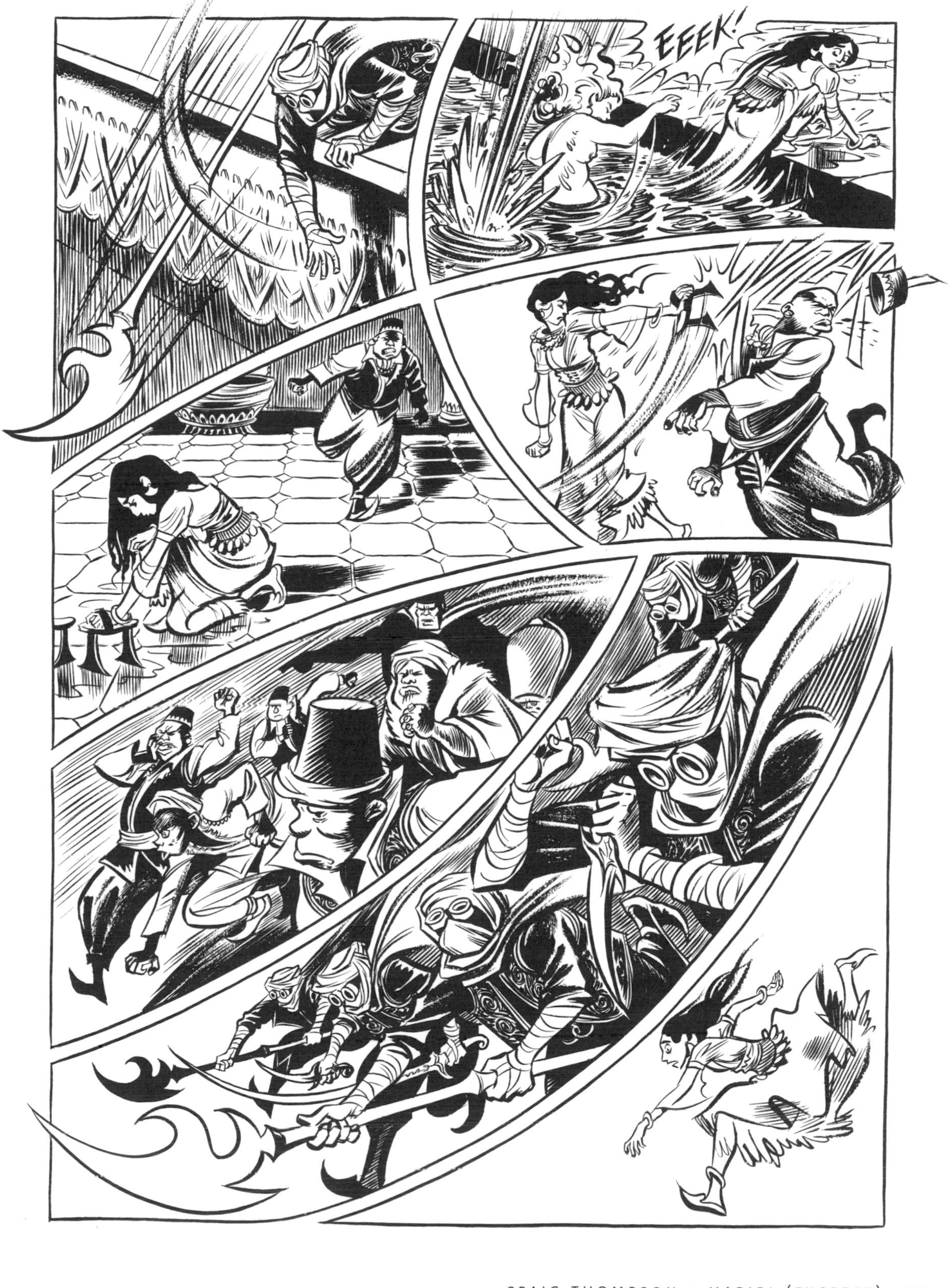
EEEK!

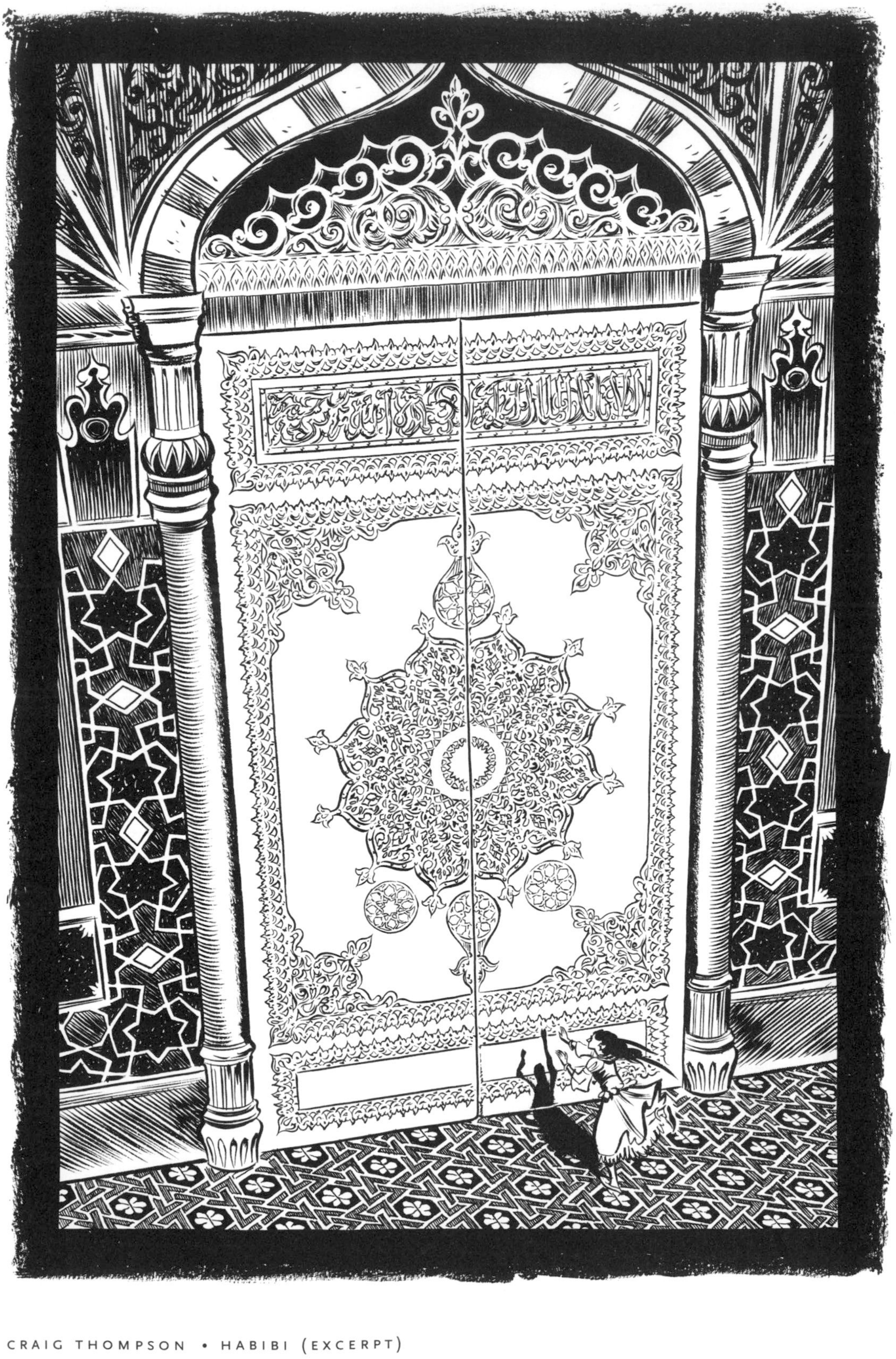

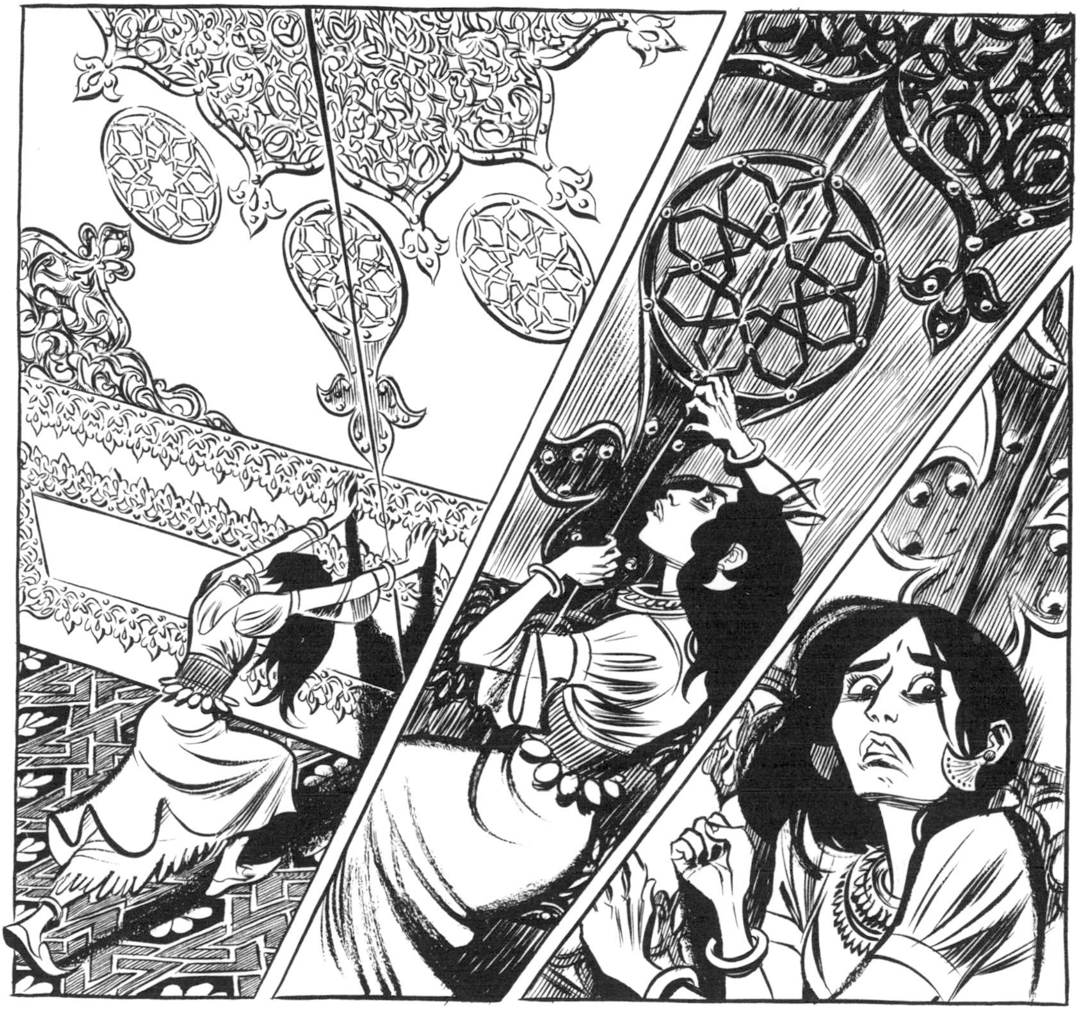

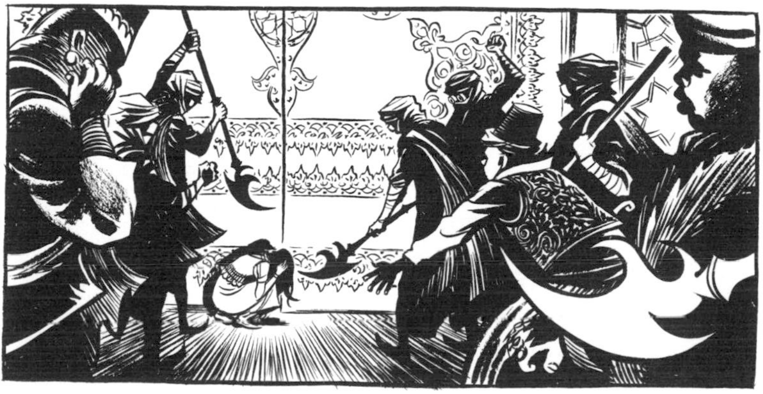

The Story of
Gráinne Ní Mháille

Excerpt from
Gone to Amerikay

Colleen Doran and Derek McCulloch

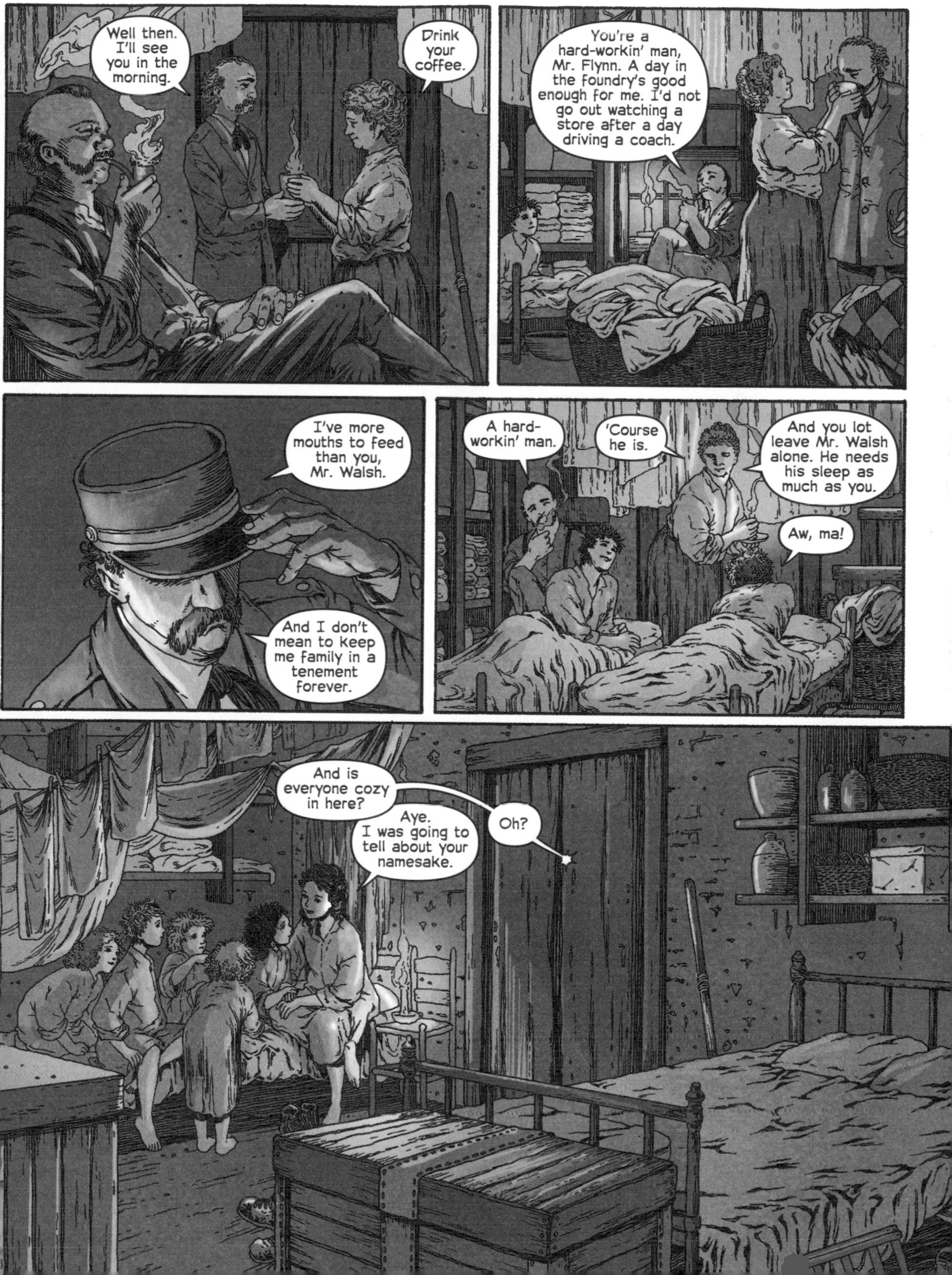
Well then. I'll see you in the morning.
Drink your coffee.
You're a hard-workin' man, Mr. Flynn. A day in the foundry's good enough for me. I'd not go out watching a store after a day driving a coach.
I've more mouths to feed than you, Mr. Walsh.
And I don't mean to keep me family in a tenement forever.
A hard-workin' man.
'Course he is.
And you lot leave Mr. Walsh alone. He needs his sleep as much as you.
Aw, ma!
And is everyone cozy in here?
Aye. I was going to tell about your namesake.
Oh?

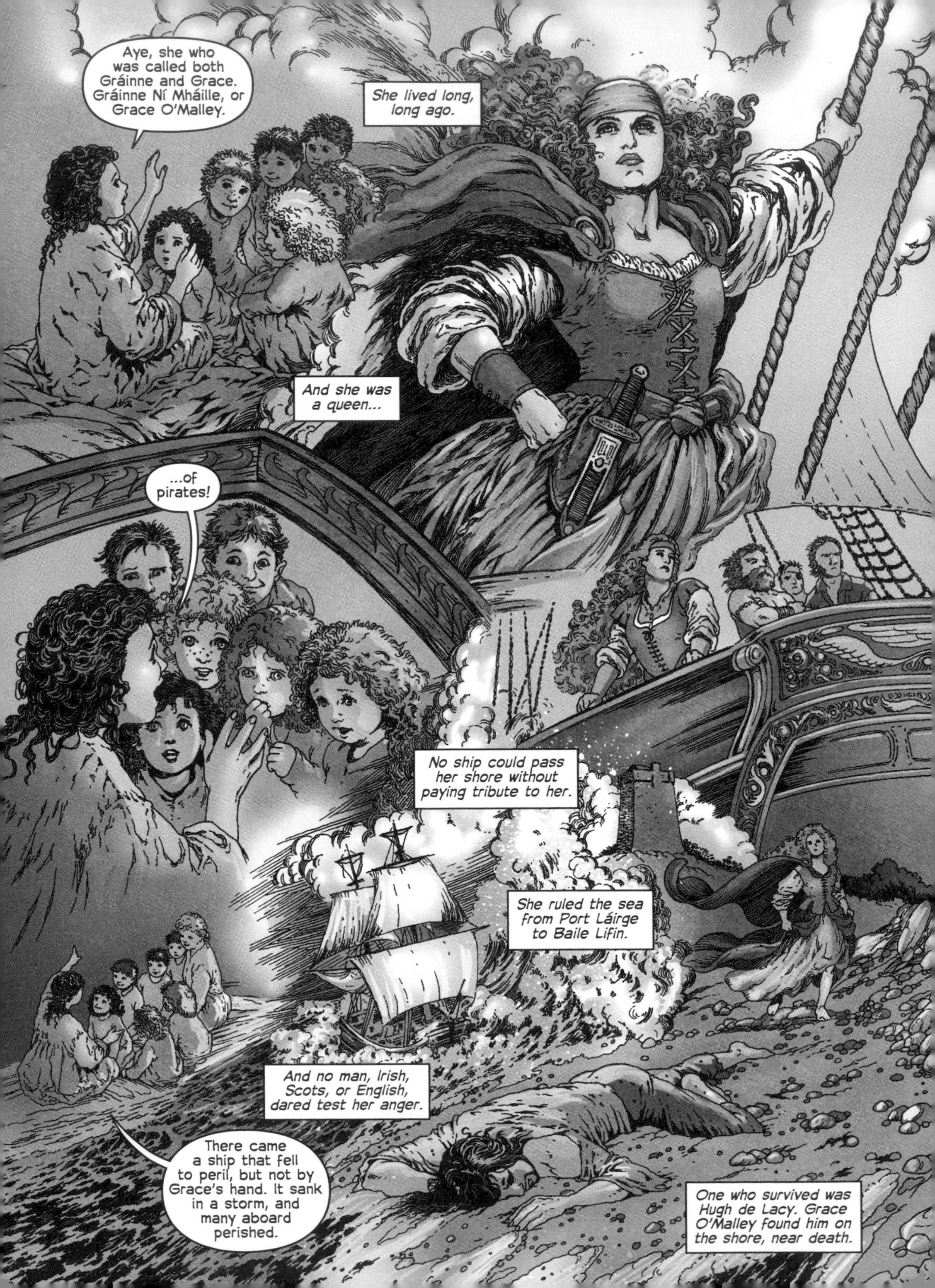
Aye, she who was called both Gráinne and Grace. Gráinne Ní Mháille, or Grace O'Malley.
She lived long, long ago.
And she was a queen...
...of pirates!
No ship could pass her shore without paying tribute to her.
She ruled the sea from Port Láirge to Baile Lifin.
And no man, Irish, Scots, or English, dared test her anger.
There came a ship that fell to peril, but not by Grace's hand. It sank in a storm, and many aboard perished.
One who survived was Hugh de Lacy. Grace O'Malley found him on the shore, near death.

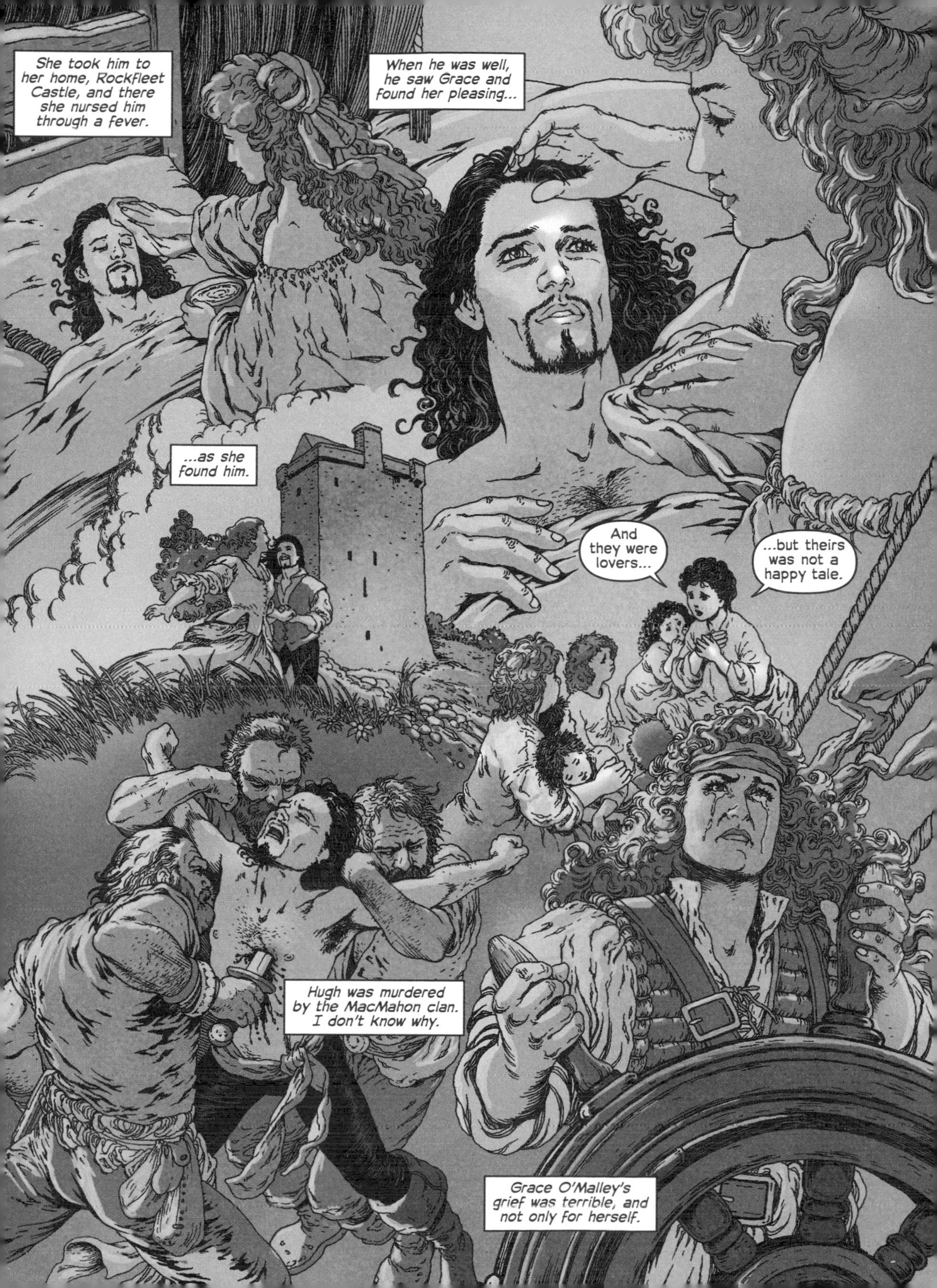
She took him to her home, Rockfleet Castle, and there she nursed him through a fever.
When he was well, he saw Grace and found her pleasing...
...as she found him.
And they were lovers...
...but theirs was not a happy tale.
Hugh was murdered by the MacMahon clan. I don't know why.
Grace O'Malley's grief was terrible, and not only for herself.

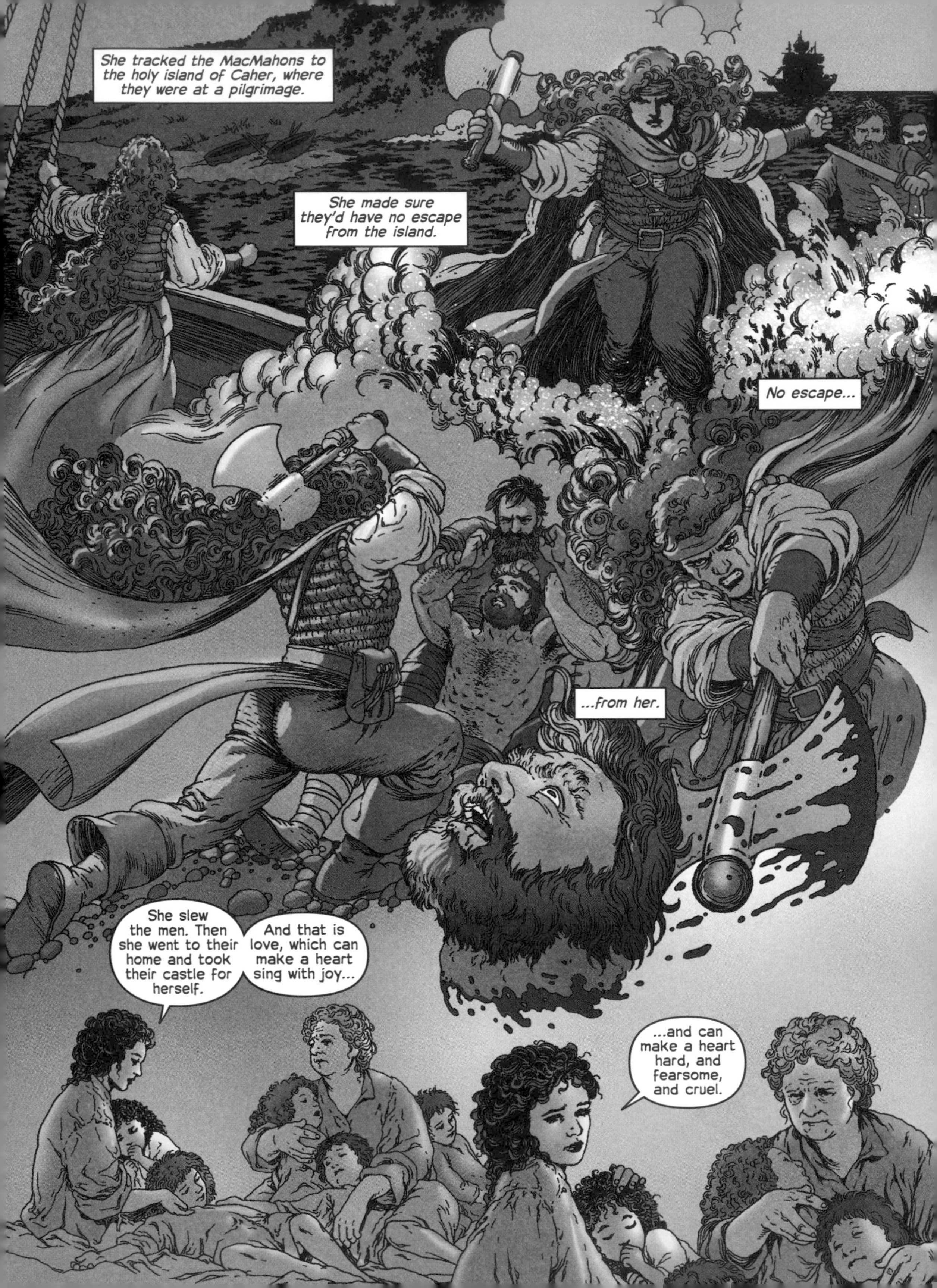
She tracked the MacMahons to the holy island of Caher, where they were at a pilgrimage.
She made sure they'd have no escape from the island.
No escape...
...from her.
She slew the men. Then she went to their home and took their castle for herself.
And that is love, which can make a heart sing with joy...
...and can make a heart hard, and fearsome, and cruel.

excerpts from

AMERICAN ELF

James Kochalka

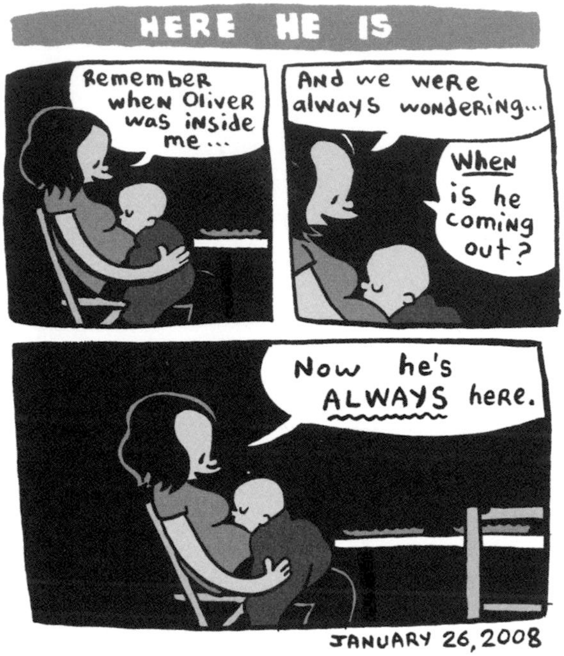
HERE HE IS
Remember when Oliver was inside me...
And we were always wondering...
When is he coming out?
Now he's ALWAYS here.
JANUARY 26, 2008

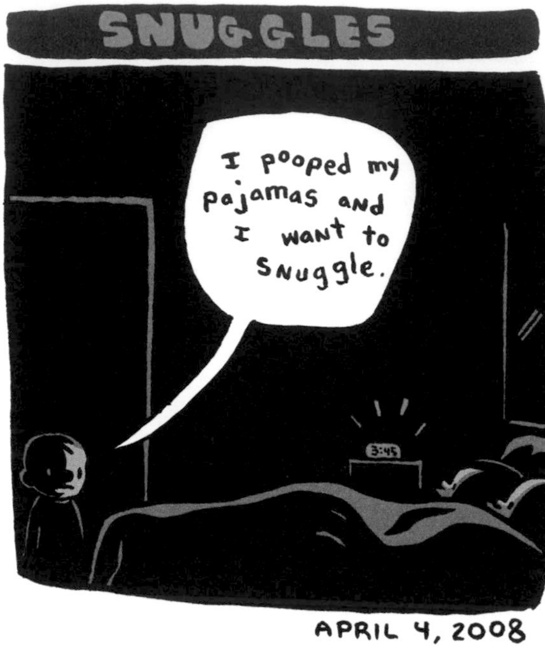
SNUGGLES
I pooped my pajamas and I want to snuggle.
3:45
APRIL 4, 2008

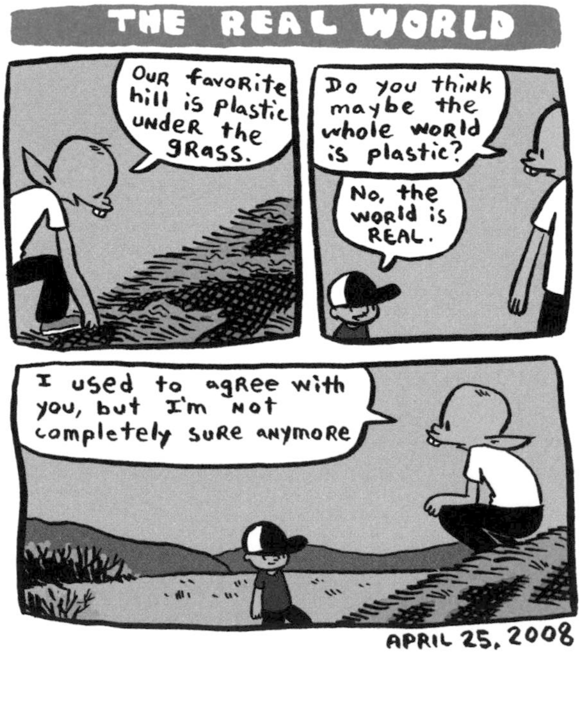
THE REAL WORLD
Our favorite hill is plastic under the grass.
Do you think maybe the whole world is plastic?
No, the world is REAL.
I used to agree with you, but I'm not completely sure anymore
APRIL 25, 2008

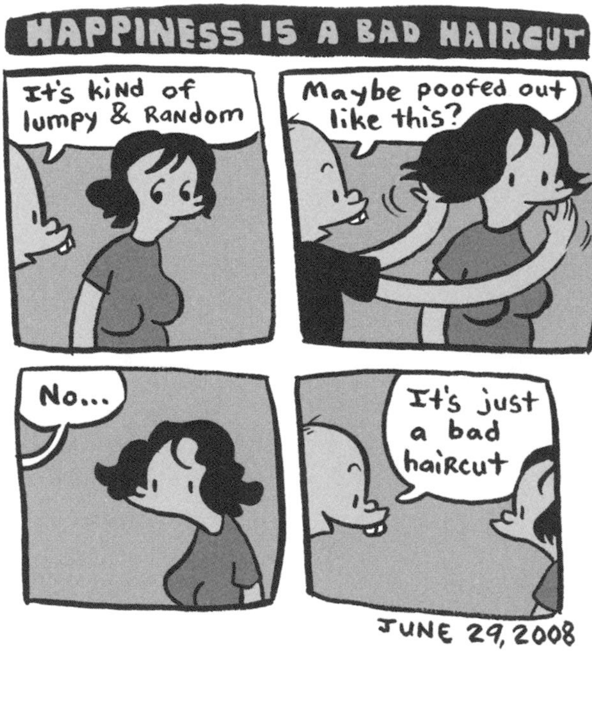
HAPPINESS IS A BAD HAIRCUT
It's kind of lumpy & Random
Maybe poofed out like this?
No...
It's just a bad haircut
JUNE 29, 2008

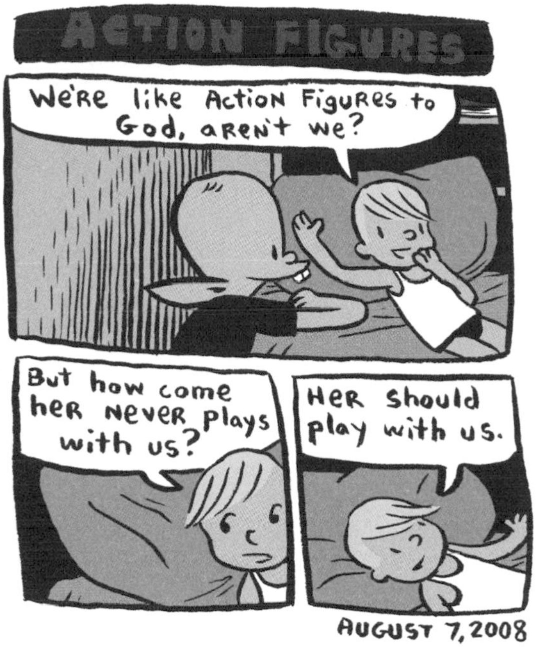
ACTION FIGURES
We're like Action Figures to God, aren't we?
But how come her never plays with us?
Her should play with us.
AUGUST 7, 2008

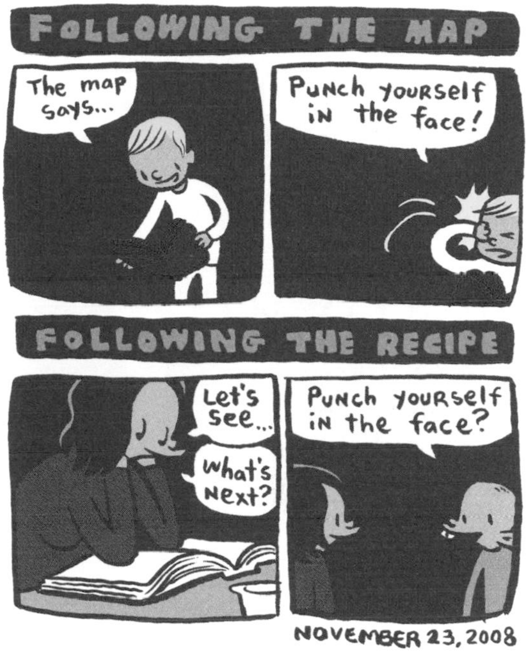
FOLLOWING THE MAP
The map says...
Punch yourself in the face!
FOLLOWING THE RECIPE
Let's see...
What's next?
Punch yourself in the face?
NOVEMBER 23, 2008

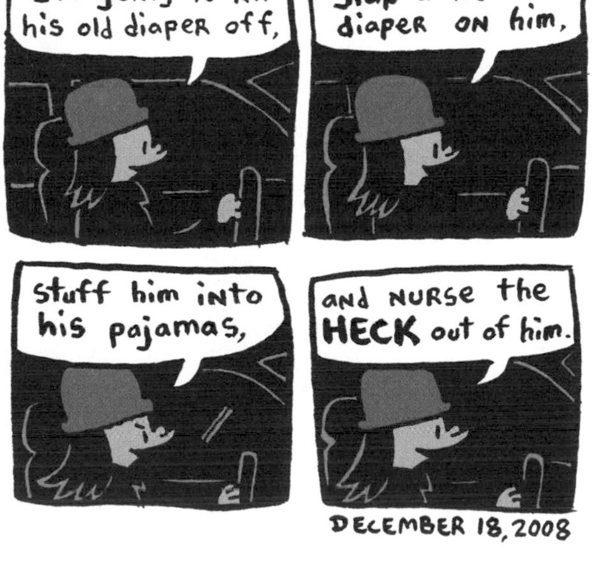
AMY'S PLAN
(FOR OLIVER, WHEN WE GET HOME)
I'm going to RIP his old diaper off,
Slap a new diaper on him,
stuff him into his pajamas,
and nurse the HECK out of him.
DECEMBER 18, 2008

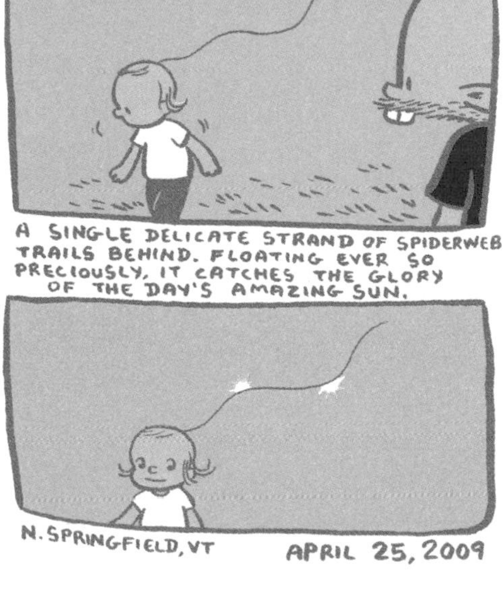
MY SUNSHINE
AS OLIVER EXPLORES GRANDMA'S YARD
A SINGLE DELICATE STRAND OF SPIDERWEB TRAILS BEHIND. FLOATING EVER SO PRECIOUSLY, IT CATCHES THE GLORY OF THE DAY'S AMAZING SUN.
N. SPRINGFIELD, VT
APRIL 25, 2009

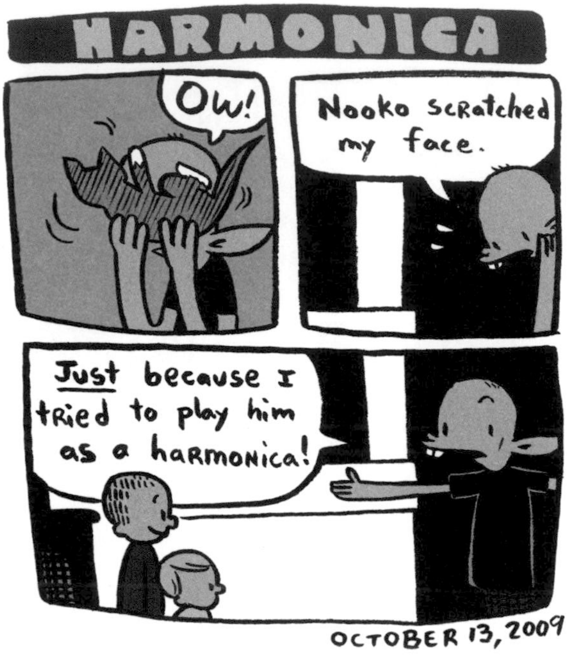
HARMONICA
OW!
Nooko scratched my face.
Just because I tried to play him as a harmonica!
OCTOBER 13, 2009

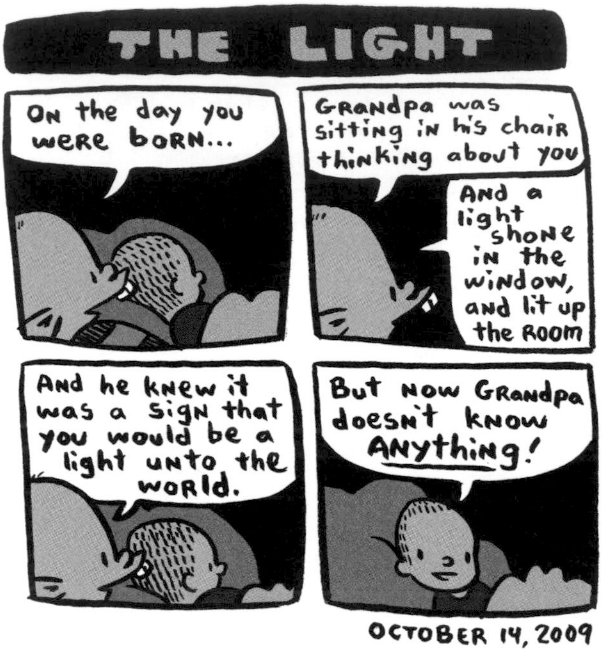
THE LIGHT
On the day you were born...
Grandpa was sitting in his chair thinking about you
And a light shone in the window, and lit up the room
And he knew it was a sign that you would be a light unto the world.
But now Grandpa doesn't know ANYTHING!
OCTOBER 14, 2009

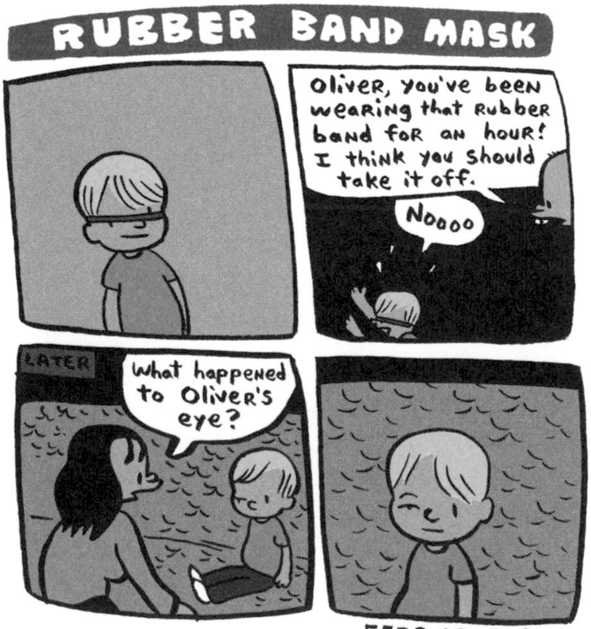
RUBBER BAND MASK
Oliver, you've been wearing that rubber band for an hour! I think you should take it off.
Noooo
LATER
What happened to Oliver's eye?
FEBRUARY 26, 2010

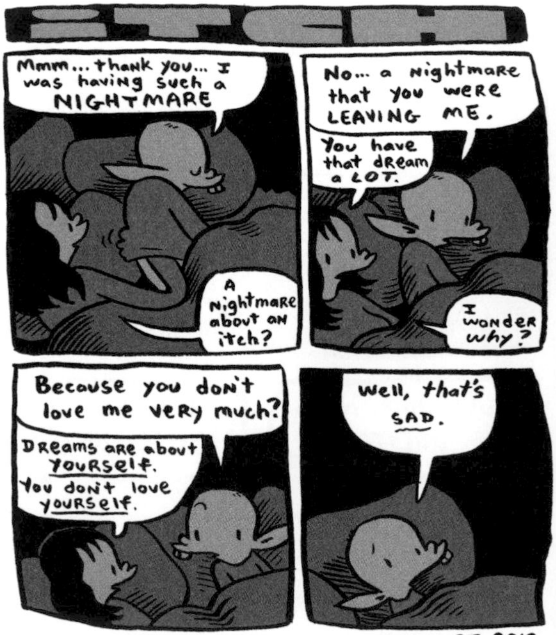
Mmm... thank you... I was having such a NIGHTMARE
A nightmare about an itch?
No... a nightmare that you were LEAVING ME.
You have that dream a LOT.
I wonder why?
Because you don't love me very much?
Dreams are about YOURSELF.
You don't love YOURSELF.
Well, that's SAD.
MARCH 25, 2010

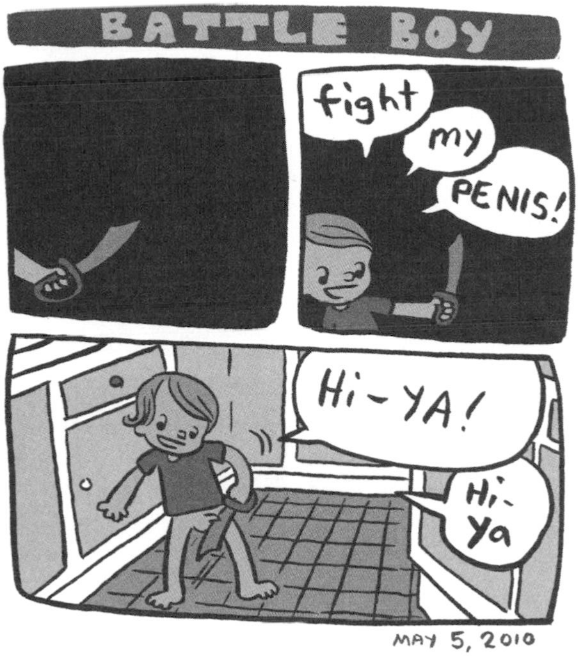
BATTLE BOY
fight
my
PENIS!
Hi-YA!
Hi-Ya
MAY 5, 2010

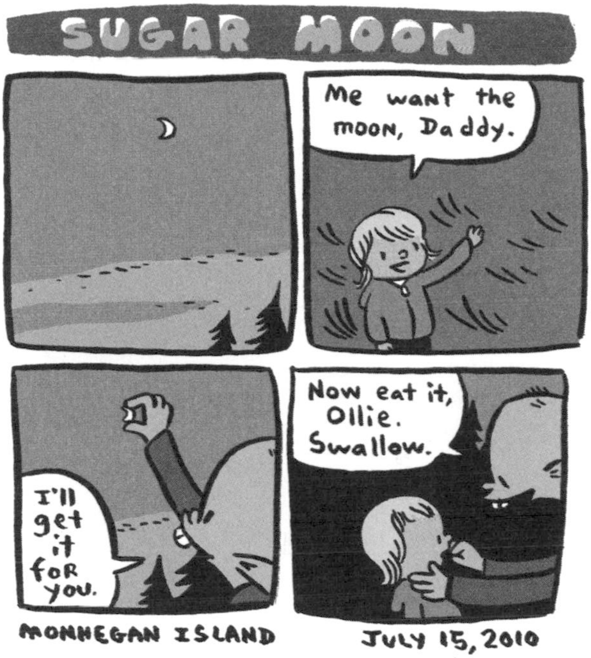
SUGAR MOON
Me want the moon, Daddy.
I'll get it for you.
Now eat it, Ollie. Swallow.
MONHEGAN ISLAND
JULY 15, 2010

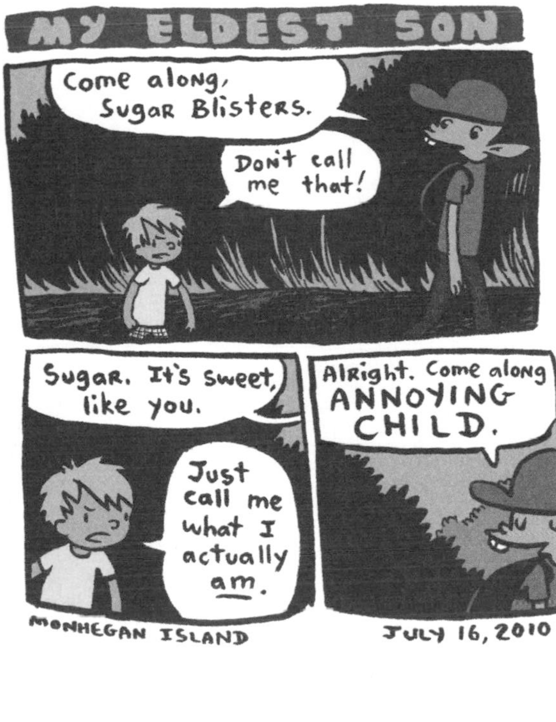
MY ELDEST SON
Come along, Sugar Blisters.
Don't call me that!
Sugar. It's sweet, like you.
Just call me what I actually am.
Alright. Come along ANNOYING CHILD.
MONHEGAN ISLAND
JULY 16, 2010

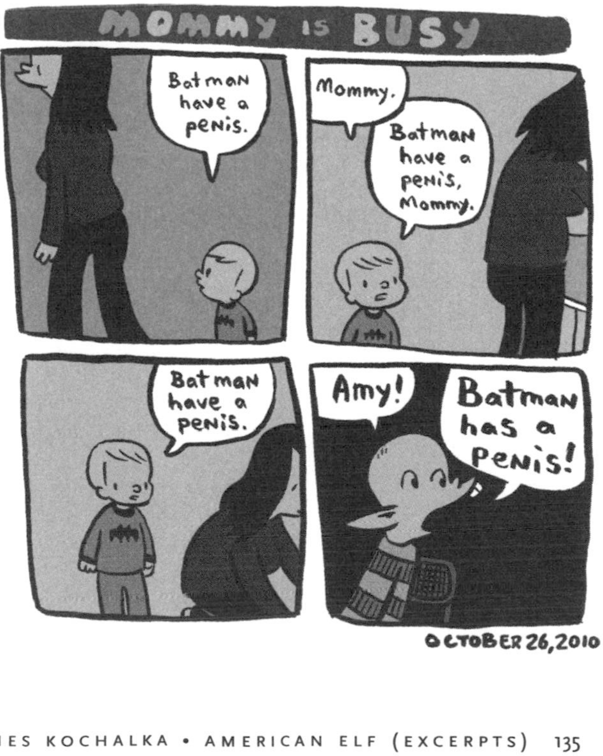
MOMMY IS BUSY
Batman have a penis.
Mommy.
Batman have a penis, Mommy.
Batman have a penis.
Amy!
Batman has a penis!
OCTOBER 26, 2010

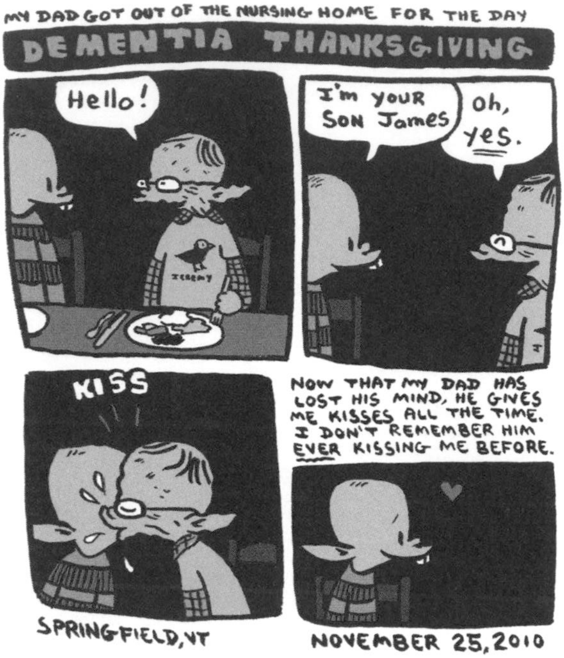
MY DAD GOT OUT OF THE NURSING HOME FOR THE DAY
DEMENTIA THANKSGIVING
Hello!
I'm your Son James
Oh, yes.
KISS
NOW THAT MY DAD HAS LOST HIS MIND, HE GIVES ME KISSES ALL THE TIME. I DON'T REMEMBER HIM EVER KISSING ME BEFORE.
SPRINGFIELD, VT
NOVEMBER 25, 2010

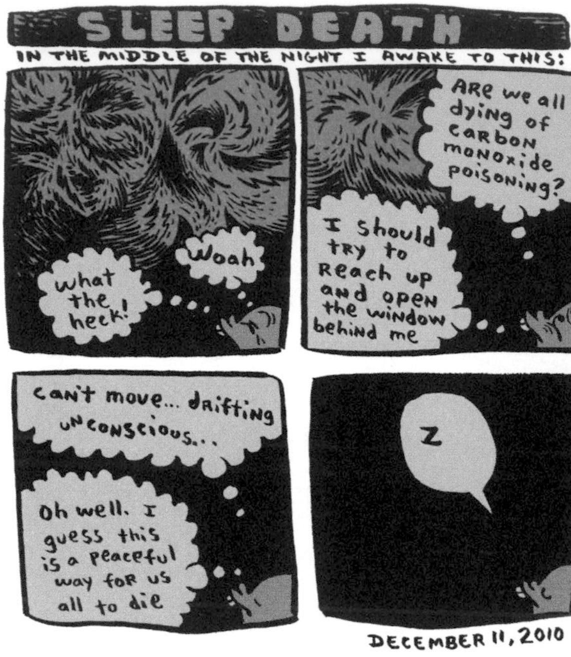
SLEEP DEATH
IN THE MIDDLE OF THE NIGHT I AWAKE TO THIS:
what the heck!
Woah
Are we all dying of carbon monoxide poisoning?
I should try to reach up and open the window behind me
can't move... drifting unconscious...
Oh well. I guess this is a peaceful way for us all to die
Z
DECEMBER 11, 2010

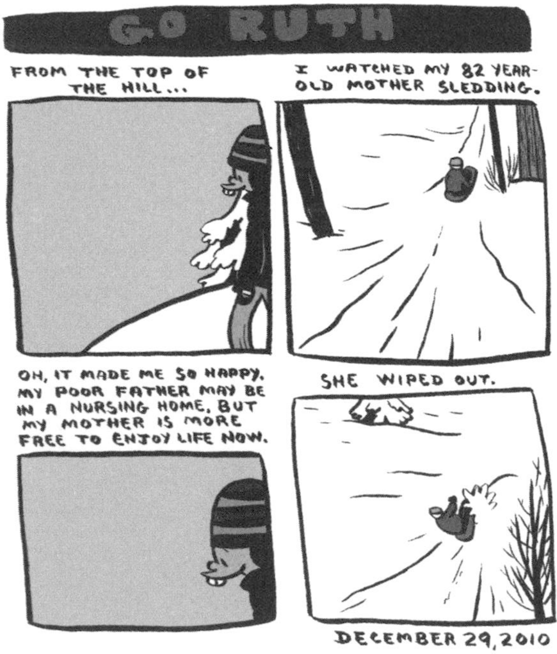
GO RUTH
FROM THE TOP OF THE HILL...
I WATCHED MY 82 YEAR-OLD MOTHER SLEDDING.
OH, IT MADE ME SO HAPPY. MY POOR FATHER MAY BE IN A NURSING HOME, BUT MY MOTHER IS MORE FREE TO ENJOY LIFE NOW.
SHE WIPED OUT.
DECEMBER 29, 2010

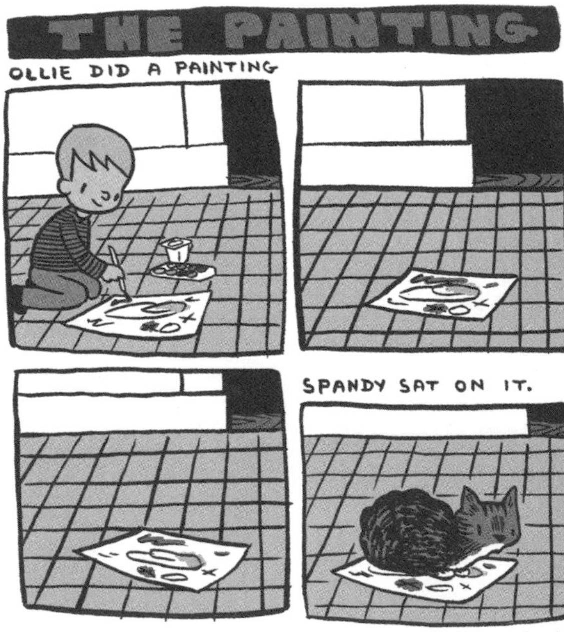
THE PAINTING
OLLIE DID A PAINTING
SPANDY SAT ON IT.
MAY 15, 2011

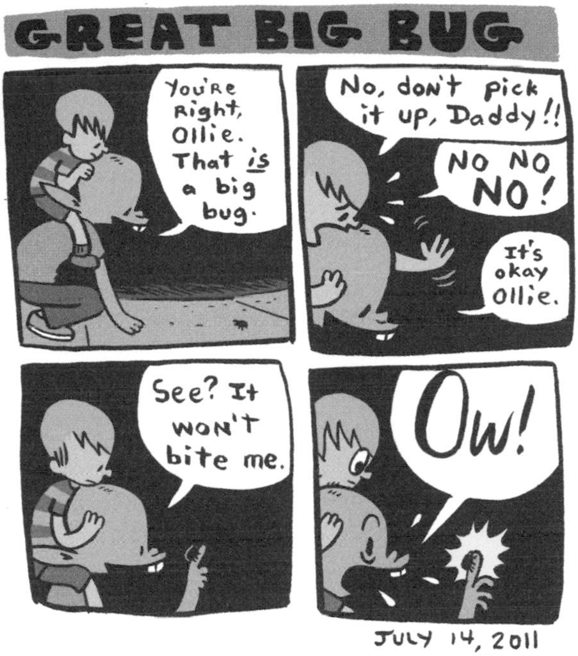
GREAT BIG BUG
You're right, Ollie. That is a big bug.
No, don't pick it up, Daddy!!
NO NO NO!
It's okay Ollie.
See? It won't bite me.
Ow!
JULY 14, 2011

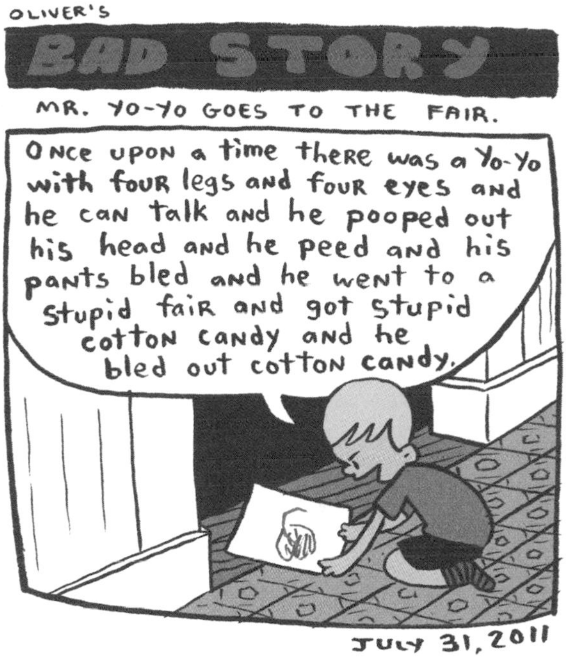
OLIVER'S
BAD STORY
MR. YO-YO GOES TO THE FAIR.
Once upon a time there was a Yo-Yo with four legs and four eyes and he can talk and he pooped out his head and he peed and his pants bled and he went to a stupid fair and got stupid cotton candy and he bled out cotton candy.
JULY 31, 2011

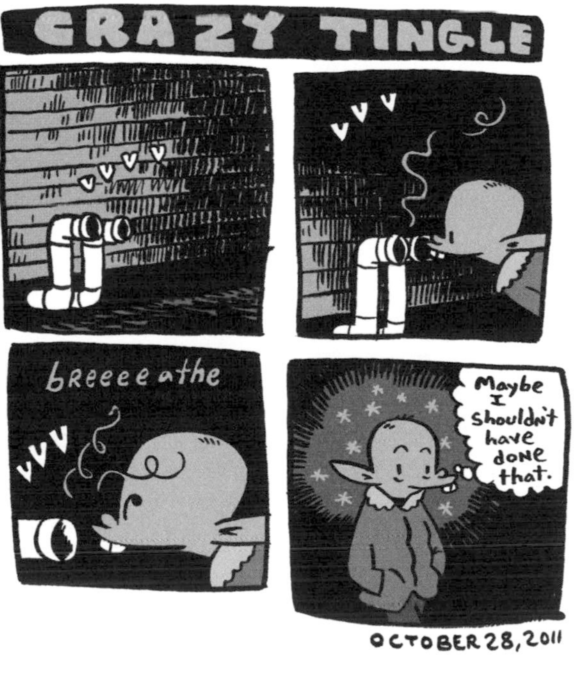
CRAZY TINGLE
breeeeathe
Maybe I shouldn't have done that.
OCTOBER 28, 2011

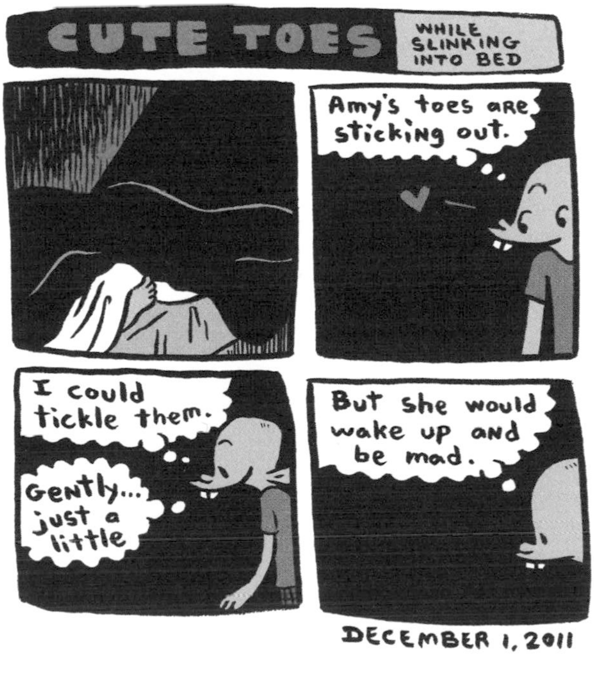
CUTE TOES
WHILE SLINKING INTO BED
Amy's toes are sticking out.
I could tickle them.
Gently... just a little
But she would wake up and be mad.
DECEMBER 1, 2011

You Lied to Us!

excerpt from

Giants, Beware!

Jorge Aguirre and Rafael Rosado

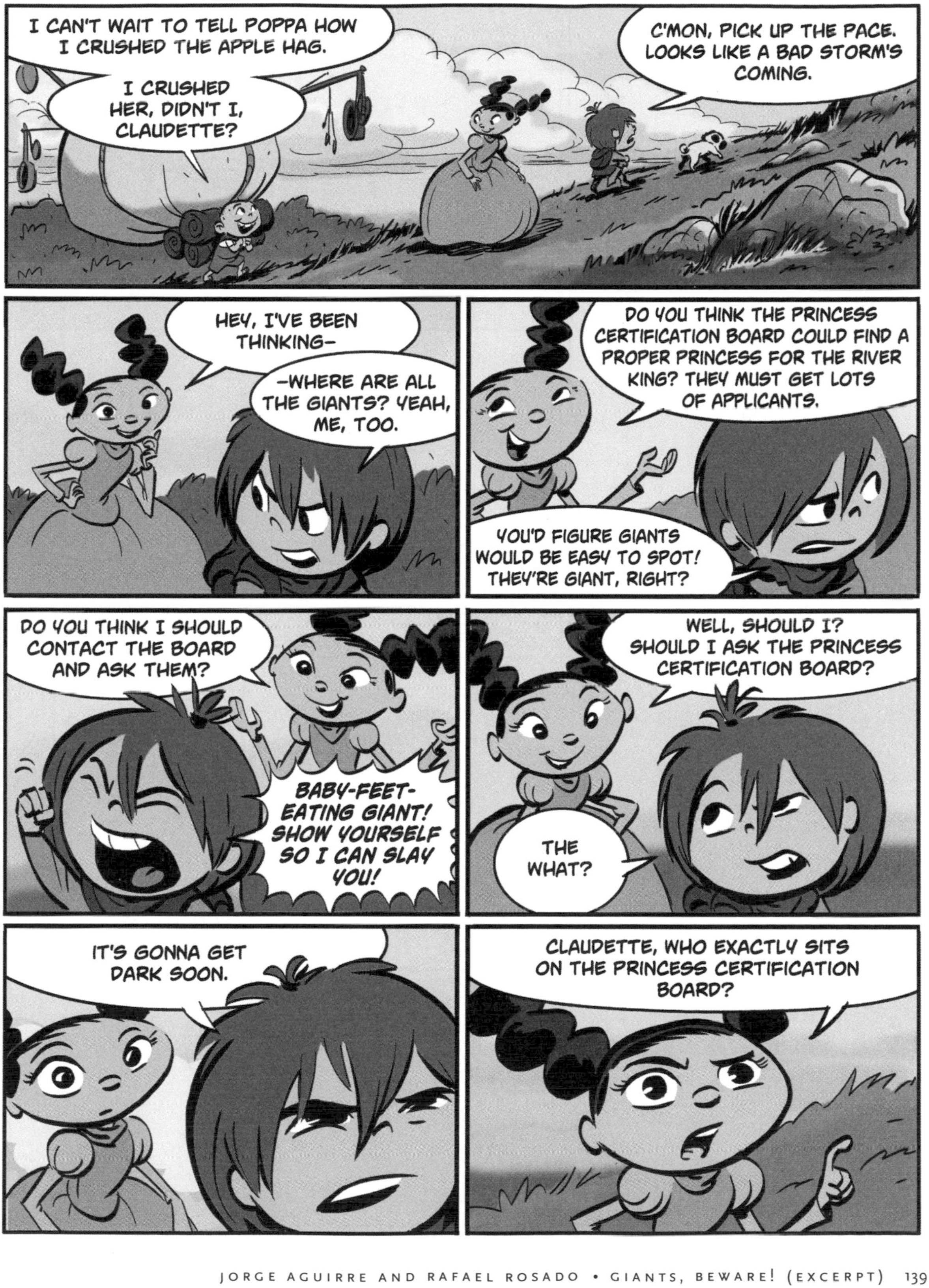
I CAN'T WAIT TO TELL POPPA HOW I CRUSHED THE APPLE HAG.
I CRUSHED HER, DIDN'T I, CLAUDETTE?
C'MON, PICK UP THE PACE. LOOKS LIKE A BAD STORM'S COMING.
HEY, I'VE BEEN THINKING–
–WHERE ARE ALL THE GIANTS? YEAH, ME, TOO.
DO YOU THINK THE PRINCESS CERTIFICATION BOARD COULD FIND A PROPER PRINCESS FOR THE RIVER KING? THEY MUST GET LOTS OF APPLICANTS.
YOU'D FIGURE GIANTS WOULD BE EASY TO SPOT! THEY'RE GIANT, RIGHT?
DO YOU THINK I SHOULD CONTACT THE BOARD AND ASK THEM?
BABY-FEET-EATING GIANT! SHOW YOURSELF SO I CAN SLAY YOU!
WELL, SHOULD I? SHOULD I ASK THE PRINCESS CERTIFICATION BOARD?
THE WHAT?
IT'S GONNA GET DARK SOON.
CLAUDETTE, WHO EXACTLY SITS ON THE PRINCESS CERTIFICATION BOARD?

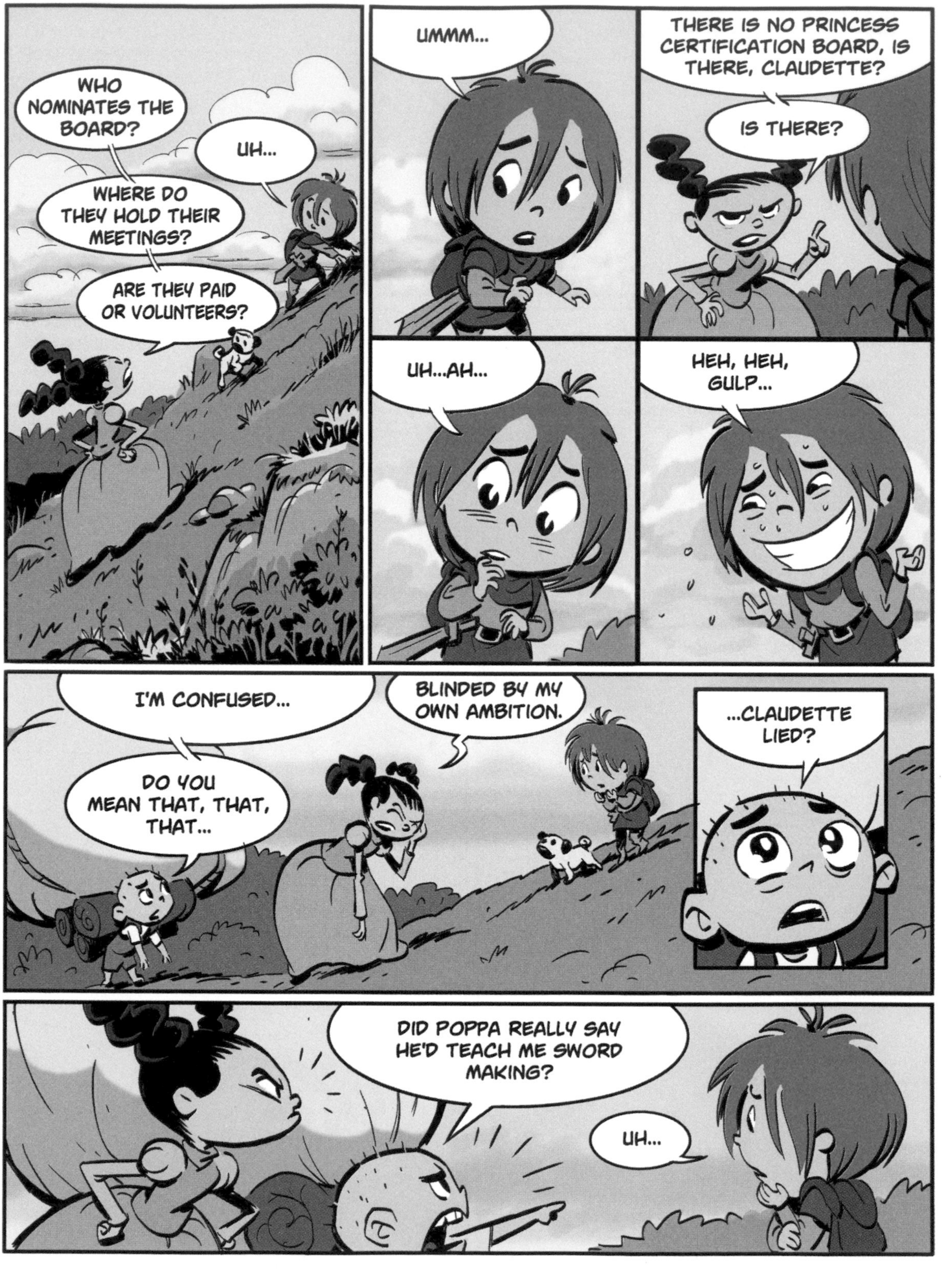
WHO NOMINATES THE BOARD?
UH...
WHERE DO THEY HOLD THEIR MEETINGS?
ARE THEY PAID OR VOLUNTEERS?
UMMM...
THERE IS NO PRINCESS CERTIFICATION BOARD, IS THERE, CLAUDETTE?
IS THERE?
UH...AH...
HEH, HEH, GULP...
I'M CONFUSED...
DO YOU MEAN THAT, THAT, THAT...
BLINDED BY MY OWN AMBITION.
...CLAUDETTE LIED?
DID POPPA REALLY SAY HE'D TEACH ME SWORD MAKING?
UH...

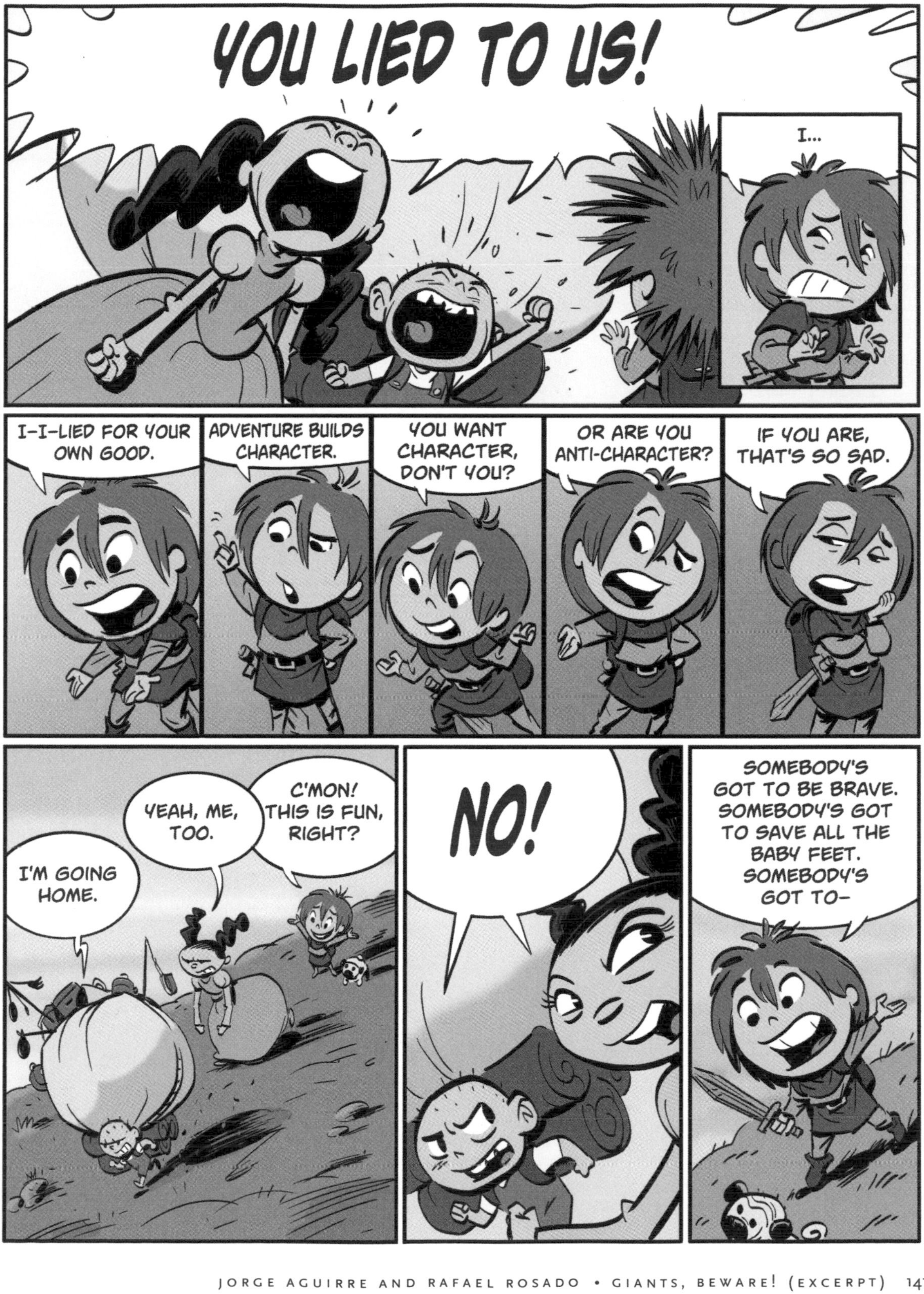
YOU LIED TO US!
I...
I-I-LIED FOR YOUR OWN GOOD.
ADVENTURE BUILDS CHARACTER.
YOU WANT CHARACTER, DON'T YOU?
OR ARE YOU ANTI-CHARACTER?
IF YOU ARE, THAT'S SO SAD.
I'M GOING HOME.
YEAH, ME, TOO.
C'MON! THIS IS FUN, RIGHT?
NO!
SOMEBODY'S GOT TO BE BRAVE. SOMEBODY'S GOT TO SAVE ALL THE BABY FEET. SOMEBODY'S GOT TO–

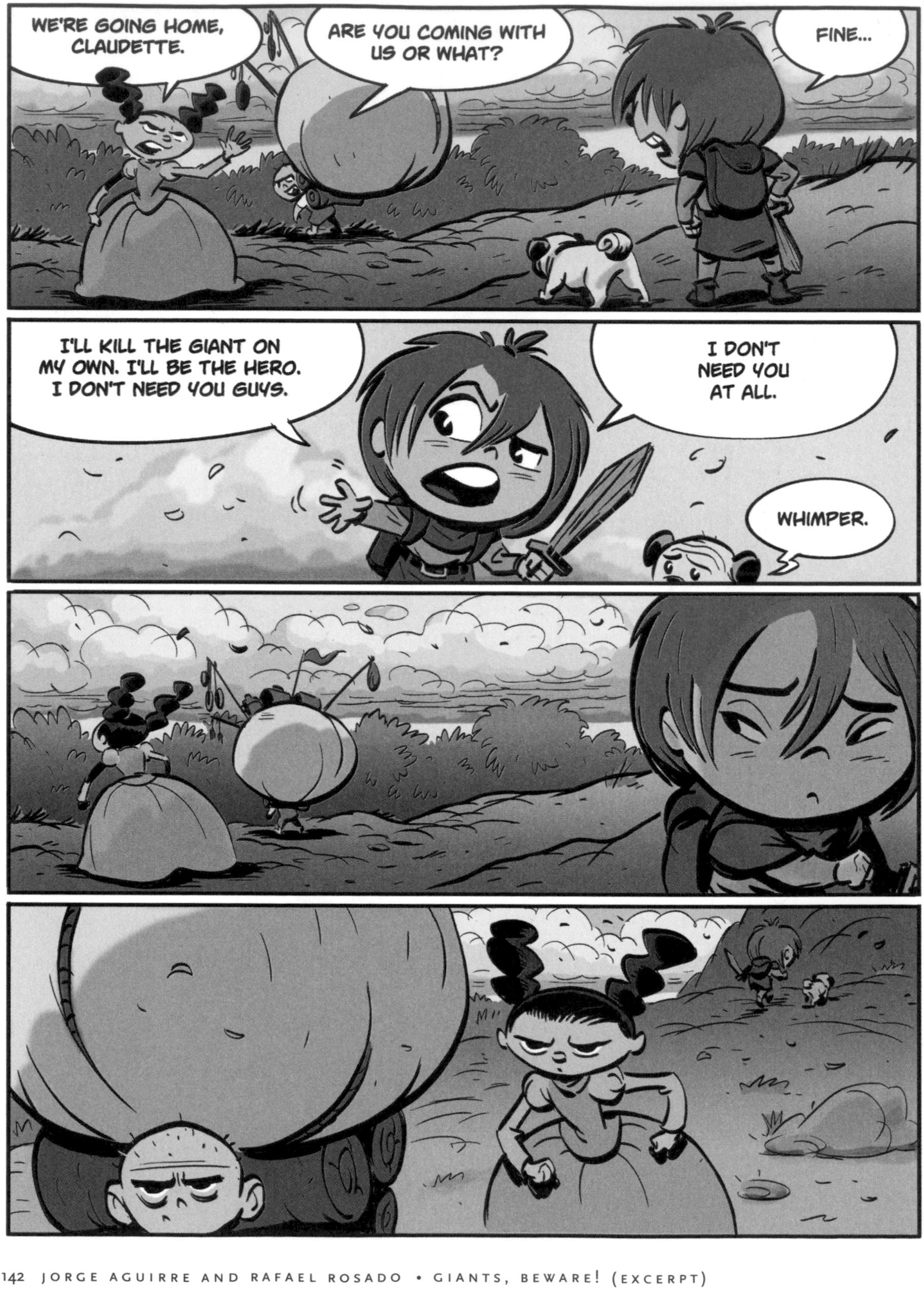
WE'RE GOING HOME, CLAUDETTE.
ARE YOU COMING WITH US OR WHAT?
FINE...
I'LL KILL THE GIANT ON MY OWN. I'LL BE THE HERO. I DON'T NEED YOU GUYS.
I DON'T NEED YOU AT ALL.
WHIMPER.

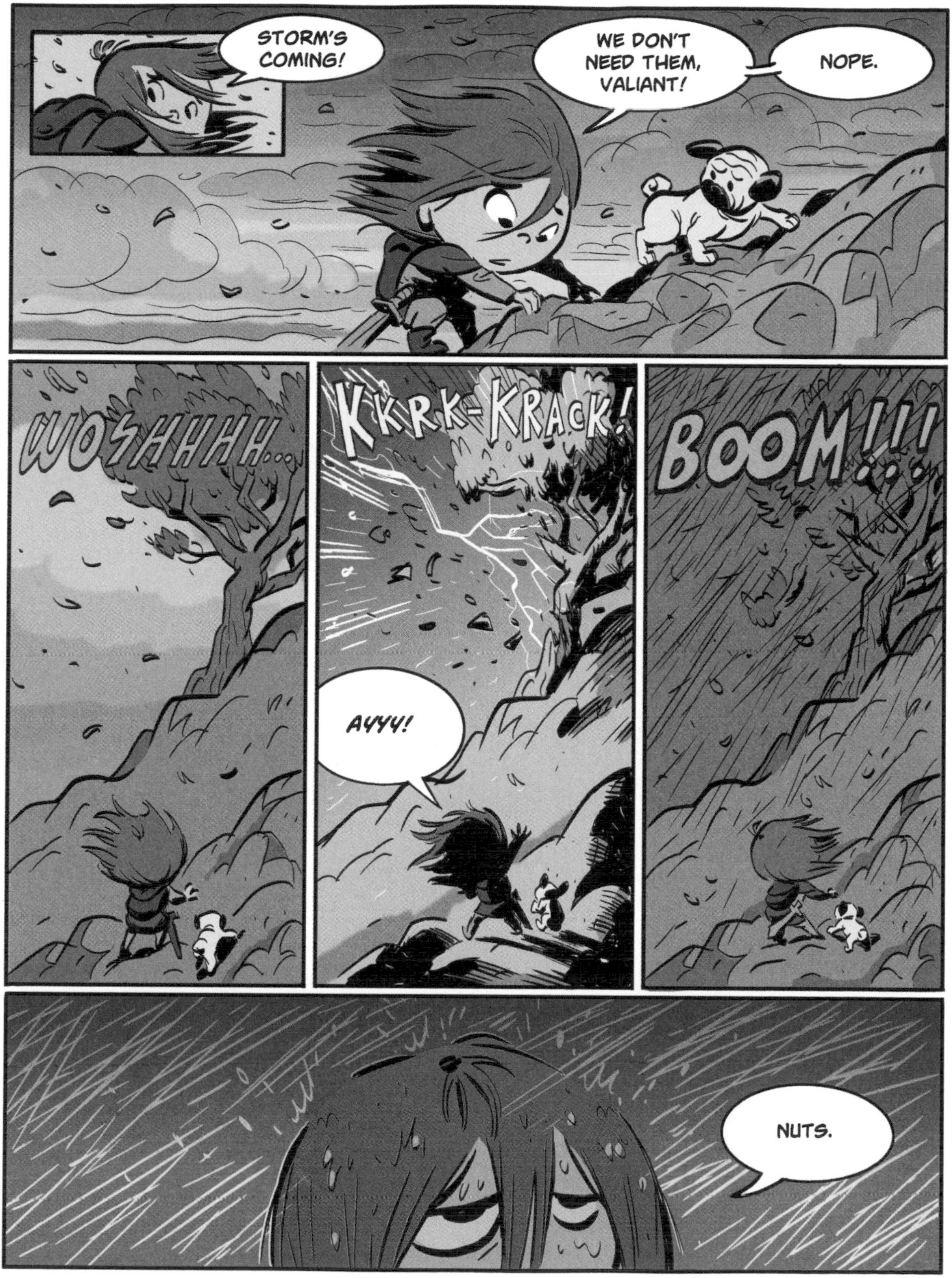
STORM'S COMING!
WE DON'T NEED THEM, VALIANT!
NOPE.
WOSHHHH...
KKRK-KRACK!
AYYY!
BOOM!!!
NUTS.

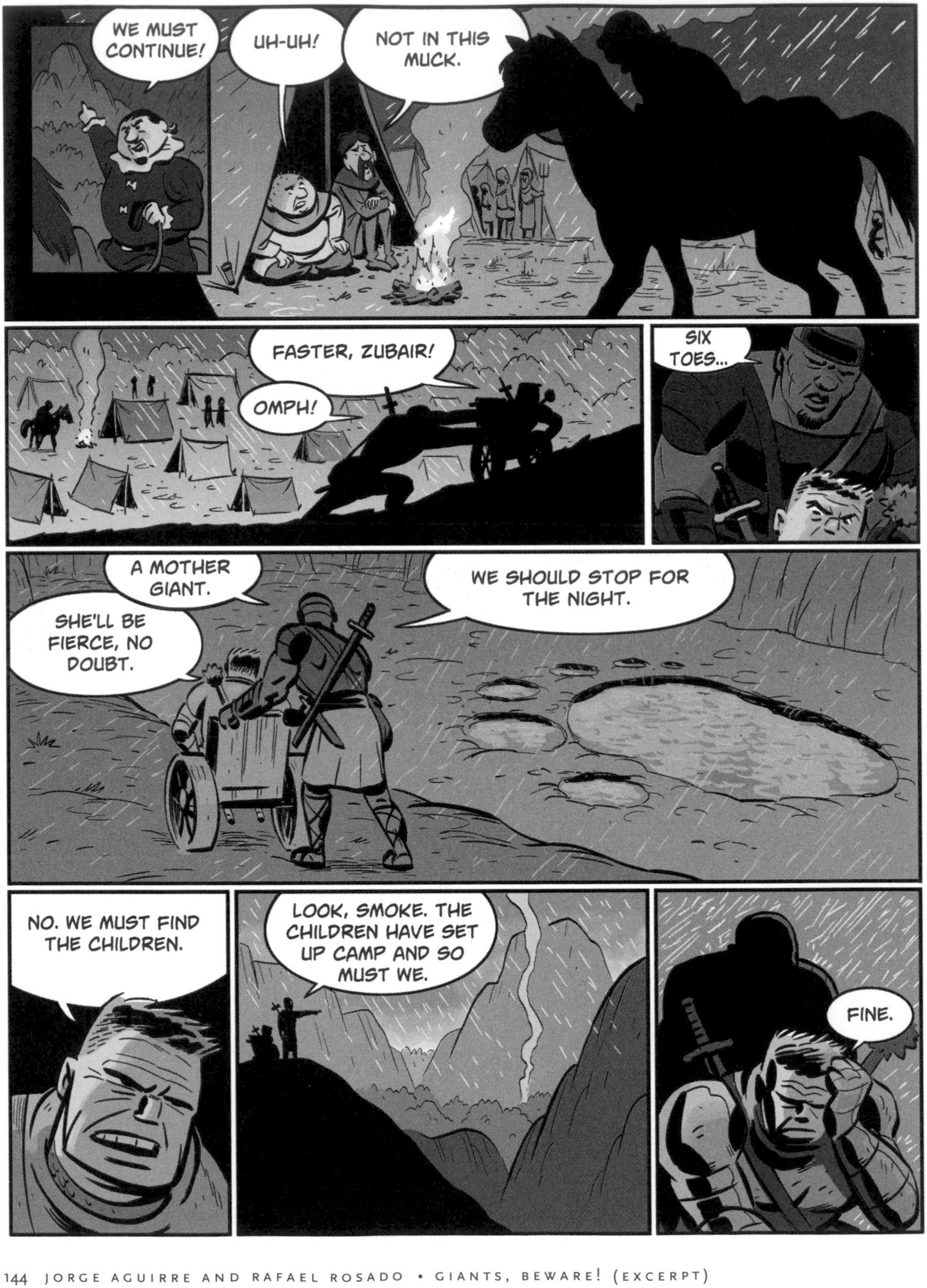
WE MUST CONTINUE!
UH-UH!
NOT IN THIS MUCK.
FASTER, ZUBAIR!
OMPH!
SIX TOES...
A MOTHER GIANT.
SHE'LL BE FIERCE, NO DOUBT.
WE SHOULD STOP FOR THE NIGHT.
NO. WE MUST FIND THE CHILDREN.
LOOK, SMOKE. THE CHILDREN HAVE SET UP CAMP AND SO MUST WE.
FINE.

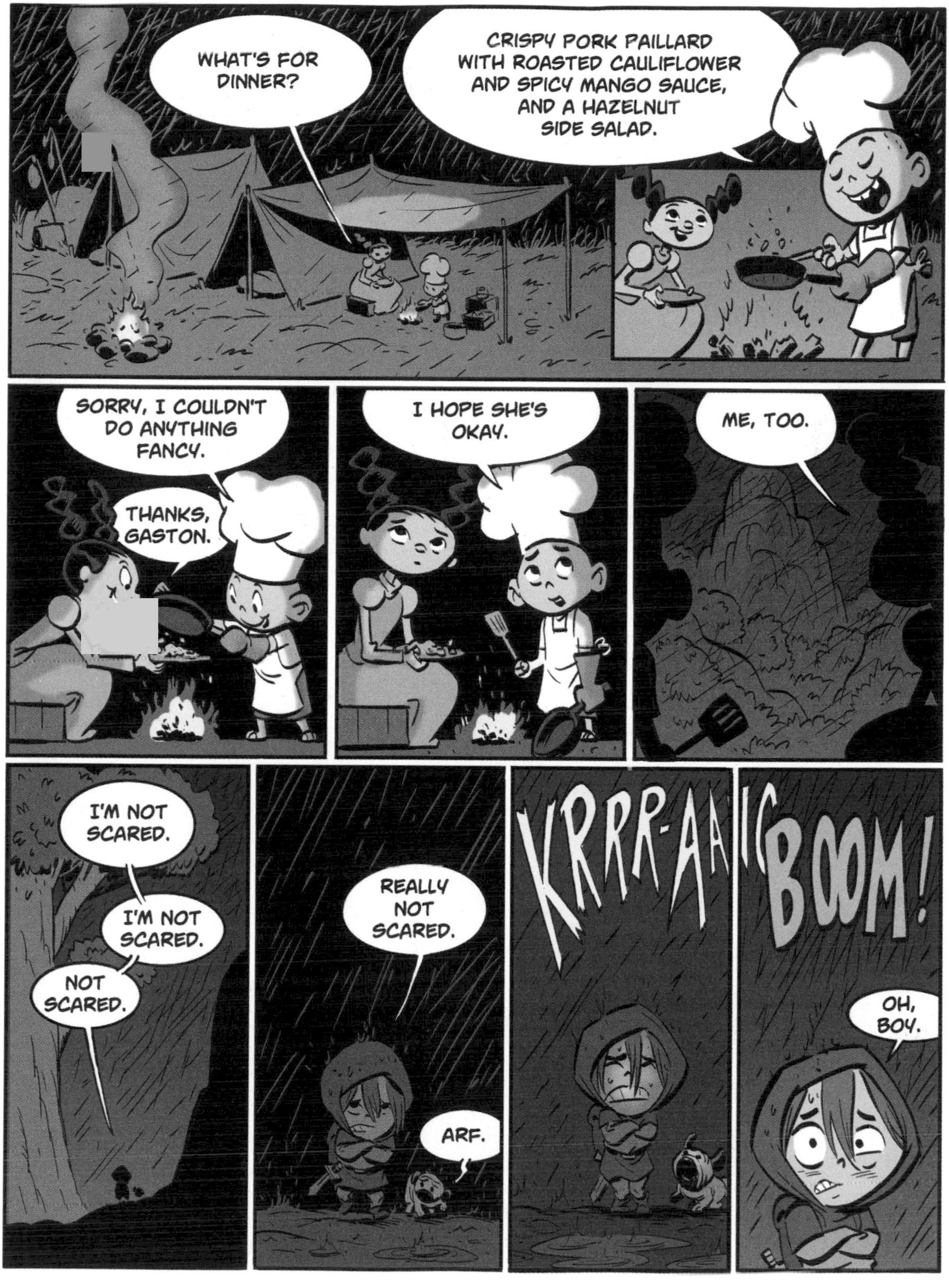
WHAT'S FOR DINNER?
CRISPY PORK PAILLARD WITH ROASTED CAULIFLOWER AND SPICY MANGO SAUCE, AND A HAZELNUT SIDE SALAD.
SORRY, I COULDN'T DO ANYTHING FANCY.
THANKS, GASTON.
I HOPE SHE'S OKAY.
ME, TOO.
I'M NOT SCARED.
I'M NOT SCARED.
NOT SCARED.
REALLY NOT SCARED.
ARF.
KRRR-AAAC
BOOM!
OH, BOY.

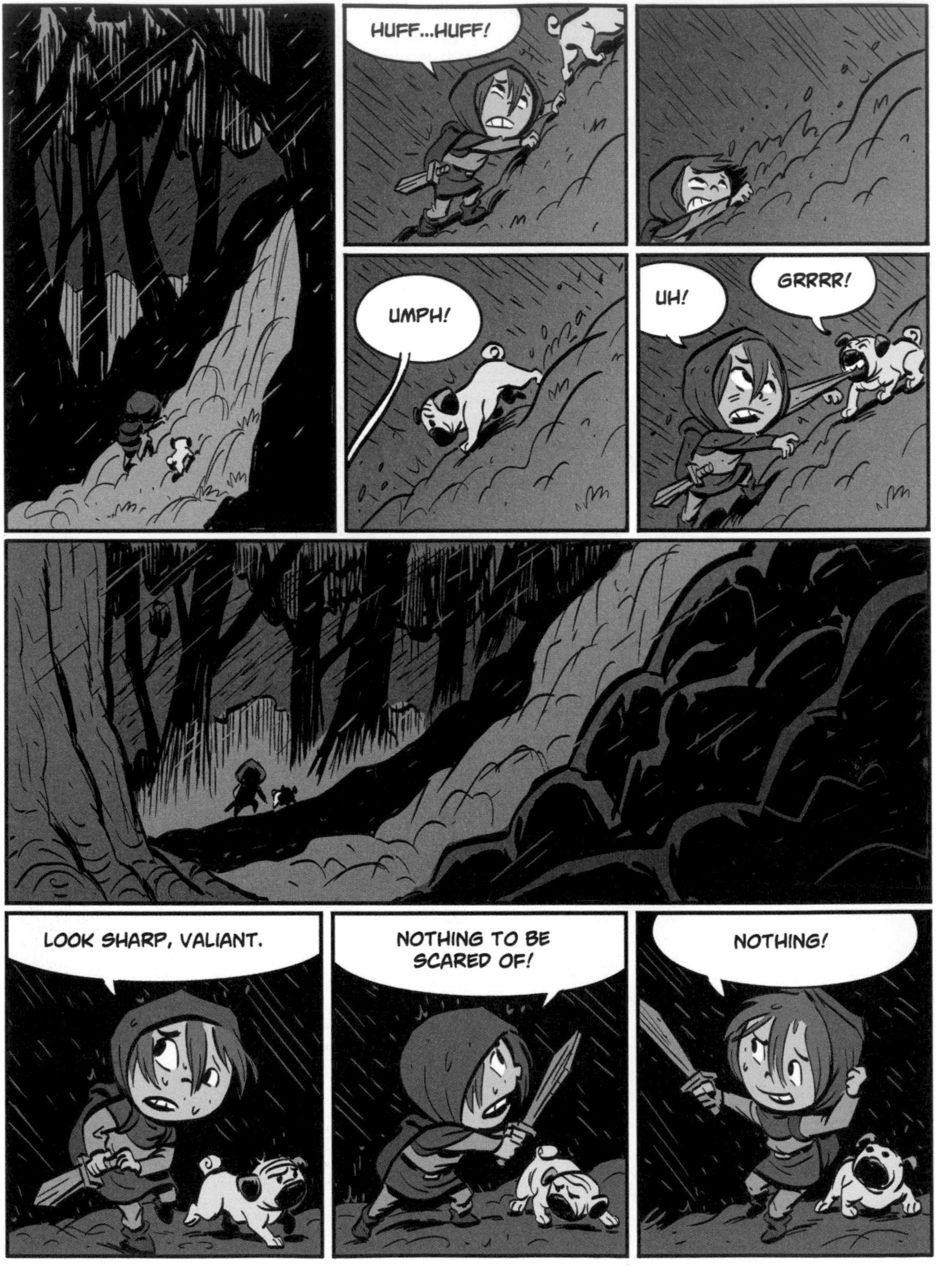
HUFF...HUFF!
UMPH!
UH!
GRRRR!
LOOK SHARP, VALIANT.
NOTHING TO BE SCARED OF!
NOTHING!

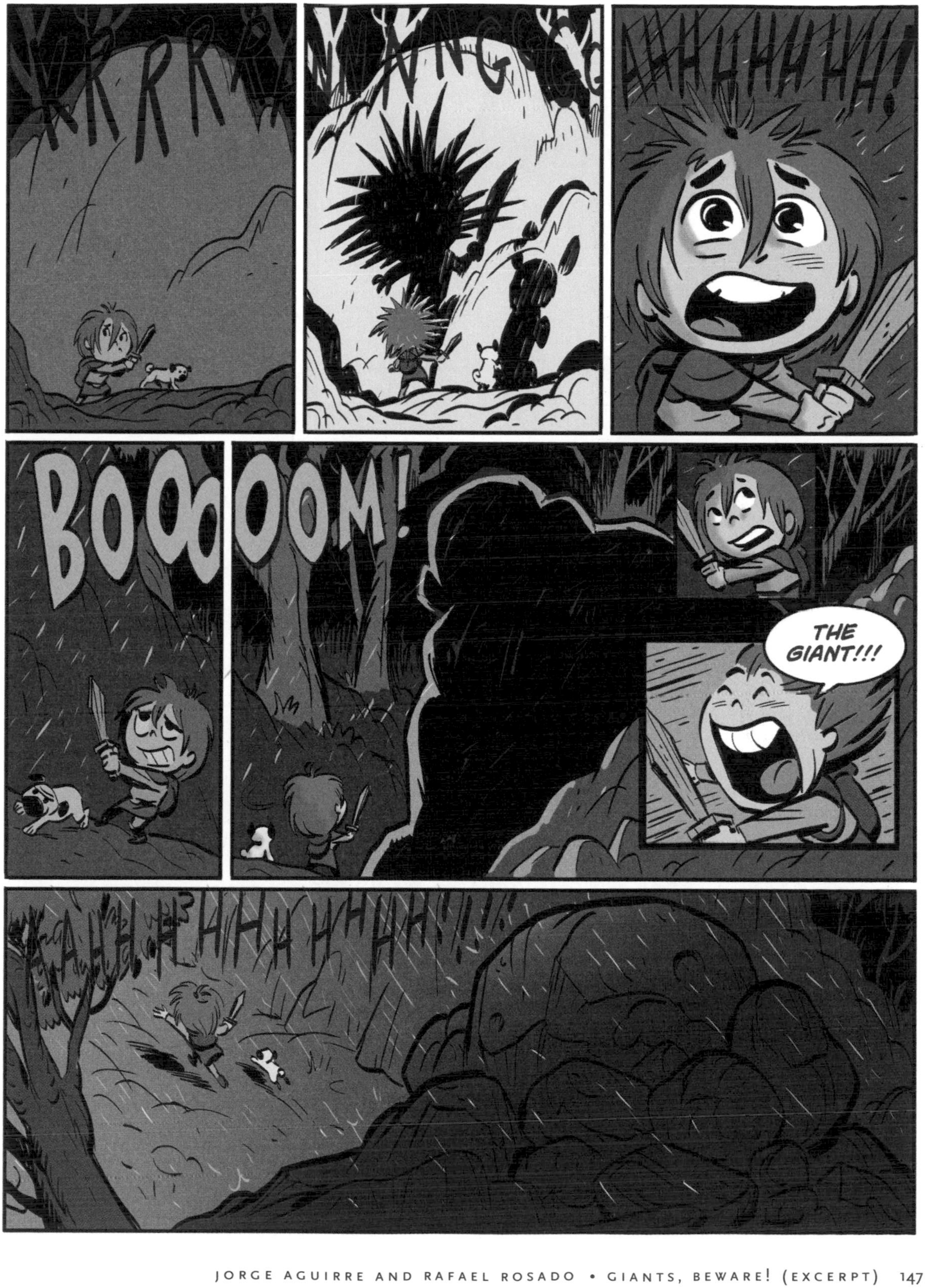
KRRRR
VNNGGG
AHHHHHHH!
BOOOOOM!
THE GIANT!!!
AHHHHHHHHHH!!!

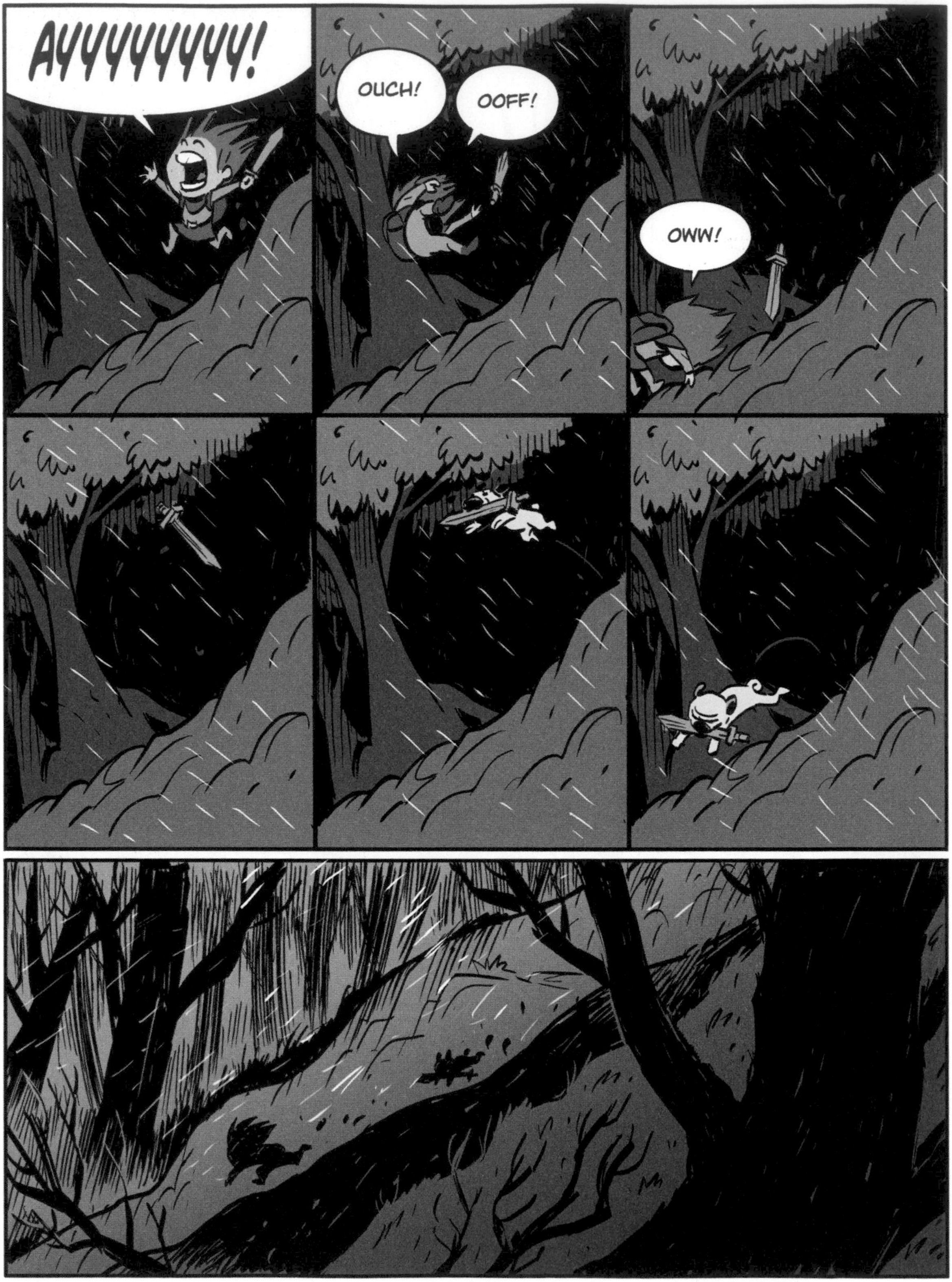
AYYYYYYYY!
OUCH!
OOFF!
OWW!

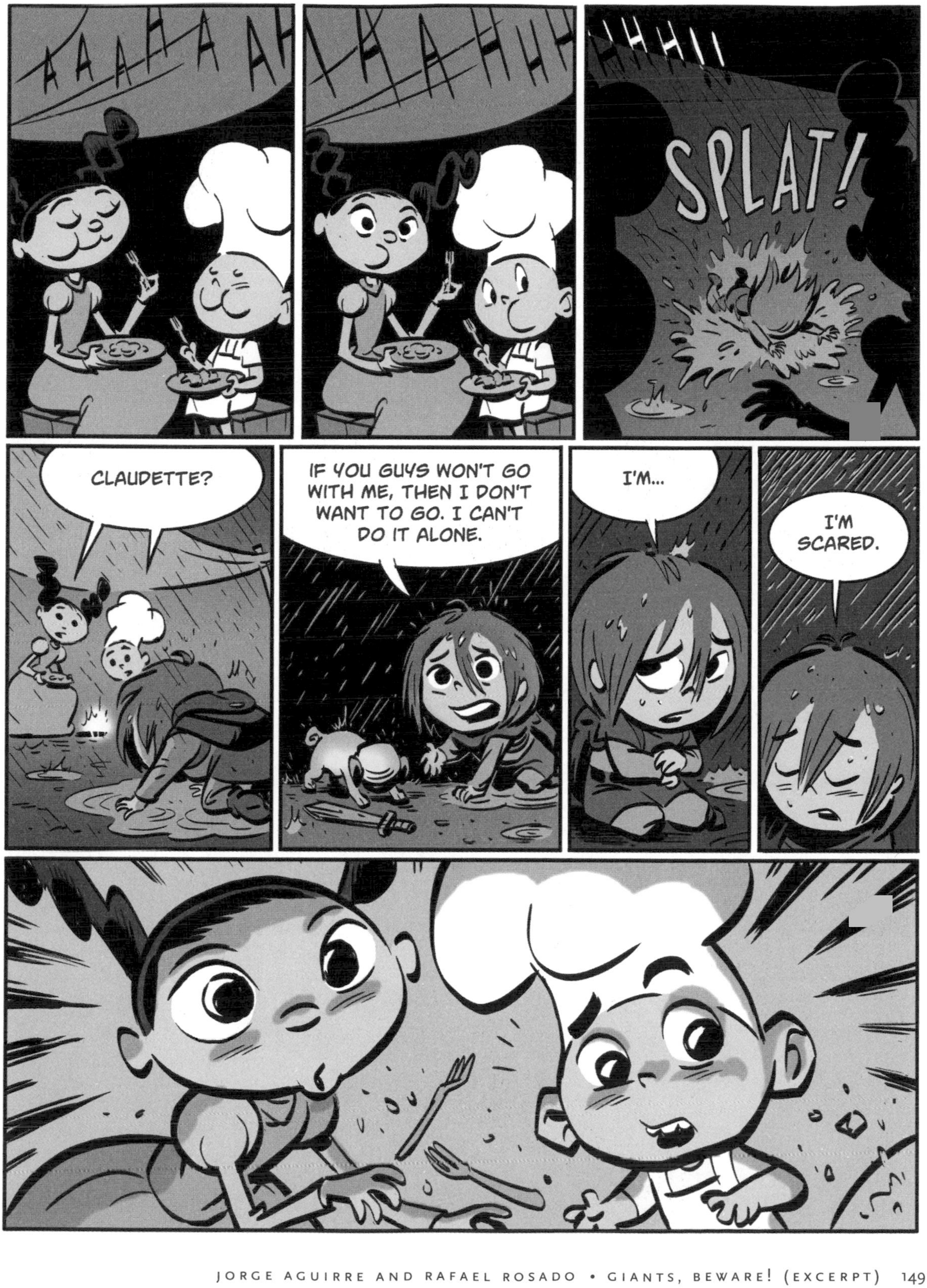
SPLAT!
CLAUDETTE?
IF YOU GUYS WON'T GO WITH ME, THEN I DON'T WANT TO GO. I CAN'T DO IT ALONE.
I'M...
I'M SCARED.

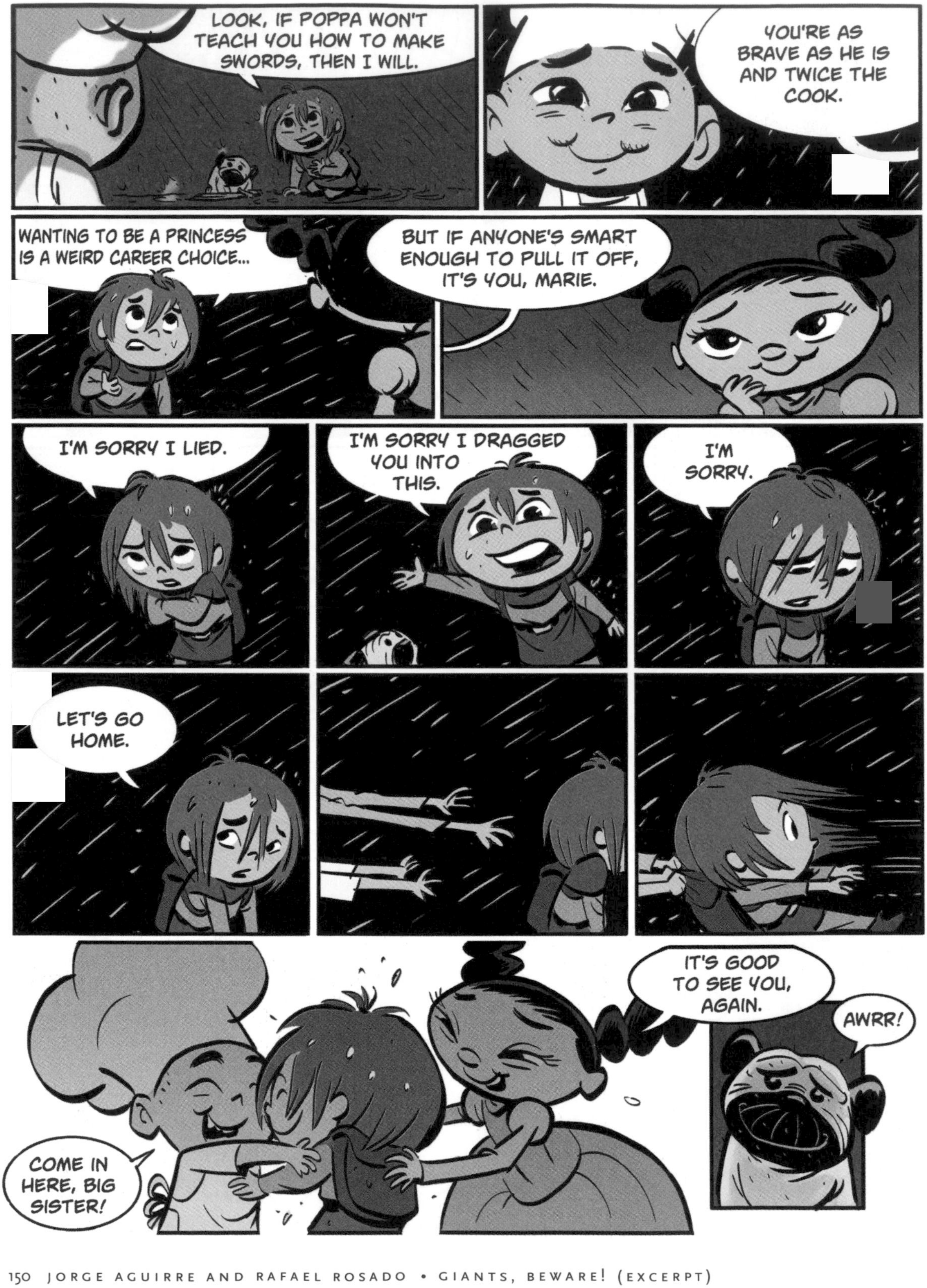
LOOK, IF POPPA WON'T TEACH YOU HOW TO MAKE SWORDS, THEN I WILL.
YOU'RE AS BRAVE AS HE IS AND TWICE THE COOK.
WANTING TO BE A PRINCESS IS A WEIRD CAREER CHOICE...
BUT IF ANYONE'S SMART ENOUGH TO PULL IT OFF, IT'S YOU, MARIE.
I'M SORRY I LIED.
I'M SORRY I DRAGGED YOU INTO THIS.
I'M SORRY.
LET'S GO HOME.
IT'S GOOD TO SEE YOU, AGAIN.
AWRR!
COME IN HERE, BIG SISTER!

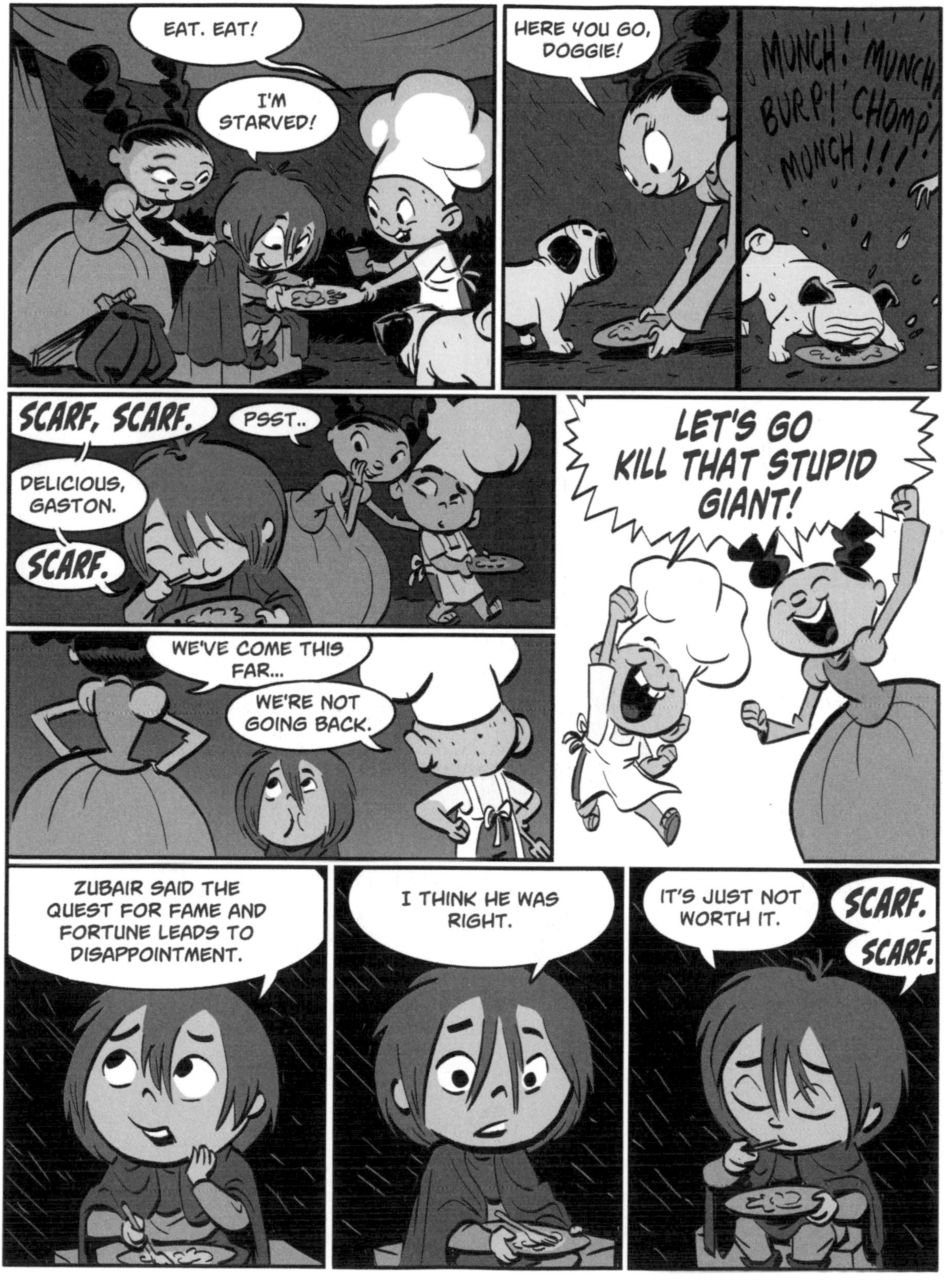
EAT. EAT!
I'M STARVED!
HERE YOU GO, DOGGIE!
MUNCH! MUNCH! BURP! CHOMP! MUNCH!!!
SCARF, SCARF.
DELICIOUS, GASTON.
SCARF.
PSST..
LET'S GO KILL THAT STUPID GIANT!
WE'VE COME THIS FAR...
WE'RE NOT GOING BACK.
ZUBAIR SAID THE QUEST FOR FAME AND FORTUNE LEADS TO DISAPPOINTMENT.
I THINK HE WAS RIGHT.
IT'S JUST NOT WORTH IT.
SCARF.
SCARF.

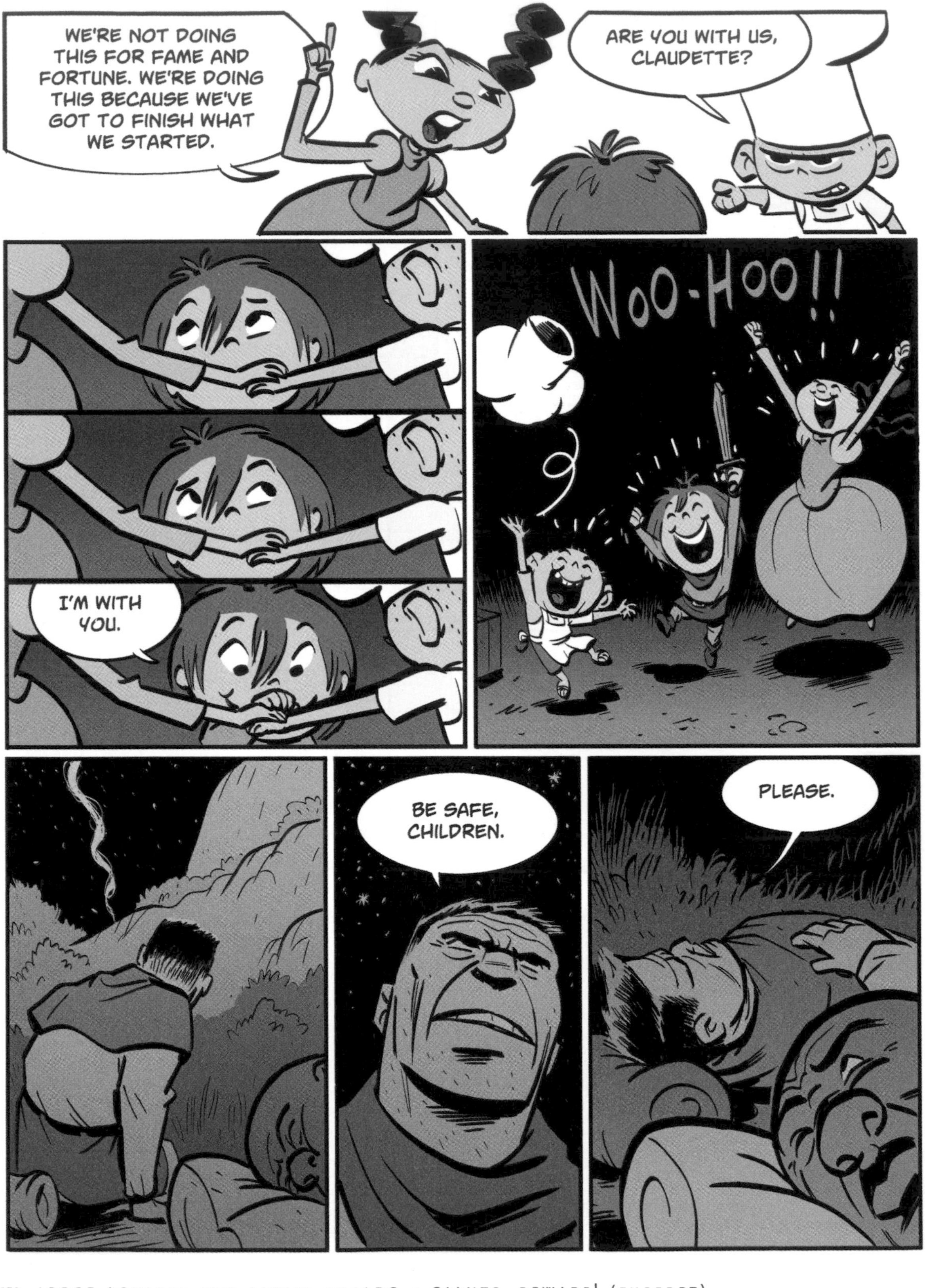
WE'RE NOT DOING THIS FOR FAME AND FORTUNE. WE'RE DOING THIS BECAUSE WE'VE GOT TO FINISH WHAT WE STARTED.
ARE YOU WITH US, CLAUDETTE?
I'M WITH YOU.
WOO-HOO!!
BE SAFE, CHILDREN.
PLEASE.

Story Time

Evan Dorkin and Jill Thompson

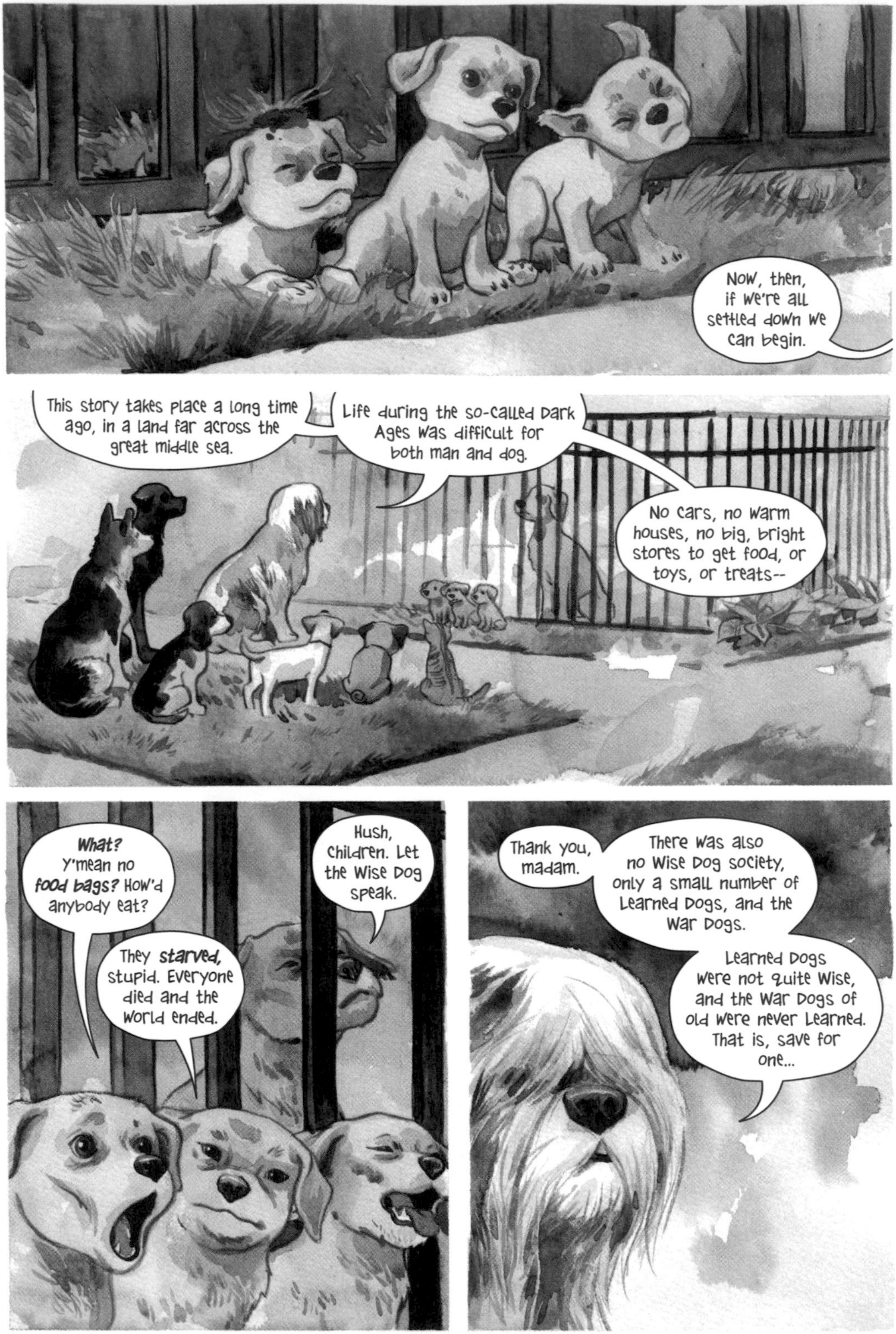
Now, then, if we're all settled down we can begin.
This story takes place a long time ago, in a land far across the great middle sea.
Life during the so-called Dark Ages was difficult for both man and dog.
No cars, no warm houses, no big, bright stores to get food, or toys, or treats--
What? Y'mean no food bags? How'd anybody eat?
They starved, stupid. Everyone died and the world ended.
Hush, Children. Let the Wise Dog speak.
Thank you, madam.
There was also no Wise Dog society, only a small number of Learned Dogs, and the War Dogs.
Learned Dogs were not quite Wise, and the War Dogs of old were never Learned. That is, save for one...

Story Time - by Evan Dorkin & Jill Thompson with Jason Arthur

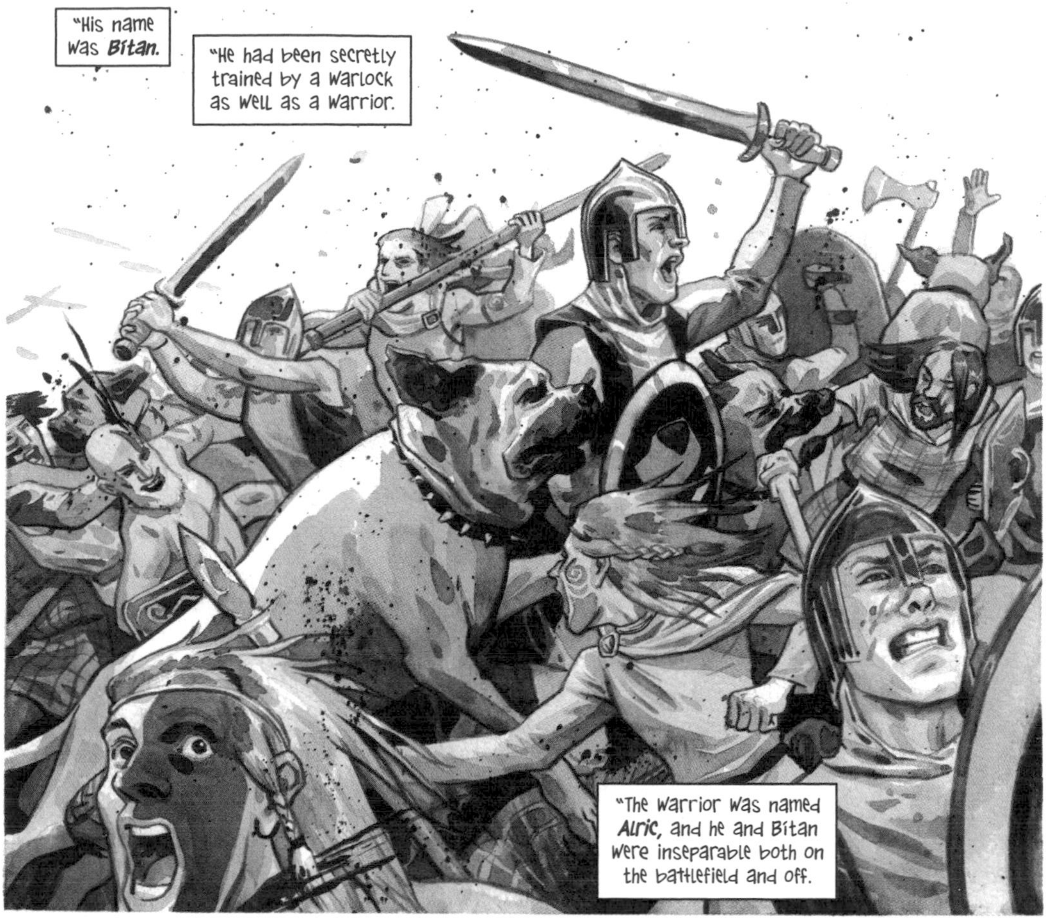
"His name was Bitan.
"He had been secretly trained by a warlock as well as a warrior.
"The warrior was named Alric, and he and Bitan were inseparable both on the battlefield and off.

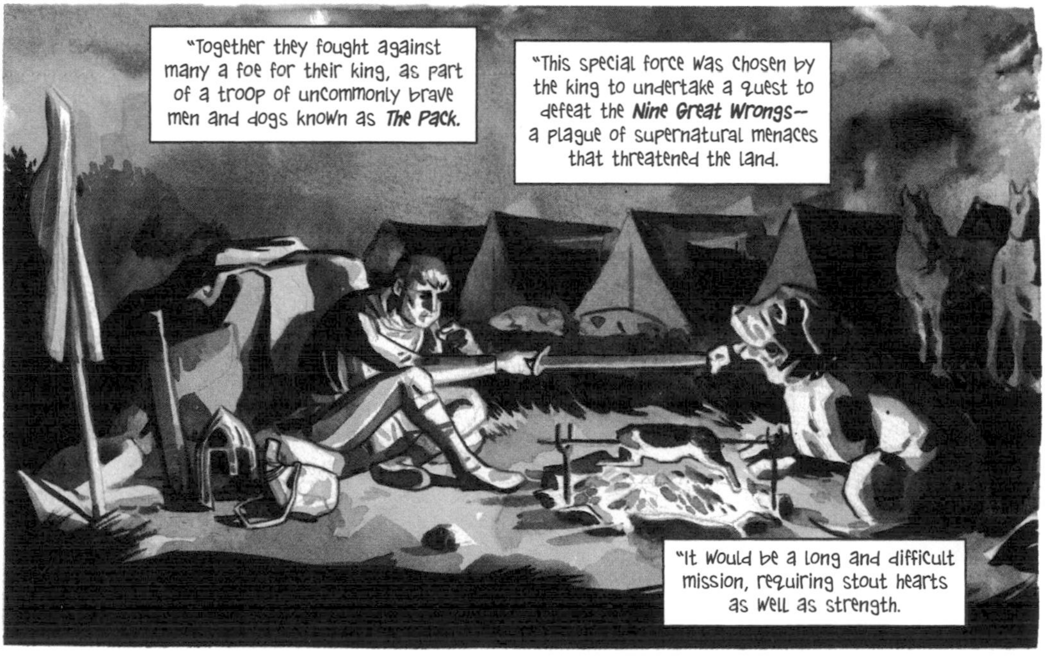
"Together they fought against many a foe for their king, as part of a troop of uncommonly brave men and dogs known as The Pack.
"This special force was chosen by the king to undertake a quest to defeat the Nine Great Wrongs— a plague of supernatural menaces that threatened the land.
"It would be a long and difficult mission, requiring stout hearts as well as strength.

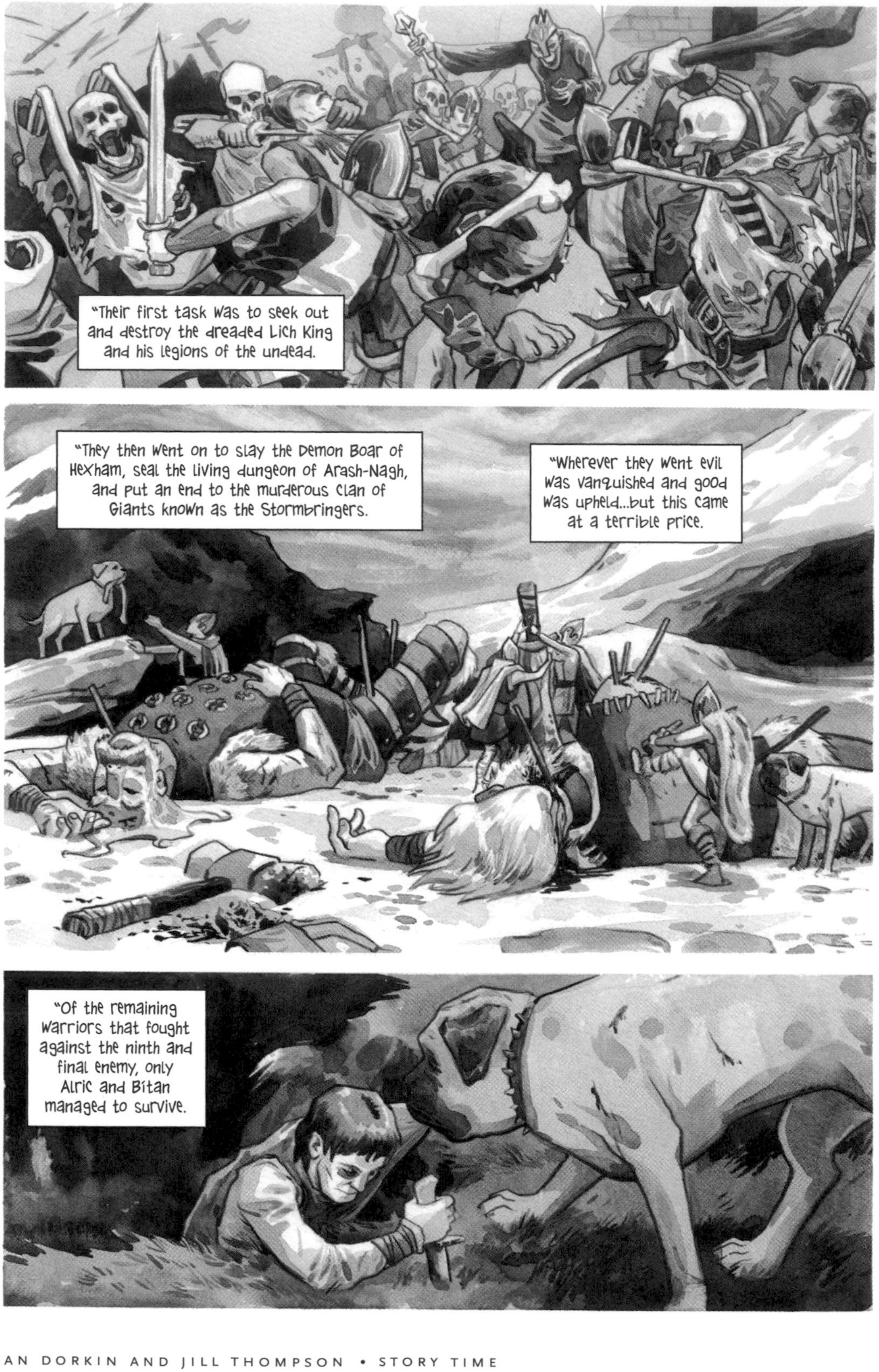
"Their first task was to seek out and destroy the dreaded Lich King and his legions of the undead.
"They then went on to slay the Demon Boar of Hexham, seal the living dungeon of Arash-Nagh, and put an end to the murderous clan of Giants known as the Stormbringers.
"Wherever they went evil was vanquished and good was upheld...but this came at a terrible price.
"Of the remaining warriors that fought against the ninth and final enemy, only Alric and Bitan managed to survive.

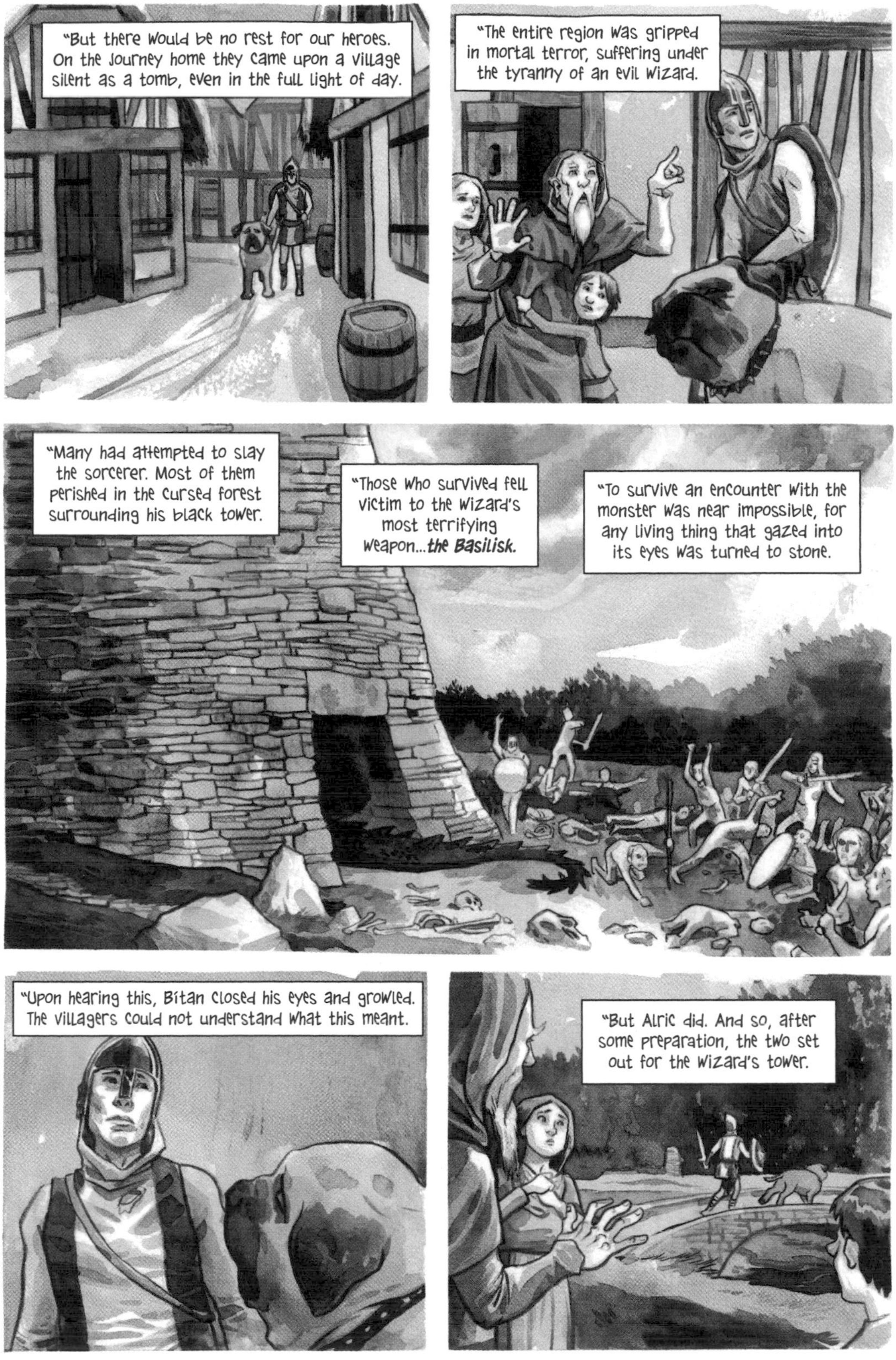
"But there would be no rest for our heroes. On the journey home they came upon a village silent as a tomb, even in the full light of day.
"The entire region was gripped in mortal terror, suffering under the tyranny of an evil wizard.
"Many had attempted to slay the sorcerer. Most of them perished in the cursed forest surrounding his black tower.
"Those who survived fell victim to the wizard's most terrifying weapon...*the Basilisk.*
"To survive an encounter with the monster was near impossible, for any living thing that gazed into its eyes was turned to stone.
"Upon hearing this, Bitan closed his eyes and growled. The villagers could not understand what this meant.
"But Alric did. And so, after some preparation, the two set out for the wizard's tower.

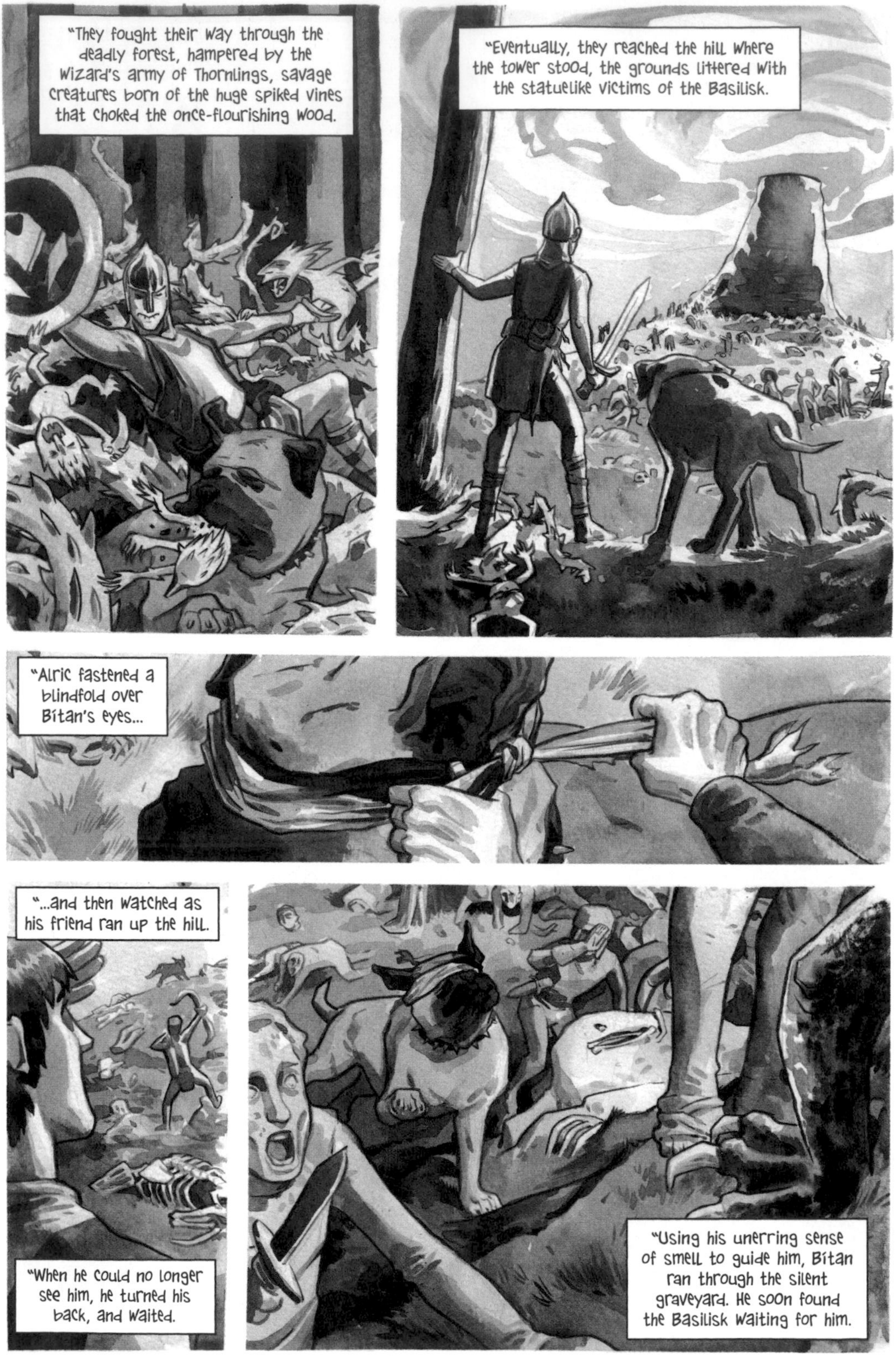
"They fought their way through the deadly forest, hampered by the Wizard's army of Thornlings, savage creatures born of the huge spiked vines that choked the once-flourishing wood.
"Eventually, they reached the hill where the tower stood, the grounds littered with the statuelike victims of the Basilisk.
"Alric fastened a blindfold over Bitan's eyes...
"...and then watched as his friend ran up the hill.
"When he could no longer see him, he turned his back, and waited.
"Using his unerring sense of smell to guide him, Bitan ran through the silent graveyard. He soon found the Basilisk waiting for him.

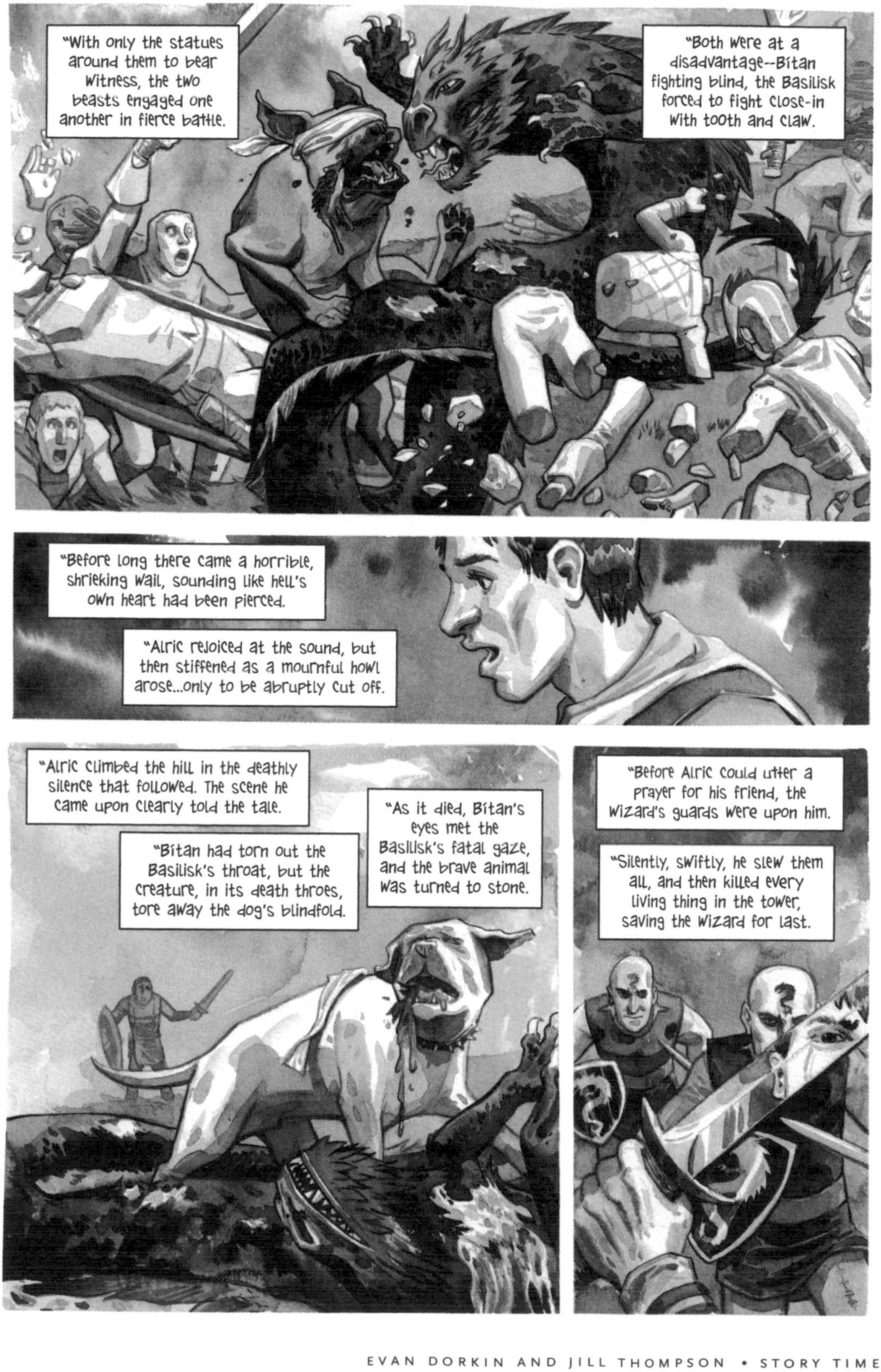
"With only the statues around them to bear witness, the two beasts engaged one another in fierce battle.
"Both were at a disadvantage--Bitan fighting blind, the Basilisk forced to fight close-in with tooth and claw.
"Before long there came a horrible, shrieking wail, sounding like hell's own heart had been pierced.
"Alric rejoiced at the sound, but then stiffened as a mournful howl arose...only to be abruptly cut off.
"Alric climbed the hill in the deathly silence that followed. The scene he came upon clearly told the tale.
"Bitan had torn out the Basilisk's throat, but the creature, in its death throes, tore away the dog's blindfold.
"As it died, Bitan's eyes met the Basilisk's fatal gaze, and the brave animal was turned to stone.
"Before Alric could utter a prayer for his friend, the wizard's guards were upon him.
"Silently, swiftly, he slew them all, and then killed every living thing in the tower, saving the wizard for last.

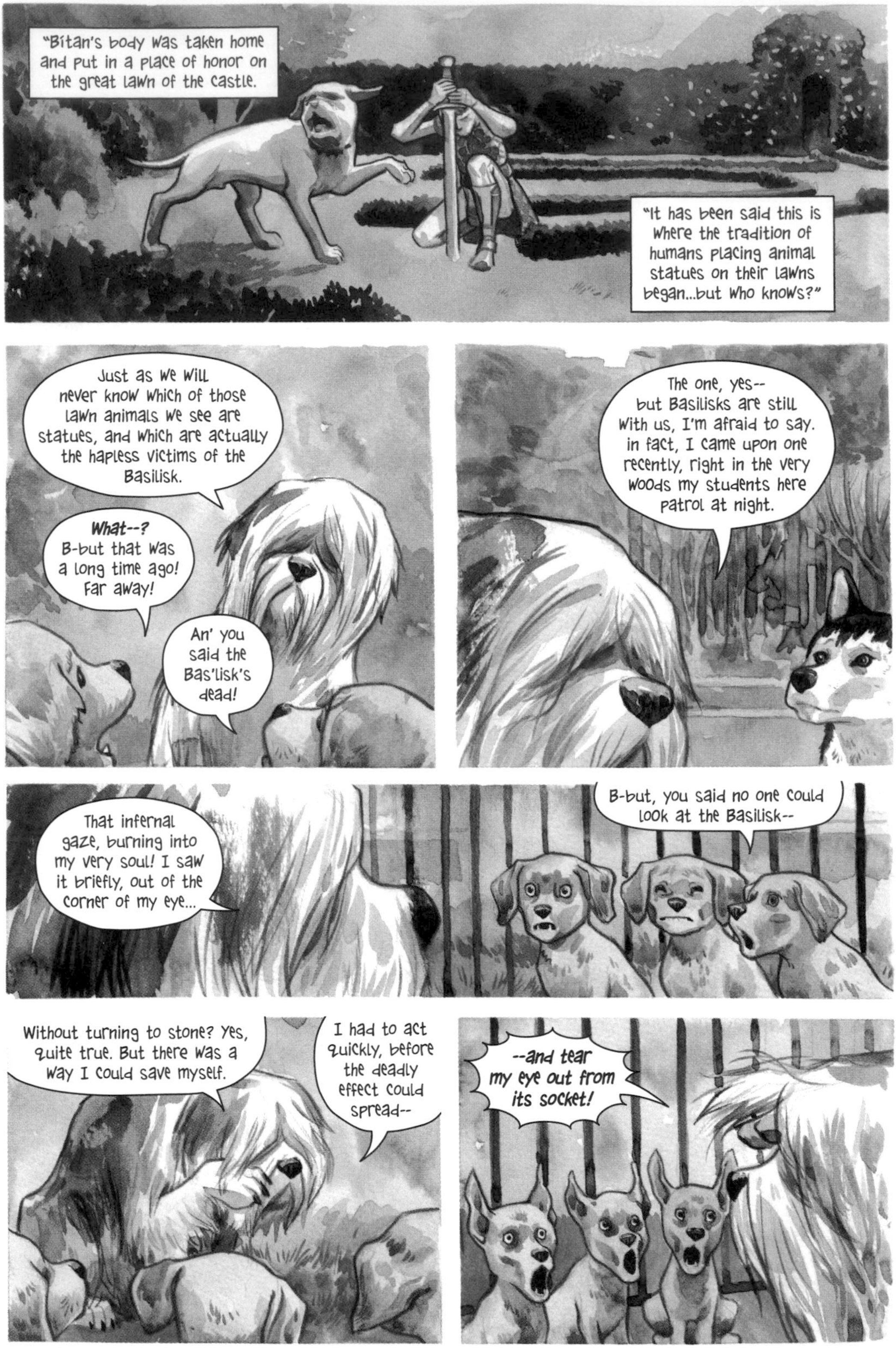
"Bitan's body was taken home and put in a place of honor on the great lawn of the castle.
"It has been said this is where the tradition of humans placing animal statues on their lawns began...but who knows?"
Just as we will never know which of those lawn animals we see are statues, and which are actually the hapless victims of the Basilisk.
What--? B-but that was a long time ago! Far away!
An' you said the Bas'lisk's dead!
The one, yes-- but Basilisks are still with us, I'm afraid to say. in fact, I came upon one recently, right in the very woods my students here patrol at night.
That infernal gaze, burning into my very soul! I saw it briefly, out of the corner of my eye...
B-but, you said no one could look at the Basilisk--
Without turning to stone? Yes, quite true. But there was a way I could save myself.
I had to act quickly, before the deadly effect could spread--
--and tear my eye out from its socket!

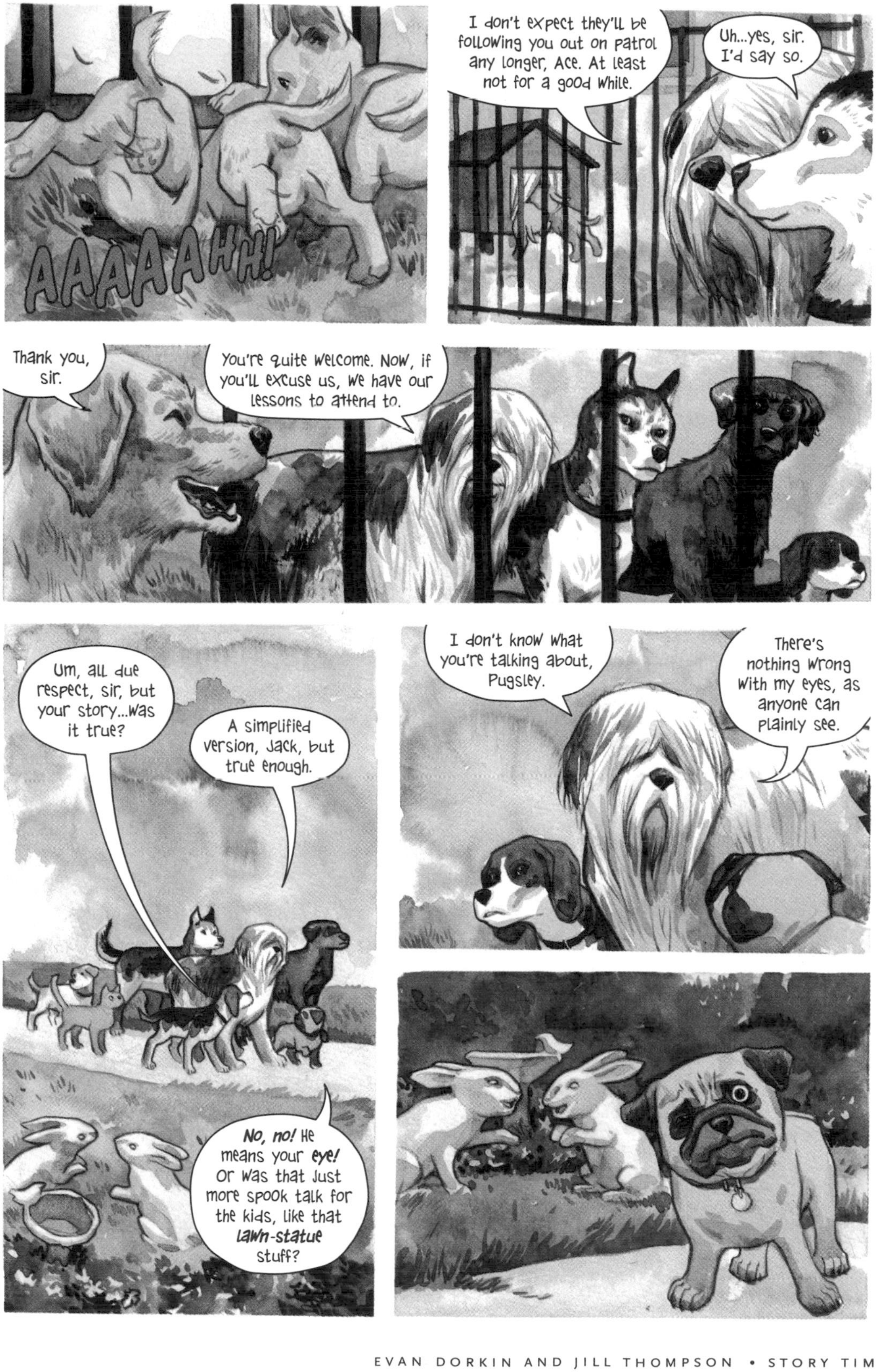
AAAAAHH!
I don't expect they'll be following you out on patrol any longer, Ace. At least not for a good while.
Uh...yes, sir. I'd say so.
Thank you, sir.
You're quite welcome. Now, if you'll excuse us, we have our lessons to attend to.
Um, all due respect, sir, but your story...was it true?
A simplified version, Jack, but true enough.
No, no! He means your eye! Or was that just more spook talk for the kids, like that lawn-statue stuff?
I don't know what you're talking about, Pugsley.
There's nothing wrong with my eyes, as anyone can plainly see.

FAITH ERIN HICKS

RAIDERS

excerpt from

FRIENDS WITH BOYS

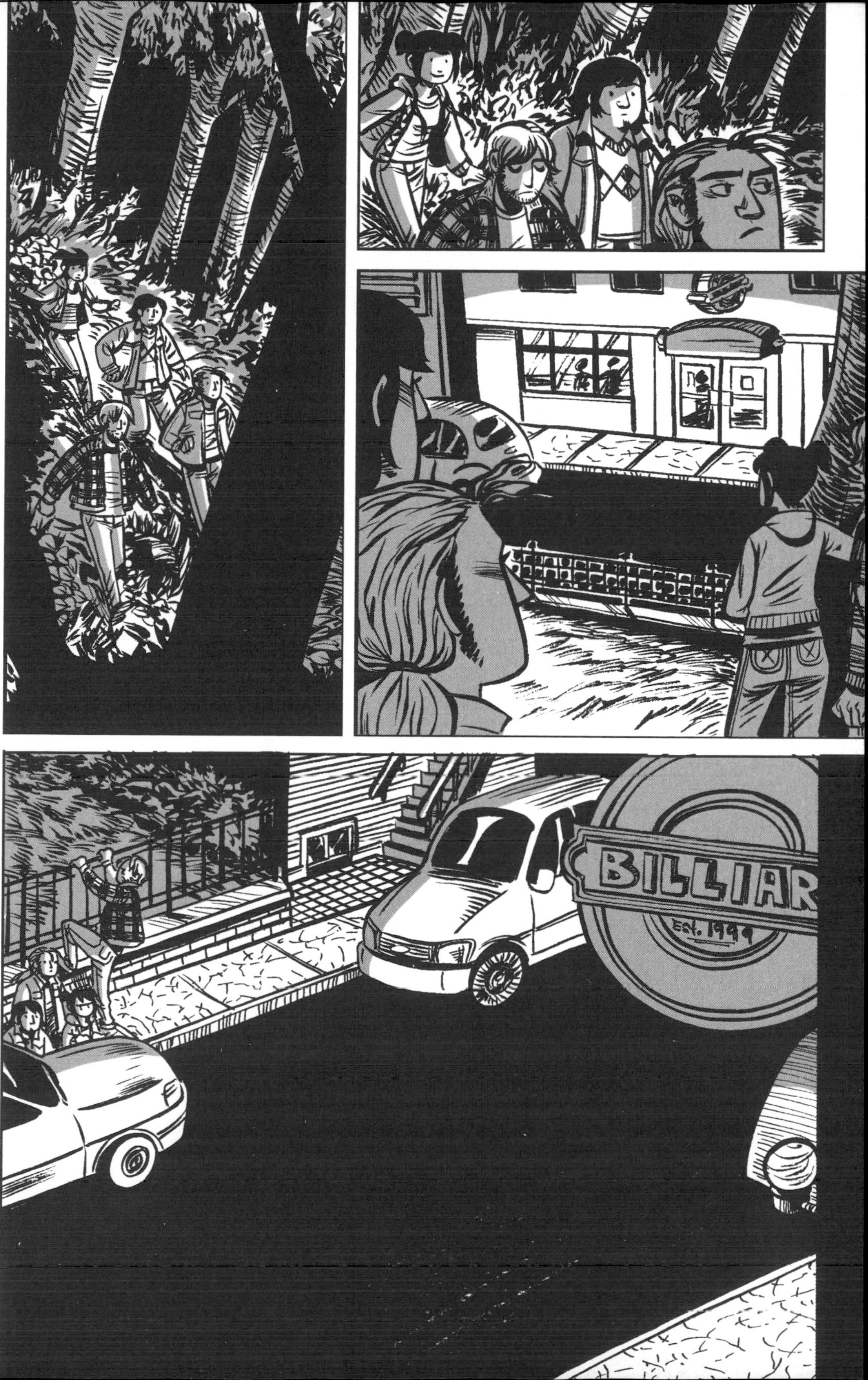
BILLIAR
Est. 1999

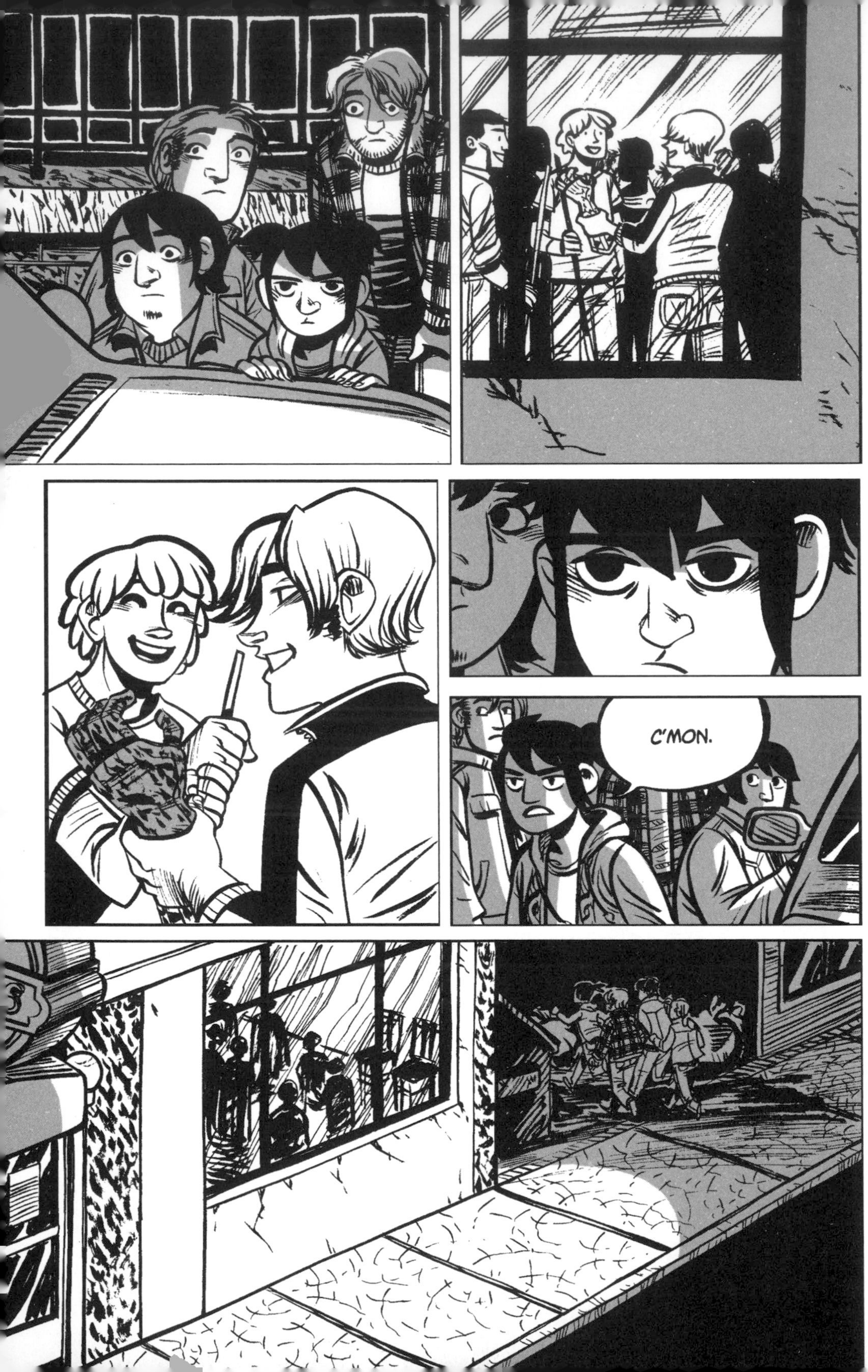
C'MON.

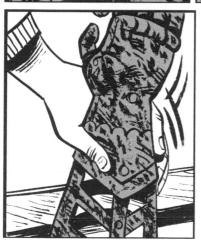

MOVE.

THIS IS A JOB FOR SOMEONE WHO'S SEEN "RAIDERS OF THE LOST ARK" THREE HUNDRED AND FOURTEEN TIMES.

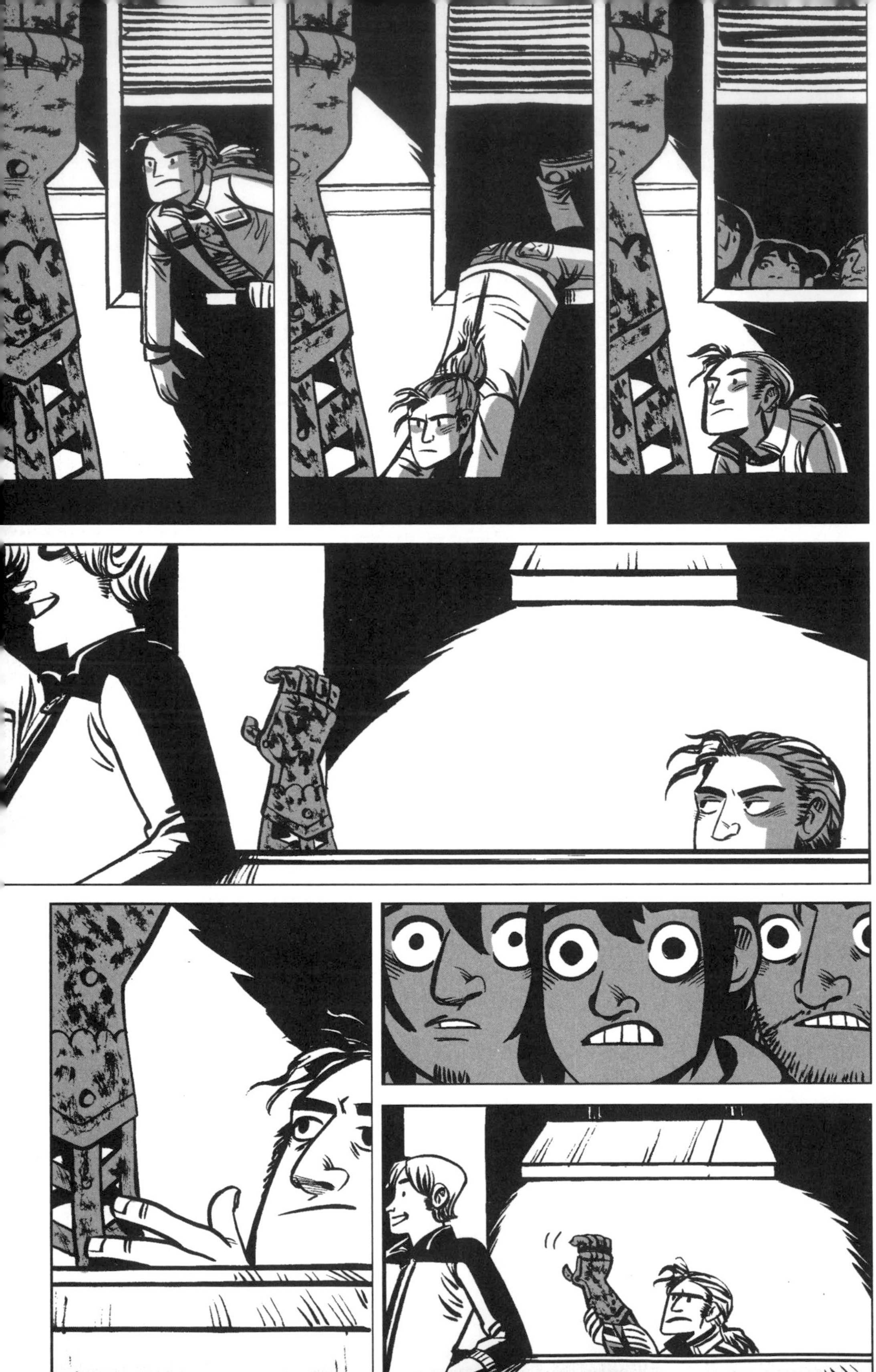

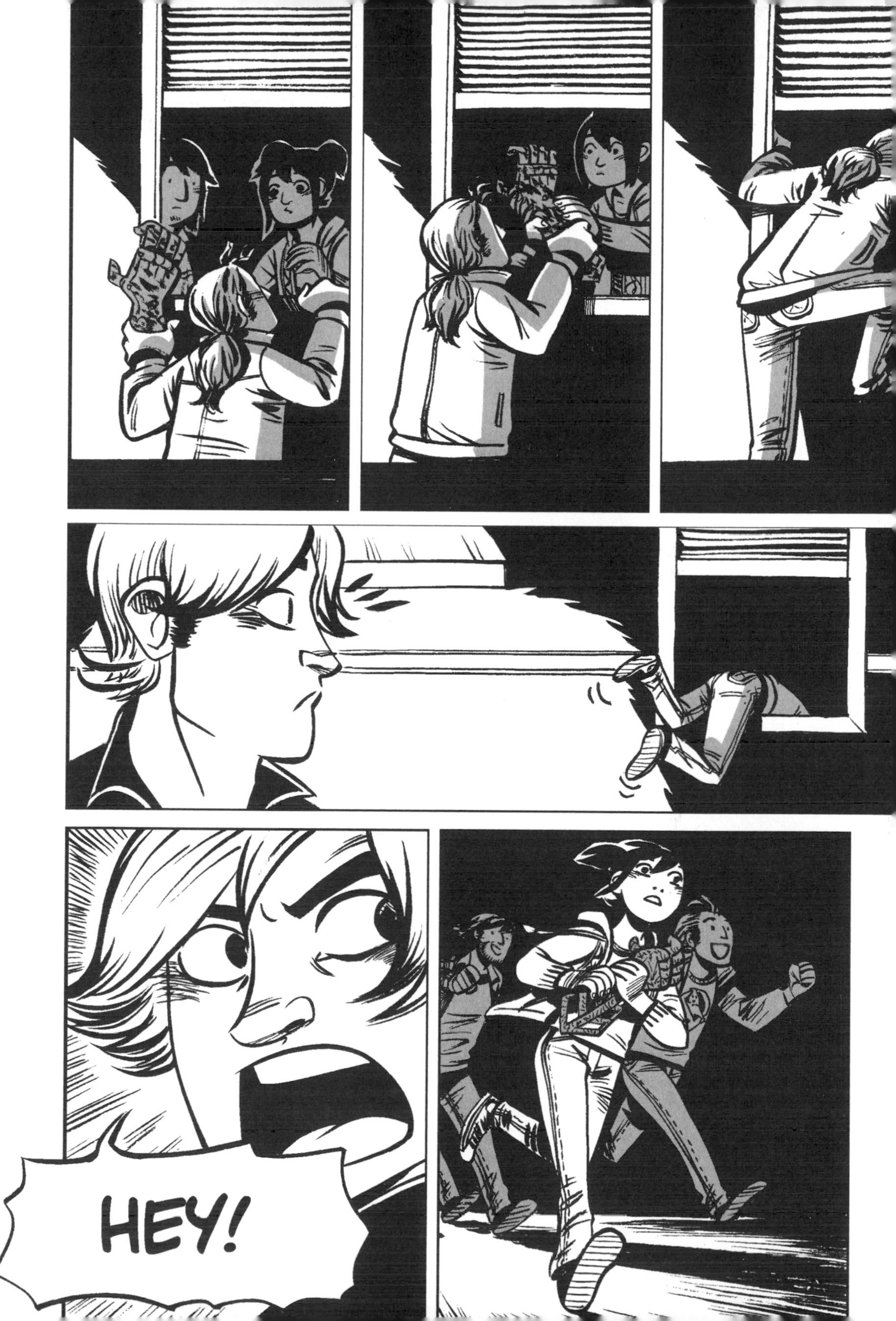
HEY!

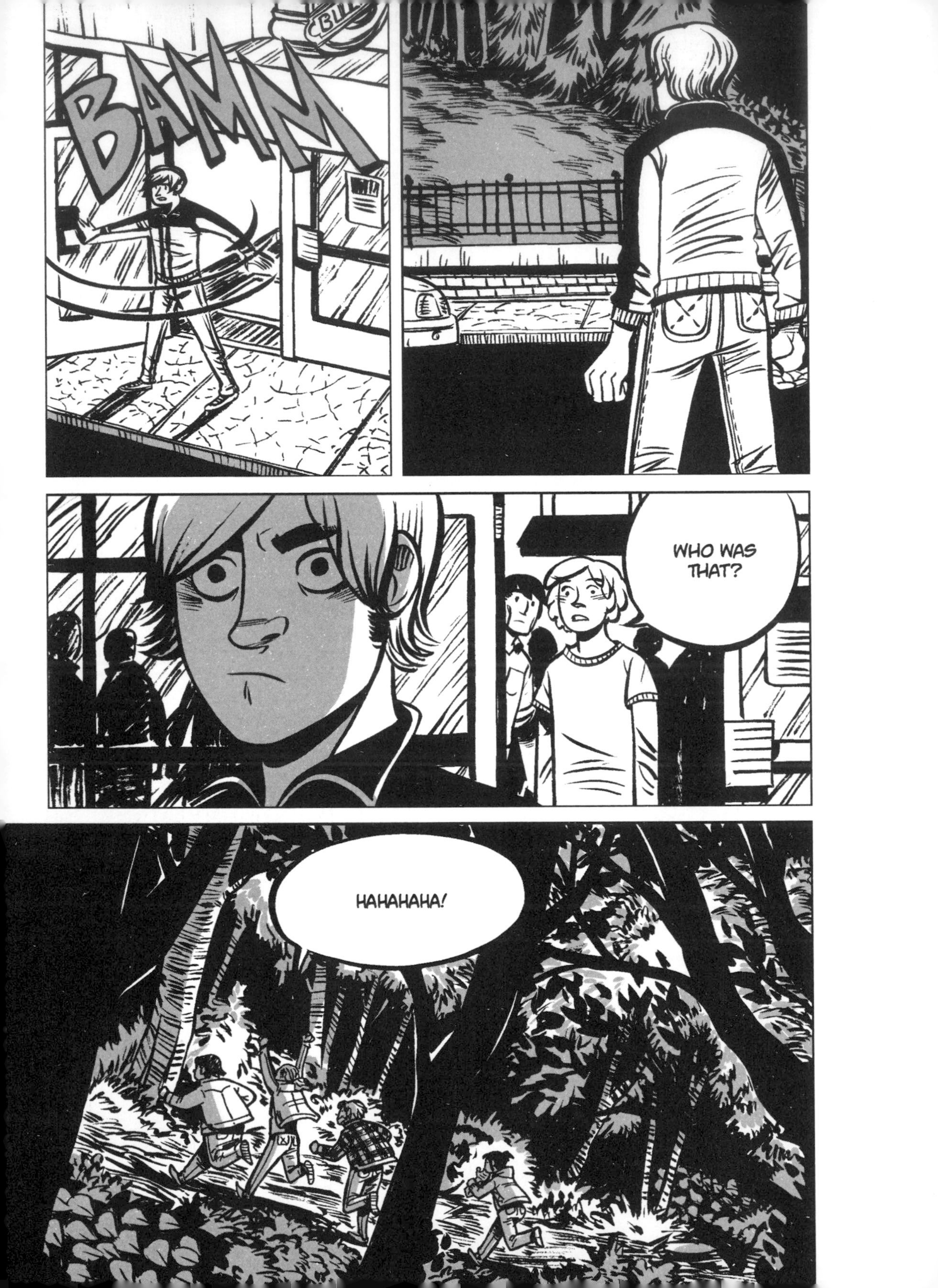
BAMM
WHO WAS THAT?
HAHAHAHA!

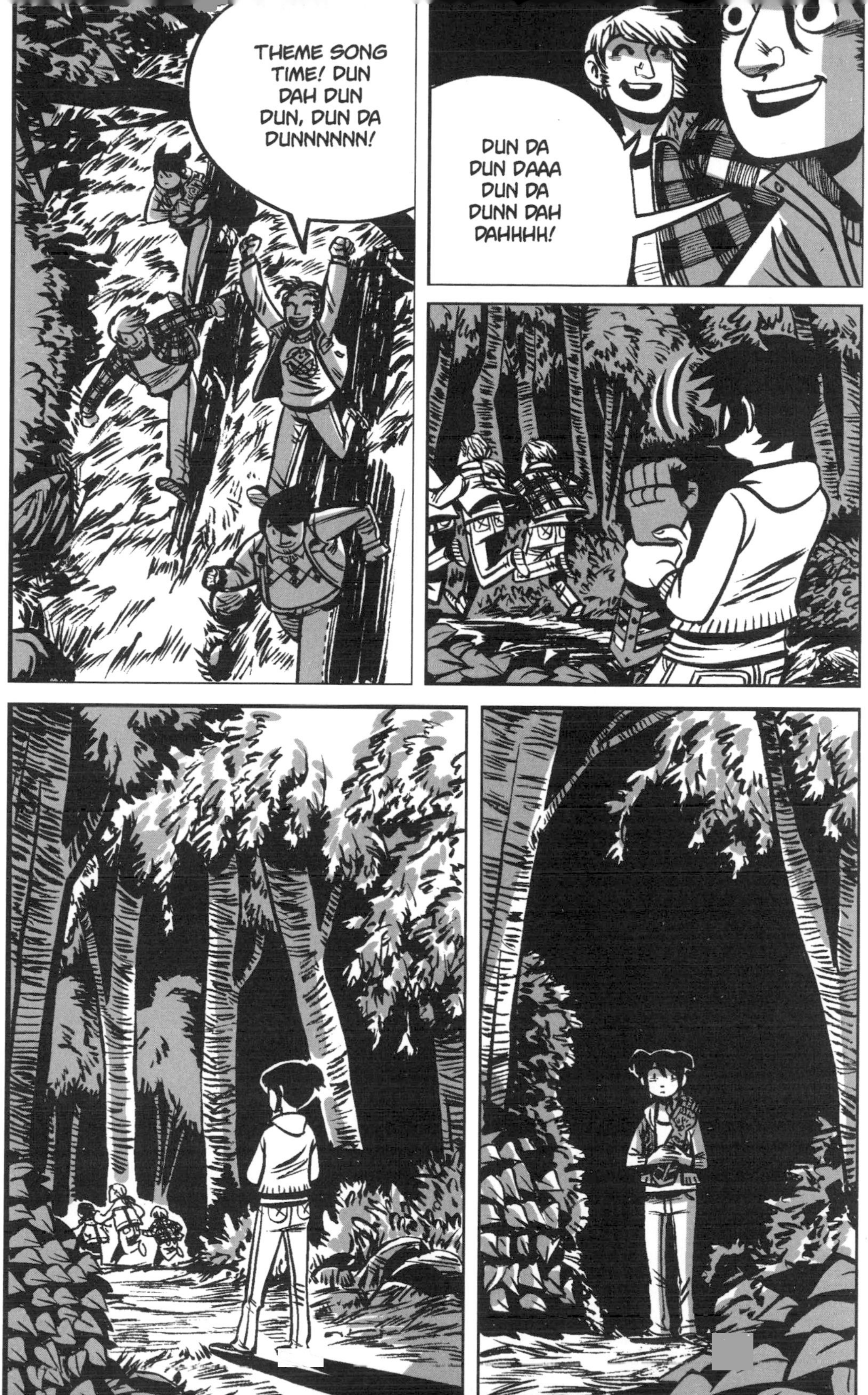
THEME SONG TIME! DUN DAH DUN DUN, DUN DA DUNNNNNN!
DUN DA DUN DAAA DUN DA DUNN DAH DAHHHH!

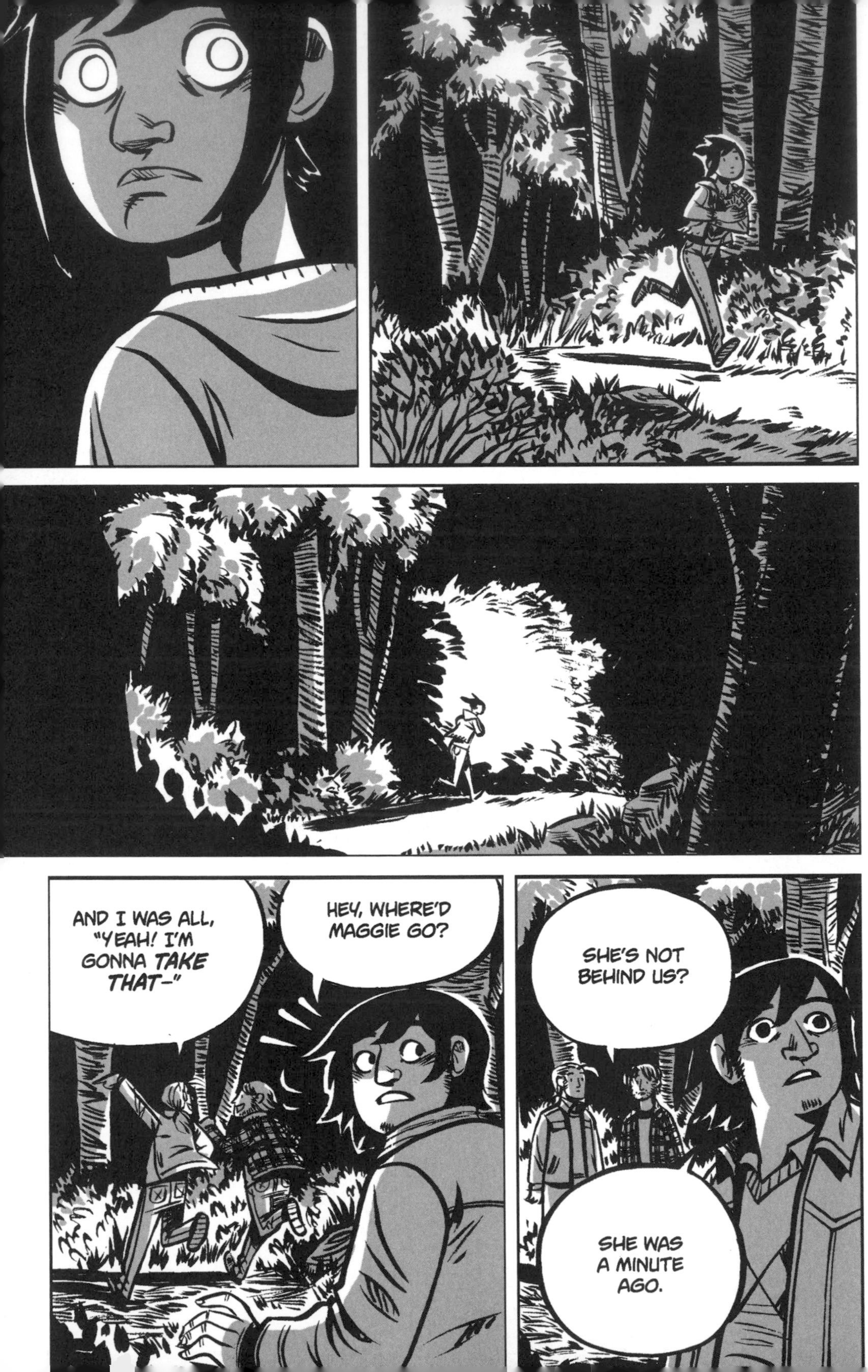
AND I WAS ALL, "YEAH! I'M GONNA *TAKE THAT*–"
HEY, WHERE'D MAGGIE GO?
SHE'S NOT BEHIND US?
SHE WAS A MINUTE AGO.

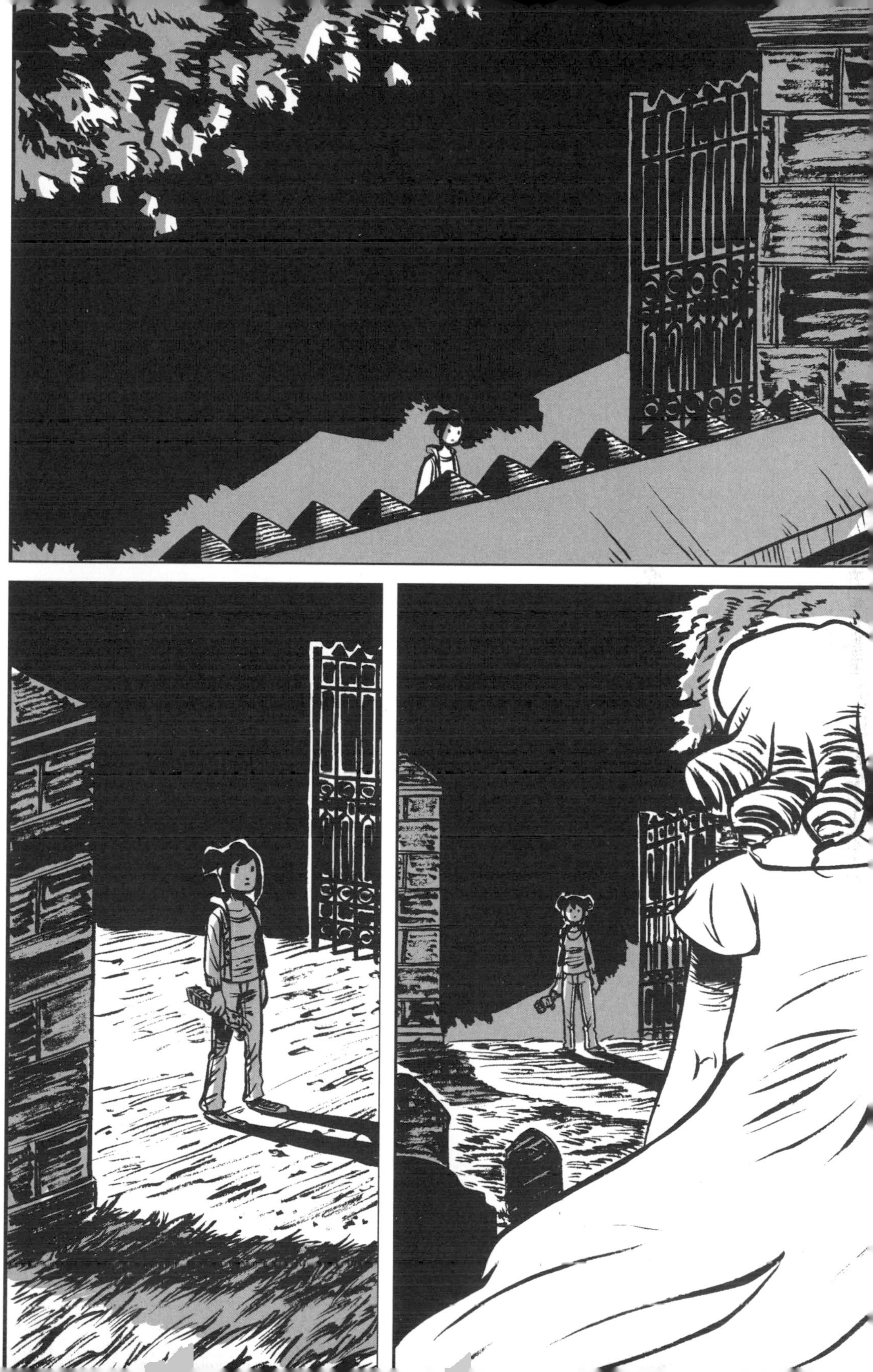

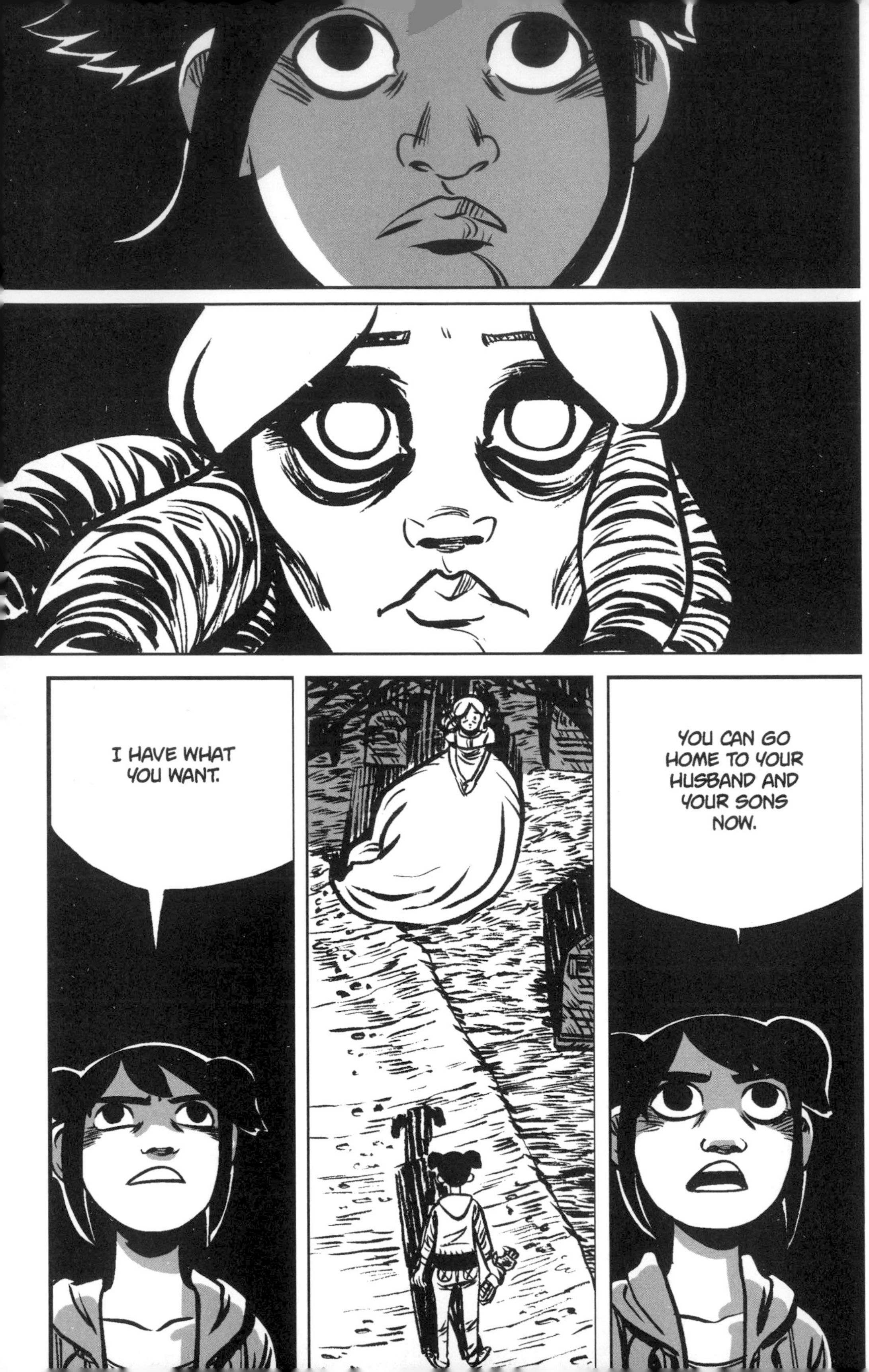

I HAVE WHAT YOU WANT.
YOU CAN GO HOME TO YOUR HUSBAND AND YOUR SONS NOW.

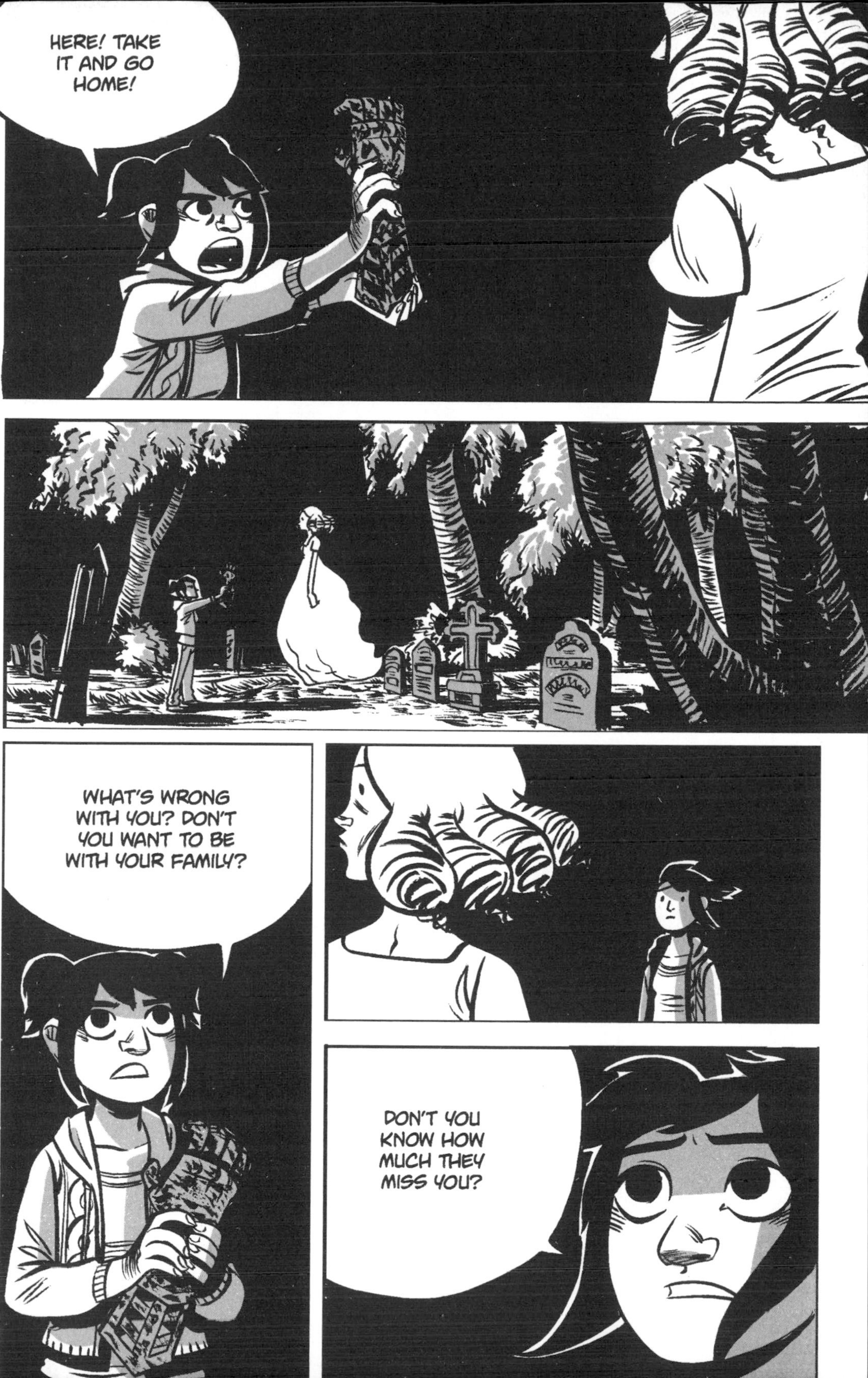
HERE! TAKE IT AND GO HOME!
WHAT'S WRONG WITH YOU? DON'T YOU WANT TO BE WITH YOUR FAMILY?
DON'T YOU KNOW HOW MUCH THEY MISS YOU?

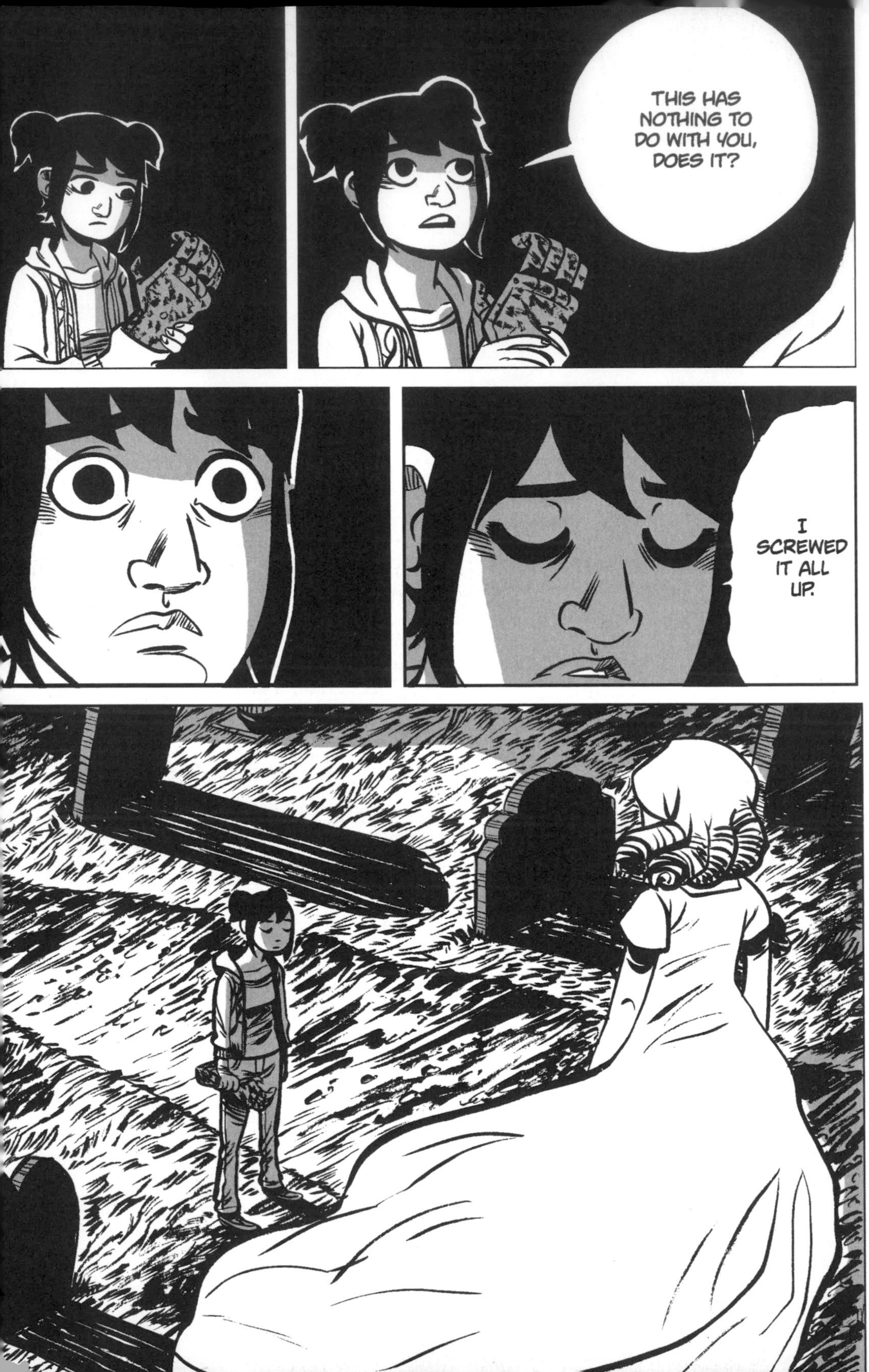
THIS HAS NOTHING TO DO WITH YOU, DOES IT?
I SCREWED IT ALL UP.

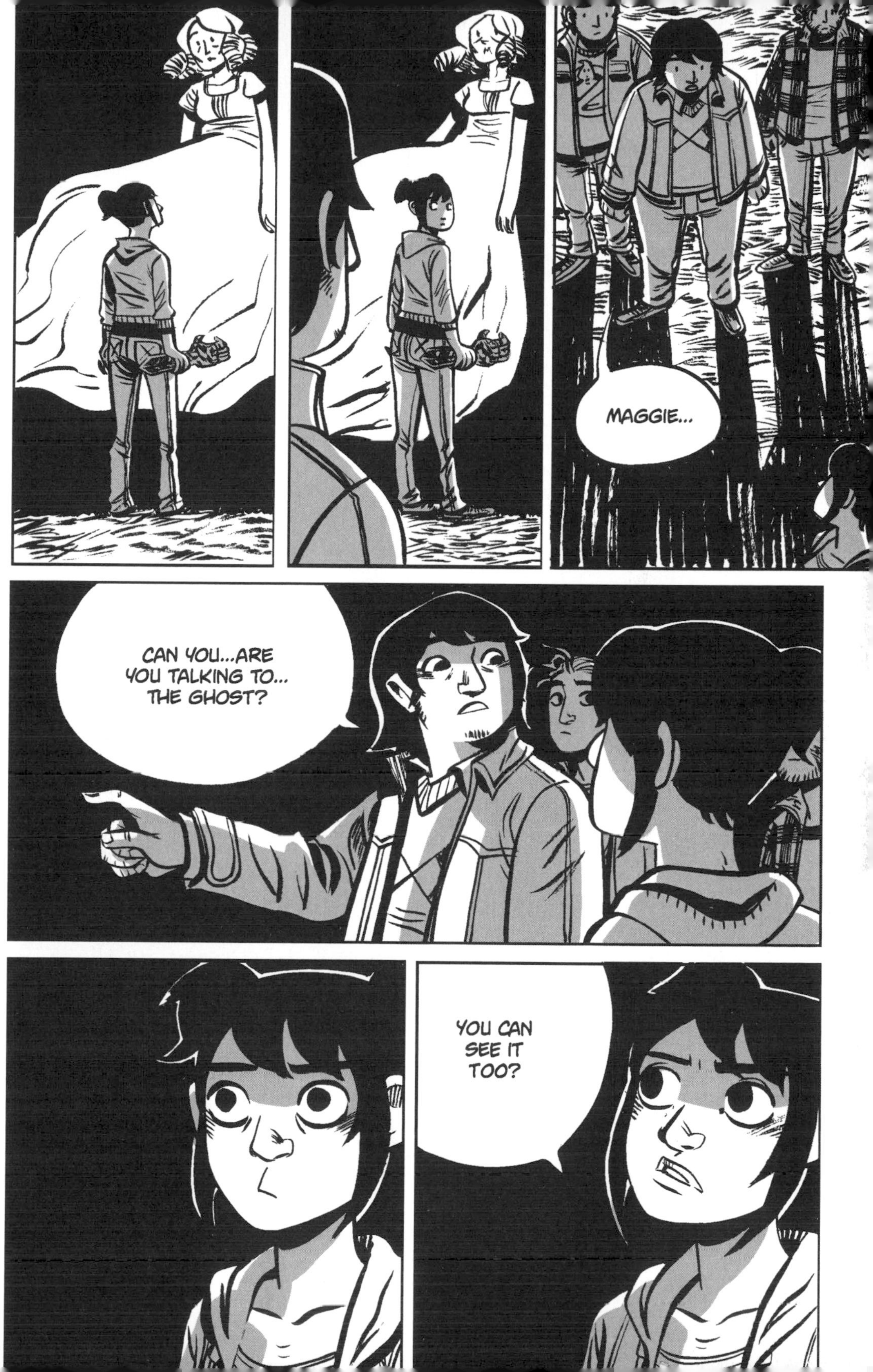
MAGGIE...
CAN YOU...ARE YOU TALKING TO... THE GHOST?
YOU CAN SEE IT TOO?

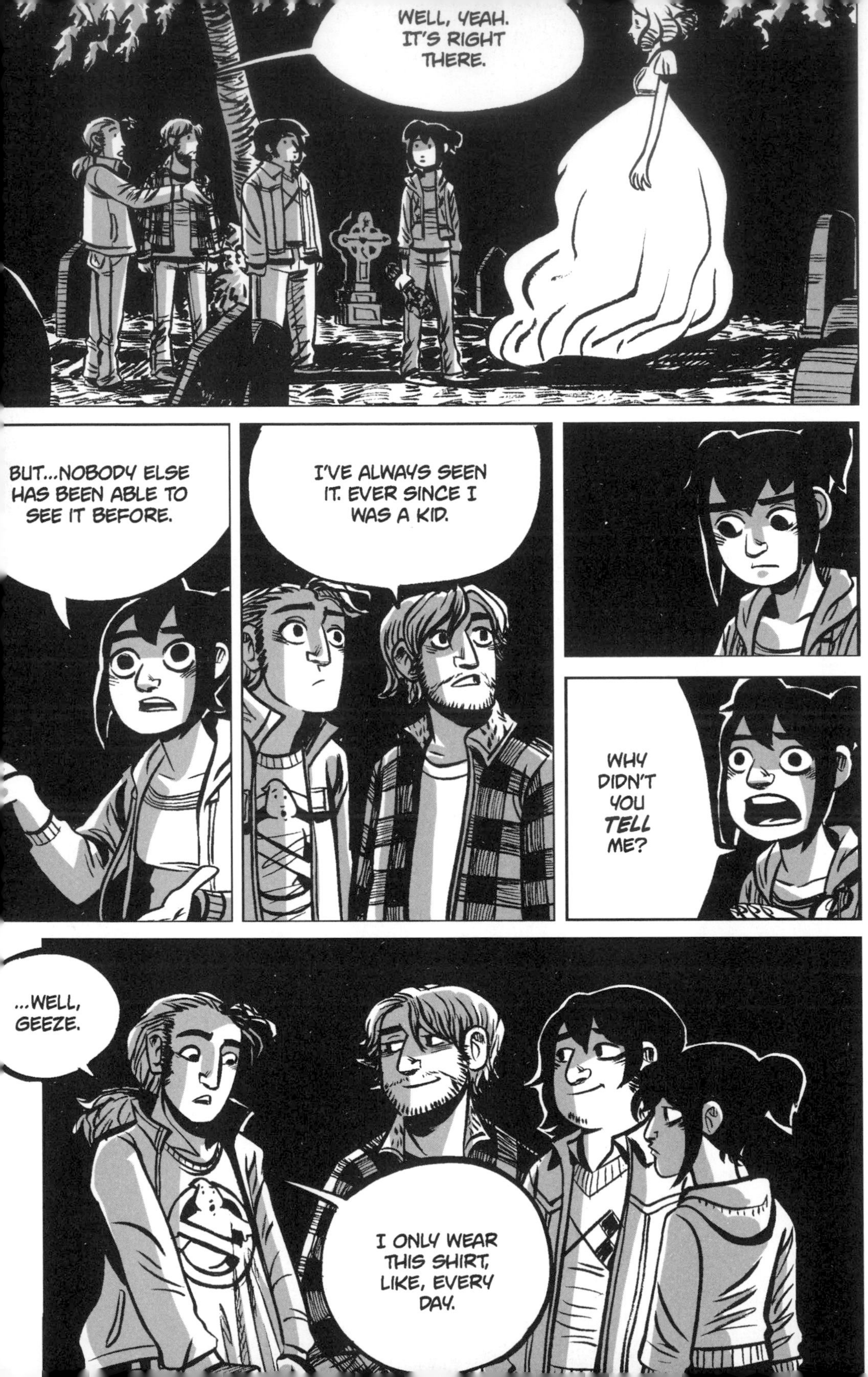
WELL, YEAH. IT'S RIGHT THERE.
BUT...NOBODY ELSE HAS BEEN ABLE TO SEE IT BEFORE.
I'VE ALWAYS SEEN IT. EVER SINCE I WAS A KID.
WHY DIDN'T YOU TELL ME?
...WELL, GEEZE.
I ONLY WEAR THIS SHIRT, LIKE, EVERY DAY.

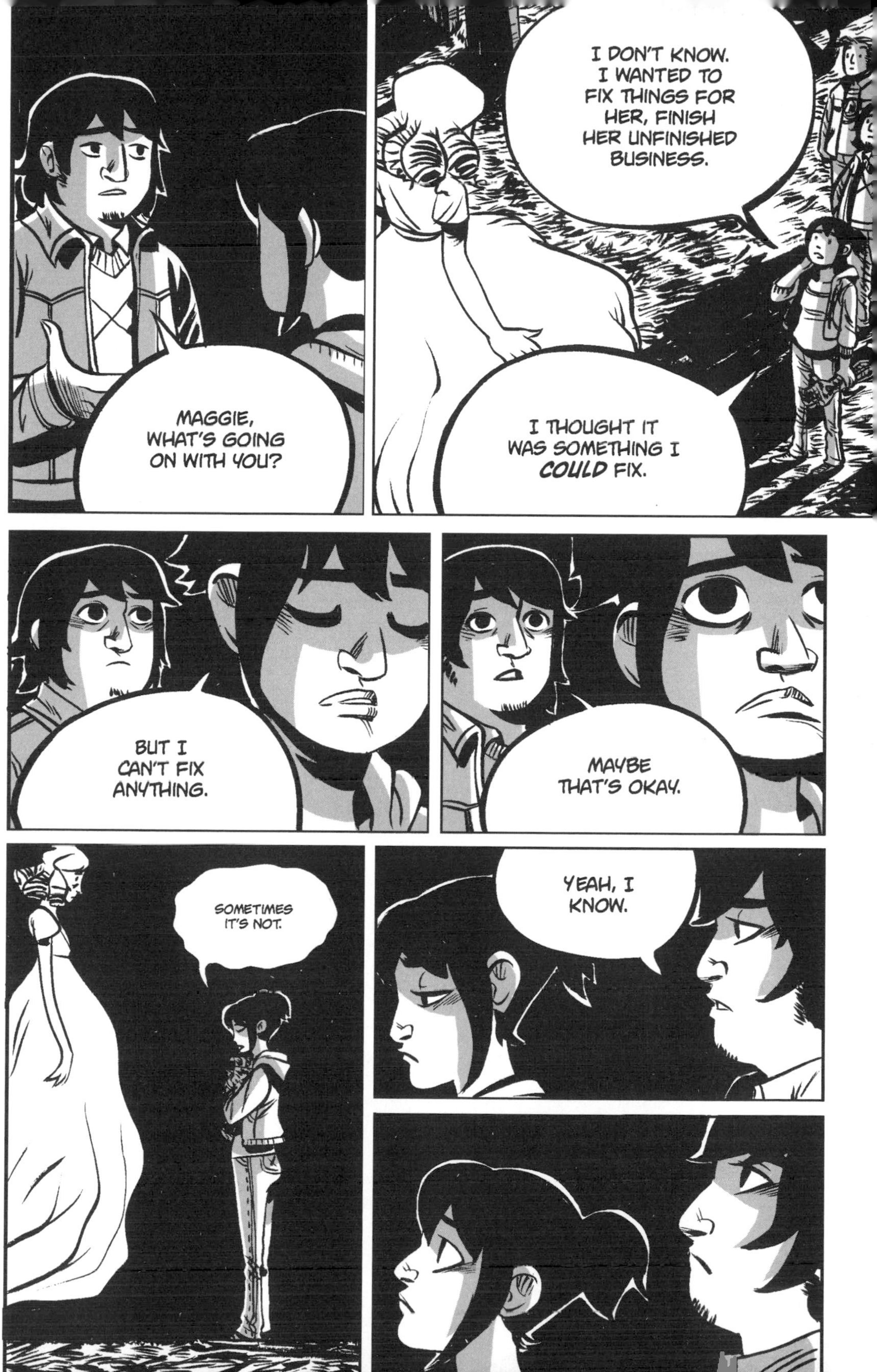
MAGGIE, WHAT'S GOING ON WITH YOU?
I DON'T KNOW. I WANTED TO FIX THINGS FOR HER, FINISH HER UNFINISHED BUSINESS.
I THOUGHT IT WAS SOMETHING I COULD FIX.
BUT I CAN'T FIX ANYTHING.
MAYBE THAT'S OKAY.
SOMETIMES IT'S NOT.
YEAH, I KNOW.

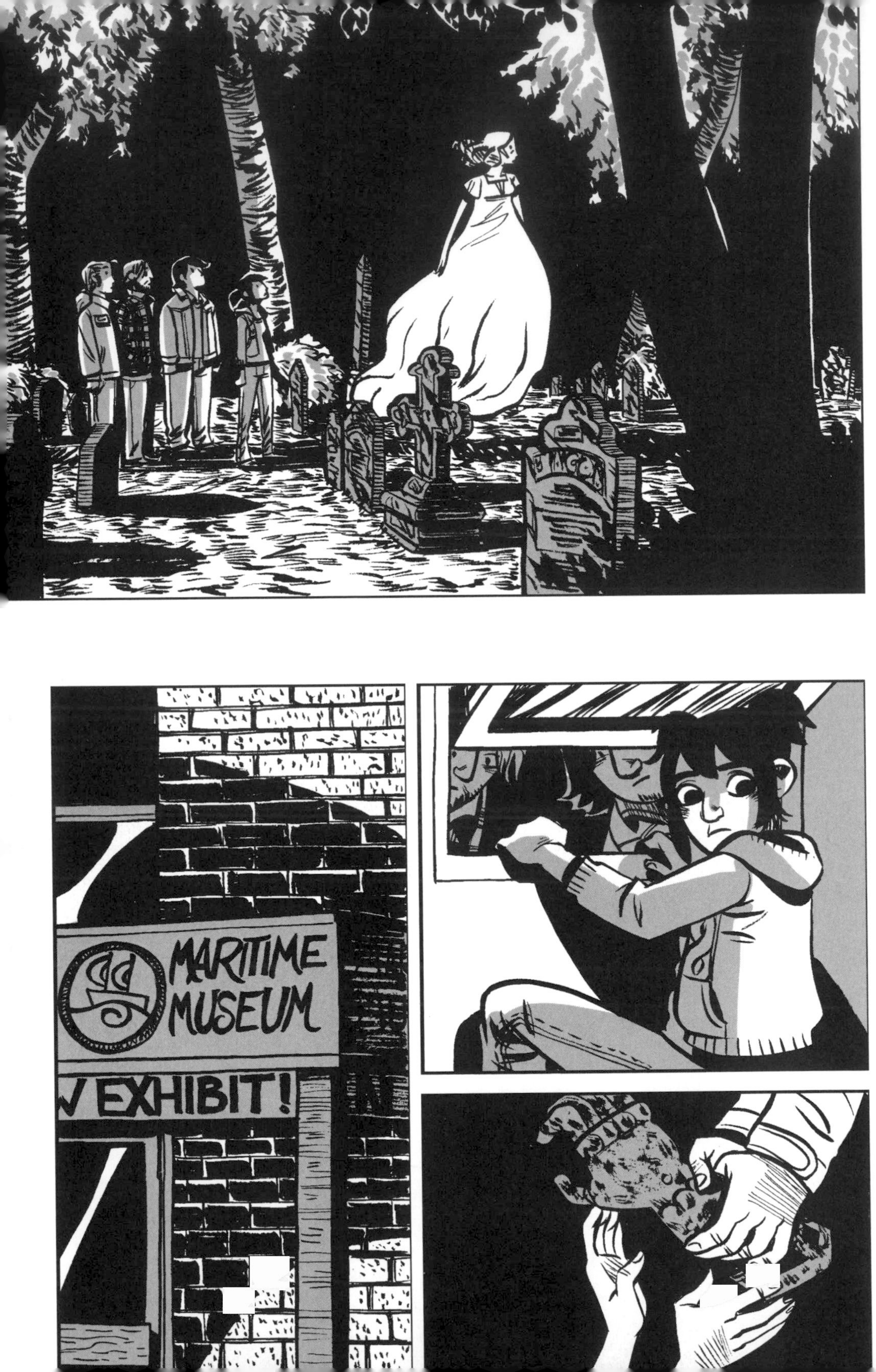
MARITIME
MUSEUM
W EXHIBIT!

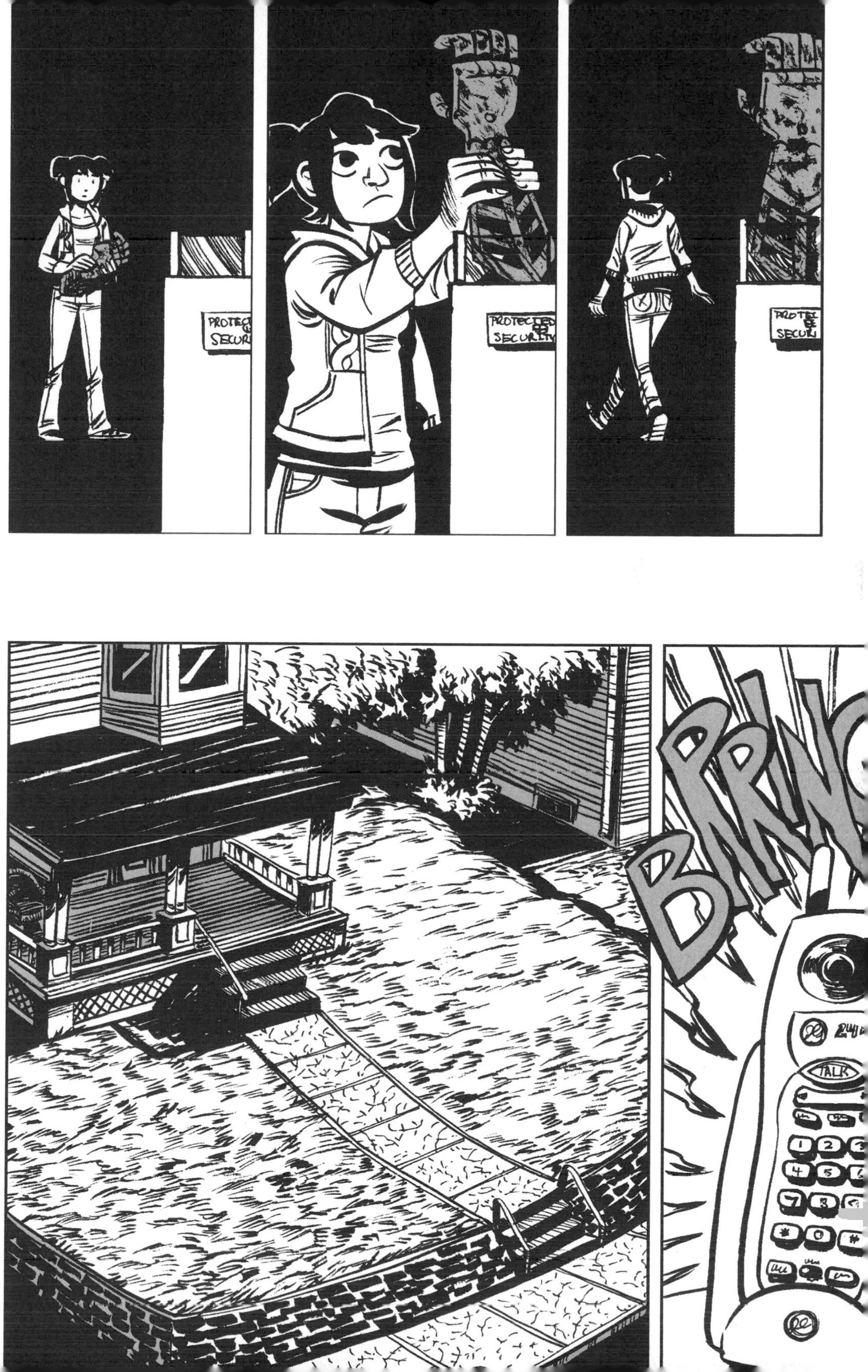
PROTECTED
SECURITY
TALK

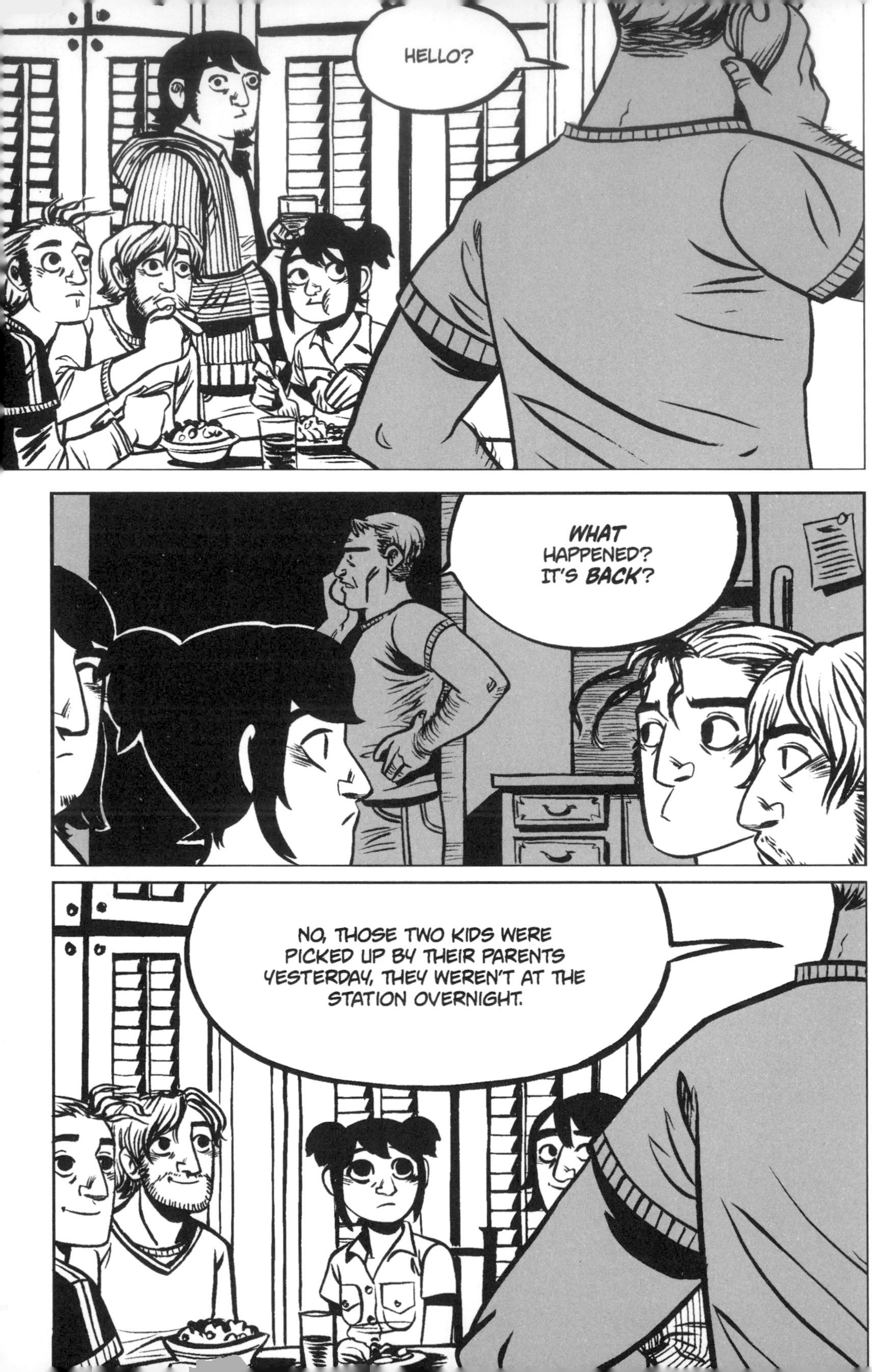
HELLO?
WHAT HAPPENED? IT'S BACK?
NO, THOSE TWO KIDS WERE PICKED UP BY THEIR PARENTS YESTERDAY, THEY WEREN'T AT THE STATION OVERNIGHT.

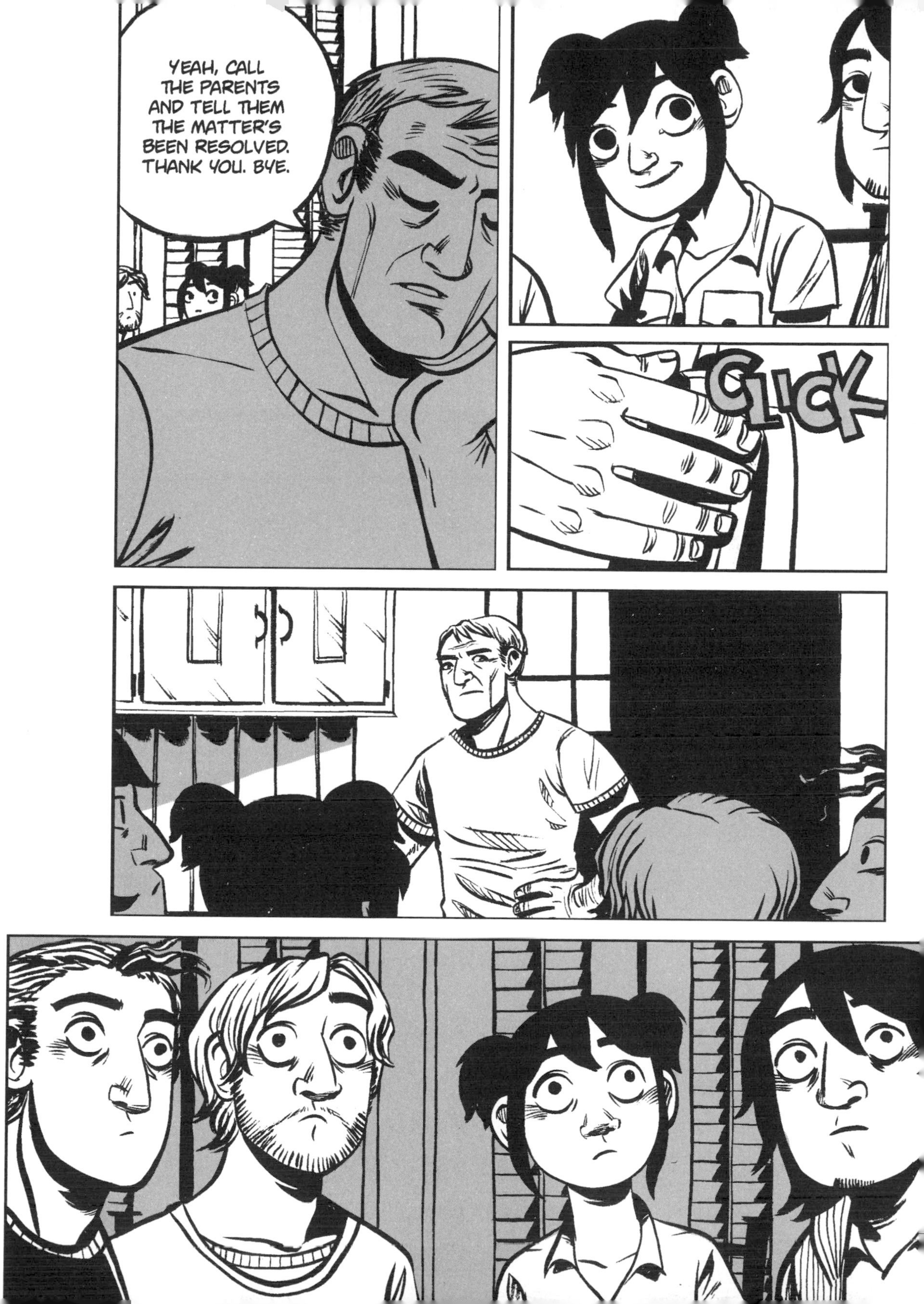
YEAH, CALL THE PARENTS AND TELL THEM THE MATTER'S BEEN RESOLVED. THANK YOU. BYE.
CLICK

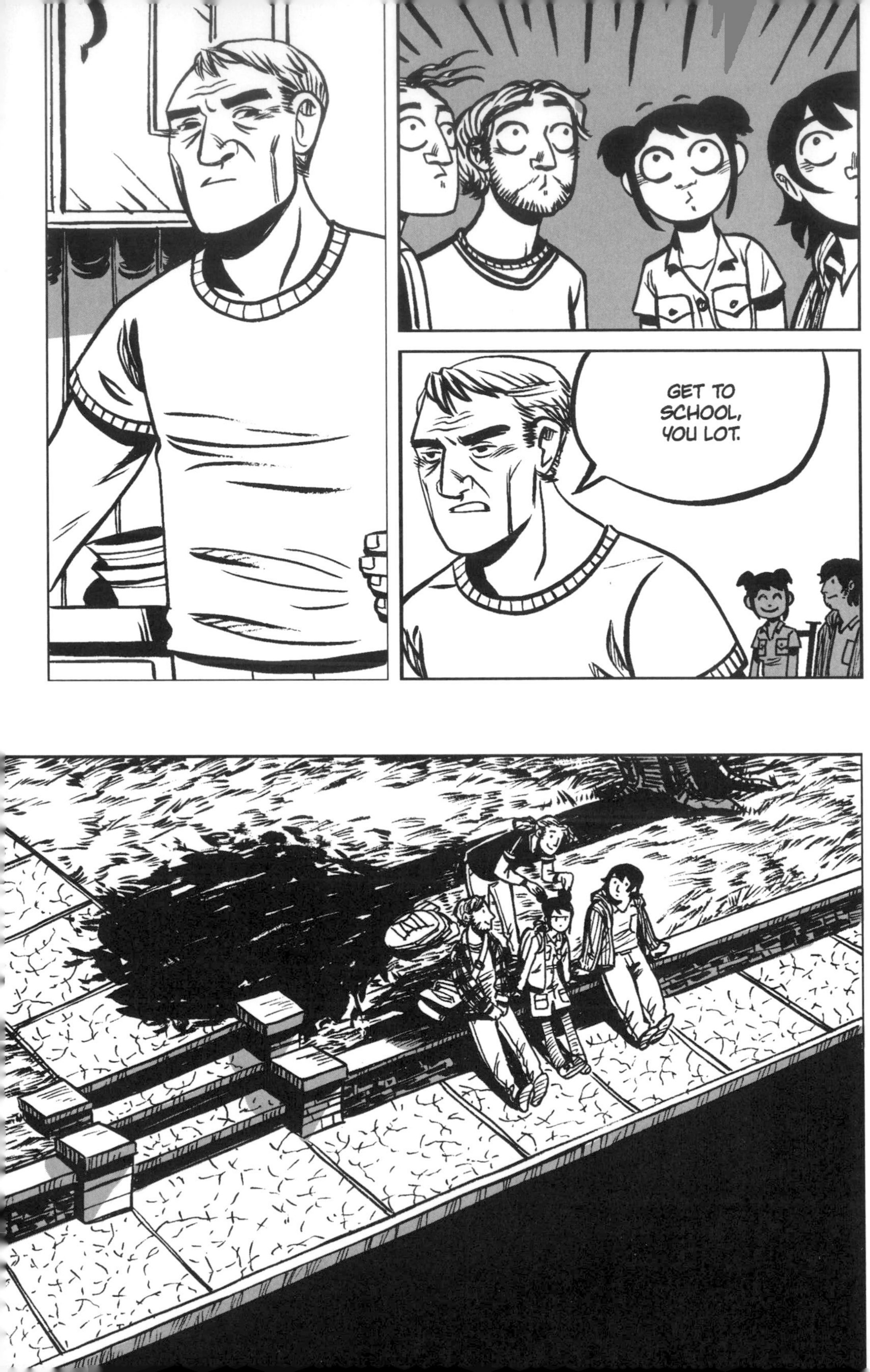
GET TO SCHOOL, YOU LOT.

1912

excerpt from

UNTERZAKHN

Leela Corman

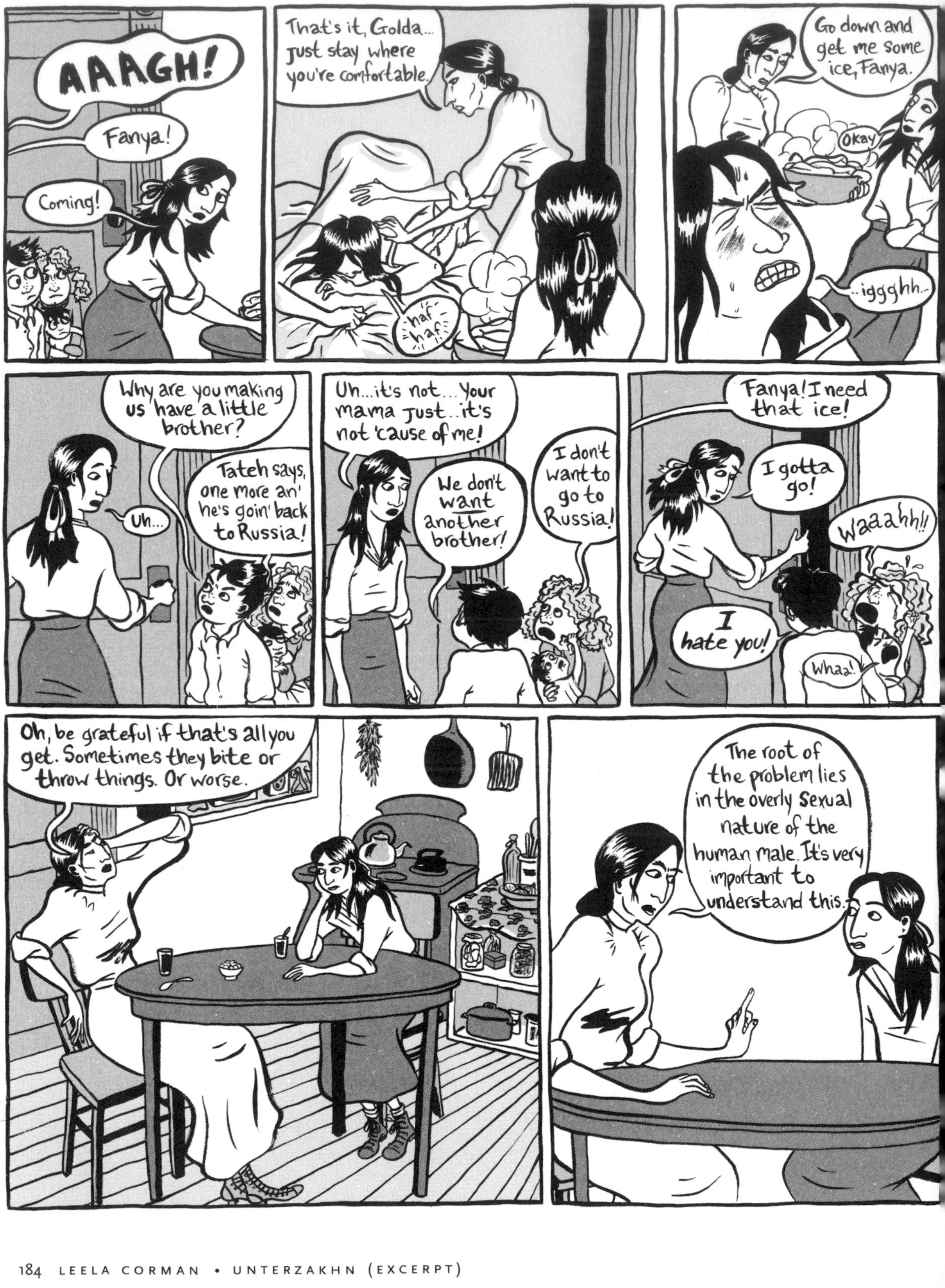
AAAGH!
Fanya!
Coming!
That's it, Golda... just stay where you're comfortable.
haf haf
Go down and get me some ice, Fanya.
Okay
..iggghh..
Why are you making us have a little brother?
Uh...
Tateh says, one more an' he's goin' back to Russia!
Uh...it's not... Your mama just...it's not 'cause of me!
We don't want another brother!
I don't want to go to Russia!
Fanya! I need that ice!
I gotta go!
Waaahh!!
I hate you!
Whaa!
Oh, be grateful if that's all you get. Sometimes they bite or throw things. Or worse.
The root of the problem lies in the overly sexual nature of the human male. It's very important to understand this.

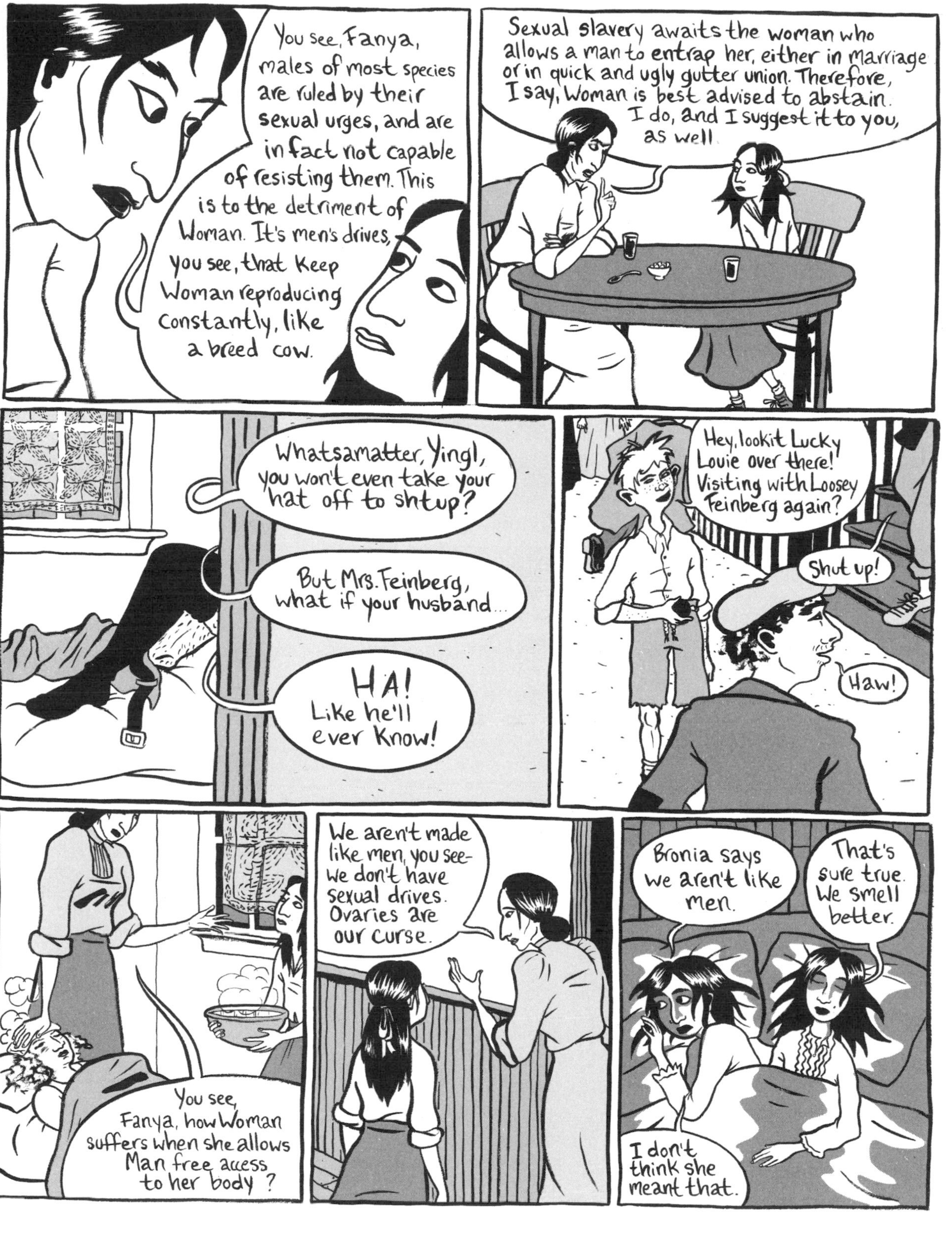

You see, Fanya, males of most species are ruled by their sexual urges, and are in fact not capable of resisting them. This is to the detriment of Woman. It's men's drives, you see, that keep Woman reproducing constantly, like a breed cow.
Sexual slavery awaits the woman who allows a man to entrap her, either in marriage or in quick and ugly gutter union. Therefore, I say, Woman is best advised to abstain. I do, and I suggest it to you, as well.
Whatsamatter, Yingl, you won't even take your hat off to shtup?
But Mrs. Feinberg, what if your husband...
HA! Like he'll ever know!
Hey, lookit Lucky Louie over there! Visiting with Loosey Feinberg again?
Shut up!
Haw!
You see, Fanya, how Woman suffers when she allows Man free access to her body?
We aren't made like men, you see- we don't have sexual drives. Ovaries are our curse.
Bronia says we aren't like men.
That's sure true. We smell better.
I don't think she meant that.

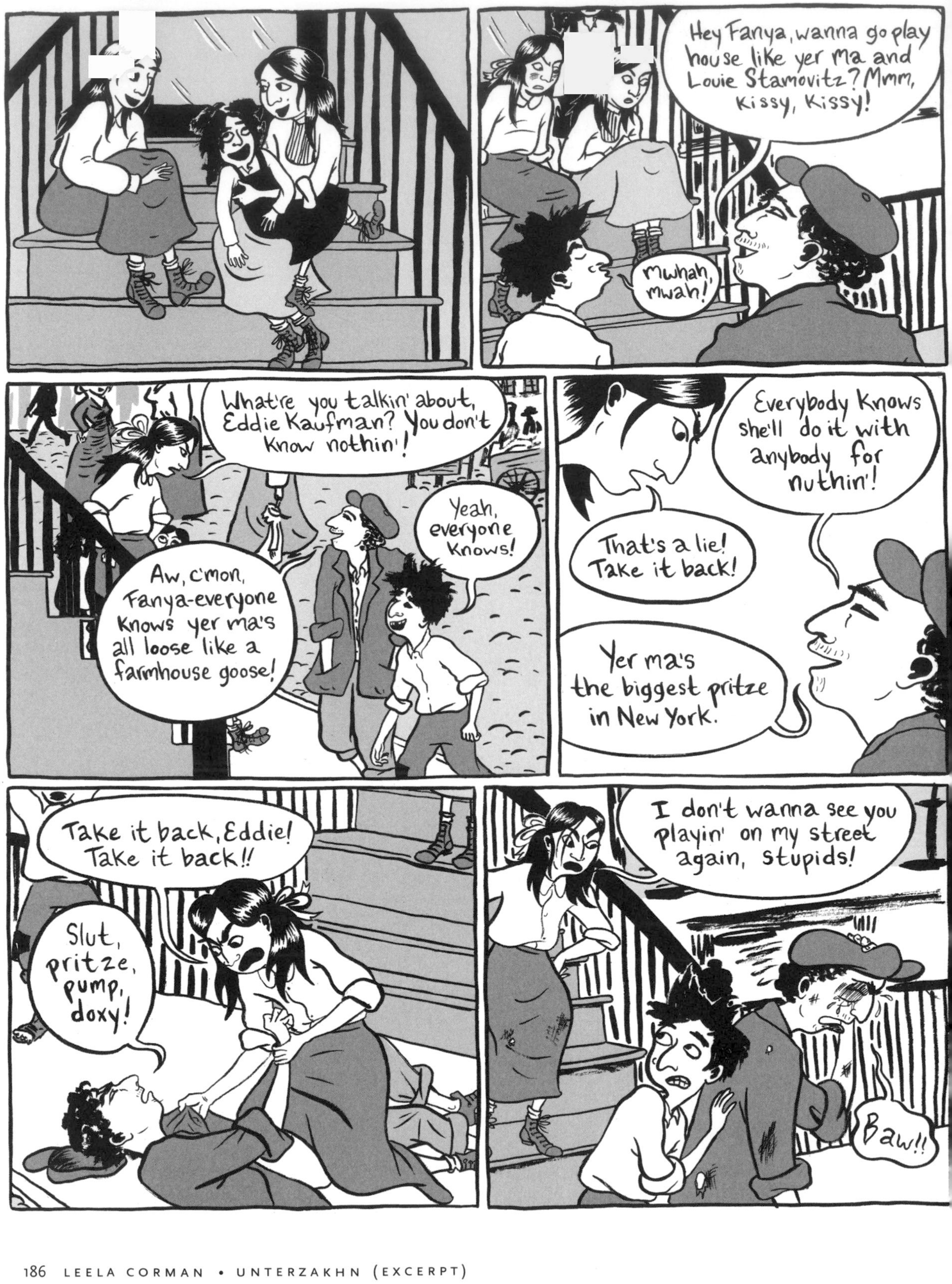
Hey Fanya, wanna go play house like yer ma and Louie Stamovitz? Mmm, kissy, kissy!
mwhah, mwah!
What're you talkin' about, Eddie Kaufman? You don't know nothin'!
Aw, c'mon, Fanya-everyone knows yer ma's all loose like a farmhouse goose!
Yeah, everyone knows!
Everybody knows she'll do it with anybody for nuthin'!
That's a lie! Take it back!
Yer ma's the biggest pritze in New York.
Take it back, Eddie! Take it back!!
Slut, pritze, pump, doxy!
I don't wanna see you playin' on my street again, stupids!
Baw!!

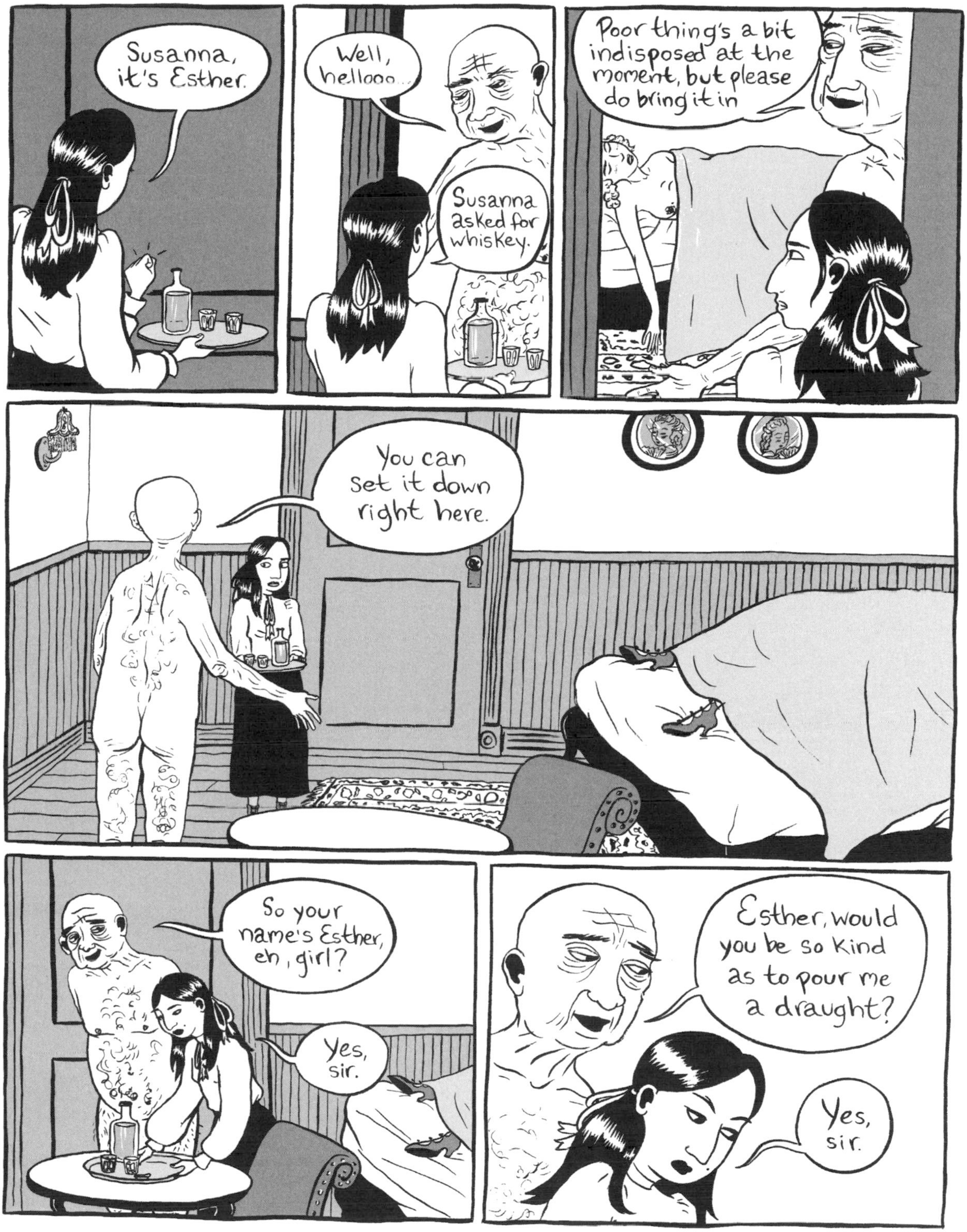
Susanna, it's Esther.
Well, hellooo...
Susanna asked for whiskey.
Poor thing's a bit indisposed at the moment, but please do bring it in
You can set it down right here.
So your name's Esther, eh, girl?
Yes, sir.
Esther, would you be so kind as to pour me a draught?
Yes, sir.

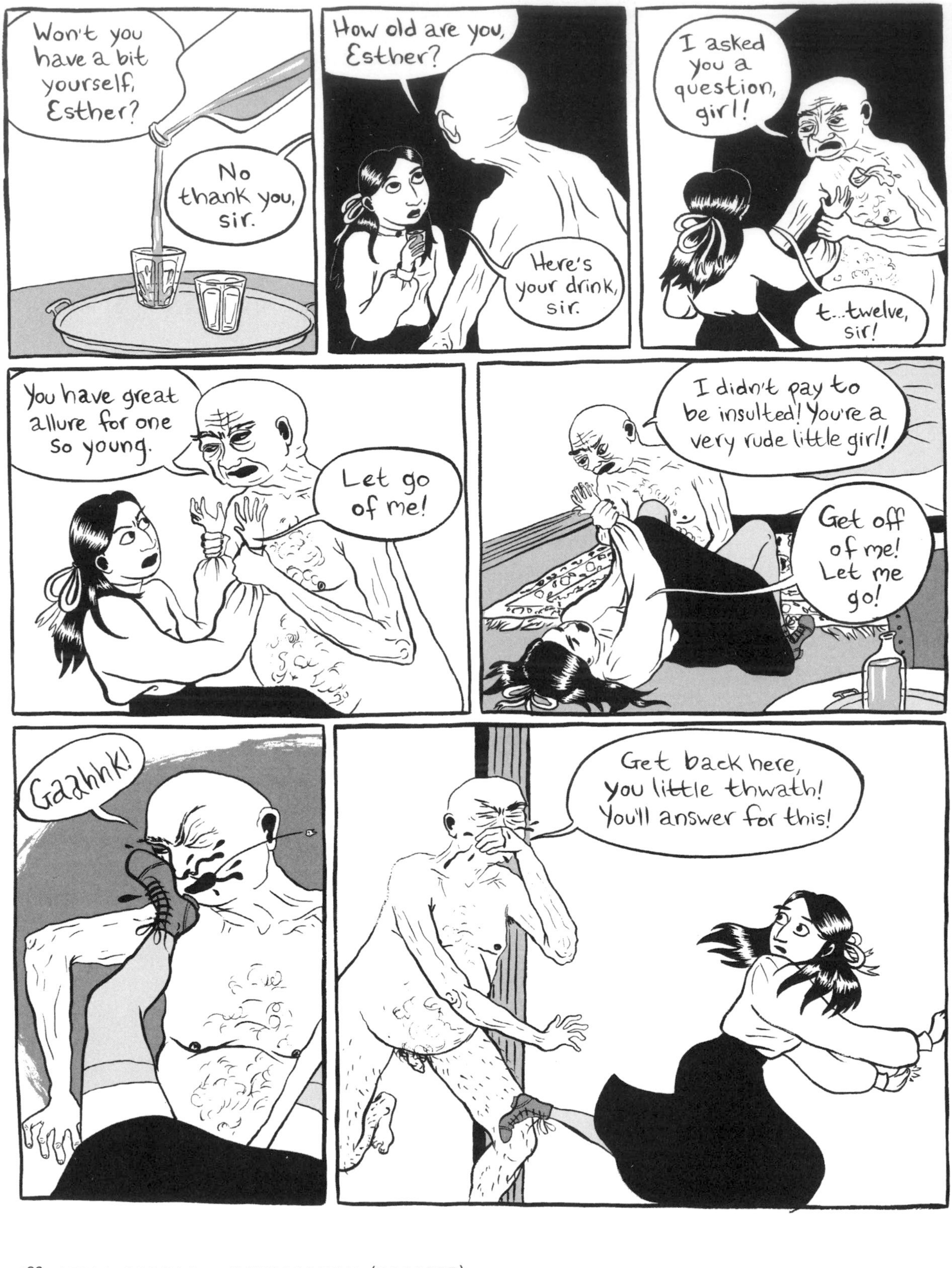
Won't you have a bit yourself, Esther?
No thank you, sir.
How old are you, Esther?
Here's your drink, sir.
I asked you a question, girl!
t...twelve, sir!
You have great allure for one so young.
Let go of me!
I didn't pay to be insulted! You're a very rude little girl!
Get off of me! Let me go!
Gaahhk!
Get back here, you little thwath! You'll answer for this!

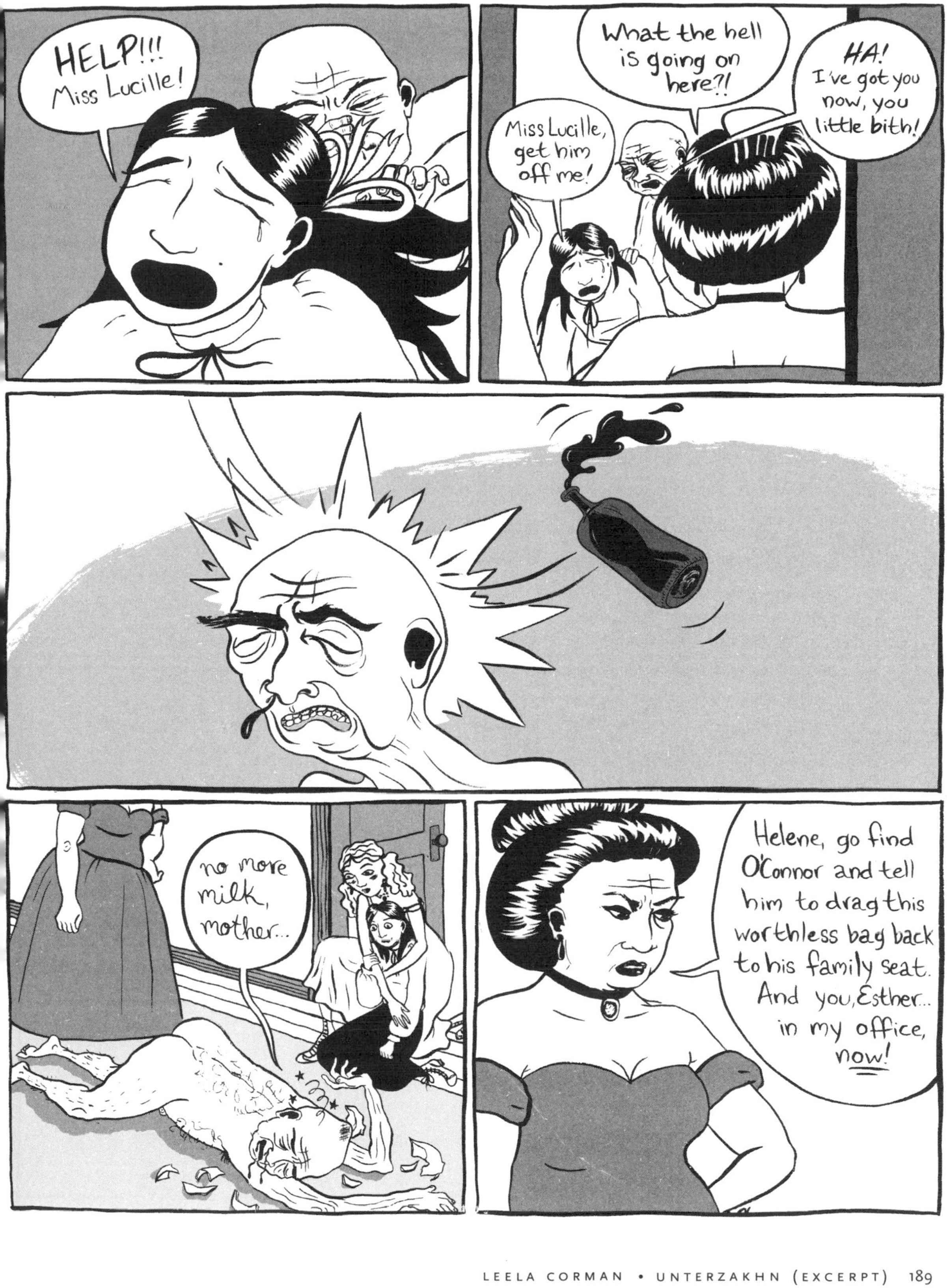
HELP!!! Miss Lucille!
What the hell is going on here?!
HA! I've got you now, you little bith!
Miss Lucille, get him off me!
no more milk, mother...
Helene, go find O'Connor and tell him to drag this worthless bag back to his family seat. And you, Esther... in my office, now!

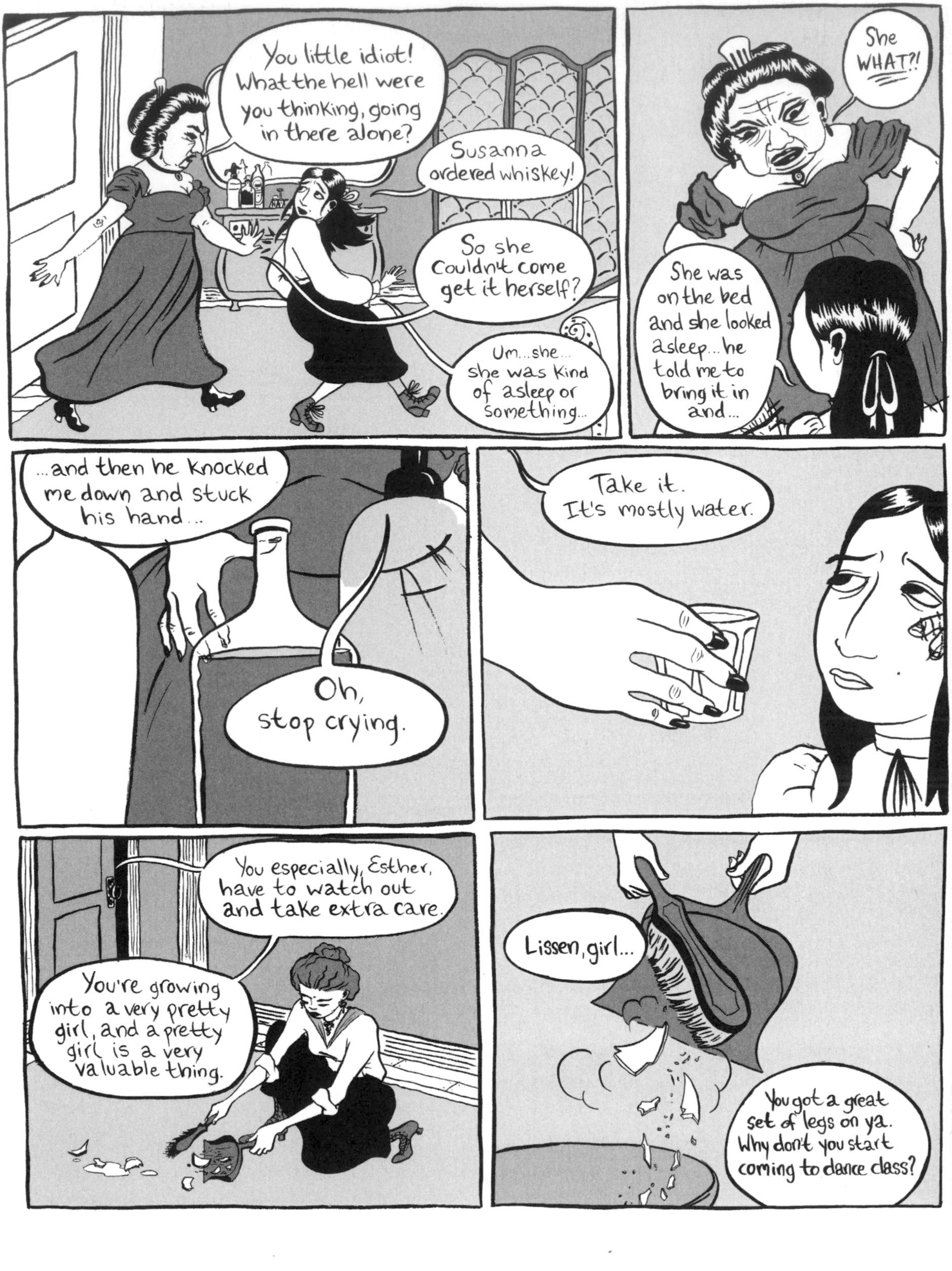
You little idiot! What the hell were you thinking, going in there alone?
Susanna ordered whiskey!
So she couldn't come get it herself?
Um...she... she was kind of asleep or something...
She WHAT?!
She was on the bed and she looked asleep... he told me to bring it in and...
...and then he knocked me down and stuck his hand...
Oh, stop crying.
Take it. It's mostly water.
You especially, Esther, have to watch out and take extra care.
You're growing into a very pretty girl, and a pretty girl is a very valuable thing.
Lissen, girl...
You got a great set of legs on ya. Why don't you start coming to dance class?

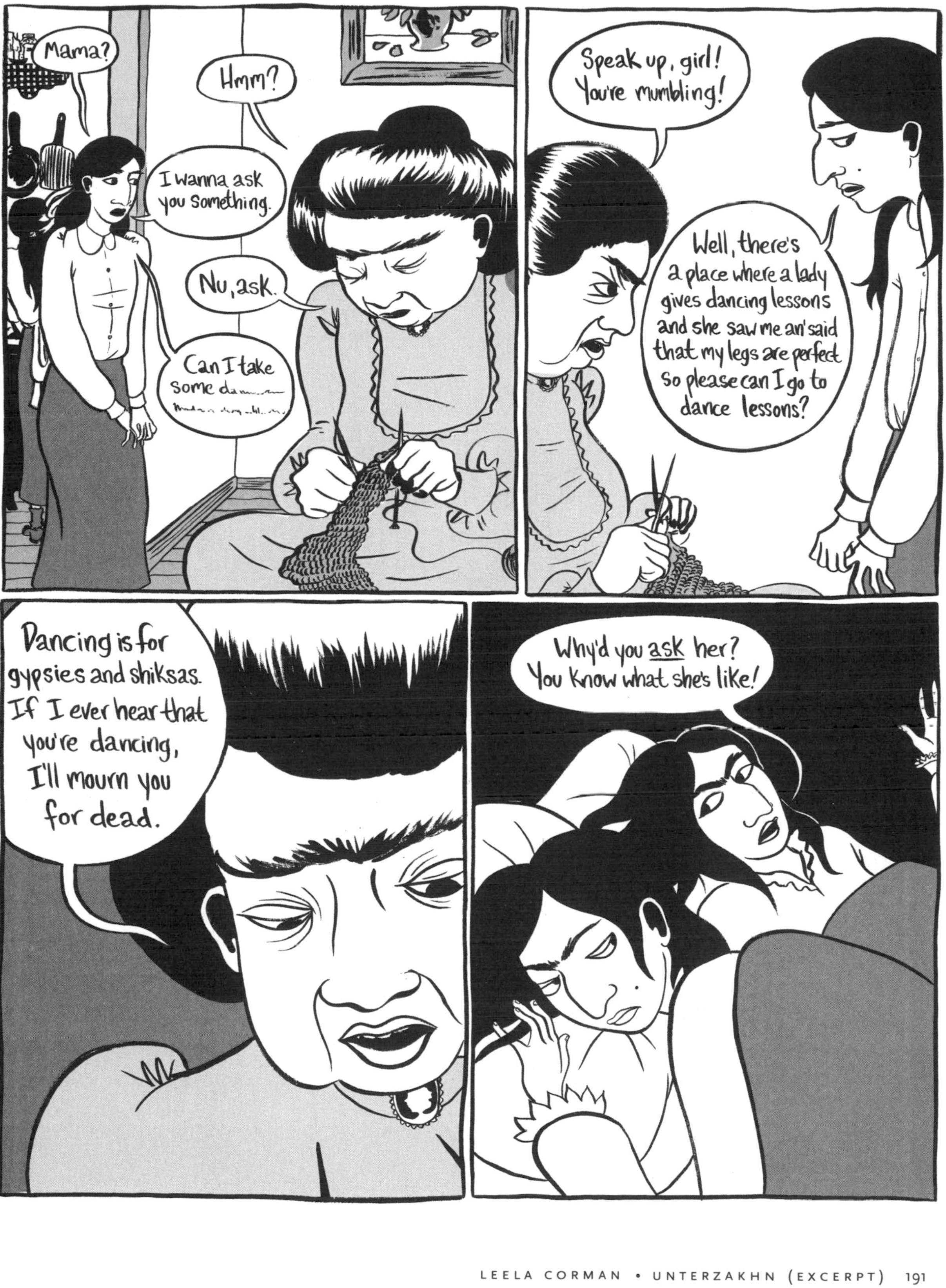
Mama?
Hmm?
I wanna ask you something.
Nu, ask.
Can I take some da
Speak up, girl! You're mumbling!
Well, there's a place where a lady gives dancing lessons and she saw me an' said that my legs are perfect so please can I go to dance lessons?
Dancing is for gypsies and shiksas. If I ever hear that you're dancing, I'll mourn you for dead.
Why'd you ask her? You know what she's like!

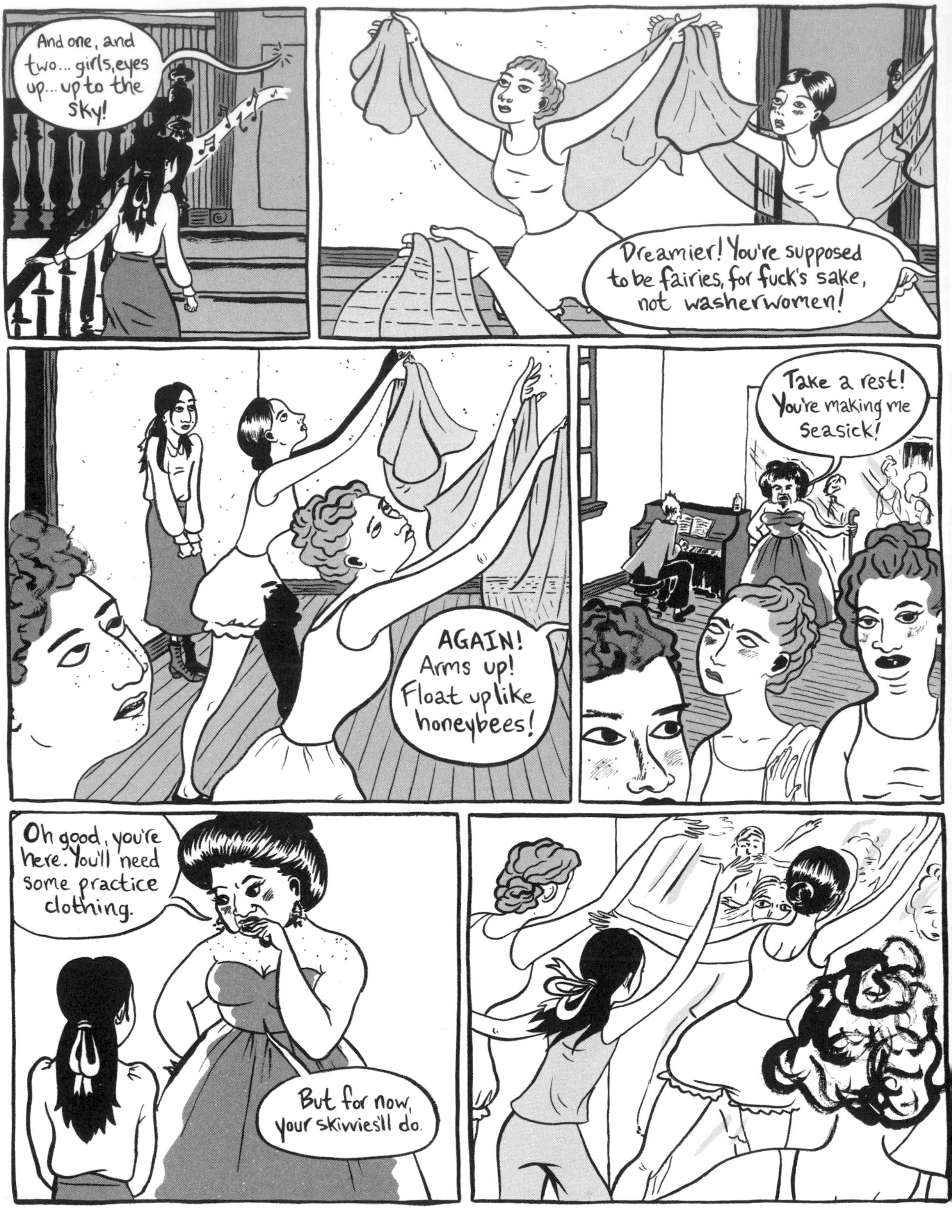

And one, and two... girls, eyes up... up to the sky!
Dreamier! You're supposed to be fairies, for fuck's sake, not washerwomen!
AGAIN! Arms up! Float up like honeybees!
Take a rest! You're making me seasick!
Oh good, you're here. You'll need some practice clothing.
But for now, your skivvies'll do.

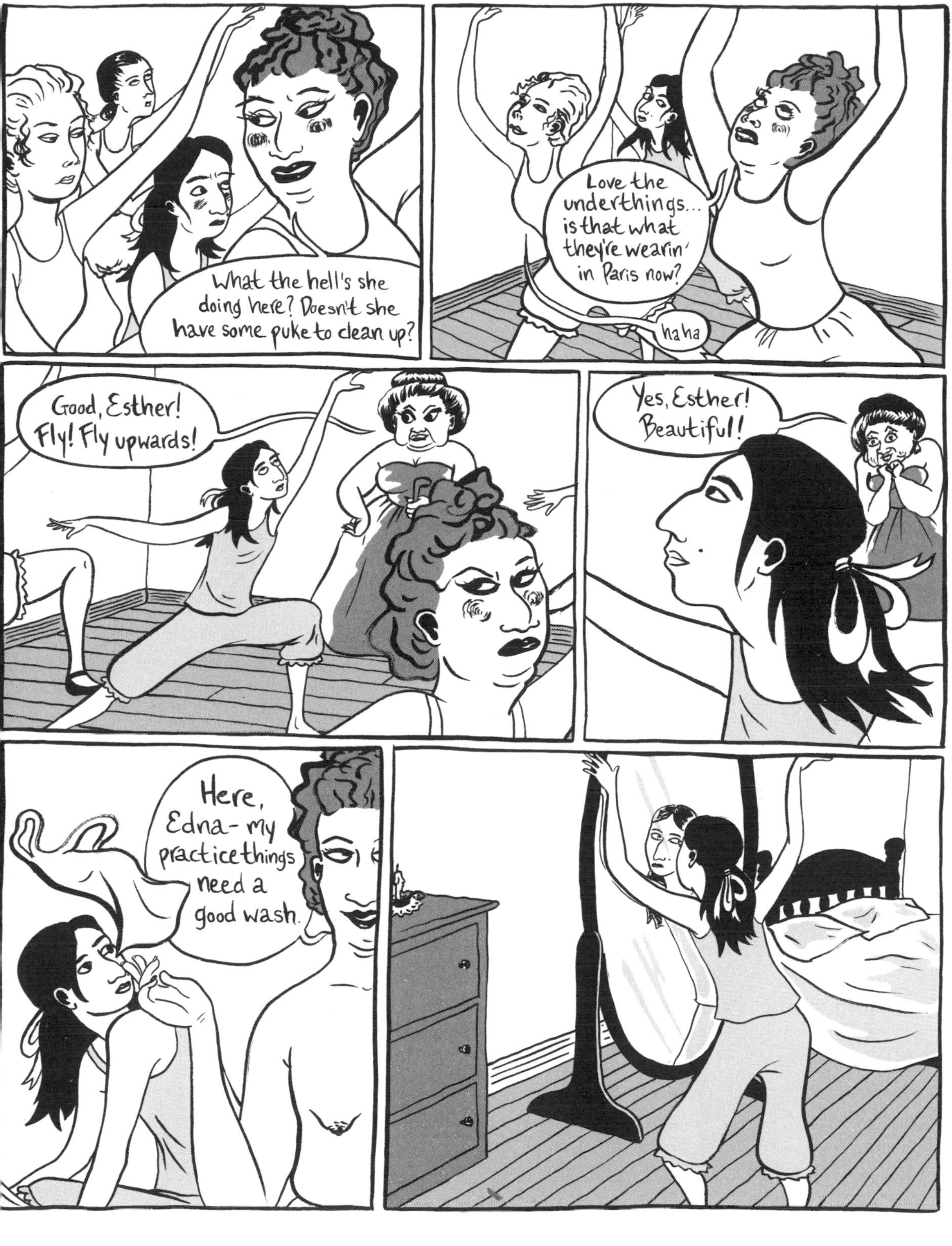
What the hell's she doing here? Doesn't she have some puke to clean up?
Love the underthings... is that what they're wearin' in Paris now?
haha
Good, Esther! Fly! Fly upwards!
Yes, Esther! Beautiful!
Here, Edna- my practice things need a good wash.

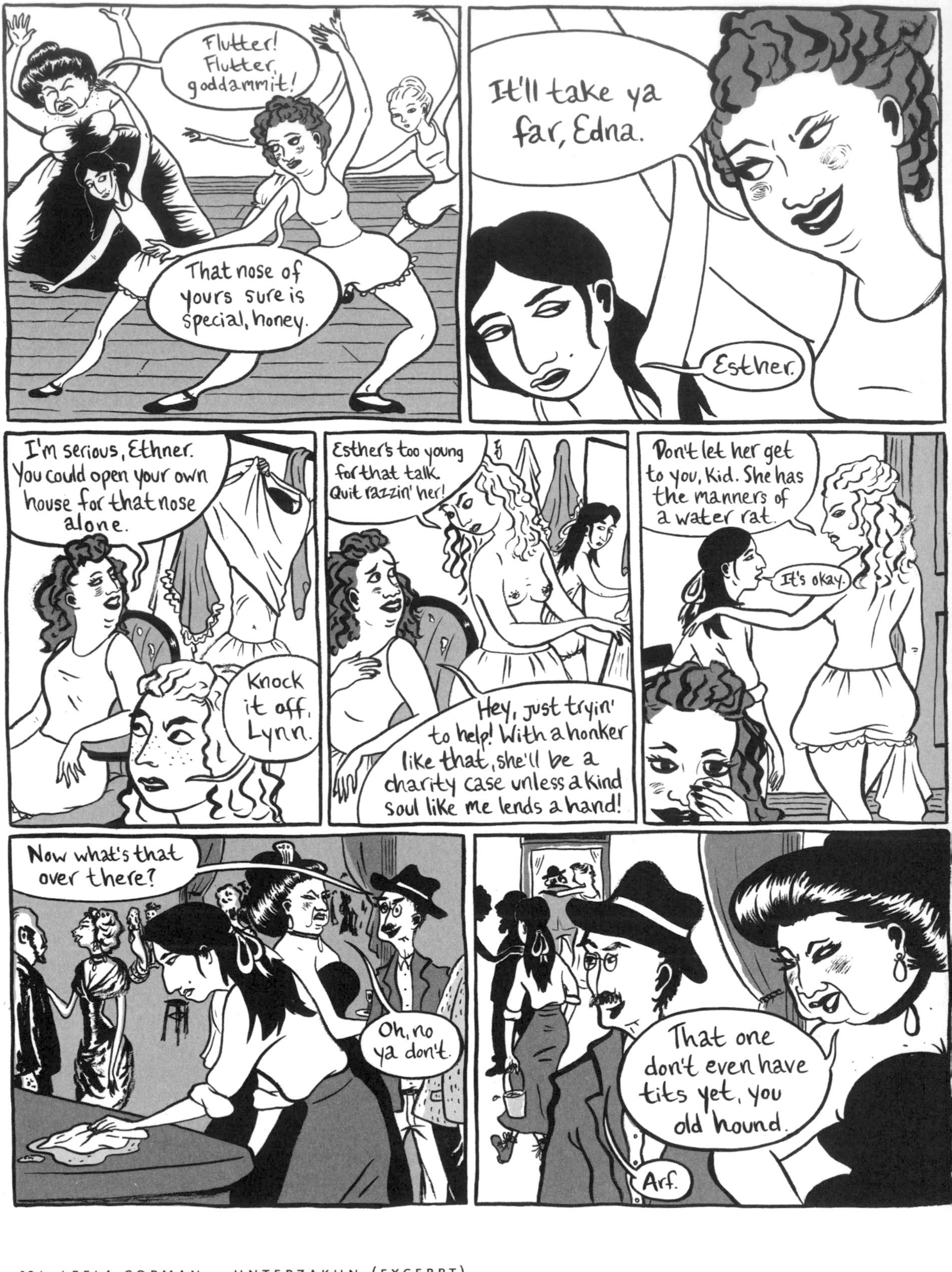
Flutter! Flutter, goddammit!
That nose of yours sure is special, honey.
It'll take ya far, Edna.
Esther.
I'm serious, Ethner. You could open your own house for that nose alone.
Knock it off, Lynn.
Esther's too young for that talk. Quit razzin' her!
Hey, just tryin' to help! With a honker like that, she'll be a charity case unless a kind soul like me lends a hand!
Don't let her get to you, Kid. She has the manners of a water rat.
It's okay.
Now what's that over there?
Oh, no ya don't.
That one don't even have tits yet, you old hound.
Arf.

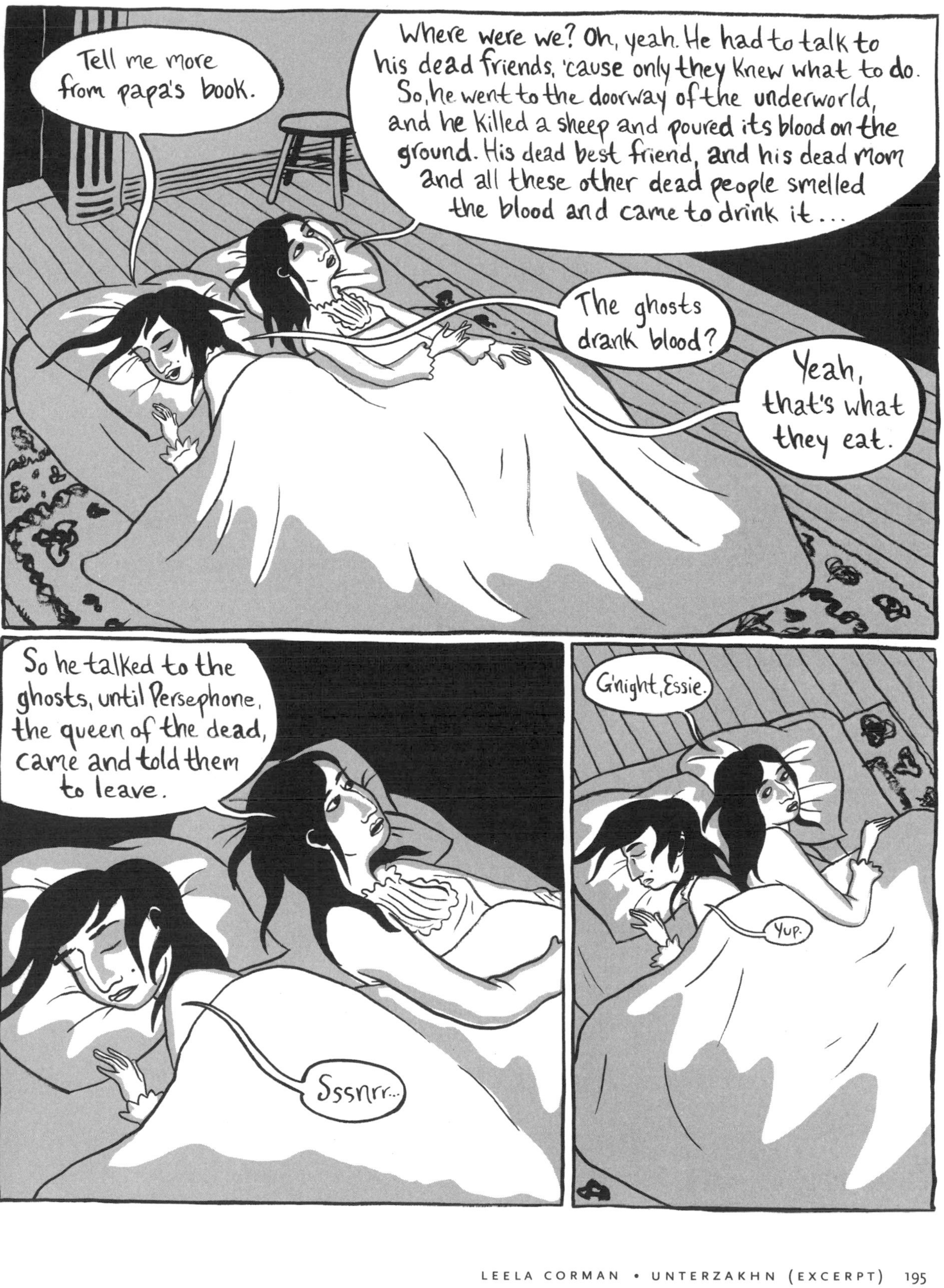
Tell me more from papa's book.
Where were we? Oh, yeah. He had to talk to his dead friends, 'cause only they knew what to do. So, he went to the doorway of the underworld, and he killed a sheep and poured its blood on the ground. His dead best friend, and his dead mom and all these other dead people smelled the blood and came to drink it...
The ghosts drank blood?
Yeah, that's what they eat.
So he talked to the ghosts, until Persephone, the queen of the dead, came and told them to leave.
Sssnrr...
G'night, Essie.
Yup.

SAMMY HARKHAM

A HUSBAND
AND A WIFE

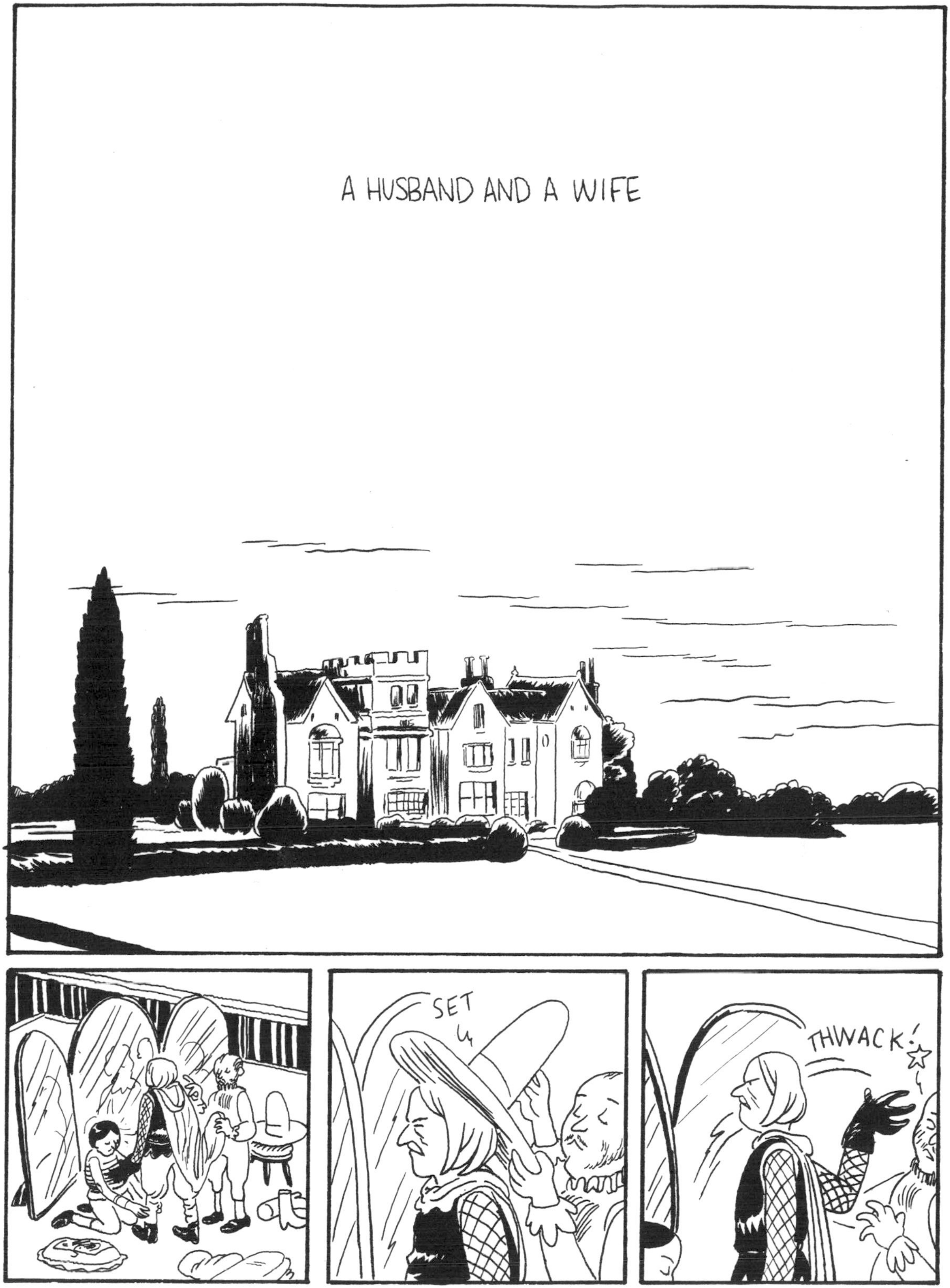
A HUSBAND AND A WIFE
SET
THWACK!

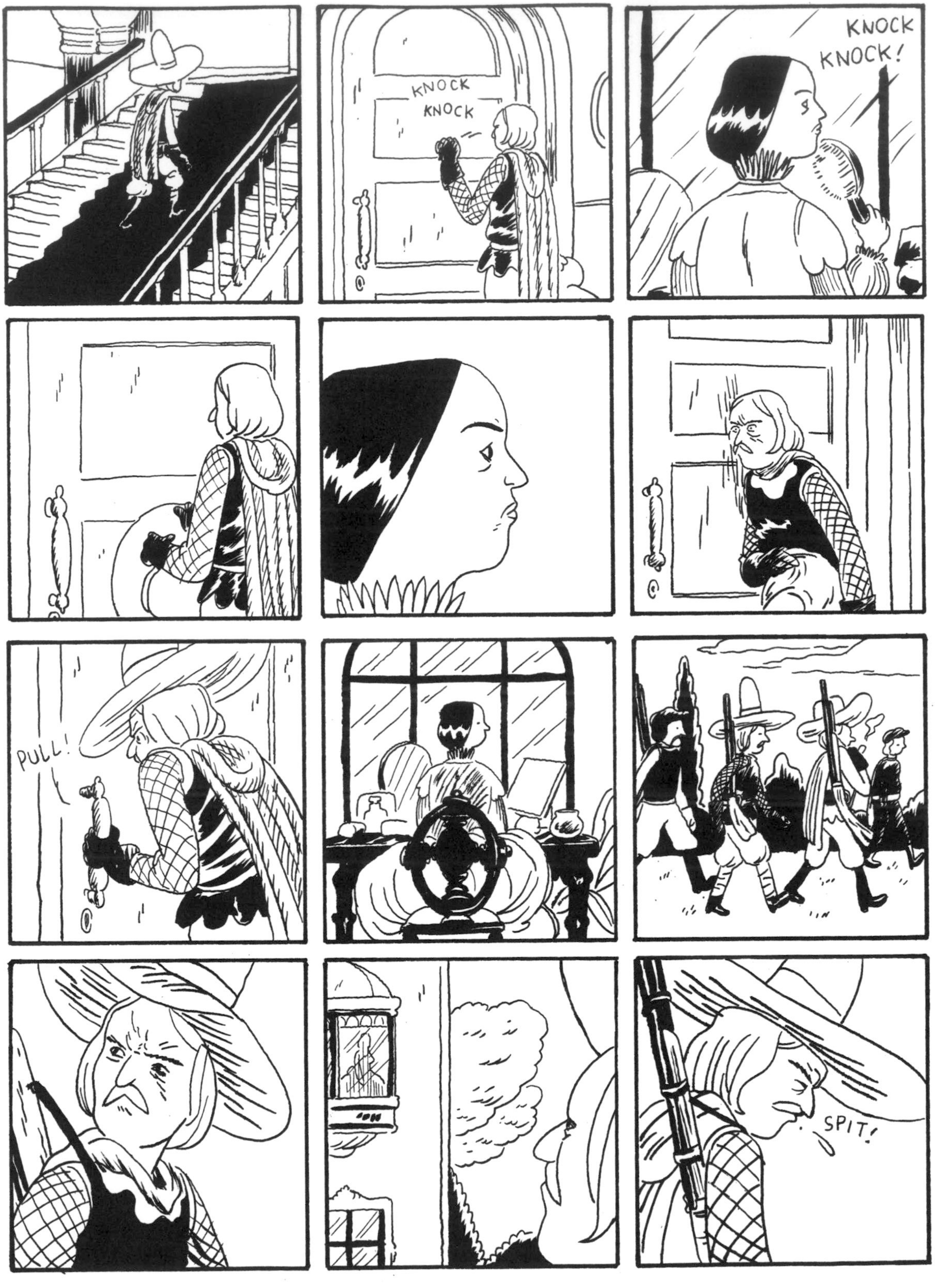
KNOCK
KNOCK
KNOCK
KNOCK!
PULL!
SPIT!

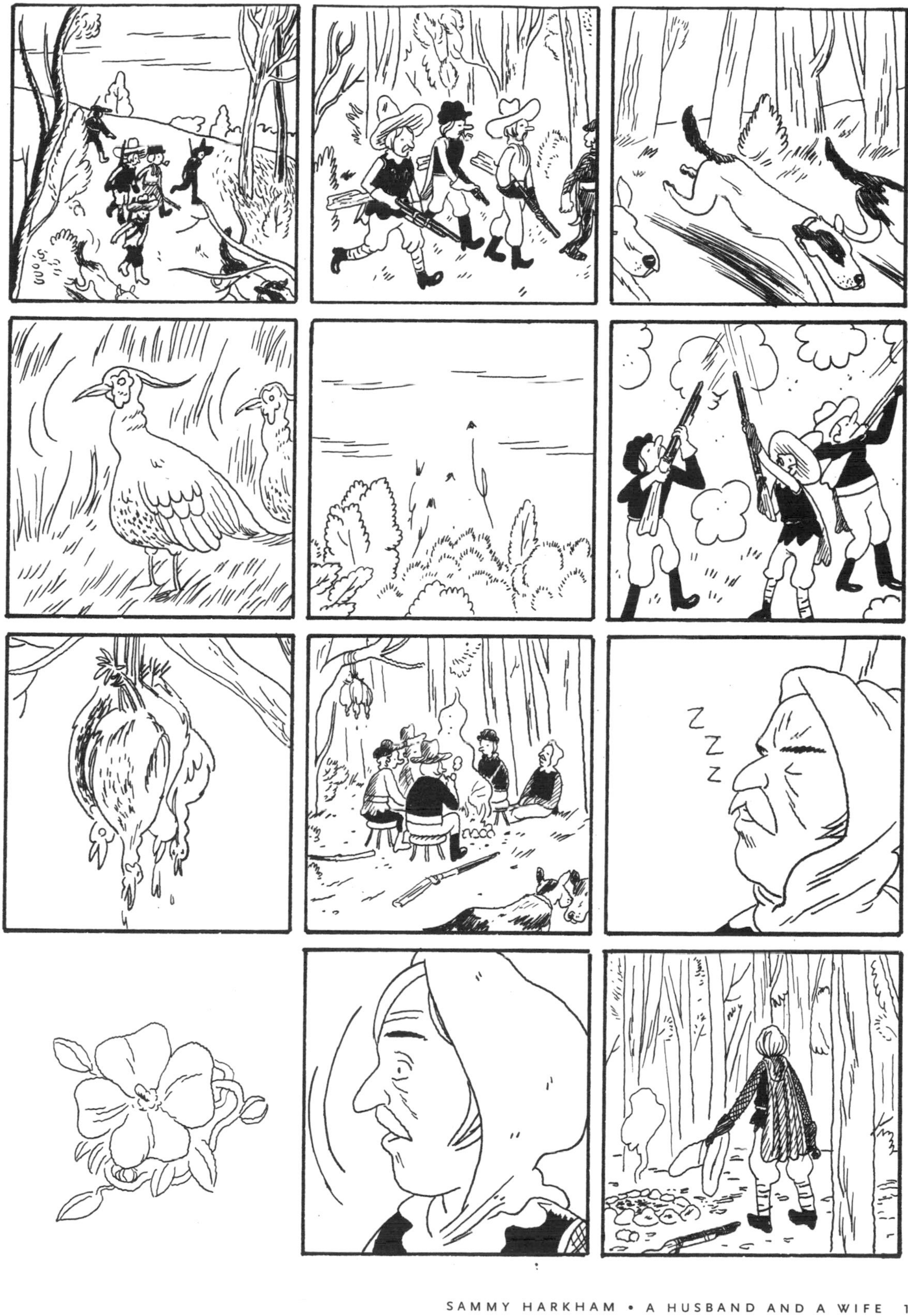
Z
Z
Z

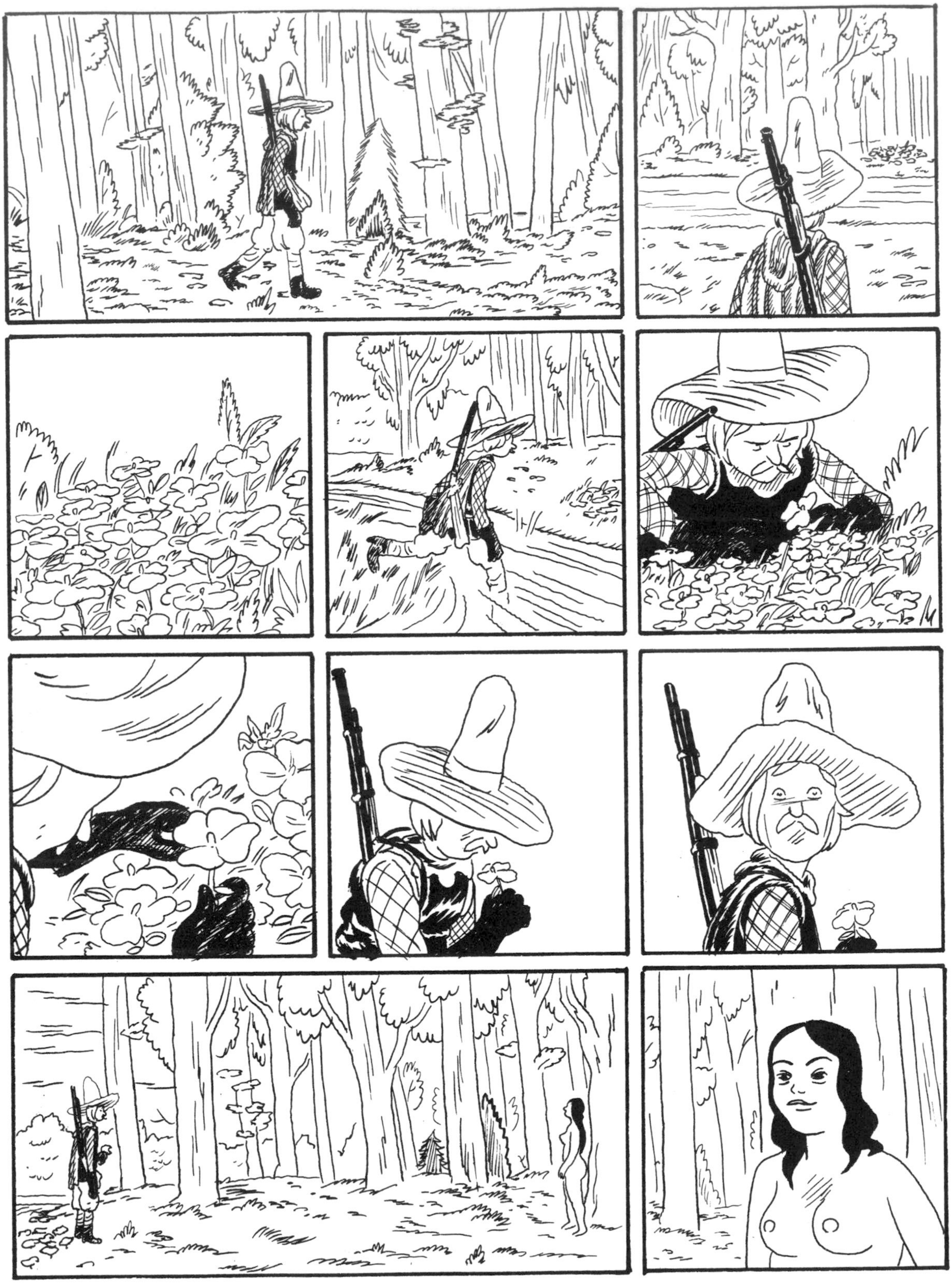

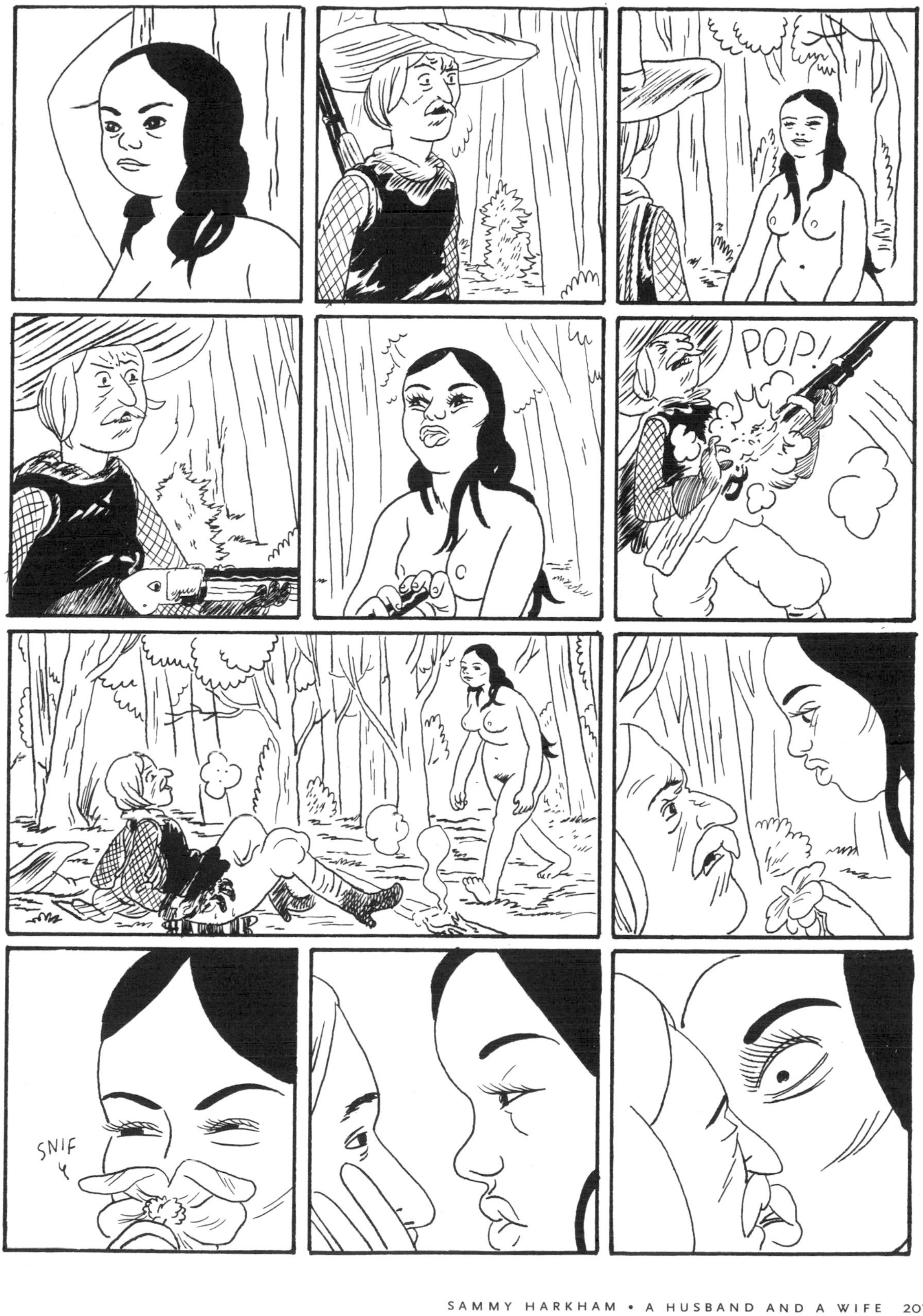
POP!
SNIF

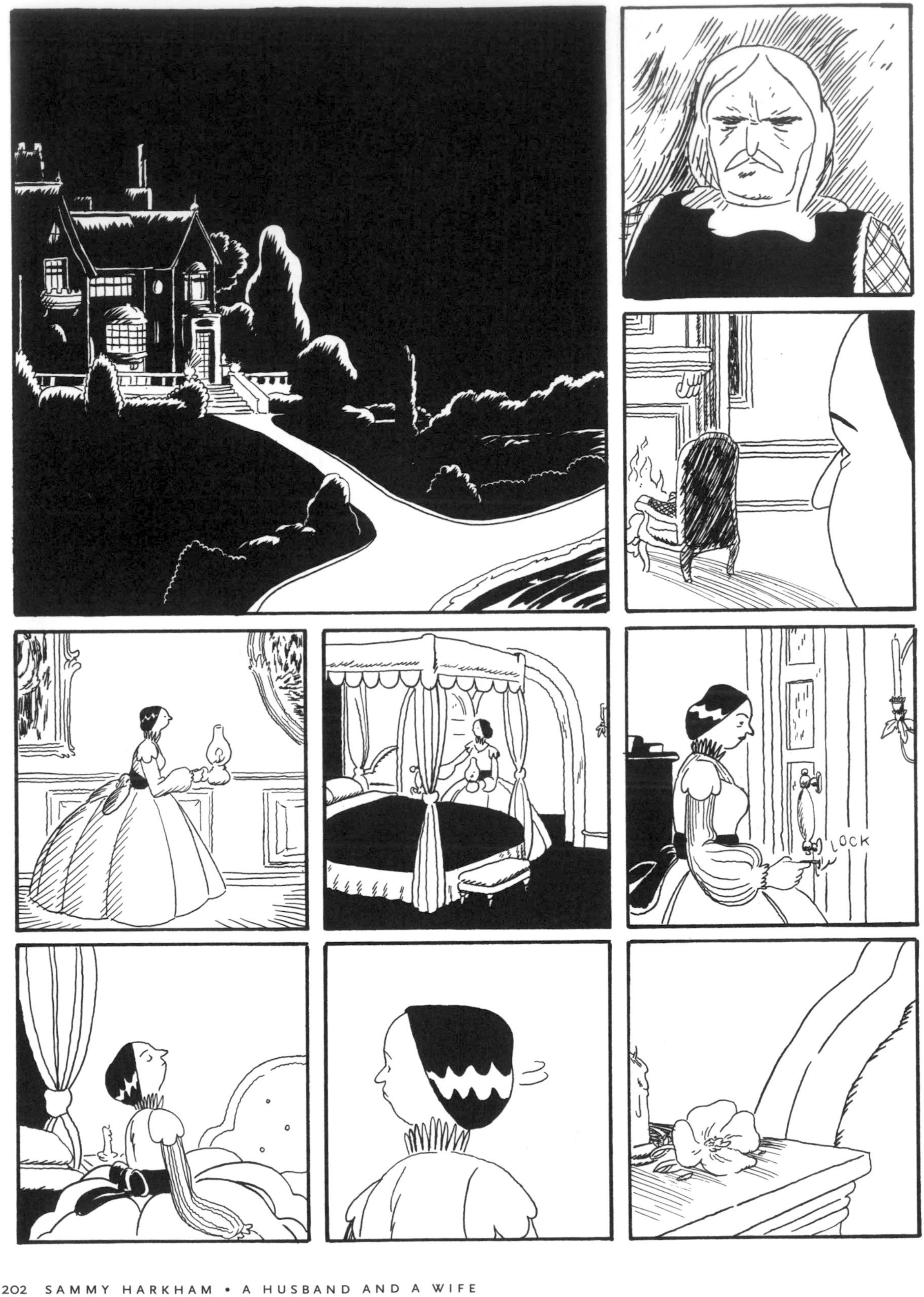
LOCK

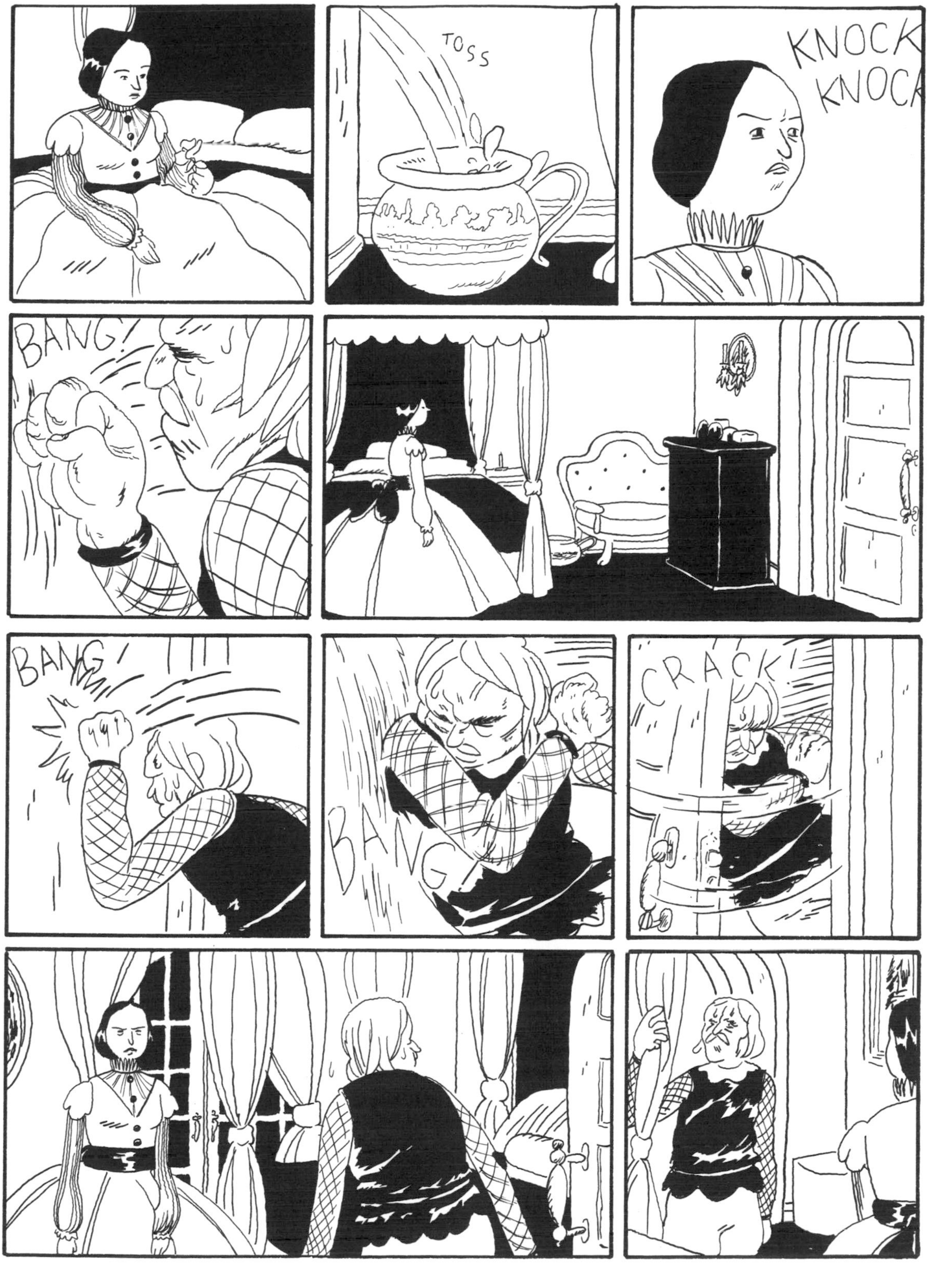
TOSS
KNOCK KNOCK
BANG!
BANG!
BANG
CRACK!

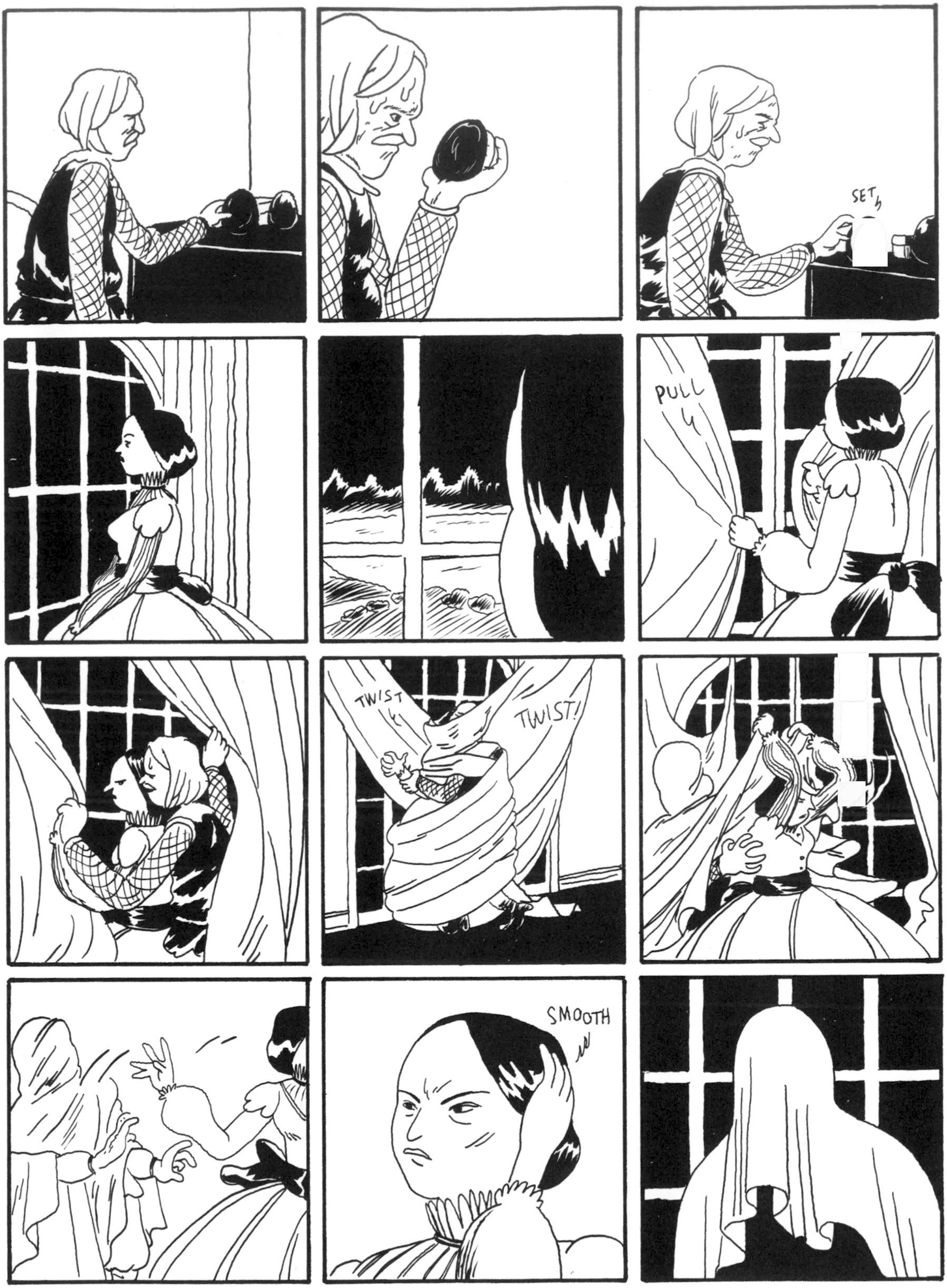
SET
PULL
TWIST
TWIST!
SMOOTH

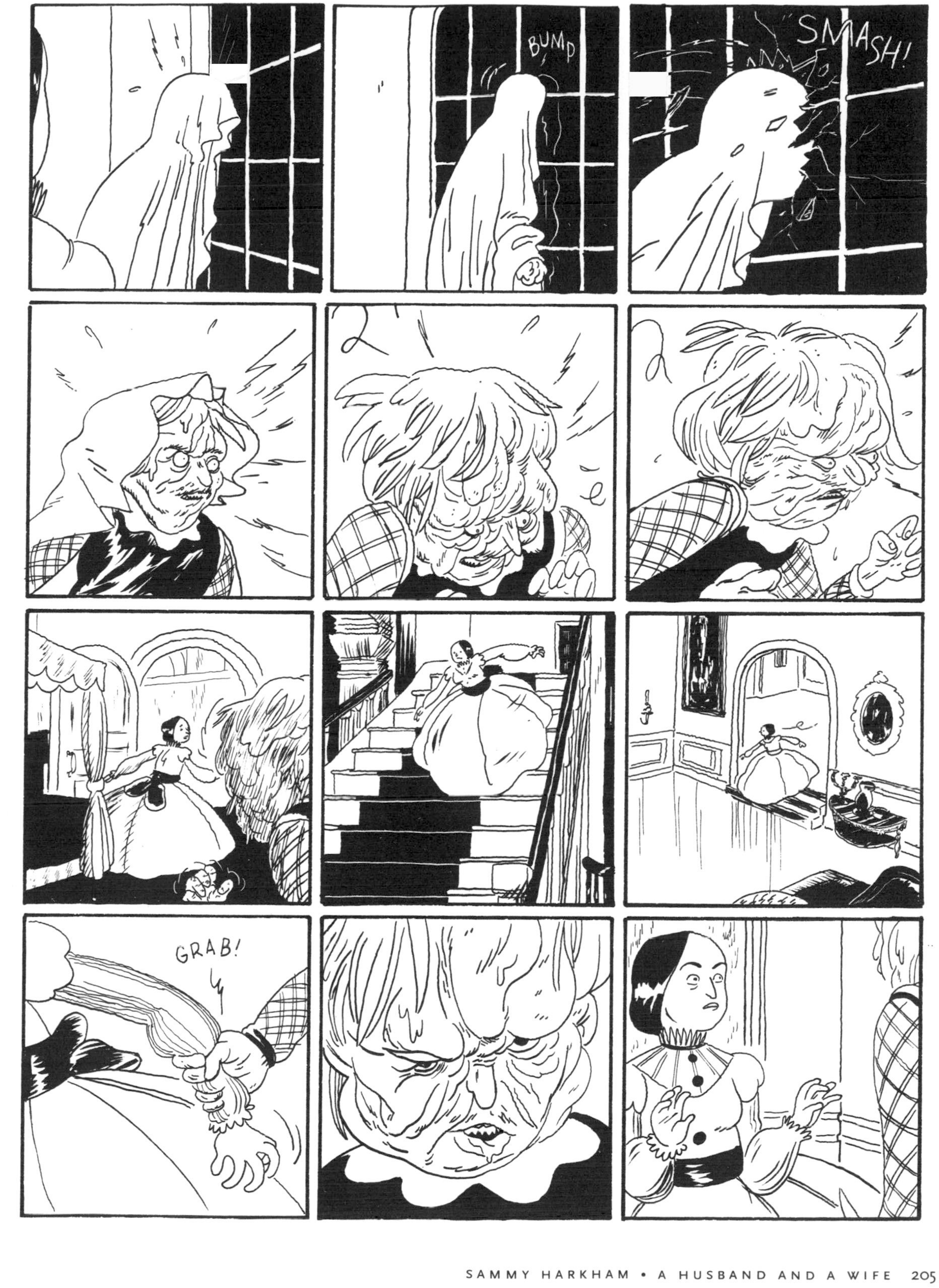
BUMP
SMASH!
GRAB!

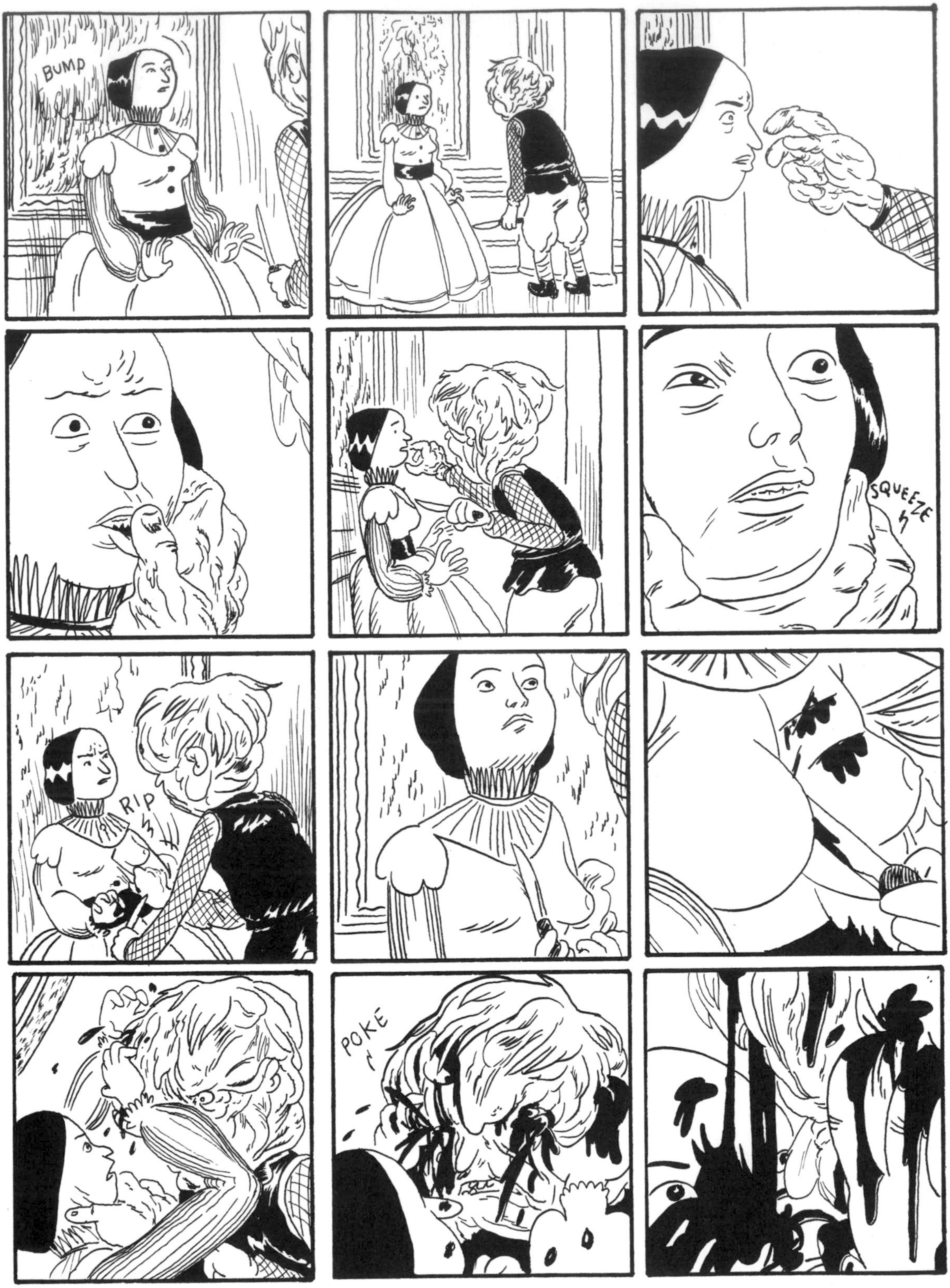
BUMP
SQUEEZE
RIP
POKE

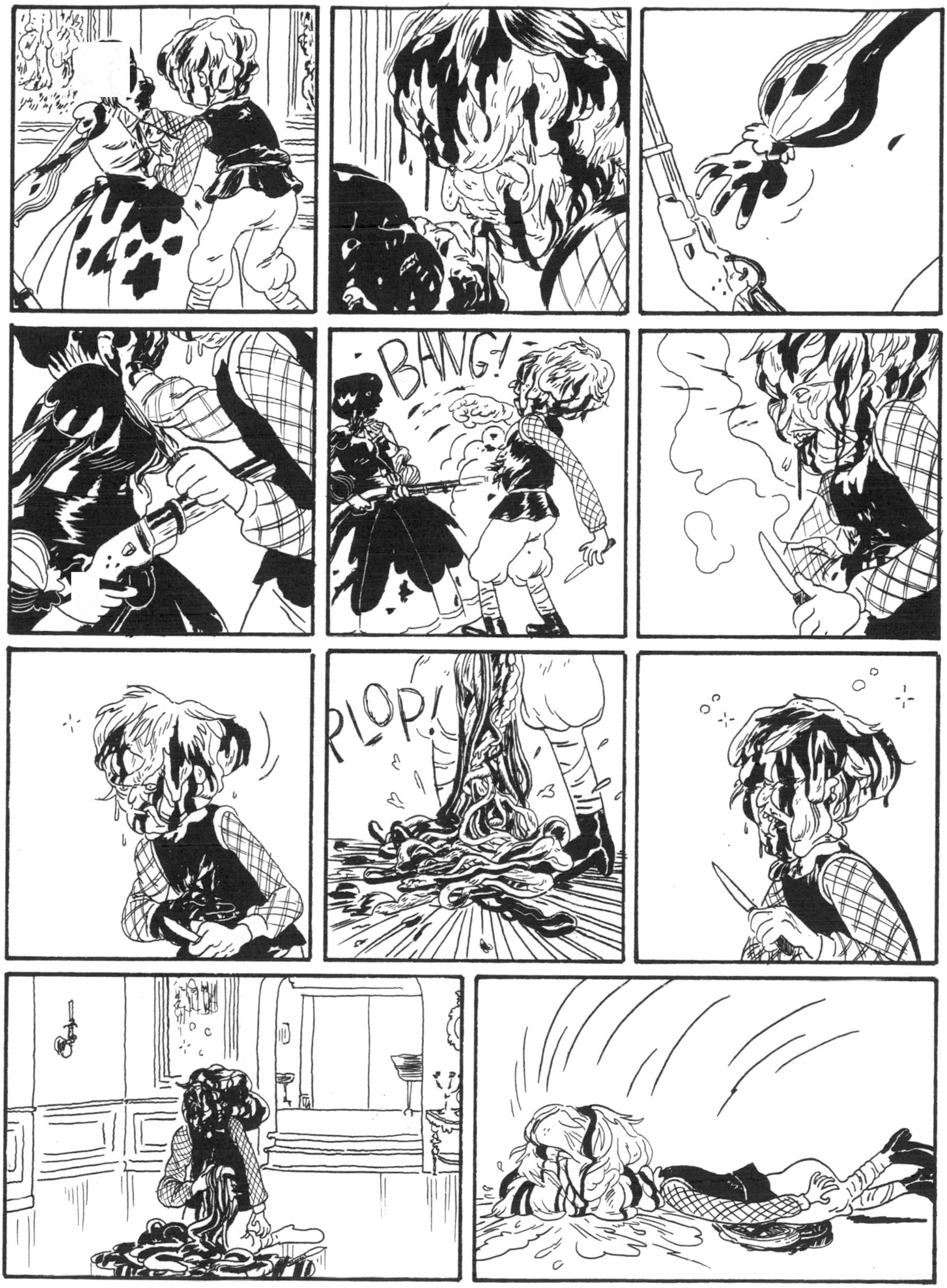
BANG!
PLOP!

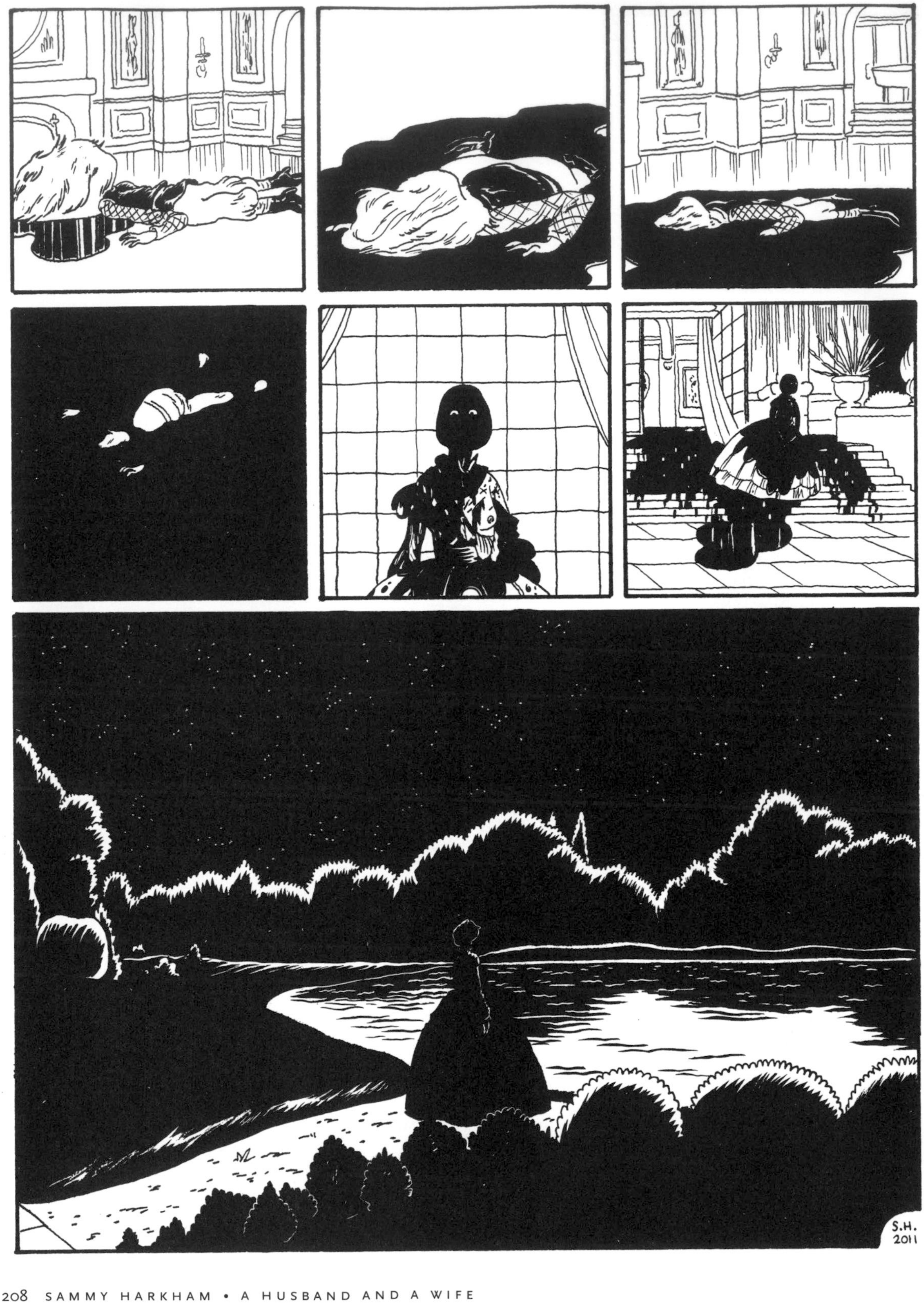
S.H.
2011

GRANT SNIDER

FOUR COMICS

FROM INCIDENTALCOMICS.COM

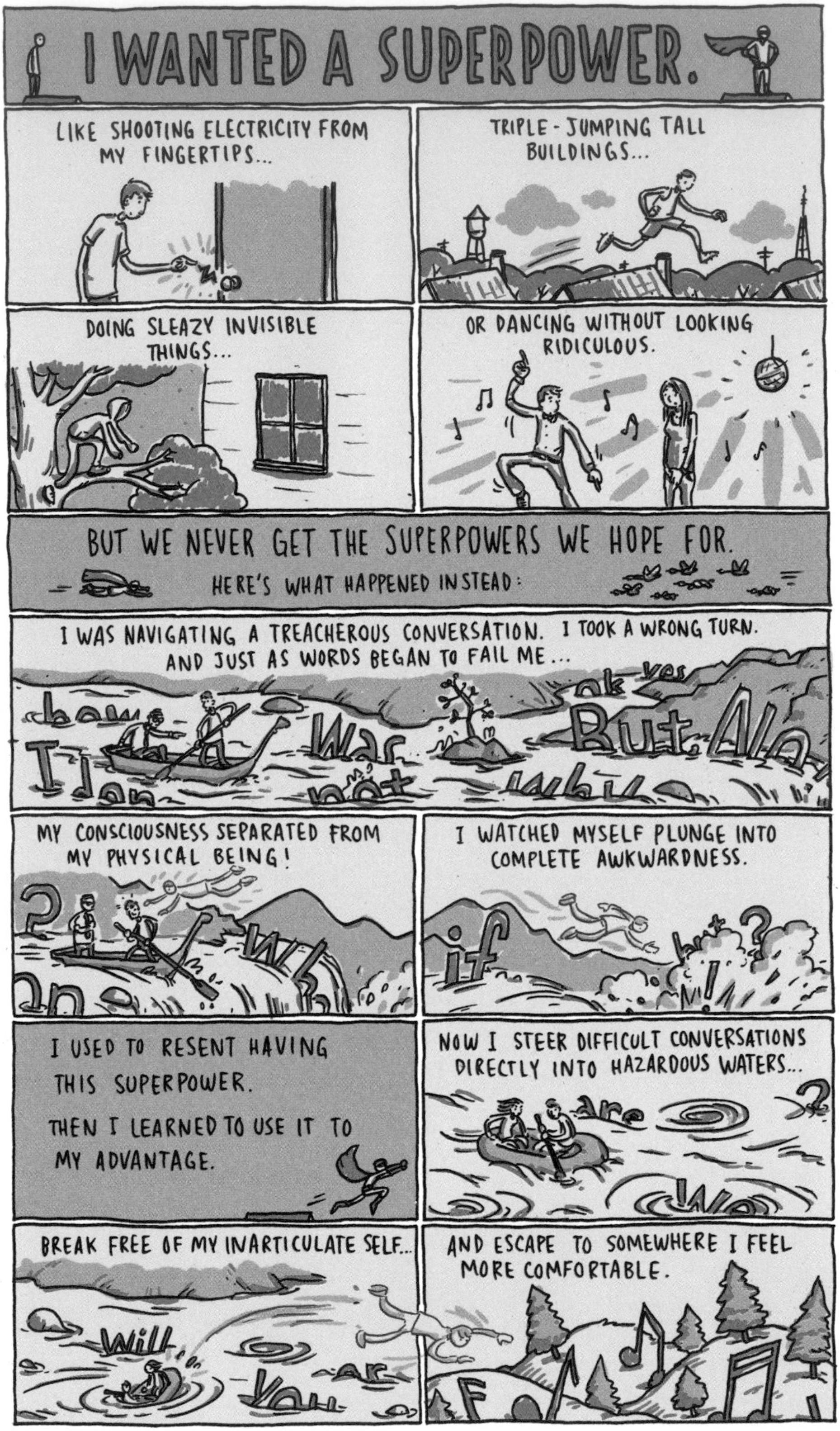
I WANTED A SUPERPOWER.
LIKE SHOOTING ELECTRICITY FROM MY FINGERTIPS...
TRIPLE-JUMPING TALL BUILDINGS...
DOING SLEAZY INVISIBLE THINGS...
OR DANCING WITHOUT LOOKING RIDICULOUS.
BUT WE NEVER GET THE SUPERPOWERS WE HOPE FOR.
HERE'S WHAT HAPPENED INSTEAD:
I WAS NAVIGATING A TREACHEROUS CONVERSATION. I TOOK A WRONG TURN. AND JUST AS WORDS BEGAN TO FAIL ME...
MY CONSCIOUSNESS SEPARATED FROM MY PHYSICAL BEING!
I WATCHED MYSELF PLUNGE INTO COMPLETE AWKWARDNESS.
I USED TO RESENT HAVING THIS SUPERPOWER.
THEN I LEARNED TO USE IT TO MY ADVANTAGE.
NOW I STEER DIFFICULT CONVERSATIONS DIRECTLY INTO HAZARDOUS WATERS...
BREAK FREE OF MY INARTICULATE SELF...
AND ESCAPE TO SOMEWHERE I FEEL MORE COMFORTABLE.

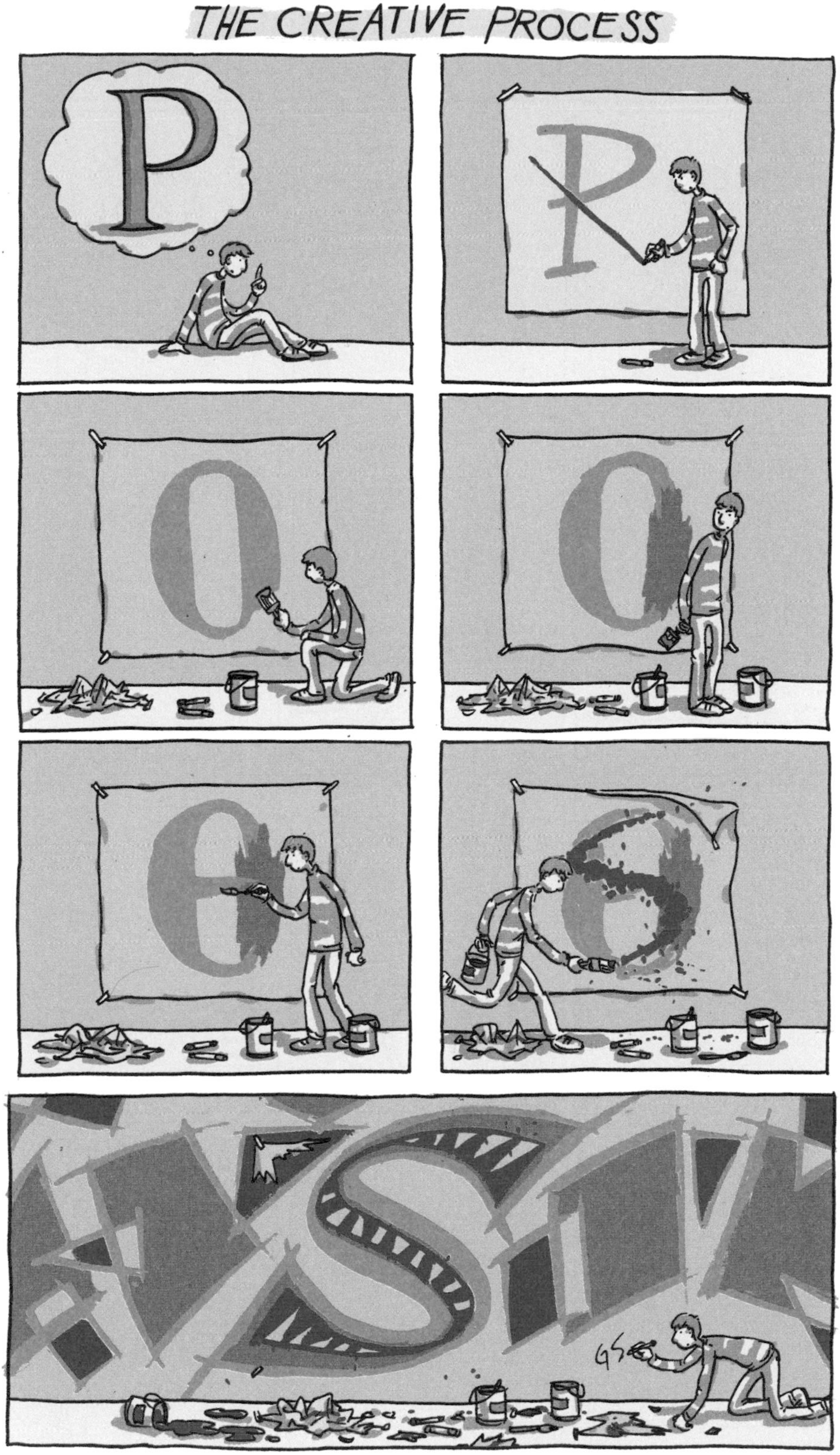
THE CREATIVE PROCESS

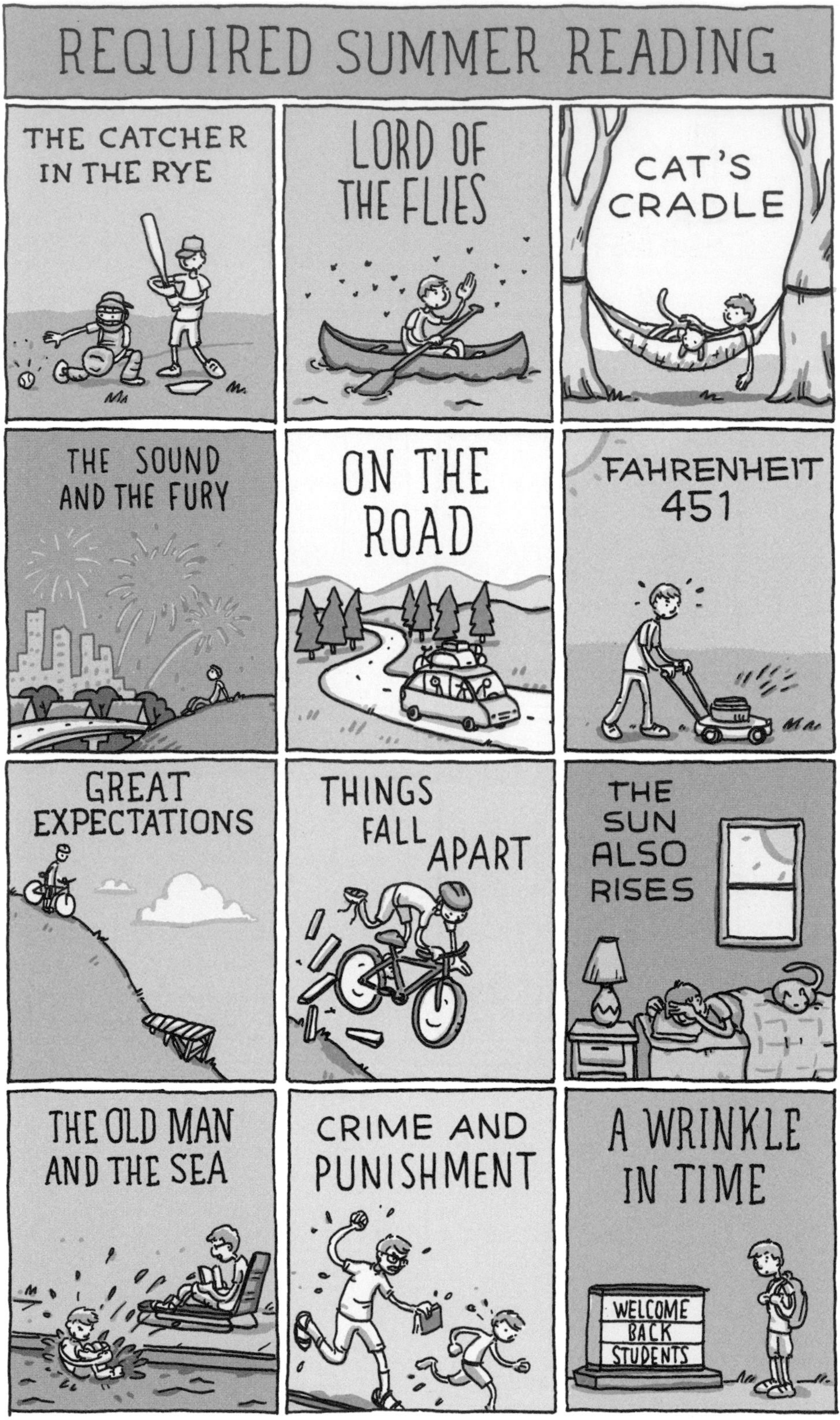
REQUIRED SUMMER READING
THE CATCHER IN THE RYE
LORD OF THE FLIES
CAT'S CRADLE
THE SOUND AND THE FURY
ON THE ROAD
FAHRENHEIT 451
GREAT EXPECTATIONS
THINGS FALL APART
THE SUN ALSO RISES
THE OLD MAN AND THE SEA
CRIME AND PUNISHMENT
A WRINKLE IN TIME
WELCOME BACK STUDENTS

SUMMER NIGHT

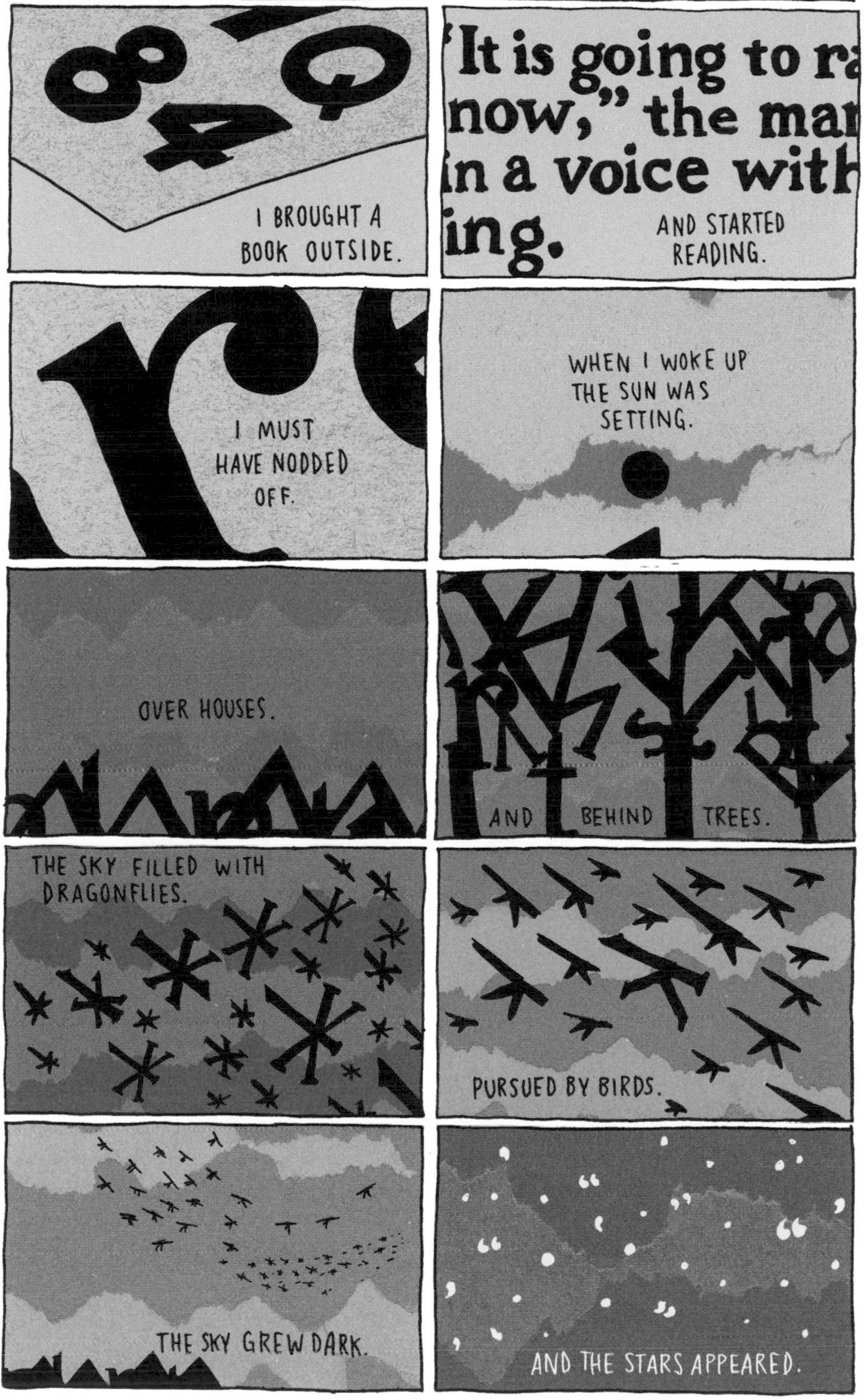
I BROUGHT A BOOK OUTSIDE.
"It is going to ra
now," the mar
in a voice with
ing.
AND STARTED READING.
I MUST HAVE NODDED OFF.
WHEN I WOKE UP THE SUN WAS SETTING.
OVER HOUSES.
AND BEHIND TREES.
THE SKY FILLED WITH DRAGONFLIES.
PURSUED BY BIRDS.
THE SKY GREW DARK.
AND THE STARS APPEARED.

ELEANOR DAVIS

NITA GOES HOME

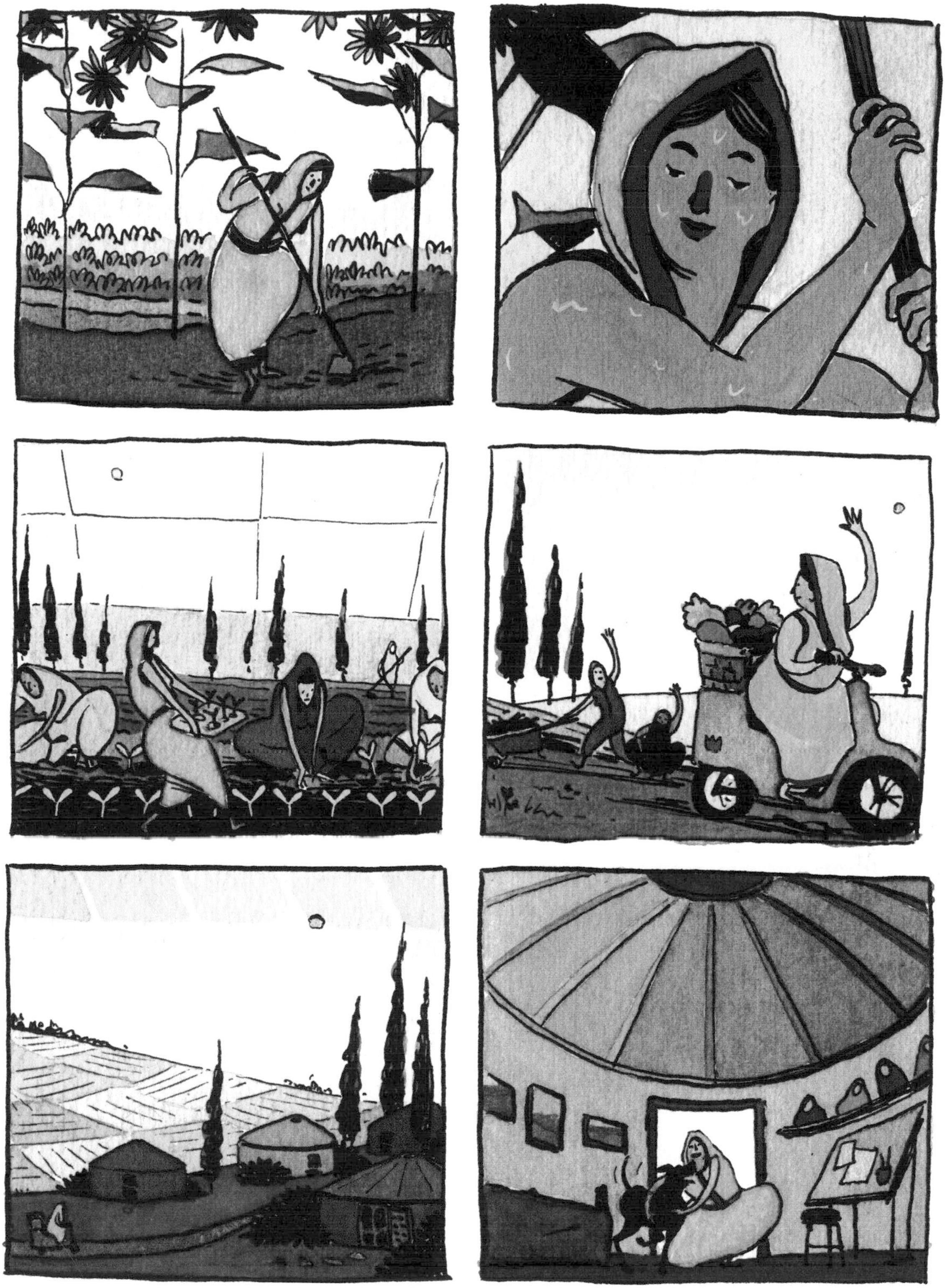

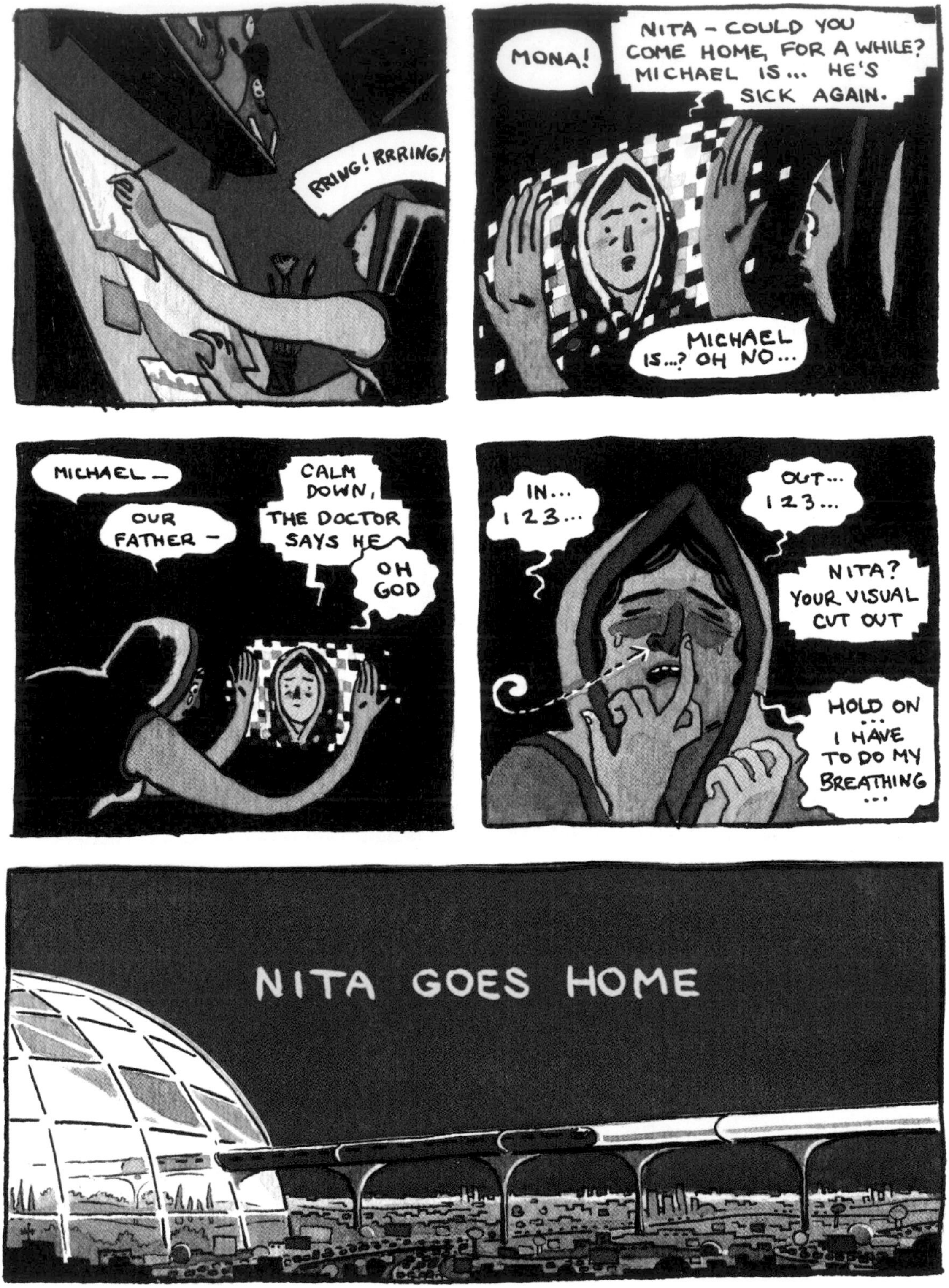
RRING! RRRING!
MONA!
NITA - COULD YOU COME HOME, FOR A WHILE? MICHAEL IS... HE'S SICK AGAIN.
MICHAEL IS...? OH NO...
MICHAEL—
OUR FATHER —
CALM DOWN, THE DOCTOR SAYS HE
OH GOD
IN... 1 2 3...
OUT... 1 2 3...
NITA? YOUR VISUAL CUT OUT
HOLD ON ... I HAVE TO DO MY BREATHING ...
NITA GOES HOME

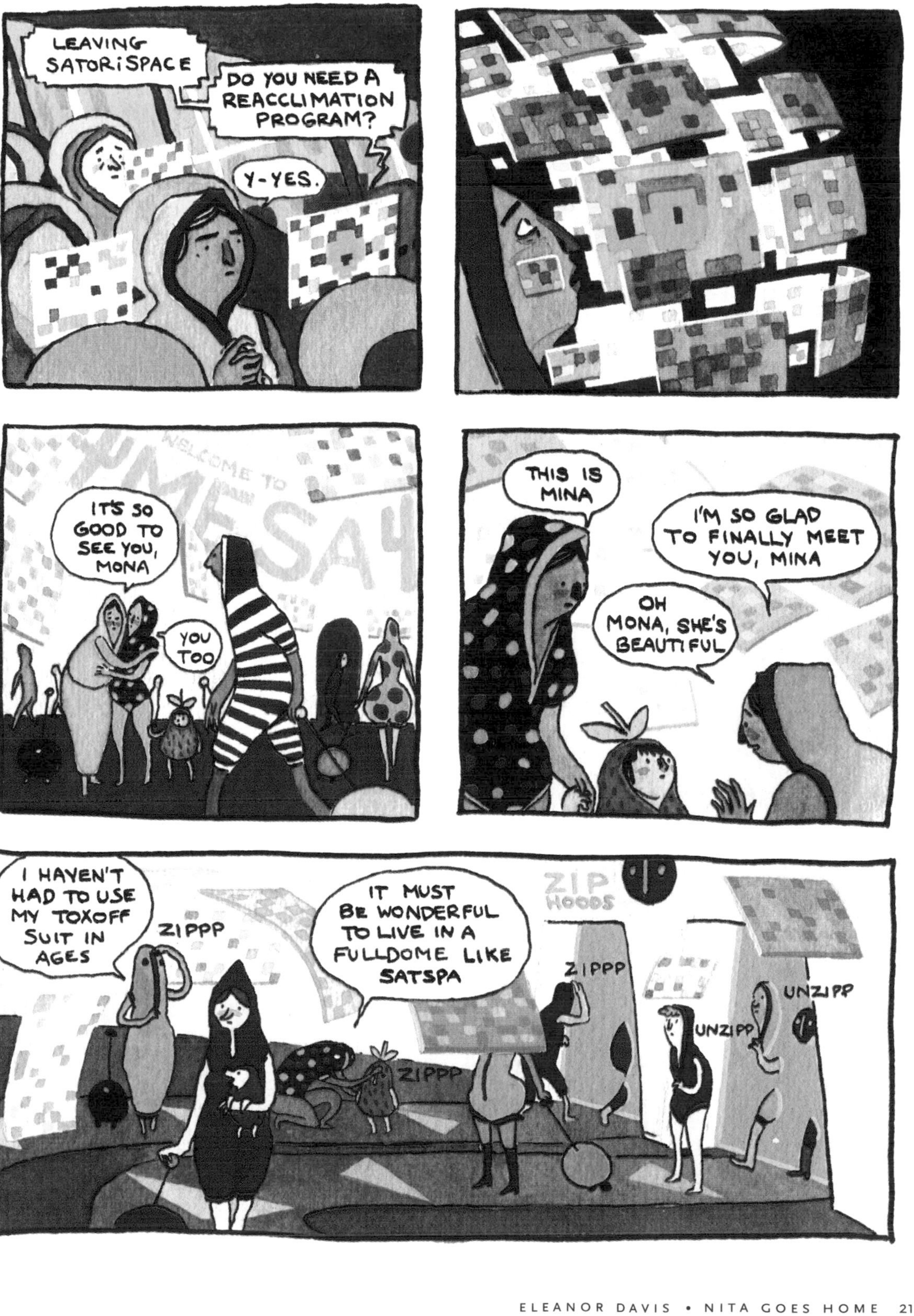
LEAVING SATORISPACE
DO YOU NEED A REACCLIMATION PROGRAM?
Y-YES.
WELCOME TO MESA4
IT'S SO GOOD TO SEE YOU, MONA
YOU TOO
THIS IS MINA
I'M SO GLAD TO FINALLY MEET YOU, MINA
OH MONA, SHE'S BEAUTIFUL
I HAVEN'T HAD TO USE MY TOXOFF SUIT IN AGES
ZIPPP
IT MUST BE WONDERFUL TO LIVE IN A FULLDOME LIKE SATSPA
ZIP HOODS
ZIPPP
ZIPPP
UNZIPP
UNZIPP

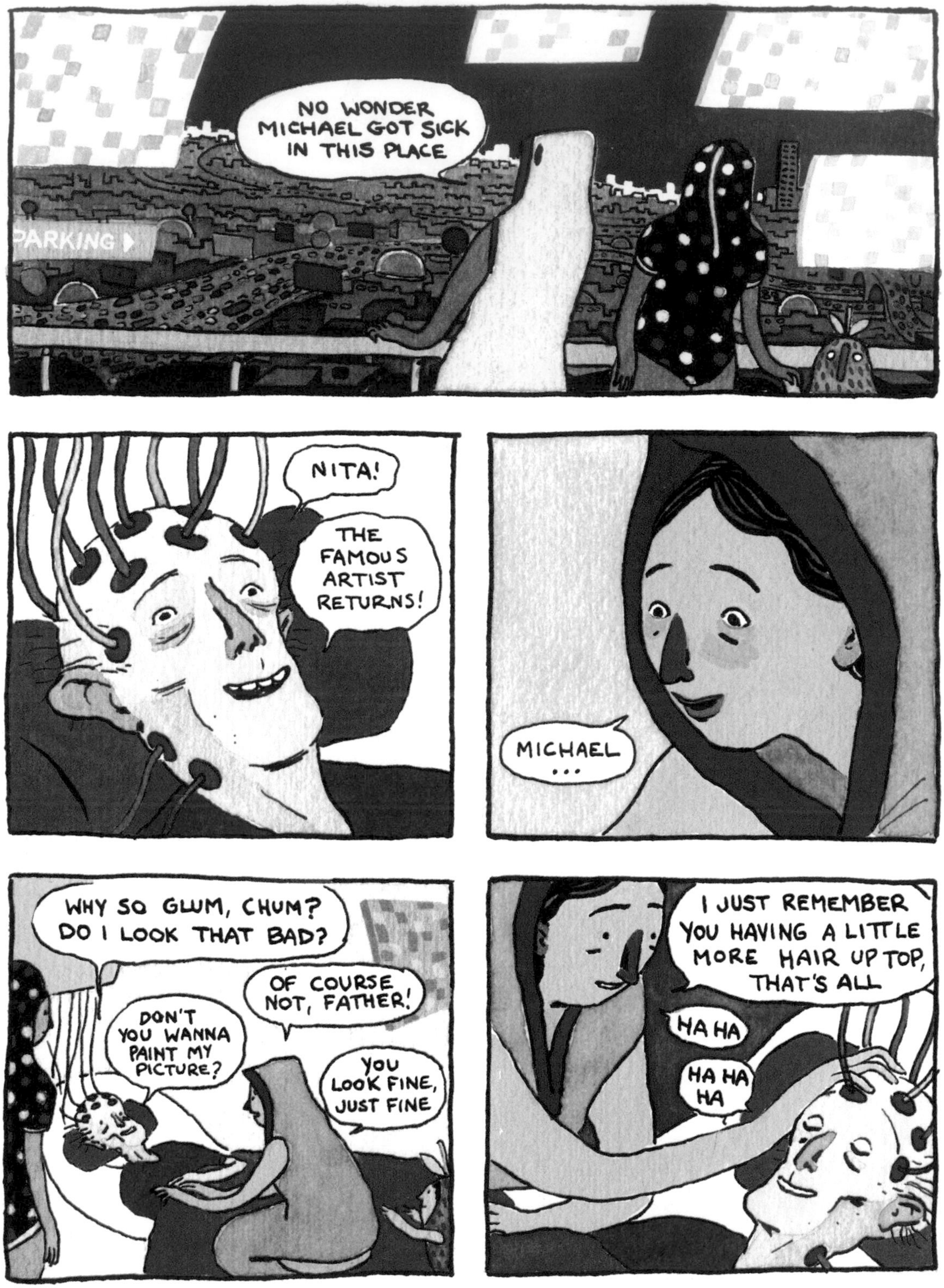
PARKING
NO WONDER MICHAEL GOT SICK IN THIS PLACE
NITA!
THE FAMOUS ARTIST RETURNS!
MICHAEL ...
WHY SO GLUM, CHUM? DO I LOOK THAT BAD?
OF COURSE NOT, FATHER!
DON'T YOU WANNA PAINT MY PICTURE?
YOU LOOK FINE, JUST FINE
I JUST REMEMBER YOU HAVING A LITTLE MORE HAIR UP TOP, THAT'S ALL
HA HA
HA HA HA

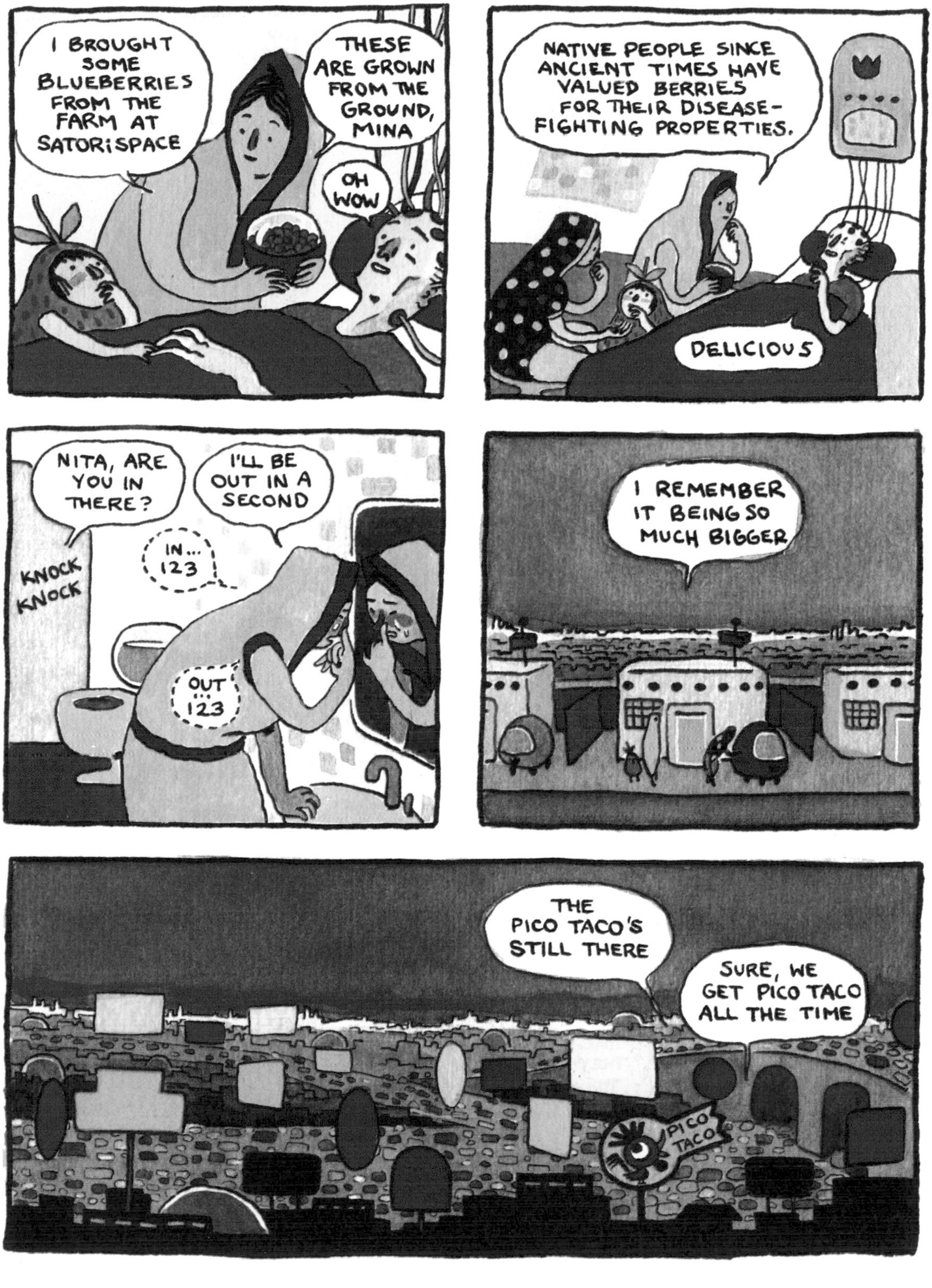

I BROUGHT SOME BLUEBERRIES FROM THE FARM AT SATORiSPACE
THESE ARE GROWN FROM THE GROUND, MINA
OH WOW
NATIVE PEOPLE SINCE ANCIENT TIMES HAVE VALUED BERRIES FOR THEIR DISEASE-FIGHTING PROPERTIES.
DELICIOUS
NITA, ARE YOU IN THERE?
I'LL BE OUT IN A SECOND
KNOCK KNOCK
IN... 123
OUT ... 123
I REMEMBER IT BEING SO MUCH BIGGER
THE PICO TACO'S STILL THERE
SURE, WE GET PICO TACO ALL THE TIME
PICO TACO

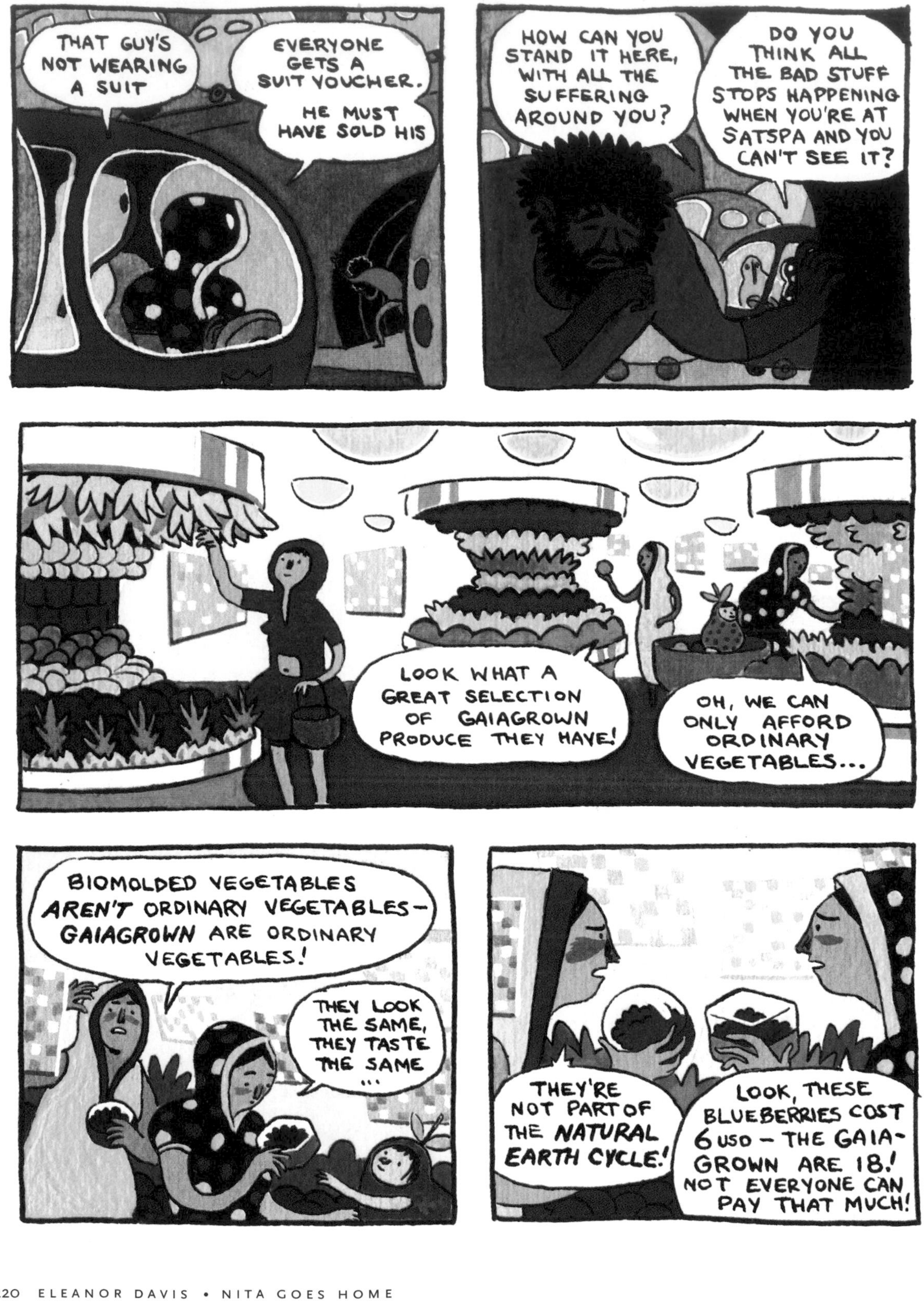
THAT GUY'S NOT WEARING A SUIT
EVERYONE GETS A SUIT VOUCHER.
HE MUST HAVE SOLD HIS
HOW CAN YOU STAND IT HERE, WITH ALL THE SUFFERING AROUND YOU?
DO YOU THINK ALL THE BAD STUFF STOPS HAPPENING WHEN YOU'RE AT SATSPA AND YOU CAN'T SEE IT?
LOOK WHAT A GREAT SELECTION OF GAIAGROWN PRODUCE THEY HAVE!
OH, WE CAN ONLY AFFORD ORDINARY VEGETABLES...
BIOMOLDED VEGETABLES *AREN'T* ORDINARY VEGETABLES— *GAIAGROWN* ARE ORDINARY VEGETABLES!
THEY LOOK THE SAME, THEY TASTE THE SAME ...
THEY'RE NOT PART OF THE *NATURAL EARTH CYCLE!*
LOOK, THESE BLUEBERRIES COST 6 USD — THE GAIA-GROWN ARE 18! NOT EVERYONE CAN PAY THAT MUCH!

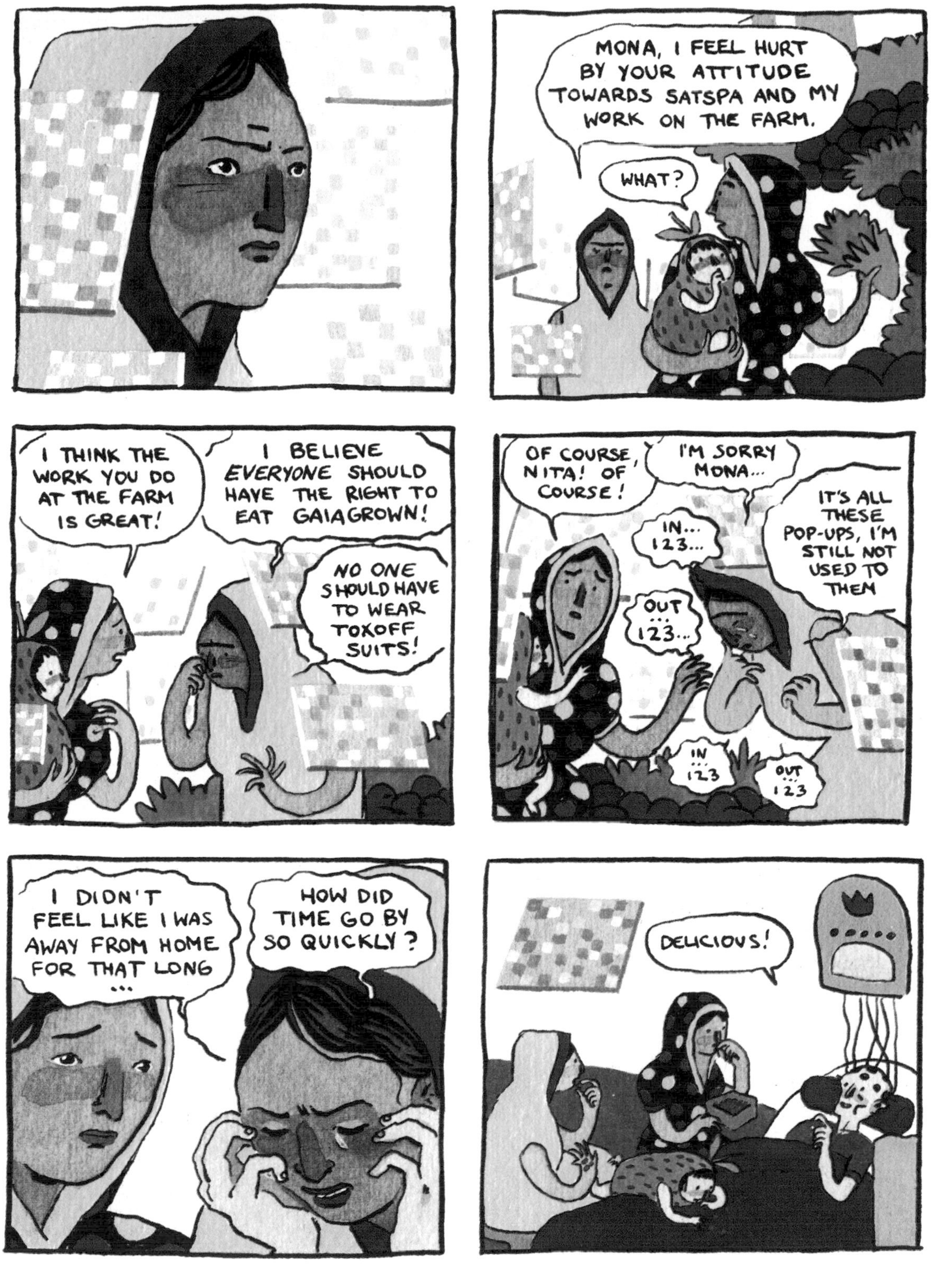

MONA, I FEEL HURT BY YOUR ATTITUDE TOWARDS SATSPA AND MY WORK ON THE FARM.
WHAT?
I THINK THE WORK YOU DO AT THE FARM IS GREAT!
I BELIEVE *EVERYONE* SHOULD HAVE THE RIGHT TO EAT GAIAGROWN!
NO ONE SHOULD HAVE TO WEAR TOXOFF SUITS!
OF COURSE, NITA! OF COURSE!
I'M SORRY MONA...
IN... 123...
IT'S ALL THESE POP-UPS, I'M STILL NOT USED TO THEM
OUT... 123...
IN... 123
OUT... 123
I DIDN'T FEEL LIKE I WAS AWAY FROM HOME FOR THAT LONG...
HOW DID TIME GO BY SO QUICKLY?
DELICIOUS!

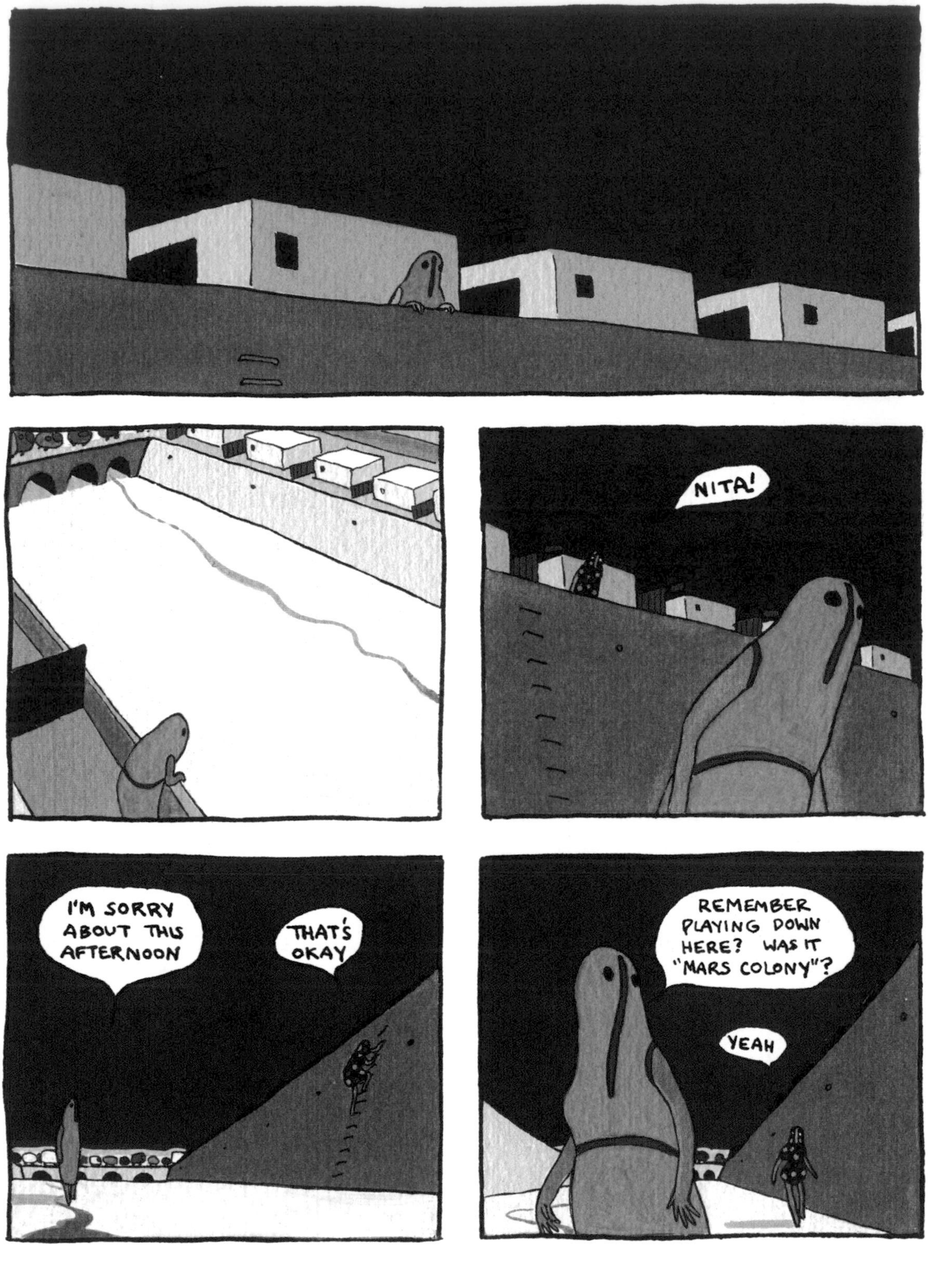
NITA!
I'M SORRY ABOUT THIS AFTERNOON
THAT'S OKAY
REMEMBER PLAYING DOWN HERE? WAS IT "MARS COLONY"?
YEAH

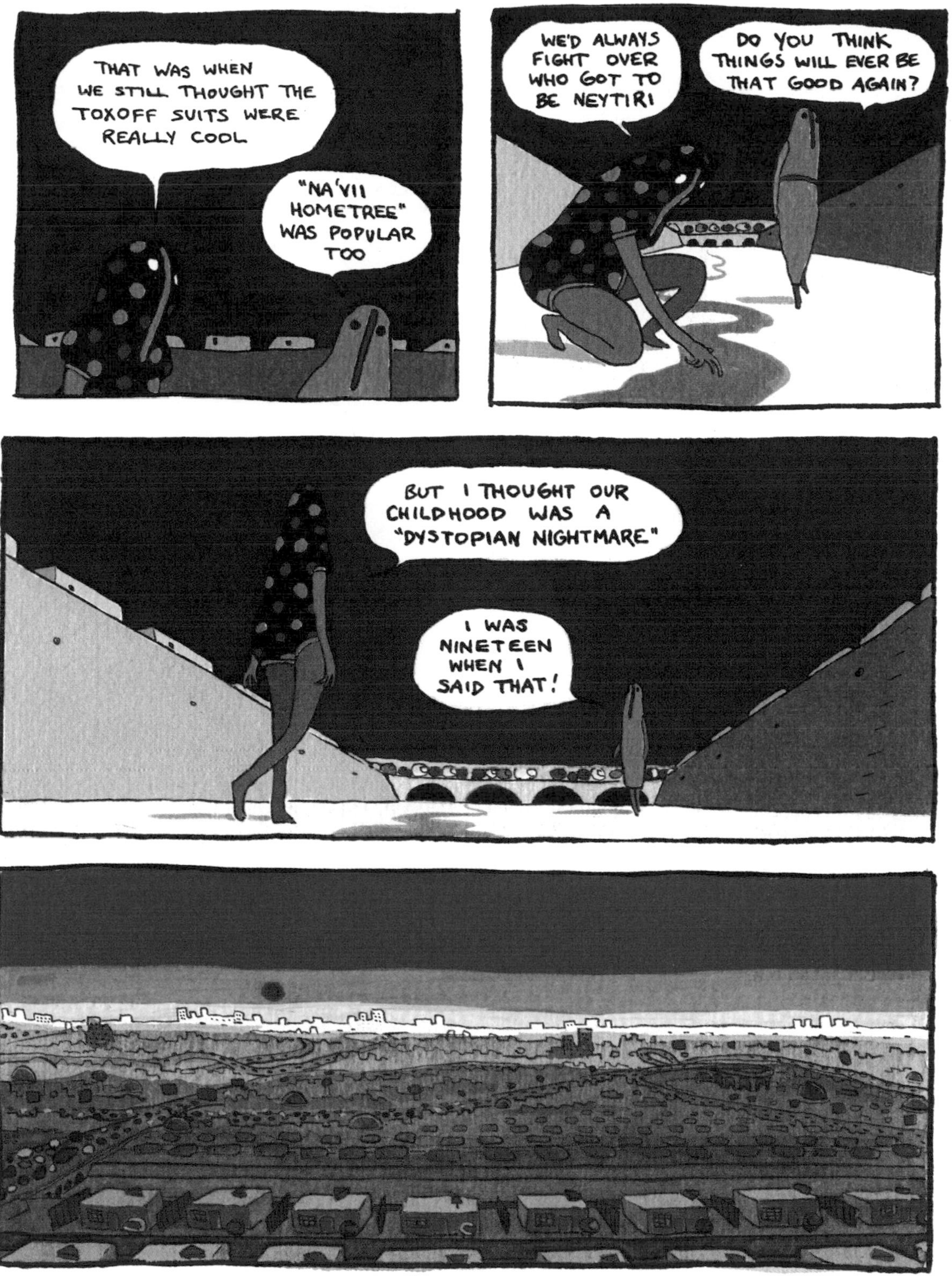
THAT WAS WHEN WE STILL THOUGHT THE TOXOFF SUITS WERE REALLY COOL
"NA'VII HOMETREE" WAS POPULAR TOO
WE'D ALWAYS FIGHT OVER WHO GOT TO BE NEYTIRI
DO YOU THINK THINGS WILL EVER BE THAT GOOD AGAIN?
BUT I THOUGHT OUR CHILDHOOD WAS A "DYSTOPIAN NIGHTMARE"
I WAS NINETEEN WHEN I SAID THAT!

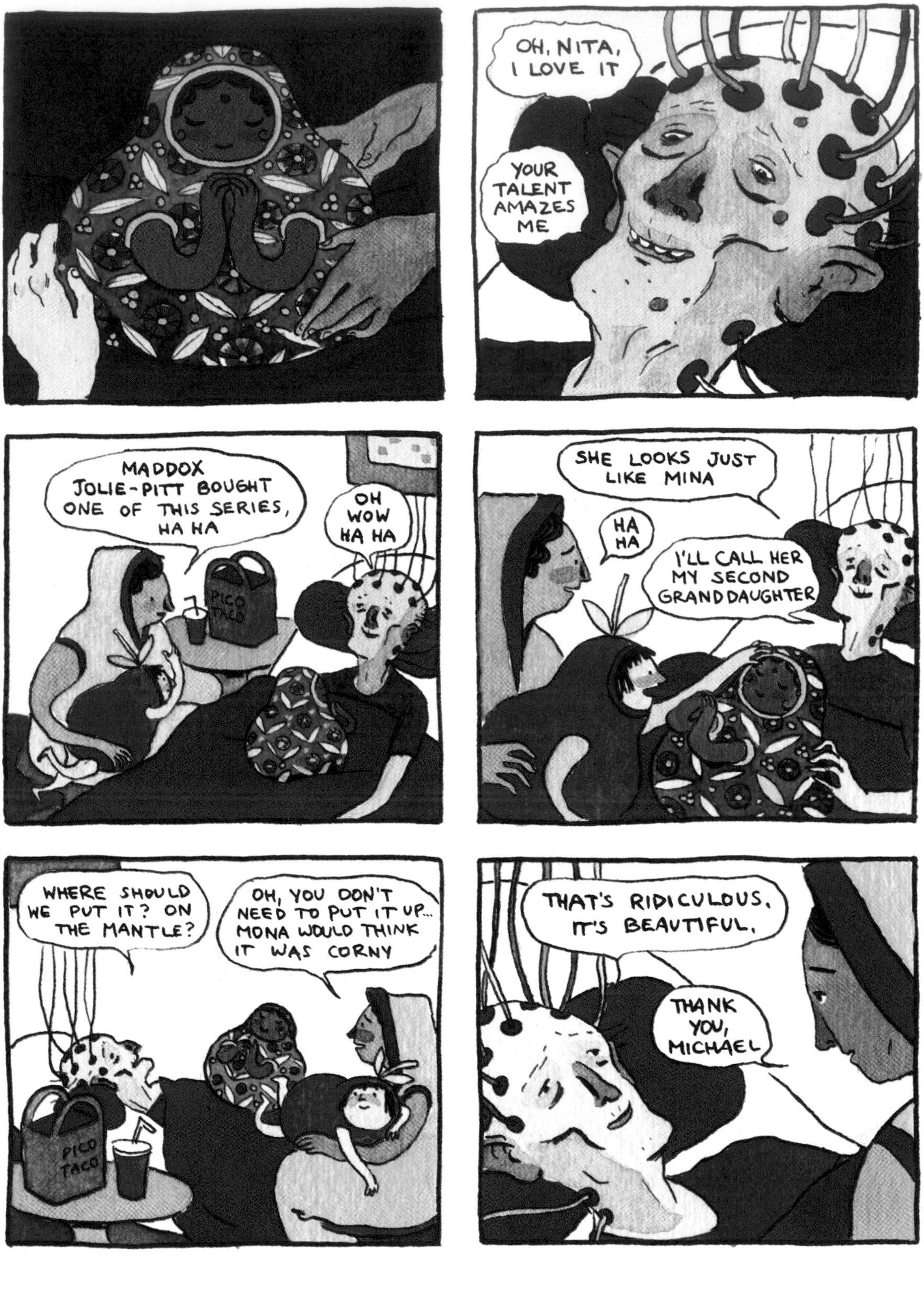

OH, NITA, I LOVE IT
YOUR TALENT AMAZES ME
MADDOX JOLIE-PITT BOUGHT ONE OF THIS SERIES, HA HA
OH WOW HA HA
PICO TACO
SHE LOOKS JUST LIKE MINA
HA HA
I'LL CALL HER MY SECOND GRANDDAUGHTER
WHERE SHOULD WE PUT IT? ON THE MANTLE?
OH, YOU DON'T NEED TO PUT IT UP... MONA WOULD THINK IT WAS CORNY
PICO TACO
THAT'S RIDICULOUS, IT'S BEAUTIFUL,
THANK YOU, MICHAEL

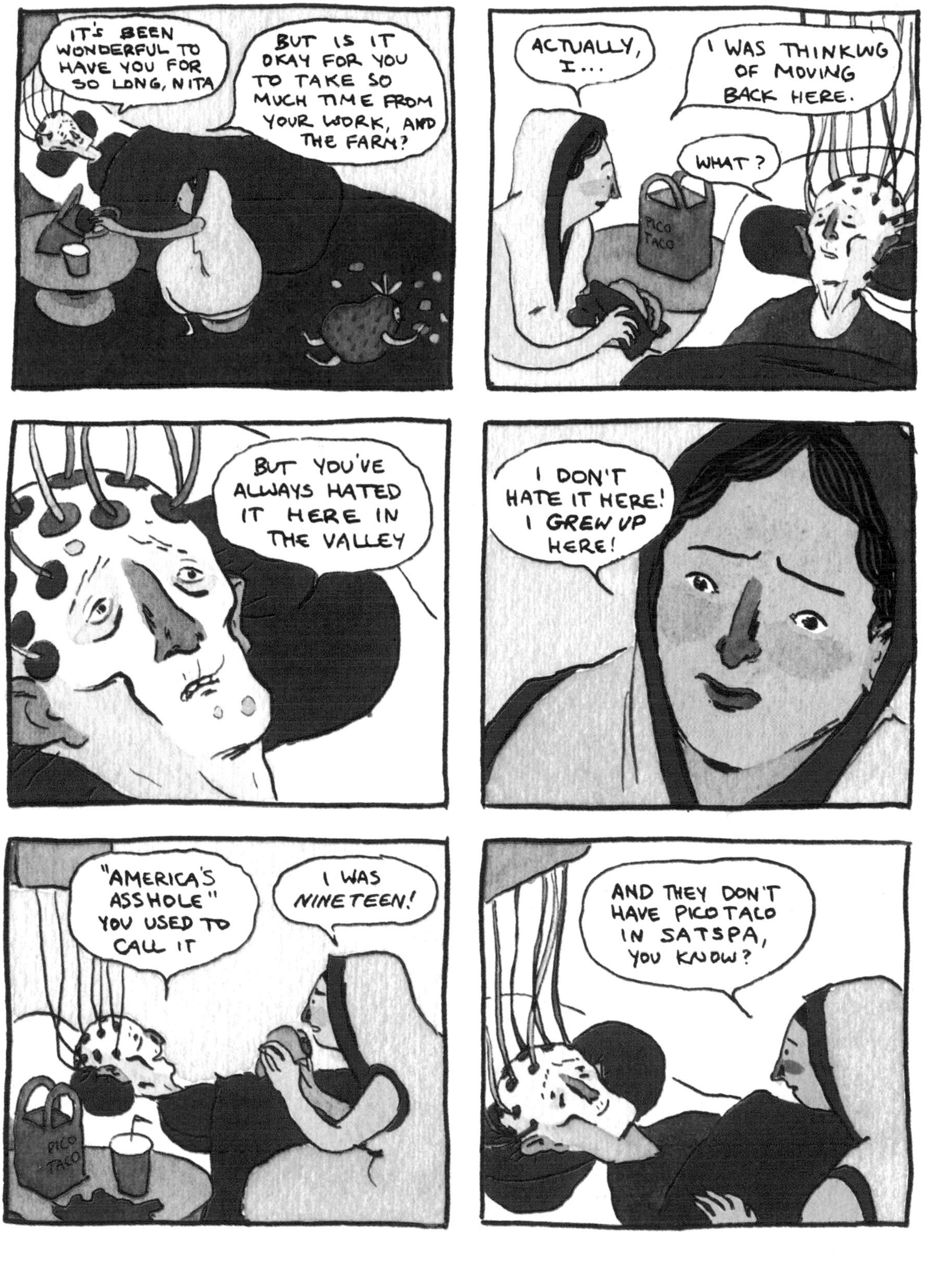
IT'S BEEN WONDERFUL TO HAVE YOU FOR SO LONG, NITA
BUT IS IT OKAY FOR YOU TO TAKE SO MUCH TIME FROM YOUR WORK, AND THE FARM?
ACTUALLY, I...
I WAS THINKWG OF MOVING BACK HERE.
WHAT?
PICO TACO
BUT YOU'VE ALWAYS HATED IT HERE IN THE VALLEY
I DON'T HATE IT HERE! I GREW UP HERE!
"AMERICA'S ASSHOLE" YOU USED TO CALL IT
I WAS NINETEEN!
PICO TACO
AND THEY DON'T HAVE PICO TACO IN SATSPA, YOU KNOW?

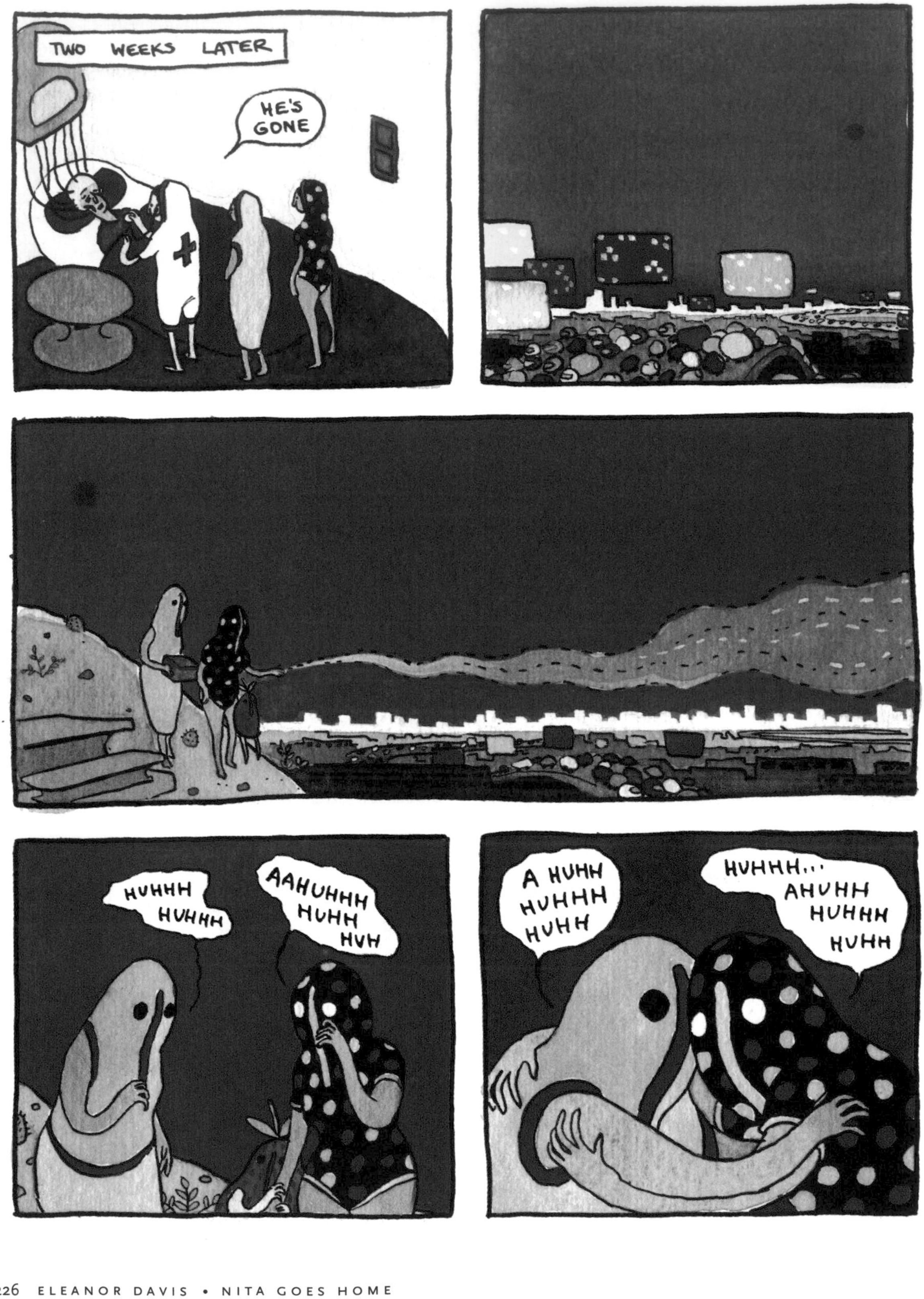
TWO WEEKS LATER
HE'S GONE
HUHHH HUHHH
AAHUHHH HUHH HUH
A HUHH HUHHH HUHH
HUHHH... AHUHH HUHHH HUHH

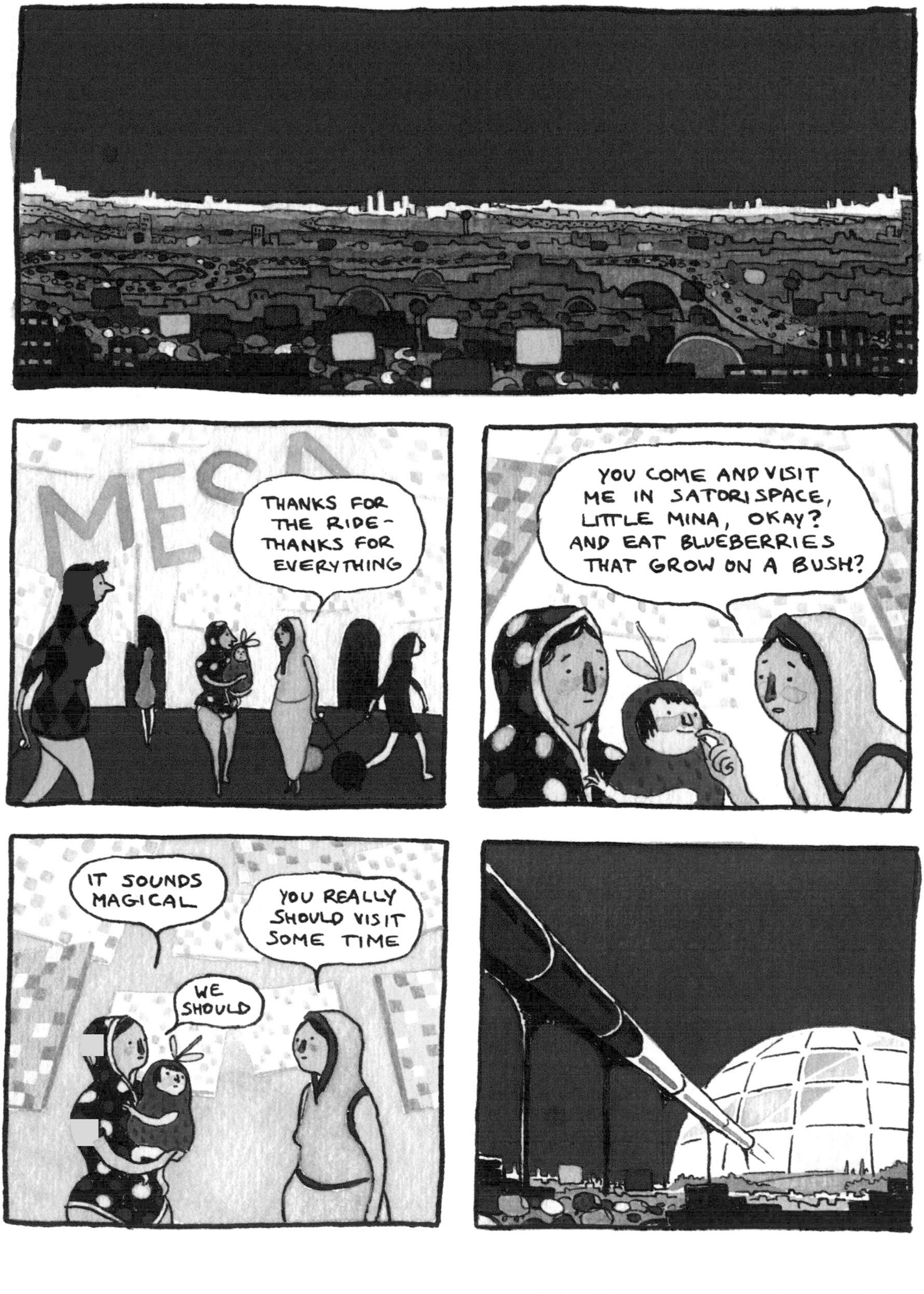
MES
THANKS FOR THE RIDE- THANKS FOR EVERYTHING
YOU COME AND VISIT ME IN SATORISPACE, LITTLE MINA, OKAY? AND EAT BLUEBERRIES THAT GROW ON A BUSH?
IT SOUNDS MAGICAL
YOU REALLY SHOULD VISIT SOME TIME
WE SHOULD

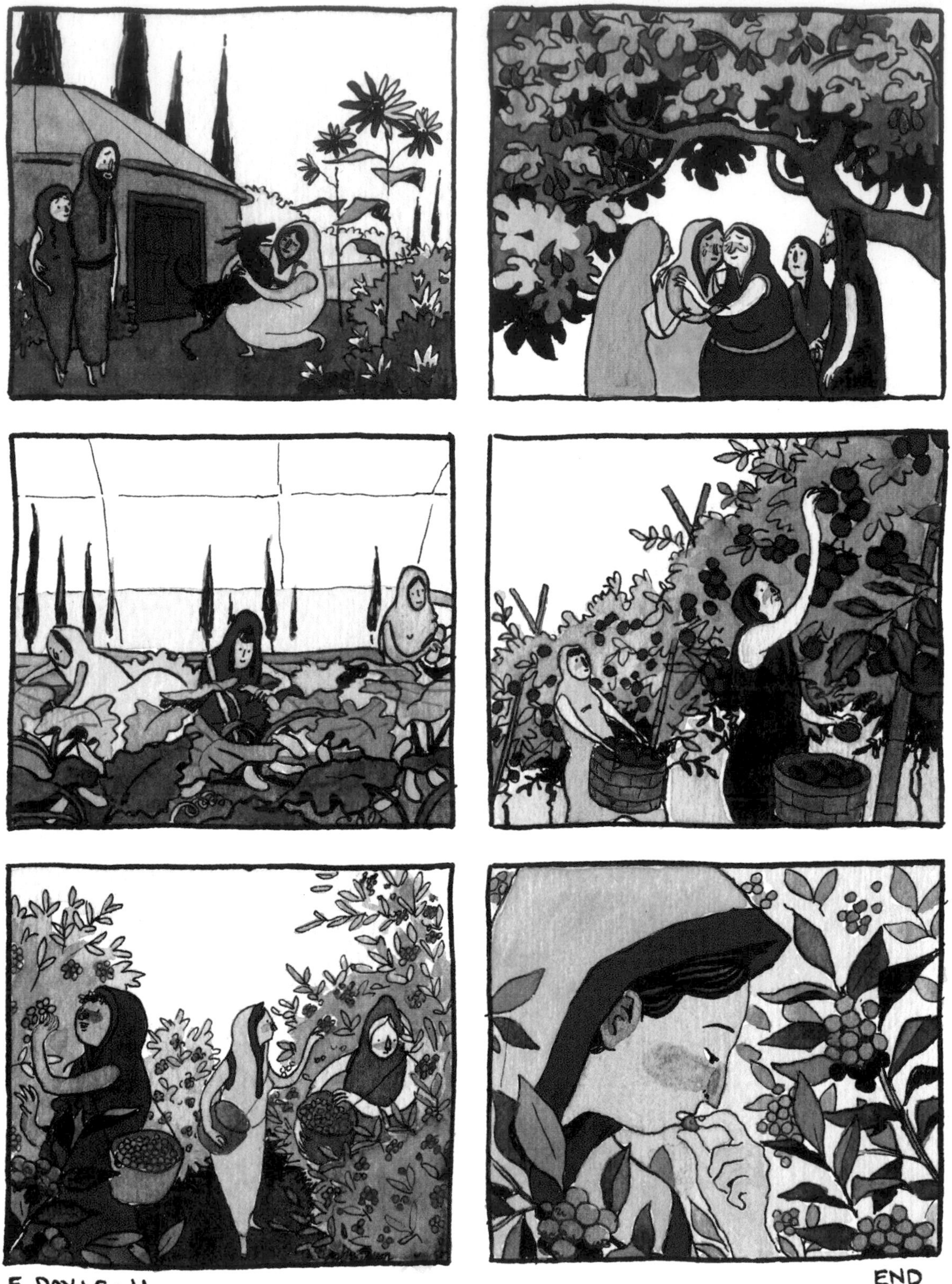
E DAVIS · 11
END

TONY PURYEAR

CONCRETE PARK

BOOK 1: CHAPTER 1

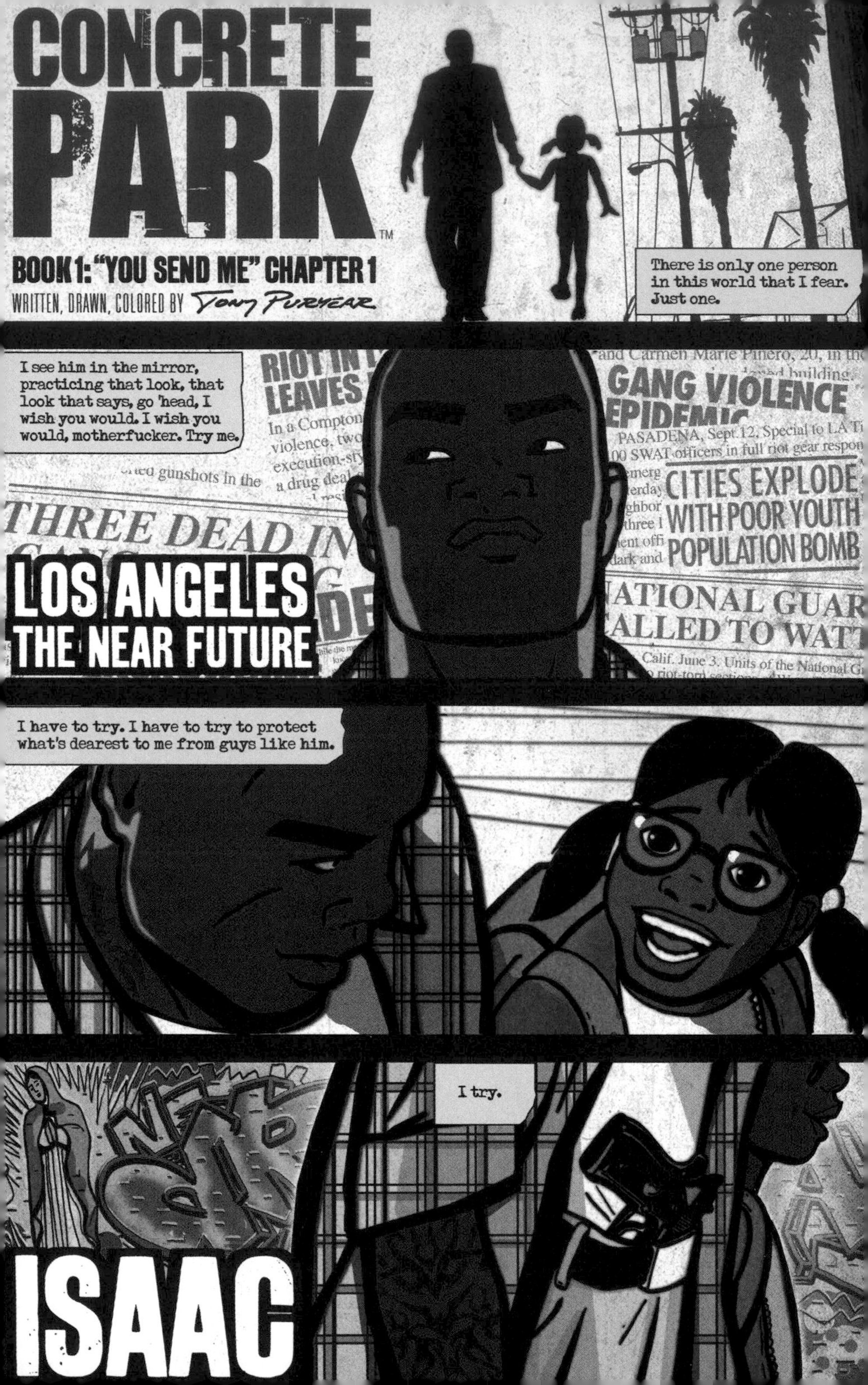
CONCRETE PARK™
BOOK 1: "YOU SEND ME" CHAPTER 1
WRITTEN, DRAWN, COLORED BY TONY PURYEAR
There is only one person in this world that I fear. Just one.
I see him in the mirror, practicing that look, that look that says, go 'head, I wish you would. I wish you would, motherfucker. Try me.
GANG VIOLENCE EPIDEMIC
CITIES EXPLODE WITH POOR YOUTH POPULATION BOMB
THREE DEAD IN
NATIONAL GUARD CALLED TO WATT
LOS ANGELES THE NEAR FUTURE
I have to try. I have to try to protect what's dearest to me from guys like him.
I try.
ISAAC

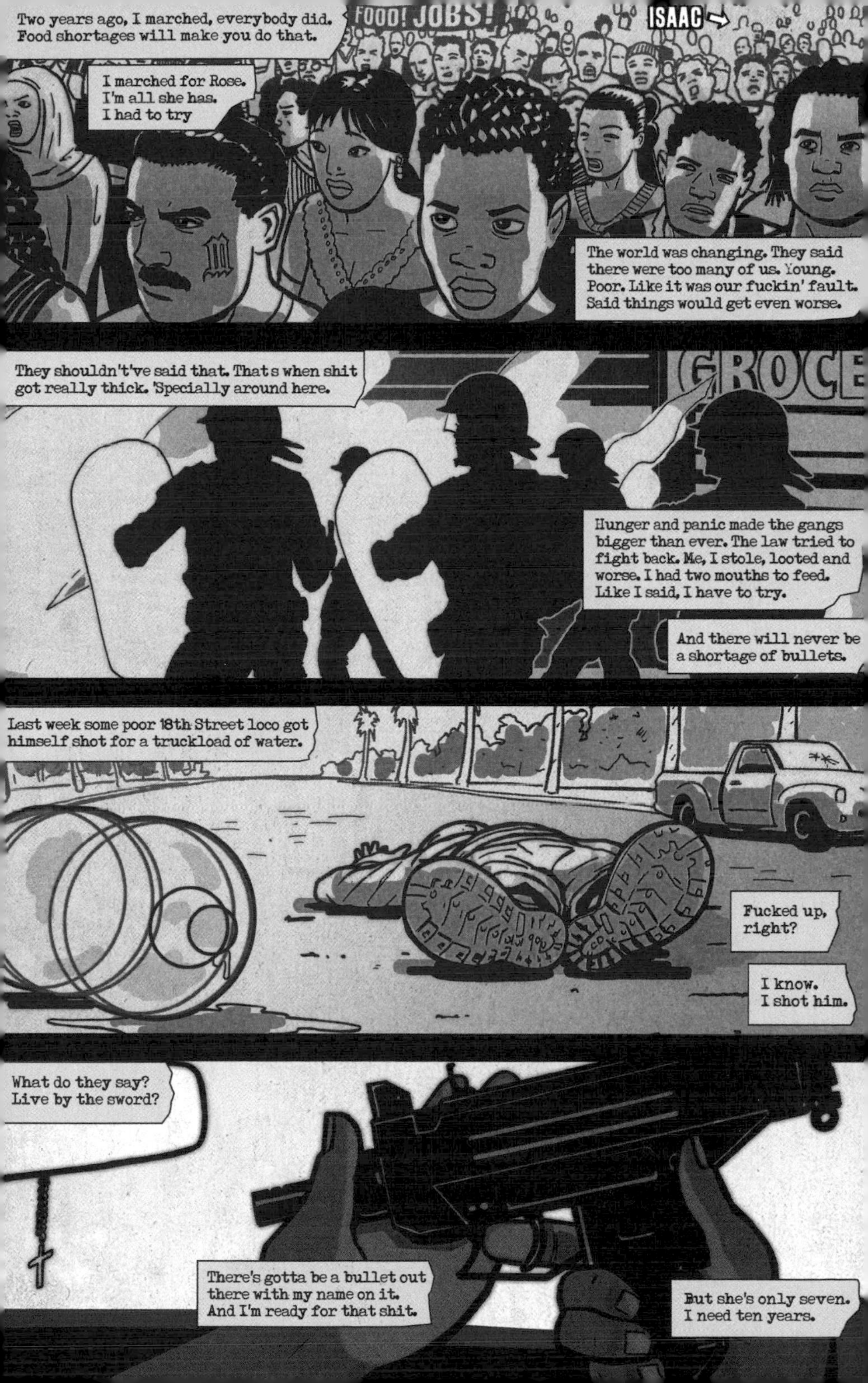
Two years ago, I marched, everybody did. Food shortages will make you do that.
FOOD! JOBS!
ISAAC
I marched for Rose. I'm all she has. I had to try
The world was changing. They said there were too many of us. Young. Poor. Like it was our fuckin' fault. Said things would get even worse.
They shouldn't've said that. That s when shit got really thick. 'Specially around here.
GROCE
Hunger and panic made the gangs bigger than ever. The law tried to fight back. Me, I stole, looted and worse. I had two mouths to feed. Like I said, I have to try.
And there will never be a shortage of bullets.
Last week some poor 18th Street loco got himself shot for a truckload of water.
Fucked up, right?
I know. I shot him.
What do they say? Live by the sword?
There's gotta be a bullet out there with my name on it. And I'm ready for that shit.
But she's only seven. I need ten years.

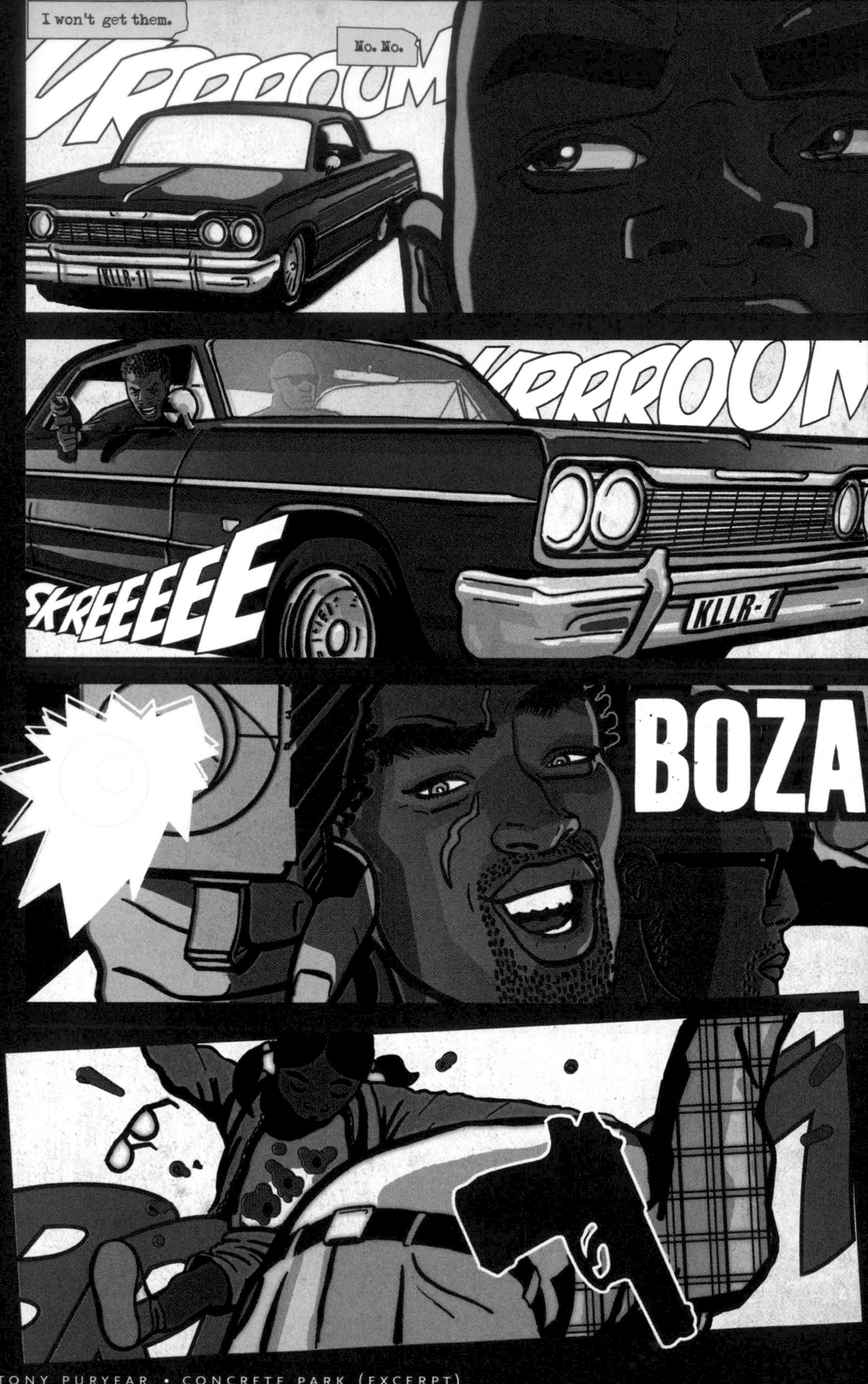
I won't get them.
No. No.
VRRROOM
VRRROOM
SKREEEEE
KLLR-1
BOZA

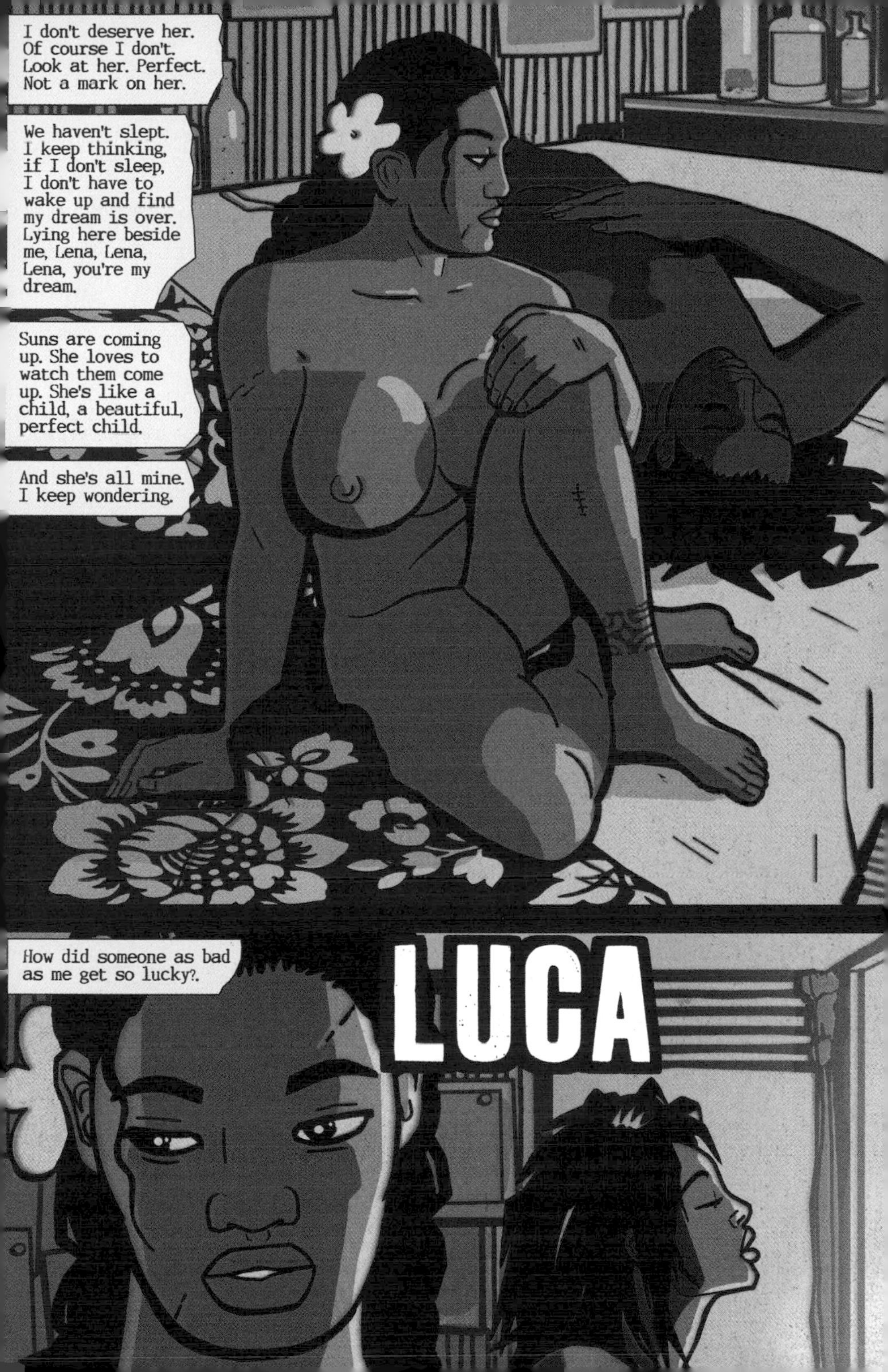
I don't deserve her. Of course I don't. Look at her. Perfect. Not a mark on her.
We haven't slept. I keep thinking, if I don't sleep, I don't have to wake up and find my dream is over. Lying here beside me, Lena, Lena, Lena, you're my dream.
Suns are coming up. She loves to watch them come up. She's like a child, a beautiful, perfect child.
And she's all mine. I keep wondering.
How did someone as bad as me get so lucky?.
LUCA

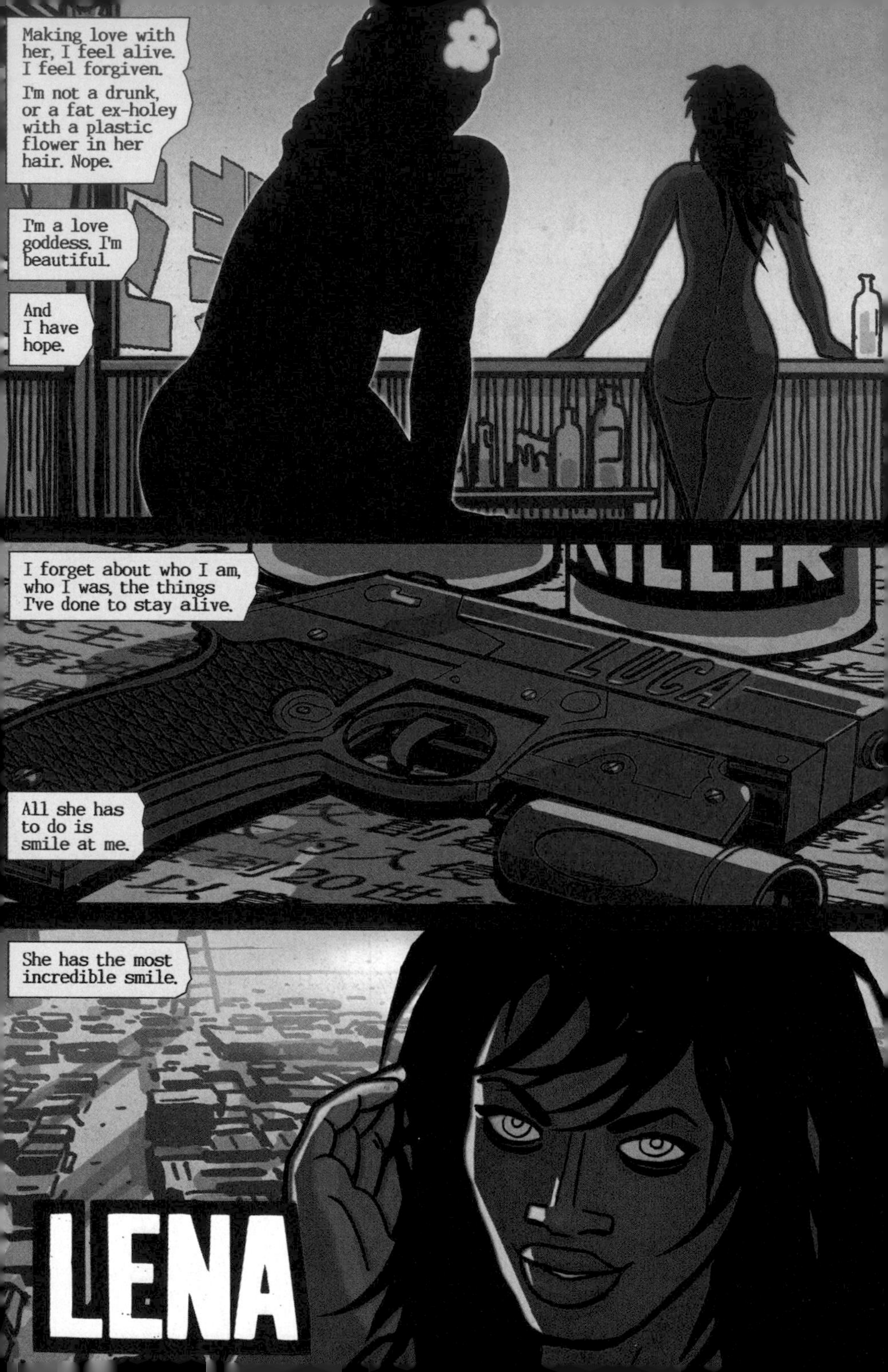
Making love with her, I feel alive. I feel forgiven.
I'm not a drunk, or a fat ex-holey with a plastic flower in her hair. Nope.
I'm a love goddess. I'm beautiful.
And I have hope.
I forget about who I am, who I was, the things I've done to stay alive.
LUCA
All she has to do is smile at me.
She has the most incredible smile.
LENA

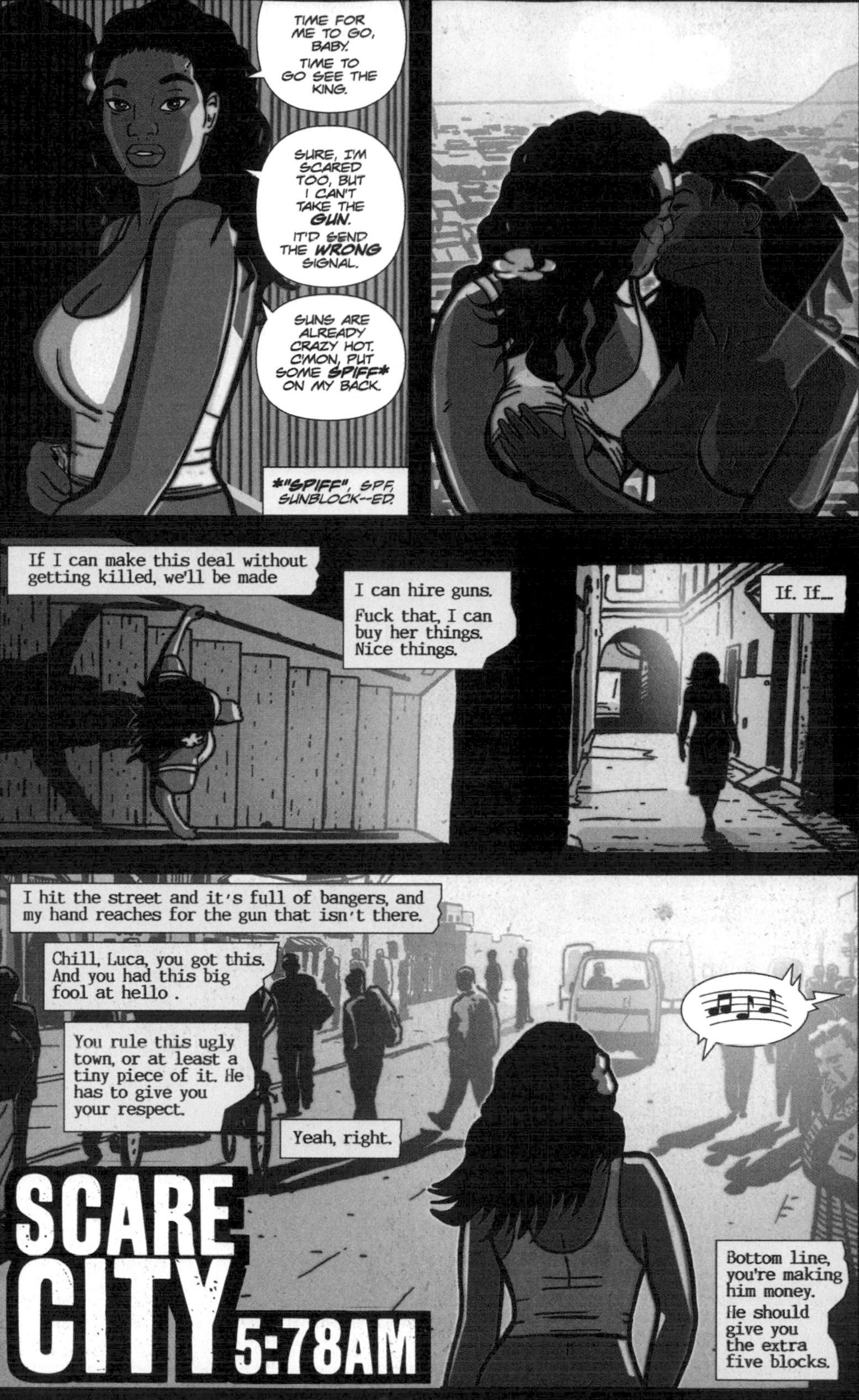
TIME FOR ME TO GO, BABY.
TIME TO GO SEE THE KING.
SURE, I'M SCARED TOO, BUT I CAN'T TAKE THE GUN.
IT'D SEND THE WRONG SIGNAL.
SUNS ARE ALREADY CRAZY HOT. C'MON, PUT SOME SPIFF* ON MY BACK.
*"SPIFF", SPF, SUNBLOCK--ED.
If I can make this deal without getting killed, we'll be made
I can hire guns.
Fuck that, I can buy her things. Nice things.
If. If...
I hit the street and it's full of bangers, and my hand reaches for the gun that isn't there.
Chill, Luca, you got this. And you had this big fool at hello .
You rule this ugly town, or at least a tiny piece of it. He has to give you your respect.
Yeah, right.
SCARE CITY 5:78AM
Bottom line, you're making him money.
He should give you the extra five blocks.

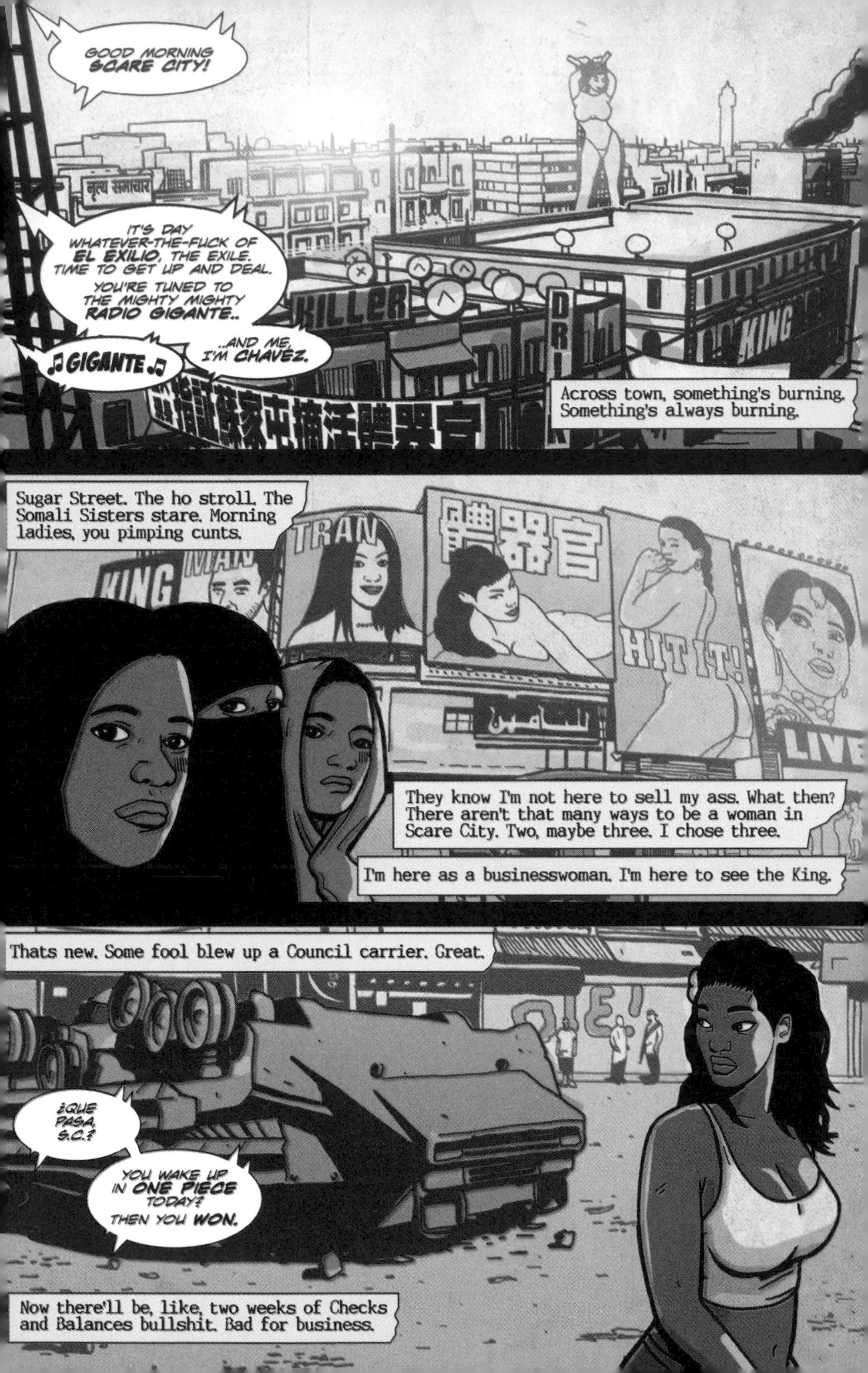
GOOD MORNING SCARE CITY!
IT'S DAY WHATEVER-THE-FUCK OF EL EXILIO, THE EXILE. TIME TO GET UP AND DEAL.
YOU'RE TUNED TO THE MIGHTY MIGHTY RADIO GIGANTE..
♫ GIGANTE ♫
..AND ME, I'M CHAVEZ.
KILLER
KING
Across town, something's burning. Something's always burning.
Sugar Street. The ho stroll. The Somali Sisters stare. Morning ladies, you pimping cunts.
KING
TRAN
體器官
HIT IT!
LIVE
They know I'm not here to sell my ass. What then? There aren't that many ways to be a woman in Scare City. Two, maybe three. I chose three.
I'm here as a businesswoman. I'm here to see the King.
Thats new. Some fool blew up a Council carrier. Great.
¿QUE PASA, S.C.?
YOU WAKE UP IN ONE PIECE TODAY? THEN YOU WON.
Now there'll be, like, two weeks of Checks and Balances bullshit. Bad for business.

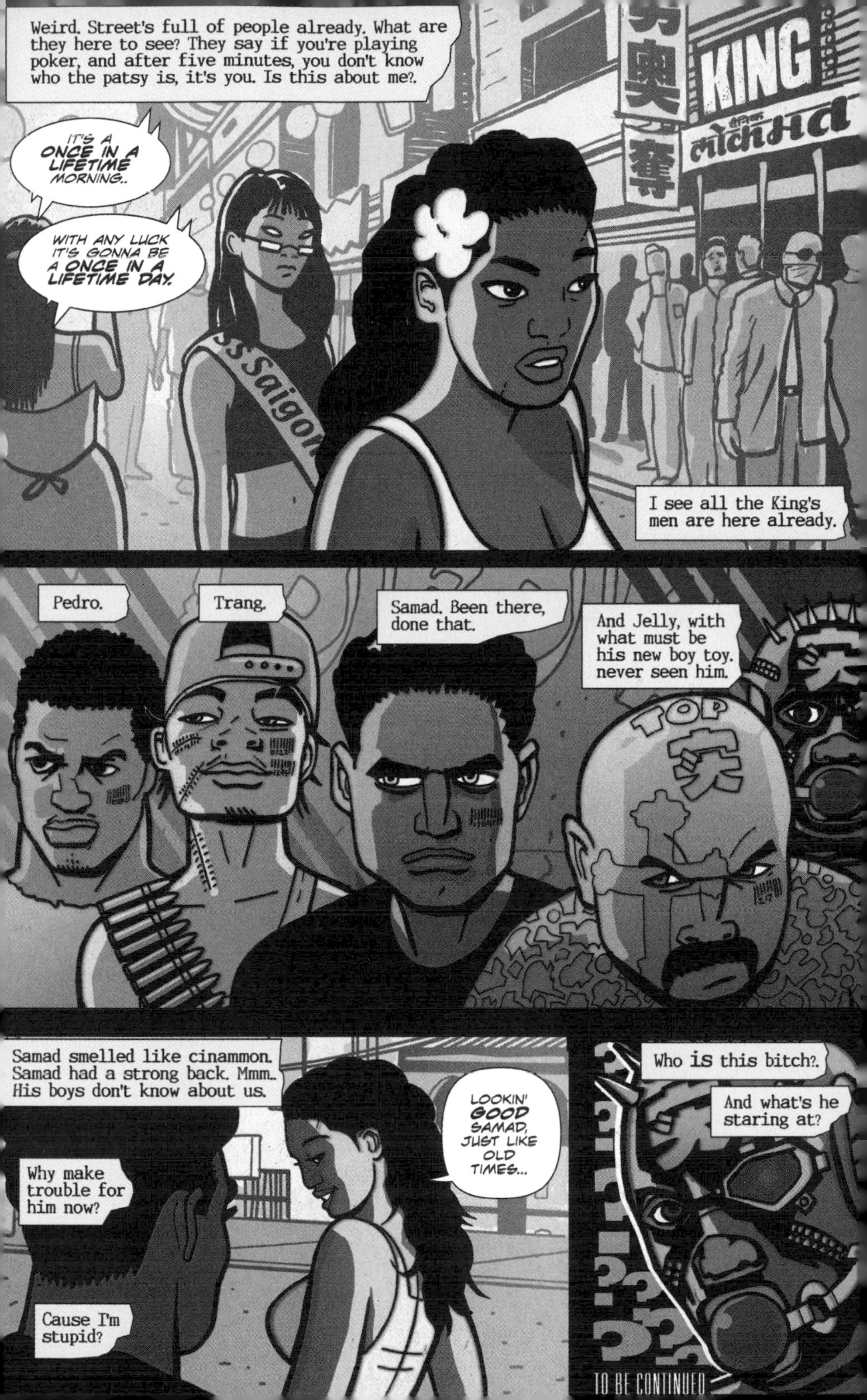
Weird. Street's full of people already. What are they here to see? They say if you're playing poker, and after five minutes, you don't know who the patsy is, it's you. Is this about me?.
KING
IT'S A ONCE IN A LIFETIME MORNING..
WITH ANY LUCK IT'S GONNA BE A ONCE IN A LIFETIME DAY.
I see all the King's men are here already.
Pedro.
Trang.
Samad. Been there, done that.
And Jelly, with what must be his new boy toy. never seen him.
TOP
Samad smelled like cinammon. Samad had a strong back. Mmm.. His boys don't know about us.
LOOKIN' GOOD SAMAD, JUST LIKE OLD TIMES...
Why make trouble for him now?
Cause I'm stupid?
Who is this bitch?.
And what's he staring at?
TO BE CONTINUED

TOP FIVE
MALACHI WARD

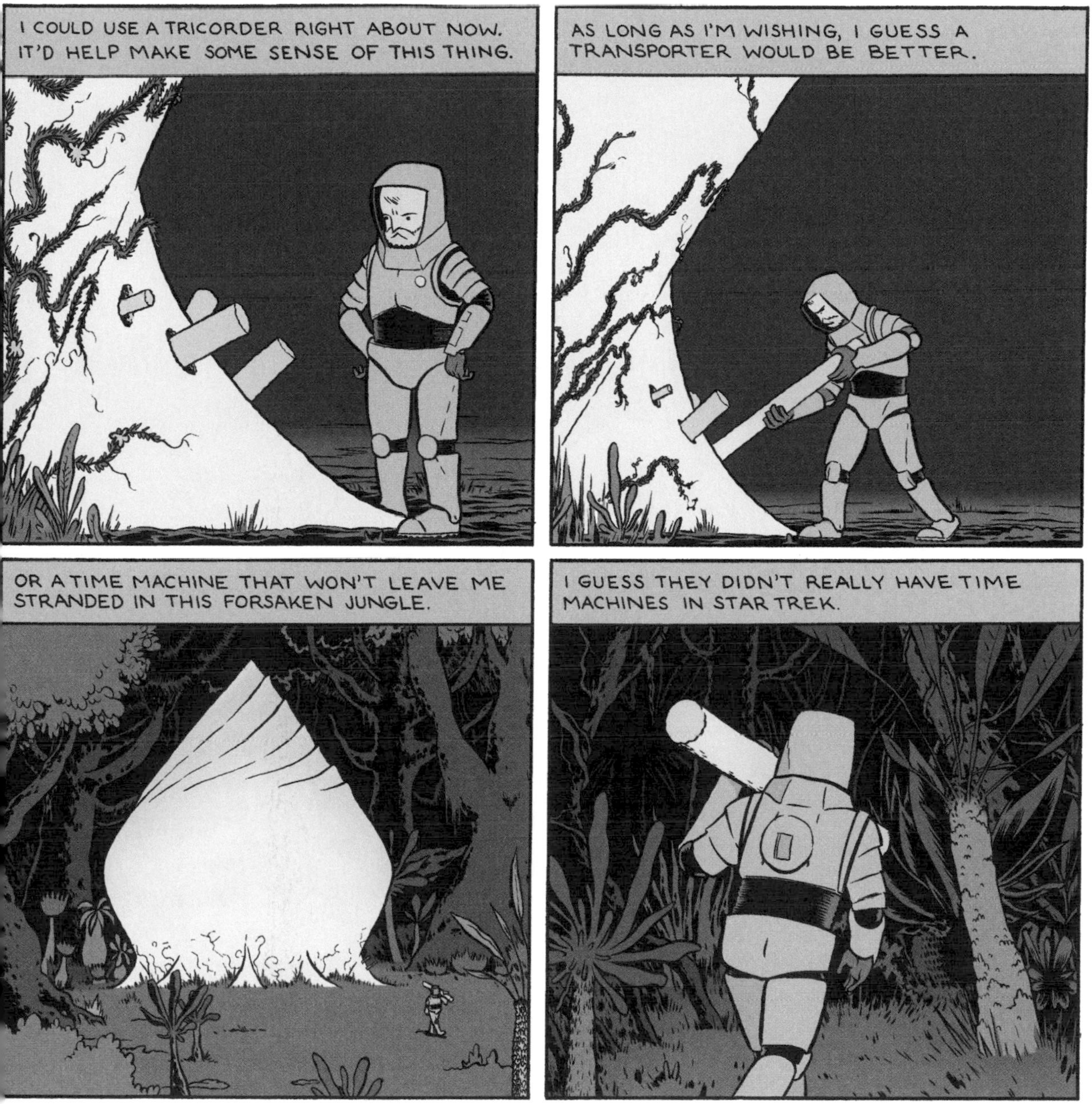
I COULD USE A TRICORDER RIGHT ABOUT NOW. IT'D HELP MAKE SOME SENSE OF THIS THING.
AS LONG AS I'M WISHING, I GUESS A TRANSPORTER WOULD BE BETTER.
OR A TIME MACHINE THAT WON'T LEAVE ME STRANDED IN THIS FORSAKEN JUNGLE.
I GUESS THEY DIDN'T REALLY HAVE TIME MACHINES IN STAR TREK.

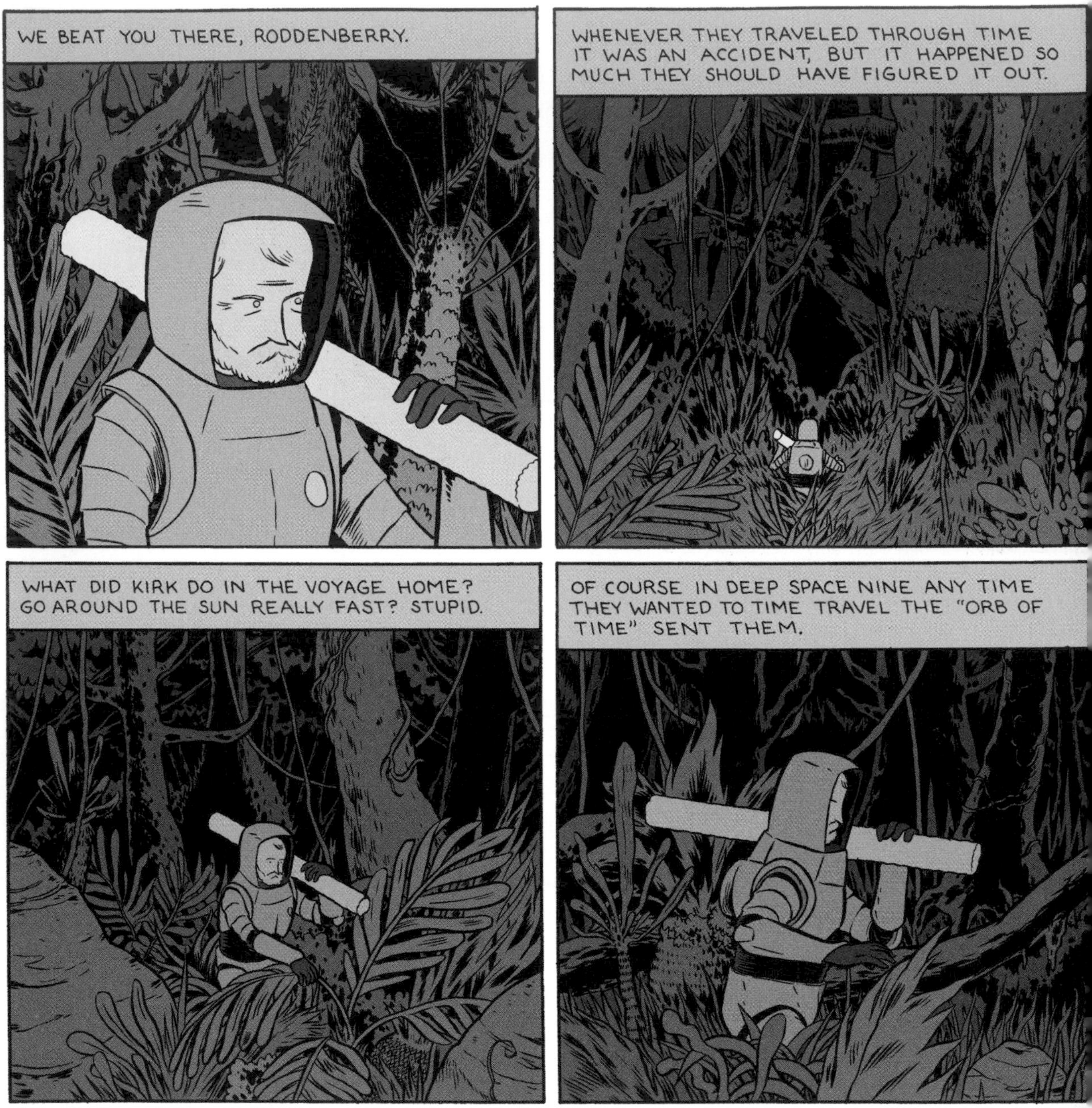
WE BEAT YOU THERE, RODDENBERRY.
WHENEVER THEY TRAVELED THROUGH TIME IT WAS AN ACCIDENT, BUT IT HAPPENED SO MUCH THEY SHOULD HAVE FIGURED IT OUT.
WHAT DID KIRK DO IN THE VOYAGE HOME? GO AROUND THE SUN REALLY FAST? STUPID.
OF COURSE IN DEEP SPACE NINE ANY TIME THEY WANTED TO TIME TRAVEL THE "ORB OF TIME" SENT THEM.

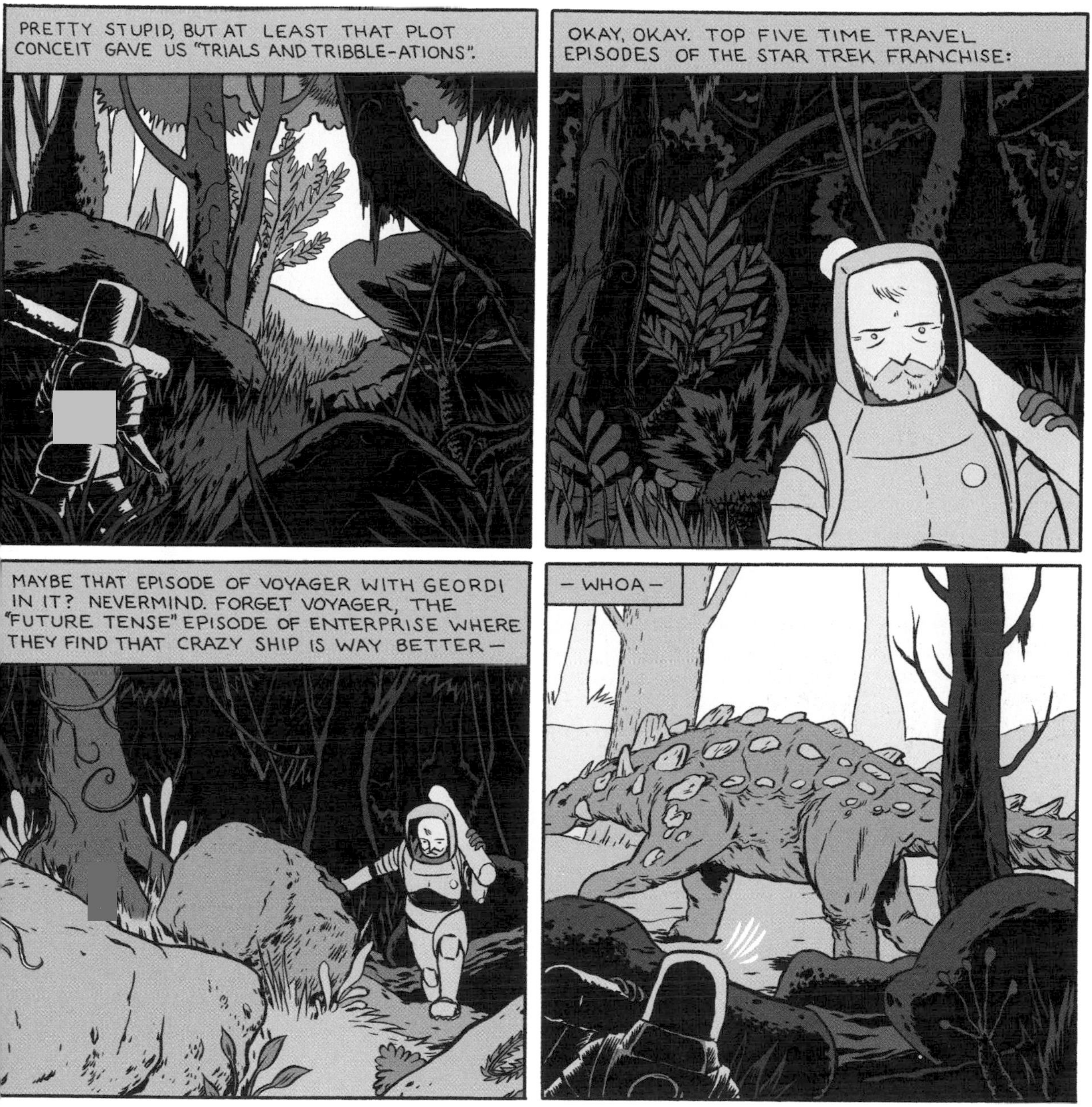
PRETTY STUPID, BUT AT LEAST THAT PLOT CONCEIT GAVE US "TRIALS AND TRIBBLE-ATIONS".
OKAY, OKAY. TOP FIVE TIME TRAVEL EPISODES OF THE STAR TREK FRANCHISE:
MAYBE THAT EPISODE OF VOYAGER WITH GEORDI IN IT? NEVERMIND. FORGET VOYAGER, THE "FUTURE TENSE" EPISODE OF ENTERPRISE WHERE THEY FIND THAT CRAZY SHIP IS WAY BETTER—
—WHOA—

VOYAGER WAS SUCH A CRAPPY SHOW.

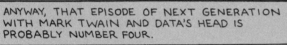
ANYWAY, THAT EPISODE OF NEXT GENERATION WITH MARK TWAIN AND DATA'S HEAD IS PROBABLY NUMBER FOUR.

NEXT GENERATION'S "ALL GOOD THINGS", I'D PUT THAT AT NUMBER THREE.

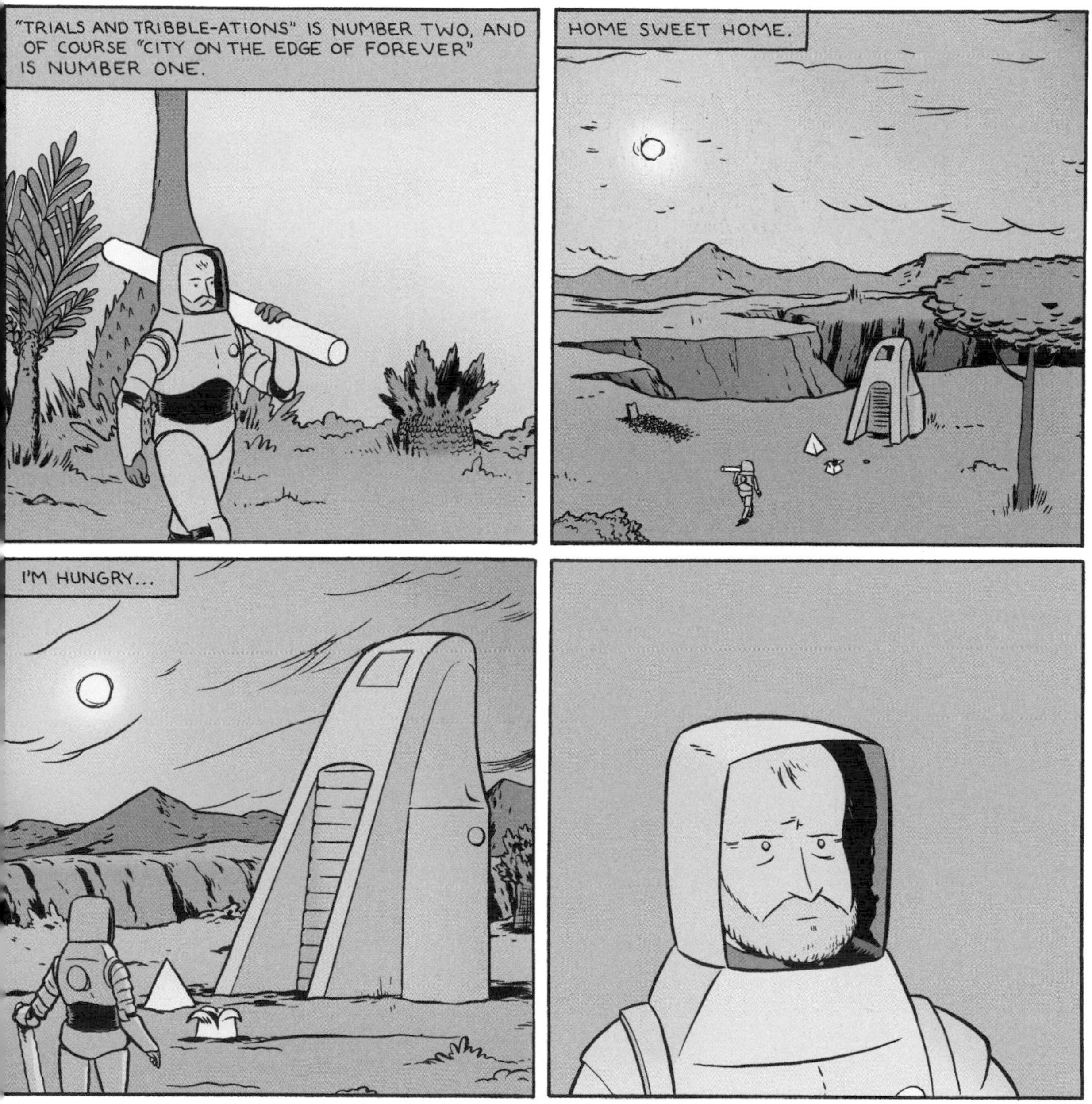
"TRIALS AND TRIBBLE-ATIONS" IS NUMBER TWO, AND OF COURSE "CITY ON THE EDGE OF FOREVER" IS NUMBER ONE.
HOME SWEET HOME.
I'M HUNGRY...

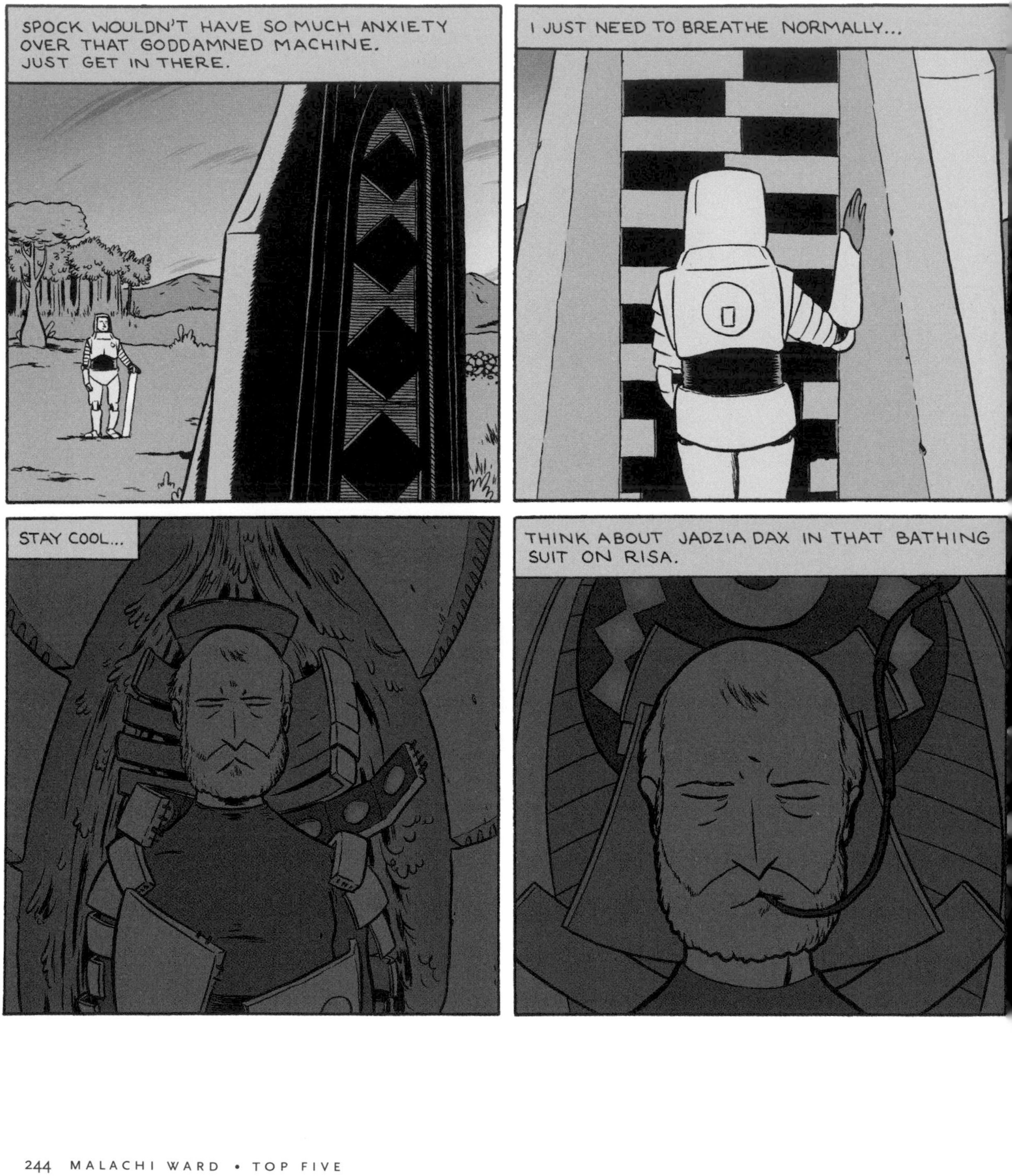
SPOCK WOULDN'T HAVE SO MUCH ANXIETY OVER THAT GODDAMNED MACHINE. JUST GET IN THERE.
I JUST NEED TO BREATHE NORMALLY...
STAY COOL...
THINK ABOUT JADZIA DAX IN THAT BATHING SUIT ON RISA.

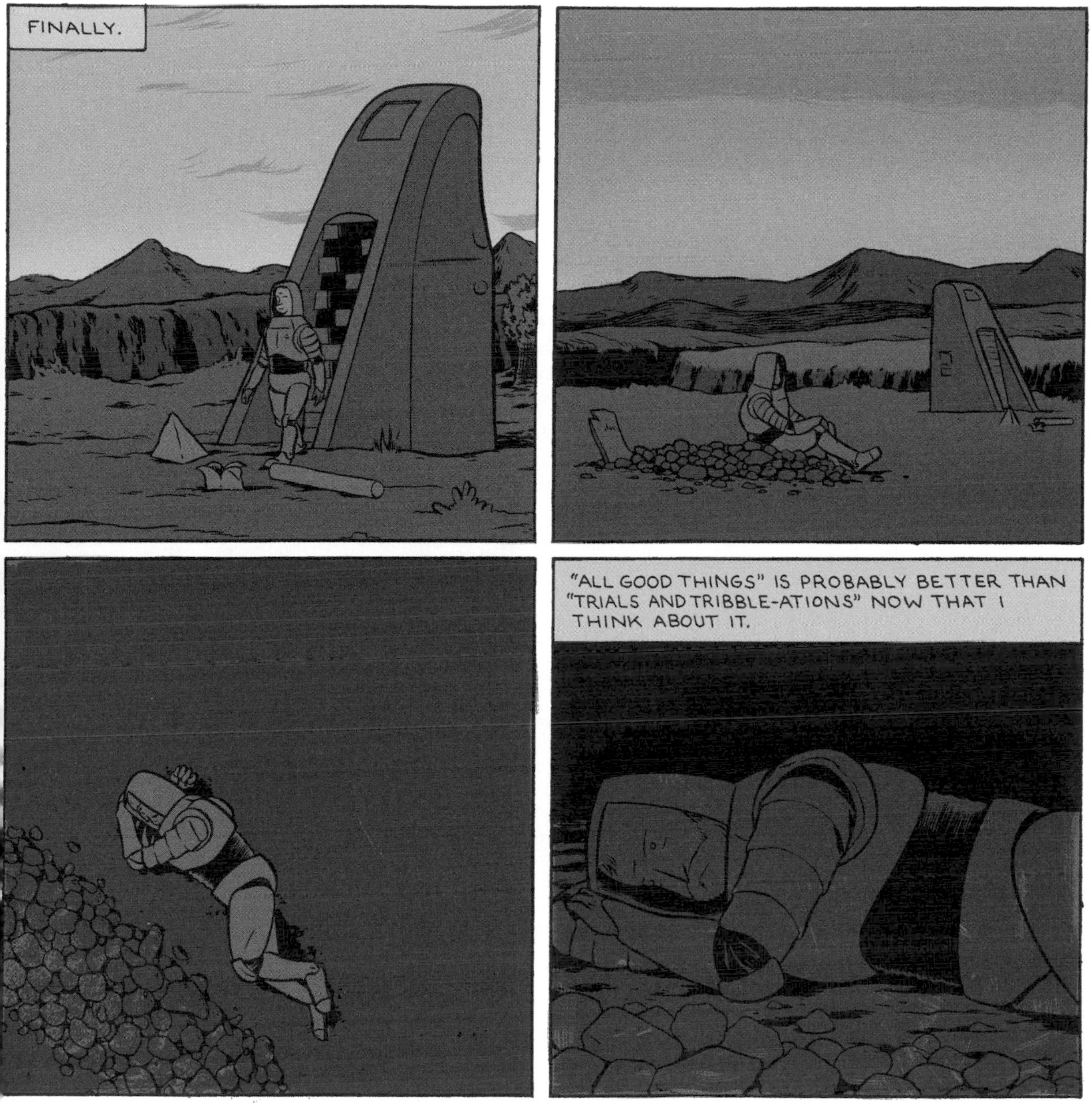
FINALLY.
"ALL GOOD THINGS" IS PROBABLY BETTER THAN "TRIALS AND TRIBBLE-ATIONS" NOW THAT I THINK ABOUT IT.

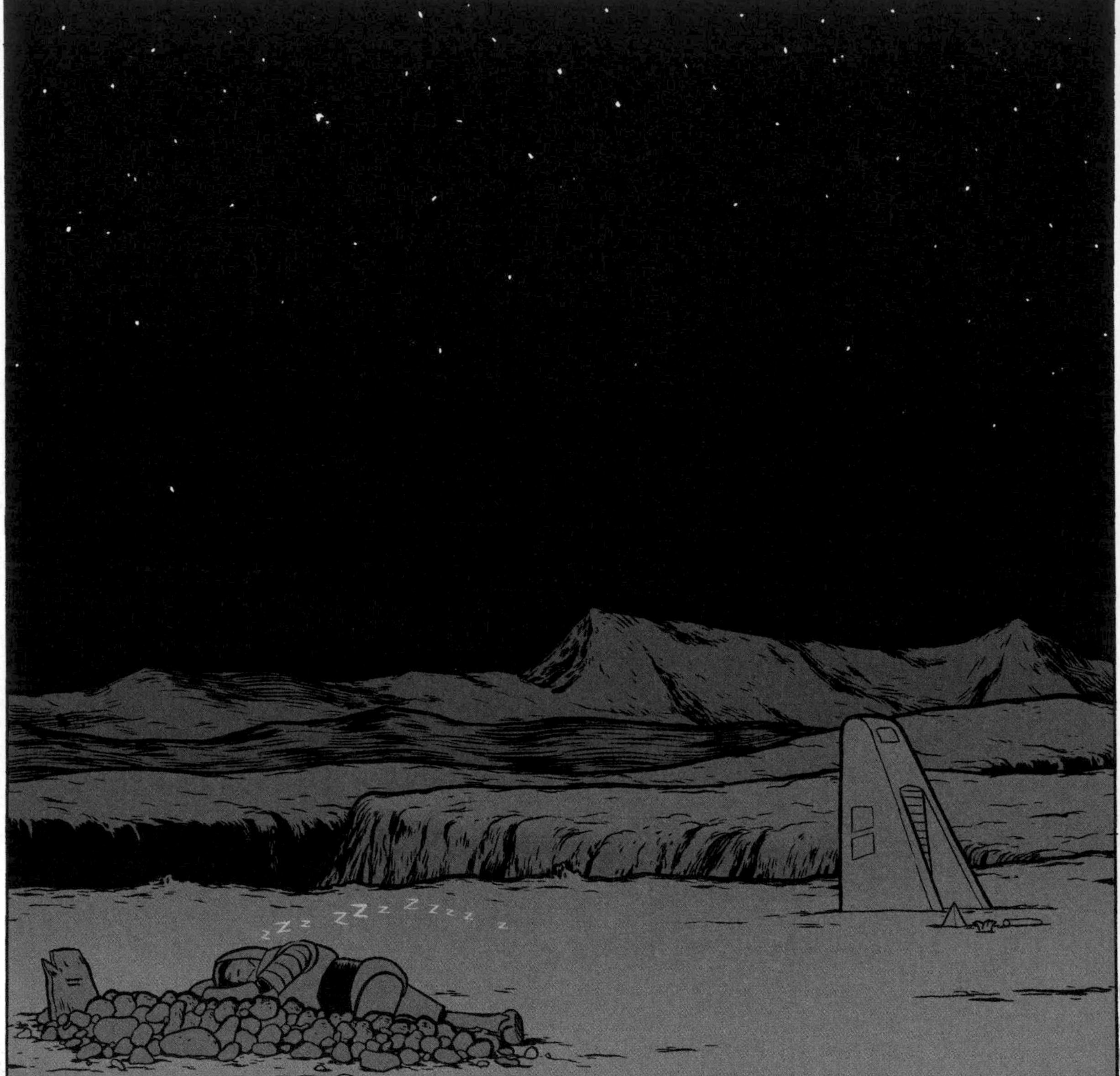

DERF BACKDERF

The Strange Boy

EXCERPT FROM

MY FRIEND DAHMER

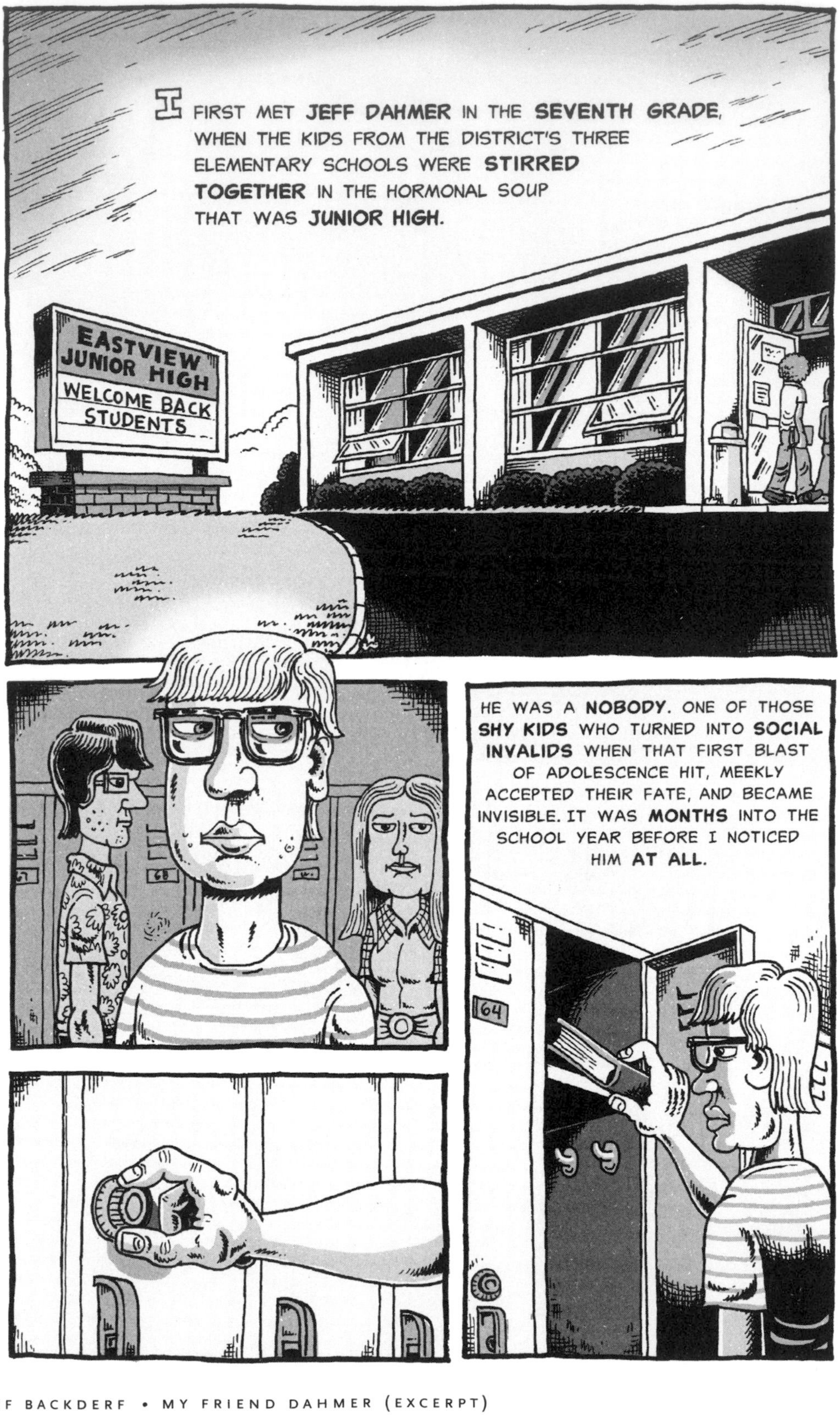
I FIRST MET JEFF DAHMER IN THE SEVENTH GRADE, WHEN THE KIDS FROM THE DISTRICT'S THREE ELEMENTARY SCHOOLS WERE STIRRED TOGETHER IN THE HORMONAL SOUP THAT WAS JUNIOR HIGH.
EASTVIEW JUNIOR HIGH
WELCOME BACK STUDENTS
HE WAS A NOBODY. ONE OF THOSE SHY KIDS WHO TURNED INTO SOCIAL INVALIDS WHEN THAT FIRST BLAST OF ADOLESCENCE HIT, MEEKLY ACCEPTED THEIR FATE, AND BECAME INVISIBLE. IT WAS MONTHS INTO THE SCHOOL YEAR BEFORE I NOTICED HIM AT ALL.
64

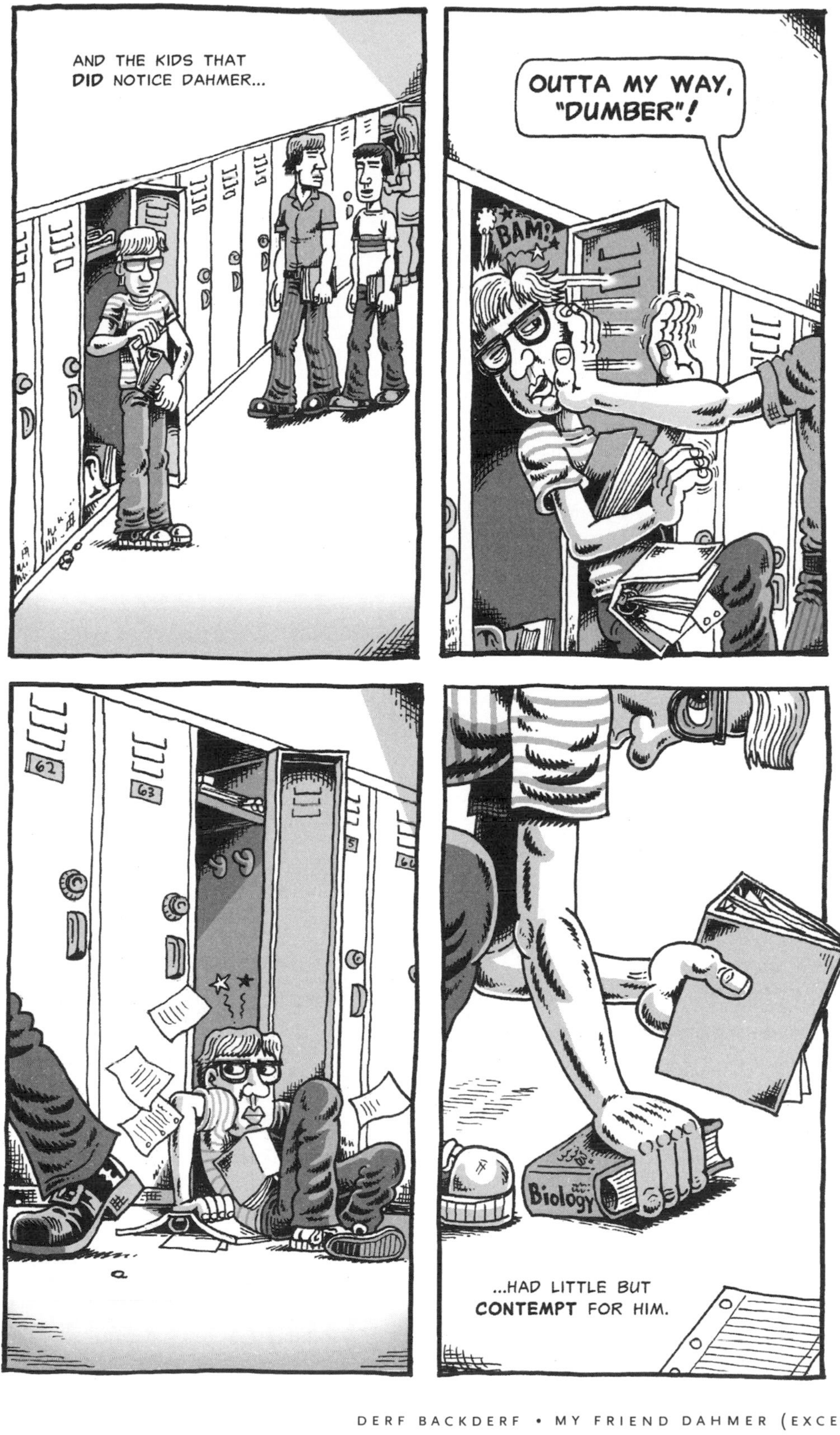
AND THE KIDS THAT DID NOTICE DAHMER...
OUTTA MY WAY, "DUMBER"!
BAM!
62
63
Biology
...HAD LITTLE BUT CONTEMPT FOR HIM.

TEN MINUTES, PEOPLE! YOU SHOULD BE DONE WITH YOUR LEAF DIAGRAM, MR. BACKDERF.
OK, OK.
HOW MANY CHLOROPLASTS DID YOU GET?
THIRTY.
WHAT!?! I'M NOT EVEN CLOSE TO THAT!
OK! LET'S CLEAN UP!
DANG IT! I HAVE TOTALLY BLOWN THIS ASSIGNMENT.
FETAL PIG
TAPEWORM

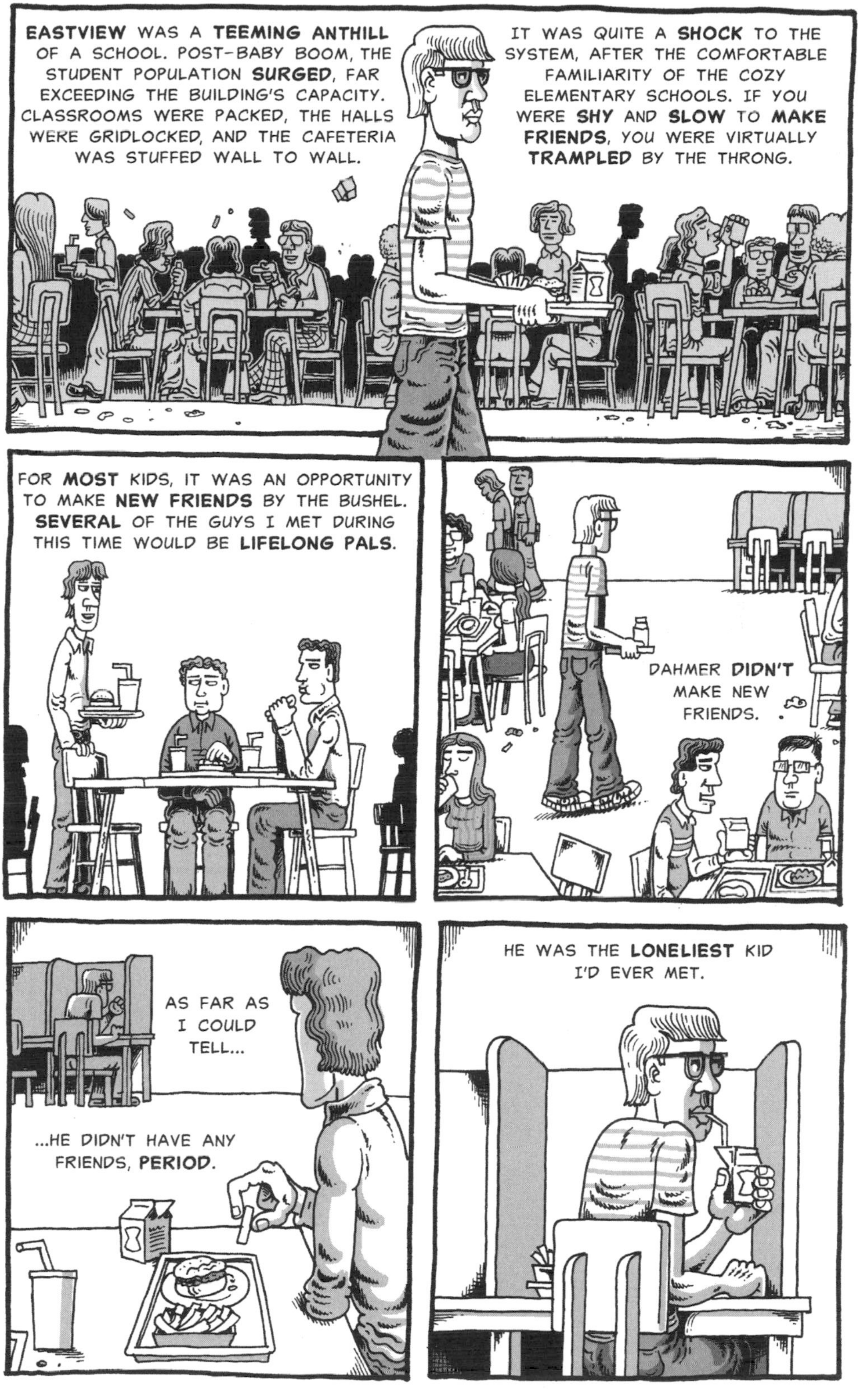
EASTVIEW WAS A TEEMING ANTHILL OF A SCHOOL. POST-BABY BOOM, THE STUDENT POPULATION SURGED, FAR EXCEEDING THE BUILDING'S CAPACITY. CLASSROOMS WERE PACKED, THE HALLS WERE GRIDLOCKED, AND THE CAFETERIA WAS STUFFED WALL TO WALL.
IT WAS QUITE A SHOCK TO THE SYSTEM, AFTER THE COMFORTABLE FAMILIARITY OF THE COZY ELEMENTARY SCHOOLS. IF YOU WERE SHY AND SLOW TO MAKE FRIENDS, YOU WERE VIRTUALLY TRAMPLED BY THE THRONG.
FOR MOST KIDS, IT WAS AN OPPORTUNITY TO MAKE NEW FRIENDS BY THE BUSHEL. SEVERAL OF THE GUYS I MET DURING THIS TIME WOULD BE LIFELONG PALS.
DAHMER DIDN'T MAKE NEW FRIENDS.
AS FAR AS I COULD TELL...
...HE DIDN'T HAVE ANY FRIENDS, PERIOD.
HE WAS THE LONELIEST KID I'D EVER MET.

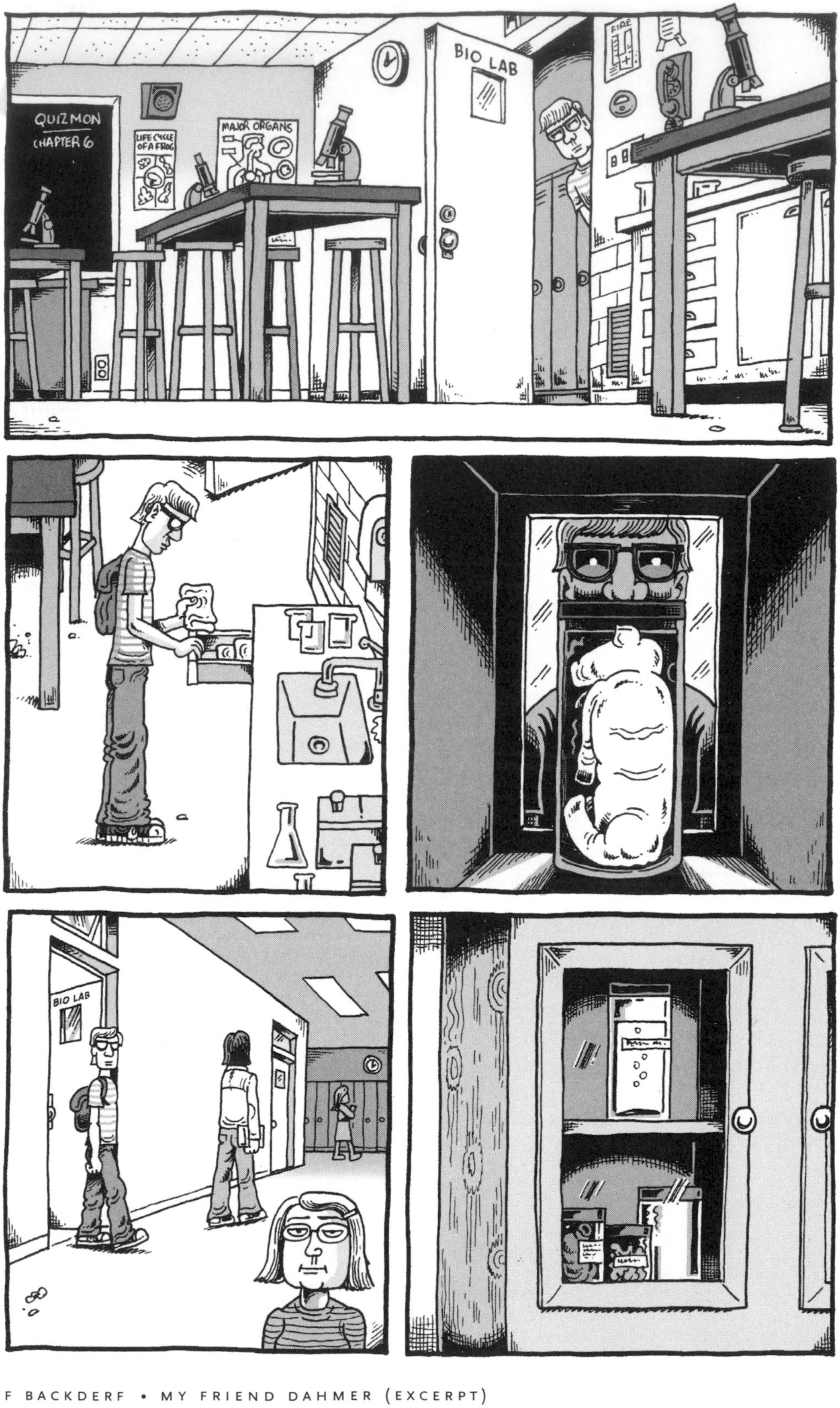
QUIZMON
CHAPTER 6
LIFE CYCLE OF A FROG
MAJOR ORGANS
BIO LAB
BIO LAB

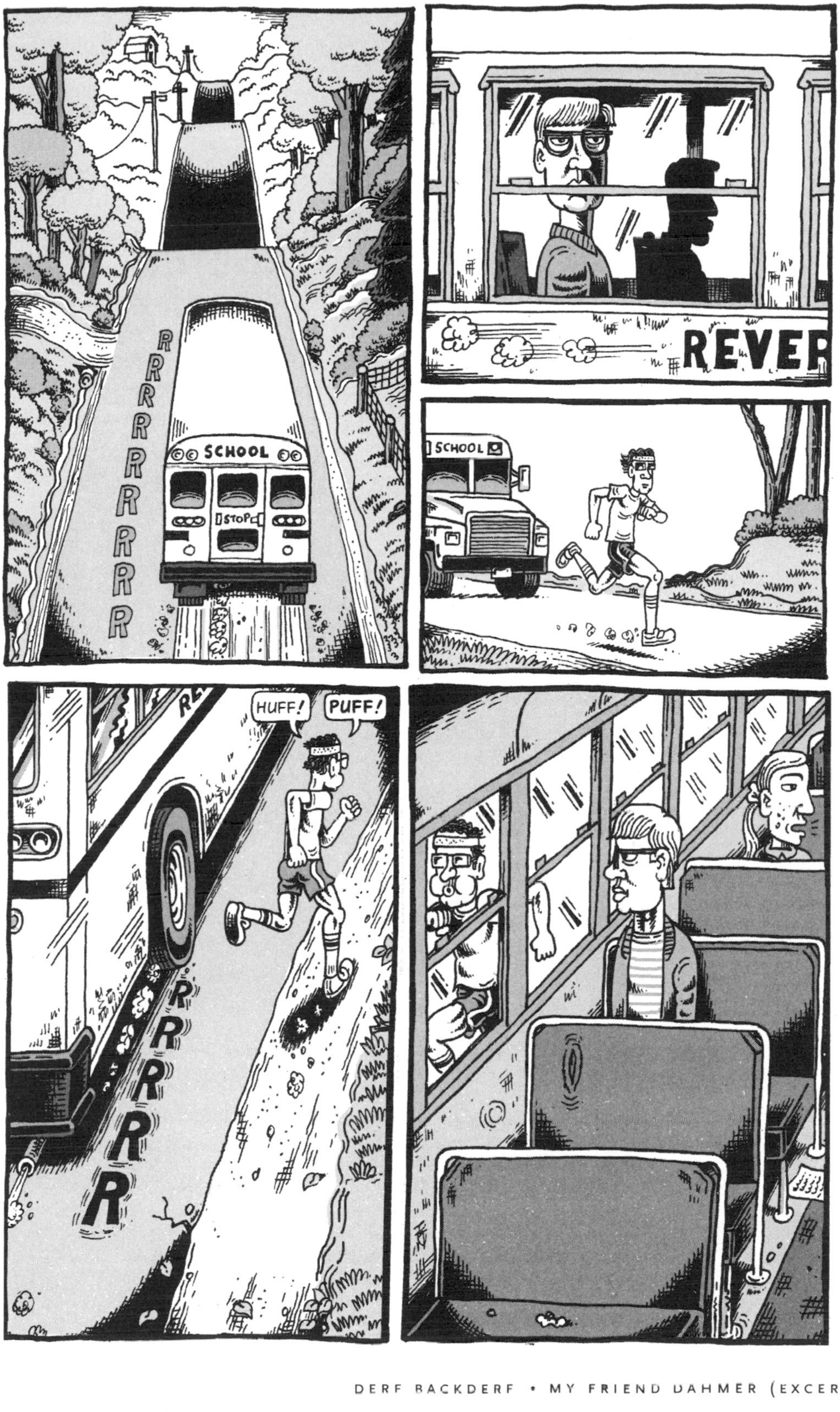
RRRRRRRRRRR
SCHOOL
STOP
REVER
SCHOOL
HUFF!
PUFF!
RRRRRR

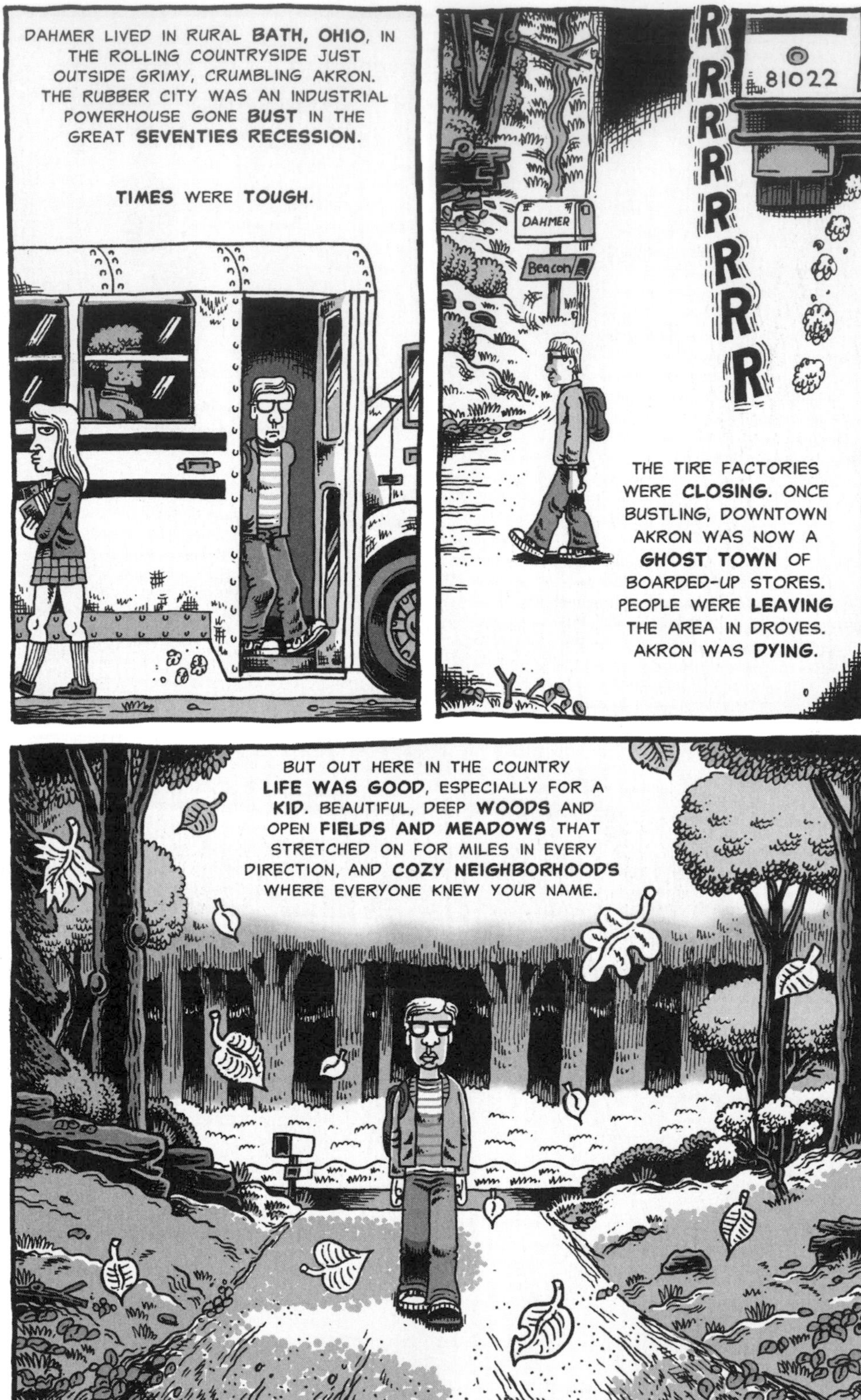
DAHMER LIVED IN RURAL BATH, OHIO, IN THE ROLLING COUNTRYSIDE JUST OUTSIDE GRIMY, CRUMBLING AKRON. THE RUBBER CITY WAS AN INDUSTRIAL POWERHOUSE GONE BUST IN THE GREAT SEVENTIES RECESSION.
TIMES WERE TOUGH.
RRRRRRRRR
81022
DAHMER
Beacon
THE TIRE FACTORIES WERE CLOSING. ONCE BUSTLING, DOWNTOWN AKRON WAS NOW A GHOST TOWN OF BOARDED-UP STORES. PEOPLE WERE LEAVING THE AREA IN DROVES. AKRON WAS DYING.
BUT OUT HERE IN THE COUNTRY LIFE WAS GOOD, ESPECIALLY FOR A KID. BEAUTIFUL, DEEP WOODS AND OPEN FIELDS AND MEADOWS THAT STRETCHED ON FOR MILES IN EVERY DIRECTION, AND COZY NEIGHBORHOODS WHERE EVERYONE KNEW YOUR NAME.

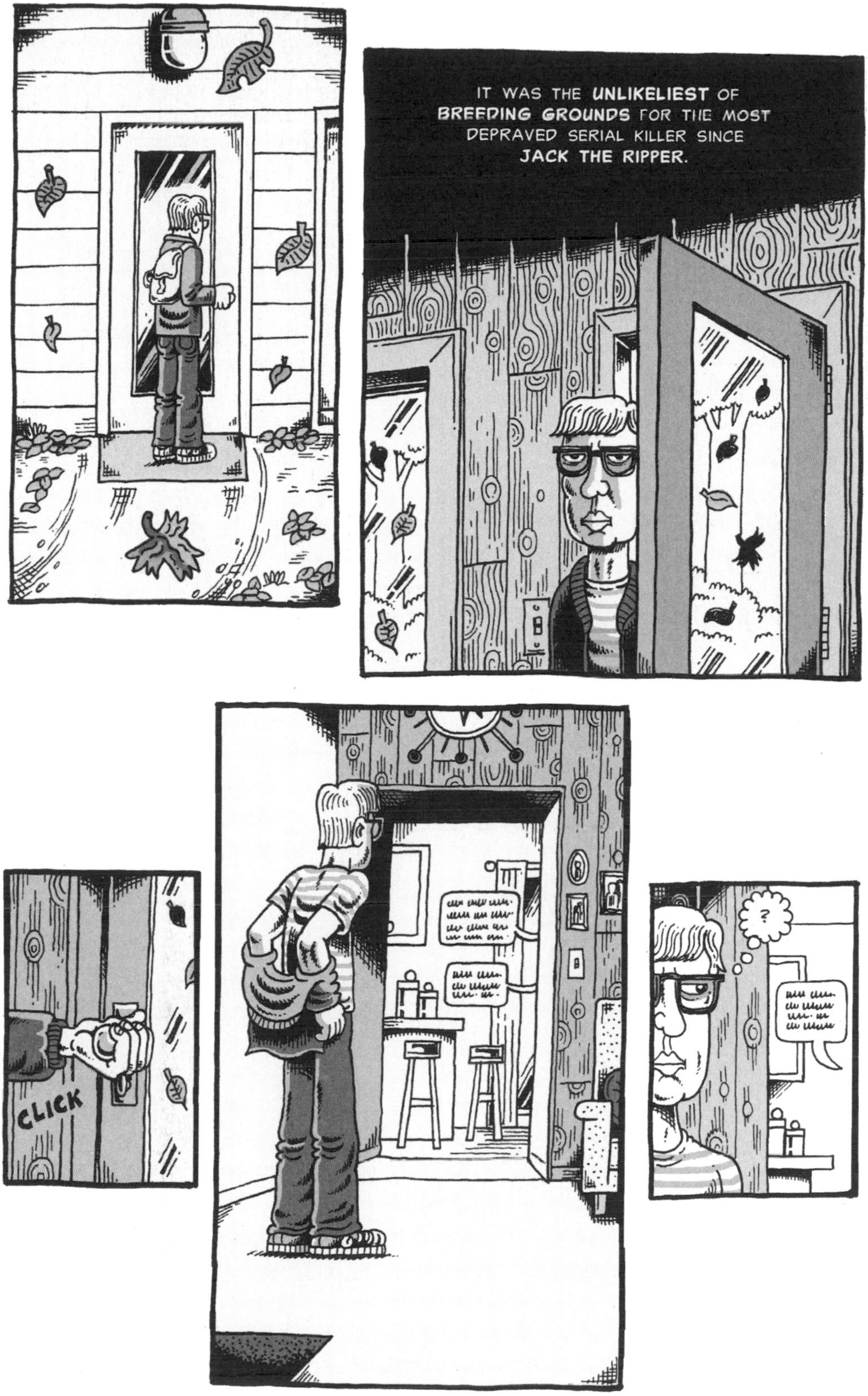
IT WAS THE UNLIKELIEST OF BREEDING GROUNDS FOR THE MOST DEPRAVED SERIAL KILLER SINCE JACK THE RIPPER.
CLICK

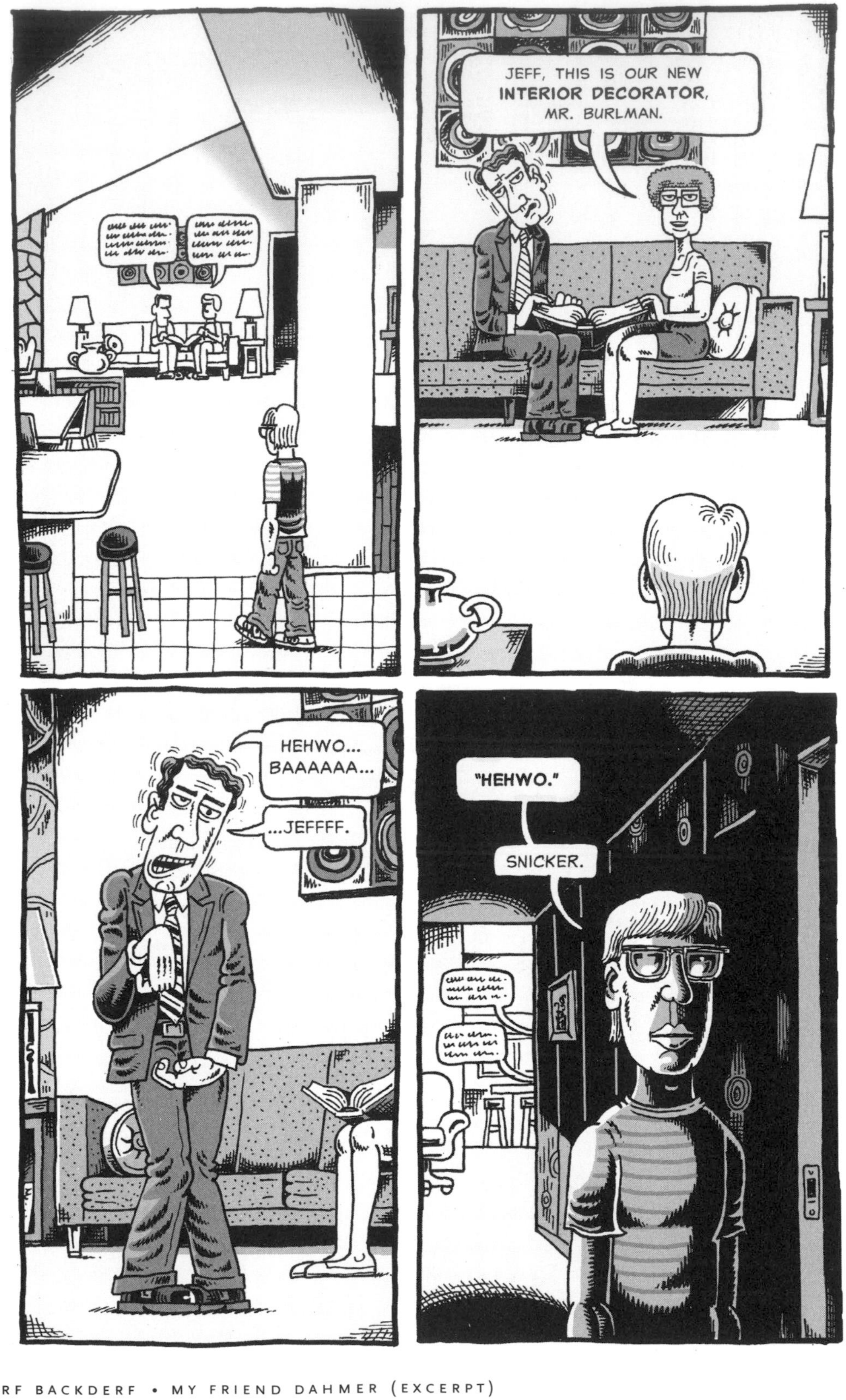
JEFF, THIS IS OUR NEW INTERIOR DECORATOR, MR. BURLMAN.
HEHWO... BAAAAAA...
...JEFFFF.
"HEHWO."
SNICKER.

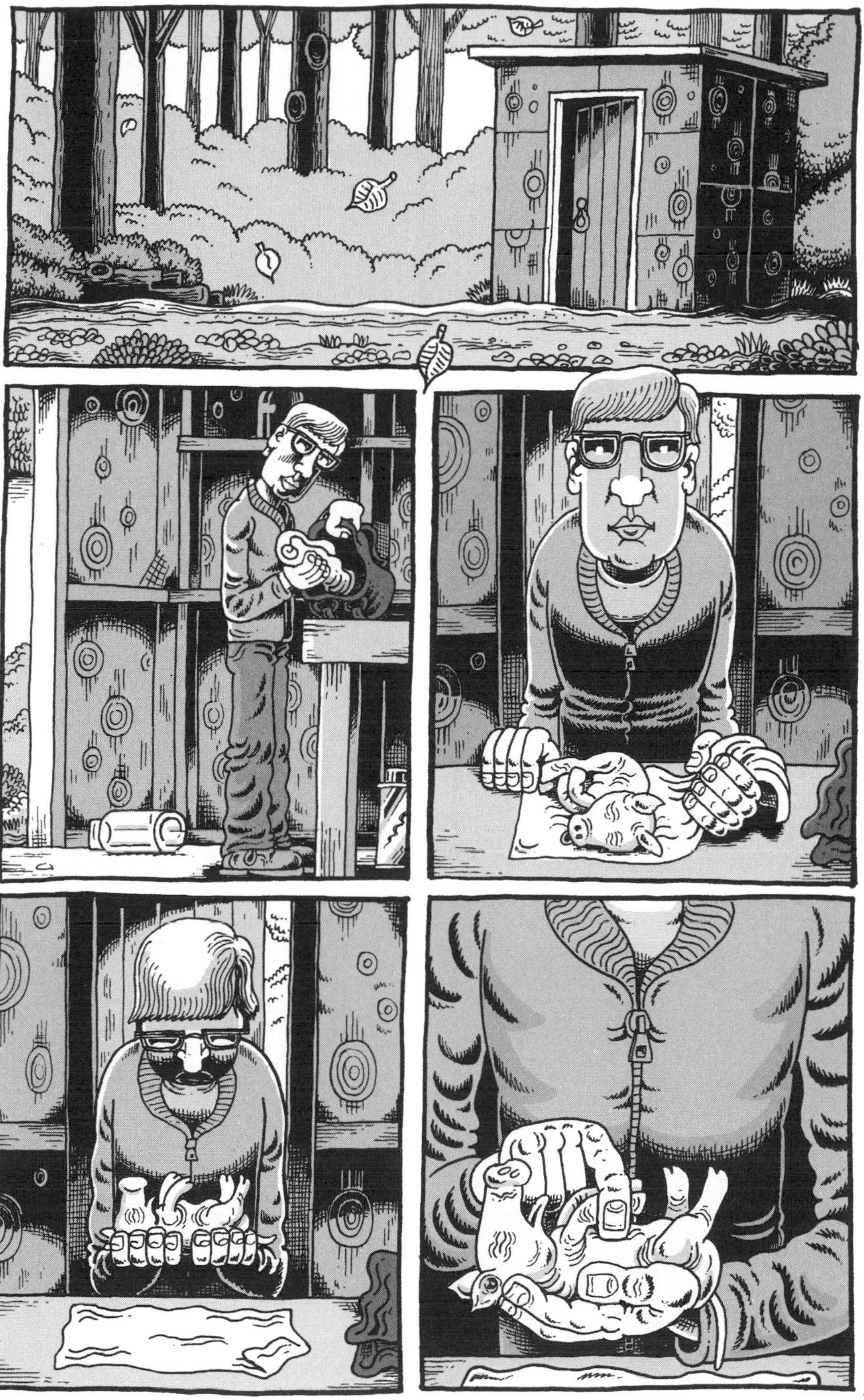

JEFF LIVED IN A SMALL HOUSE WITH HIS PARENTS, **LIONEL** AND **JOYCE**, AND HIS BROTHER, **DAVE**, NEARLY SEVEN YEARS YOUNGER.

DAVE **ISN'T** PART OF **THIS** STORY. HE WAS JUST A KID AND BENEATH MY NOTICE.

HE CERTAINLY HAD A **BIG ROLE** IN JEFF'S LIFE, BUT **I** DIDN'T WITNESS IT.

HOW DO YOU LIKE EASTVIEW, JEFF?

S'OKAY.

LIONEL WAS A CHEMIST, HARDWORKING AND DRIVEN. HE WAS A **NICE MAN**, BUT HAD A FORCEFUL PERSONALITY AND AN INTIMIDATING INTELLECT.

MY DAD WAS A CHEMIST, TOO, SO I KNOW WELL **THE TYPE**, MORE COMFORTABLE WITH **TEST TUBES** THAN WITH **TEENAGE SONS**. I NEVER SAW THAT MUCH OF LIONEL EITHER.

JOYCE WAS A HOUSEWIFE WHO WAS **CHAFING** IN THAT ROLE, LIKE **MANY** MOMS IN THE EARLY SEVENTIES.

SHE WAS ALWAYS PLEASANT TO ME, BUT SHE WAS **ODD**. VERY **MOODY** AND **FRAGILE**. IT WAS OBVIOUS SHE WAS LUGGING AROUND SOME **HEAVY BAGGAGE**.

BUT THERE WERE LOTS OF **DAMAGED MOMS** IN TOWN.

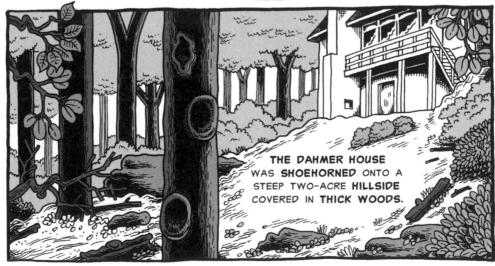

THE DAHMER HOUSE WAS **SHOEHORNED** ONTO A STEEP TWO-ACRE **HILLSIDE** COVERED IN **THICK WOODS**.

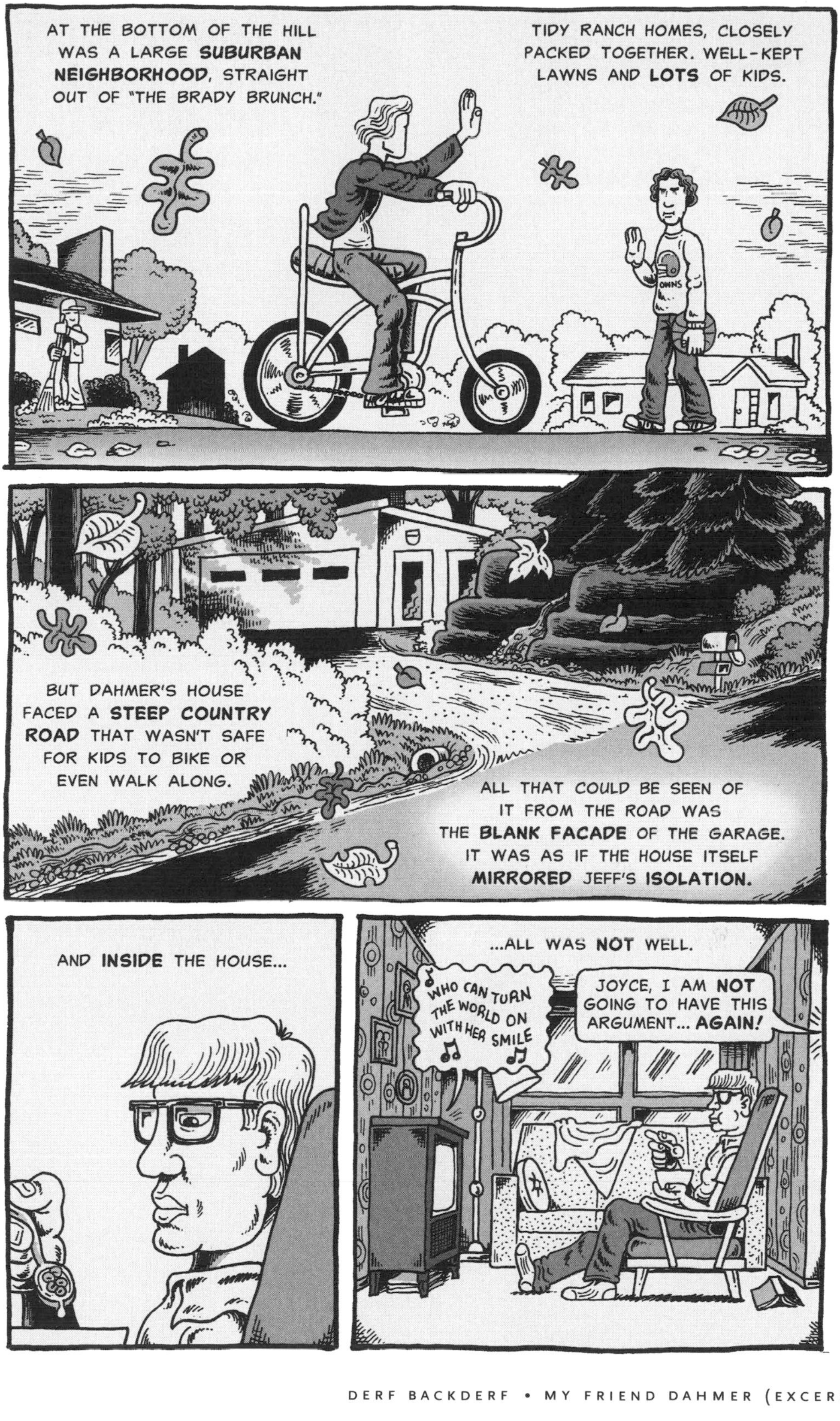

AT THE BOTTOM OF THE HILL WAS A LARGE SUBURBAN NEIGHBORHOOD, STRAIGHT OUT OF "THE BRADY BRUNCH."
TIDY RANCH HOMES, CLOSELY PACKED TOGETHER. WELL-KEPT LAWNS AND LOTS OF KIDS.
BUT DAHMER'S HOUSE FACED A STEEP COUNTRY ROAD THAT WASN'T SAFE FOR KIDS TO BIKE OR EVEN WALK ALONG.
ALL THAT COULD BE SEEN OF IT FROM THE ROAD WAS THE BLANK FACADE OF THE GARAGE. IT WAS AS IF THE HOUSE ITSELF MIRRORED JEFF'S ISOLATION.
AND INSIDE THE HOUSE...
...ALL WAS NOT WELL.
WHO CAN TURN THE WORLD ON WITH HER SMILE
JOYCE, I AM NOT GOING TO HAVE THIS ARGUMENT... AGAIN!

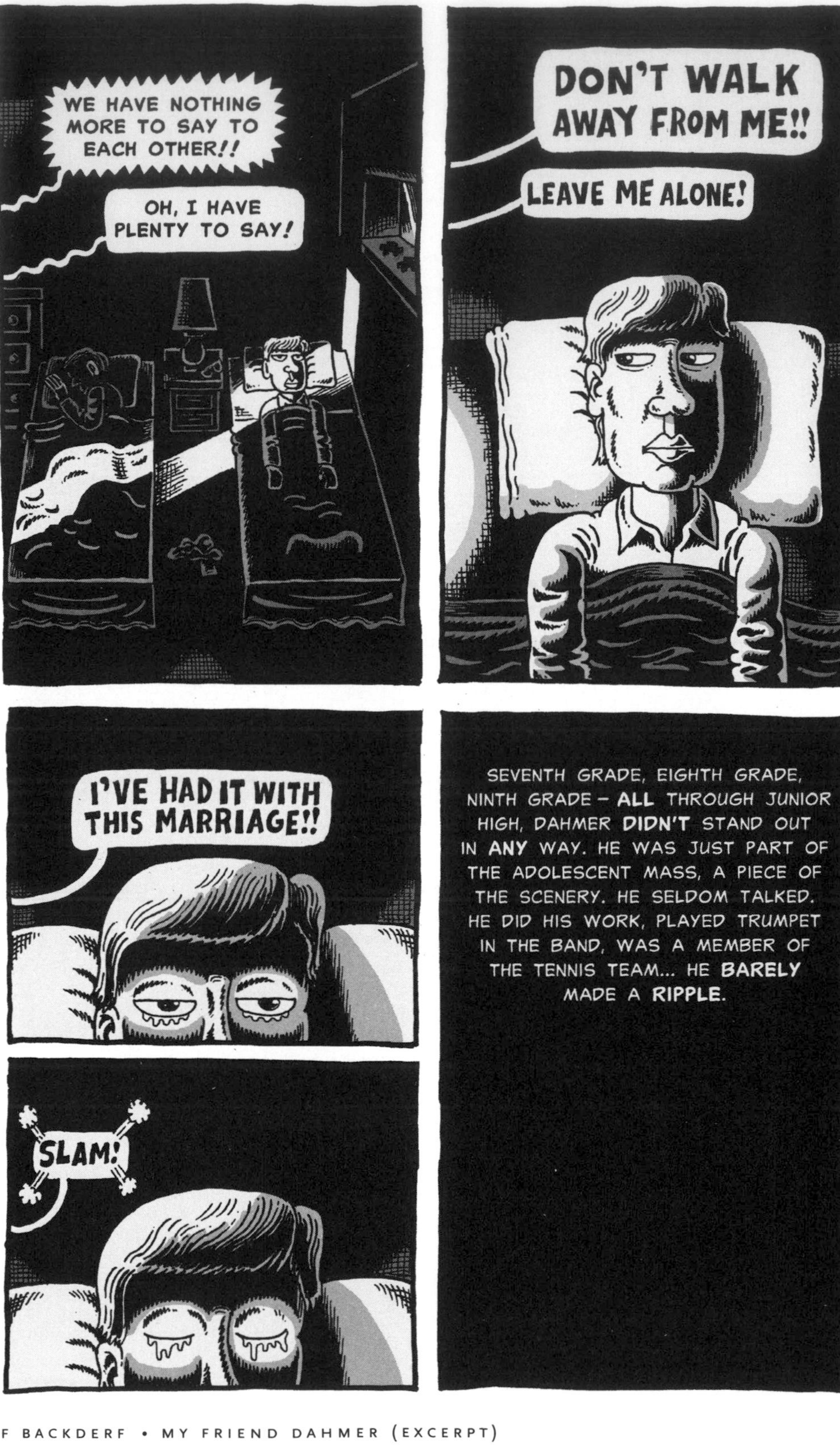
WE HAVE NOTHING MORE TO SAY TO EACH OTHER!!
OH, I HAVE PLENTY TO SAY!
DON'T WALK AWAY FROM ME!!
LEAVE ME ALONE!
I'VE HAD IT WITH THIS MARRIAGE!!
SEVENTH GRADE, EIGHTH GRADE, NINTH GRADE – ALL THROUGH JUNIOR HIGH, DAHMER DIDN'T STAND OUT IN ANY WAY. HE WAS JUST PART OF THE ADOLESCENT MASS, A PIECE OF THE SCENERY. HE SELDOM TALKED. HE DID HIS WORK, PLAYED TRUMPET IN THE BAND, WAS A MEMBER OF THE TENNIS TEAM... HE BARELY MADE A RIPPLE.
SLAM!

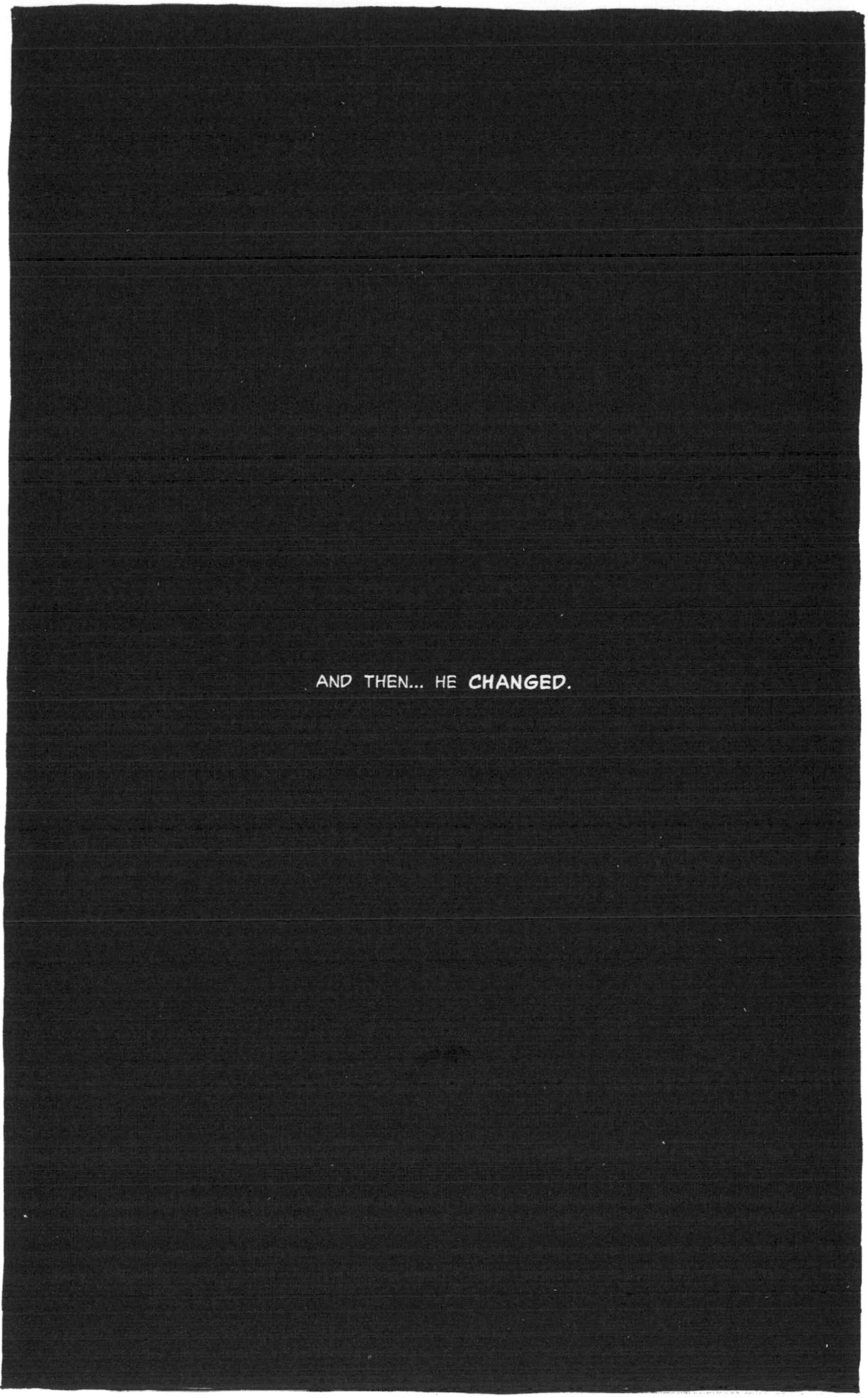
AND THEN... HE **CHANGED.**

Terry Moore

A Killer's Surprise

Excerpt from

Rachel Rising

FROM MY ROTTING BODY, FLOWERS
SHALL GROW AND I AM IN THEM
AND THAT IS ETERNITY.
—EDWARD MUNCH

UNDERWOOD
MORTUARY

SCREEECH!

AUTHORIZED
PERSONNEL
ONLY

BZZT!

WHO IS IT?

IT'S ME,
RACHEL.

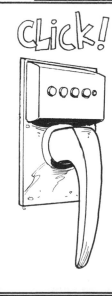

CLICK!

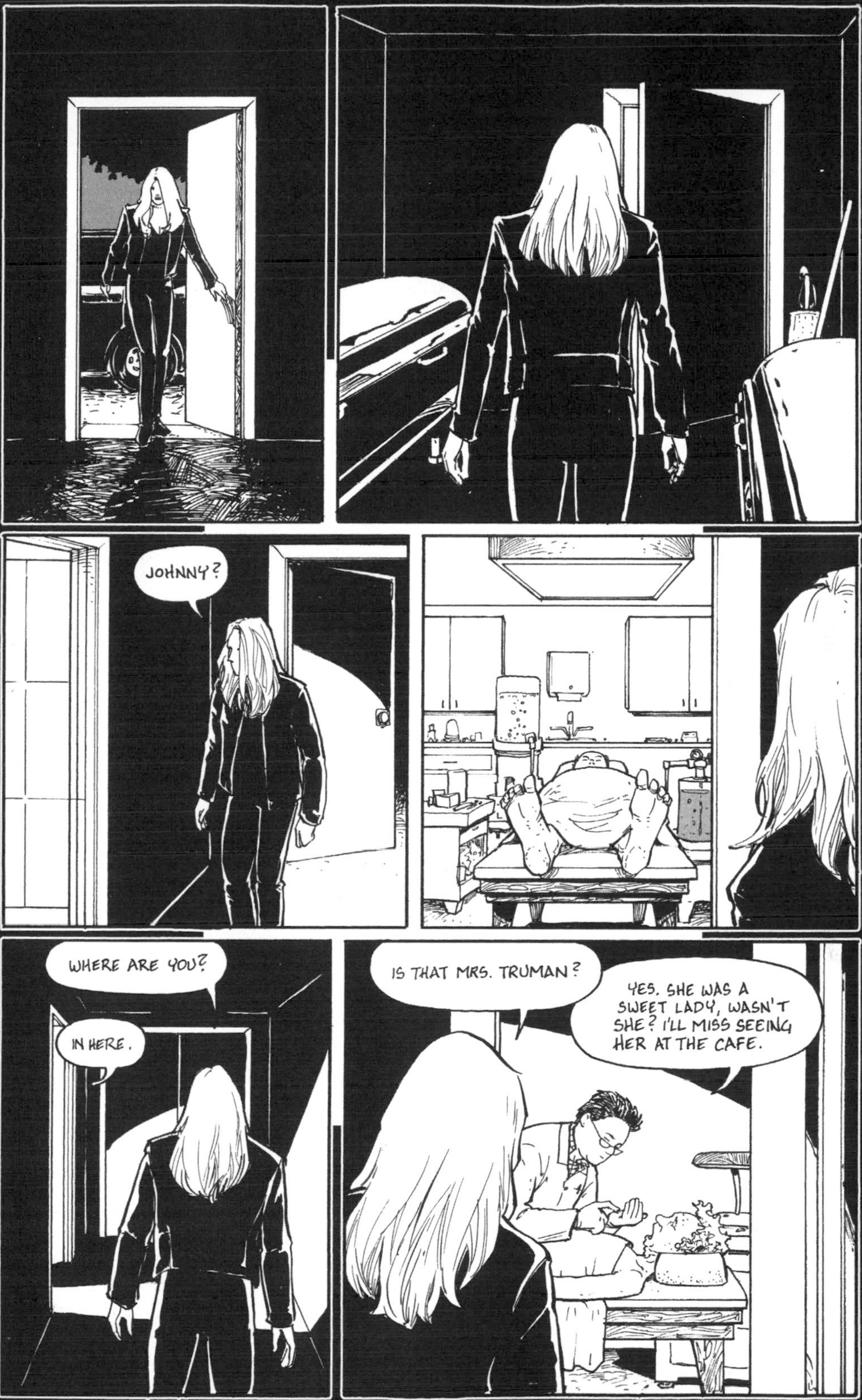
JOHNNY?
WHERE ARE YOU?
IN HERE.
IS THAT MRS. TRUMAN?
YES. SHE WAS A SWEET LADY, WASN'T SHE? I'LL MISS SEEING HER AT THE CAFE.

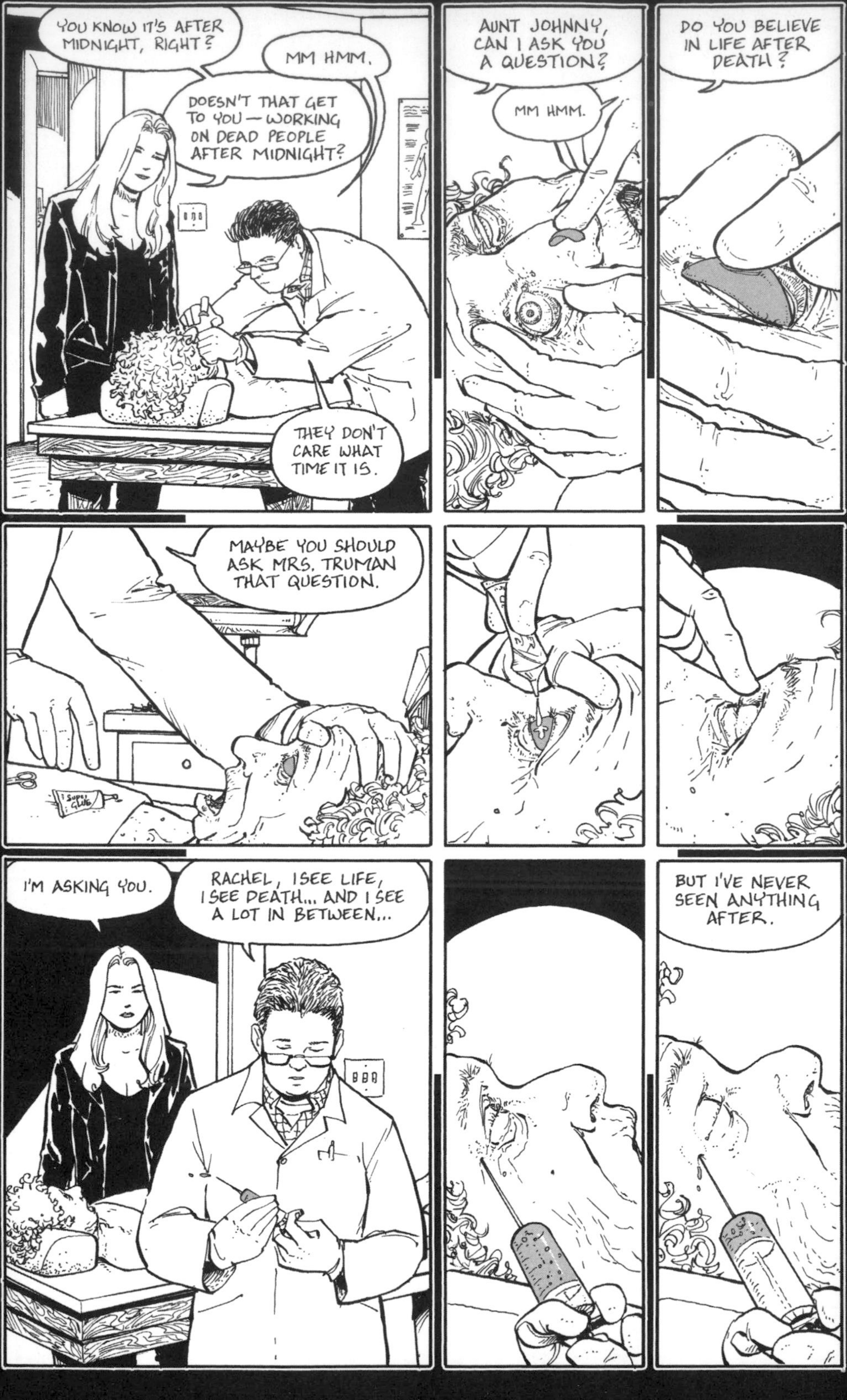
YOU KNOW IT'S AFTER MIDNIGHT, RIGHT?
MM HMM.
DOESN'T THAT GET TO YOU—WORKING ON DEAD PEOPLE AFTER MIDNIGHT?
THEY DON'T CARE WHAT TIME IT IS.
AUNT JOHNNY, CAN I ASK YOU A QUESTION?
MM HMM.
DO YOU BELIEVE IN LIFE AFTER DEATH?
MAYBE YOU SHOULD ASK MRS. TRUMAN THAT QUESTION.
SUPER GLUE
I'M ASKING YOU.
RACHEL, I SEE LIFE, I SEE DEATH... AND I SEE A LOT IN BETWEEN...
BUT I'VE NEVER SEEN ANYTHING AFTER.

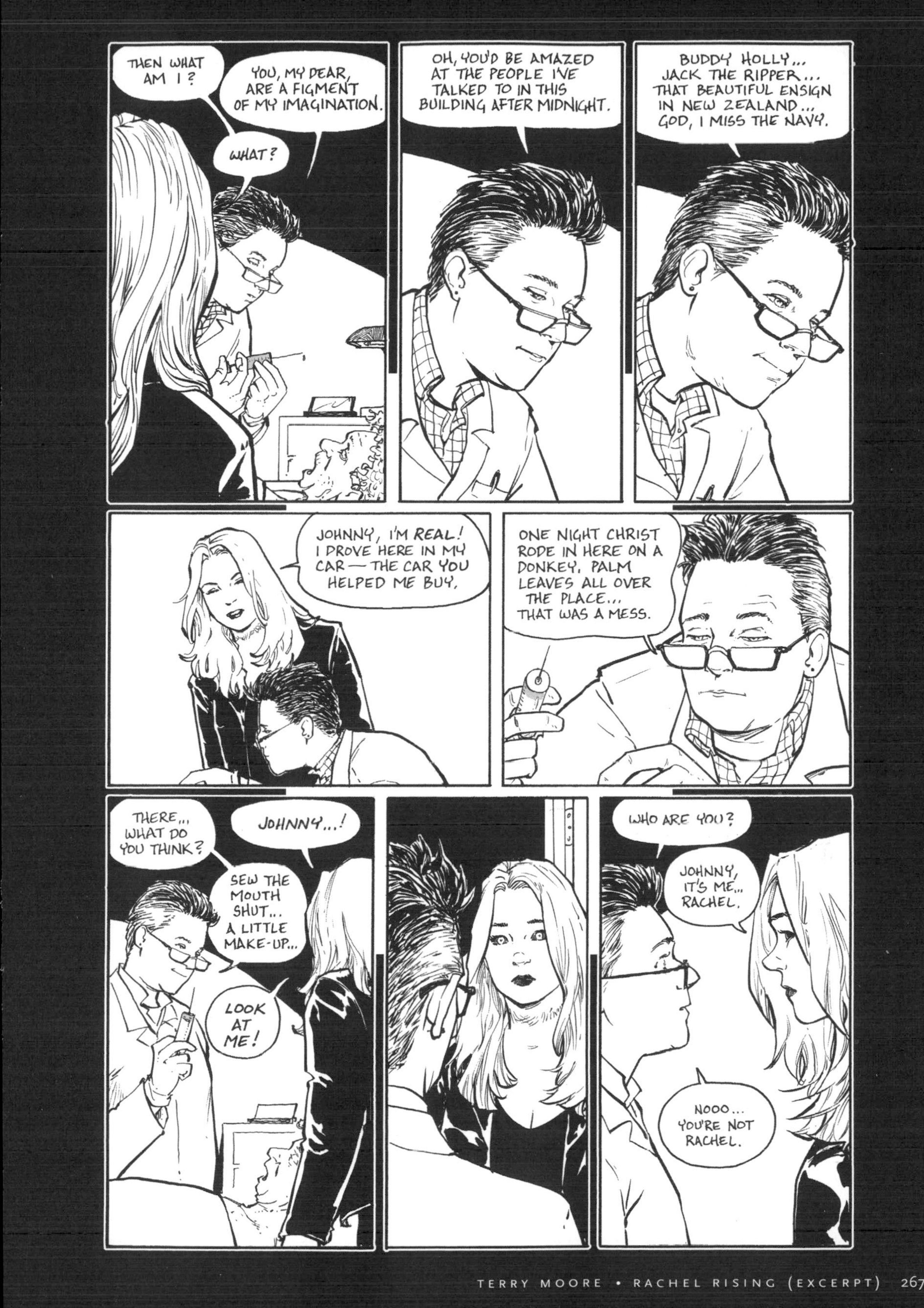
THEN WHAT AM I?
YOU, MY DEAR, ARE A FIGMENT OF MY IMAGINATION.
WHAT?
OH, YOU'D BE AMAZED AT THE PEOPLE I'VE TALKED TO IN THIS BUILDING AFTER MIDNIGHT.
BUDDY HOLLY... JACK THE RIPPER... THAT BEAUTIFUL ENSIGN IN NEW ZEALAND... GOD, I MISS THE NAVY.
JOHNNY, I'M REAL! I DROVE HERE IN MY CAR — THE CAR YOU HELPED ME BUY.
ONE NIGHT CHRIST RODE IN HERE ON A DONKEY. PALM LEAVES ALL OVER THE PLACE... THAT WAS A MESS.
THERE... WHAT DO YOU THINK?
JOHNNY...!
SEW THE MOUTH SHUT... A LITTLE MAKE-UP...
LOOK AT ME!
WHO ARE YOU?
JOHNNY, IT'S ME... RACHEL.
NOOO... YOU'RE NOT RACHEL.

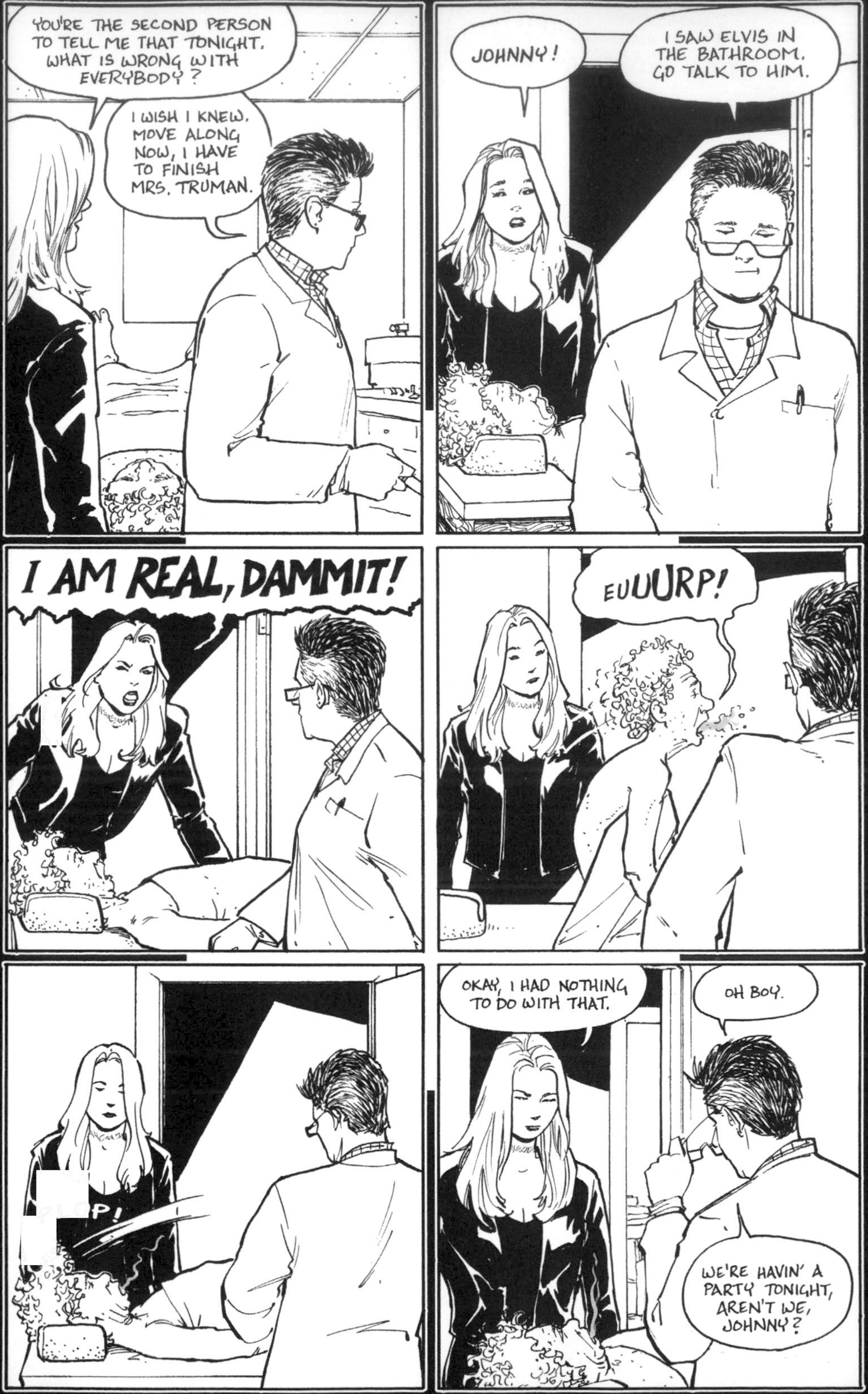

YOU'RE THE SECOND PERSON TO TELL ME THAT TONIGHT. WHAT IS WRONG WITH EVERYBODY?
I WISH I KNEW. MOVE ALONG NOW, I HAVE TO FINISH MRS. TRUMAN.
JOHNNY!
I SAW ELVIS IN THE BATHROOM. GO TALK TO HIM.
I AM REAL, DAMMIT!
EUUURP!
OKAY, I HAD NOTHING TO DO WITH THAT.
OH BOY.
WE'RE HAVIN' A PARTY TONIGHT, AREN'T WE, JOHNNY?

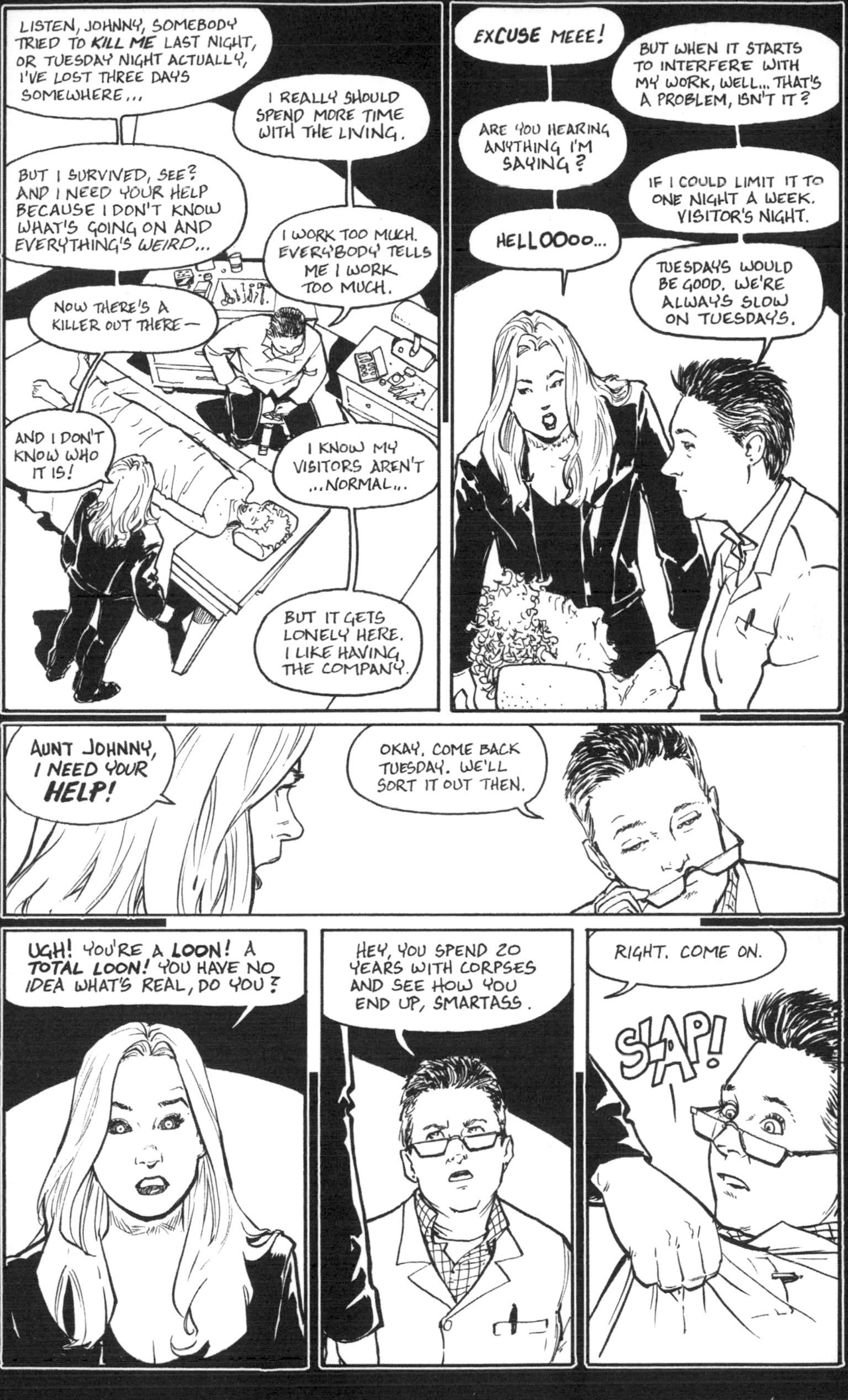
LISTEN, JOHNNY, SOMEBODY TRIED TO KILL ME LAST NIGHT, OR TUESDAY NIGHT ACTUALLY, I'VE LOST THREE DAYS SOMEWHERE...
I REALLY SHOULD SPEND MORE TIME WITH THE LIVING.
BUT I SURVIVED, SEE? AND I NEED YOUR HELP BECAUSE I DON'T KNOW WHAT'S GOING ON AND EVERYTHING'S WEIRD...
I WORK TOO MUCH. EVERYBODY TELLS ME I WORK TOO MUCH.
NOW THERE'S A KILLER OUT THERE—
AND I DON'T KNOW WHO IT IS!
I KNOW MY VISITORS AREN'T ...NORMAL...
BUT IT GETS LONELY HERE. I LIKE HAVING THE COMPANY.
EXCUSE MEEE!
BUT WHEN IT STARTS TO INTERFERE WITH MY WORK, WELL... THAT'S A PROBLEM, ISN'T IT?
ARE YOU HEARING ANYTHING I'M SAYING?
IF I COULD LIMIT IT TO ONE NIGHT A WEEK. VISITOR'S NIGHT.
HELLOOoo...
TUESDAYS WOULD BE GOOD. WE'RE ALWAYS SLOW ON TUESDAYS.
AUNT JOHNNY, I NEED YOUR HELP!
OKAY. COME BACK TUESDAY. WE'LL SORT IT OUT THEN.
UGH! YOU'RE A LOON! A TOTAL LOON! YOU HAVE NO IDEA WHAT'S REAL, DO YOU?
HEY, YOU SPEND 20 YEARS WITH CORPSES AND SEE HOW YOU END UP, SMARTASS.
RIGHT. COME ON.
SLAP!

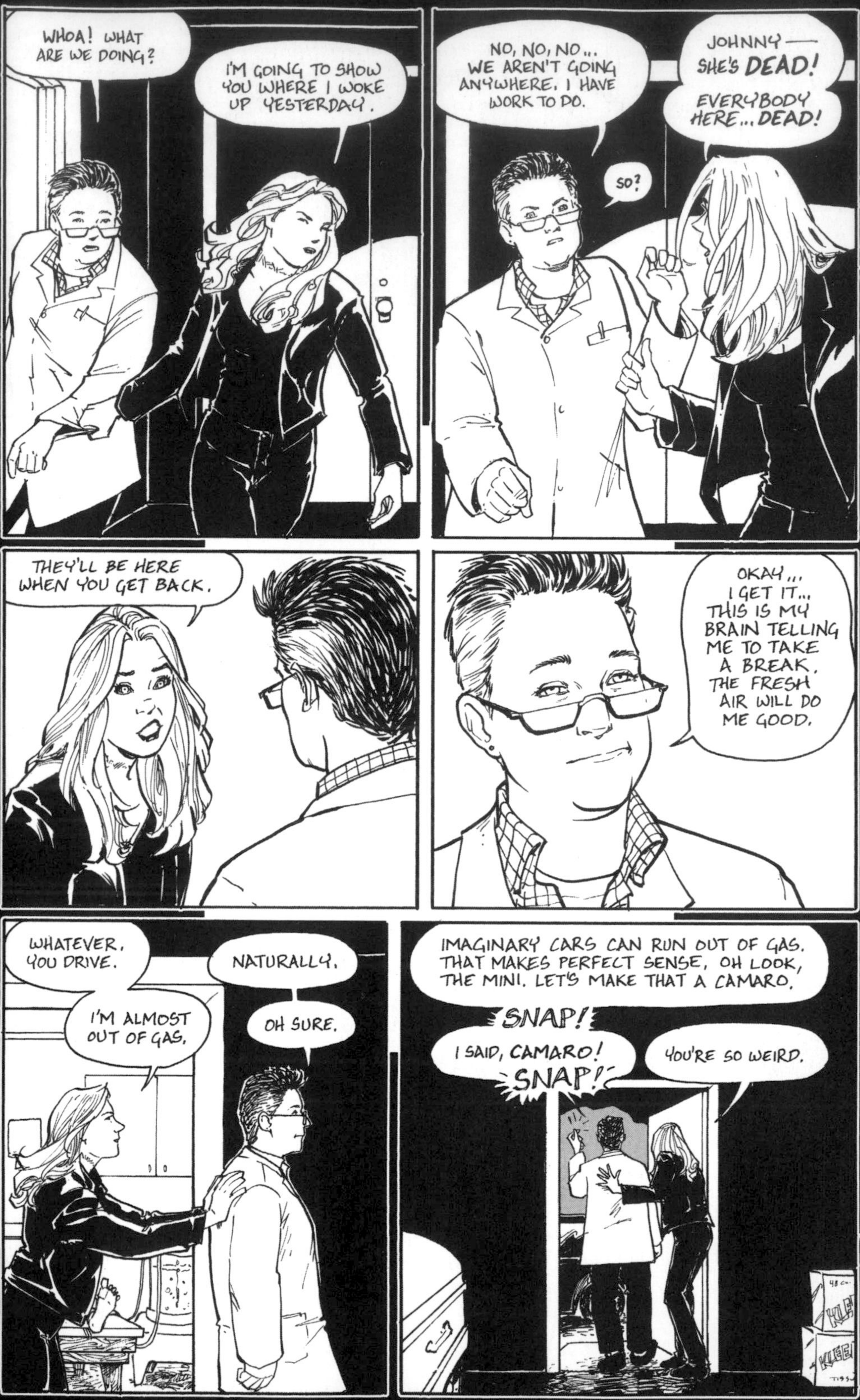
WHOA! WHAT ARE WE DOING?
I'M GOING TO SHOW YOU WHERE I WOKE UP YESTERDAY.
NO, NO, NO... WE AREN'T GOING ANYWHERE. I HAVE WORK TO DO.
JOHNNY— SHE'S DEAD!
EVERYBODY HERE... DEAD!
SO?
THEY'LL BE HERE WHEN YOU GET BACK.
OKAY... I GET IT... THIS IS MY BRAIN TELLING ME TO TAKE A BREAK. THE FRESH AIR WILL DO ME GOOD.
WHATEVER. YOU DRIVE.
NATURALLY.
I'M ALMOST OUT OF GAS.
OH SURE.
IMAGINARY CARS CAN RUN OUT OF GAS. THAT MAKES PERFECT SENSE. OH LOOK, THE MINI. LET'S MAKE THAT A CAMARO.
SNAP!
I SAID, CAMARO!
SNAP!
YOU'RE SO WEIRD.

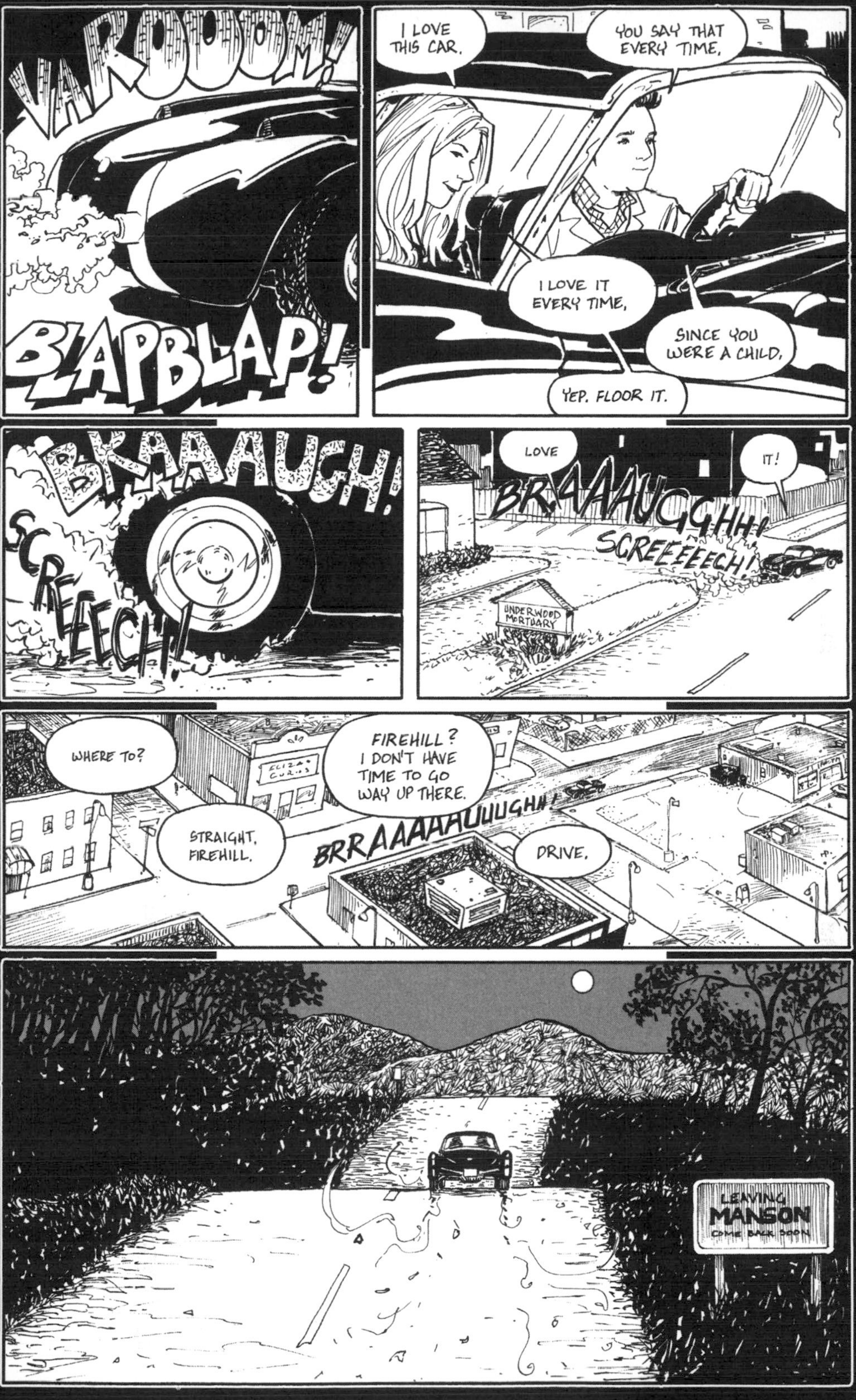
VAROOOOM!
BLAPBLAP!
I LOVE THIS CAR.
YOU SAY THAT EVERY TIME.
I LOVE IT EVERY TIME.
SINCE YOU WERE A CHILD.
YEP. FLOOR IT.
BRAAAAUGH!
SCREEEECH!
LOVE
IT!
BRAAAAUGGHH!
SCREEEEECH!
UNDERWOOD MORTUARY
WHERE TO?
FIREHILL? I DON'T HAVE TIME TO GO WAY UP THERE.
STRAIGHT. FIREHILL.
BRRAAAAAUUUGHH!
DRIVE.
LEAVING MANSON COME BACK SOON

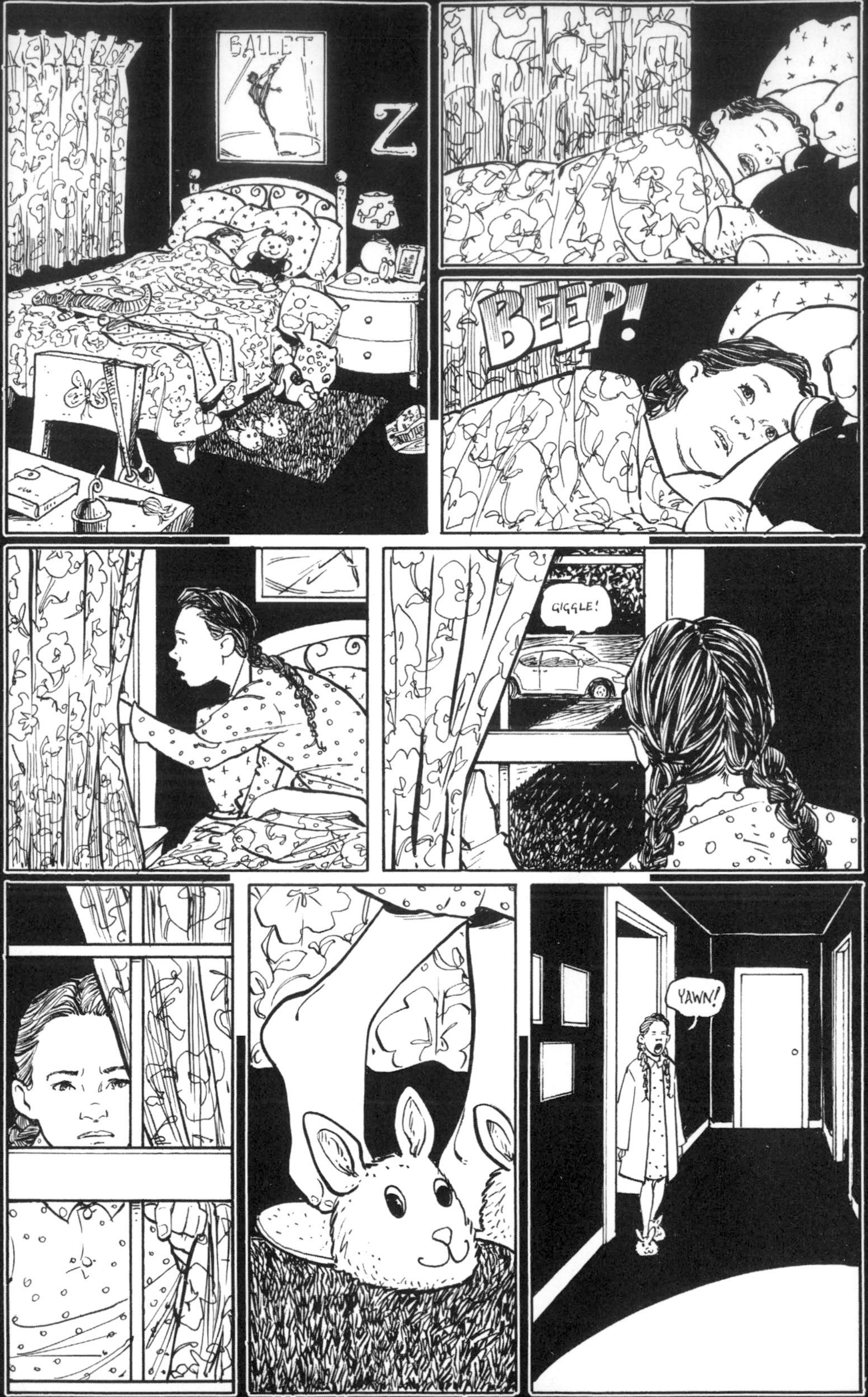
BALLET
Z
BEEP!
GIGGLE!
YAWN!

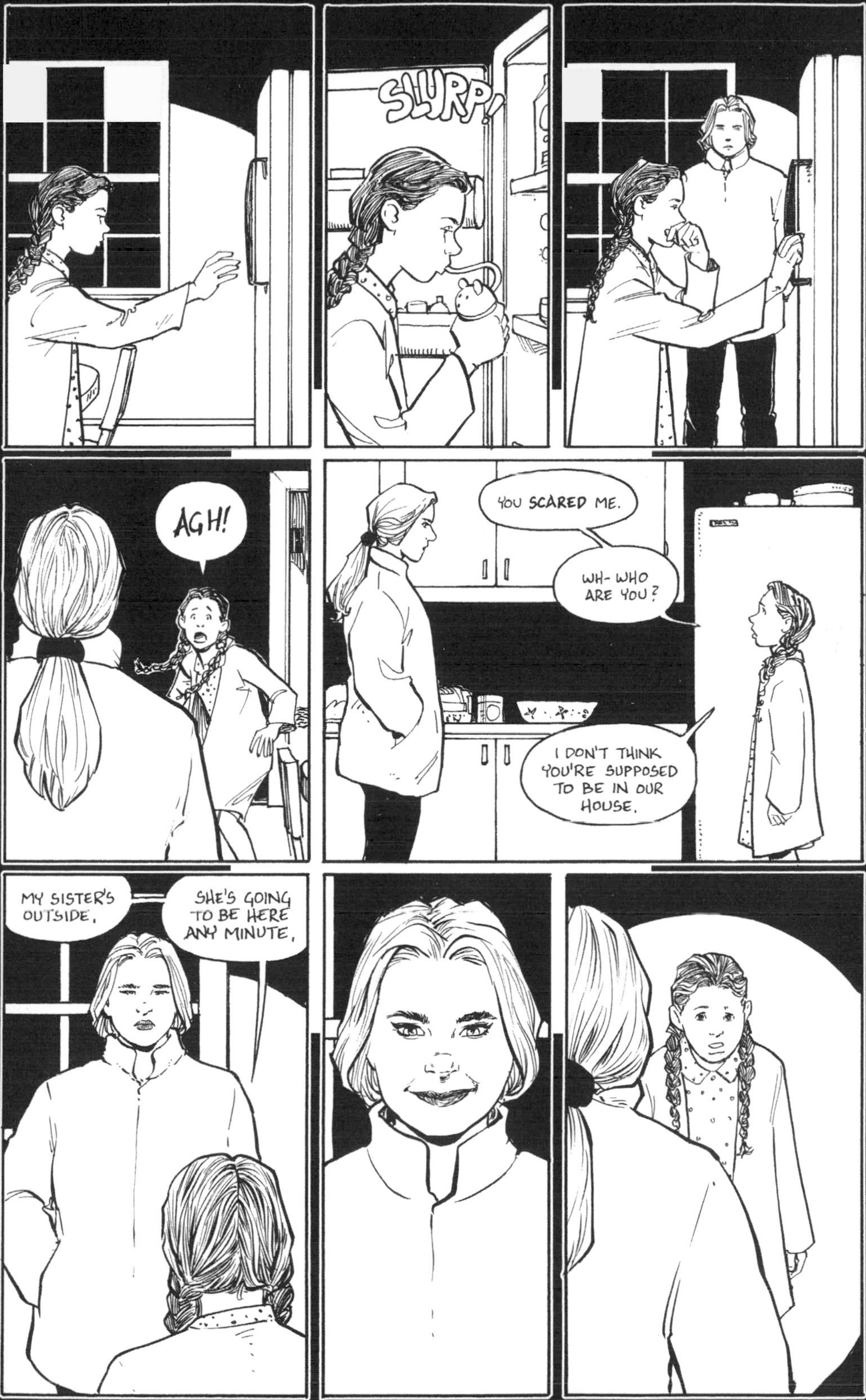
SLURP!
AGH!
YOU SCARED ME.
WH- WHO ARE YOU?
I DON'T THINK YOU'RE SUPPOSED TO BE IN OUR HOUSE.
MY SISTER'S OUTSIDE.
SHE'S GOING TO BE HERE ANY MINUTE.

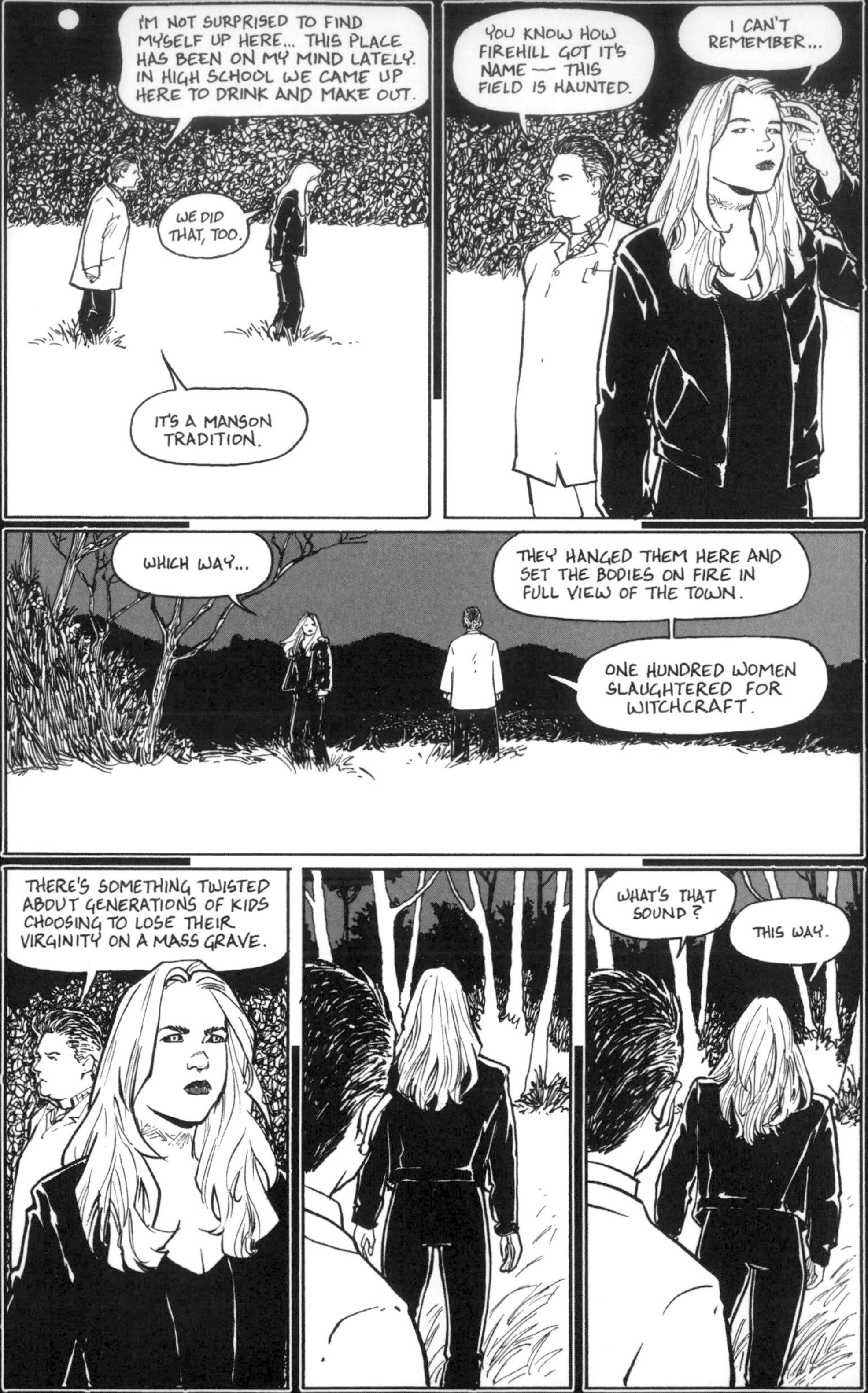
I'M NOT SURPRISED TO FIND MYSELF UP HERE... THIS PLACE HAS BEEN ON MY MIND LATELY. IN HIGH SCHOOL WE CAME UP HERE TO DRINK AND MAKE OUT.
WE DID THAT, TOO.
IT'S A MANSON TRADITION.
YOU KNOW HOW FIREHILL GOT IT'S NAME — THIS FIELD IS HAUNTED.
I CAN'T REMEMBER...
WHICH WAY...
THEY HANGED THEM HERE AND SET THE BODIES ON FIRE IN FULL VIEW OF THE TOWN.
ONE HUNDRED WOMEN SLAUGHTERED FOR WITCHCRAFT.
THERE'S SOMETHING TWISTED ABOUT GENERATIONS OF KIDS CHOOSING TO LOSE THEIR VIRGINITY ON A MASS GRAVE.
WHAT'S THAT SOUND?
THIS WAY.

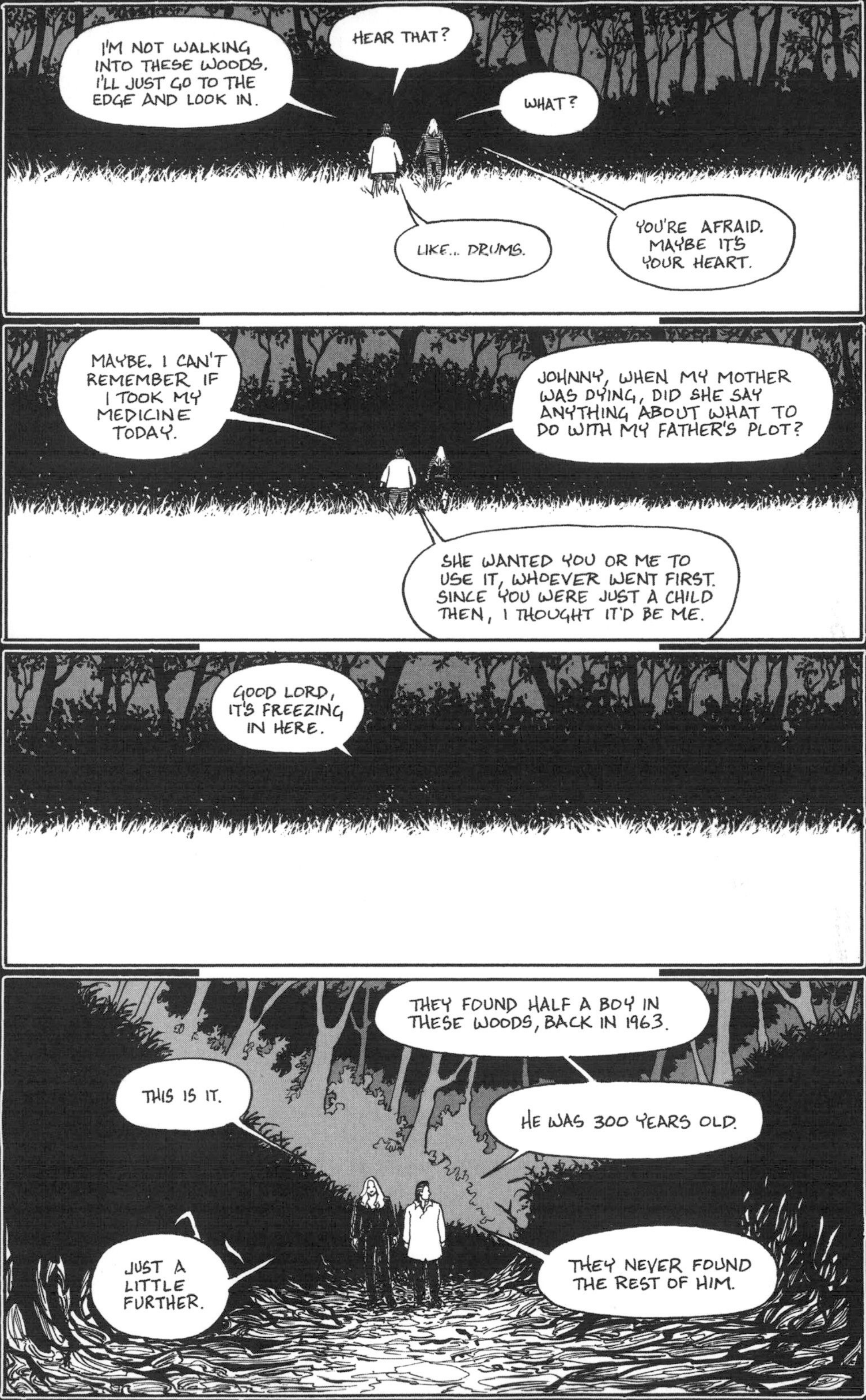

I'M NOT WALKING INTO THESE WOODS. I'LL JUST GO TO THE EDGE AND LOOK IN.
HEAR THAT?
WHAT?
LIKE... DRUMS.
YOU'RE AFRAID. MAYBE IT'S YOUR HEART.
MAYBE. I CAN'T REMEMBER IF I TOOK MY MEDICINE TODAY.
JOHNNY, WHEN MY MOTHER WAS DYING, DID SHE SAY ANYTHING ABOUT WHAT TO DO WITH MY FATHER'S PLOT?
SHE WANTED YOU OR ME TO USE IT, WHOEVER WENT FIRST. SINCE YOU WERE JUST A CHILD THEN, I THOUGHT IT'D BE ME.
GOOD LORD, IT'S FREEZING IN HERE.
THEY FOUND HALF A BOY IN THESE WOODS, BACK IN 1963.
THIS IS IT.
HE WAS 300 YEARS OLD.
JUST A LITTLE FURTHER.
THEY NEVER FOUND THE REST OF HIM.

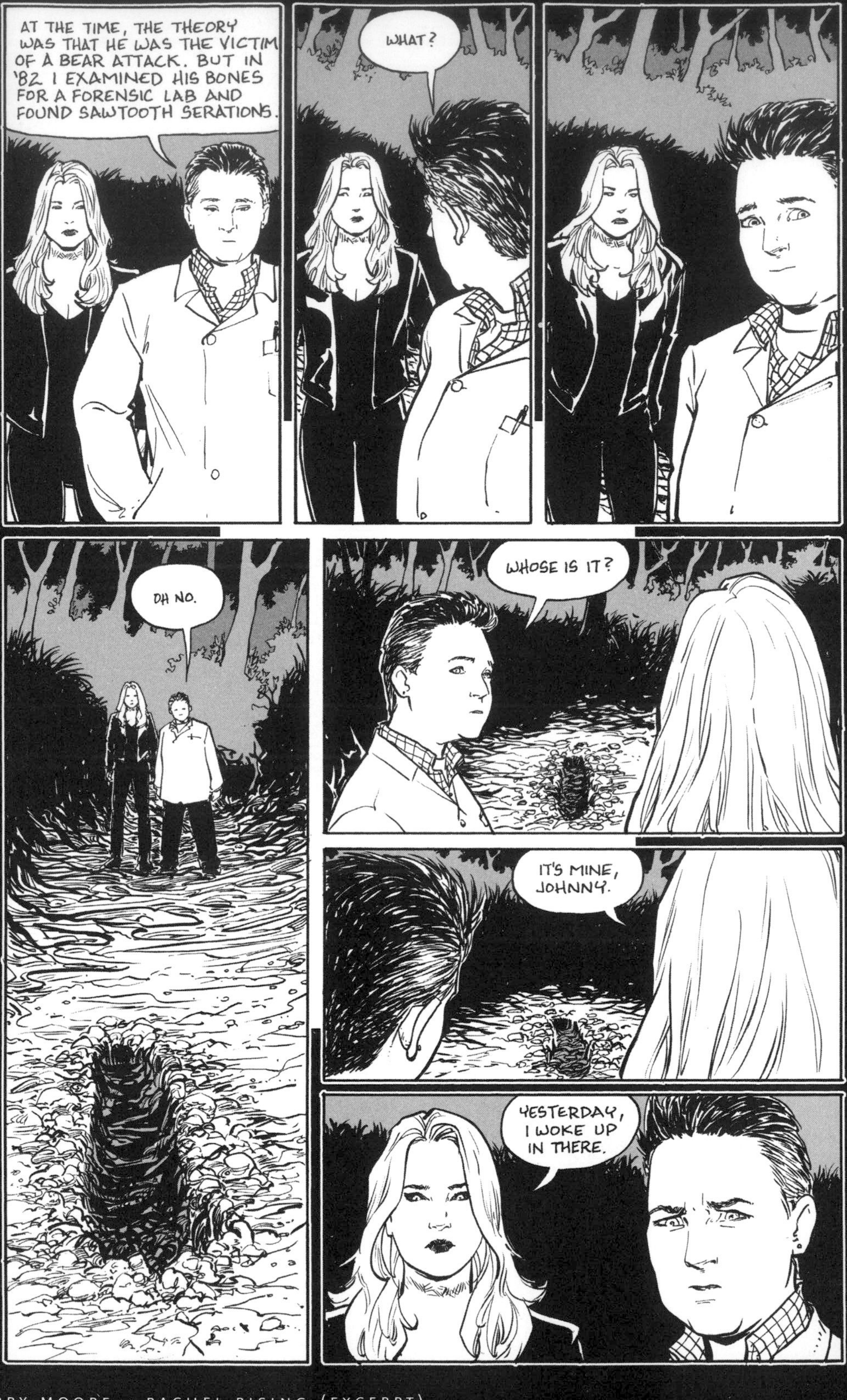
AT THE TIME, THE THEORY WAS THAT HE WAS THE VICTIM OF A BEAR ATTACK. BUT IN '82 I EXAMINED HIS BONES FOR A FORENSIC LAB AND FOUND SAWTOOTH SERATIONS.
WHAT?
OH NO.
WHOSE IS IT?
IT'S MINE, JOHNNY.
YESTERDAY, I WOKE UP IN THERE.

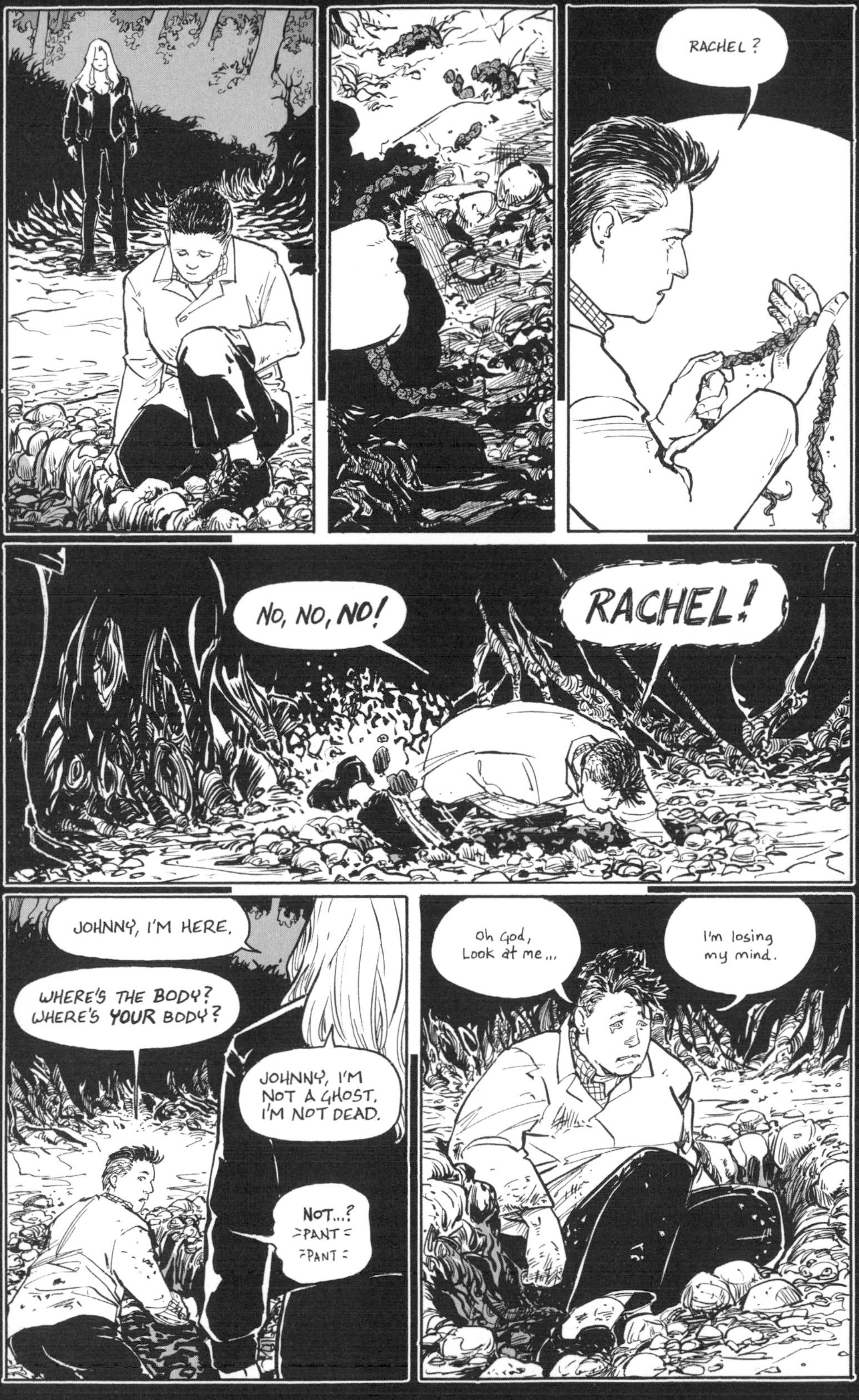
RACHEL?
NO, NO, NO!
RACHEL!
JOHNNY, I'M HERE.
WHERE'S THE BODY? WHERE'S YOUR BODY?
JOHNNY, I'M NOT A GHOST. I'M NOT DEAD.
NOT...? PANT PANT
Oh God, Look at me...
I'm losing my mind.

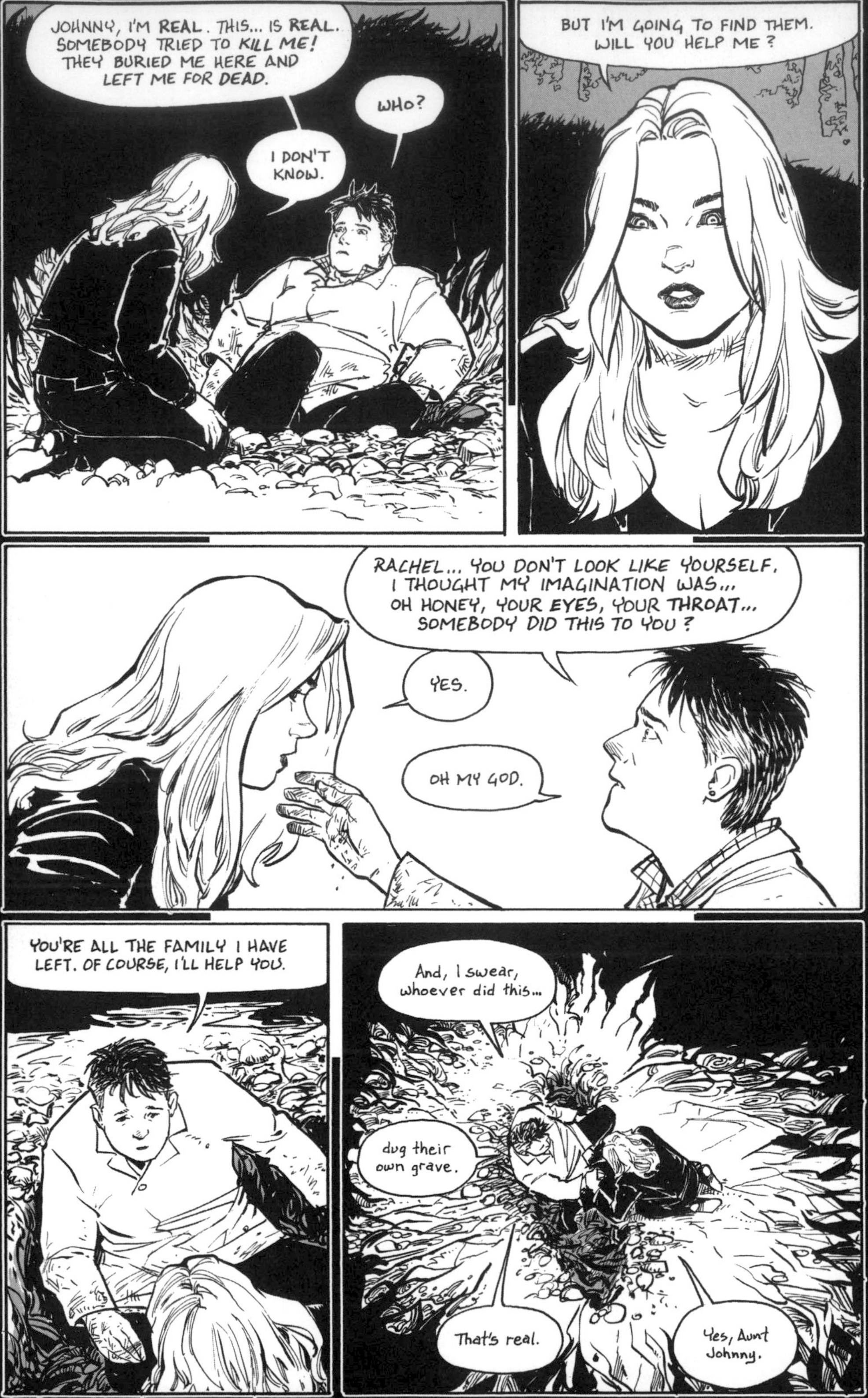
JOHNNY, I'M REAL. THIS... IS REAL. SOMEBODY TRIED TO KILL ME! THEY BURIED ME HERE AND LEFT ME FOR DEAD.
WHO?
I DON'T KNOW.
BUT I'M GOING TO FIND THEM. WILL YOU HELP ME?
RACHEL... YOU DON'T LOOK LIKE YOURSELF. I THOUGHT MY IMAGINATION WAS... OH HONEY, YOUR EYES, YOUR THROAT... SOMEBODY DID THIS TO YOU?
YES.
OH MY GOD.
YOU'RE ALL THE FAMILY I HAVE LEFT. OF COURSE, I'LL HELP YOU.
And, I swear, whoever did this...
dug their own grave.
That's real.
Yes, Aunt Johnny.

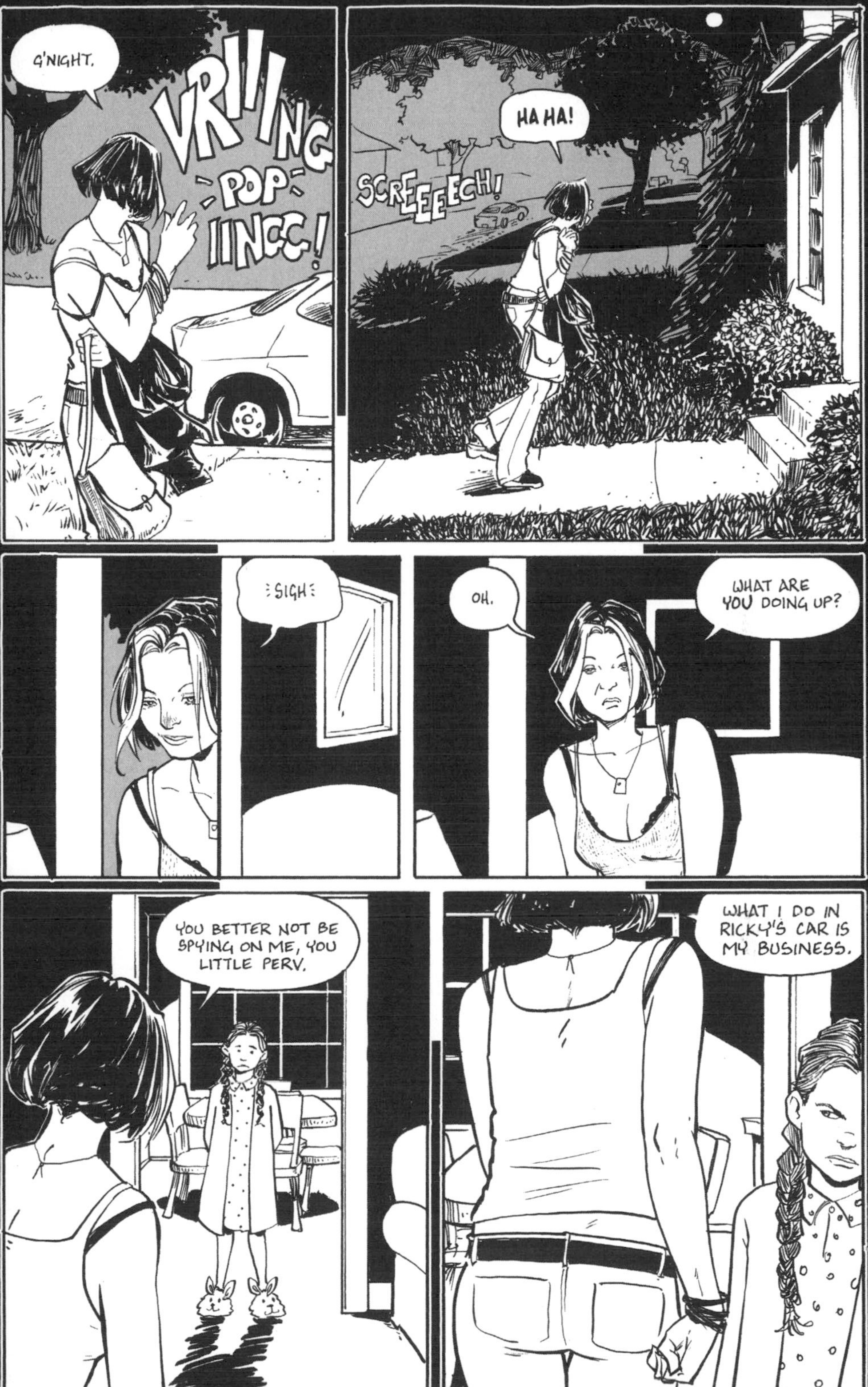
G'NIGHT.
VRIIING
-POP-
IINGG!
HA HA!
SCREEEEECH!
SIGH
OH.
WHAT ARE YOU DOING UP?
YOU BETTER NOT BE SPYING ON ME, YOU LITTLE PERV.
WHAT I DO IN RICKY'S CAR IS MY BUSINESS.

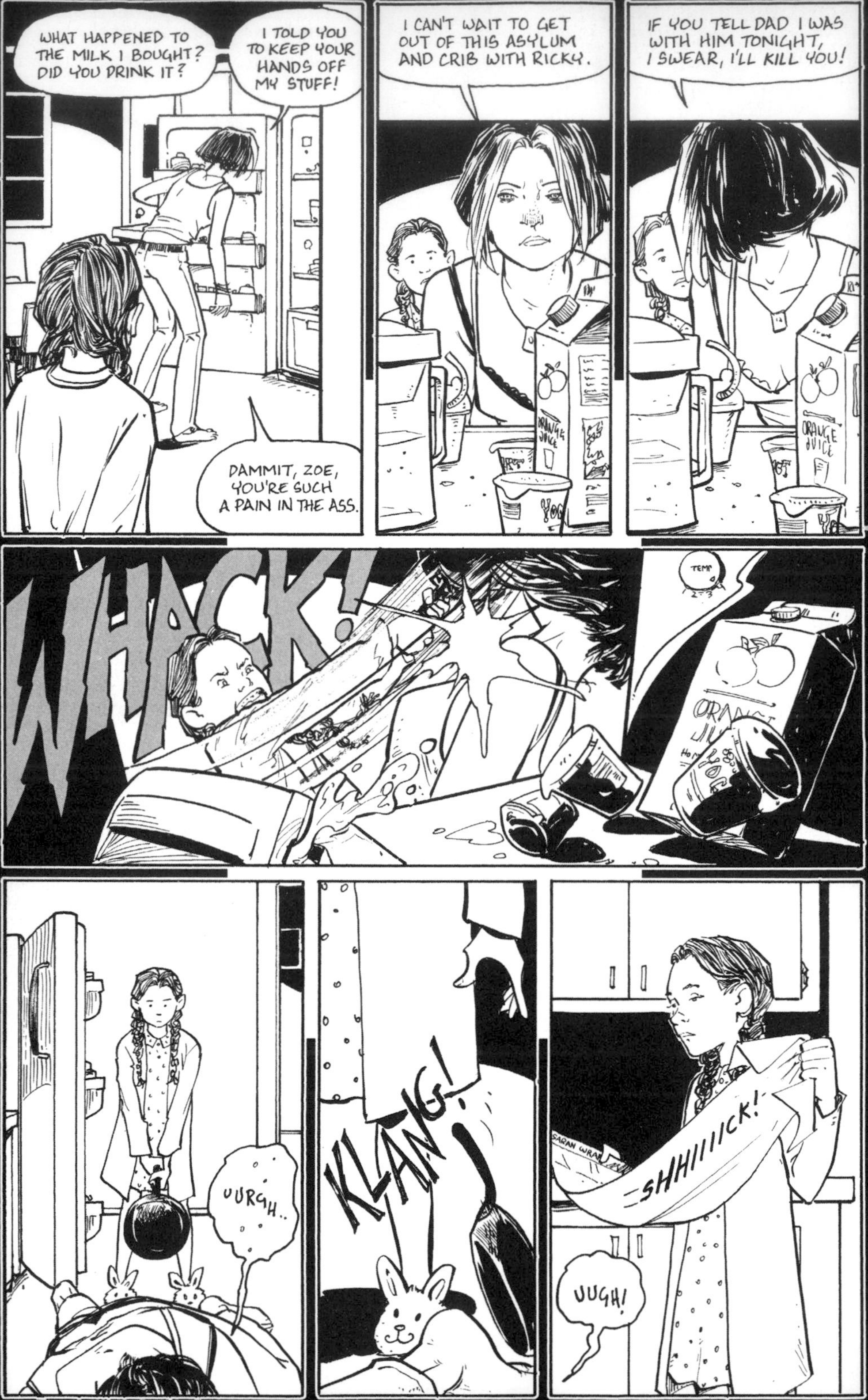
WHAT HAPPENED TO THE MILK I BOUGHT? DID YOU DRINK IT?
I TOLD YOU TO KEEP YOUR HANDS OFF MY STUFF!
DAMMIT, ZOE, YOU'RE SUCH A PAIN IN THE ASS.
I CAN'T WAIT TO GET OUT OF THIS ASYLUM AND CRIB WITH RICKY.
ORANGE JUICE
IF YOU TELL DAD I WAS WITH HIM TONIGHT, I SWEAR, I'LL KILL YOU!
ORANGE JUICE
WHACK!
TEMP
UURGH..
KLANG!
SARAN WRAP
SHHIIIIICK!
UUGH!

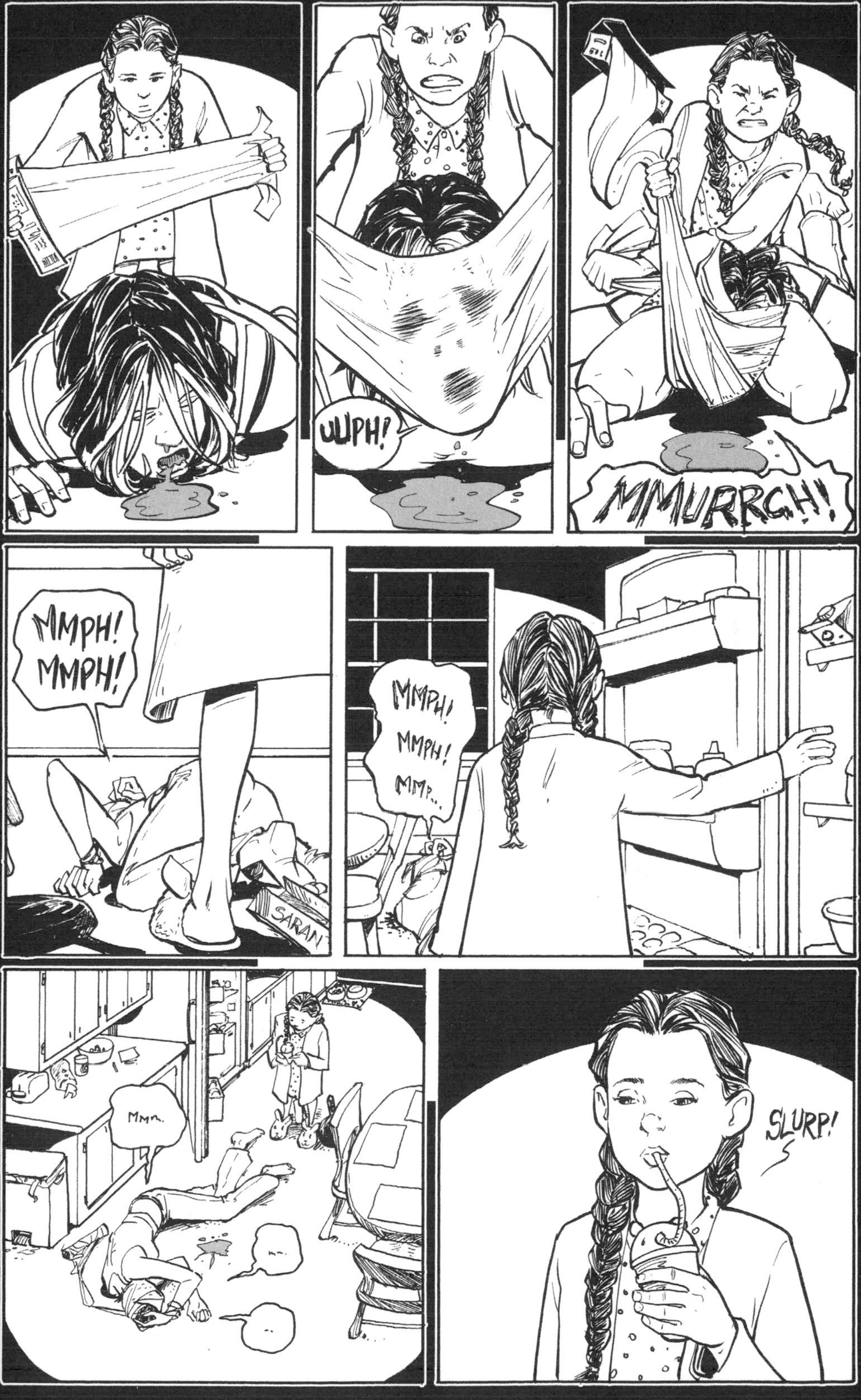
UUPH!
MMURRGH!
MMPH! MMPH!
MMPH! MMPH! MMP...
SARAN
Mmn.
SLURP!

Laura PARK

GEORGE

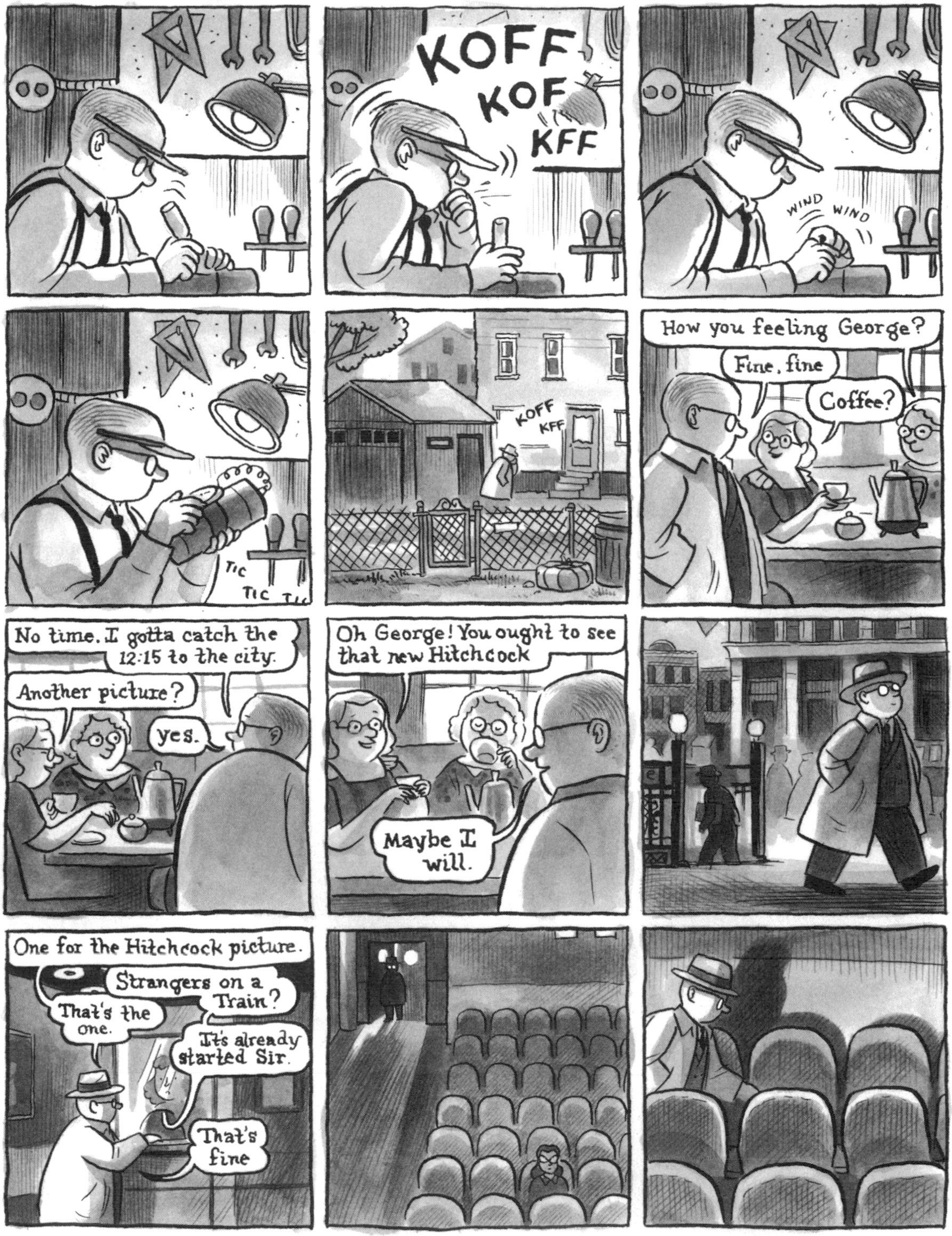
KOFF
KOF
KFF
WIND WIND
TIC TIC TIC
KOFF
KFF
How you feeling George?
Fine, fine
Coffee?
No time. I gotta catch the 12:15 to the city.
Another picture?
yes.
Oh George! You ought to see that new Hitchcock
Maybe I will.
One for the Hitchcock picture.
Strangers on a Train?
That's the one.
It's already started Sir.
That's fine

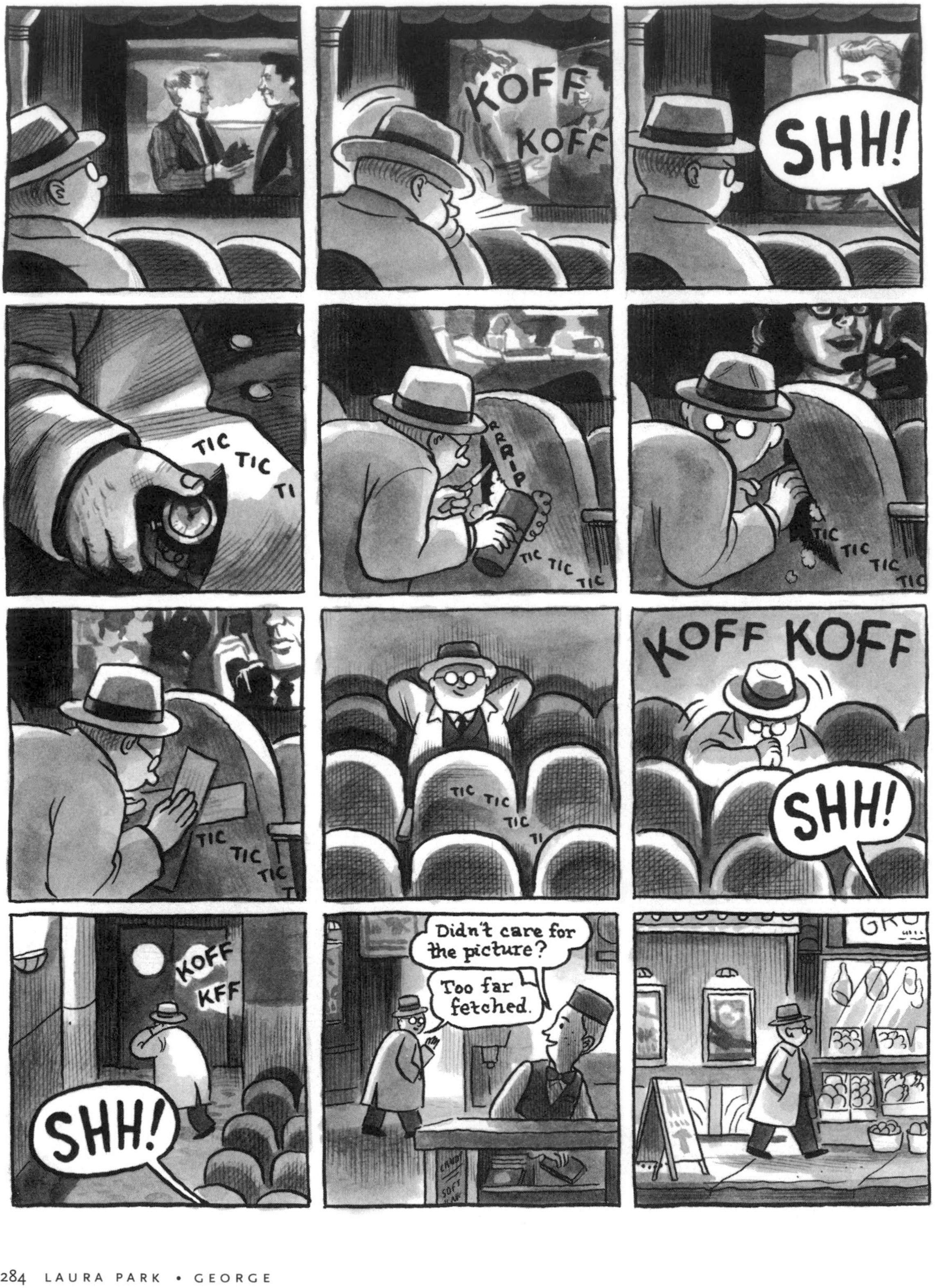
KOFF
KOFF
SHH!
TIC
TIC
TI
RRRIP
TIC TIC TIC
TIC
TIC
TIC
TIC
TIC
TIC
TIC
T
TIC TIC
TIC
TI
KOFF KOFF
SHH!
KOFF
KFF
SHH!
Didn't care for the picture?
Too far fetched.

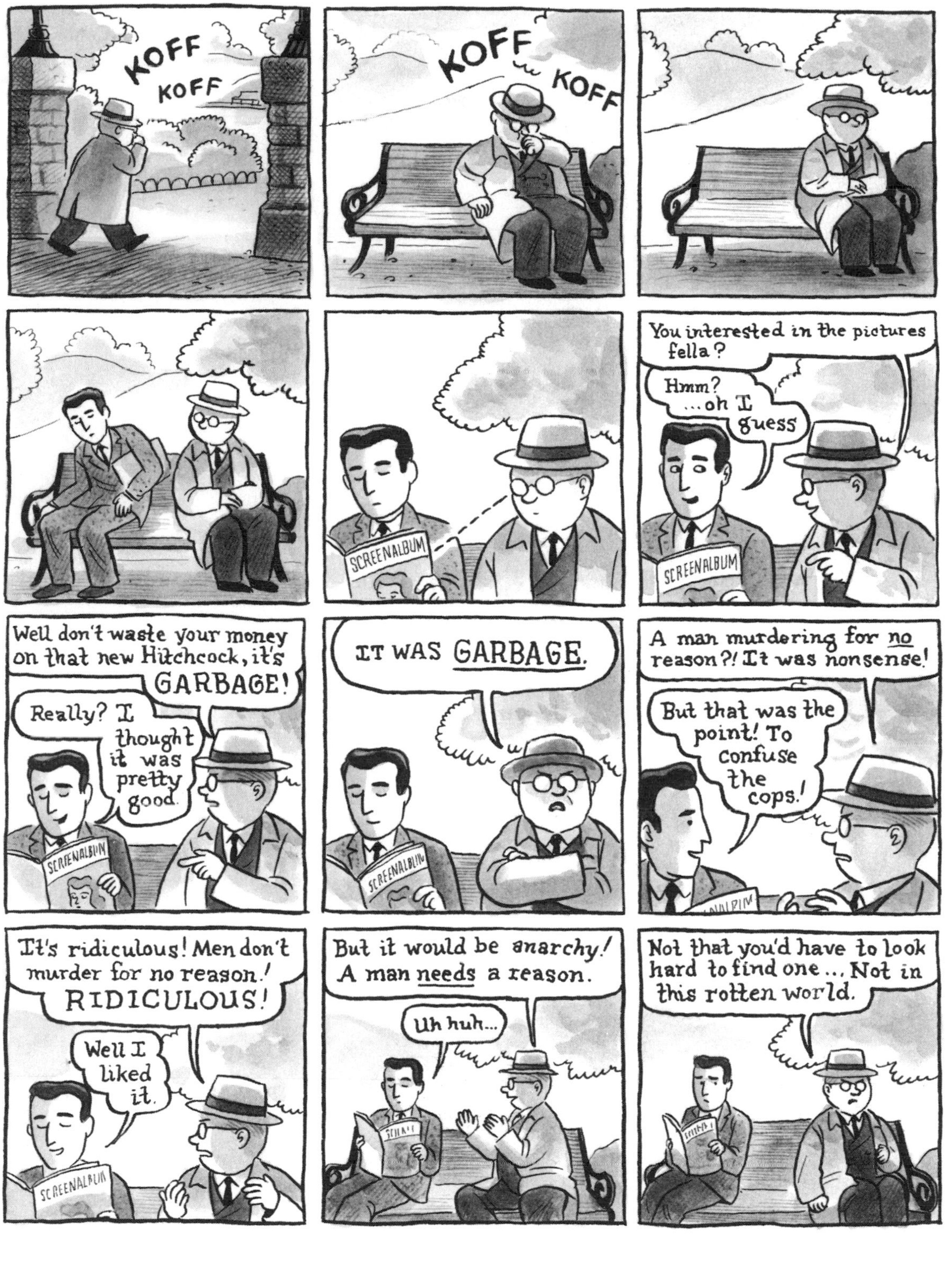
KOFF
KOFF
KOFF
KOFF
You interested in the pictures fella?
Hmm? ...oh I guess
SCREENALBUM
Well don't waste your money on that new Hitchcock, it's GARBAGE!
Really? I thought it was pretty good.
IT WAS GARBAGE.
A man murdering for no reason?! It was nonsense!
But that was the point! To confuse the cops!
It's ridiculous! Men don't murder for no reason! RIDICULOUS!
Well I liked it.
But it would be anarchy! A man needs a reason.
Uh huh...
Not that you'd have to look hard to find one... Not in this rotten world.

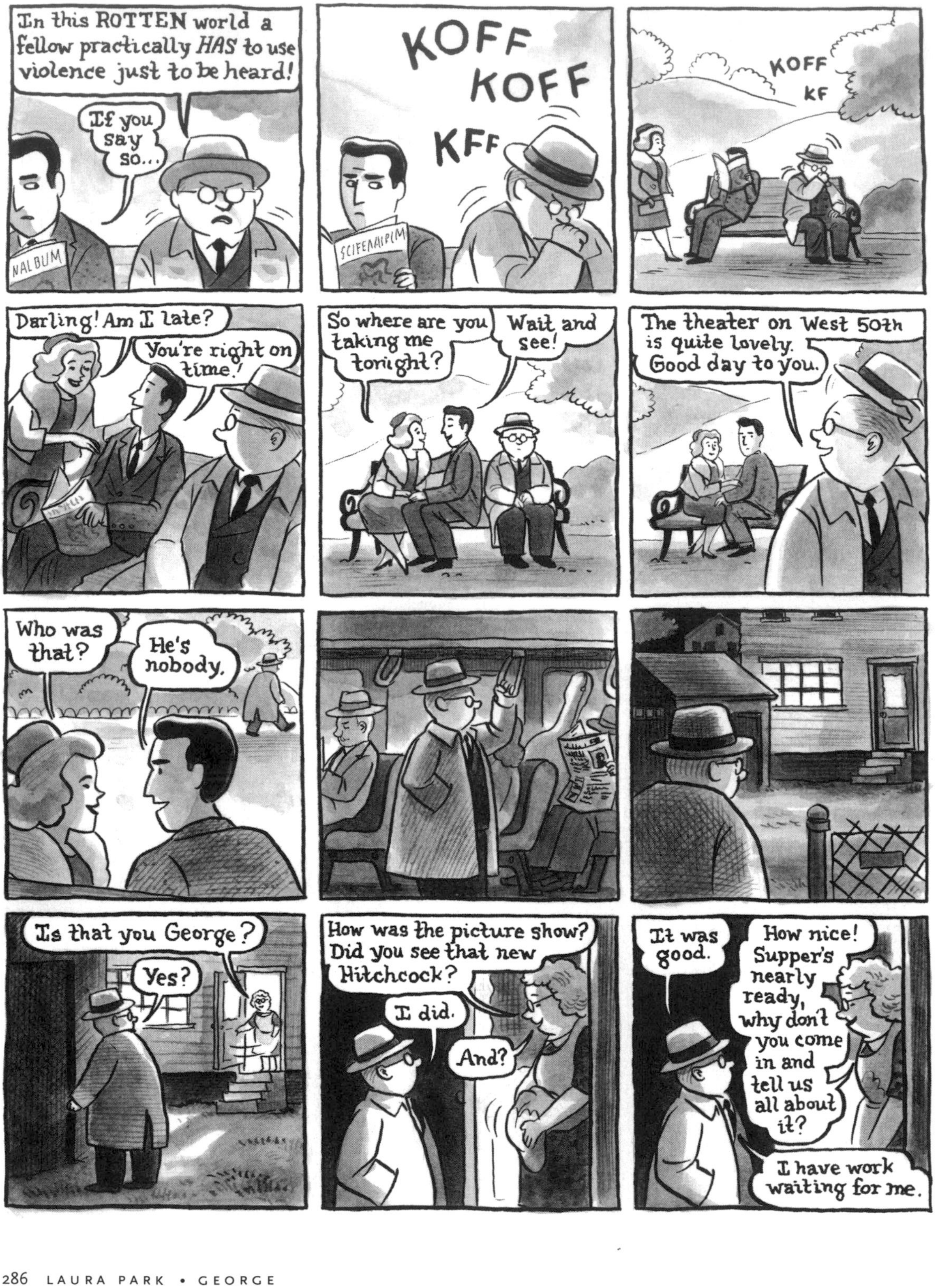
In this ROTTEN world a fellow practically HAS to use violence just to be heard!
If you say so...
NALBUM
KOFF
KOFF
KFF
SCIFEΛΛIPIM
KOFF
KF
Darling! Am I late?
You're right on time!
So where are you taking me tonight?
Wait and see!
The theater on West 50th is quite lovely. Good day to you.
Who was that?
He's nobody.
Is that you George?
Yes?
How was the picture show? Did you see that new Hitchcock?
I did.
And?
It was good.
How nice! Supper's nearly ready, why don't you come in and tell us all about it?
I have work waiting for me.

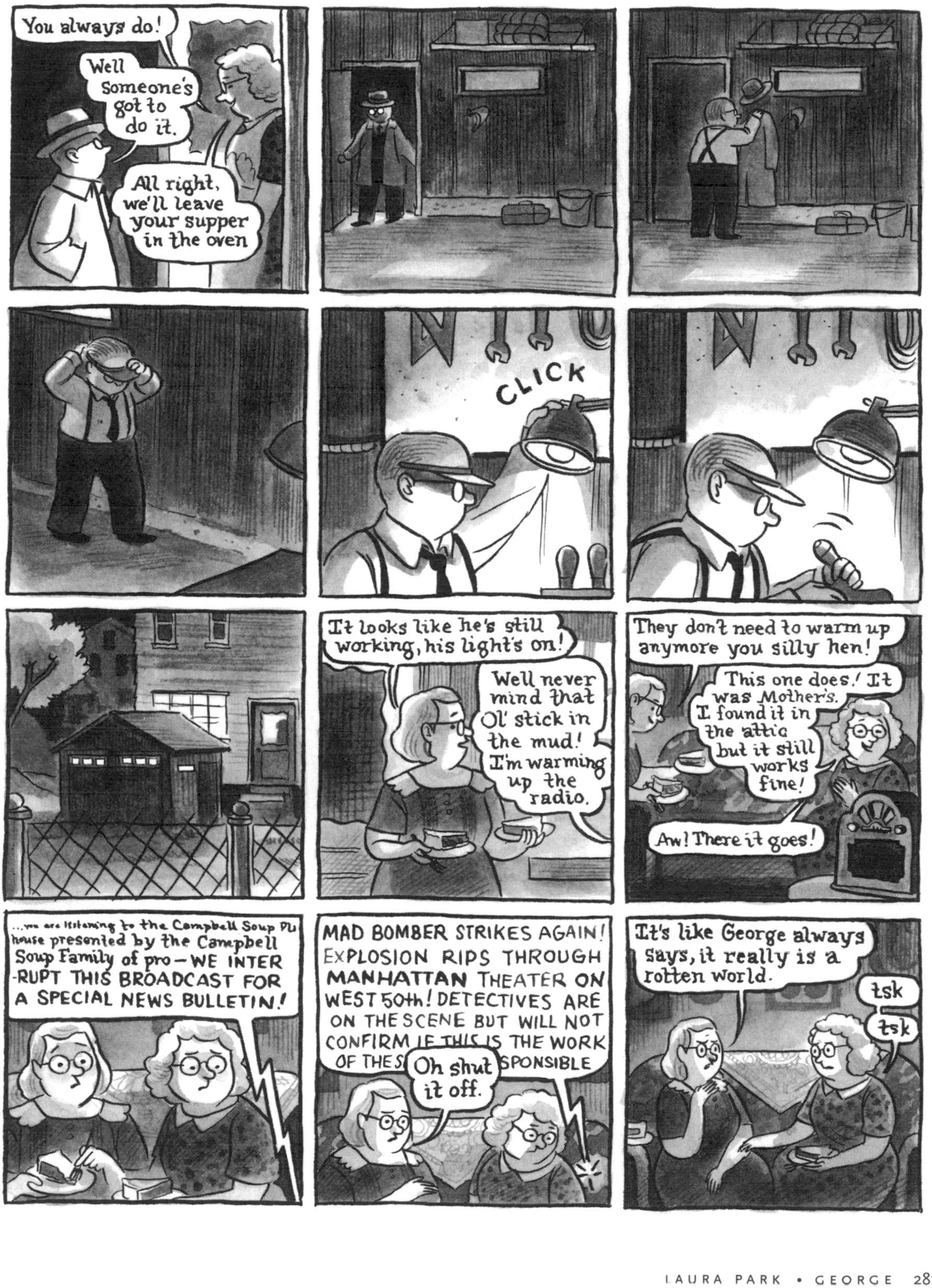
You always do!
Well someone's got to do it.
All right, we'll leave your supper in the oven
CLICK
It looks like he's still working, his light's on!
Well never mind that Ol' stick in the mud! I'm warming up the radio.
They don't need to warm up anymore you silly hen!
This one does! It was Mother's. I found it in the attic but it still works fine!
Aw! There it goes!
...you are listening to the Campbell Soup Pl- house presented by the Campbell Soup Family of pro—WE INTER-RUPT THIS BROADCAST FOR A SPECIAL NEWS BULLETIN!
MAD BOMBER STRIKES AGAIN! EXPLOSION RIPS THROUGH MANHATTAN THEATER ON WEST 50th! DETECTIVES ARE ON THE SCENE BUT WILL NOT CONFIRM IF THIS IS THE WORK OF THE S SPONSIBLE
Oh shut it off.
It's like George always says, it really is a rotten world.
tsk
tsk

Kate Beaton

VELOCIPEDE

from *Hark! A Vagrant*

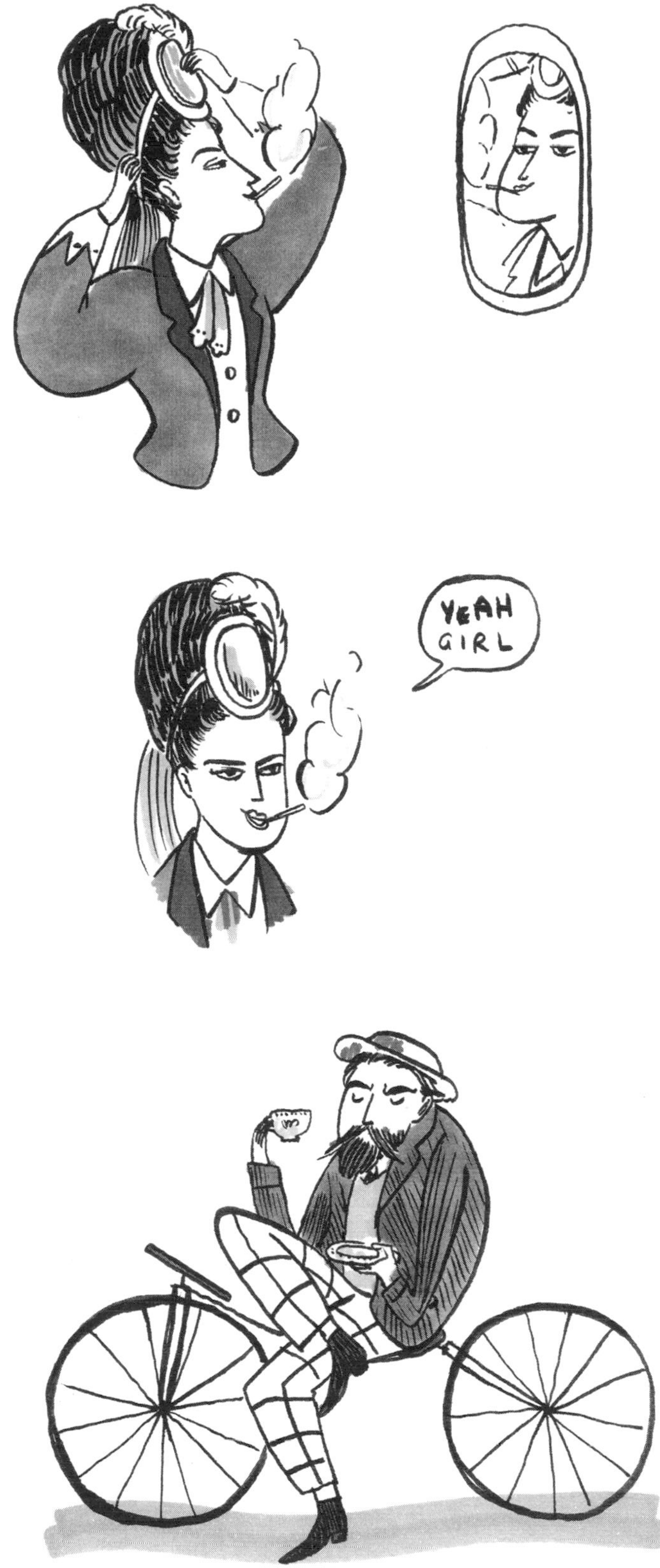
YEAH GIRL

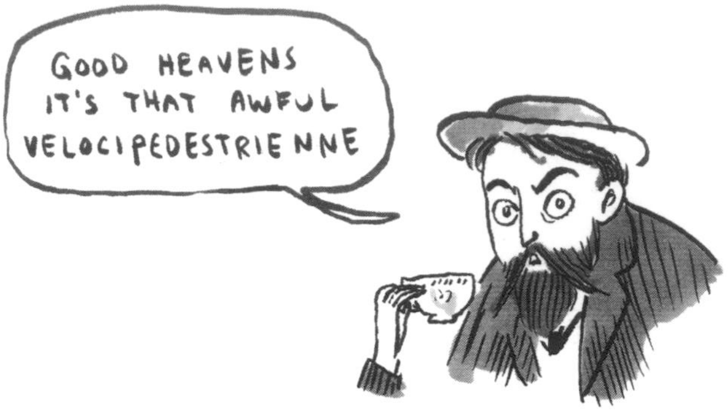
GOOD HEAVENS IT'S THAT AWFUL VELOCIPEDESTRIENNE

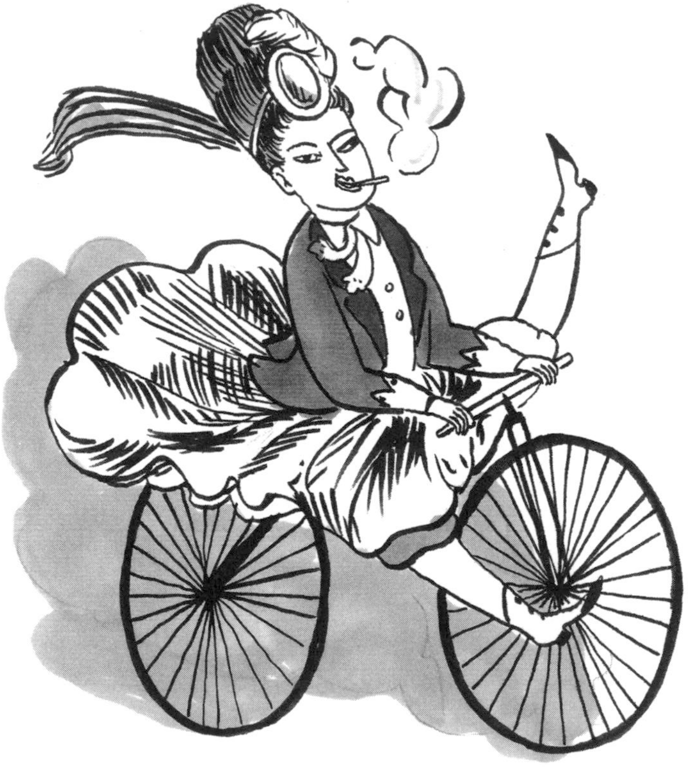

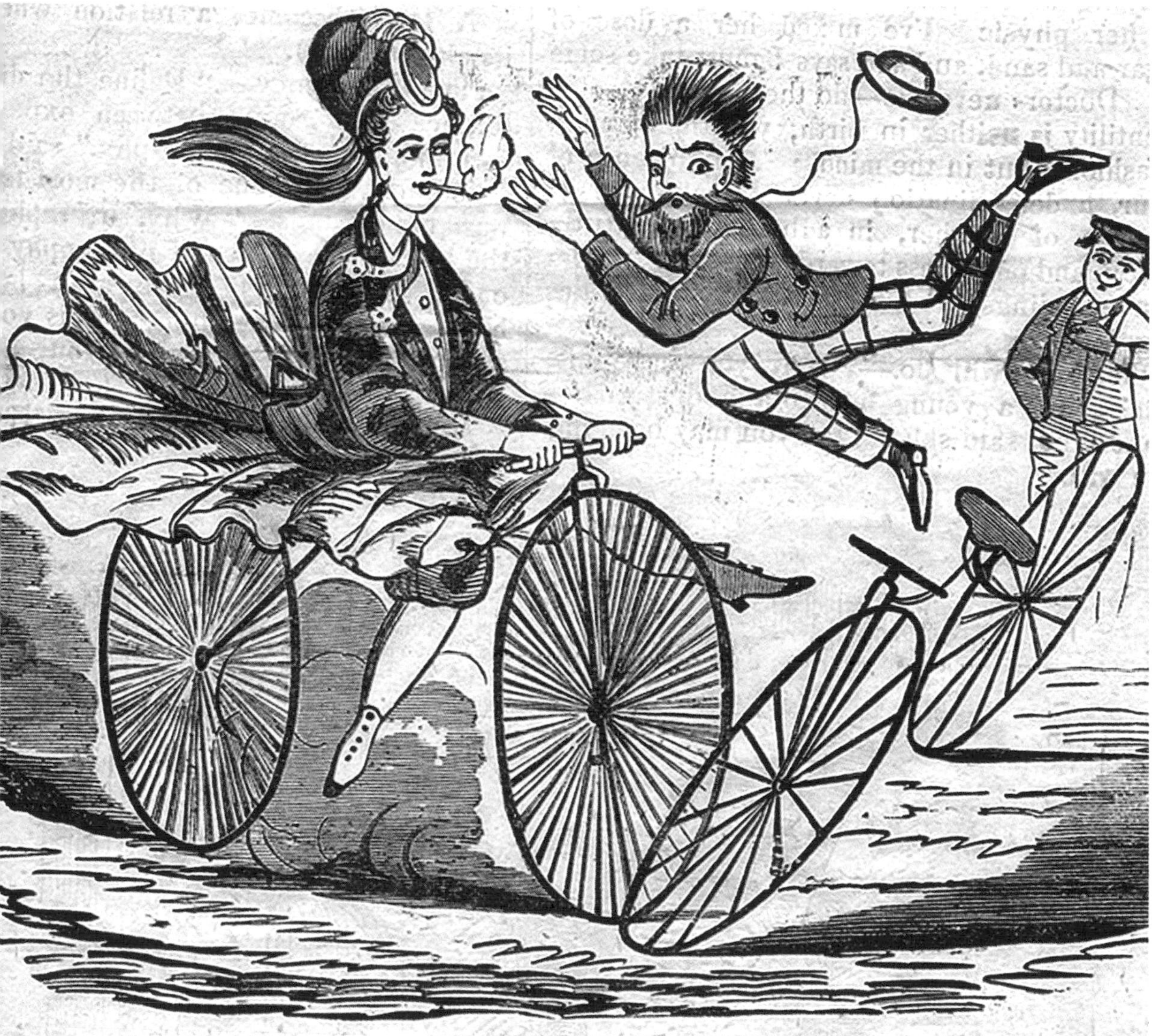

THE AWFUL EFFECTS OF VELOCIPEDING.

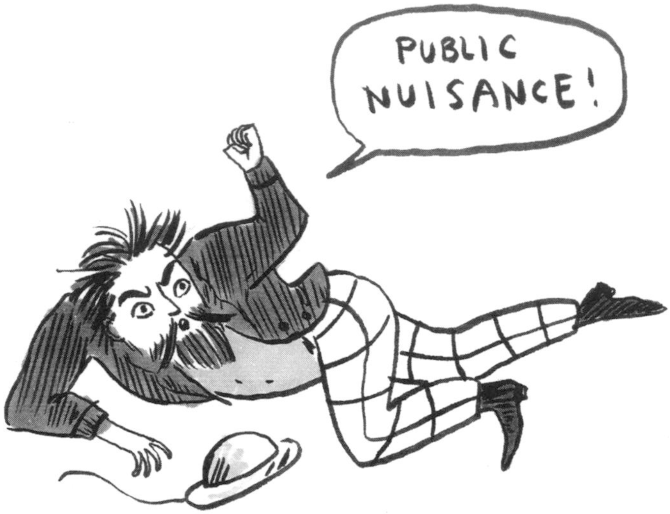
PUBLIC NUISANCE!

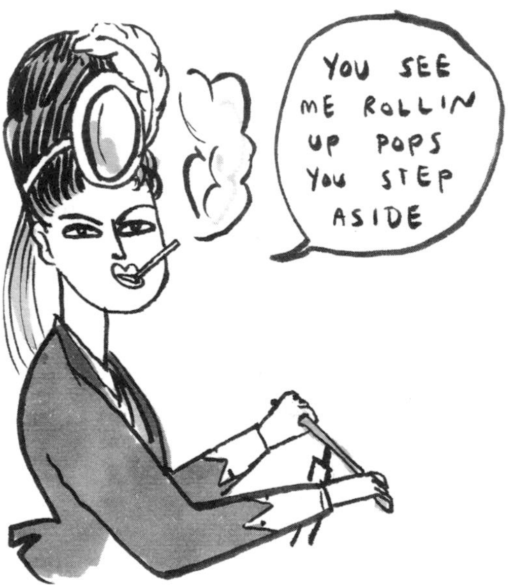
YOU SEE ME ROLLIN UP POPS YOU STEP ASIDE

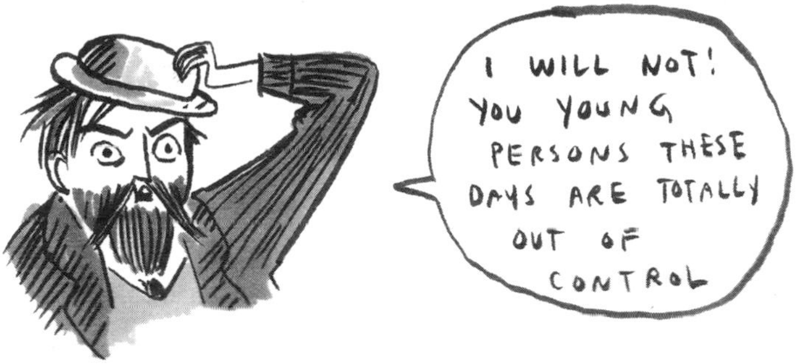
I WILL NOT! YOU YOUNG PERSONS THESE DAYS ARE TOTALLY OUT OF CONTROL

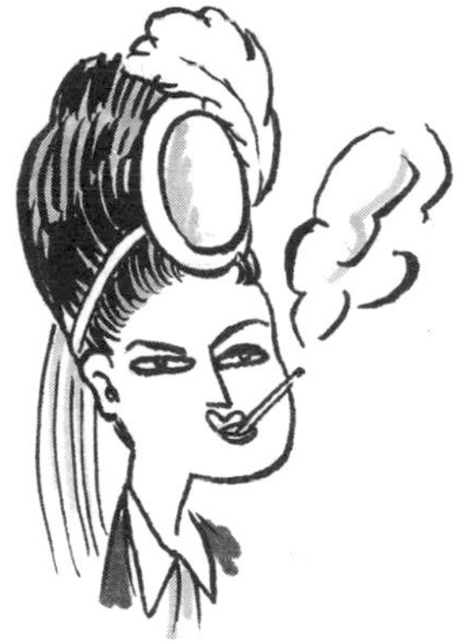

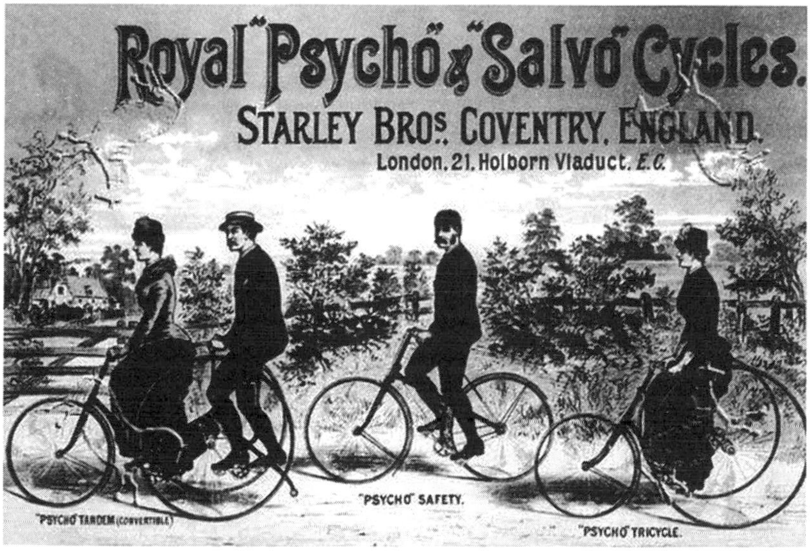
Royal "Psycho" & "Salvo" Cycles.
STARLEY BROS. COVENTRY, ENGLAND.
London, 21, Holborn Viaduct, E.C.
"PSYCHO" TANDEM (CONVERTIBLE)
"PSYCHO" SAFETY.
"PSYCHO" TRICYCLE.

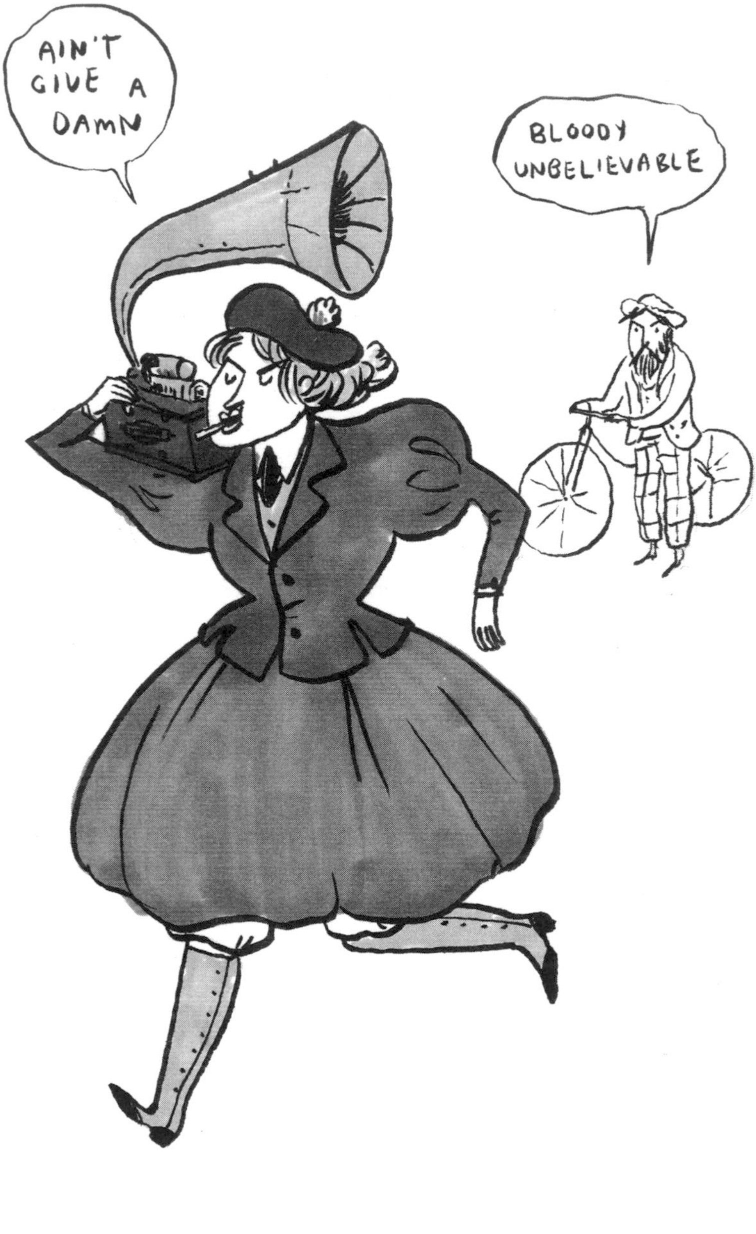
AIN'T GIVE A DAMN
BLOODY UNBELIEVABLE

EVAN DORKIN

FUN STRIPS

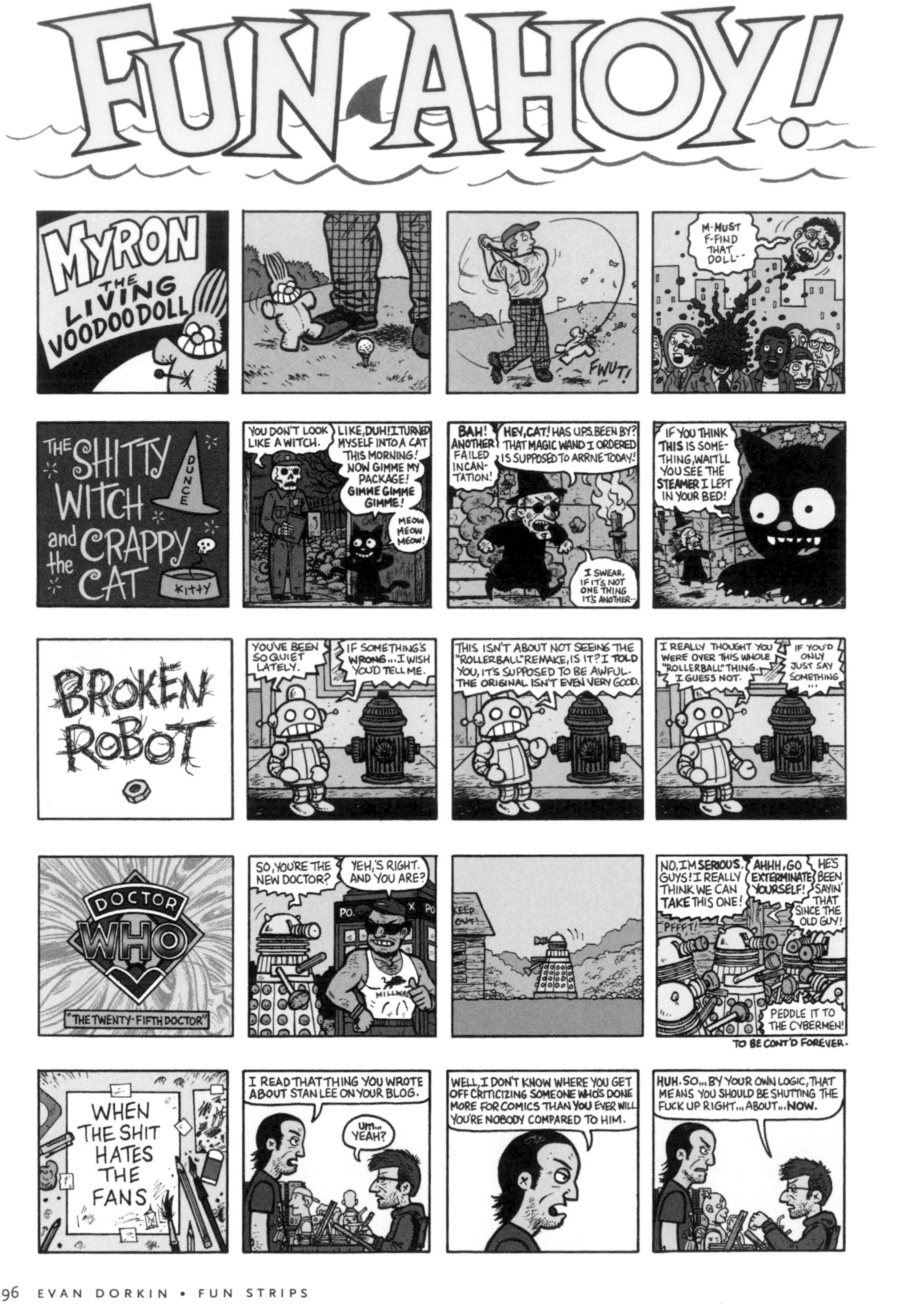

FUN AHOY!
MYRON THE LIVING VOODOO DOLL
FWUT!
M-MUST F-FIND THAT DOLL--
THE SHITTY WITCH and the CRAPPY CAT
DUNCE
KITTY
YOU DON'T LOOK LIKE A WITCH.
LIKE, DUH! I TURNED MYSELF INTO A CAT THIS MORNING! NOW GIMME MY PACKAGE! GIMME GIMME GIMME!
MEOW MEOW MEOW!
BAH! ANOTHER FAILED INCANTATION!
HEY, CAT! HAS U.P.S. BEEN BY? THAT MAGIC WAND I ORDERED IS SUPPOSED TO ARRIVE TODAY!
I SWEAR, IF IT'S NOT ONE THING IT'S ANOTHER--
IF YOU THINK THIS IS SOMETHING, WAIT'LL YOU SEE THE STEAMER I LEFT IN YOUR BED!
BROKEN ROBOT
YOU'VE BEEN SO QUIET LATELY.
IF SOMETHING'S WRONG... I WISH YOU'D TELL ME.
THIS ISN'T ABOUT NOT SEEING THE "ROLLERBALL" REMAKE, IS IT? I TOLD YOU, IT'S SUPPOSED TO BE AWFUL. THE ORIGINAL ISN'T EVEN VERY GOOD.
I REALLY THOUGHT YOU WERE OVER THIS WHOLE "ROLLERBALL" THING. I GUESS NOT.
IF YOU'D ONLY JUST SAY SOMETHING ...
DOCTOR WHO
"THE TWENTY-FIFTH DOCTOR"
SO, YOU'RE THE NEW DOCTOR?
YEH, 'S RIGHT. AND YOU ARE?
PO.
MILLWALL
KEEP OUT!
NO, I'M SERIOUS, GUYS! I REALLY THINK WE CAN TAKE THIS ONE!
AHHH, GO EXTERMINATE YOURSELF!
HE'S BEEN SAYIN' THAT SINCE THE OLD GUY!
PFFFT!
PEDDLE IT TO THE CYBERMEN!
TO BE CONT'D FOREVER.
WHEN THE SHIT HATES THE FANS
I READ THAT THING YOU WROTE ABOUT STAN LEE ON YOUR BLOG.
UM... YEAH?
WELL, I DON'T KNOW WHERE YOU GET OFF CRITICIZING SOMEONE WHO'S DONE MORE FOR COMICS THAN YOU EVER WILL. YOU'RE NOBODY COMPARED TO HIM.
HUH. SO... BY YOUR OWN LOGIC, THAT MEANS YOU SHOULD BE SHUTTING THE FUCK UP RIGHT... ABOUT... NOW.

MONSTROUS FUN

MYSTERIES OF COMICS

WHY DID JACK COLE KILL HIMSELF?

TO DOROTHY / TO HEF

WHY DOESN'T ANYONE WANT TO TALK PUBLICLY ABOUT WHERE THE "HUMBUG" ART DISAPPEARED TO FOR ALL THOSE YEARS?

WAIT, WASN'T THAT ART OWNED BY THE CREATORS?

YEP. IRONIC, HUH? NOW WAIT'LL YOU HEAR HOW THEY FOUND OUT WHERE THE ART WAS THE WHOLE TIME—

WHAT ARE "ROYALTY CHECKS"?

USELESS MEMBER OF SOCIETY— PLEASE GIVE

I MUST KNOW.

VETERINARIAN'S OFFICE, 10:25 A.M.

DO YOU PUT DOWN CHILDREN?

GOOD DOG

DO YOU KNOW ANYBODY WHO DOES?

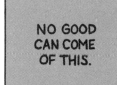

NO GOOD CAN COME OF THIS.

LEPER BOWLING LEAGUE

AMATEUR BOMB DEFUSERS CLUB

YOUR TURN, AL!

VOLUNTEER HOSTAGE NEGOTIATORS OF AMERICA

GIVE IT UP, ASSHOLE!

WE GOT YOU SURROUNDED! HA HA HA HA HA HA!

BROKEN ROBOT

1011011001001100100 0110101100001101110111

1001110111001011 100111110001110000 1101--? 0111001101--?

1101? 1101?! 1101?!?

EAST MEETS WORST

UM, ARNIE? STICKING YOUR CHOPSTICKS IN YOUR BOWL OF RICE IS CONSIDERED VERY BAD LUCK HERE.

WHAT? YOU SHITTIN' ME? WHAT CENTURY IS THIS? "BAD LUCK"! WHAT A LOAD OF SUPERSTITIOUS BULL--

I'VE LOST FACE, HAVEN'T I?

FUNZAPOPPIN!

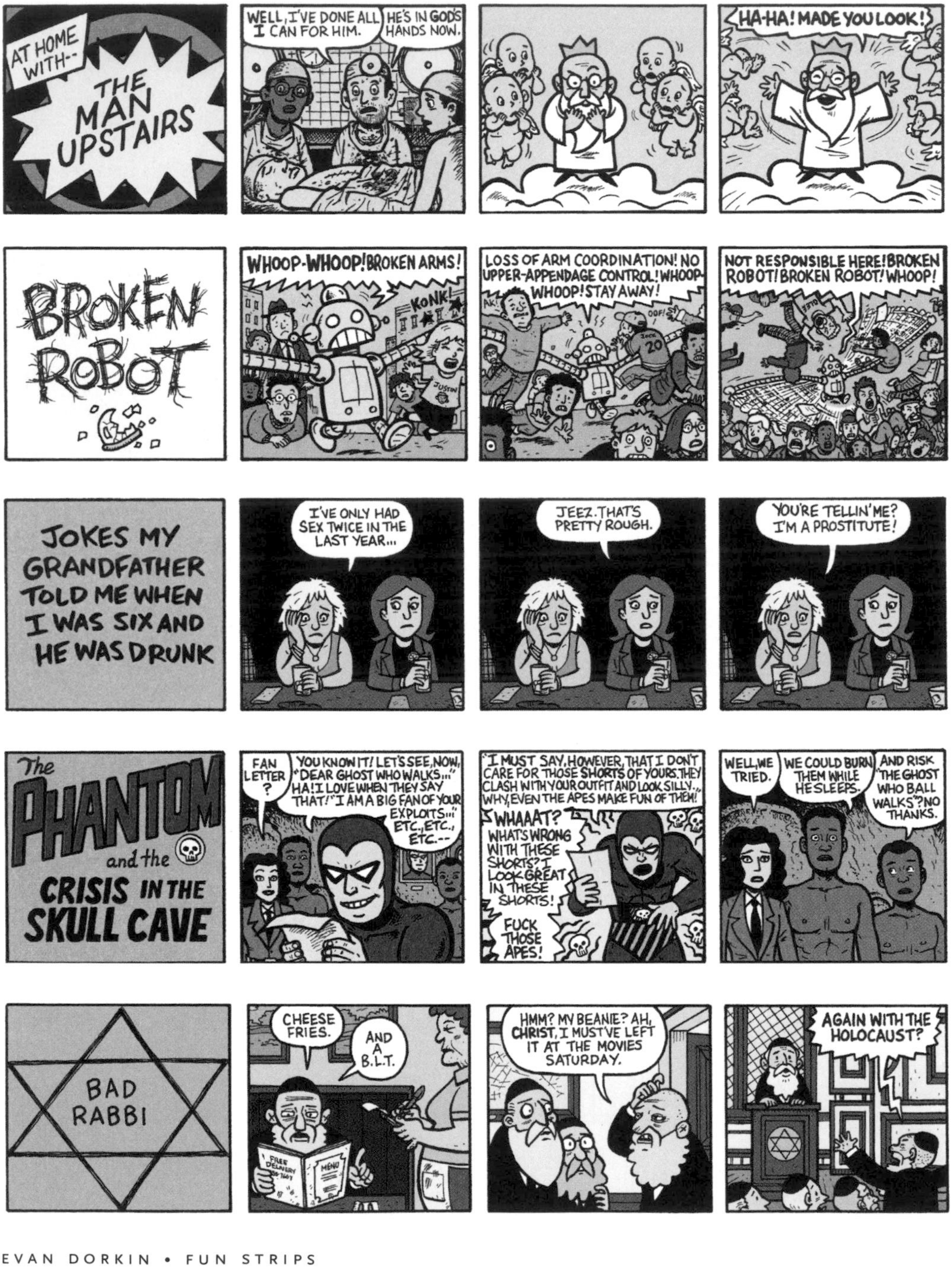
AT HOME WITH--
THE MAN UPSTAIRS
WELL, I'VE DONE ALL I CAN FOR HIM.
HE'S IN GOD'S HANDS NOW.
HA-HA! MADE YOU LOOK!
BROKEN ROBOT
WHOOP-WHOOP! BROKEN ARMS!
KONK!
LOSS OF ARM COORDINATION! NO UPPER-APPENDAGE CONTROL! WHOOP-WHOOP! STAY AWAY!
AK!
OOF!
NOT RESPONSIBLE HERE! BROKEN ROBOT! BROKEN ROBOT! WHOOP!
JOKES MY GRANDFATHER TOLD ME WHEN I WAS SIX AND HE WAS DRUNK
I'VE ONLY HAD SEX TWICE IN THE LAST YEAR...
JEEZ. THAT'S PRETTY ROUGH.
YOU'RE TELLIN' ME? I'M A PROSTITUTE!
The PHANTOM and the CRISIS IN THE SKULL CAVE
FAN LETTER?
YOU KNOW IT! LET'S SEE, NOW, "DEAR GHOST WHO WALKS..." HA! I LOVE WHEN THEY SAY THAT! "I AM A BIG FAN OF YOUR EXPLOITS..." ETC., ETC., ETC.--
"I MUST SAY, HOWEVER, THAT I DON'T CARE FOR THOSE SHORTS OF YOURS. THEY CLASH WITH YOUR OUTFIT AND LOOK SILLY... WHY, EVEN THE APES MAKE FUN OF THEM!"
WHAAAT? WHAT'S WRONG WITH THESE SHORTS? I LOOK GREAT IN THESE SHORTS!
FUCK THOSE APES!
WELL, WE TRIED.
WE COULD BURN THEM WHILE HE SLEEPS.
AND RISK "THE GHOST WHO BALL WALKS"? NO THANKS.
BAD RABBI
CHEESE FRIES.
AND A B.L.T.
HMM? MY BEANIE? AH, CHRIST, I MUST'VE LEFT IT AT THE MOVIES SATURDAY.
AGAIN WITH THE HOLOCAUST?

SOME FUN, eh?

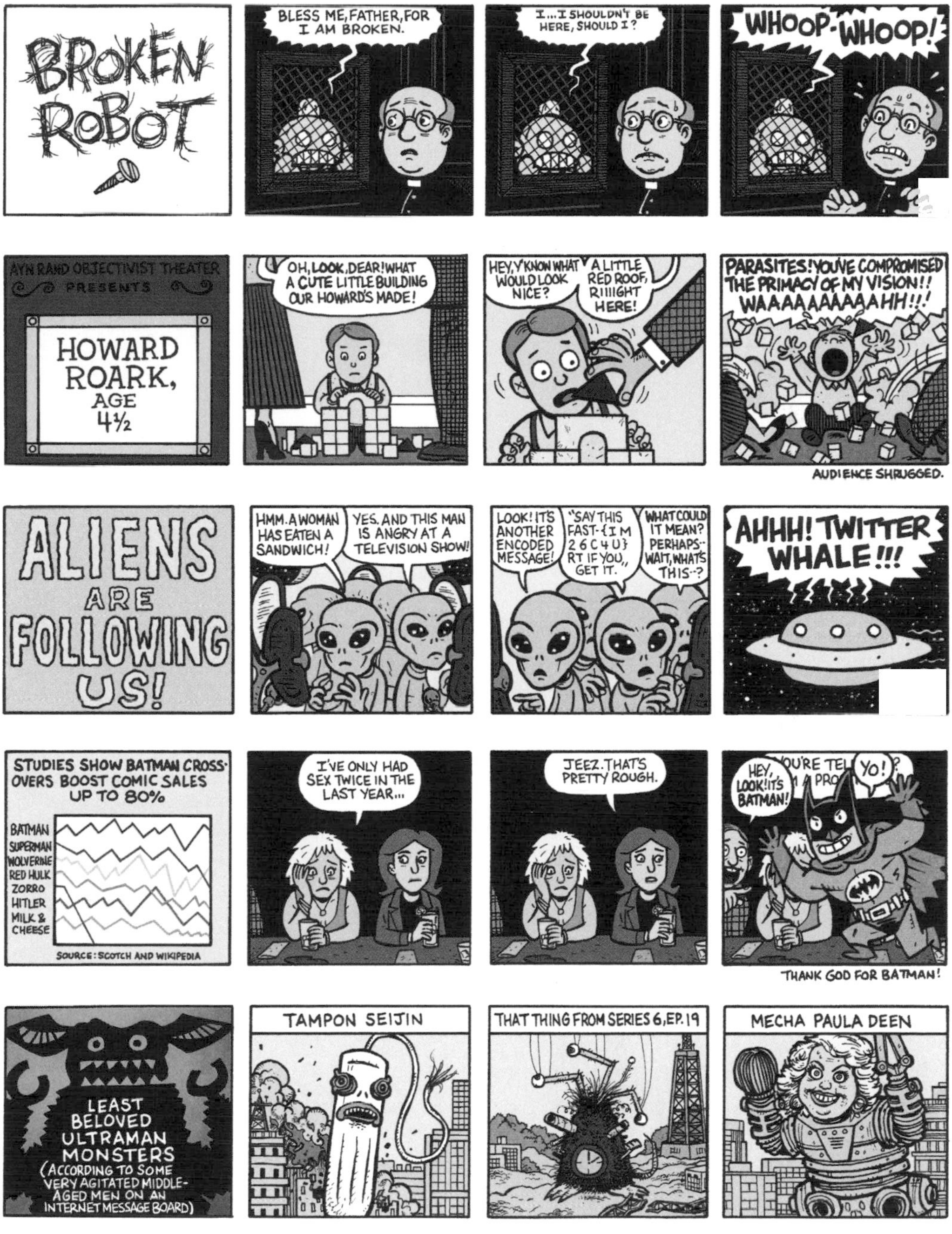

BROKEN ROBOT
BLESS ME, FATHER, FOR I AM BROKEN.
I... I SHOULDN'T BE HERE, SHOULD I?
WHOOP-WHOOP!
AYN RAND OBJECTIVIST THEATER PRESENTS
HOWARD ROARK, AGE 4½
OH, LOOK, DEAR! WHAT A CUTE LITTLE BUILDING OUR HOWARD'S MADE!
HEY, Y'KNOW WHAT WOULD LOOK NICE?
A LITTLE RED ROOF, RIIIIGHT HERE!
PARASITES! YOU'VE COMPROMISED THE PRIMACY OF MY VISION!! WAAAAAAAAAAHH!!!
AUDIENCE SHRUGGED.
ALIENS ARE FOLLOWING US!
HMM. A WOMAN HAS EATEN A SANDWICH!
YES. AND THIS MAN IS ANGRY AT A TELEVISION SHOW!
LOOK! IT'S ANOTHER ENCODED MESSAGE!
"SAY THIS FAST-{I M 2 6 C 4 U} RT IF YOU GET IT."
WHAT COULD IT MEAN? PERHAPS-- WAIT, WHAT'S THIS--?
AHHH! TWITTER WHALE!!!
STUDIES SHOW BATMAN CROSS-OVERS BOOST COMIC SALES UP TO 80%
BATMAN
SUPERMAN
WOLVERINE
RED HULK
ZORRO
HITLER
MILK & CHEESE
SOURCE: SCOTCH AND WIKIPEDIA
I'VE ONLY HAD SEX TWICE IN THE LAST YEAR...
JEEZ. THAT'S PRETTY ROUGH.
HEY, LOOK! IT'S BATMAN!
YO!
THANK GOD FOR BATMAN!
LEAST BELOVED ULTRAMAN MONSTERS (ACCORDING TO SOME VERY AGITATED MIDDLE-AGED MEN ON AN INTERNET MESSAGE BOARD)
TAMPON SEIJIN
THAT THING FROM SERIES 6, EP. 19
MECHA PAULA DEEN

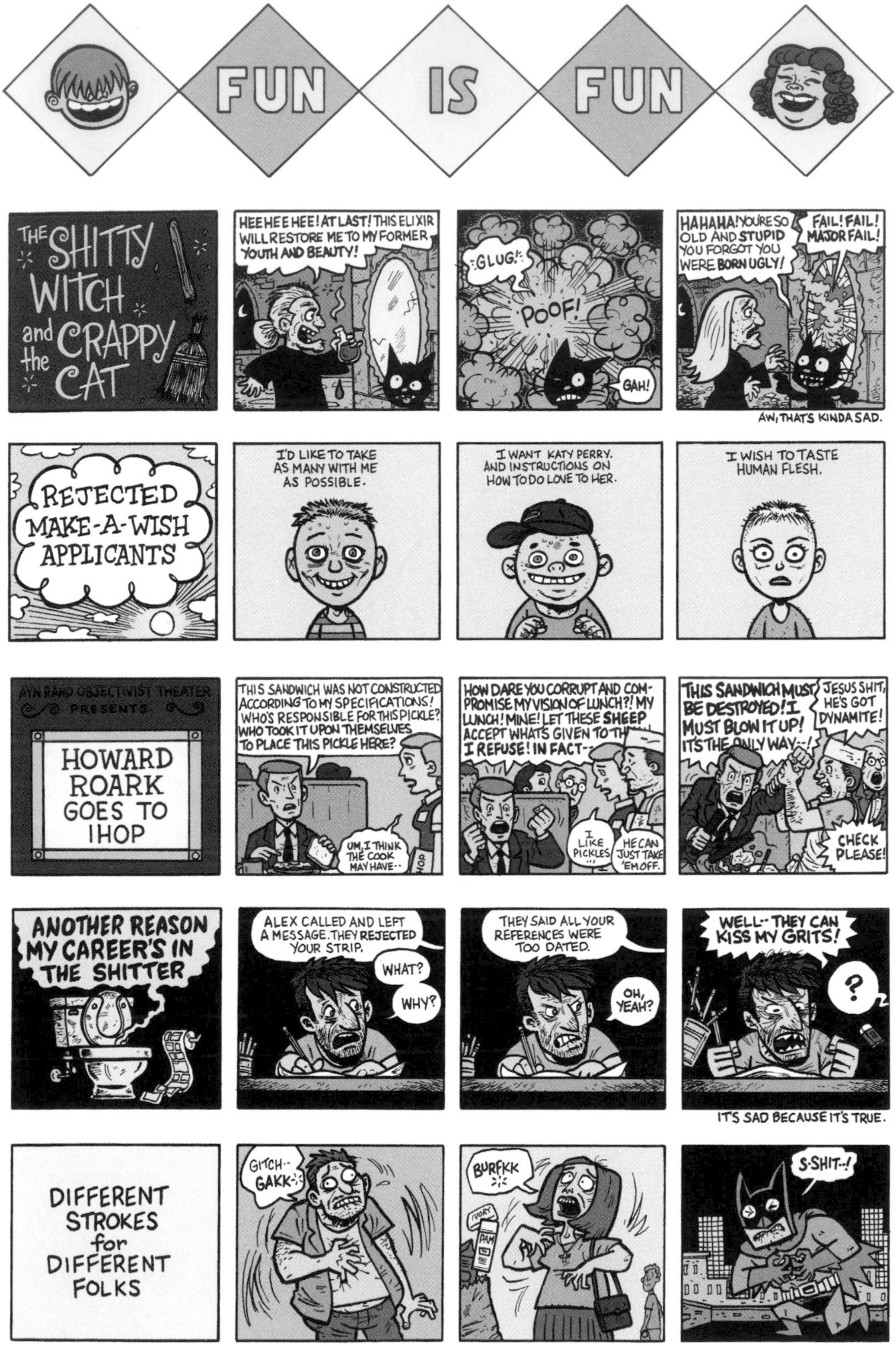
FUN IS FUN
THE SHITTY WITCH and the CRAPPY CAT
HEEHEEHEE! AT LAST! THIS ELIXIR WILL RESTORE ME TO MY FORMER YOUTH AND BEAUTY!
GLUG!
POOF!
GAH!
HAHAHA! YOU'RE SO OLD AND STUPID YOU FORGOT YOU WERE BORN UGLY!
FAIL! FAIL! MAJOR FAIL!
AW, THAT'S KINDA SAD.
REJECTED MAKE-A-WISH APPLICANTS
I'D LIKE TO TAKE AS MANY WITH ME AS POSSIBLE.
I WANT KATY PERRY. AND INSTRUCTIONS ON HOW TO DO LOVE TO HER.
I WISH TO TASTE HUMAN FLESH.
AYN RAND OBJECTIVIST THEATER PRESENTS
HOWARD ROARK GOES TO IHOP
THIS SANDWICH WAS NOT CONSTRUCTED ACCORDING TO MY SPECIFICATIONS! WHO'S RESPONSIBLE FOR THIS PICKLE? WHO TOOK IT UPON THEMSELVES TO PLACE THIS PICKLE HERE?
UM, I THINK THE COOK MAY HAVE--
HOW DARE YOU CORRUPT AND COMPROMISE MY VISION OF LUNCH?! MY LUNCH! MINE! LET THESE SHEEP ACCEPT WHAT'S GIVEN TO TH--- I REFUSE! IN FACT--
I LIKE PICKLES...
HE CAN JUST TAKE 'EM OFF.
THIS SANDWICH MUST BE DESTROYED! I MUST BLOW IT UP! IT'S THE ONLY WAY--!
JESUS SHIT, HE'S GOT DYNAMITE!
CHECK PLEASE!
ANOTHER REASON MY CAREER'S IN THE SHITTER
ALEX CALLED AND LEFT A MESSAGE. THEY REJECTED YOUR STRIP.
WHAT?
WHY?
THEY SAID ALL YOUR REFERENCES WERE TOO DATED.
OH, YEAH?
WELL-- THEY CAN KISS MY GRITS!
?
IT'S SAD BECAUSE IT'S TRUE.
DIFFERENT STROKES for DIFFERENT FOLKS
GITCH-- GAKK-
BURFKK
IVORY
PAM
S-SHIT--!

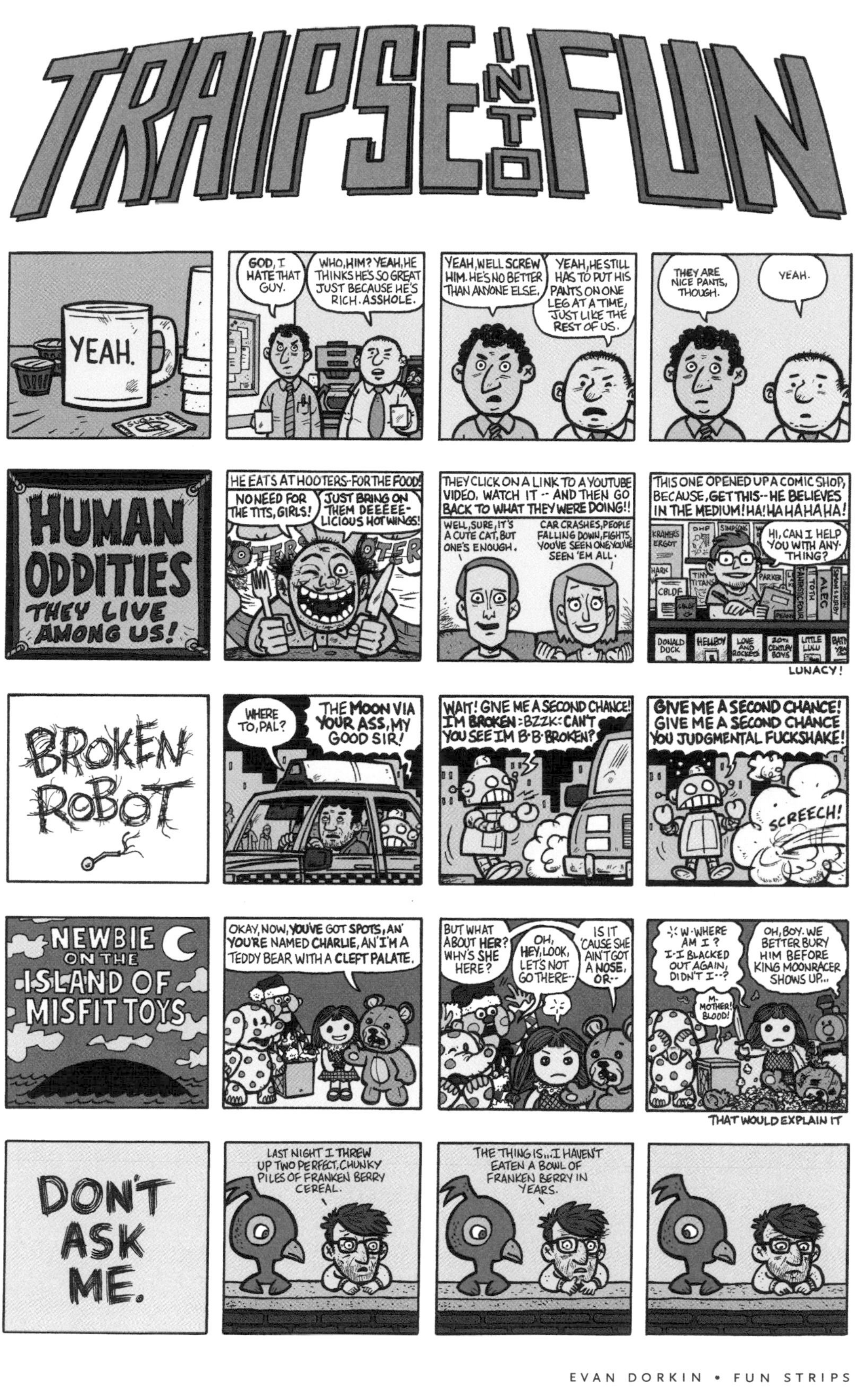
TRAIPSE INTO FUN
YEAH.
GOD, I HATE THAT GUY.
WHO, HIM? YEAH, HE THINKS HE'S SO GREAT JUST BECAUSE HE'S RICH. ASSHOLE.
YEAH, WELL SCREW HIM. HE'S NO BETTER THAN ANYONE ELSE.
YEAH, HE STILL HAS TO PUT HIS PANTS ON ONE LEG AT A TIME, JUST LIKE THE REST OF US.
THEY ARE NICE PANTS, THOUGH.
YEAH.
HUMAN ODDITIES
THEY LIVE AMONG US!
HE EATS AT HOOTERS--FOR THE FOOD!
NO NEED FOR THE TITS, GIRLS!
JUST BRING ON THEM DEEEEE-LICIOUS HOT WINGS!
THEY CLICK ON A LINK TO A YOUTUBE VIDEO, WATCH IT -- AND THEN GO BACK TO WHAT THEY WERE DOING!!
WELL, SURE, IT'S A CUTE CAT, BUT ONE'S ENOUGH.
CAR CRASHES, PEOPLE FALLING DOWN, FIGHTS, YOU'VE SEEN ONE YOU'VE SEEN 'EM ALL.
THIS ONE OPENED UP A COMIC SHOP, BECAUSE, GET THIS-- HE BELIEVES IN THE MEDIUM! HA! HA HA HA HA!
HI, CAN I HELP YOU WITH ANYTHING?
DONALD DUCK
HELLBOY
LOVE AND ROCKETS
20TH CENTURY BOYS
LITTLE LULU
LUNACY!
BROKEN ROBOT
WHERE TO, PAL?
THE MOON VIA YOUR ASS, MY GOOD SIR!
WAIT! GIVE ME A SECOND CHANCE! I'M BROKEN :BZZK: CAN'T YOU SEE I'M B-B-BROKEN?
GIVE ME A SECOND CHANCE! GIVE ME A SECOND CHANCE YOU JUDGMENTAL FUCKSHAKE!
SCREECH!
NEWBIE ON THE ISLAND OF MISFIT TOYS
OKAY, NOW, YOU'VE GOT SPOTS, AN' YOU'RE NAMED CHARLIE, AN' I'M A TEDDY BEAR WITH A CLEFT PALATE.
BUT WHAT ABOUT HER? WHY'S SHE HERE?
OH, HEY, LOOK, LET'S NOT GO THERE--
IS IT 'CAUSE SHE AIN'T GOT A NOSE, OR--
W-WHERE AM I? I-I BLACKED OUT AGAIN, DIDN'T I--?
OH, BOY. WE BETTER BURY HIM BEFORE KING MOONRACER SHOWS UP...
M-MOTHER! BLOOD!
THAT WOULD EXPLAIN IT
DON'T ASK ME.
LAST NIGHT I THREW UP TWO PERFECT, CHUNKY PILES OF FRANKEN BERRY CEREAL.
THE THING IS... I HAVEN'T EATEN A BOWL OF FRANKEN BERRY IN YEARS.

SAINTS
in the
STORE

Jennifer Hayden

Saints in the Store

BY Jennifer Hayden

2010

TWENTY MILES OUTSIDE QUEBEC CITY, WE STOPPED AT THE SHRINE OF SAINTE-ANNE-DE-BEAUPRÉ.

St. Lawrence River

Avenue Royale

ice

St. Anne's

our tour bus

Snow ?!

French class trip

Quebec City

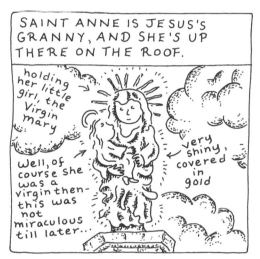

SAINT ANNE IS JESUS'S GRANNY, AND SHE'S UP THERE ON THE ROOF.

holding her little girl, the Virgin Mary

very shiny, covered in gold

Well, of course she was a virgin then—this was not miraculous till later...

THE LOCAL FISHERMEN DEDICATED THEIR CHURCH TO ANNE BECAUSE SHE IS THE PATRON SAINT OF SAILORS.

SHIPWRECK 1658

Holy Merde!! We made it, eh? *

Only because we pray to Saint Anne and she save us! *

But now we gotta build a church, eh? *

* Translated from the French.

After a workman fell from the roof and recovered, the shrine was thought to have healing powers.

Crutches left by cured pilgrims

our guide, Andrée

AND THERE WAS DEFINITELY A GOOD ENERGY ABOUT THE PLACE. CHARLOTTE WANTED TO LIGHT A CANDLE.

Well, we're agnostic, but I guess that's okay. Who's it for?

The people in Haiti.

5$

Jesus, Char. You really are a much better person than I am.

a moment of silence for those who are suffering...

WE HAD JUST ENOUGH TIME LEFT TO VISIT THE GIFT SHOP.

there were saints in plastic baskets

Sanctuary snow-globes

SHAKE!

white plaster mini-statues of Leonardo's Last Supper (I bought one)

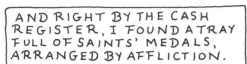

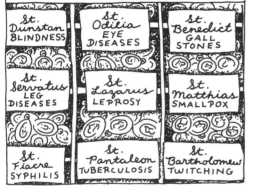

AND RIGHT BY THE CASH REGISTER, I FOUND A TRAY FULL OF SAINTS' MEDALS, ARRANGED BY AFFLICTION.

St. Dunstan BLINDNESS	St. Odilia EYE DISEASES	St. Benedict GALL STONES
St. Servatus LEG DISEASES	St. Lazarus LEPROSY	St. Matthias SMALLPOX
St. Fiacre SYPHILIS	St. Pantaleon TUBERCULOSIS	St. Bartholomew TWITCHING

I PICKED UP SAINT DYMPHNA.

Nervous disorders... Well, I'm pretty nervous about the gig next weekend...

Okay, Dymphna, I'm not a believer, but I do believe in something.

SAINT DYMPHNA

Would you be willing to work with someone like me?

THE MEDAL WARMED IN MY HAND.

QUEBEC CITY

I bought it

END

MICHAEL KUPPERMAN

SCARY BATHTUB STORIES

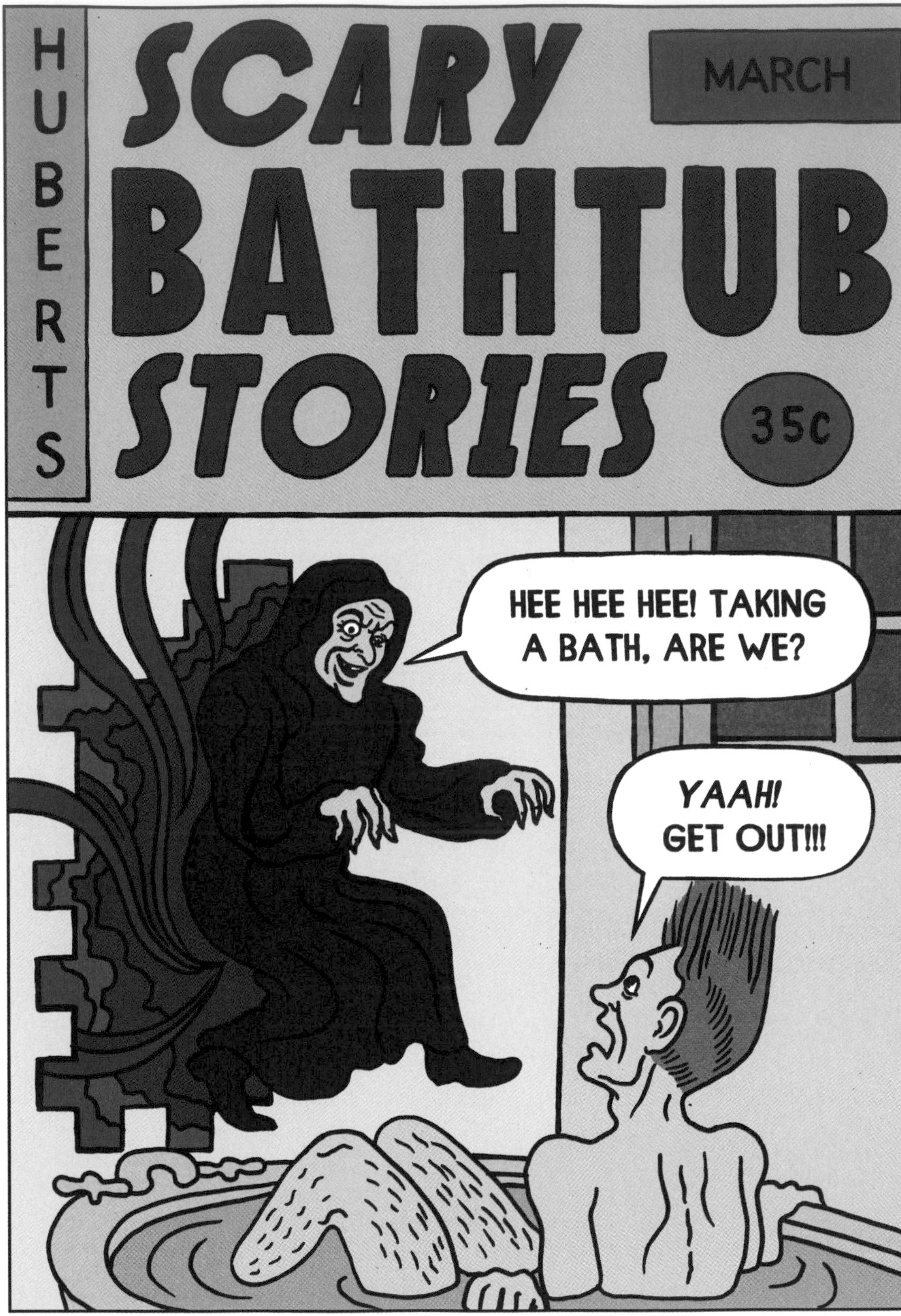
HUBERTS
SCARY BATHTUB STORIES
MARCH
35¢
HEE HEE HEE! TAKING A BATH, ARE WE?
YAAH! GET OUT!!!

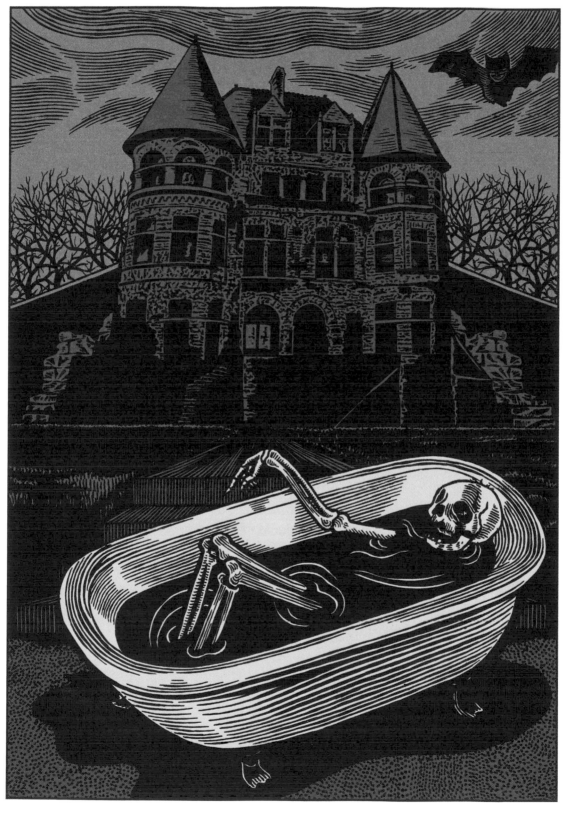

DID YOU KNOW MORE PEOPLE DIE IN BATHTUBS EVERY YEAR THAN IN ANY OTHER FORM OF BATHING TUB? NO WONDER TUBS HAVE A BAD REPUTATION— THEY'RE DEADLY!

EVERY YEAR, HUNDREDS OF PEOPLE ARE FOUND DEAD IN BATHTUBS, SOME OF THEM LOOKING LIKE THEY HAD SUFFERED UNSPEAKABLE HORROR BEFORE SHUFFLING OFF THIS MORTAL COIL.

SOME SAY THAT THE BATHTUB WAS INVENTED IN HELL, BY THE DEVIL HIMSELF!

OTHERS BELIEVE THAT IT REPRESENTS A SUBCONSCIOUS DESIRE OF MAN TO SUBMERGE HIMSELF IN HIS OWN EXCREMENT!

WHATEVER THE TRUE STORY, IT IS NOT UNREASONABLE TO FEEL SHEER NAKED TERROR WHEN CONTEMPLATING THIS UNHOLY VESSEL!

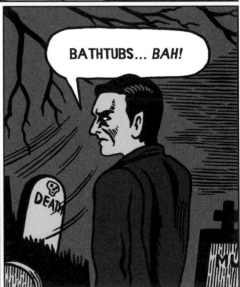

BATHTUBS... *BAH!*

DEATH

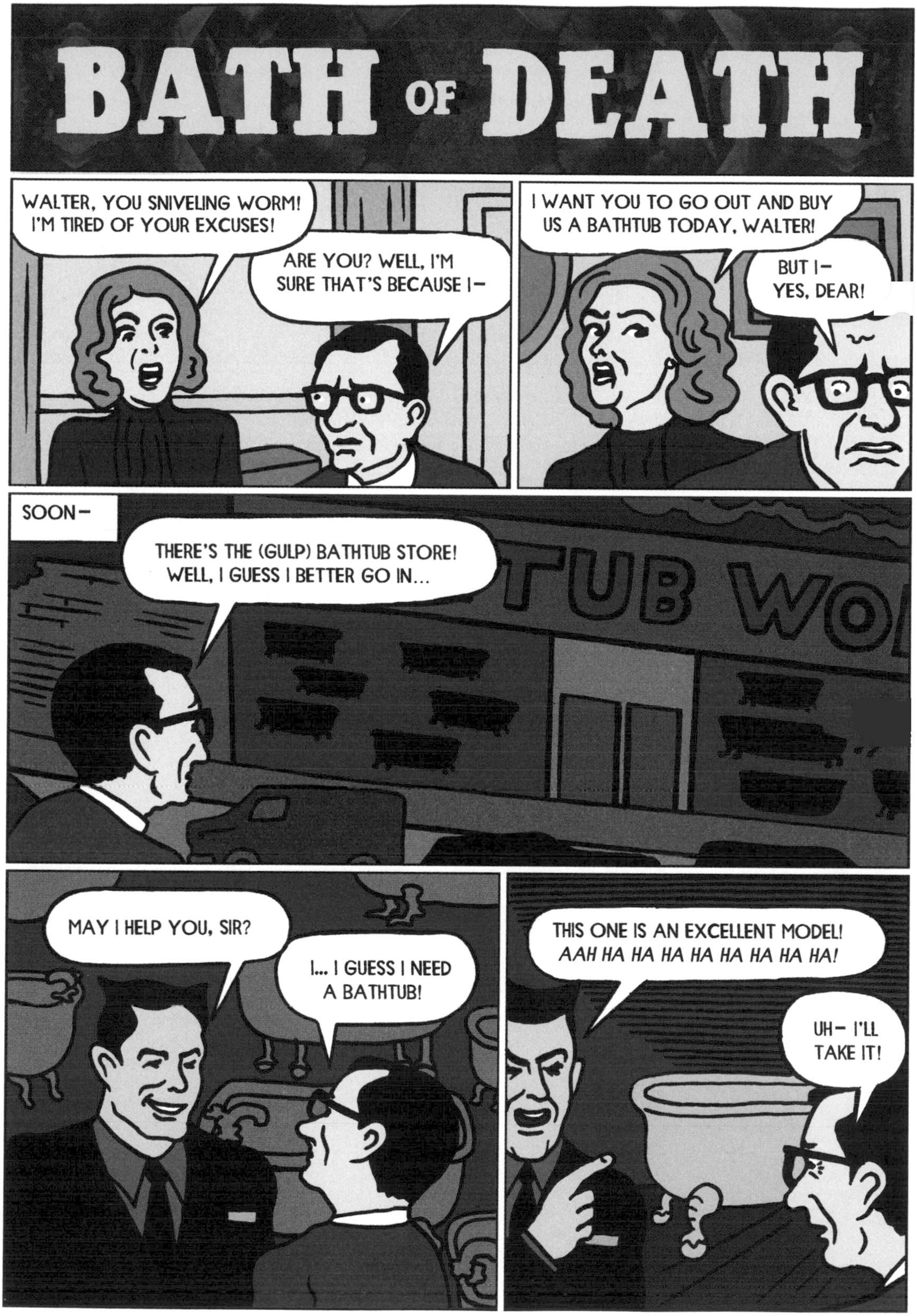
BATH OF DEATH
WALTER, YOU SNIVELING WORM! I'M TIRED OF YOUR EXCUSES!
ARE YOU? WELL, I'M SURE THAT'S BECAUSE I—
I WANT YOU TO GO OUT AND BUY US A BATHTUB TODAY, WALTER!
BUT I— YES, DEAR!
SOON—
THERE'S THE (GULP) BATHTUB STORE! WELL, I GUESS I BETTER GO IN...
TUB WO
MAY I HELP YOU, SIR?
I... I GUESS I NEED A BATHTUB!
THIS ONE IS AN EXCELLENT MODEL! *AAH HA HA HA HA HA HA HA HA!*
UH— I'LL TAKE IT!

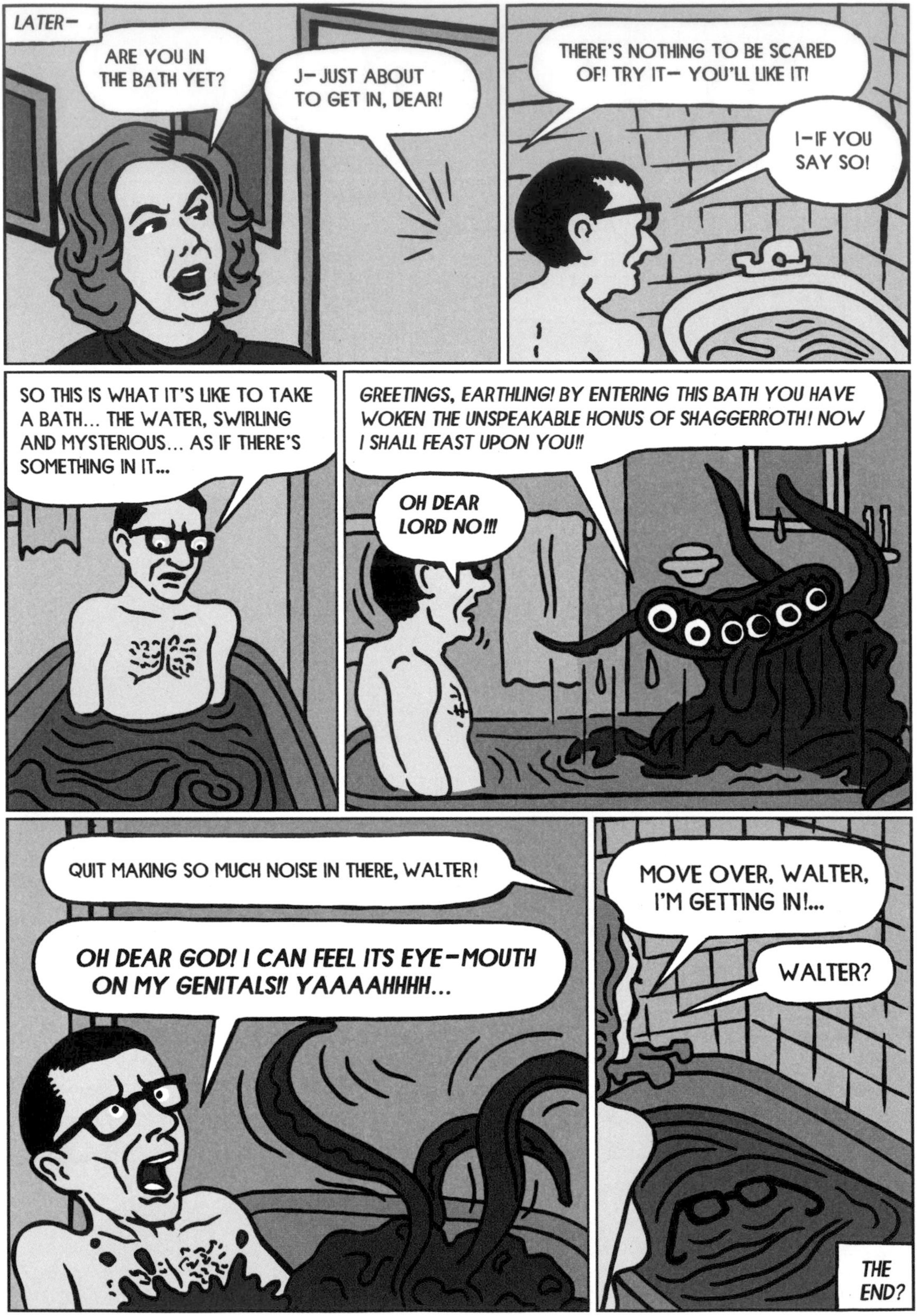
LATER—
ARE YOU IN THE BATH YET?
J— JUST ABOUT TO GET IN, DEAR!
THERE'S NOTHING TO BE SCARED OF! TRY IT— YOU'LL LIKE IT!
I—IF YOU SAY SO!
SO THIS IS WHAT IT'S LIKE TO TAKE A BATH... THE WATER, SWIRLING AND MYSTERIOUS... AS IF THERE'S SOMETHING IN IT...
GREETINGS, EARTHLING! BY ENTERING THIS BATH YOU HAVE WOKEN THE UNSPEAKABLE HONUS OF SHAGGERROTH! NOW I SHALL FEAST UPON YOU!!
OH DEAR LORD NO!!!
QUIT MAKING SO MUCH NOISE IN THERE, WALTER!
OH DEAR GOD! I CAN FEEL ITS EYE-MOUTH ON MY GENITALS!! YAAAAHHHH...
MOVE OVER, WALTER, I'M GETTING IN!...
WALTER?
THE END?

AVOID THE NIGHTMARE OF BATHS
VISIT HUBERT'S SHOWER WORLD AND
CHOOSE FROM ONE OF OUR THOUSANDS
OF SPECIALTY SHOWER HEADS

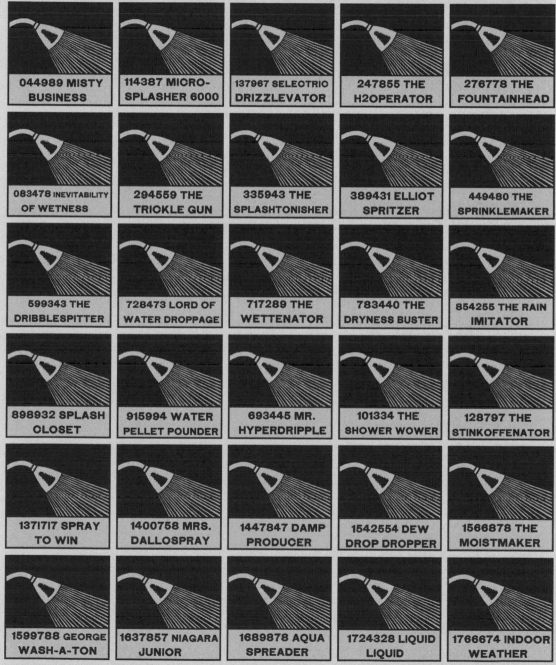

044989 MISTY BUSINESS	114387 MICRO-SPLASHER 6000	137967 SELECTRIC DRIZZLEVATOR	247855 THE H2OPERATOR	276778 THE FOUNTAINHEAD
083478 INEVITABILITY OF WETNESS	294559 THE TRICKLE GUN	335943 THE SPLASHTONISHER	389431 ELLIOT SPRITZER	449480 THE SPRINKLEMAKER
599343 THE DRIBBLESPITTER	728473 LORD OF WATER DROPPAGE	717289 THE WETTENATOR	783440 THE DRYNESS BUSTER	854255 THE RAIN IMITATOR
898932 SPLASH CLOSET	915994 WATER PELLET POUNDER	693445 MR. HYPERDRIPPLE	101334 THE SHOWER WOWER	128797 THE STINKOFFENATOR
1371717 SPRAY TO WIN	1400758 MRS. DALLOSPRAY	1447847 DAMP PRODUCER	1542554 DEW DROP DROPPER	1566878 THE MOISTMAKER
1599788 GEORGE WASH-A-TON	1637857 NIAGARA JUNIOR	1689878 AQUA SPREADER	1724328 LIQUID LIQUID	1766674 INDOOR WEATHER

HUBERT'S SHOWER WORLD - NOW WITH 17 CONVENIENT LOCATIONS

GABRIELLE BELL

Cody

CODY

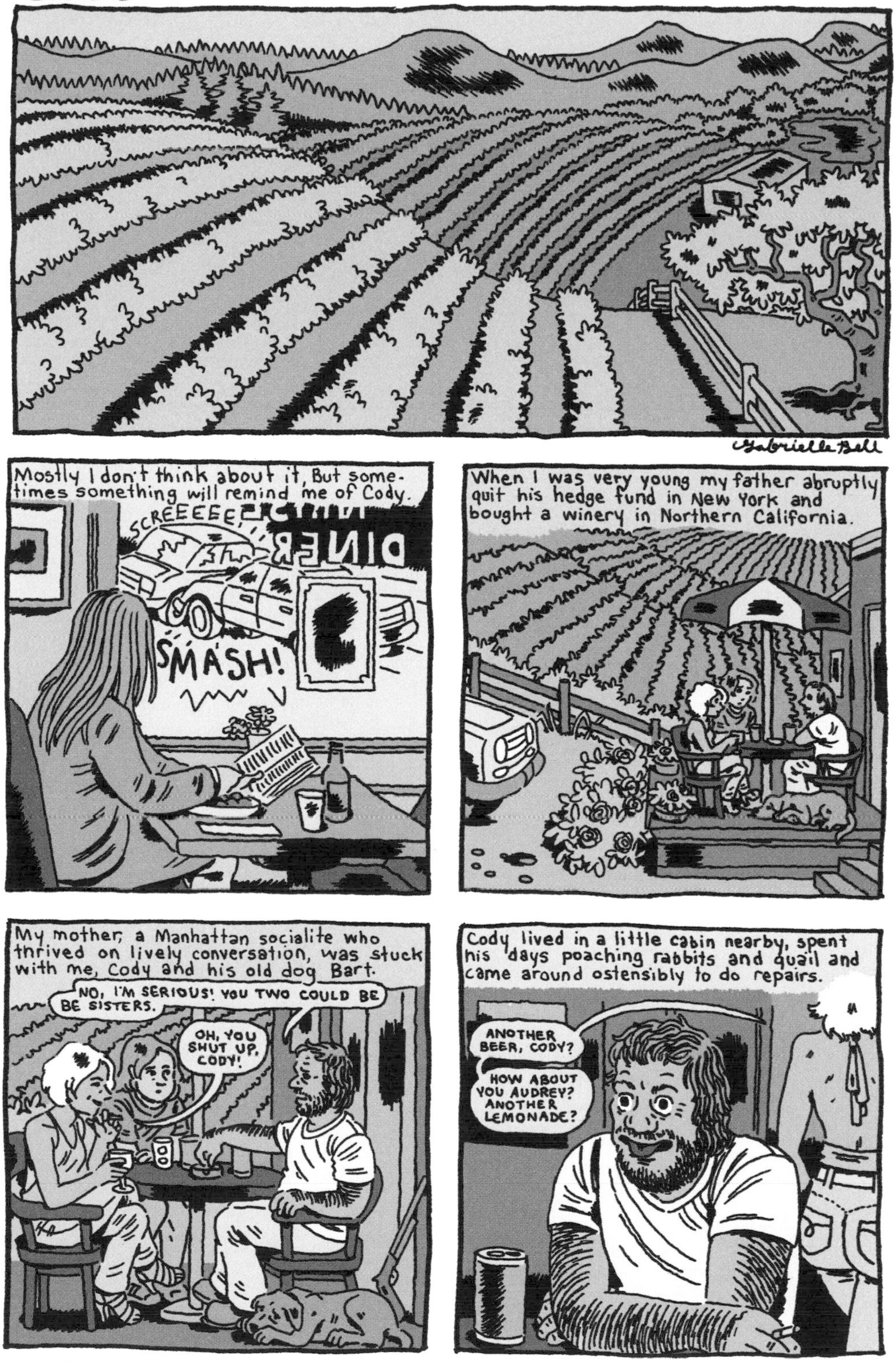
Gabrielle Bell
Mostly I don't think about it, But sometimes something will remind me of Cody.
SCREEEEEE
DINER
SMASH!
When I was very young my father abruptly quit his hedge fund in New York and bought a winery in Northern California.
My mother, a Manhattan socialite who thrived on lively conversation, was stuck with me, Cody and his old dog Bart.
NO, I'M SERIOUS! YOU TWO COULD BE BE SISTERS.
OH, YOU SHUT UP, CODY!
Cody lived in a little cabin nearby, spent his days poaching rabbits and quail and came around ostensibly to do repairs.
ANOTHER BEER, CODY?
HOW ABOUT YOU AUDREY? ANOTHER LEMONADE?

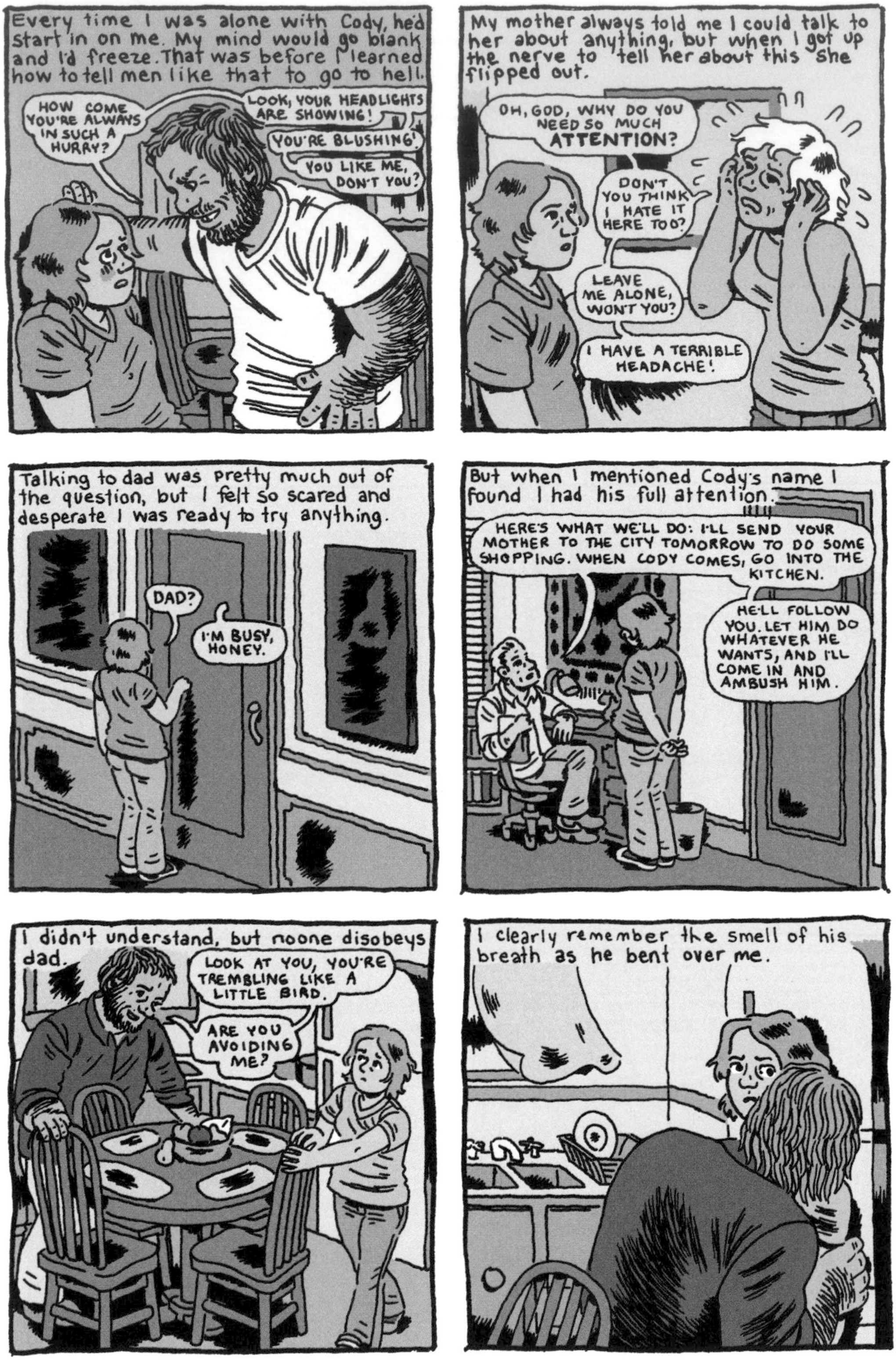
Every time I was alone with Cody, he'd start in on me. My mind would go blank and I'd freeze. That was before I learned how to tell men like that to go to hell.
HOW COME YOU'RE ALWAYS IN SUCH A HURRY?
LOOK, YOUR HEADLIGHTS ARE SHOWING!
YOU'RE BLUSHING!
YOU LIKE ME, DON'T YOU?
My mother always told me I could talk to her about anything, but when I got up the nerve to tell her about this she flipped out.
OH, GOD, WHY DO YOU NEED SO MUCH ATTENTION?
DON'T YOU THINK I HATE IT HERE TOO?
LEAVE ME ALONE, WON'T YOU?
I HAVE A TERRIBLE HEADACHE!
Talking to dad was pretty much out of the question, but I felt so scared and desperate I was ready to try anything.
DAD?
I'M BUSY, HONEY.
But when I mentioned Cody's name I found I had his full attention.
HERE'S WHAT WE'LL DO: I'LL SEND YOUR MOTHER TO THE CITY TOMORROW TO DO SOME SHOPPING. WHEN CODY COMES, GO INTO THE KITCHEN.
HE'LL FOLLOW YOU. LET HIM DO WHATEVER HE WANTS, AND I'LL COME IN AND AMBUSH HIM.
I didn't understand, but noone disobeys dad.
LOOK AT YOU, YOU'RE TREMBLING LIKE A LITTLE BIRD.
ARE YOU AVOIDING ME?
I clearly remember the smell of his breath as he bent over me.

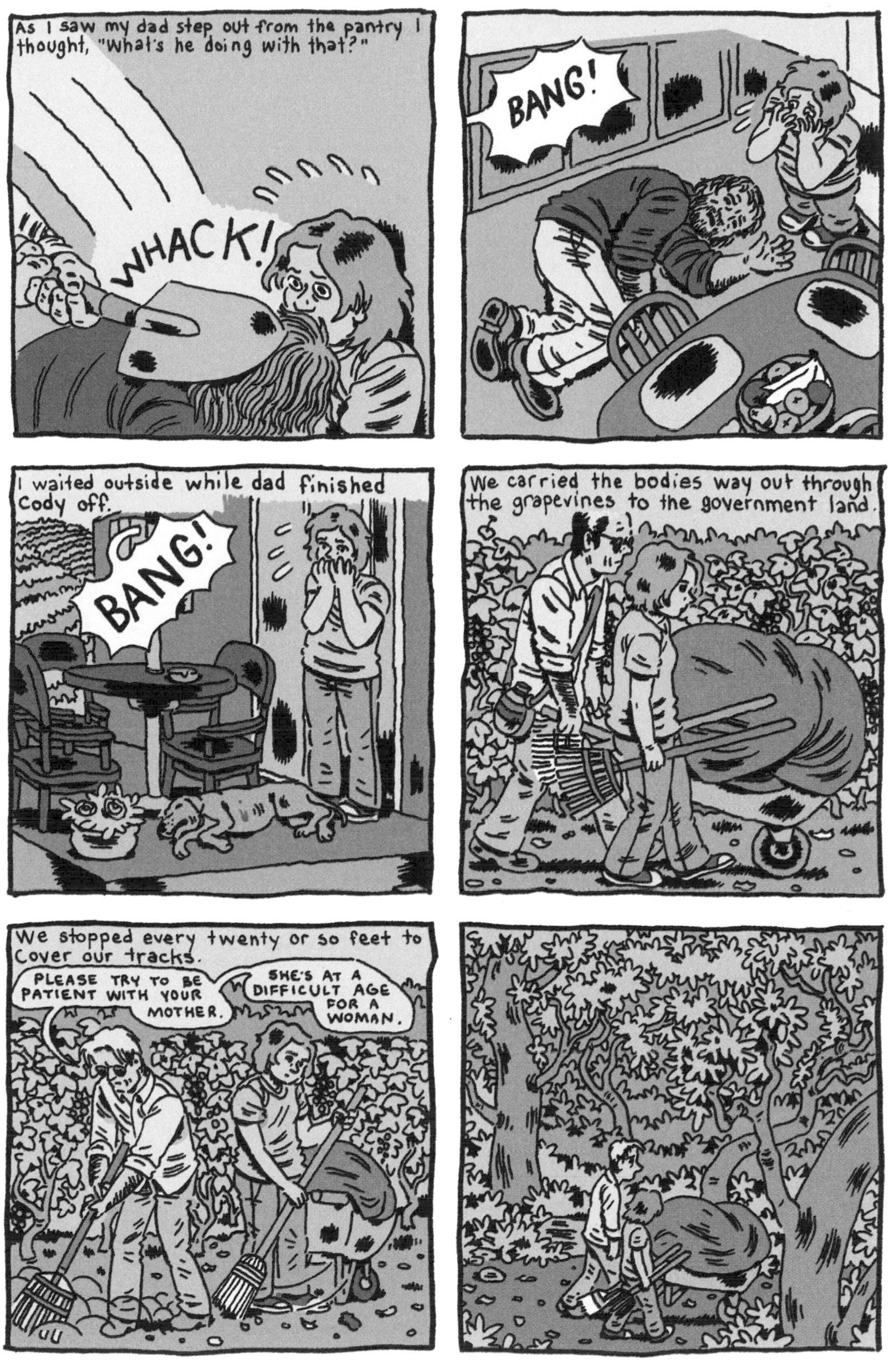
As I saw my dad step out from the pantry I thought, "What's he doing with that?"
WHACK!
BANG!
I waited outside while dad finished Cody off.
BANG!
We carried the bodies way out through the grapevines to the government land.
We stopped every twenty or so feet to cover our tracks.
PLEASE TRY TO BE PATIENT WITH YOUR MOTHER.
SHE'S AT A DIFFICULT AGE FOR A WOMAN.

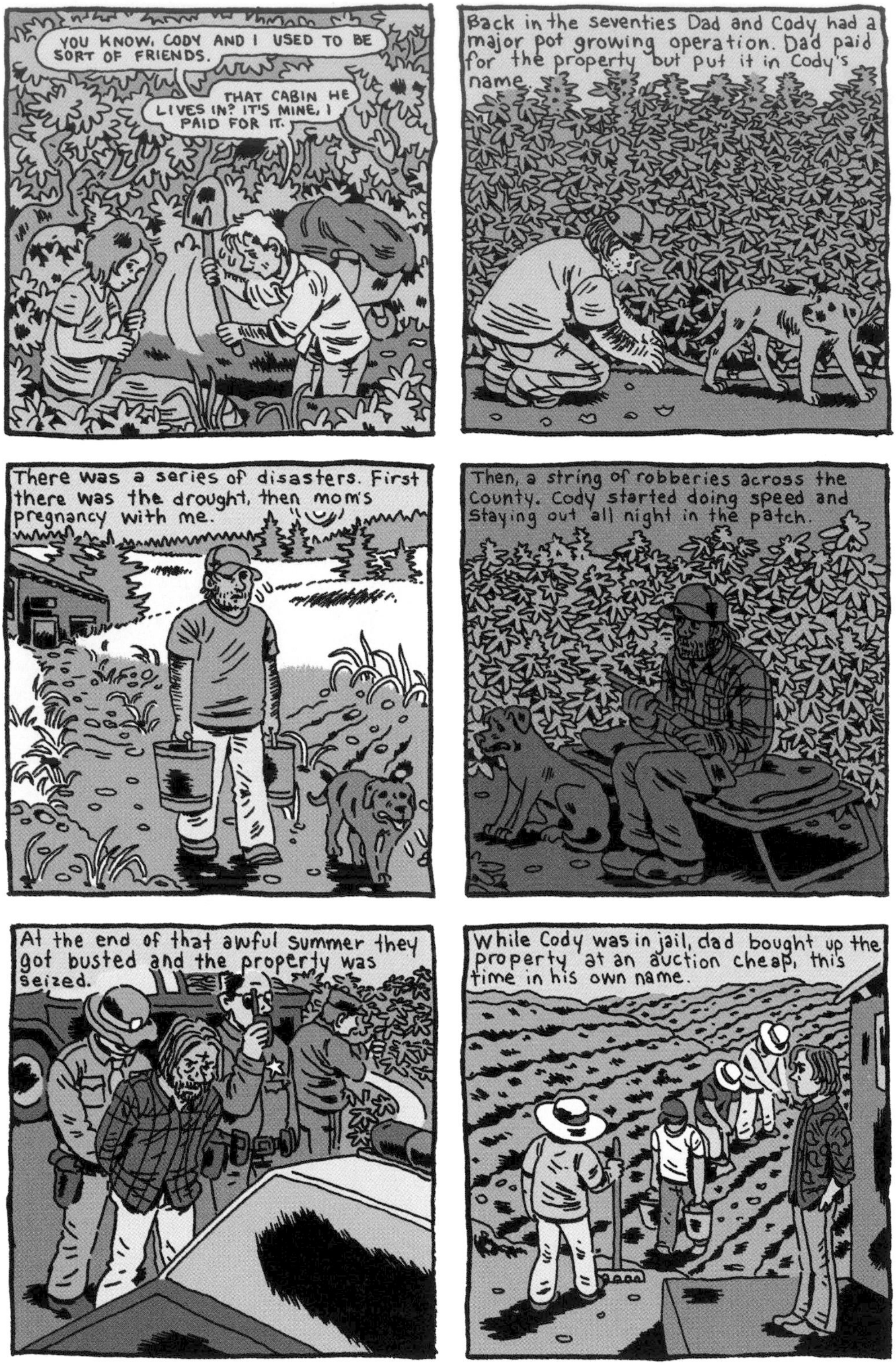
YOU KNOW, CODY AND I USED TO BE SORT OF FRIENDS.
THAT CABIN HE LIVES IN? IT'S MINE, I PAID FOR IT.
Back in the seventies Dad and Cody had a major pot growing operation. Dad paid for the property but put it in Cody's name.
There was a series of disasters. First there was the drought, then mom's pregnancy with me.
Then, a string of robberies across the County. Cody started doing speed and staying out all night in the patch.
At the end of that awful summer they got busted and the property was seized.
While Cody was in jail, dad bought up the property at an auction cheap, this time in his own name.

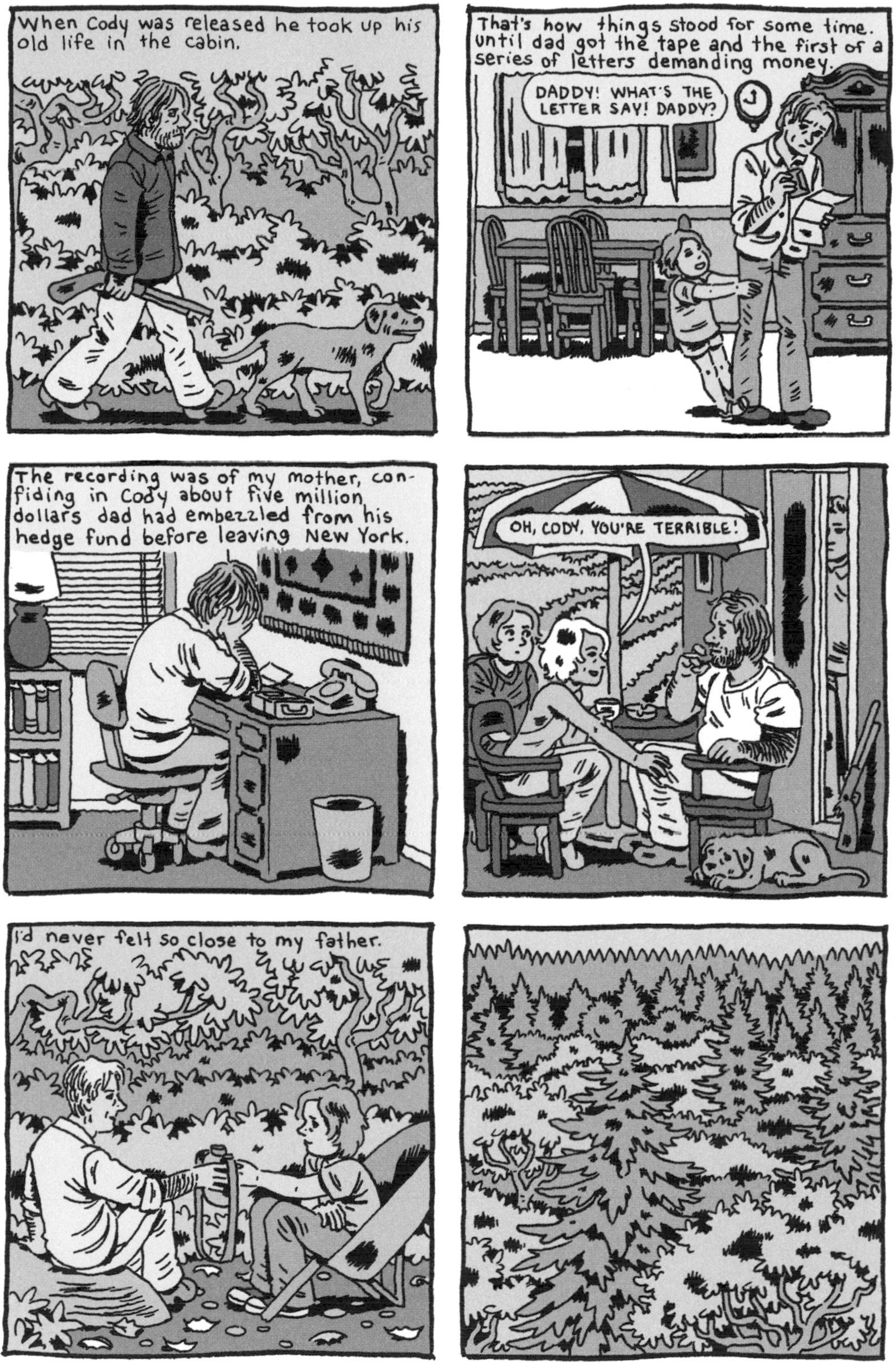
When Cody was released he took up his old life in the cabin.
That's how things stood for some time. until dad got the tape and the first of a series of letters demanding money.
DADDY! WHAT'S THE LETTER SAY! DADDY?
The recording was of my mother, confiding in Cody about five million dollars dad had embezzled from his hedge fund before leaving New York.
OH, CODY, YOU'RE TERRIBLE!
I'd never felt so close to my father.

Vanessa Davis

IN THE ROUGH

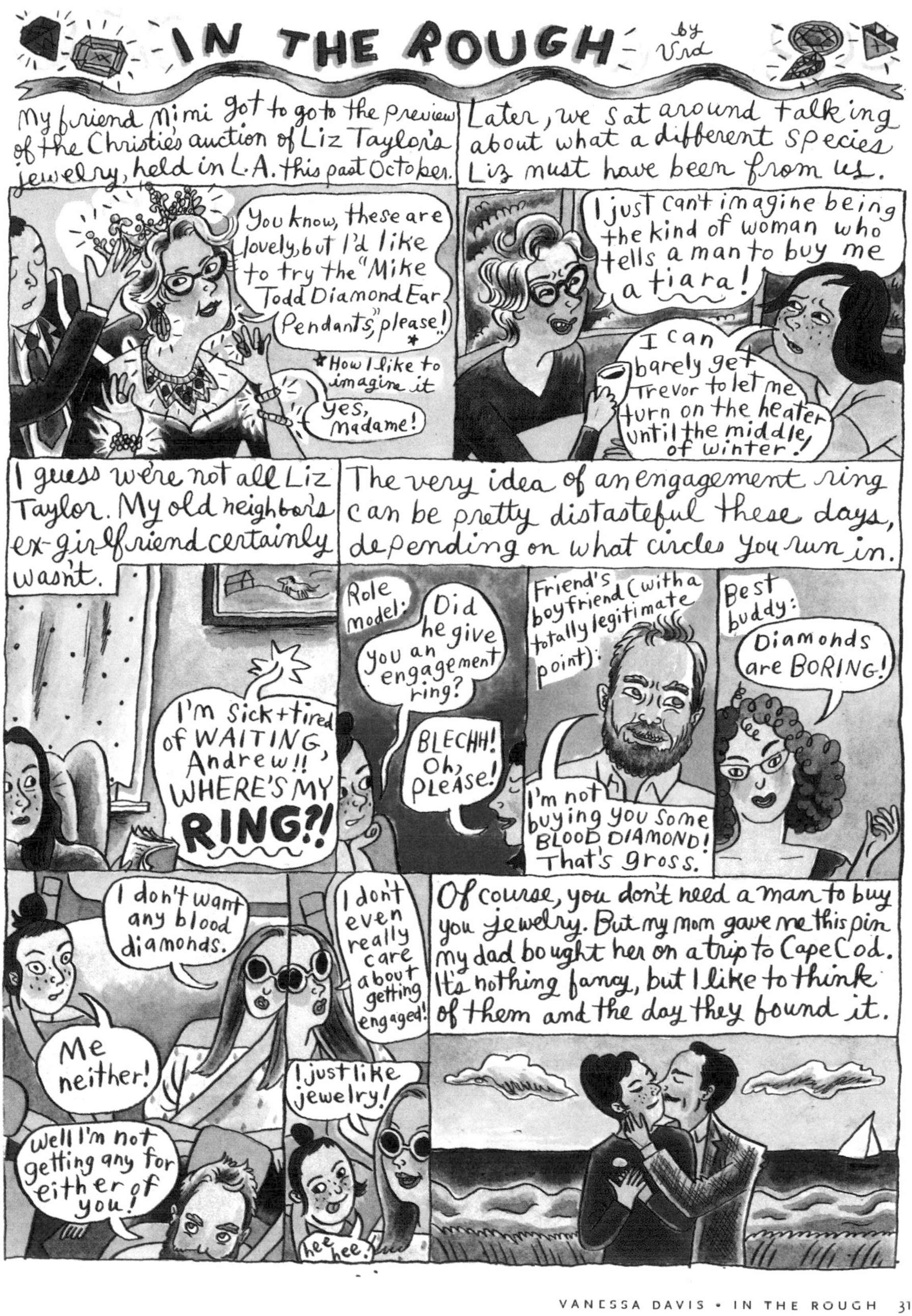
IN THE ROUGH
by Vnd
My friend Mimi got to go to the preview of the Christie's auction of Liz Taylor's jewelry, held in L.A. this past October.
You know, these are lovely, but I'd like to try the "Mike Todd Diamond Ear Pendants," please! *
* How I like to imagine it
Yes, Madame!
Later, we sat around talking about what a different species Liz must have been from us.
I just can't imagine being the kind of woman who tells a man to buy me a tiara!
I can barely get Trevor to let me turn on the heater until the middle of winter!
I guess we're not all Liz Taylor. My old neighbor's ex-girlfriend certainly wasn't.
I'm sick + tired of WAITING, Andrew!! WHERE'S MY RING?!
The very idea of an engagement ring can be pretty distasteful these days, depending on what circles you run in.
Role model:
Did he give you an engagement ring?
BLECHH! Oh, PLEASE!
Friend's boyfriend (with a totally legitimate point):
I'm not buying you some BLOOD DIAMOND! That's gross.
Best buddy:
Diamonds are BORING!
I don't want any blood diamonds.
Me neither!
Well I'm not getting any for either of you!
I don't even really care about getting engaged!
I just like jewelry!
hee hee.
Of course, you don't need a man to buy you jewelry. But my mom gave me this pin my dad bought her on a trip to Cape Cod. It's nothing fancy, but I like to think of them and the day they found it.

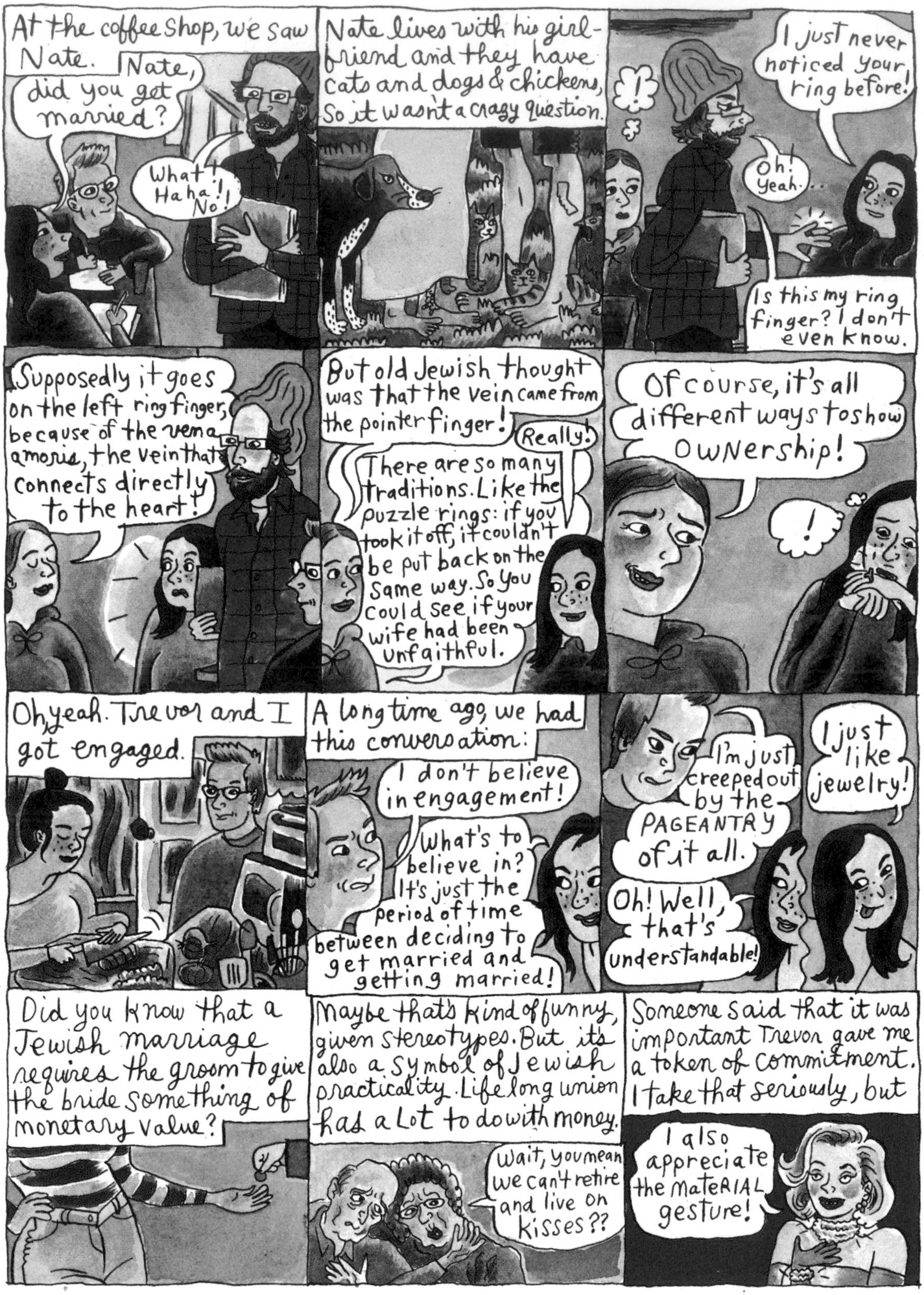
At the coffee shop, we saw Nate.
Nate, did you get married?
What! Haha! No!
Nate lives with his girlfriend and they have cats and dogs & chickens, so it wasn't a crazy question.
!
I just never noticed your ring before!
Oh! Yeah...
Is this my ring finger? I don't even know.
Supposedly it goes on the left ring finger, because of the vena amoris, the vein that connects directly to the heart!
But old Jewish thought was that the vein came from the pointer finger!
Really!
There are so many traditions. Like the puzzle rings: if you took it off, it couldn't be put back on the same way. So you could see if your wife had been unfaithful.
Of course, it's all different ways to show OWNERSHIP!
!
Oh, yeah. Trevor and I got engaged.
A long time ago, we had this conversation:
I don't believe in engagement!
What's to believe in? It's just the period of time between deciding to get married and getting married!
I'm just creeped out by the PAGEANTRY of it all.
Oh! Well, that's understandable!
I just like jewelry!
Did you know that a Jewish marriage requires the groom to give the bride something of monetary value?
Maybe that's kind of funny, given stereotypes. But it's also a symbol of Jewish practicality. Life long union has a lot to do with money.
Wait, you mean we can't retire and live on kisses??
Someone said that it was important Trevor gave me a token of commitment. I take that seriously, but
I also appreciate the MATERIAL gesture!

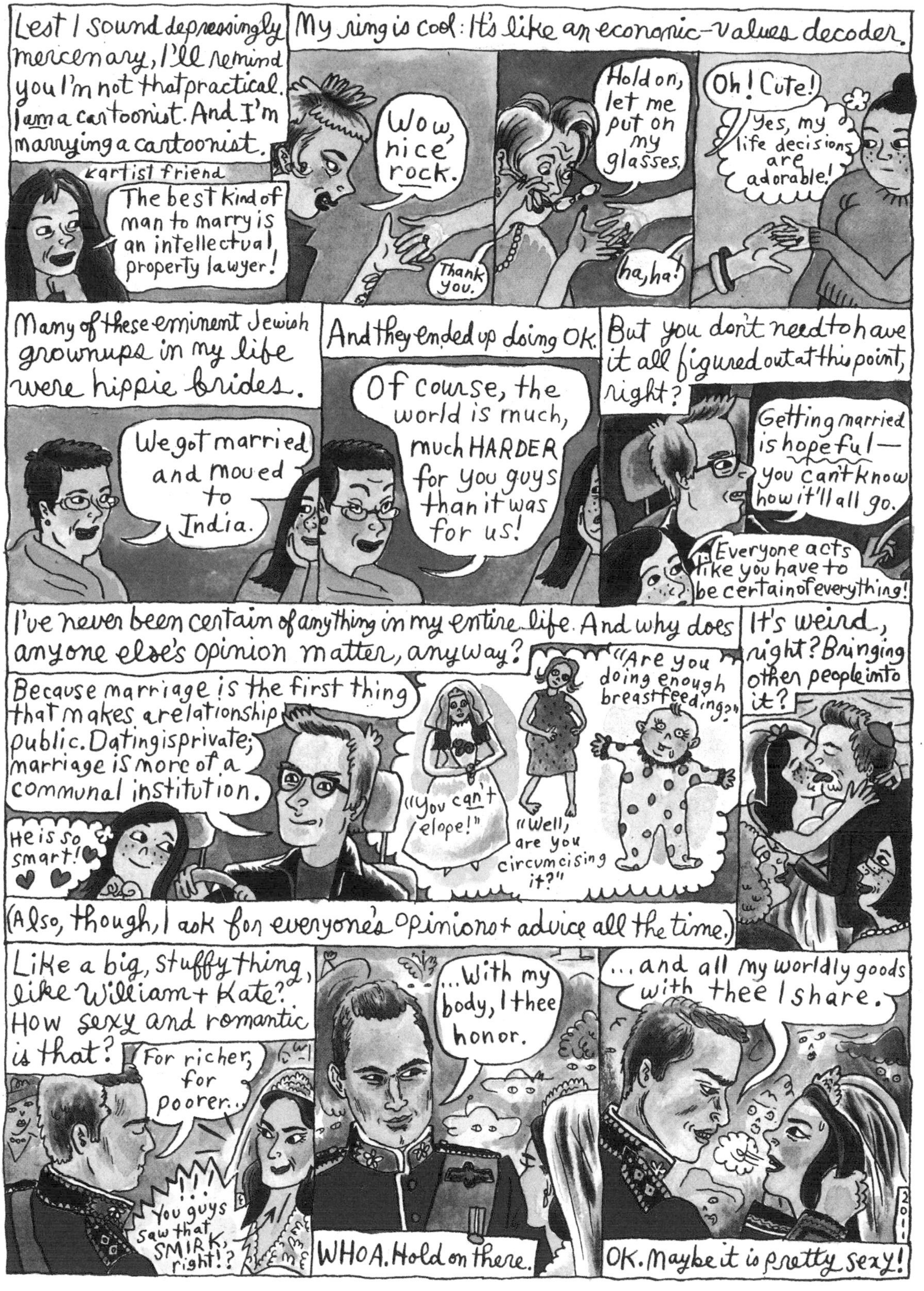

Lest I sound depressingly mercenary, I'll remind you I'm not that practical. I am a cartoonist. And I'm marrying a cartoonist.
artist friend
The best kind of man to marry is an intellectual property lawyer!
My ring is cool: It's like an economic-values decoder.
Wow, nice rock.
Thank you.
Hold on, let me put on my glasses.
ha, ha!
Oh! Cute!
Yes, my life decisions are adorable!
Many of these eminent Jewish grownups in my life were hippie brides.
We got married and moved to India.
And they ended up doing OK.
Of course, the world is much, much HARDER for you guys than it was for us!
But you don't need to have it all figured out at this point, right?
Getting married is hopeful— you can't know how it'll all go.
Everyone acts like you have to be certain of everything!
I've never been certain of anything in my entire life. And why does anyone else's opinion matter, anyway?
Because marriage is the first thing that makes a relationship public. Dating is private; marriage is more of a communal institution.
He is so smart!
"You can't elope!"
"Are you doing enough breastfeeding?"
"Well, are you circumcising it?"
(Also, though, I ask for everyone's opinions + advice all the time.)
It's weird, right? Bringing other people into it?
Like a big, stuffy thing, like William + Kate? How sexy and romantic is that?
For richer, for poorer...
!!! You guys saw that SMIRK, right!?
...With my body, I thee honor.
WHOA. Hold on there.
...and all my worldly goods with thee I share.
OK. Maybe it is pretty sexy!
2011

JEREMY SORESE

Love Me Forever! Oh! Oh! Oh!

from

LITTLE HEART: A COMIC ANTHOLOGY
FOR MARRIAGE EQUALITY

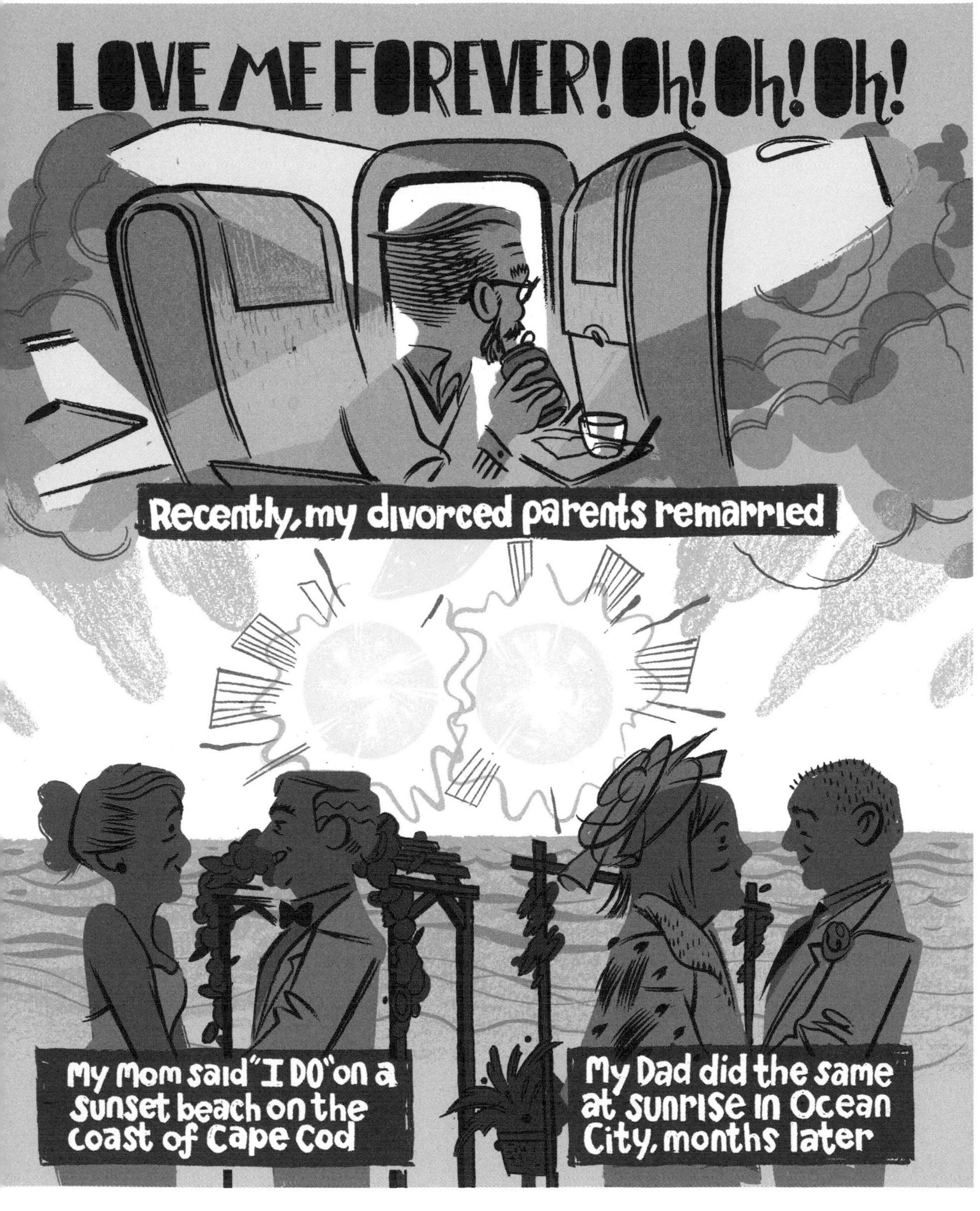
LOVE ME FOREVER! Oh! Oh! Oh!
Recently, my divorced parents remarried
My Mom said "I DO" on a sunset beach on the coast of Cape Cod
My Dad did the same at sunrise in Ocean City, months later

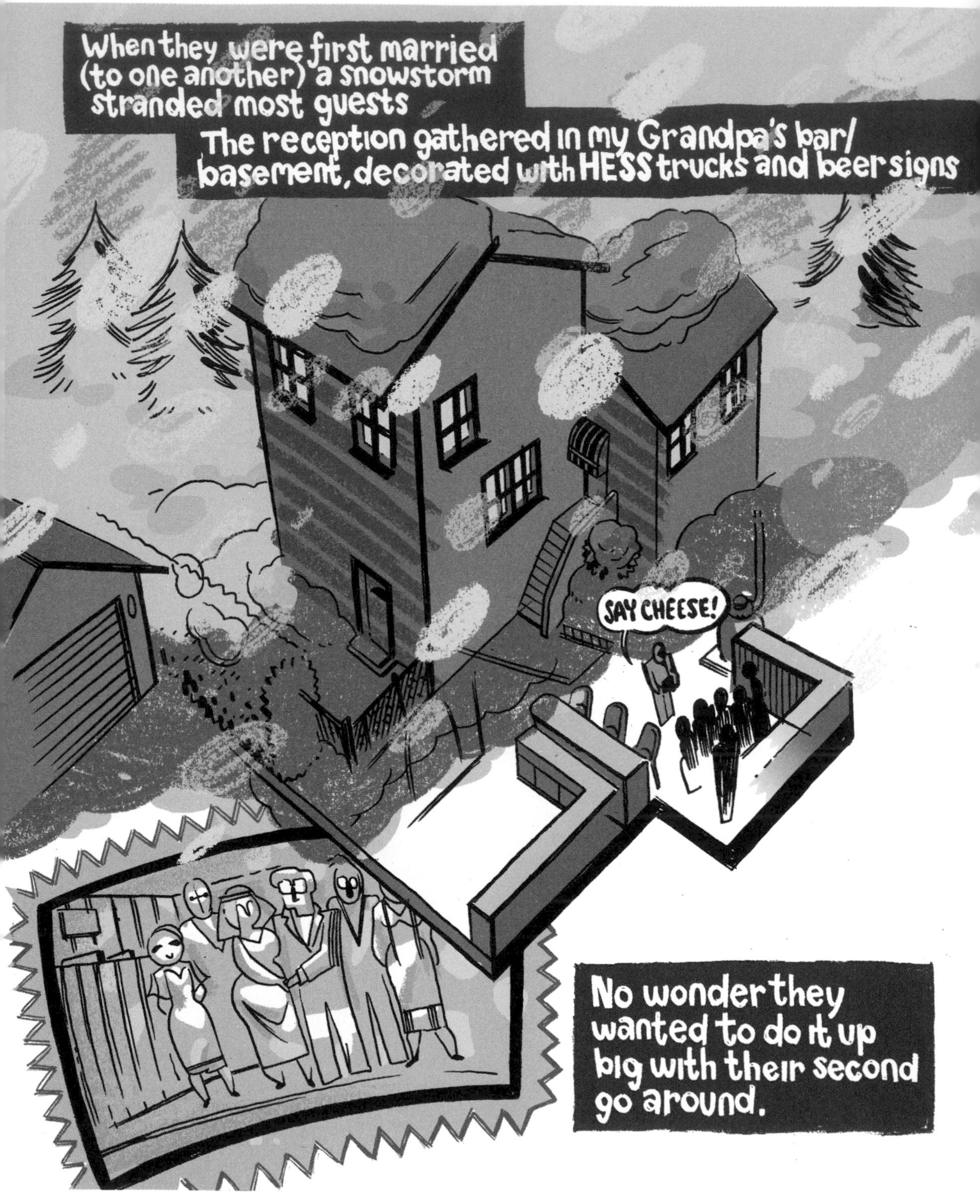
When they were first married (to one another) a snowstorm stranded most guests
The reception gathered in my Grandpa's bar/basement, decorated with HESS trucks and beer signs
SAY CHEESE!
No wonder they wanted to do it up big with their second go around.

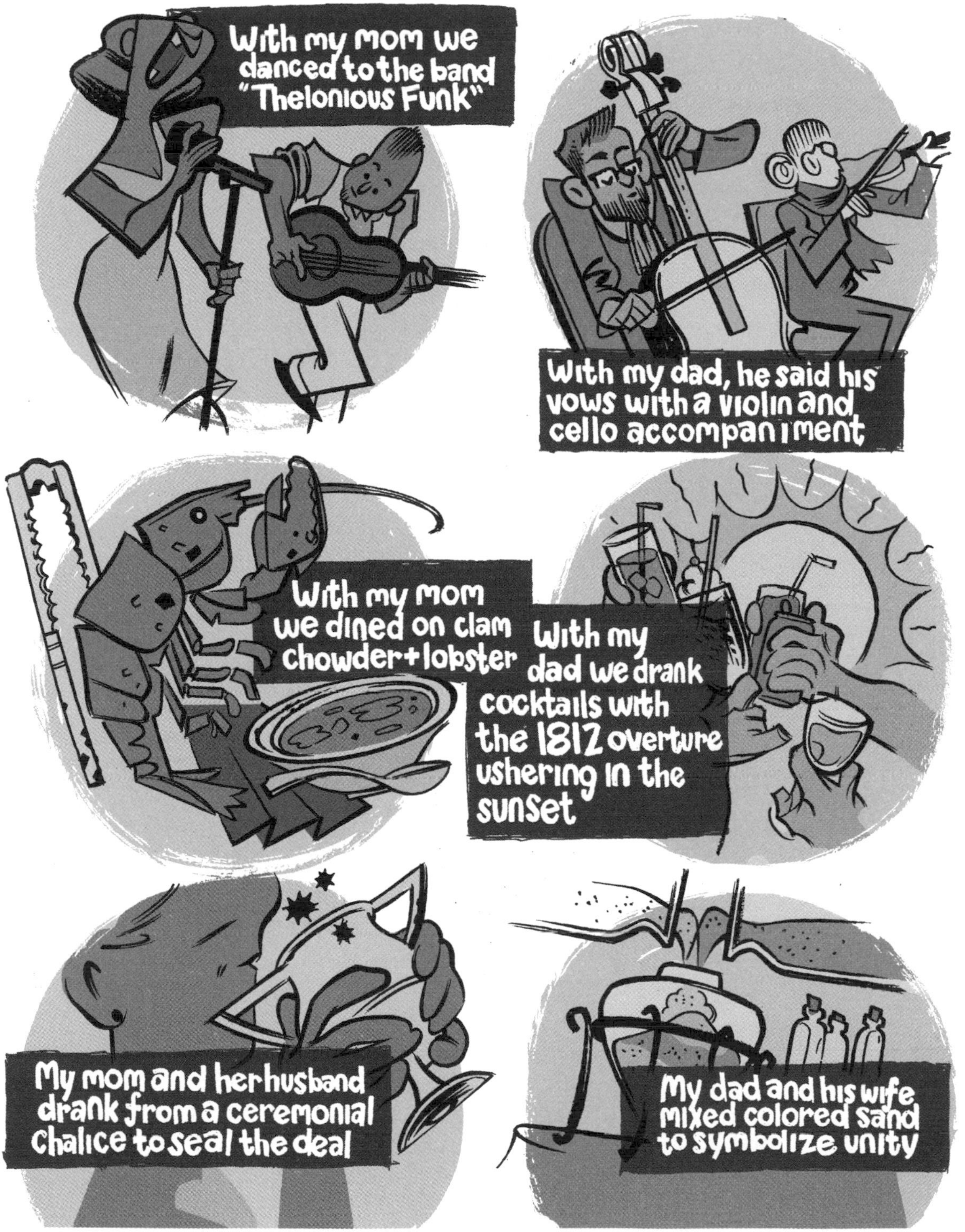
With my mom we danced to the band "Thelonious Funk"
With my dad, he said his vows with a violin and cello accompaniment
With my mom we dined on clam chowder+lobster
With my dad we drank cocktails with the 1812 overture ushering in the sunset
My mom and her husband drank from a ceremonial chalice to seal the deal
My dad and his wife mixed colored sand to symbolize unity

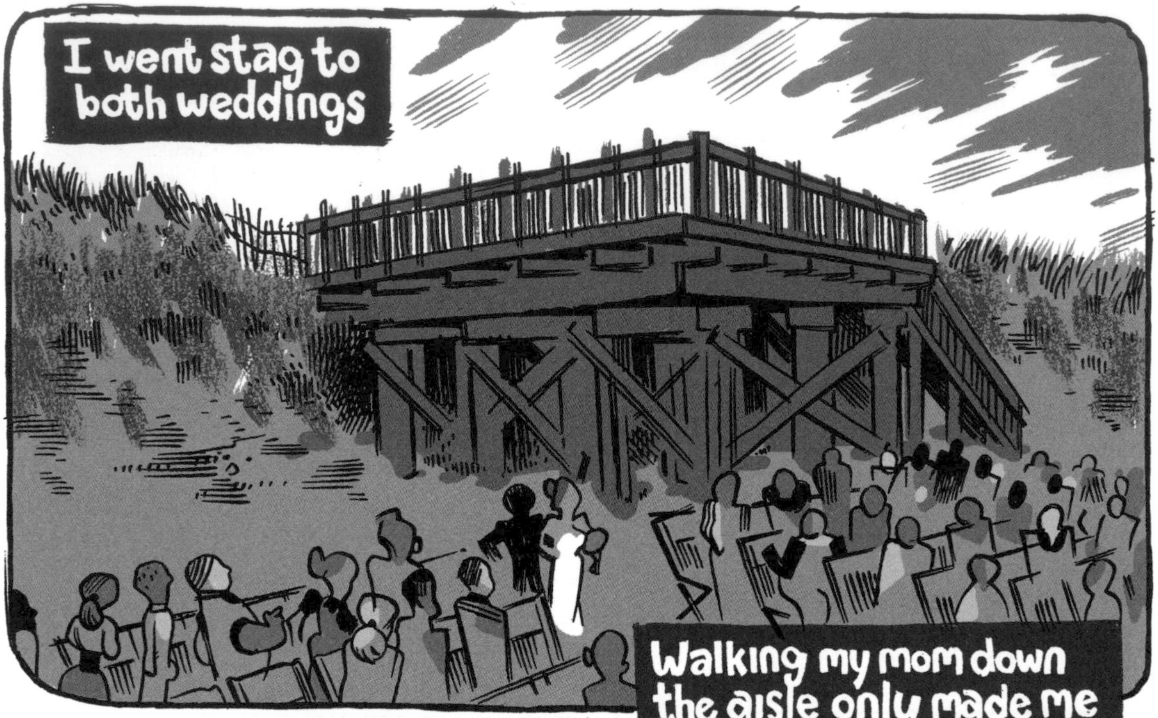
I went stag to both weddings
Walking my mom down the aisle only made me feel more single

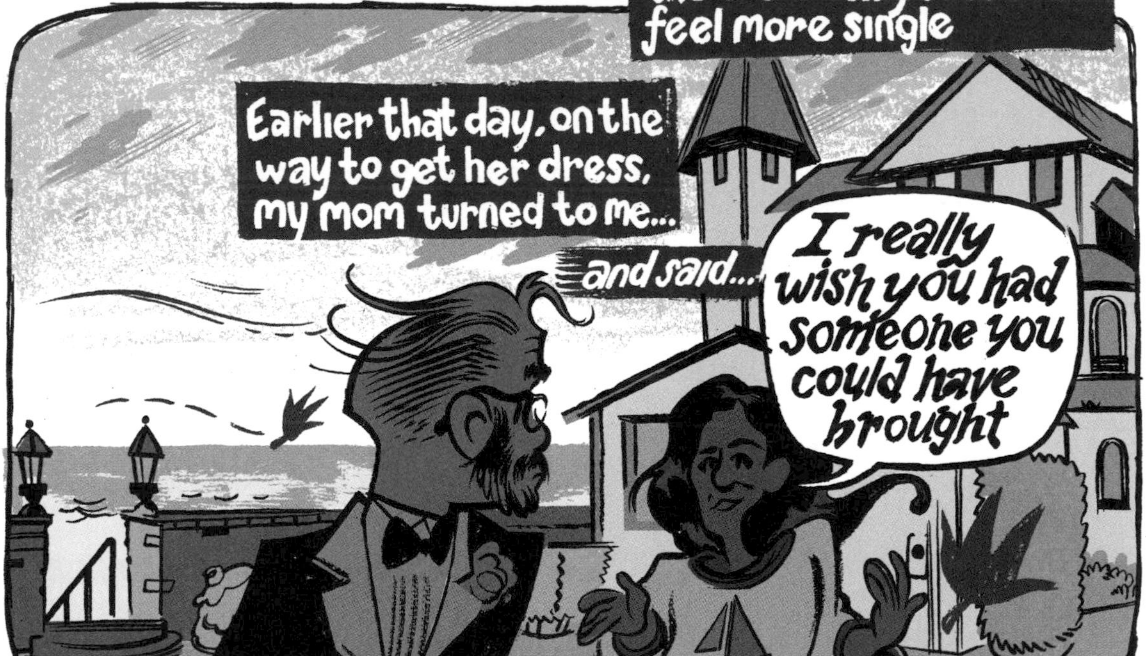
Earlier that day, on the way to get her dress, my mom turned to me...
and said...
I really wish you had someone you could have brought

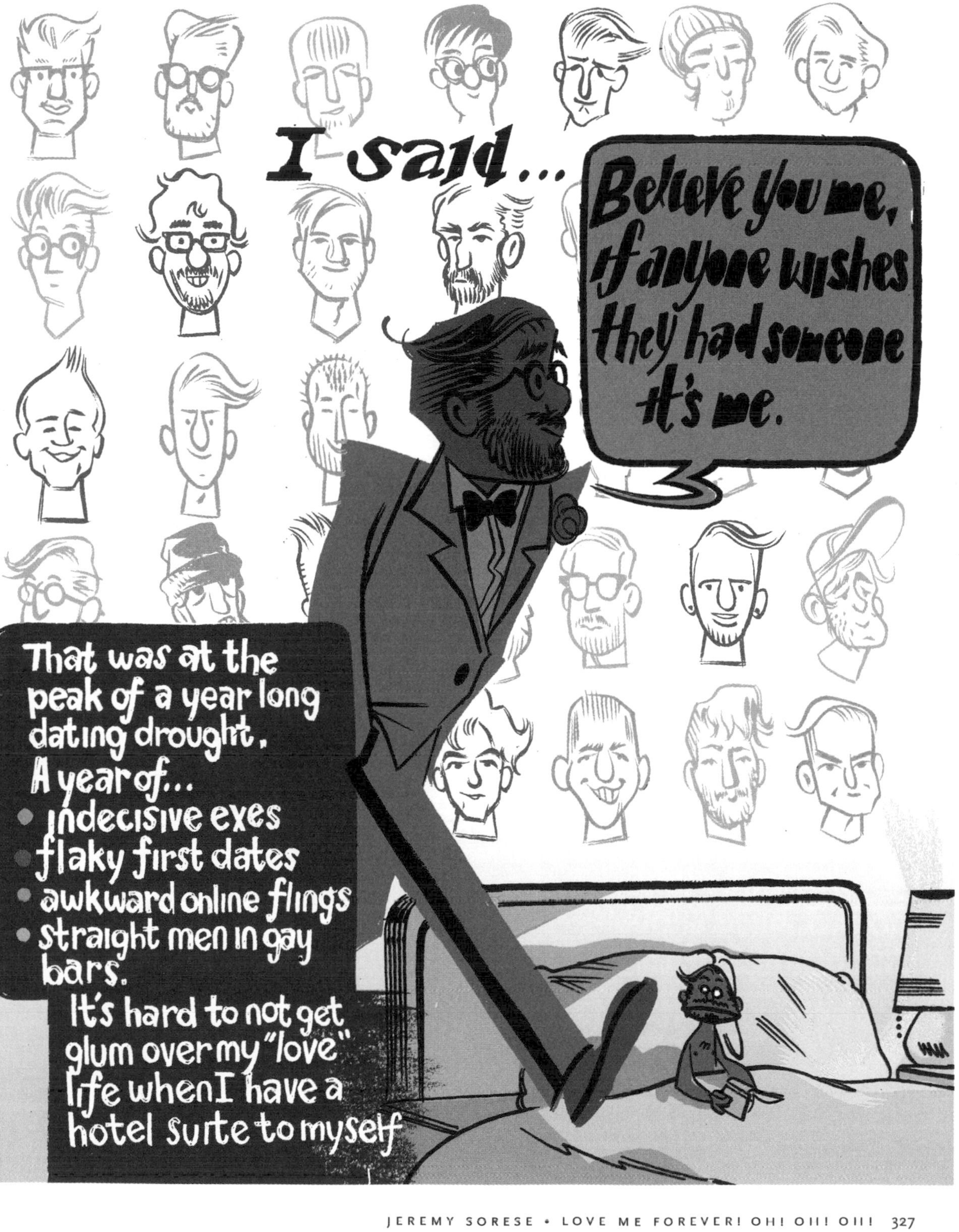
I said...
Believe you me, if anyone wishes they had someone it's me.
That was at the peak of a year long dating drought. A year of...
• indecisive exes
• flaky first dates
• awkward online flings
• straight men in gay bars.
It's hard to not get glum over my "love" life when I have a hotel suite to myself

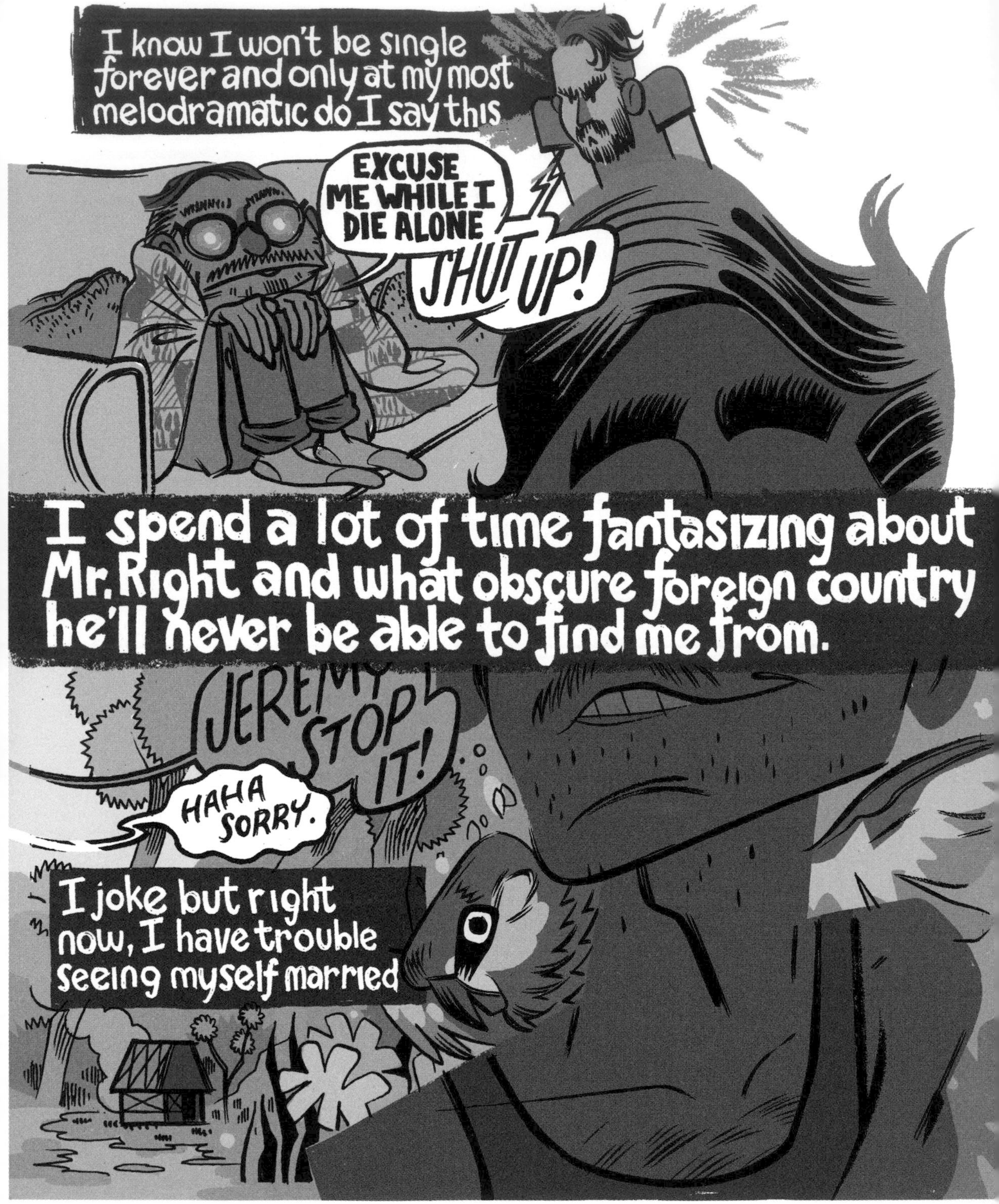
I know I won't be single forever and only at my most melodramatic do I say this
EXCUSE ME WHILE I DIE ALONE
SHUT UP!
I spend a lot of time fantasizing about Mr. Right and what obscure foreign country he'll never be able to find me from.
JEREMY STOP IT!
HAHA SORRY.
I joke but right now, I have trouble seeing myself married

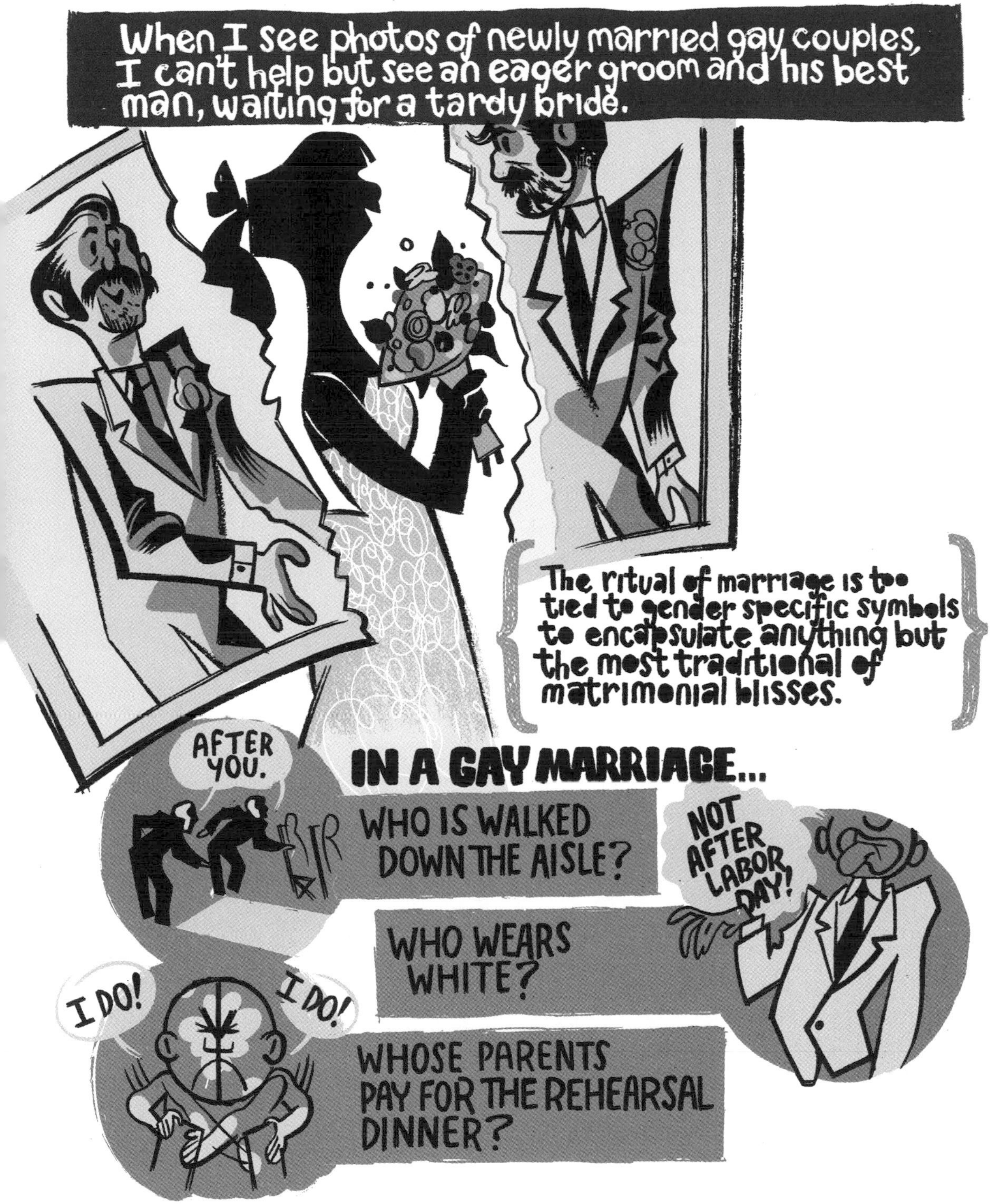
When I see photos of newly married gay couples, I can't help but see an eager groom and his best man, waiting for a tardy bride.
The ritual of marriage is too tied to gender specific symbols to encapsulate anything but the most traditional of matrimonial blisses.
AFTER YOU.
IN A GAY MARRIAGE...
WHO IS WALKED DOWN THE AISLE?
NOT AFTER LABOR DAY!
WHO WEARS WHITE?
I DO!
I DO!
WHOSE PARENTS PAY FOR THE REHEARSAL DINNER?

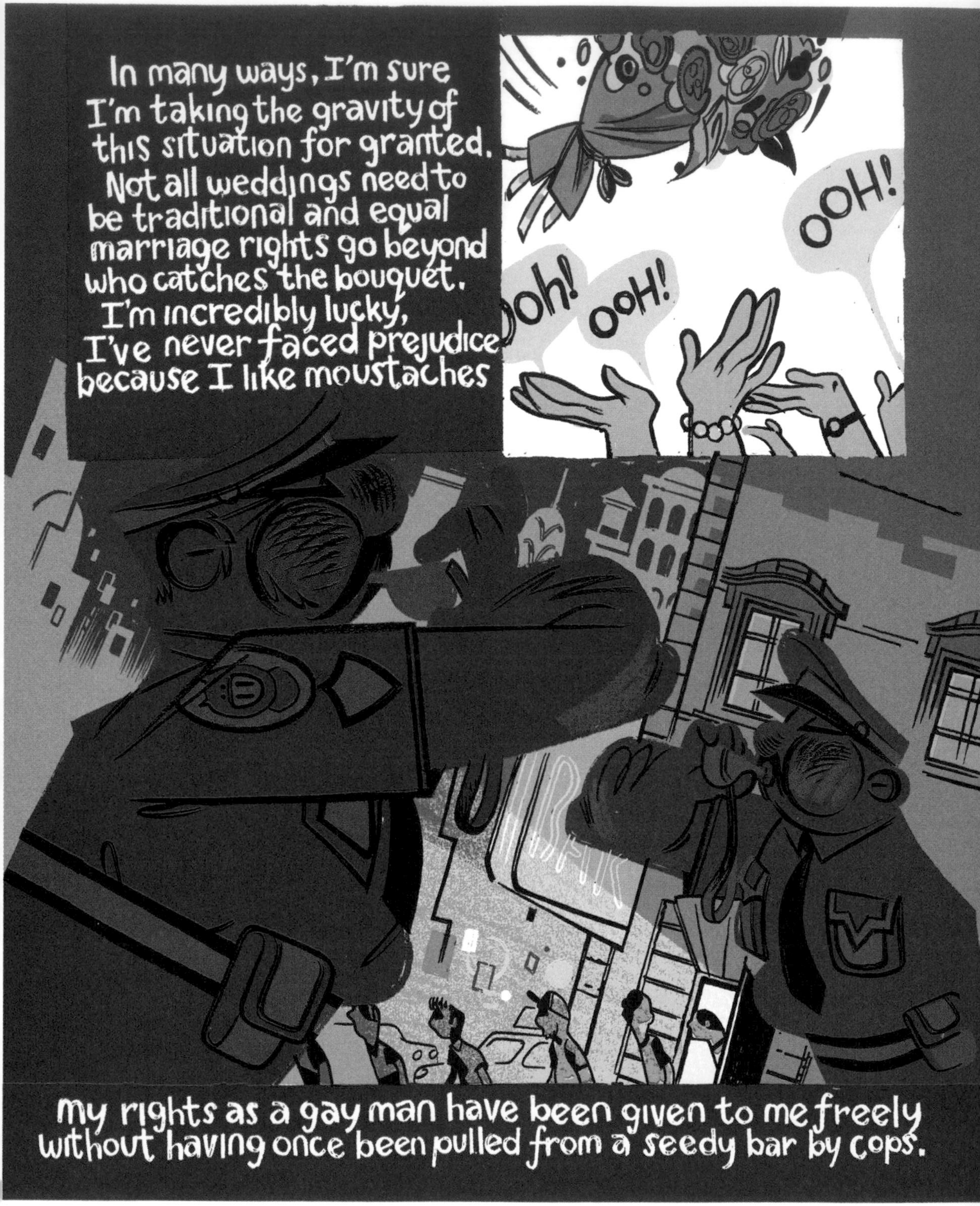
In many ways, I'm sure I'm taking the gravity of this situation for granted. Not all weddings need to be traditional and equal marriage rights go beyond who catches the bouquet. I'm incredibly lucky, I've never faced prejudice because I like moustaches
OOH!
OOH!
OOH!
my rights as a gay man have been given to me freely without having once been pulled from a seedy bar by cops.

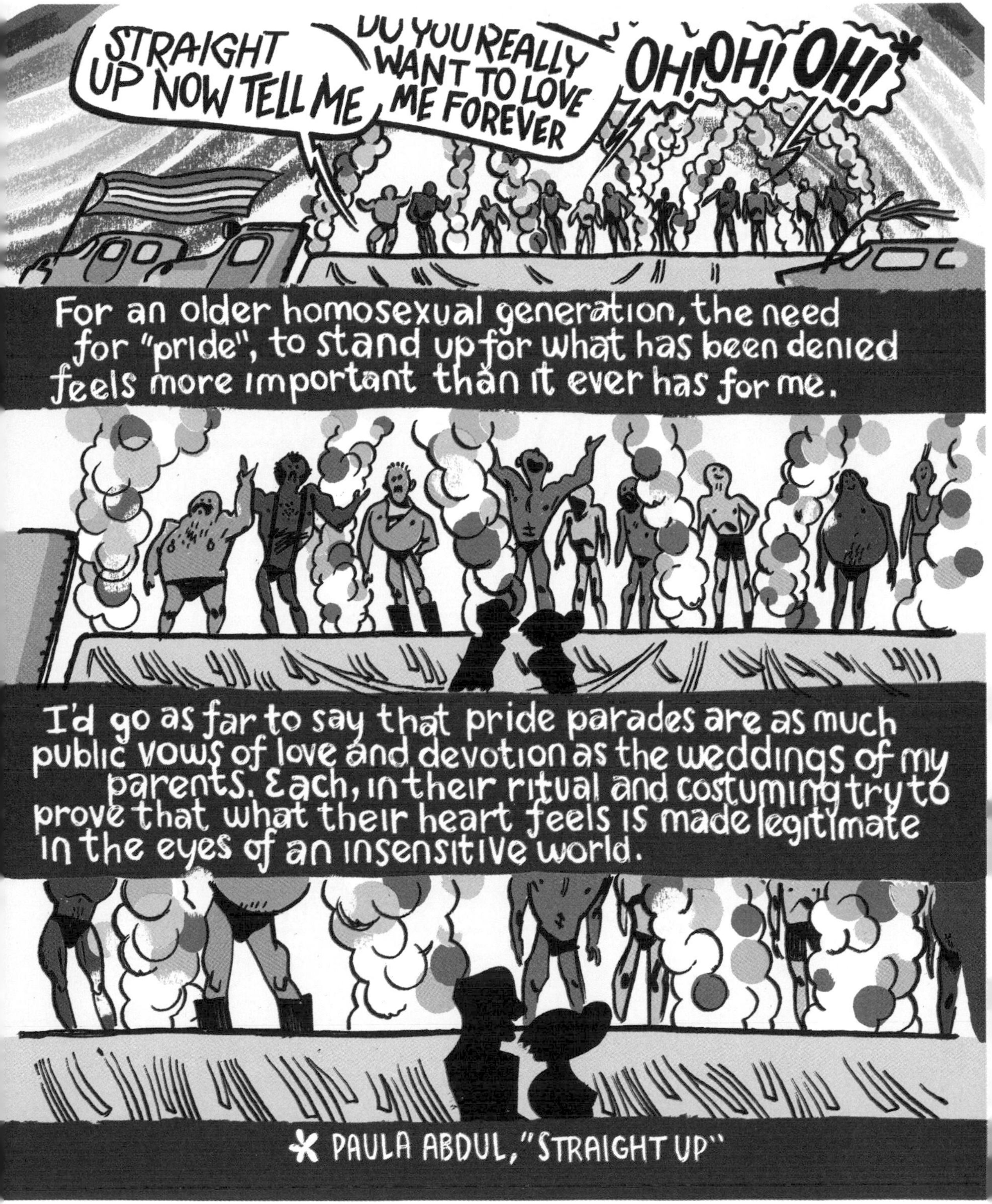
STRAIGHT UP NOW TELL ME
DO YOU REALLY WANT TO LOVE ME FOREVER
OH! OH! OH!*
For an older homosexual generation, the need for "pride", to stand up for what has been denied feels more important than it ever has for me.
I'd go as far to say that pride parades are as much public vows of love and devotion as the weddings of my parents. Each, in their ritual and costuming try to prove that what their heart feels is made legitimate in the eyes of an insensitive world.
* PAULA ABDUL, "STRAIGHT UP"

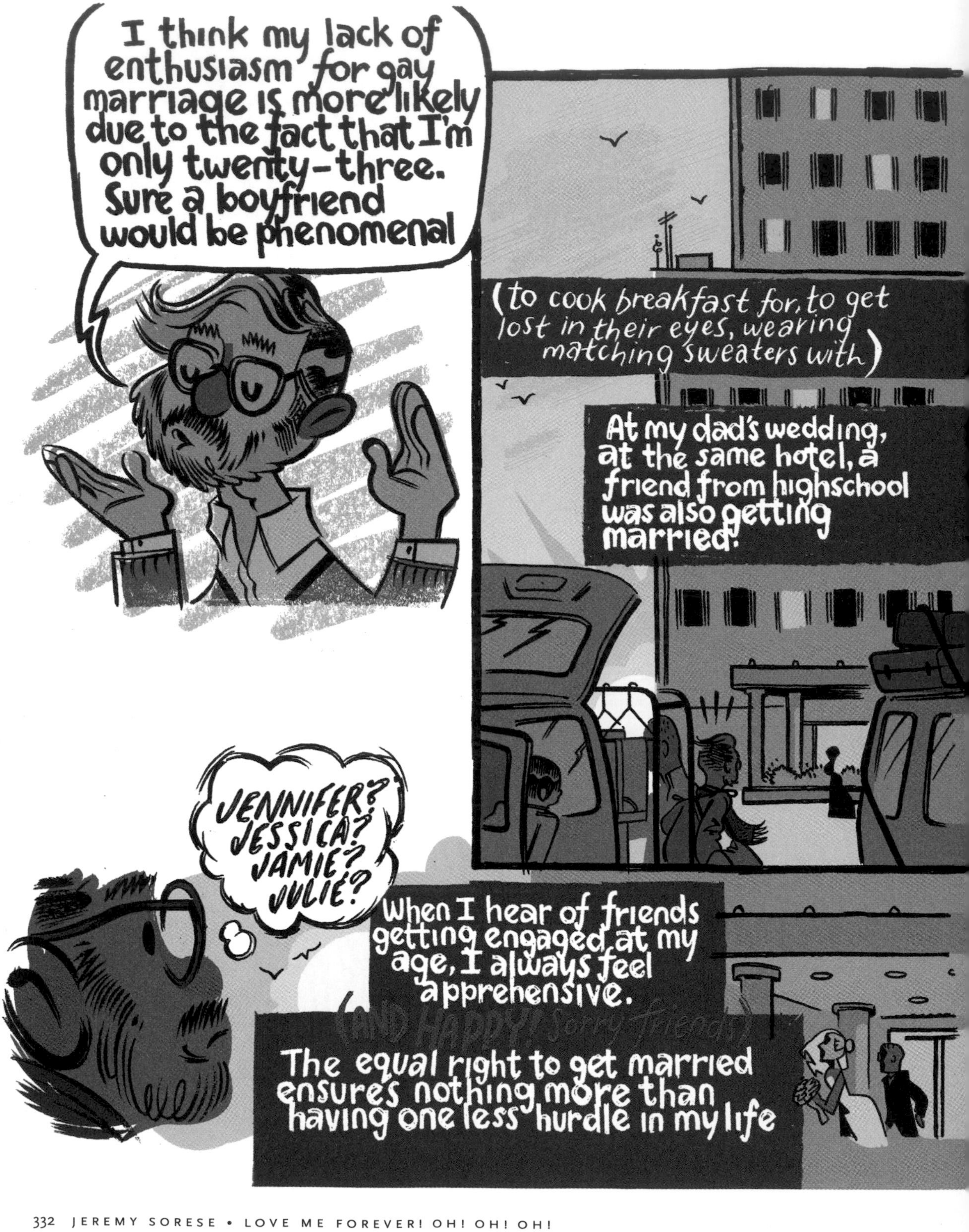
I think my lack of enthusiasm for gay marriage is more likely due to the fact that I'm only twenty-three. Sure a boyfriend would be phenomenal
(to cook breakfast for, to get lost in their eyes, wearing matching sweaters with)
At my dad's wedding, at the same hotel, a friend from highschool was also getting married.
JENNIFER? JESSICA? JAMIE? JULIE?
When I hear of friends getting engaged at my age, I always feel apprehensive.
(AND HAPPY! Sorry friends)
The equal right to get married ensures nothing more than having one less hurdle in my life

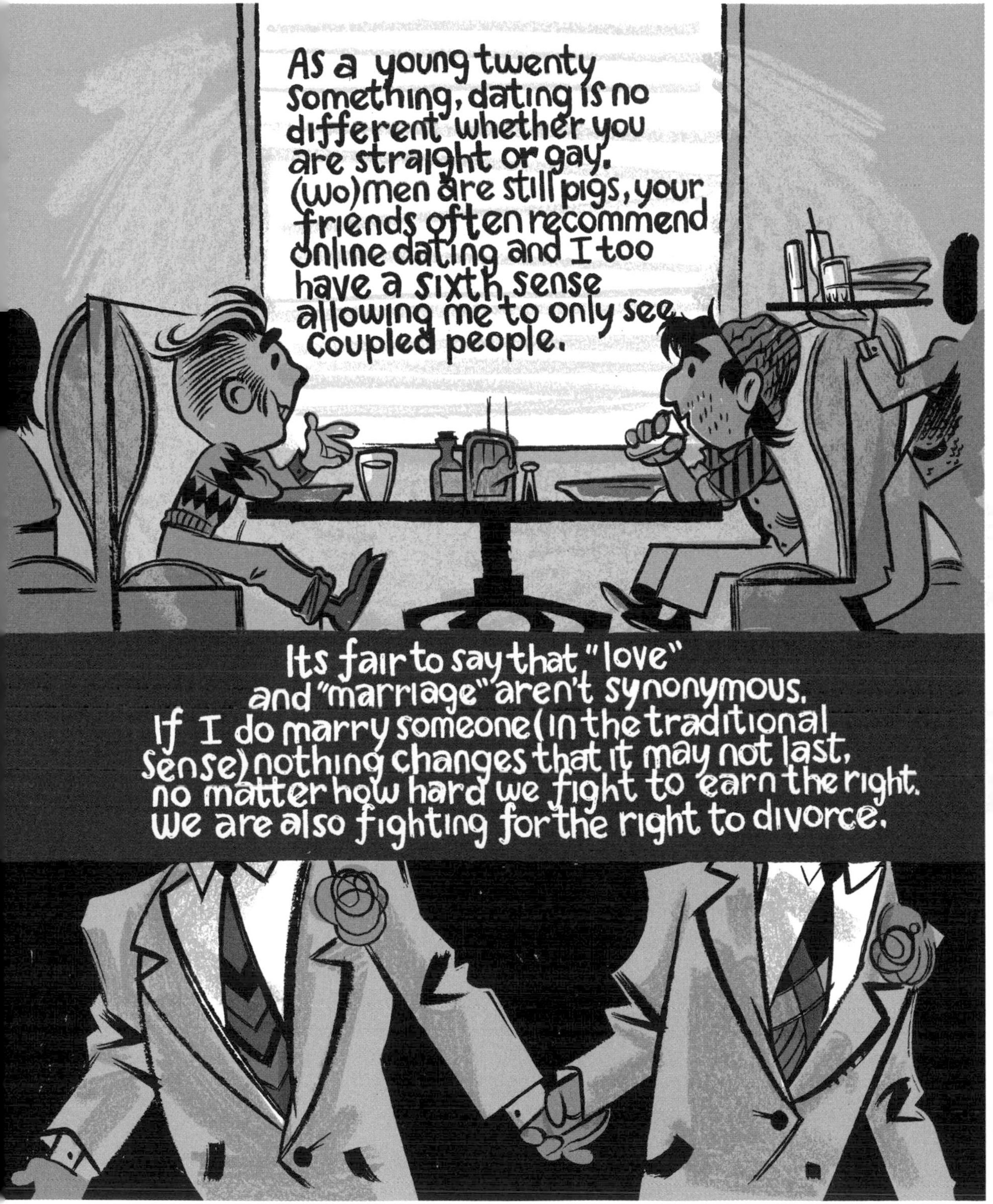
As a young twenty something, dating is no different whether you are straight or gay. (wo)men are still pigs, your friends often recommend online dating and I too have a sixth sense allowing me to only see coupled people.
Its fair to say that "love" and "marriage" aren't synonymous. If I do marry someone (in the traditional sense) nothing changes that it may not last, no matter how hard we fight to earn the right. We are also fighting for the right to divorce.

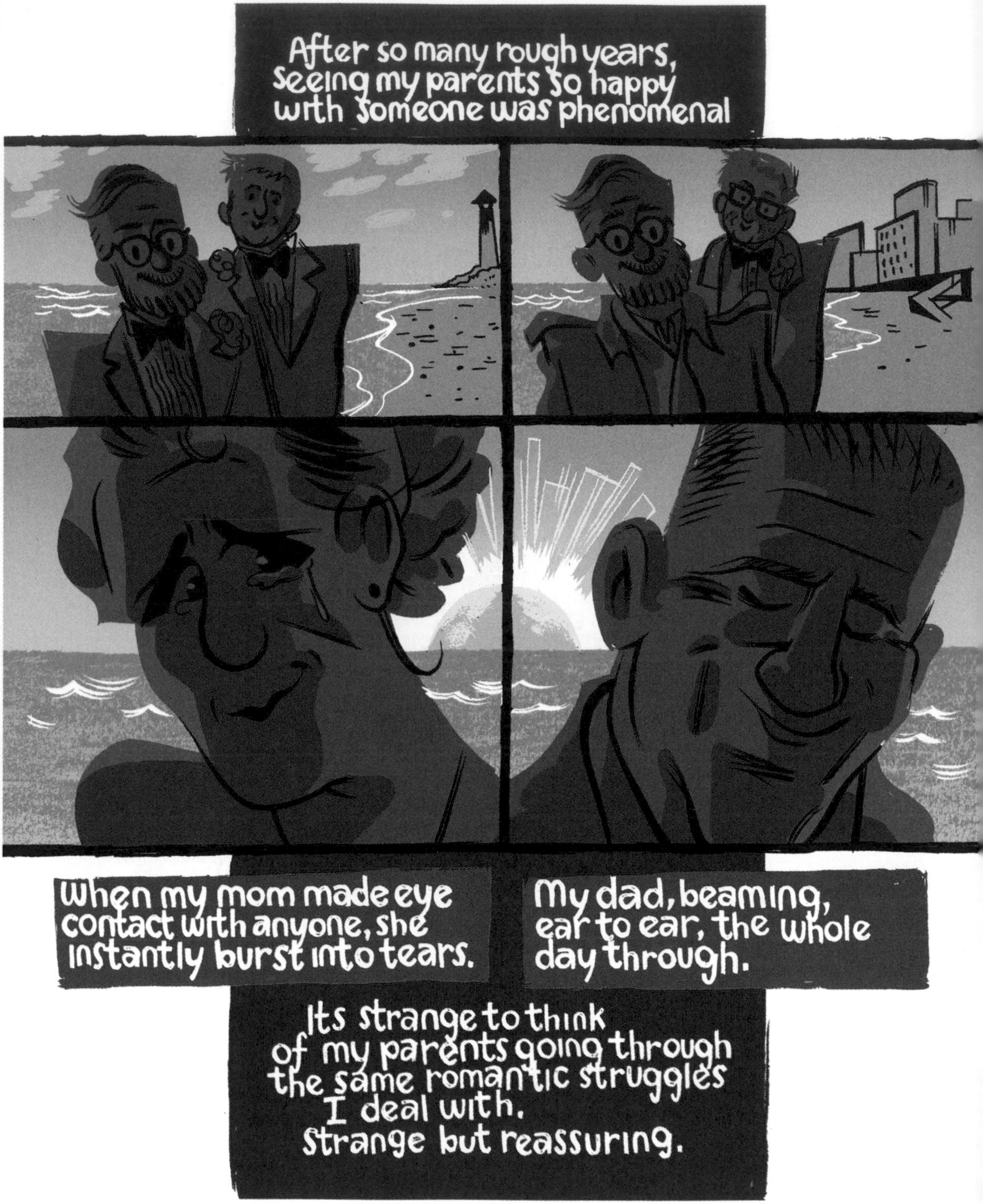
After so many rough years, seeing my parents so happy with someone was phenomenal
When my mom made eye contact with anyone, she instantly burst into tears.
My dad, beaming, ear to ear, the whole day through.
Its strange to think of my parents going through the same romantic struggles I deal with.
Strange but reassuring.

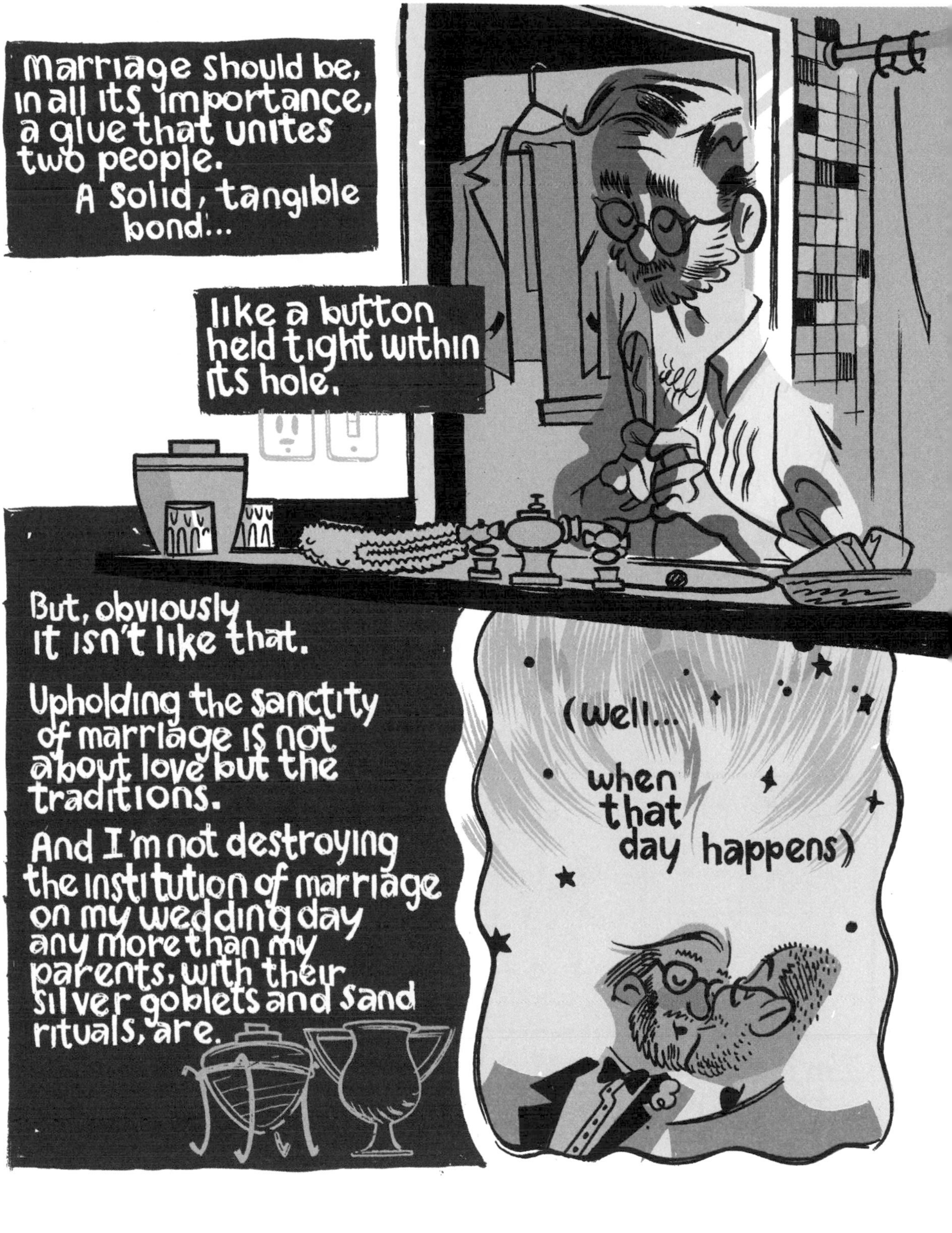
Marriage should be, in all its importance, a glue that unites two people.
A solid, tangible bond...
like a button held tight within its hole.
But, obviously it isn't like that.
Upholding the sanctity of marriage is not about love but the traditions.
And I'm not destroying the institution of marriage on my wedding day any more than my parents, with their silver goblets and sand rituals, are.
(well... when that day happens)

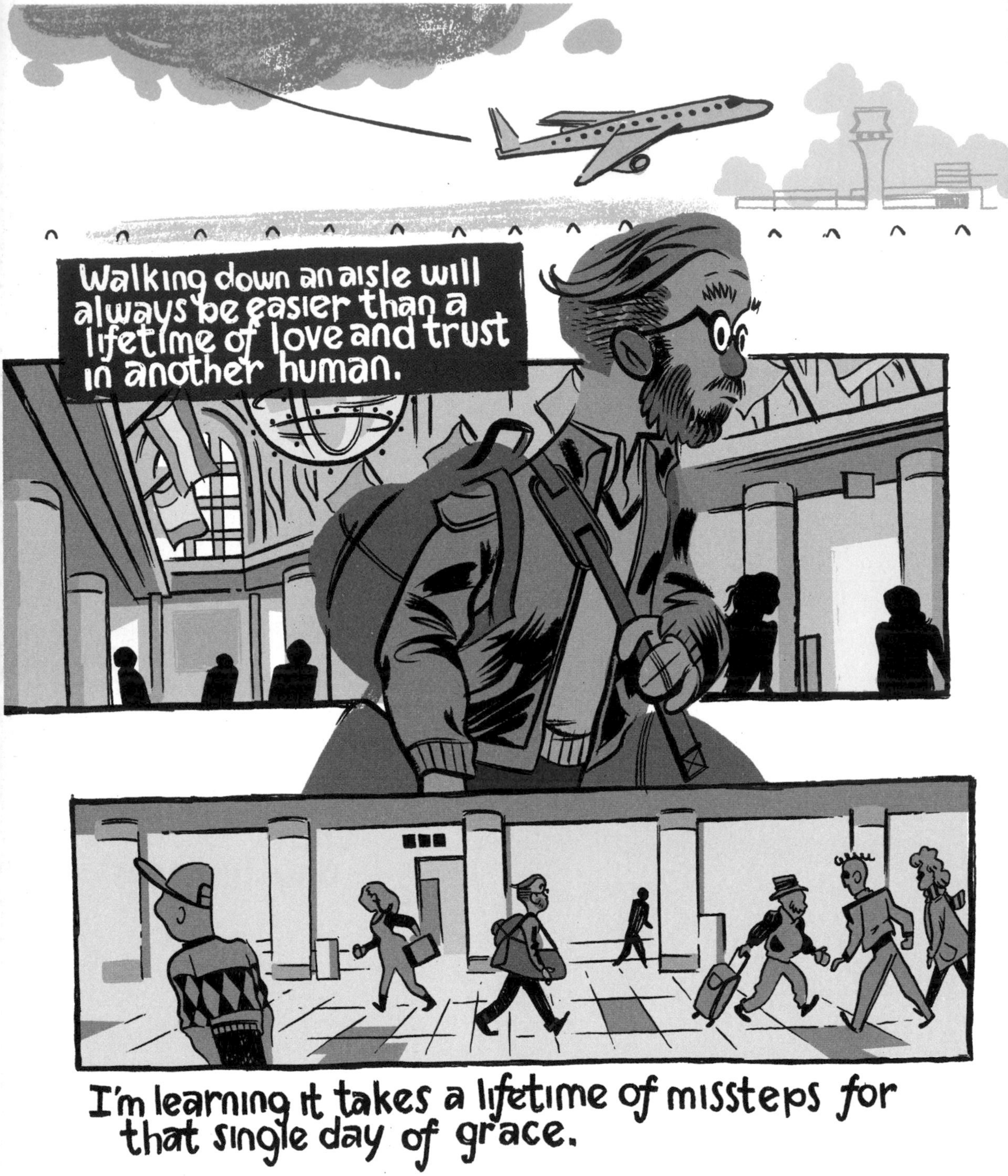
Walking down an aisle will always be easier than a lifetime of love and trust in another human.
I'm learning it takes a lifetime of missteps for that single day of grace.
J. Sorese '11 for my family

Discipline

excerpt from

Annie Sullivan and the Trials of Helen Keller

Joseph Lambert

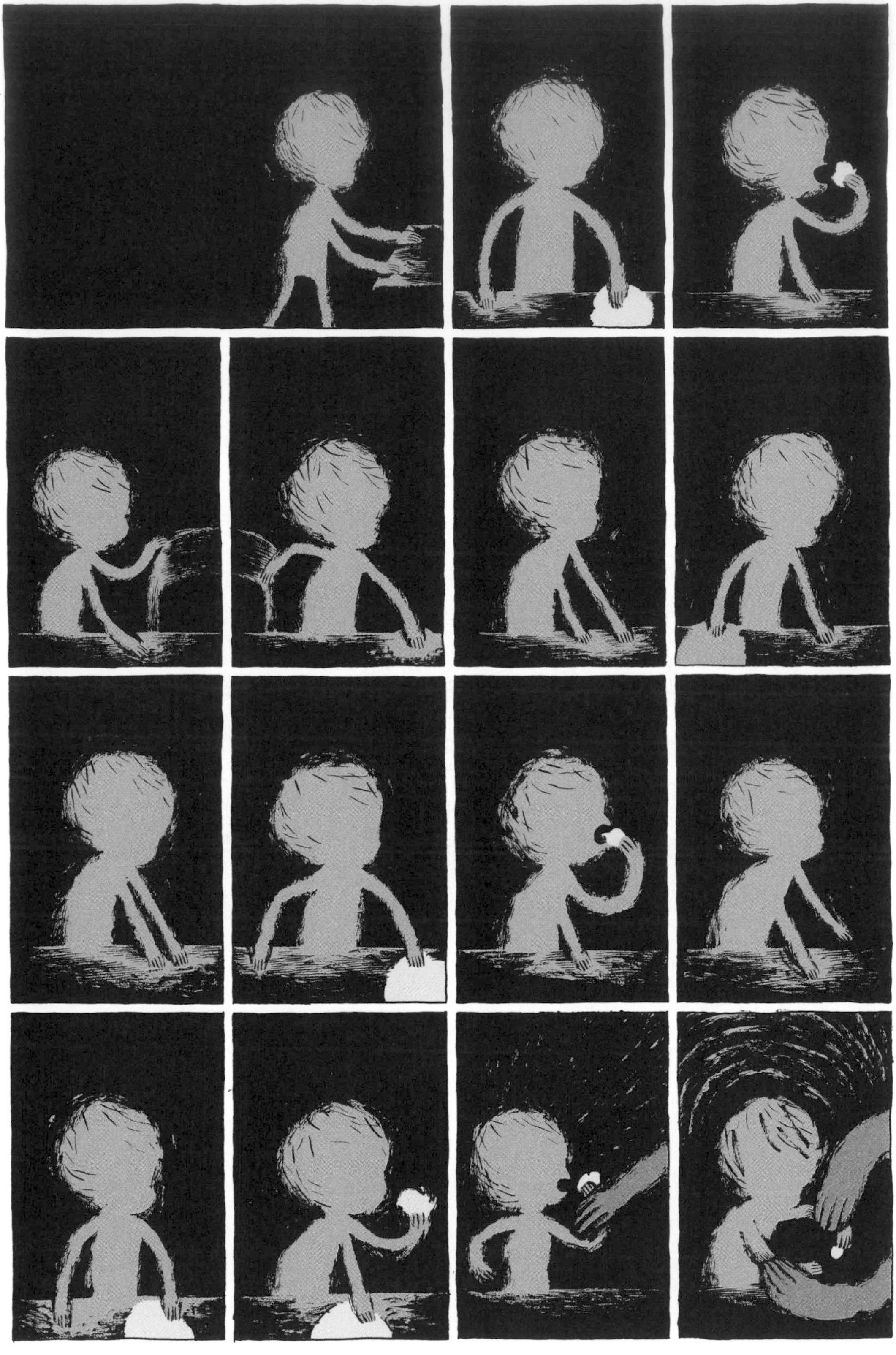

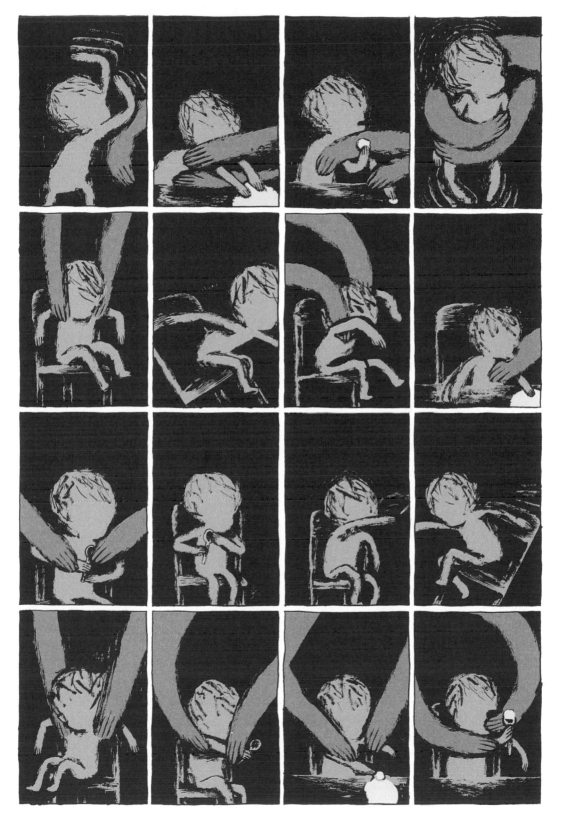

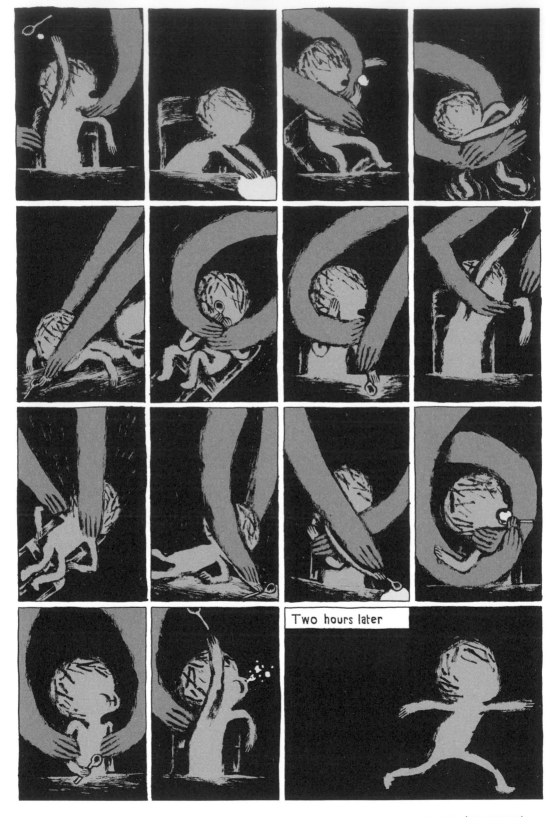

Two hours later

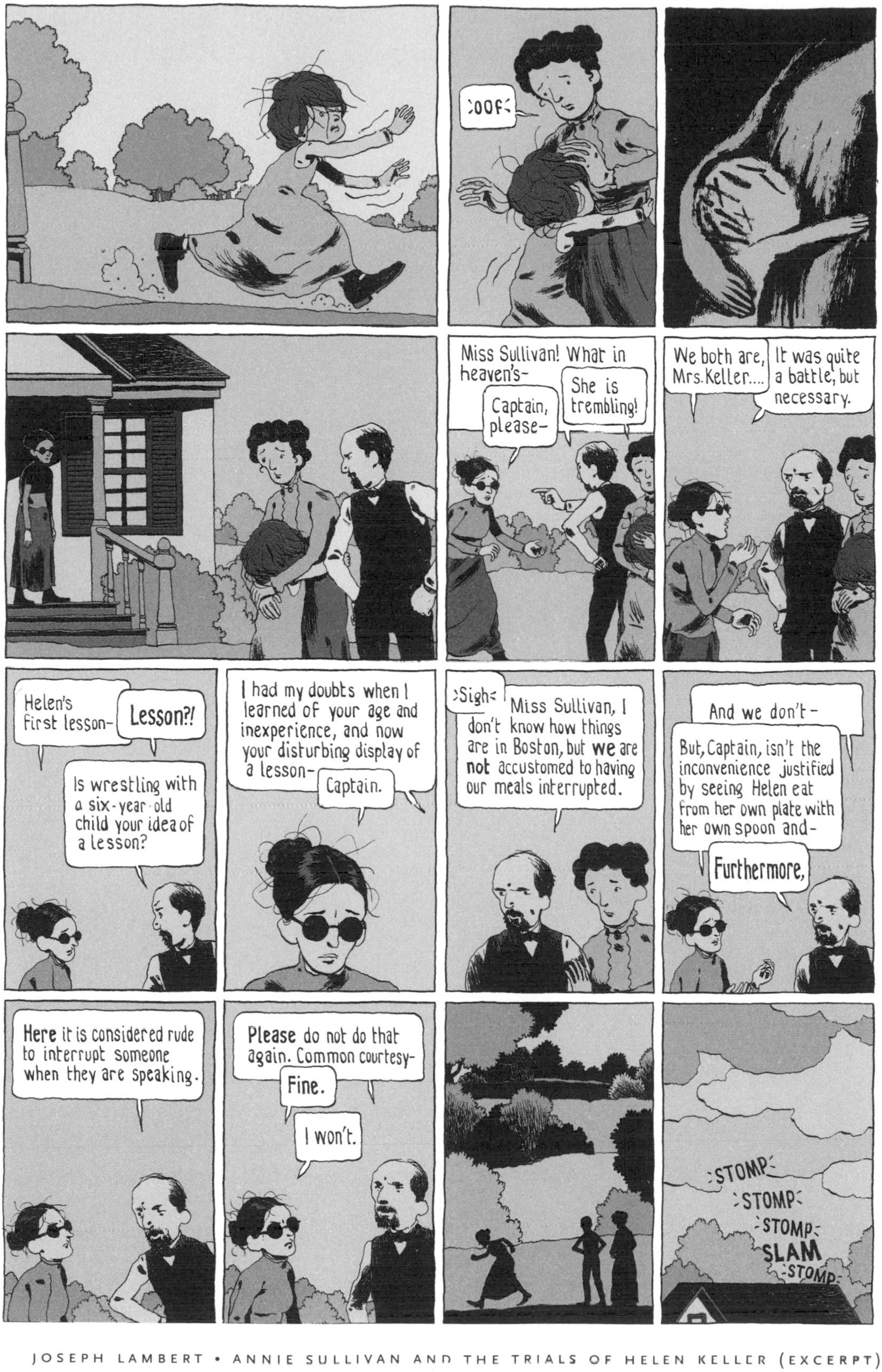

OOF
Miss Sullivan! What in heaven's-
Captain, please-
She is trembling!
We both are, Mrs. Keller....
It was quite a battle, but necessary.
Helen's first lesson-
Lesson?!
Is wrestling with a six-year-old child your idea of a lesson?
I had my doubts when I learned of your age and inexperience, and now your disturbing display of a lesson-
Captain.
Sigh
Miss Sullivan, I don't know how things are in Boston, but we are not accustomed to having our meals interrupted.
And we don't-
But, Captain, isn't the inconvenience justified by seeing Helen eat from her own plate with her own spoon and-
Furthermore,
Here it is considered rude to interrupt someone when they are speaking.
Please do not do that again. Common courtesy-
Fine.
I won't.
STOMP
STOMP
STOMP
SLAM
STOMP

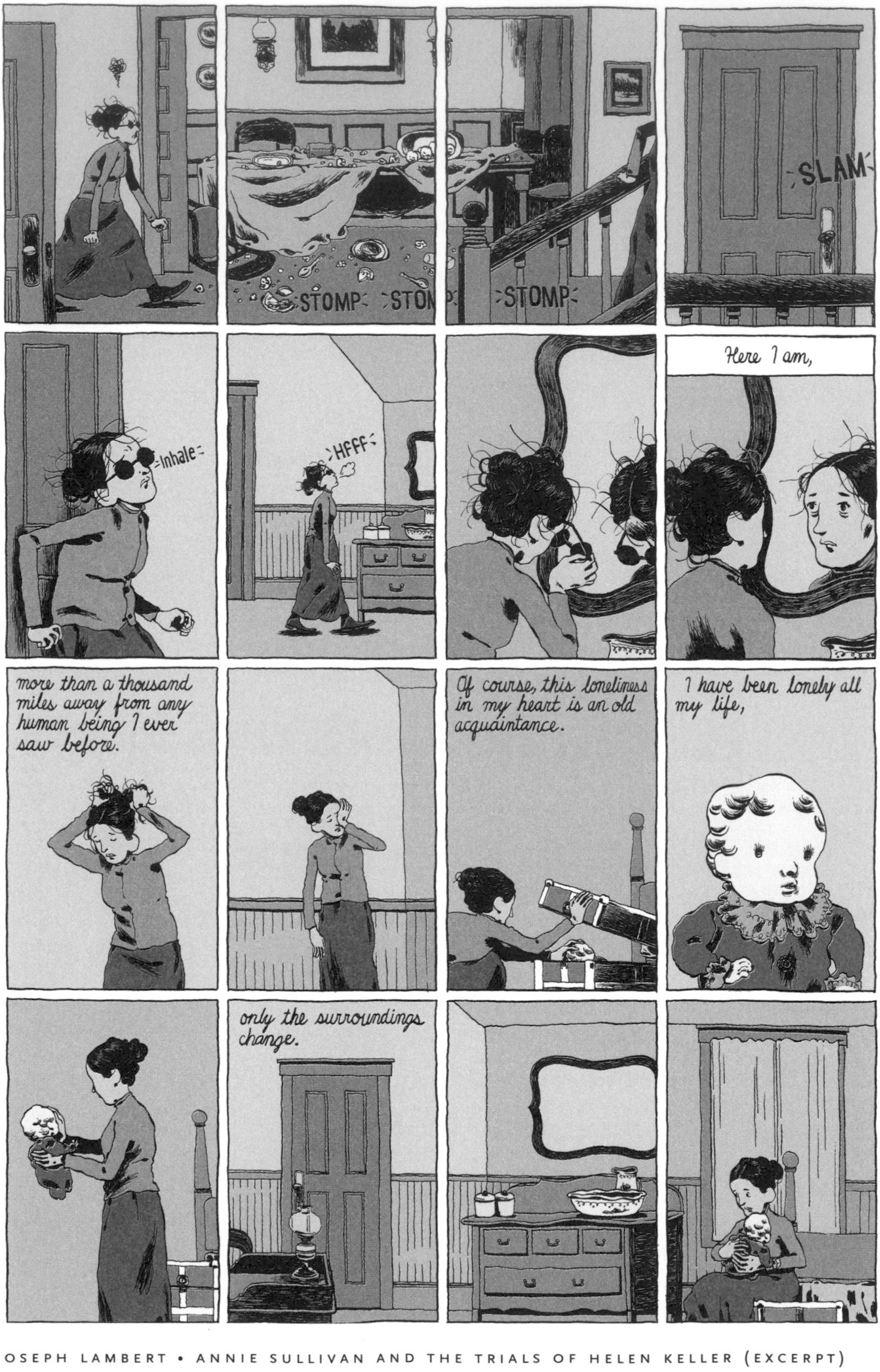
STOMP
STOMP
STOMP
SLAM
Inhale
HFFF
Here I am,
more than a thousand miles away from any human being I ever saw before.
Of course, this loneliness in my heart is an old acquaintance.
I have been lonely all my life,
only the surroundings change.

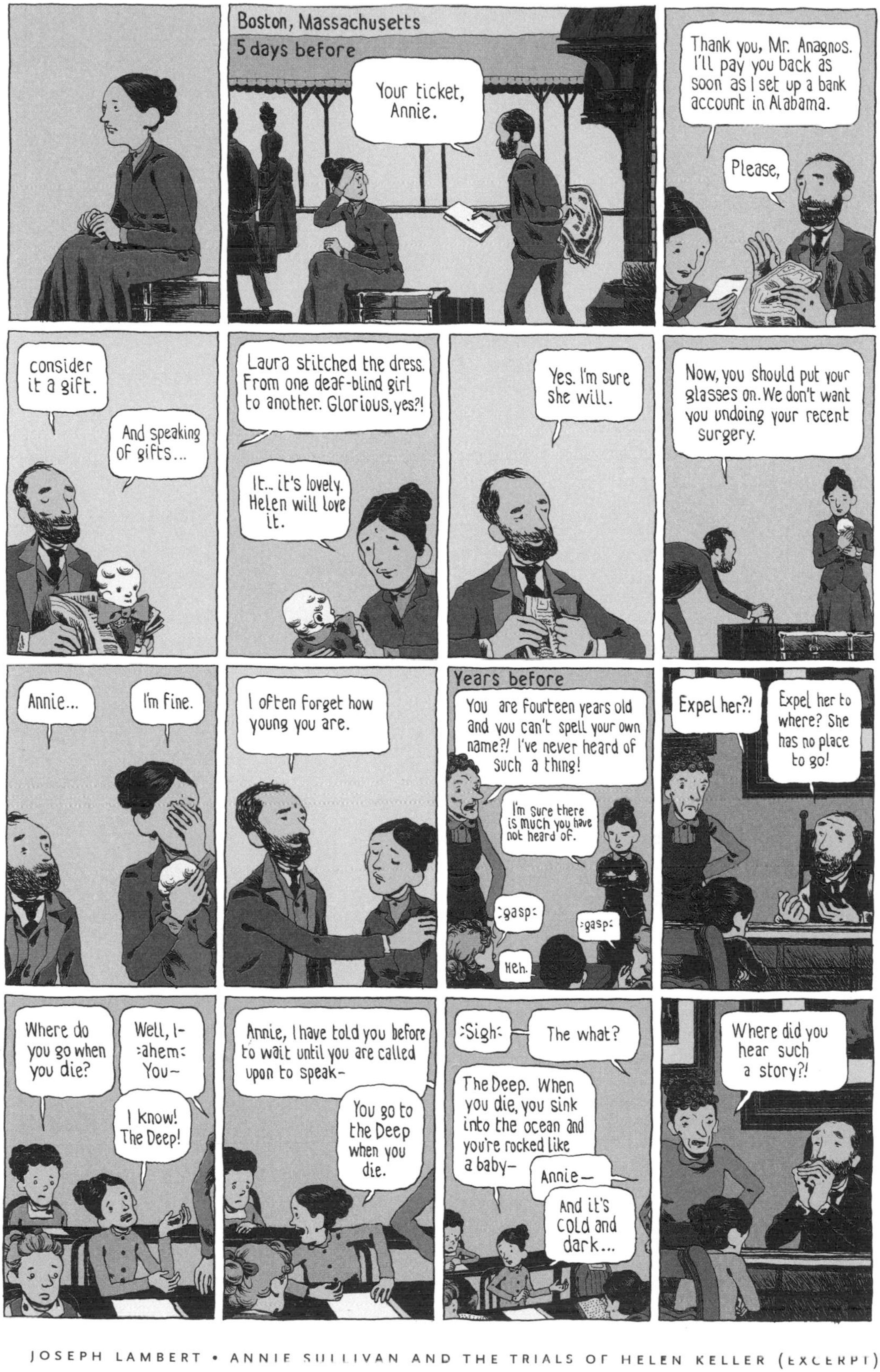

Boston, Massachusetts
5 days before
Your ticket, Annie.
Thank you, Mr. Anagnos. I'll pay you back as soon as I set up a bank account in Alabama.
Please,
consider it a gift.
And speaking of gifts...
Laura stitched the dress. From one deaf-blind girl to another. Glorious, yes?!
It.. it's lovely. Helen will love it.
Yes. I'm sure she will.
Now, you should put your glasses on. We don't want you undoing your recent surgery.
Annie...
I'm fine.
I often forget how young you are.
Years before
You are fourteen years old and you can't spell your own name?! I've never heard of such a thing!
I'm sure there is much you have not heard of.
:gasp:
:gasp:
Heh.
Expel her?!
Expel her to where? She has no place to go!
Where do you go when you die?
Well, I- :ahem: You-
I know! The Deep!
Annie, I have told you before to wait until you are called upon to speak-
You go to the Deep when you die.
:Sigh:
The what?
The Deep. When you die, you sink into the ocean and you're rocked like a baby-
Annie—
And it's cold and dark...
Where did you hear such a story?!

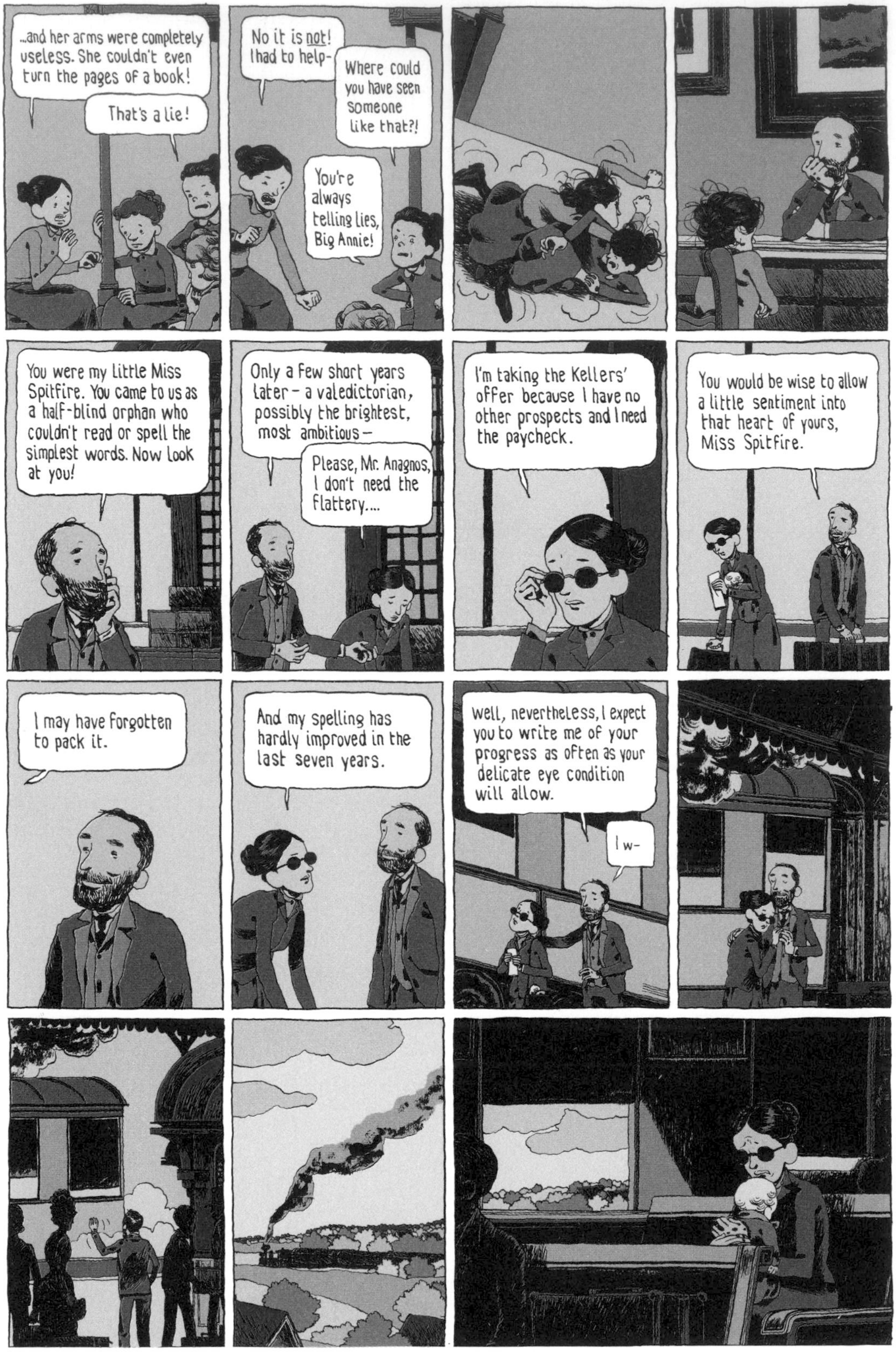
...and her arms were completely useless. She couldn't even turn the pages of a book!
That's a lie!
No it is not! I had to help-
Where could you have seen someone like that?!
You're always telling lies, Big Annie!
You were my little Miss Spitfire. You came to us as a half-blind orphan who couldn't read or spell the simplest words. Now look at you!
Only a few short years later - a valedictorian, possibly the brightest, most ambitious -
Please, Mr. Anagnos, I don't need the flattery....
I'm taking the Kellers' offer because I have no other prospects and I need the paycheck.
You would be wise to allow a little sentiment into that heart of yours, Miss Spitfire.
I may have forgotten to pack it.
And my spelling has hardly improved in the last seven years.
Well, nevertheless, I expect you to write me of your progress as often as your delicate eye condition will allow.
I w-

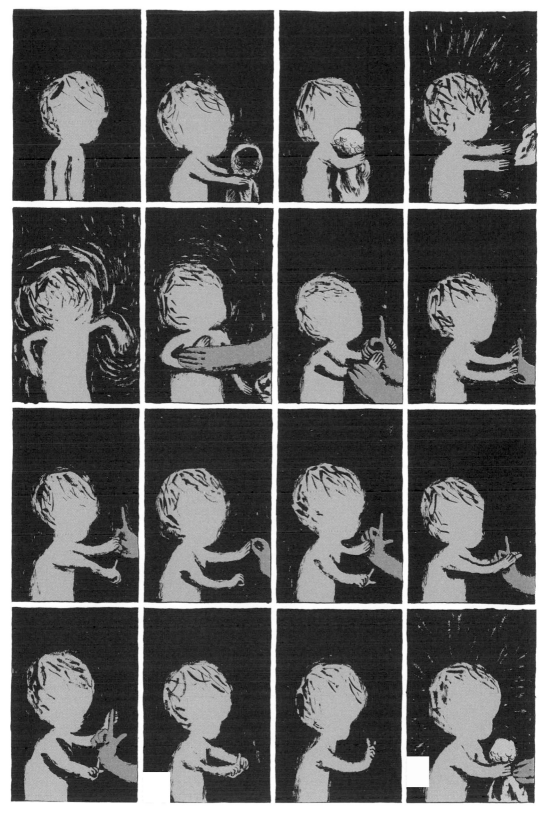

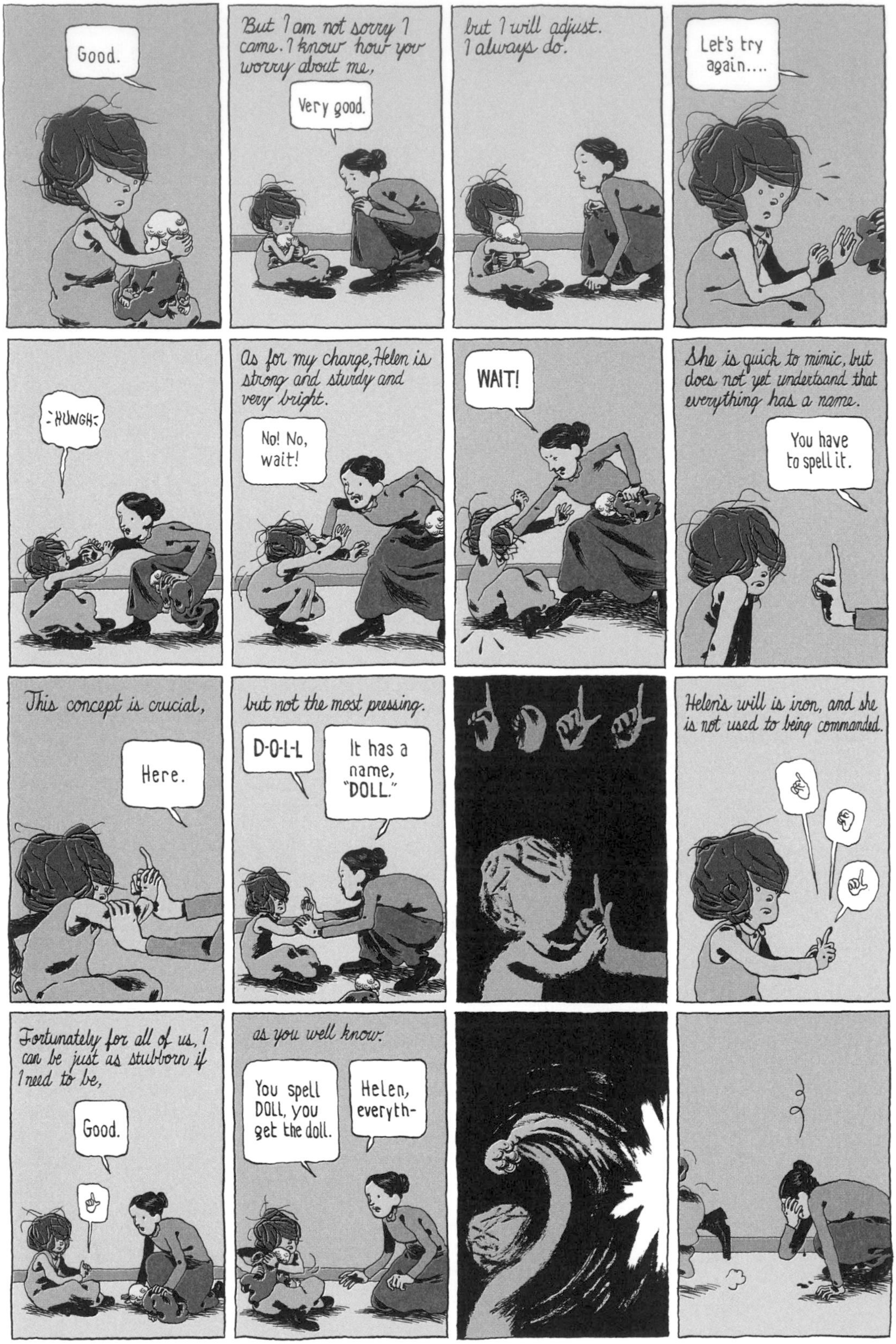
Good.
But I am not sorry I came. I know how you worry about me,
Very good.
but I will adjust. I always do.
Let's try again....
HUNGH
As for my charge, Helen is strong and sturdy and very bright.
No! No, wait!
WAIT!
She is quick to mimic, but does not yet undertsand that everything has a name.
You have to spell it.
This concept is crucial,
Here.
but not the most pressing.
D-O-L-L
It has a name, "DOLL."
Helen's will is iron, and she is not used to being commanded.
Fortunately for all of us, I can be just as stubborn if I need to be,
Good.
as you well know.
You spell DOLL, you get the doll.
Helen, everyth-

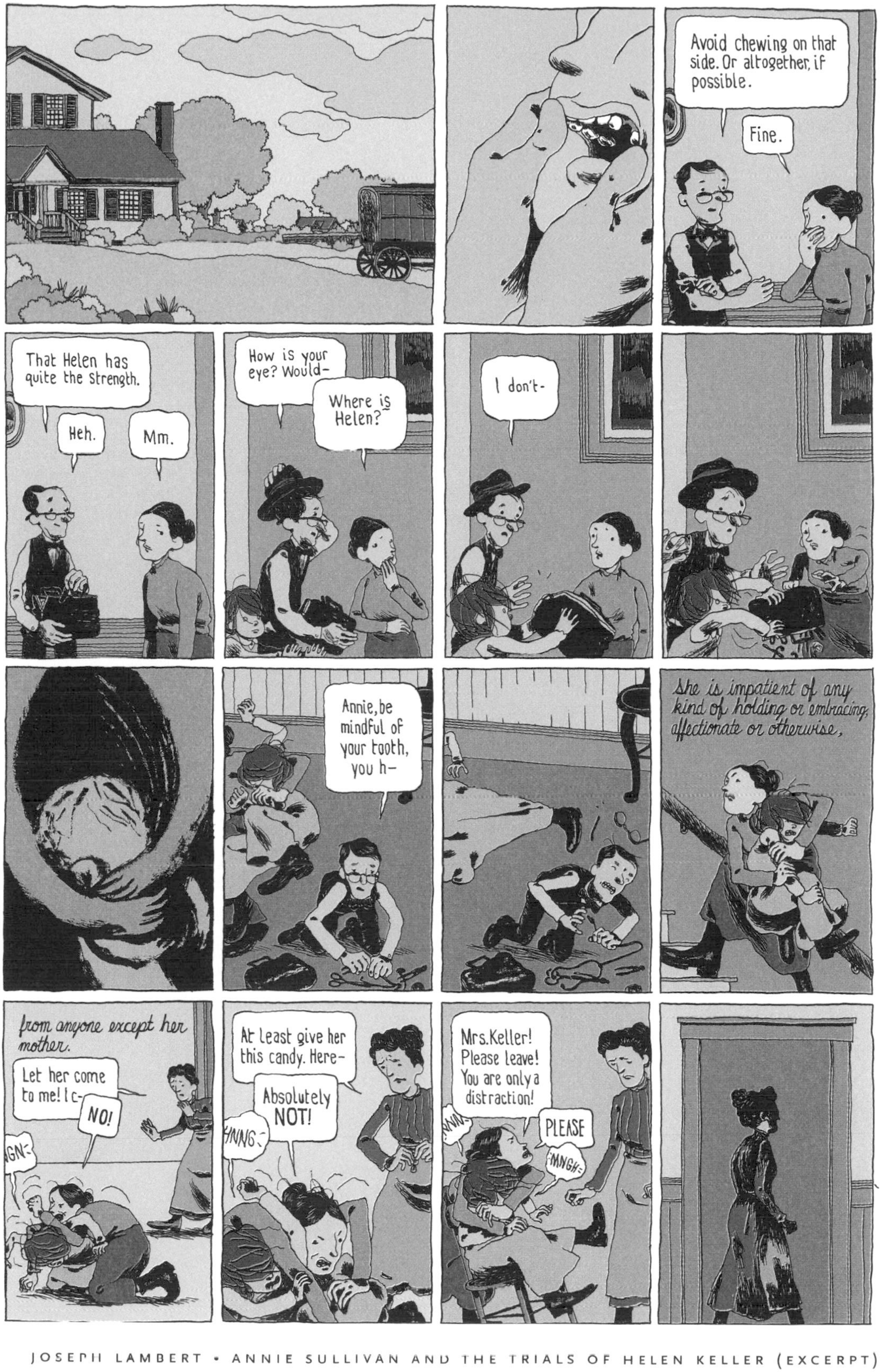
Avoid chewing on that side. Or altogether, if possible.
Fine.
That Helen has quite the strength.
Heh.
Mm.
How is your eye? Would-
Where is Helen?
I don't-
Annie, be mindful of your tooth, you h-
She is impatient of any kind of holding or embracing, affectionate or otherwise,
from anyone except her mother.
Let her come to me! I c-
NO!
GN-
At least give her this candy. Here-
Absolutely NOT!
HNNG-
Mrs. Keller! Please leave! You are only a distraction!
PLEASE
MNGH-

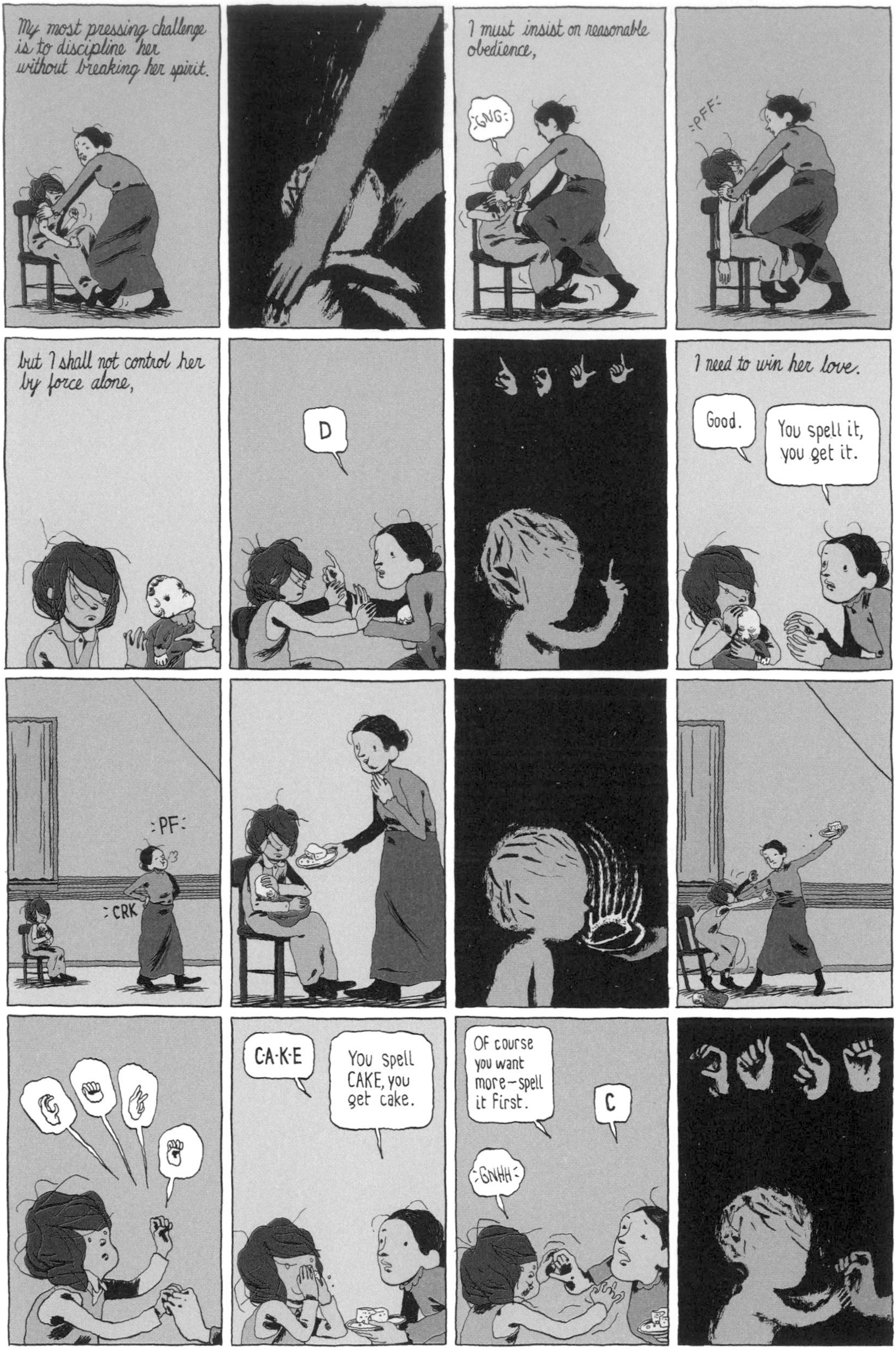
My most pressing challenge is to discipline her without breaking her spirit.
I must insist on reasonable obedience,
GNG
PFF
but I shall not control her by force alone,
D
I need to win her love.
Good.
You spell it, you get it.
PF
CRK
C·A·K·E
You spell CAKE, you get cake.
Of course you want more—spell it first.
C
GNHH

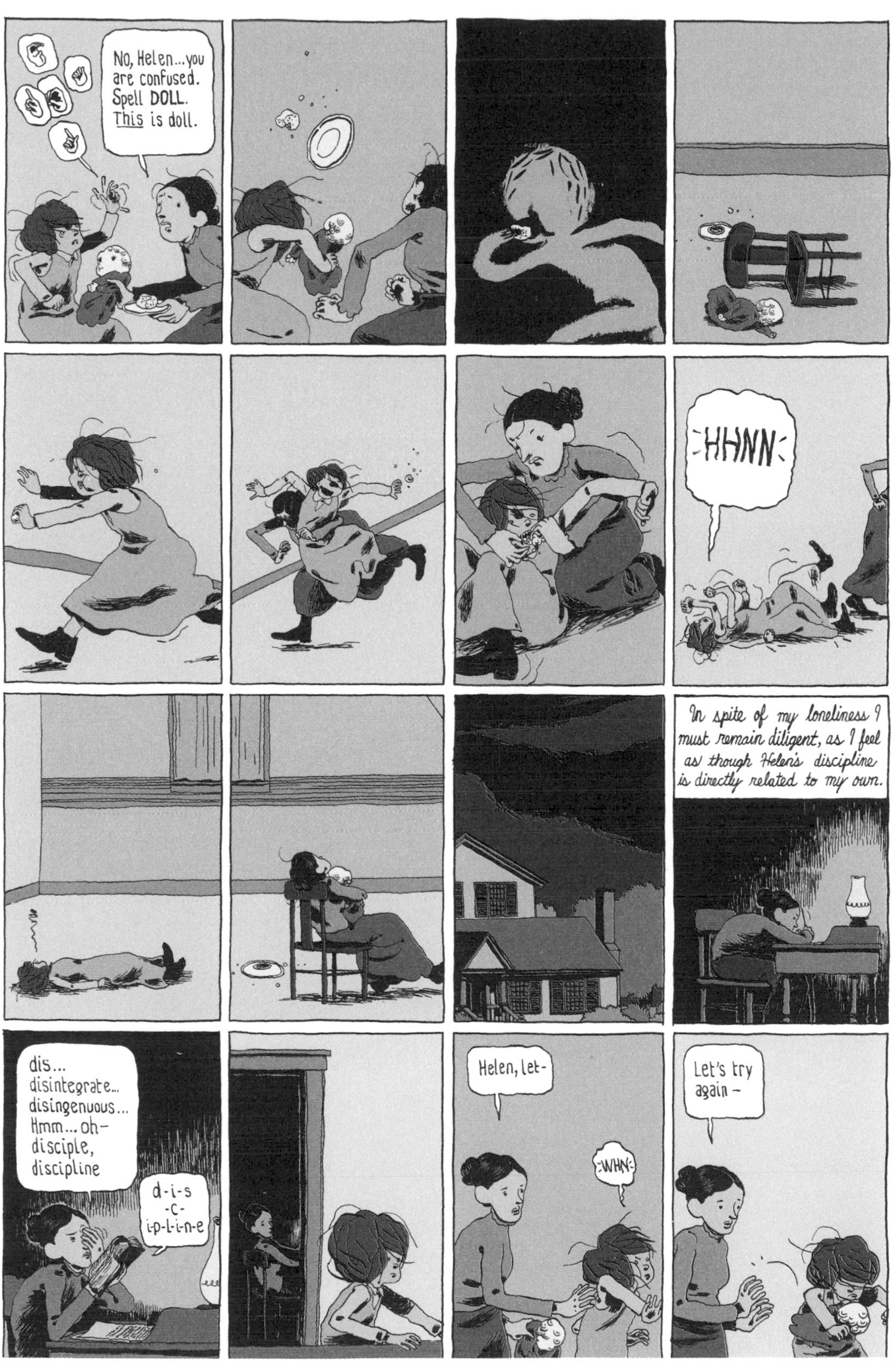
No, Helen... you are confused. Spell DOLL. This is doll.
HHNN
In spite of my loneliness I must remain diligent, as I feel as though Helen's discipline is directly related to my own.
dis... disintegrate... disingenuous... Hmm... oh- disciple, discipline
d-i-s -c- i-p-l-i-n-e
Helen, let-
WHN
Let's try again -

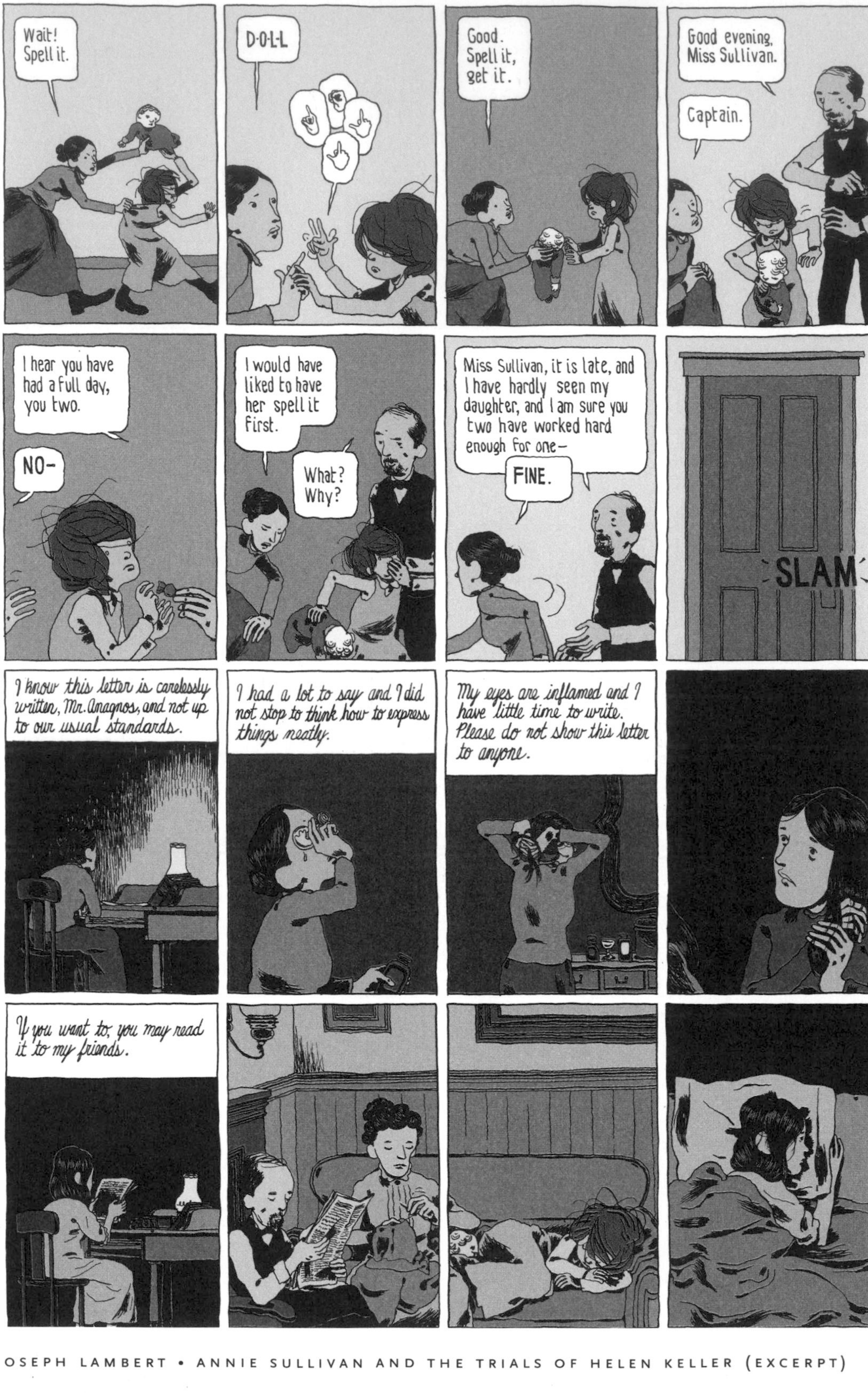
Wait! Spell it.
D-O-L-L
Good. Spell it, get it.
Good evening, Miss Sullivan.
Captain.
I hear you have had a full day, you two.
NO-
I would have liked to have her spell it first.
What? Why?
Miss Sullivan, it is late, and I have hardly seen my daughter, and I am sure you two have worked hard enough for one-
FINE.
SLAM
I know this letter is carelessly written, Mr. Anagnos, and not up to our usual standards.
I had a lot to say and I did not stop to think how to express things neatly.
My eyes are inflamed and I have little time to write. Please do not show this letter to anyone.
If you want to, you may read it to my friends.

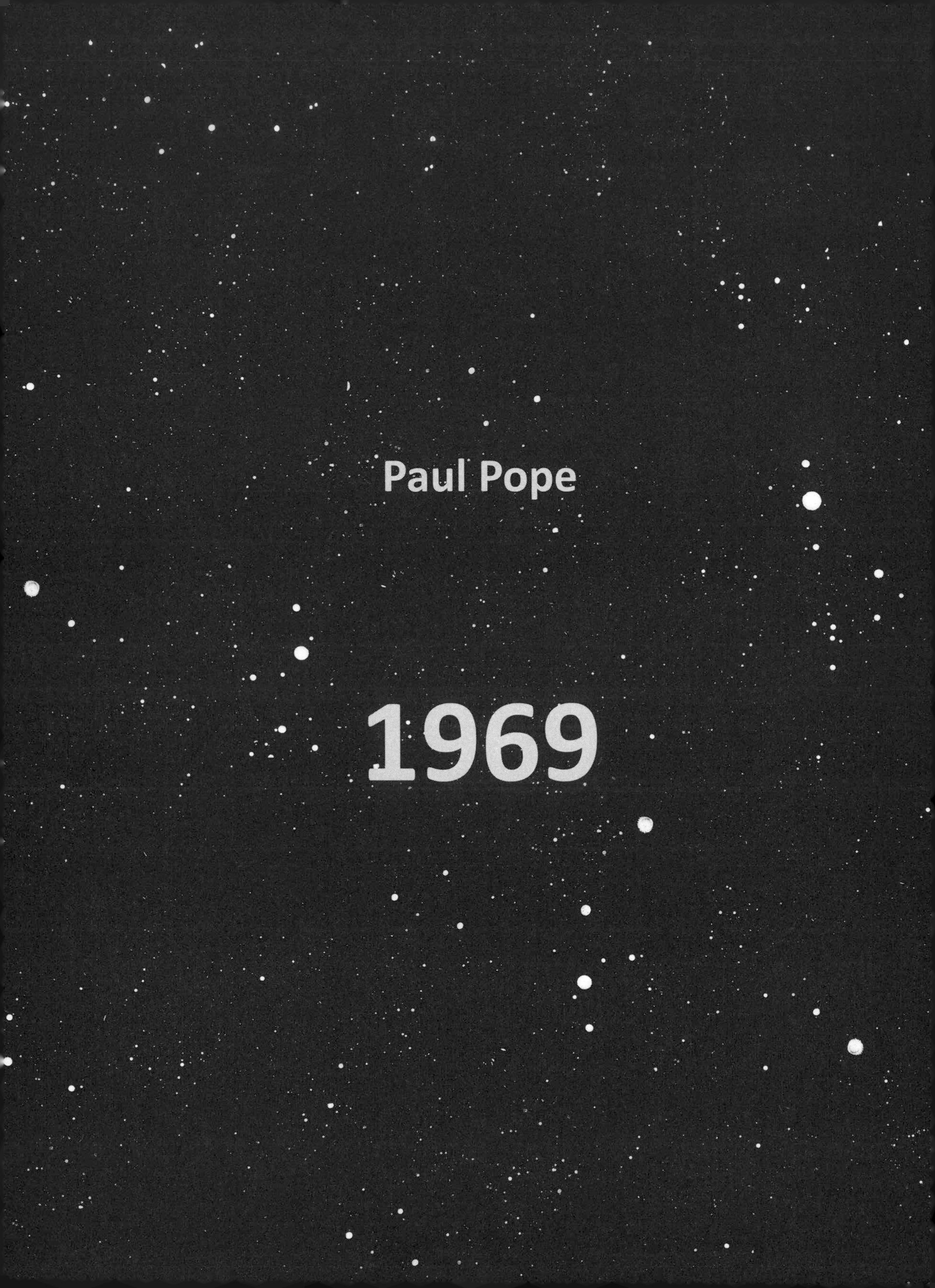
Paul Pope
1969

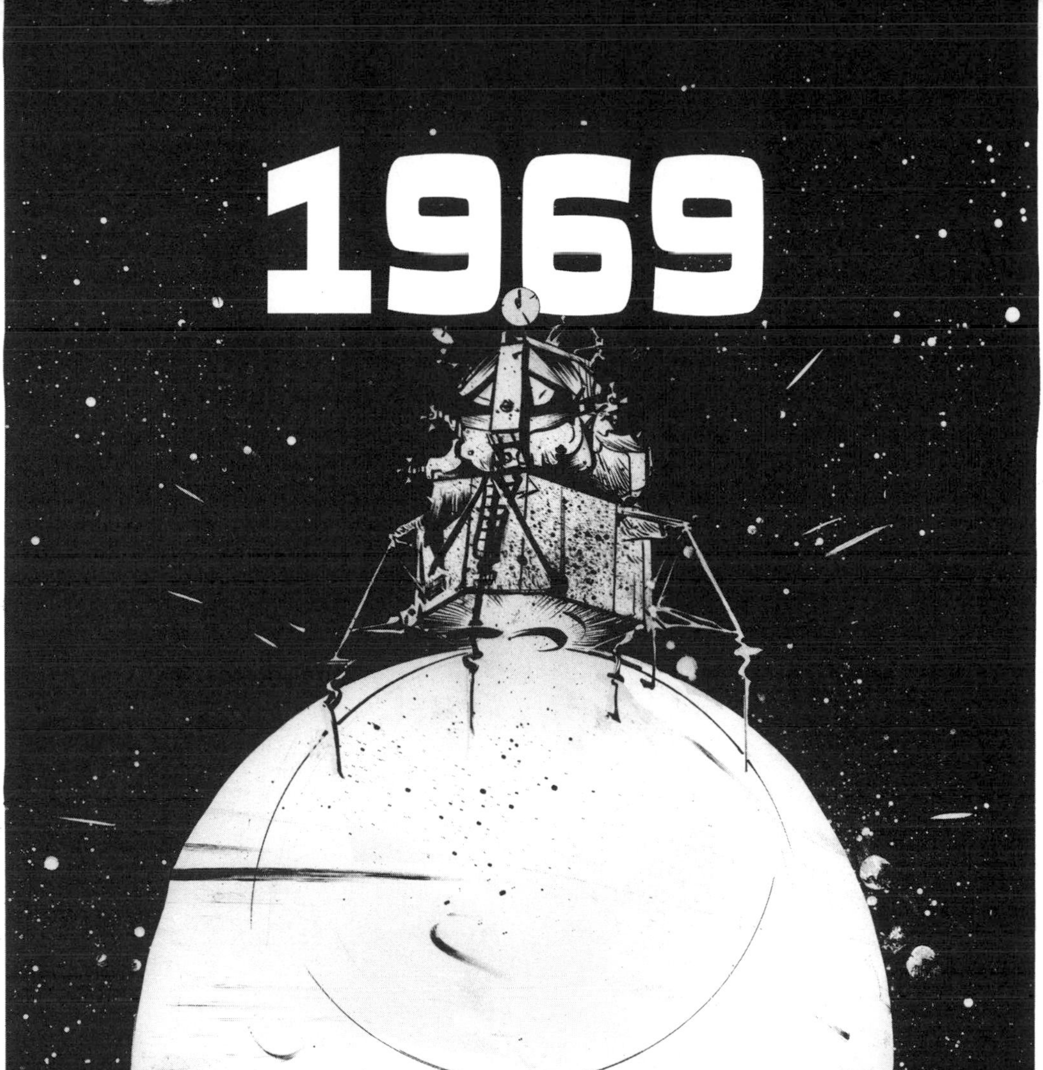
1969

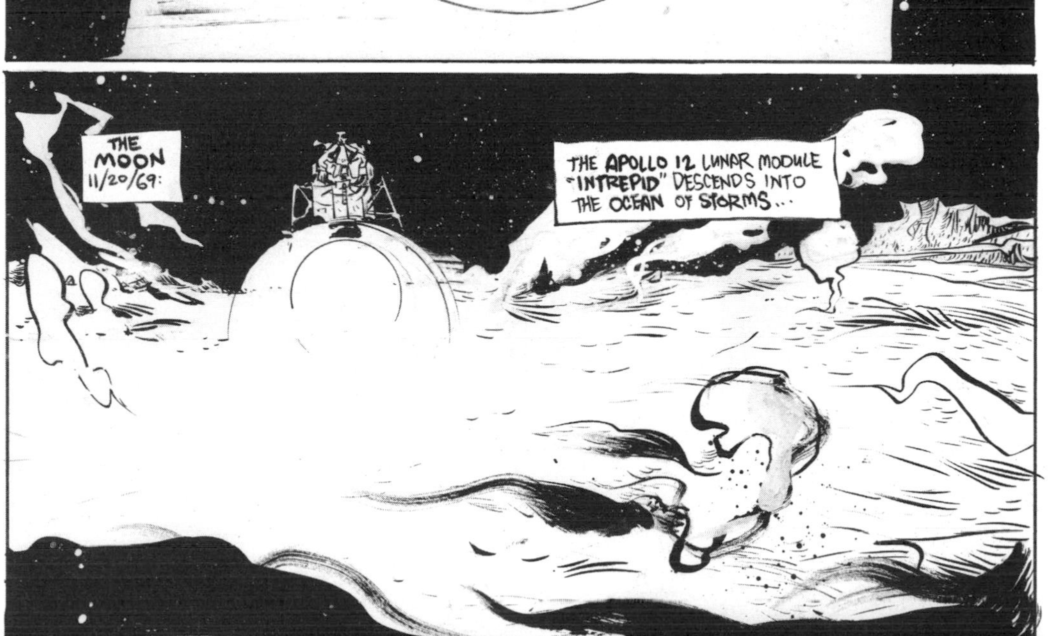
THE MOON 11/20/69:
THE APOLLO 12 LUNAR MODULE "INTREPID" DESCENDS INTO THE OCEAN OF STORMS...

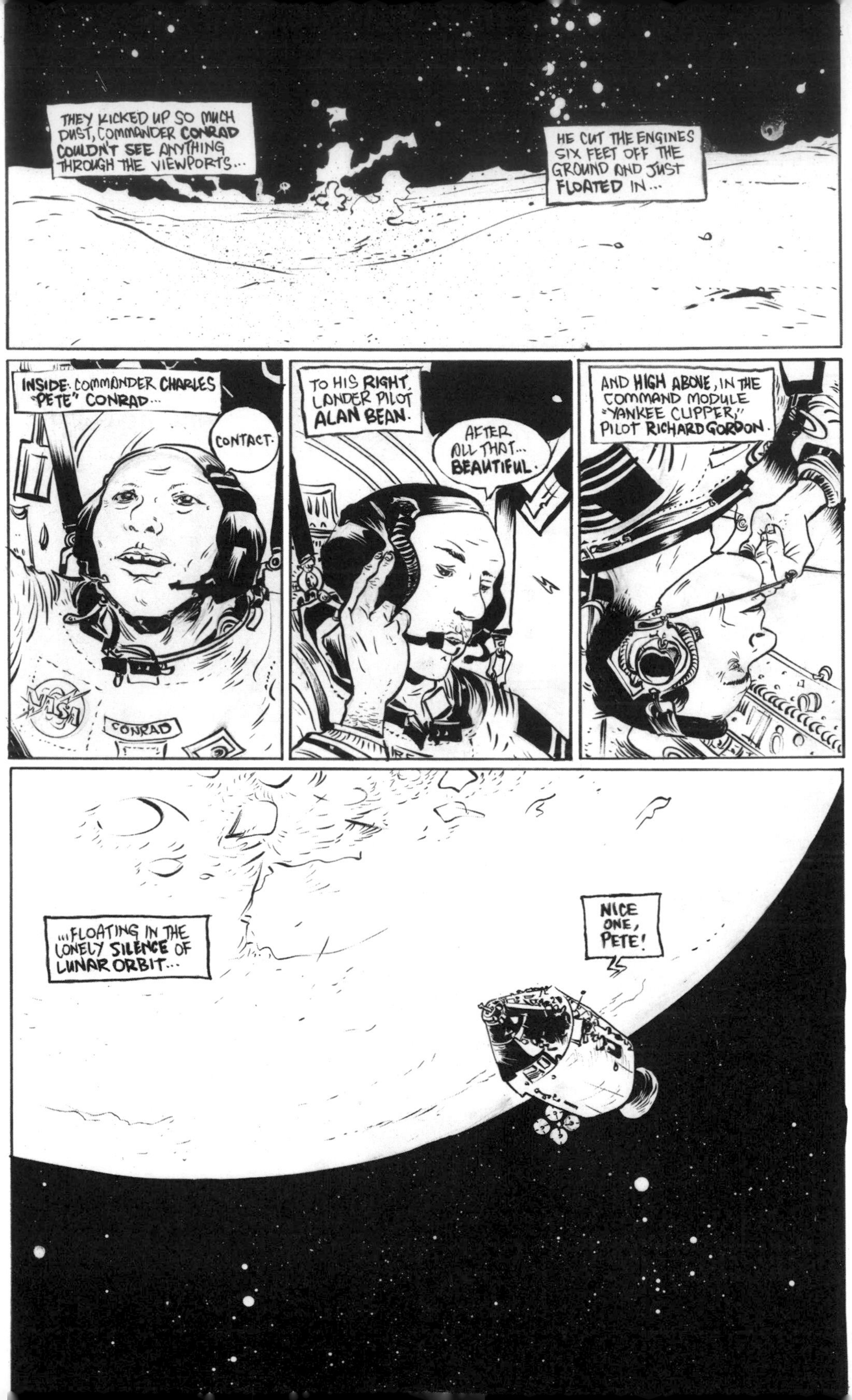
THEY KICKED UP SO MUCH DUST, COMMANDER CONRAD COULDN'T SEE ANYTHING THROUGH THE VIEWPORTS...
HE CUT THE ENGINES SIX FEET OFF THE GROUND AND JUST FLOATED IN...
INSIDE: COMMANDER CHARLES "PETE" CONRAD...
CONTACT.
NASA
CONRAD
TO HIS RIGHT, LANDER PILOT ALAN BEAN.
AFTER ALL THAT... BEAUTIFUL.
AND HIGH ABOVE, IN THE COMMAND MODULE "YANKEE CLIPPER," PILOT RICHARD GORDON.
...FLOATING IN THE LONELY SILENCE OF LUNAR ORBIT...
NICE ONE, PETE!

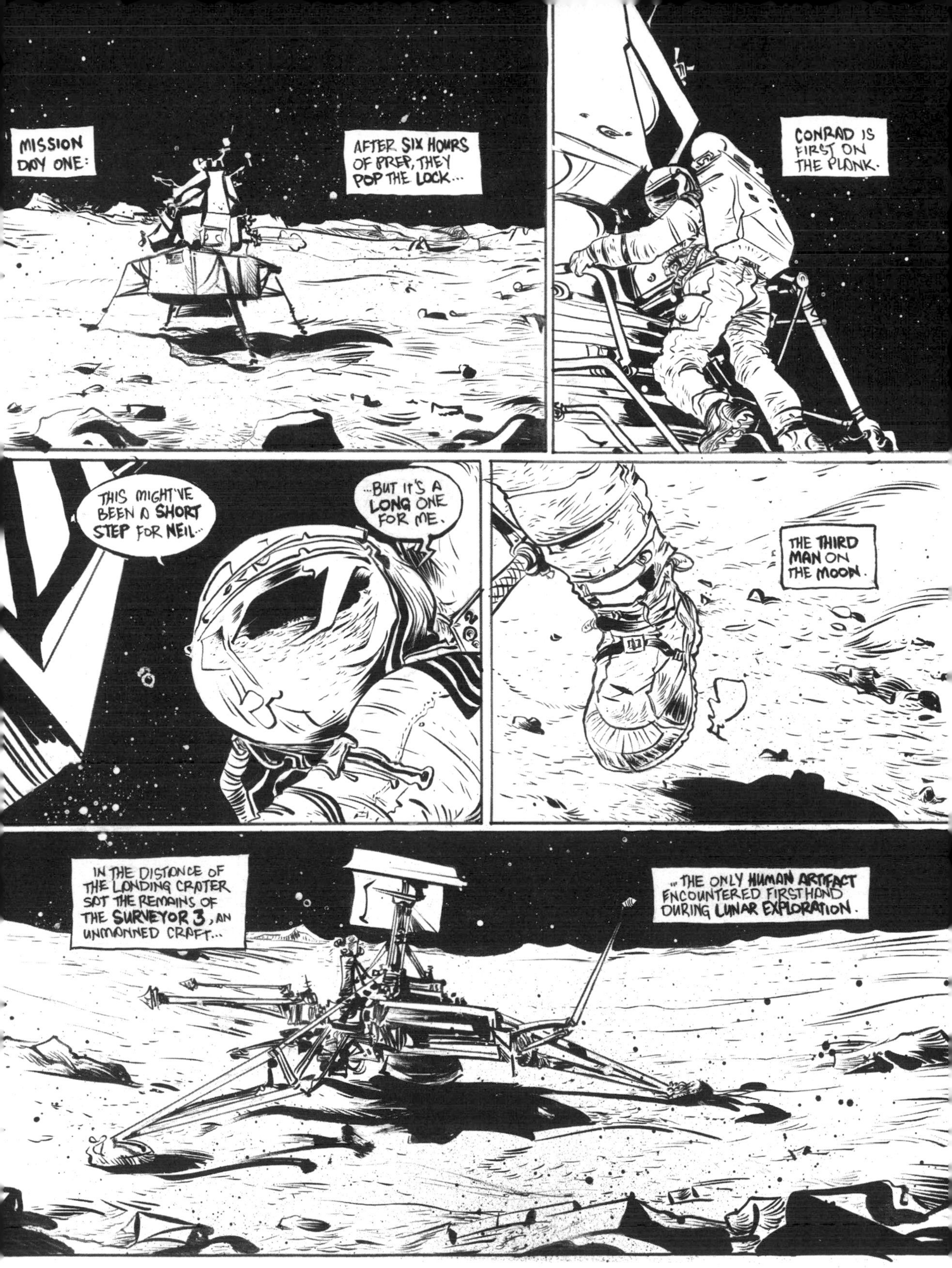
MISSION DAY ONE:
AFTER SIX HOURS OF PREP, THEY POP THE LOCK...
CONRAD IS FIRST ON THE PLANK.
THIS MIGHT'VE BEEN A SHORT STEP FOR NEIL...
...BUT IT'S A LONG ONE FOR ME.
THE THIRD MAN ON THE MOON.
IN THE DISTANCE OF THE LANDING CRATER SAT THE REMAINS OF THE SURVEYOR 3, AN UNMANNED CRAFT...
...THE ONLY HUMAN ARTIFACT ENCOUNTERED FIRSTHAND DURING LUNAR EXPLORATION.

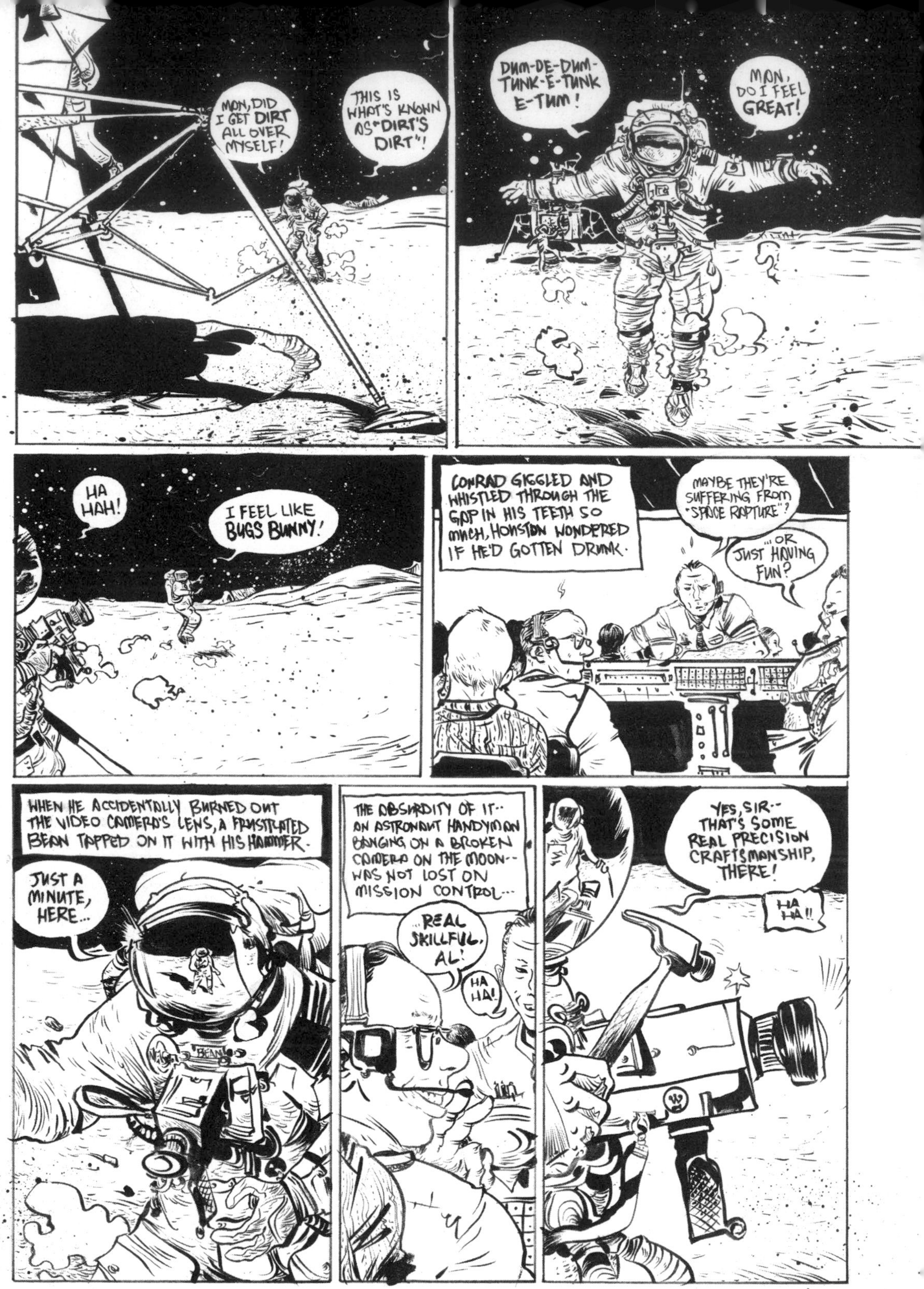
MAN, DID I GET DIRT ALL OVER MYSELF!
THIS IS WHAT'S KNOWN AS "DIRT'S DIRT"!
DUM-DE-DUM-TUNK-E-TUNK E-TUM!
MAN, DO I FEEL GREAT!
HA HAH!
I FEEL LIKE BUGS BUNNY!
CONRAD GIGGLED AND WHISTLED THROUGH THE GAP IN HIS TEETH SO MUCH, HOUSTON WONDERED IF HE'D GOTTEN DRUNK.
MAYBE THEY'RE SUFFERING FROM "SPACE RAPTURE"?
"...OR JUST HAVING FUN?
WHEN HE ACCIDENTALLY BURNED OUT THE VIDEO CAMERA'S LENS, A FRUSTRATED BEAN TAPPED ON IT WITH HIS HAMMER.
JUST A MINUTE, HERE...
BEAN
THE ABSURDITY OF IT-- AN ASTRONAUT HANDYMAN BANGING ON A BROKEN CAMERA ON THE MOON-- WAS NOT LOST ON MISSION CONTROL...
...REAL SKILLFUL, AL!
HA HA!
YES, SIR-- THAT'S SOME REAL PRECISION CRAFTSMANSHIP, THERE!
HA HA!!

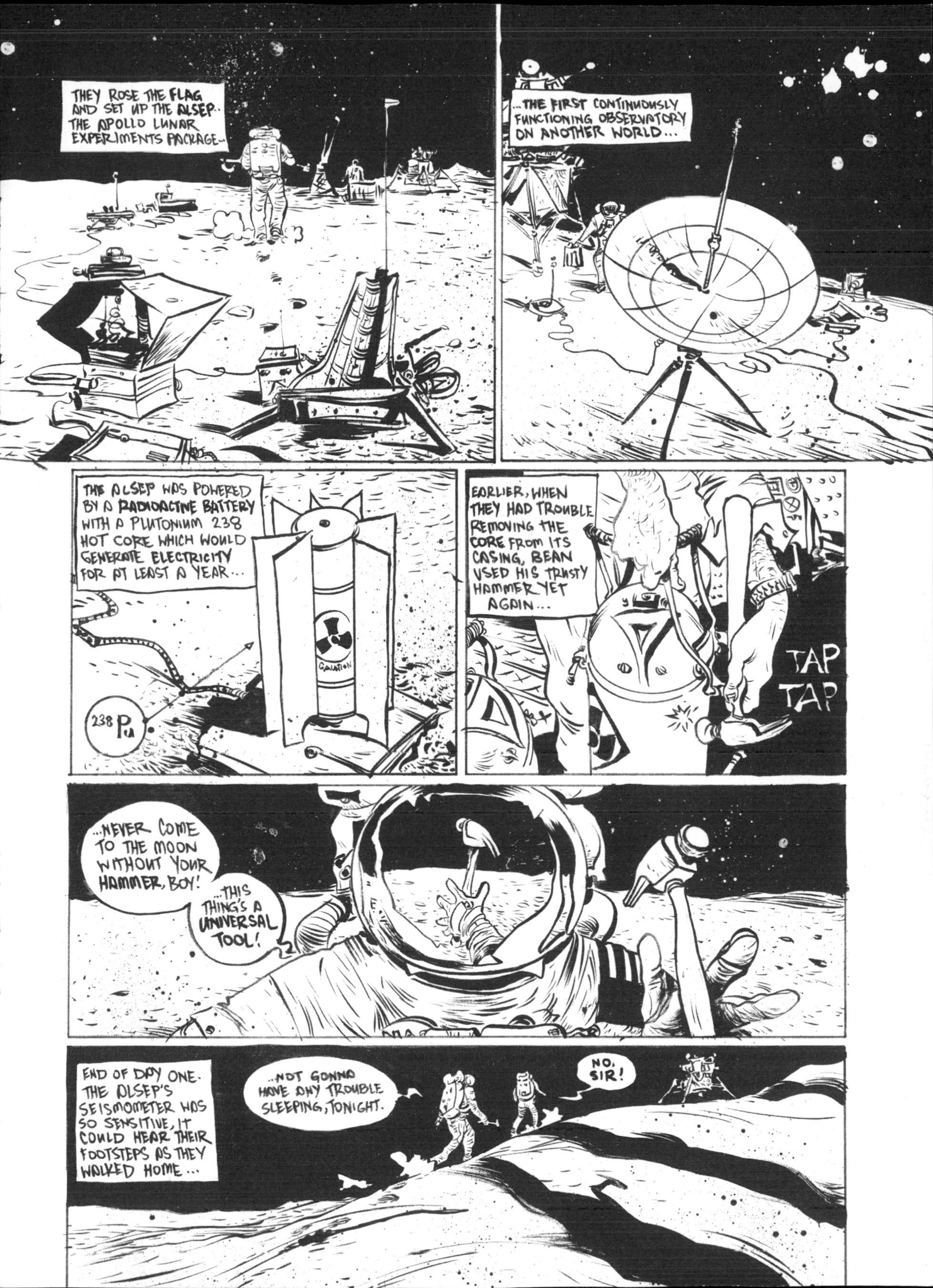
THEY ROSE THE FLAG AND SET UP THE ALSEP.. THE APOLLO LUNAR EXPERIMENTS PACKAGE...
...THE FIRST CONTINUOUSLY FUNCTIONING OBSERVATORY ON ANOTHER WORLD...
THE ALSEP WAS POWERED BY A RADIOACTIVE BATTERY WITH A PLUTONIUM 238 HOT CORE WHICH WOULD GENERATE ELECTRICITY FOR AT LEAST A YEAR...
CAUTION
238 Pu
EARLIER, WHEN THEY HAD TROUBLE REMOVING THE CORE FROM ITS CASING, BEAN USED HIS TRUSTY HAMMER YET AGAIN...
TAP TAP
...NEVER COME TO THE MOON WITHOUT YOUR HAMMER, BOY!
...THIS THING'S A UNIVERSAL TOOL!
END OF DAY ONE. THE ALSEP'S SEISMOMETER WAS SO SENSITIVE, IT COULD HEAR THEIR FOOTSTEPS AS THEY WALKED HOME...
...NOT GONNA HAVE ANY TROUBLE SLEEPING, TONIGHT.
NO, SIR!

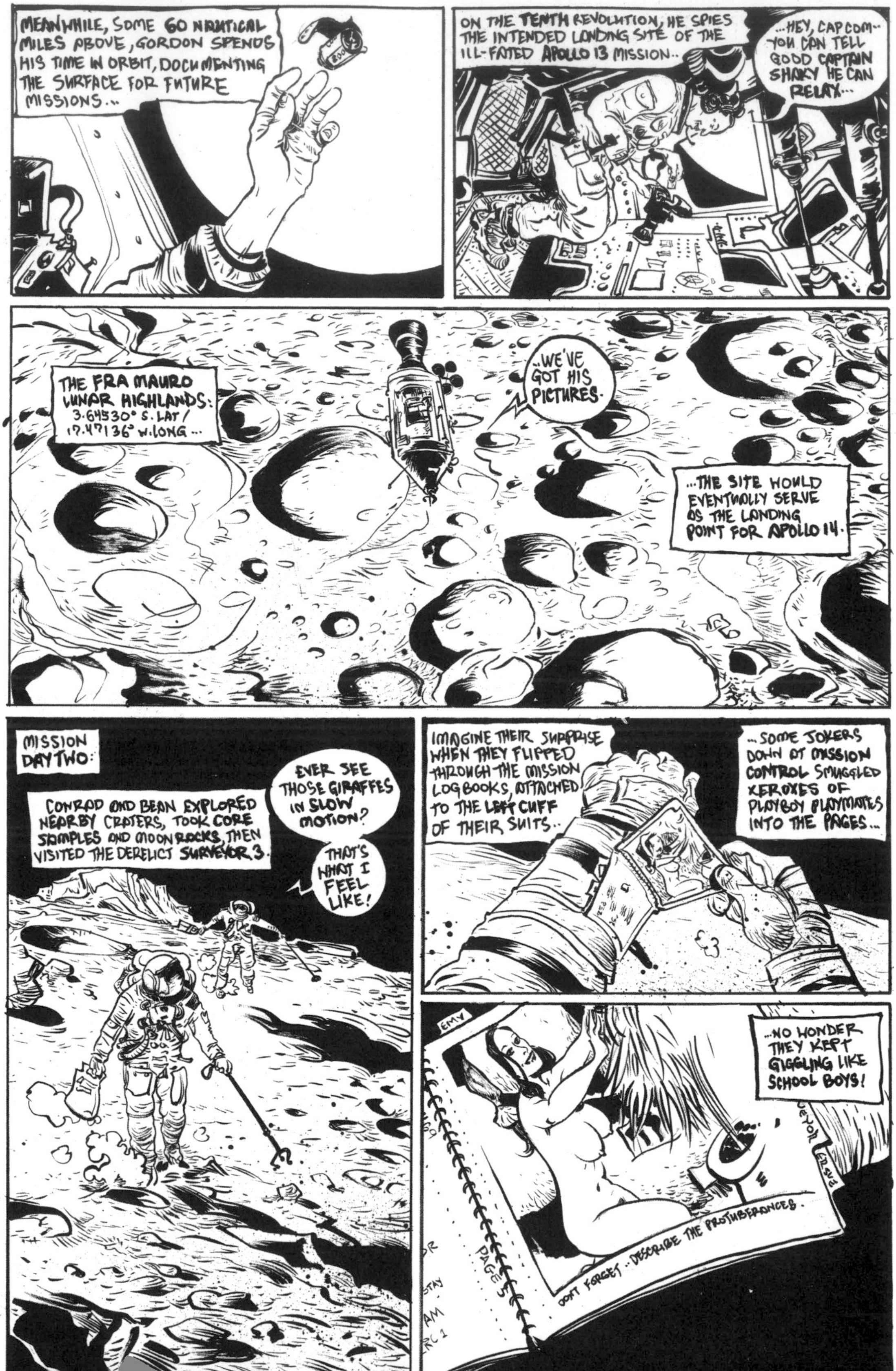
MEANWHILE, SOME 60 NAUTICAL MILES ABOVE, GORDON SPENDS HIS TIME IN ORBIT, DOCUMENTING THE SURFACE FOR FUTURE MISSIONS...
ON THE TENTH REVOLUTION, HE SPIES THE INTENDED LANDING SITE OF THE ILL-FATED APOLLO 13 MISSION...
...HEY, CAP COM-- YOU CAN TELL GOOD CAPTAIN SHAKY HE CAN RELAX...
THE FRA MAURO LUNAR HIGHLANDS: 3.64530° S. LAT / 17.47136° W. LONG...
...WE'VE GOT HIS PICTURES.
...THE SITE WOULD EVENTUALLY SERVE AS THE LANDING POINT FOR APOLLO 14.
MISSION DAY TWO:
CONRAD AND BEAN EXPLORED NEARBY CRATERS, TOOK CORE SAMPLES AND MOON ROCKS, THEN VISITED THE DERELICT SURVEYOR 3.
EVER SEE THOSE GIRAFFES IN SLOW MOTION?
THAT'S WHAT I FEEL LIKE!
IMAGINE THEIR SURPRISE WHEN THEY FLIPPED THROUGH THE MISSION LOG BOOKS, ATTACHED TO THE LEFT CUFF OF THEIR SUITS...
...SOME JOKERS DOWN AT MISSION CONTROL SMUGGLED XEROXES OF PLAYBOY PLAYMATES INTO THE PAGES...
EMY
PAGE 5
DON'T FORGET .. DESCRIBE THE PROTUBERANCES.
...NO WONDER THEY KEPT GIGGLING LIKE SCHOOL BOYS!

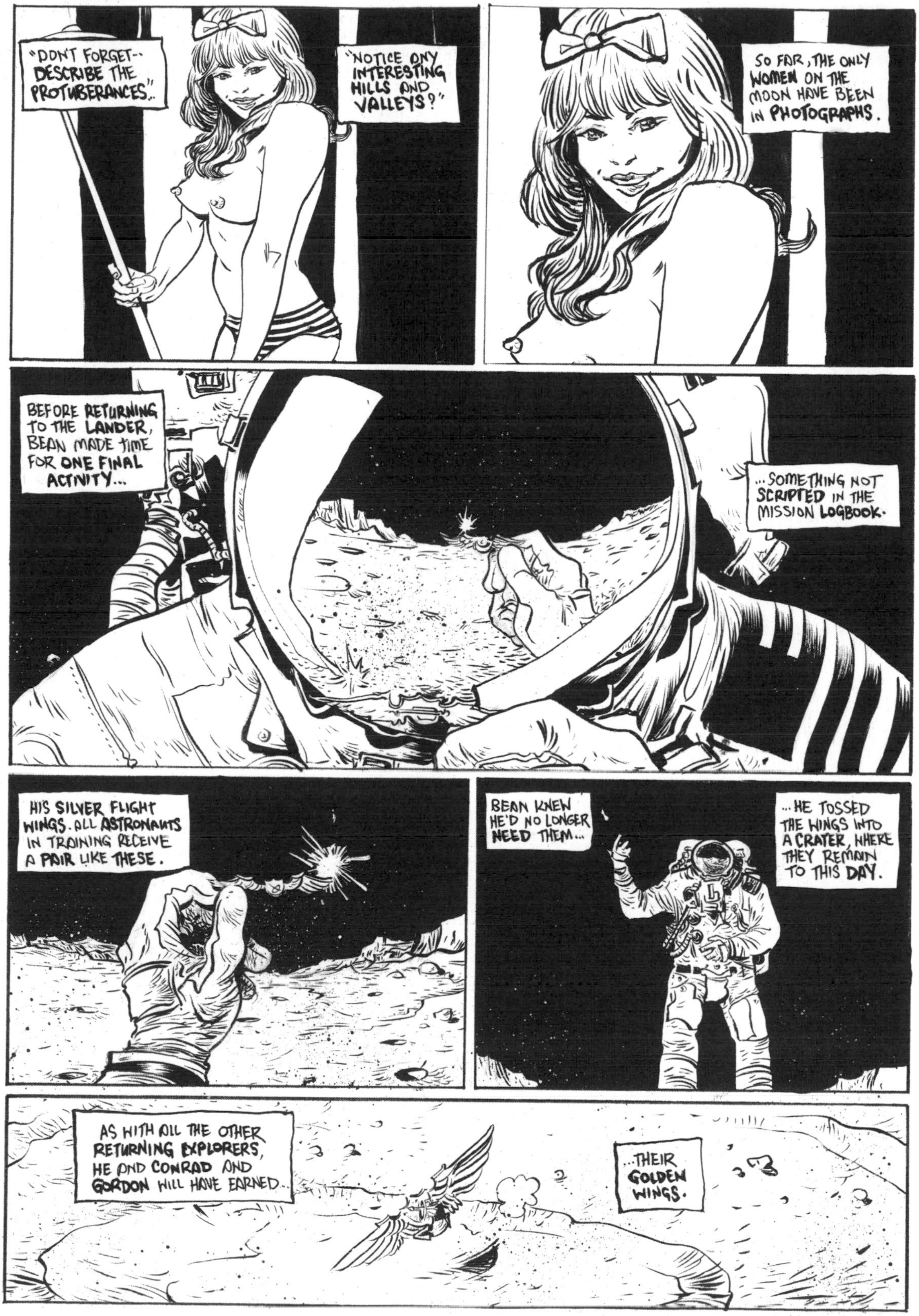
"DON'T FORGET--DESCRIBE THE PROTUBERANCES"..
"NOTICE ANY INTERESTING HILLS AND VALLEYS?"
SO FAR, THE ONLY WOMEN ON THE MOON HAVE BEEN IN PHOTOGRAPHS.
BEFORE RETURNING TO THE LANDER, BEAN MADE TIME FOR ONE FINAL ACTIVITY...
...SOMETHING NOT SCRIPTED IN THE MISSION LOGBOOK.
HIS SILVER FLIGHT WINGS. ALL ASTRONAUTS IN TRAINING RECEIVE A PAIR LIKE THESE.
BEAN KNEW HE'D NO LONGER NEED THEM...
...HE TOSSED THE WINGS INTO A CRATER, WHERE THEY REMAIN TO THIS DAY.
AS WITH ALL THE OTHER RETURNING EXPLORERS, HE AND CONRAD AND GORDON WILL HAVE EARNED...
...THEIR GOLDEN WINGS.

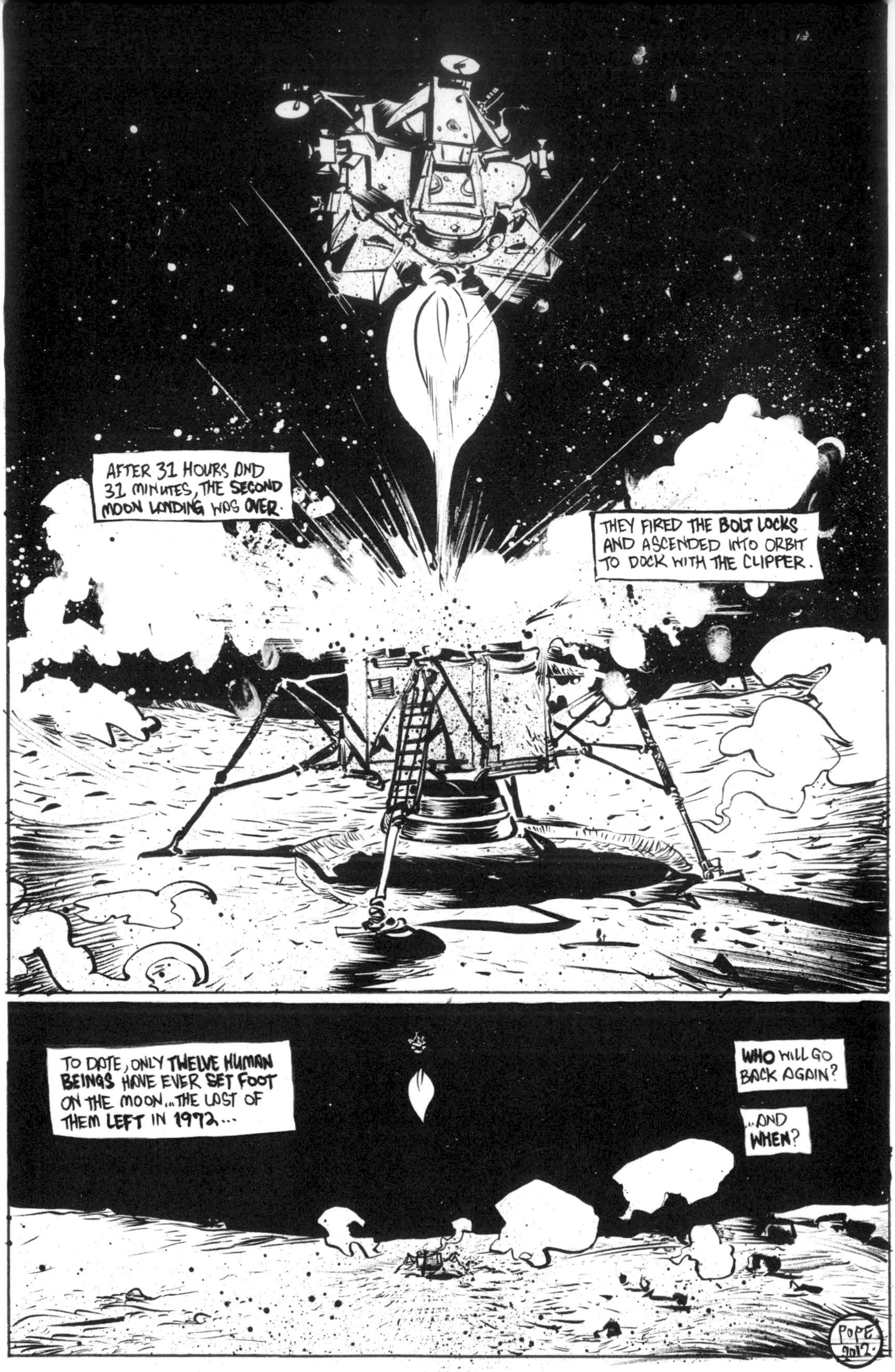
AFTER 31 HOURS AND 31 MINUTES, THE SECOND MOON LANDING WAS OVER.
THEY FIRED THE BOLT LOCKS AND ASCENDED INTO ORBIT TO DOCK WITH THE CLIPPER.
TO DATE, ONLY TWELVE HUMAN BEINGS HAVE EVER SET FOOT ON THE MOON... THE LAST OF THEM LEFT IN 1972...
WHO WILL GO BACK AGAIN?
...AND WHEN?
POPE 2012

Contributors' Notes

Jorge Aguirre writes for kids' TV, books, and digital media. Originally from Columbus, Ohio, he's based in New Jersey.

Born in Puerto Rico and based in Columbus, Ohio, **Rafael Rosado** is a veteran of the animation industry. He is currently a freelance storyboard artist.

▪ RAFAEL: I kept going back to a sketch of three kids I'd drawn and a tale of a giant. And Jorge and I have been friends for a long time . . .

JORGE: I've known Rafael since we were at Ohio State University. I took Raf's idea and fleshed out the world, the characters, and story.

RAFAEL: I think it's safe to say that making *Giants Beware* is the most fun either of us has ever had creatively.

JORGE: Definitely, and hopefully the joy we had making the book comes through when you read it.

Sam Alden was born in 1988 in Portland, Oregon. In 2010 he studied at the Atlantic Center for the Arts's comics residency program under Craig Thompson, and he graduated from Whitman College two years later with a BA in printmaking. Sam lived in Alaska for two months as a resident artist with the 2012 Sitka Fellows Program and was an official guest at the 2013 BilBOlbul International Comics Festival in Bologna, Italy. He has a day job at a company that manufactures vast industrial shredders for metal recycling plants and spends his workday trawling Craigslist for broken appliances to purchase with company money and shred. Sam's currently drawing a comic book novel about middle school, available online at www.eighthgra.de.

▪ Most of the stylistic choices in *Haunter,* like the simple line and the watercolor washes, stemmed from wanting to draw a story very quickly. The plot was based on recurring nightmares about beautiful environments that slowly take on an atmosphere of inexplicable dread. *Haunter* was originally published on studygroupcomics.com.

Comix creator **Derf Backderf** was born and raised in the small town of Richfield, Ohio. After a brief stint at art school, he dropped out and worked on the back of a garbage truck, an experience that was the basis for his first graphic novel, *Trashed* (SLG Publishing, 2002). Backderf's second graphic novel, *Punk Rock & Trailer Parks* (SLG Publishing, 2009), was hailed by *Booklist* as "one of the standout graphic novels of the year." It was picked for inclusion in *The Best American Comics 2010.* A sampling from his freeform weekly comic strip, *The City,* was selected for *The Best American Comics 2008.* Backderf has been nominated for two Eisner Awards and an Ignatz Award and has received a host of honors for his newspaper comics, including the prestigious Robert F. Kennedy Journalism Award for political cartooning in 2006. The Derf Collection, comprising twenty-five years of Backderf's original art and papers, was established at Ohio State

University's Billy Ireland Cartoon Museum in 2009. He lives in bucolic Cleveland, for reasons he can't remember, with his wife, Sheryl, and their two children.

• *My Friend Dahmer* (Abrams Comicarts, 2012) is a project that took twenty years to complete. It began as sketchbook notes and drawings that I started in the unsettling and frantic days after Jeffrey Dahmer's shocking crimes first came to light in the summer of 1991. It grew steadily in sketchbook form until Dahmer was killed in prison in November 1994. After his death I tentatively began putting pen to paper, and from 1995 to 1997 I produced six short stories. The first of these, "Young Jeffrey Dahmer," was printed in the Fantagraphics anthology titled *Zero Zero*. Bolstered by the positive reaction to this story, I then wrote a hundred-page graphic novel in 1998, and I spent the next four years pitching it to every publisher in the comics business in vain. Finally, in 2002, I self-published a twenty-four-page sampler of the project, *My Friend Dahmer*, in hope of interesting a publisher in the larger work I envisioned. That didn't happen, but that little self-published tome became an instant cult classic. It was nominated for an Eisner Award and immortalized by author Chuck Klosterman in his bestseller *Sex, Lies & Cocoa Puffs*, which only affirmed in my mind that this was a story worth telling and that if I got it in front of the right people, it would be something special. But by then, some of the stories were seven years old and I had grown considerably as a storyteller and artist. So, when I decided to make one last push to see *My Friend Dahmer* realized, I scrapped everything and started over from scratch. I increased the scope of the project immensely, going beyond mere memoir to create both a piece of investigative journalism and a book that deals with larger issues of friendship, teenage isolation, dysfunction, and adult indifference. I combed through police and FBI files and interviewed dozens of friends, former classmates, teachers, and townspeople over several years to craft a definitive, meticulously researched portrait of my time with my strange friend. What finally emerged is the 224-page graphic novel that is excerpted here.

Kate Beaton is a cartoonist whose book *Hark! A Vagrant* was named one of *Time*'s best fiction books of 2011. Her comics often have to do with poking fun at history, and on a good day she gets to draw epaulettes.

• There's something truly irresistible about the pearl-clutching cartoons that came out during the time people thought women on bicycles were single-handedly going to bring society to ruin. You kind of wish the brassy, hardcore cyclists depicted in the drawings were real people, biking around and taking no guff from nobody.

Alison Bechdel got her start in comics in 1983 with her strip *Dykes to Watch Out For*, which she self-syndicated for many years in an ever-shifting number of ephemeral, subversive, and of-ten indecent short-run newsprint publications. In 2006 her graphic memoir *Fun Home: A Family Tragicomic* was received to surprising acclaim, which encouraged her to abandon her comic strip and plunge headlong into an autobiographical abyss, out of which she emerged in 2012 with another memoir, *Are You My Mother? A Comic Drama*. During that time she also somehow managed to guest edit *The Best American Comics 2011* and receive a Guggenheim fellowship. She lives in Vermont.

• I'm very grateful that Jeff included this excerpt from *Are You My Mother?* in *The Best Amercan Comics 2013*. I'm actually astonished that he was able to find a passage of the book that could stand fairly well on its own. *Are You My Mother?* is a very odd book that I haven't quite wrapped my mind around even a year after finishing it. What I like about writing memoir is the challenge of finding a story in the big, chaotic, ever-growing pile of material that is my life—including metalife things like dreams and therapy sessions. I also like to drag other stuff onto the pile, like—in the case of this excerpt—Donald Winnicott's psychoanalytic theories about babies and mothers, *A Little Night Music*, Freud, and Middle English love poetry. Plus a ton of other crap that got edited out. I allow myself to believe, even though I know it's not true, that there's a narrative embedded in all of this and my job is to remove everything that's not a part of it. Another challenge I like is taking a form that excels in portraying physical action and trying to get it to convey more internal and subjective kinds of experience. I'm not sure how well this book succeeds at that, but I feel very motivated to keep trying.

Gabrielle Bell's work has been selected for several previous volumes of Houghton Mifflin Harcourt's *The Best American Comics* and has been featured in the *Yale Anthology of Graphic Fiction*, *McSweeney's*, *The Believer*, and *Vice*. "Cecil and Jordan in New York," the title story of her previous book, was adapted for the screen in the film anthology *Tokyo!* by her and director Michel Gondry. Her newest book, *The Voyeurs*, was released by Uncivilized Books in September 2012. She lives in Brooklyn.

• "Cody" was based on a snippet of a dream I had, in which I was an unwitting accomplice in some sort of murder. I built the story slowly around it, adding details. I'm often asked how much of this story is autobiographical, but it's probably the least autobiographical story I've done.

Leela Corman is an illustrator, cartoonist, native New Yorker, and performer and instructor of Middle Eastern dance. *Unterzakhn* was informed by all of these things. She currently lives in Gainesville, Florida, where she teaches Egyptian dance, as well as drawing. Leela and her husband, Tom Hart, are the founders of the Sequential Artists Workshop, a nonprofit organization dedicated to the prosperity and promotion of comic art and artists and offering instruction in comic art, graphic novels, and visual storytelling. She is also an adjunct instructor at the University of Florida. Find her at www.leelacorman.com.

• *Unterzakhn* was my education in creating a long story. As such, it nearly killed me, though I'm grateful for the lessons I learned. My process begins with obsession, which leads to research; sometimes a single image appears and becomes the beginning of the next project. This was the case with *Unterzakhn*, which began when young Fanya appeared on a napkin I was doodling on, with a pillow shoved under her dress, looking in the mirror and saying "Yuck!" Knowing immediately that she lived on the LES, I then spent years researching the history of that neighborhood and of reproductive rights in America and so much more. All of my work is based in history and research; I love a really good, gritty human story set in a time we've mythologized and made sepia-toned and romantic. Puncture that romance!

Eleanor Davis lives and works.

• Arizona, where I grew up, is less desiccated and bleak than Nita's childhood home in the Valley, but not by much. Georgia, where I live now, is less absurdly bucolic than SATORiSPACE, but not by much. We have a good house and good friends, we pick wild blackberries, we bike through green fields and cool woods and over streams and rivers that have water flowing in them. We've planted a little fig tree.

My family is still in Tucson, 1,700 miles away. And Tucson still has better tacos.

When I wrote *Nita Goes Home*, I wanted to make a comic that was both serious and really funny, but it turns out no one thinks it's funny at all. I'm okay with that. It still makes me chuckle.

Michael DeForge was born in 1987 and works as a cartoonist in Toronto. His series *Lose* is published annually by Koyama Press, and his web strip, *Ant Comic*, will be collected by *Drawn and Quarterly* in 2014.

▪ The manananggal is a mythological creature from the Philippines that is able to detach its upper body from its lower half.

Colleen Doran is a cartoonist, illustrator, and conceptual artists with hundreds of credits, including *Amazing Spider-Man, Captain America, Wonder Woman,* and *Sandman.* Current works include an upcoming graphic novel by Neil Gaiman for Dark Horse, and the space opera series *A Distant Soil* for Image.

▪ *Gone to Amerikay* was a chance to fulfill two lifelong ambitions: to work on a project about the Irish-American experience and to pay homage to my greatest influence, Hal Foster, creator of *Prince Valiant.* Foster combined classic draughtsmanship with meticulous historical research. My drawing here is more fanciful than the real Gráinne Ní Mháille would have been, which is in keeping with the romantic retelling of her tale by Ciara. I omit panel borders to give a sense of fluid time and a musical feel to the images.

I started this book on an island off the coast of Morocco, and finished it on a ship off the coast of New Zealand.

Evan Dorkin is the creator of *Milk & Cheese, House of Fun,* and *Dork.* He is the cocreator of the Dark Horse Comics series *Beasts of Burden* with illustrator Jill Thompson. Cowriting with his wife, Sarah Dyer, his television credits include *Space Ghost: Coast-to-Coast, Batman Beyond,* and *Yo Gabba Gabba!.* He is a regular contributor to *MAD* magazine and usually writes funnier bios than this one.

▪ [On strips] I don't have anything much to say about these strips. You write and draw some gags and you hope some folks find them funny. That's pretty much it.

[On "Story Time"] "Story Time" was one of three Beasts of Burden stories Jill and I did showing some of the more mundane situations our animal characters deal with in the haunted town of Burden Hill. It's basically a campfire tale, only with a fable instead of a ghost story.

Sophie Goldstein is a 2013 graduate of the Center for Cartoon Studies. She was born and raised in Los Angeles and has lived in New York, Prague, South Korea, and Montreal. She currently resides in White River Junction, Vermont. For more of her work, please visit redinkradio .com.

▪ "The Good Wife" is an adaptation of the Aesop fable "The Man and the Wood." The original fable reads as follows:

> A Man came into a Wood one day with an axe in his hand, and begged all the Trees to give him a small branch which he wanted for a particular purpose. The Trees were good-natured and gave him one of their branches. What did the Man do but fix it into the axe head, and soon set to work cutting down tree after tree. Then the Trees saw how foolish they had been in giving their enemy the means of destroying themselves.

Brandon Graham was born in December 1976, the grandson of pin-up artist Bill Randall. He grew up in West Seattle around a lot of graffiti and comics. Some of his books are *King City, Escalator, Pillow Fight, Multiple Warheads,* and a sketchbook called *Walrus* that will be out in 2013. He lives in Vancouver, British Columbia, with his lady, Marian Churchland. He writes and sometimes draws the Image series *Prophet.*

• When I drew "The Speaker," I was thinking about how an artist's work can stay behind after they're gone or even become part of someone else's life in a way the artist may never know. So the parts of the dead man in the story are like his work going off without him.

At the time I did it, I thought of it as a half failure.

I had really high goals, but if anything, it's me trying to do things that are hard.

On the fifth page, I try to lead the reader's eye to the bottom of the page in the fifth panel and then back to the top. I'm still not entirely sure if it worked, but it's an attempt, and that's something.

Sammy Harkham draws the ongoing comic book series *Crickets* and edits the occasional anthology *Kramers Ergot*. A collection of short comics, *Everything Together*, was published in 2012 by PictureBox. Harkham lives in Los Angeles.

• Like most things, this strip came about from a desire to read something that moved clearly and declaratively, like large concrete blocks fitting smoothly into a solid interlocking puzzle. There is a simple pleasure in that, and one comics is killer at delivering.

Jennifer Hayden was born in New York City and shortly afterward began drawing on the wall beside her crib. As a child, she spent every summer reading Archies. She also wrote poetry, which later inspired her to write the great American novel—and fail. Recovering from breast cancer in 2004, she discovered graphic novels and never looked back. Her first book of comix, *Underwire*, was published in 2011 by Top Shelf. Her webcomic *S'crapbook* runs on Trip City, and she posts her daily diary comic *Rushes* on thegoddessrushes.blogspot.com. Jennifer is also finishing a graphic novel about her life and her breast cancer for Top Shelf. She lives in New Jersey with her husband, two teenagers, three cats, and two dogs.

• My daughter was in eighth grade when she guilt-tripped me into being a chaperone on her class trip to Quebec. As I caved, I thought, "Well, at least I'll get a comic out of it." I did this story for *Underwire* when it was still a monthly webcomic on Act-i-vate.com. At first I thought the comic would poke fun at religion, because I was raised a skeptic. But to my surprise, it ended up looking at how, in middle age, I've been cobbling together my own completely private faith.

Faith Erin Hicks started making comics for fun in 1999. In 2012 making comics is her job, something which she is astonished about regularly. Previous comics include *Demonology 101*, *Ice*, *Zombies Calling*, *The War at Ellsmere*, *Brain Camp* (with Susan Kim and Laurence Klavan), *Friends with Boys*, *Bigfoot Boy* (with J. Torres), *Nothing Can Possibly Go Wrong* (with Prudence Shen), and *The Adventures of Superhero Girl*. She lives in the mysterious Canadian province of Nova Scotia.

• Bits of *Friends with Boys* came from my own life (guess which bits—it's a fun game!), and the backgrounds in the comic are based on Halifax, Nova Scotia, where I currently live. *Friends with Boys* was the first comic I made as I was (unwillingly) leaving gainful employment and venturing out to become a full-time cartoonist. I always think about that terrifying, exciting, wonderful time whenever I look at this book.

Jesse Jacobs studied art at the Nova Scotia College of Art and Design. He currently lives in London, Ontario, where he primarily focuses on drawing comics.

• My main objective was to create a story that allowed me a lot of freedom to explore visual ideas. Using these celestial beings and their ability to manipulate molecules meant that I could pretty much draw whatever weird stuff I wanted and put in the book while maintaining some sort of narrative. It is fun to draw weird stuff.

James Kochalka is the first cartoonist laureate of Vermont. He began drawing his daily diary comic strip, *American Elf*, on October 26, 1998, and retired it approximately fourteen years later on December 31, 2012.

▪ For fourteen years I drew a daily diary comic strip called *American Elf* . . . gradually forming a complex portrait of my life and family. For this excerpt, I selected twenty-four strips from *American Elf, Book Four*, which collects the years 2008–11. I tried to pick strips that struck me as typical examples of our family life. Four years, well over a thousand strips, boiled down to just twenty-four. The flow of time is therefore highly compressed . . . you can watch my sons grow at a super-accelerated rate. My own memories of the time period are probably equally compressed, so this seems appropriate.

Michael Kupperman is an American comic artist and humorist whose words and pictures have appeared everywhere from *The New Yorker* to *Saturday Night Live*. He has written four books and illustrated many more. He lives in Brooklyn with his wife, Muire, and son, Ulysses.

▪ I wrote this comic to send a powerful message. At the time I drew it I was an actor, and I'd just landed a role on the Fox TV series *Babycops*. You may remember the tag line: "These babies don't play by the book . . . they play *with* the book!" I played second-shift desk sergeant number two, and gave the babies a resentful shake of my head about thirty-five minutes into the pilot, when they've screwed up on the Sanchez kidnapping. But then later I'm seen applauding them when they play a babyish prank on the crusty lieutenant who we all dislike. Unfortunately, the show was then cancelled.

Joseph Lambert is the author of *I Will Bite You!* and *Annie Sullivan and the Trials of Helen Keller*, published by Secret Acres and Hyperion/Disney, respectively. His work has appeared in various publications and comic anthologies. To read more of his comics, visit Submarine Submarine.com.

▪ I spent about four years, off and on, working on *Annie Sullivan and the Trials of Helen Keller*, the book this excerpt comes from. The majority of that time was spent researching and making loose thumbnail drafts. Normally a thumbnail is a loose, tiny (usually thumbnail-sized) sketch of what the page might look like, but with this book I worked at about a quarter of the print size and had to make the sketched panels legible for my publishers to review. So I felt like I drew this book three or four times before I actually started the final art, especially with these first pages. I knew what I wanted to happen on each page, and between the sixteen-panel grid and my familiarity with the flow of the story, I was able to work with loose pencils and add and omit panels as I saw fit while inking.

On the tenth page of this excerpt, the doctor is wearing a hat. I hate the way I drew that hat, and I always meant to redraw those panels, but obviously I never did for some reason. I probably forgot.

Derek McCulloch is the writer of the critically acclaimed graphic novels *Stagger Lee* (with Shepherd Hendrix) and *Pug* (with Greg Espinoza), as well as the children's book *T. Runt!* (with Jimmie Robinson). His upcoming graphic novel projects include *Displaced Persons* (with Anthony Peruzzo) and an anthology of comics adapted from stories by Damon Runyon. He is currently working as a librettist and lyricist on stage musical adaptations of *Stagger Lee* and Damon Runyon's *Madame la Gimp*.

▪ For reasons I'm not entirely sure of, music has played a big part in most of my comics work. *Gone to Amerikay* had its origins in one specific song, "Thousands Are Sailing," written by Philip Chevron of the Pogues. Our book is filled with lyrics from and references to many of the

Irish folk songs I grew up listening to. The excerpt included here was inspired by "Óró Sé Do Bheatha Abhaile," which is a song I've known my whole life but whose meaning, because I didn't know a word of Gaelic, was completely lost on me. As an adult I learned that it was a song of welcome for Gráinne Ní Mháille, the Sea Queen of Connaught, a remarkable historical figure and the subject of many folk tales. I was happy to find that the history of Gráinne Ní Mháille allowed me to include a story about her that might seem digressive on first read but would prove most thematically apt on later consideration. And I intuited, correctly, that Colleen would absolutely go to town with the opportunity to draw an Irish pirate queen.

Terry Moore has been writing and drawing critically acclaimed comic books since 1993, beginning with his classic series, *Strangers in Paradise*. Garnering numerous industry awards and published in fourteen languages, *Strangers in Paradise* remains a perennial bestseller. Celebrating its twentieth anniversary in 2013, Terry continues to reach new fans with this timeless love story.

In 2011 Moore completed the sci-fi series *Echo*, was nominated for the Eisner Award, and won the Harvey Award for Best New Series. Abstract Studio recently published Moore's *How to Draw* series as a quarterly periodical. Terry's personal take on drawing is now collected in a trade paperback and available worldwide.

He is currently working on a suspense/horror series, *Rachel Rising*, which is already a fan favorite and won the 2012 Shel Dorf Award for Self-Published Comic of the Year.

Terry is considered one of the top independent publishers in the comic book industry and continues to enthrall readers with his addictive stories and beautiful artwork.

▪ Every time I sit down to draw *Rachel Rising*, I am intimidated by the task of portraying a lush New England landscape with a fine-point pen. Only a crazy person would sit for sixteen hours every day doodling the leaves and snowflakes of a forest with a Hunt 102 dip pen. But I wanted this dense setting to suggest that the forces of nature have a strong presence in the lives of the characters. This excerpt is the second issue of the series, so every scene and setting was new to me, and I was inventing the wheel with every page—the characters, the locations, the lighting, the mood. The trick is to draw what calls to me. If I'm bored drawing it, the reader will be bored looking at it. I chase the images I'm dying to see, especially ones that can't be photographed. That gives me energy that I hope ends up on the page.

Laura Park lives in Chicago, Illinois, and is the author of the minicomics series *Do Not Disturb My Waking Dream*. She is better at drawing autobiographical details than providing them for bios.

▪ "George" was drawn for the last issue of the anthology *Mome*. The story was inspired and based on George Metesky, better known as the "Mad Bomber" during the 1940s and 1950s in New York. I've long been curious about him, and it was interesting to explore his life and mind through working on the comic.

Paul Pope is an artist living and working in New York City. He is currently drawing the second volume of *Battling Boy* for First Second Books.

▪ "1969" is the most throughly researched story I've done for comics, based entirely on actual facts. It's my first historical strip as well. Special thanks to Andrew Foster, an expert on the Apollo mission program, who helped me with many fine details for this project—including calculating the relative weight of a floating film spool in near-lunar orbit.

Cocreator and writer/artist **Tony Puryear** became the first African-American screenwriter to create a $100 million+ summer blockbuster with his script for the Arnold Schwarzenegger hit *Eraser*. He has written scripts for Mel Gibson, Oliver Stone, Jerry Bruckheimer, and Will Smith. He was born in Buffalo, New York, and raised in New York City. He now lives in Los Angeles. His design work was recently honored when his 2008 poster for Hillary Clinton's presidential campaign was included in the Smithsonian Institution's National Portrait Gallery. *Concrete Park* is his first work in comics. He is married to **Erika Alexander** (cocreator and writer), an actress perhaps best known for her roles as attorney Maxine Shaw on the hit Fox series *Living Single* and Cousin Pam on *The Cosby Show*. She has appeared in films such as *Deja Vu* with Denzel Washington and *Elsa and Fred* with Christopher Plummer and Shirley MacLaine. She most recently costarred in the critically acclaimed AMC drama series *Low Winter Sun*. She was born in Flagstaff, Arizona, and lives in Los Angeles, California. Cocreator **Robert Alexander** was born in Lovington, New Mexico. He is a writer, photographer, and digital artist. He lives in Venice, California.

- "Black people don't like science fiction. It's because they don't see themselves in the future." That's what a Hollywood studio president told us several years ago when we pitched him *Concrete Park*. He meant this as helpful advice. He was doubly misguided, firstly for the blank racism of his statement and secondly for his assumption that because we were black, because our sci-fi film pitch showed some people of color, it was a project intended solely for "the African-American market." Silly rabbit. As black writers working in Hollywood, we encounter this wack kind of thinking every day. Luckily, Mike Richardson of Dark Horse Comics had no such problem. He saw *Concrete Park*, the graphic novel, as we did: as an action-packed exploration of themes of class, race, violence, and hope in a hopeless place. We put our experience into it, of course, but we made it to move you on a dramatic level, on a human level, not a racial one. That studio president may never "get" it, but he inspired us, and we hope someday to repay him by making him famous for it.

Rafael Rosado (see Jorge Aguirre)

Grant Snider is a cartoonist, illustrator, and orthodontic resident. His strip *Incidental Comics* has appeared weekly in the *Kansas City Star* and online since 2009. It's a personal exploration of creativity, ideas, and life—and their accompanying frustrations.

- I've found that some of my best work comes after I've thrown away a few sketches out of dissatisfaction. I tried to illustrate this in "The Creative Process." For "Summer Night," I preemptively tore up and scanned sheets of construction paper to create an August sunset. I strive to keep my comics grounded in a world of books and imagination.

Jeremy Sorese was born in 1988 in Berlin, Germany, back when there was still a West Berlin. He spent his childhood in suburban Virginia before attending Savannah College of Art and Design, from which he received a BFA in sequential art in 2010. In the fall of 2012 he became a resident at La maison des auteurs in Angouleme, France. He is currently in the process of finishing his first book, a science fiction story about the energy we use in our personal relationships.

- Back in the fall of 2011, when Raighne Hogan of 2DCloud approached me about making a comic for his anthology focused on equal marriage rights, it seemed like divine intervention. The fact that both my parents had just gotten remarried in such similar fashions was all that I could talk about. In fact, marriage was all that anyone I knew could talk about. Within a few months, many of my friends had either gotten engaged or moved in with their significant others or were making plans to. That year I traveled more than I ever had before, to or from comic conventions (and weddings) via overnight Greyhound bus or discount plane tickets, always by myself. It's easy to become obsessive about what you don't have in your life when you're grumpy and restless at 30,000 feet in the air, morphing your can of in-flight Dr. Pepper into a symbol of your perpetual singledom.

Craig Thompson was born in Traverse City, Michigan, in 1975 and raised in a farming community in central Wisconsin. He attended community college for a year while working as an "ad stylist" at a newspaper. Afterward, he attended the Milwaukee Institute of Art and Design for one semester before dropping out and working as a bagel maker, telemarketer, graphic designer, house painter, stock boy at a department store and music distribution warehouse, and laser light-show animator at a children's museum. His first full-length book, *Good-bye, Chunky Rice* (Pantheon), debuted when he was twenty-three, though he is best known for his coming-of-age memoir, *Blankets* (Top Shelf Productions).

• "70 Nights of Pleasure" is a twenty-one page excerpt from my 666-page book *Habibi*, published by Pantheon Books. The graphic novel follows the relationship of two escaped child slaves, Dodola and Zam, through eighteen years of their relationship. This sequence is inspired by the bawdiness and adventure of *One Thousand and One Nights* along with historical details of the scandalous reign of Ottoman Sultan Ibrahim I (1640–1648). Drawing heavily from my obsession with Arabic calligraphy, pattern, geometric design, and architecture, these pages also employ the classic comic book tradition of the "swipe," paying tribute to Jean-Léon Gérôme's "The Harem Bath" (1889), Frederick Goodall's "A Dream of Paradise" (1889), a cutaway view of the Ottoman Mosque in Istanbul, and Agostino Veneziano's depiction of Sultan Suleyman the Magnificent wearing a Venetian helmet (1535).

Jill Thompson is the Eisner Award–winning creator of the Scary Godmother. If you're not familiar with that character, please follow these links to find two whole books of her stories:

http://www.darkhorse.com/Books/17-305/Scary-Godmother-HC
http://www.darkhorse.com/Books/17-306/Scary-Godmother-Comic-Book-Stories-TPB

She is also the creator of Magic Trixie:

http://www.amazon.com/Magic-Trixie-Jill-Thompson/dp/0061170453

Scary Godmother has been seen not only in comics but also on stage and screen. In 2001 there were twenty-six performances of *The Scary Godmother* at the Athenaeum Theater in Chicago. That play was subsequently adapted into *The Scary Godmother Holiday Spooktakular*, which is an annual treat on the Cartoon Network. In fact, it proved so popular that a request for another adaptation of a Scary Godmother story came her way, and *The Revenge of Jimmy* was also brought to animated life!

Jill is also is a cocreator of two series, *Finals,* with Will Pfeifer for DC/Vertigo, and *Beasts of Burden,* with writer Evan Dorkin for Dark Horse Comics. She has illustrated many other comics and books, including *Wonder Woman, Sandman, Death at Death's Door, The Little Endless Storybook, Delirium's Party, The Invisibles, The Dead Boy Detectives, Seekers into the Mystery, Fables, The Badger, Mick Foley's Halloween Hijinx, Tales from Wrescal Lane,* and much, much more.

Lately she's been very busy developing Scary Godmother toys and painting multiple comics stories. You can follow her on Twitter for updates on all of Jill's stuff: @theJillThompson. You can also demand her comics at finer comic shops everywhere.

▪ I draw my stories on Strathmore watercolor paper in pencil. Then I hand-letter indicators for the letterer, Jason Arthur, to follow when he digitally letters the stories with my font. I used to do all my lettering by hand on the page. Sometimes I still do. But ninety-nine percent of the time, my work is digitally lettered with a font created for me and based on my hand-lettering.

After scanning those pages for the letterer, I erase the pencil lines; tighten up the pencil drawings; tape all the panel borders and gutters with painter's tape to ensure crisp, clean edges; and then paint the art with watercolors.

Once finished, I remove the tape, scan the pages to send them to my publisher, and then send the original art.

Malachi Ward is the author of the *Ritual* series, *Utu*, and *The Scout*, and coauthor of *Expansion* with Matt Sheean. He has been published by Image Comics, Revival House Press, NoBrow, and Fantagraphics. Ward lives in South Pasadena with his wife.

▪ The main character in "Top Five" has been floating around in my comics for a while, only once before making it to a finished work. So he has a complex backstory that probably won't ever be written. I originally drew this piece in order to have something to present at a comics reading, which was a terrifying prospect to me. None of the comics I had would work in that setting, so I made "Top Five" in the hope that something with a little humor might fit.

Notable Comics

from September 1, 2011, to August 31, 2012

Selected by Jessica Abel and Matt Madden

HILARY ALLISON
Bad Words.

DERIK A. BADMAN
Untitled (The Big Sleep).

JEREMY BAUM
Postland.

JOSH BAYER
Raw Power.

BOX BROWN
The Survivalist.

JON CHAD
Bikeman.

SEYMOUR CHWAST
The Canterbury Tales.

BECKY CLOONAN
The Mire.

DARWYN COOKE
Richard Stark's Parker: The Score.

WARREN CRAGHEAD III
A Rabbit as King of the Ghosts. *Phoebe.*

ANYA DAVIDSON
Barbarian Bitch. *Kramers Ergot*, no. 8.

KRIS DRESEN
Gone.

INÉS ESTRADA
Ojitos Borrosos.

SOFIA FALKENHEM
Can I Sit Close Like This? *Rabid Rabbit*, no. 14.

A. G. (GLYNNIS) FAWKES
Thinking About Dust. *Minimum Paige.*

MICHAEL FIFFE
Zegas, no. 2.

CHARLES FORSMAN
The End of the Fucking World, Parts 1–7.

MATT FORSYTHE
Jinchalo.

EROYN FRANKLIN
Just Noise.

ELIZA FRYE
The Lady's Murder. *Regalia.*

JULIA GFRÖRER
Black Is the Color. *Study Group*, no. 12.

MYLA GOLDBERG AND JASON LITTLE
Invisible. *Bomb.*

V. A. GRAHAM AND J. A. EISENHOWER
Scaffold.

TOM HART
Daddy Lightning.

SEAMUS HEFFERNAN
Freedom, no. 1.

GILBERT HERNANDEZ
Fatima: The Blood Spinners, Issues 1 & 2.

JOE HILL AND GABRIEL RODRIGUEZ
Open the Moon. *Locke & Key.*

PETER HOEY AND MARIA HOEY
Occurrence at Pont Neuf. *Coin-Op.*

LUKE HOWARD
All Coons Look Alike to Me: The Life of Ernest Hogan, Father of Ragtime.

LEO HUSSEY AND CONOR STECHSCHULTE
Untitled (Tliug). *Weird.*

JEFF JENSEN AND JONATHAN CASE
Green River Killer.

MARK KALESNIKO
Freeway.

JEREMY KNOWLES
Look Straight Ahead.

DAVE LAPP
People Around Here.

BRENDAN LEACH
Iron Bound, no. 1.

JEFF LEMIRE
The Underwater Welder.

JASON LUTES
Berlin, no. 18.

PAUL MADONNA
Regret Trilogy. *All Over Coffee.*

JUSTIN MADSON
Breathers.
MARDOU
The Sky in Stereo.
BENJAMIN MARRA AND MICHAEL DEFORGE
Faunamancer Domination. *Smoke Signal,* no. 10.
JASON MARTIN AND CALVIN WONG
Scenes from the Fire. *Papercutter,* no. 17.
JOHN MARTZ
Machine Gum, no. 3.
DAN MAZUR AND JESSE LONERGAN
Cold Wind.
DAKOTA MCFADZEAN
Unkindness.
JESSE MCMANUS AND AUSTIN ENGLISH
Spider Monkey.
DYLAN MECONIS
Outfoxed.
TOM MOTLEY
Al Jaffee Homage Dept. *Tragic Strip.*
MARI NAOMI
Smoke in Your Eyes: Dragon's Breath. *The Rumpus.*
JOSH NEUFELD
Bahrain: Lines in Ink, Lines in the Sand. *Cartoon Movement.*
ERIC ORNER
Avi & Jihad. *The Rumpus.*
HARVEY PEKAR AND JOSEPH REMNANT
Harvey Pekar's Cleveland.
RAMON K. PEREZ, ADAPTED FROM A SCREENPLAY BY JIM HENSON AND JERRY JUHL
Tale of Sand.
J. T. PETTY AND HILARY FLORIDO
Bloody Chester.
ED PISKOR
Wizzywig.
JOHN PORCELLINO
The Strip Outsider. *Ecotone,* no. 12.
LIZ PRINCE, JOE QUINONES, AND MARIS WICKS
The Stuff of Fluff. *Minimum Paige.*
PETER QUACH
I Am a Racist (And So Can You).
MATT ROTA
Romance. *Rabid Rabbit,* no. 14.
P. CRAIG RUSSELL
Fairy Tales of Oscar Wilde.
JOE SACCO AND CHRIS HEDGES
Days of Destruction, Days of Revolt.
YUMI SAKUGAWA
Seed Bomb. *Slake,* no. 4.
WILFRED SANTIAGO
The Story of Roberto Clemente.
GABBY SCHULTZ
Sick. *Gabby's Playhouse.*
ROBERT SERGEL
Control. *Minimum Paige.*
ANUJ SHRESTHA
Genus.
GRANT SNIDER
The Book of the Future. *New York Times Book Review.*
VINCENT STALL
Things You Carry.
CONOR STECHSCHULTE
The Amateurs.
JILLIAN TAMAKI
Supermutant Magic Academy.
LAURA TERRY
Overboard.
MATTHEW THURBER
Infomaniacs. *PictureBox.*
MATTHEW THURBER AND BENJAMIN MARRA
The Transformers of Life. *Smoke Signal,* no. 10.
TIN CAN FOREST
Wax Cross.
JEREMY TINDER
Mothman, Lake Michigan. *Elephant Ear.*
BEN TOWLE
The Oyster War: Chapter 4.
ANDREA TSURUMI
Dance Party.
NOAH VAN SCIVER
1999.
VARIOUS
Suspect Device, no. 2.
VARIOUS
Cartoon Crier.
MALACHI WARD
Real Life: Ritual, Issue 1.
ANDY WARNER
The Man Who Built Beirut
LALE WESTVIND
Potent Impact. *Chromazoid.*
ERIC WILLIAMS
Wow You Are a Hungry Bottom.
JESS WORBY
A Walk in the Park.
DAN ZETTWOCH
Birdseye Bristoe.

CREDITS

"Turn Back," excerpt from *Haunter* by Sam Alden. First published in Studygroupcomics.com. Copyright © 2013 by Sam Alden. Reprinted by permission of Study Group Comics. "The Strange Boy," excerpt from *My Friend Dahmer* by Derf Backderf. Copyright © 2012 by John Backderf. Used by permission of Abrams ComicArts, an imprint of Harry N. Abrams, Inc., New York. All rights reserved. "Velocipede" by Kate Beaton. First published in *Hark! A Vagrant*. Copyright © 2012 by Kate Beaton. Reprinted by permission of Kate Beaton. "Mirror," excerpt from *Are You My Mother?: A Comic Drama* by Alison Bechdel. Copyright © 2012 by Alison Bechdel. Reprinted by permission of Houghton Mifflin Harcourt Publishing Company. All rights reserved. "The Glamorous Life" from the film version of *A Little Night Music*. Words and Music by Stephen Sondheim. © 1973 (Renewed) Rilting Music, Inc. "Liaisons" from *A Little Night Music*. Words and Music by Stephen Sondheim. © 1973 (Renewed) Rilting Music, Inc. All Rights Administered by WB Music Corp. All Rights Reserved Used by Permission. Reprinted by Permission of Hal Leonard Corporation. "Cody" by Gabrielle Bell. First published in *Kramers Ergot*. Copyright © 2013 by Gabrielle Bell. Reprinted by permission of Gabrielle Bell. "1912," excerpt from *Unterzakhn* by Leela Corman, copyright © 2012 by Leela Corman. Used by permission of Schocken Books, a division of Random House, Inc. Any third party use of this material, outside of this publication, is prohibited. Interested parties may apply directly to Random House, Inc., for permission. "Nita Goes Home" by Eleanor Davis. First published in *MOME 22*. Copyright © 2011 by Eleanor Davis. Reprinted by permission of Eleanor Davis. "In the Rough" by Vanessa Davis. First published on www.tabletmag.com. Copyright © 2013 by Vanessa Davis. Reprinted by permission of Vanessa Davis. "Manananggal" by Michael DeForge. First published in *Lose #3*, Koyama Press. Copyright © 2011 by Michael DeForge. Reprinted by permission of Michael DeForge. "Fun Strips" by Evan Dorkin. First published in *Dark Horse Presents*. Copyright © 2013 by Evan Dorkin. Reprinted by permission of Evan Dorkin. "Story Time" by Evan Dorkin and Jill Thompson. First published in *Dark Horse Presents*. Copyright © 2013 by Evan Dorkin and Jill Thompson. Reprinted by permission of Evan Dorkin and Jill Thompson. "The Good Wife" by Sophie Goldstein. First published in *The Good Wife*. Copyright © 2011 by Sophie Goldstein. Reprinted by permission of Sophie Goldstein. "The Speaker" by Brandon Graham. First published in *Dark Horse Presents*. Copyright © 2012 by Brandon Graham. Reprinted by permission of the author. "A Husband and a Wife" by Sammy Harkham. First published in *Kramers Ergot*. Copyright © 2013 by Sammy Harkham. Reprinted by permission of the author. "Saints in the Store" by Jennifer Hayden. First published in *Underwire*. Copyright © 2011 by Jennifer Hayden. Reprinted by permission of Jennifer Hayden. "Raiders," excerpt from *Friends with Boys* © 2012 by Faith Erin Hicks. Reprinted by permission of First Second, an imprint of Roaring Brook Press, a division of Holtzbrinck Publishing Holdings Limited Partnership. All Rights Reserved. "The Divine Manifestation of a Singular Impulse" by Jesse Jacobs. First published in *By This Shall You Know Him*. Copyright © 2012 by Jesse Jacobs and Koyama Press. Reprinted by permission of Jesse Jacobs and Koyama Press. Excerpts from *American Elf* by James Kochalka. First published in *American Elf*. Copyright © 2012 by James Kochalka. Reprinted by permission of James Kochalka and Top Shelf Productions. "Scary Bath Tub Stories" by Michael Kupperman. First published in *Tales Designed to Thrizzle*. Copyright © 2012 by Michael Kupperman. Reprinted by permission of Michael Kupperman. "Discipline," excerpt from *Annie Sullivan and the Trials of Helen Keller* by Joseph Lambert. Copyright © 2013 by The Center for Cartoon Studies. Reprinted by permission of The Center for Cartoon Studies. "The Story of Gráinne Ní Mháille," excerpt from *Gone to Amerikay* © 2012 Derek McCulloch and Colleen Doran. Used with Permission of DC Comics. "A Killer's Surprise," excerpt from *Rachel Rising* by Terry Moore. Copyright © 2011 by Terry Moore. Reprinted by permission ofTerry Moore. "George" by Laura Park. First published in *MOME 22*. Copyright © 2012 by Laura Park. Reprinted by permission of Laura Park. "1969" byPaul Pope. First published in *Dark Horse Presents*. Copyright © 2012 by Paul Pope. Reprinted by permission of the author. "Concrete Park (Excerpt)" by Tony Puryear. First published in *Dark Horse Presents*. Copyright © 2011 by Tony Puryear. Reprinted by permission of Tony Puryear. "You Lied to Us!," excerpt from *Giants Beware!* © 2012 by Rafael Rosado. Illustrations © 2012 by Jorge Aguirre. Reprinted by permission of First Second, an imprint of Roaring Book Press, a division of Holtzbrinck Publishing Holdings Limited Partnership. All Rights Reserved. "I Wanted a Super Power," "The Creative Process," "Required Summer Reading," and "Summer Night" by Grant Snider. First published in Incidentalcomics.com. Copyright © 2013 by Grant Snider. Reprinted by permission of Grant Snider. "Love Me Forever! Oh! Oh! Oh!," by Jeremy Sorese. First published in *Little Heart: A Comic Anthology for Marriage Equality*. Copyright © 2012 by Jeremy Sorese. Reprinted by permission of Jeremy Sorese. "70 Nights of Pleasure," excerpt from *Habibi* by Craig Thompson, copyright © 2011 by Craig Thompson. Used by permission of Pantheon Books, adivision of Random House, Inc. Any third party use of this material, outside of this publication, is prohibited. Interested parties may apply directly to Random House, Inc., for permission. "Top Five" by Malachi Ward. First published in Studygroupcomics.com. Copyright © 2012 by Malachi Ward. Reprinted by permission of Malachi Ward.

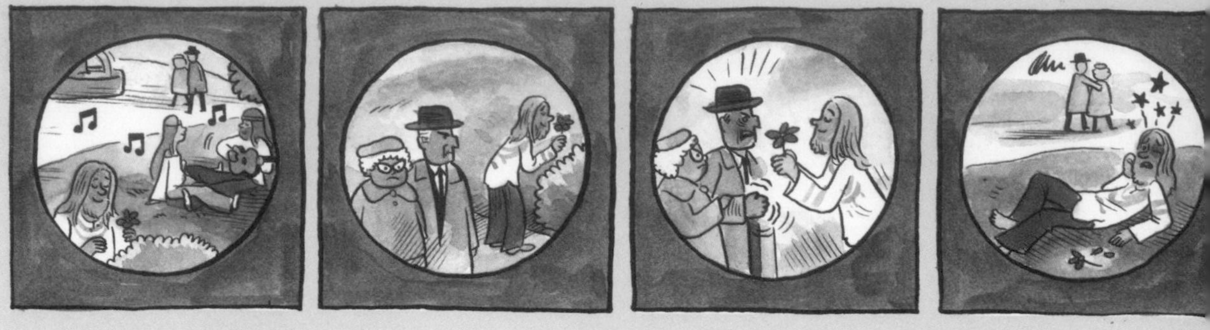

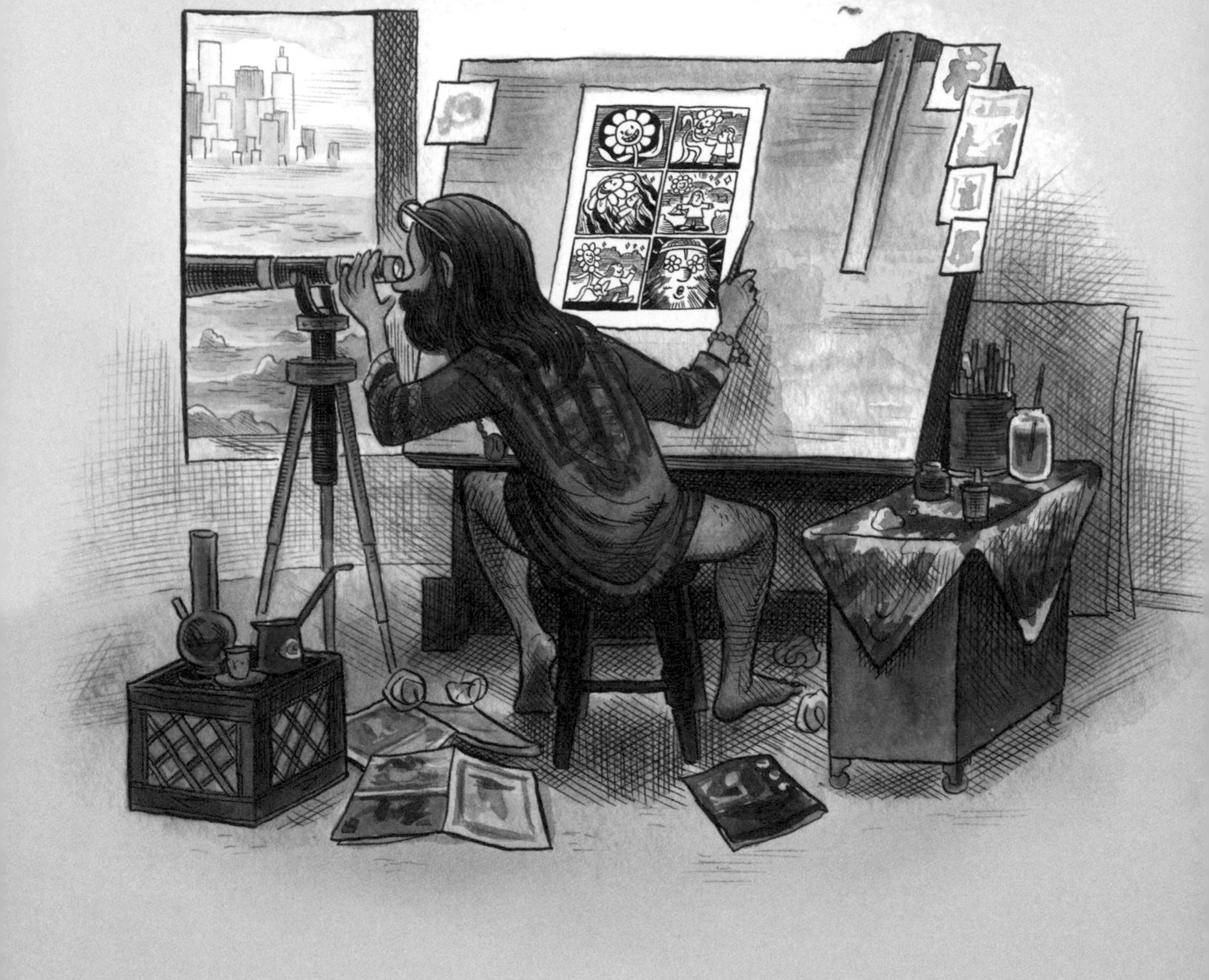